Lecture Notes in Computer Science 14445

Founding Editors

Gerhard Goos
Juris Hartmanis

Editorial Board Members

The series Lecture Notes in Computer Science (LNCS), including its subseries Lecture Notes in Artificial Intelligence (LNAI) and Lecture Notes in Bioinformatics (LNBI), has established itself as a medium for the publication of new developments in computer science and information technology research, teaching, and education.

LNCS enjoys close cooperation with the computer science R & D community, the series counts many renowned academics among its volume editors and paper authors, and collaborates with prestigious societies. Its mission is to serve this international community by providing an invaluable service, mainly focused on the publication of conference and workshop proceedings and postproceedings. LNCS commenced publication in 1973.

Jian Guo · Ron Steinfeld

Editors

Advances in Cryptology – ASIACRYPT 2023

29th International Conference on the Theory
and Application of Cryptology and Information Security
Guangzhou, China, December 4–8, 2023
Proceedings, Part VIII

Editors
Jian Guo (ID)
Nanyang Technological University
Singapore, Singapore

Ron Steinfeld (ID)
Monash University
Melbourne, VIC, Australia

ISSN 0302-9743   ISSN 1611-3349 (electronic)
Lecture Notes in Computer Science
ISBN 978-981-99-8741-2   ISBN 978-981-99-8742-9 (eBook)
https://doi.org/10.1007/978-981-99-8742-9

This Springer imprint is published by the registered company Springer Nature Singapore Pte Ltd.
The registered company address is: 152 Beach Road, #21-01/04 Gateway East, Singapore 189721, Singapore

Paper in this product is recyclable.

Preface

The 29th Annual International Conference on the Theory and Application of Cryptology and Information Security (Asiacrypt 2023) was held in Guangzhou, China, on December 4–8, 2023. The conference covered all technical aspects of cryptology, and was sponsored by the International Association for Cryptologic Research (IACR).

We received an Asiacrypt record of 376 paper submissions from all over the world, and the Program Committee (PC) selected 106 papers for publication in the proceedings of the conference. Due to this large number of papers, the Asiacrypt 2023 program had 3 tracks.

The two program chairs were supported by the great help and excellent advice of six area chairs, selected to cover the main topic areas of the conference. The area chairs were Kai-Min Chung for Information-Theoretic and Complexity-Theoretic Cryptography, Tanja Lange for Efficient and Secure Implementations, Shengli Liu for Public-Key Cryptography Algorithms and Protocols, Khoa Nguyen for Multi-Party Computation and Zero-Knowledge, Duong Hieu Phan for Public-Key Primitives with Advanced Functionalities, and Yu Sasaki for Symmetric-Key Cryptology. Each of the area chairs helped to lead discussions together with the PC members assigned as paper discussion lead. Area chairs also helped to decide on the submissions that should be accepted from their respective areas. We are very grateful for the invaluable contribution provided by the area chairs.

To review and evaluate the submissions, while keeping the load per PC member manageable, we selected a record size PC consisting of 105 leading experts from all over the world, in all six topic areas of cryptology. The two program chairs were not allowed to submit a paper, and PC members were limited to submit one single-author paper, or at most two co-authored papers, or at most three co-authored papers all with students. Each non-PC submission was reviewed by at least three reviewers consisting of either PC members or their external sub-reviewers, while each PC member submission received at least four reviews. The strong conflict of interest rules imposed by IACR ensure that papers are not handled by PC members with a close working relationship with the authors. There were approximately 420 external reviewers, whose input was critical to the selection of papers. Submissions were anonymous and their length was limited to 30 pages excluding the bibliography and supplementary materials.

The review process was conducted using double-blind peer review. The conference operated a two-round review system with a rebuttal phase. After the reviews and first round discussions the PC selected 244 submissions to proceed to the second round and the authors were then invited to participate in an interactive rebuttal phase with the reviewers to clarify questions and concerns. The remaining 131 papers were rejected, including one desk reject. The second round involved extensive discussions by the PC members. After several weeks of additional discussions, the committee selected the final 106 papers to appear in these proceedings.

The eight volumes of the conference proceedings contain the revised versions of the 106 papers that were selected. The final revised versions of papers were not reviewed again and the authors are responsible for their contents.

The PC nominated and voted for two papers to receive the Best Paper Awards, and one paper to receive the Best Early Career Paper Award. The Best Paper Awards went to Thomas Espitau, Alexandre Wallet and Yang Yu for their paper "On Gaussian Sampling, Smoothing Parameter and Application to Signatures", and to Kaijie Jiang, Anyu Wang, Hengyi Luo, Guoxiao Liu, Yang Yu, and Xiaoyun Wang for their paper "Exploiting the Symmetry of Z^n: Randomization and the Automorphism Problem". The Best Early Career Paper Award went to Maxime Plancon for the paper "Exploiting Algebraic Structure in Probing Security". The authors of those three papers were invited to submit extended versions of their papers to the Journal of Cryptology. In addition, the program of Asiacrypt 2023 also included two invited plenary talks, also nominated and voted by the PC: one talk was given by Mehdi Tibouchi and the other by Xiaoyun Wang. The conference also featured a rump session chaired by Kang Yang and Yu Yu which contained short presentations on the latest research results of the field.

Numerous people contributed to the success of Asiacrypt 2023. We would like to thank all the authors, including those whose submissions were not accepted, for submitting their research results to the conference. We are very grateful to the area chairs, PC members and external reviewers for contributing their knowledge and expertise, and for the tremendous amount of work that was done with reading papers and contributing to the discussions. We are greatly indebted to Jian Weng and Fangguo Zhang, the General Chairs, for their efforts in organizing the event and to Kevin McCurley and Kay McKelly for their help with the website and review system. We thank the Asiacrypt 2023 advisory committee members Bart Preneel, Huaxiong Wang, Kai-Min Chung, Yu Sasaki, Dongdai Lin, Shweta Agrawal and Michel Abdalla for their valuable suggestions. We are also grateful for the helpful advice and organization material provided to us by the Eurocrypt 2023 PC co-chairs Carmit Hazay and Martijn Stam and Crypto 2023 PC co-chairs Helena Handschuh and Anna Lysyanskaya. We also thank the team at Springer for handling the publication of these conference proceedings.

December 2023

Jian Guo
Ron Steinfeld

Organization

General Chairs

Jian Weng   Jinan University, China
Fangguo Zhang   Sun Yat-sen University, China

Program Committee Chairs

Jian Guo   Nanyang Technological University, Singapore
Ron Steinfeld   Monash University, Australia

Program Committee

Behzad Abdolmaleki   University of Sheffield, UK
Masayuki Abe   NTT Social Informatics Laboratories, Japan
Miguel Ambrona   Input Output Global (IOHK), Spain
Daniel Apon   MITRE Labs, USA
Shi Bai   Florida Atlantic University, USA
Gustavo Banegas   Qualcomm, France
Zhenzhen Bao   Tsinghua University, China
Andrea Basso   University of Bristol, UK
Ward Beullens   IBM Research Europe, Switzerland
Katharina Boudgoust   Aarhus University, Denmark
Matteo Campanelli   Protocol Labs, Denmark
Ignacio Cascudo   IMDEA Software Institute, Spain
Wouter Castryck   imec-COSIC, KU Leuven, Belgium
Jie Chen   East China Normal University, China
Yilei Chen   Tsinghua University, China
Jung Hee Cheon   Seoul National University and Cryptolab Inc, South Korea
Sherman S. M. Chow   Chinese University of Hong Kong, China
Kai-Min Chung   Academia Sinica, Taiwan
Michele Ciampi   University of Edinburgh, UK
Bernardo David   IT University of Copenhagen, Denmark
Yi Deng   Institute of Information Engineering, Chinese Academy of Sciences, China

Patrick Derbez	University of Rennes, France
Xiaoyang Dong	Tsinghua University, China
Rafael Dowsley	Monash University, Australia
Nico Döttling	Helmholtz Center for Information Security, Germany
Maria Eichlseder	Graz University of Technology, Austria
Muhammed F. Esgin	Monash University, Australia
Thomas Espitau	PQShield, France
Jun Furukawa	NEC Corporation, Japan
Aron Gohr	Independent Researcher, New Zealand
Junqing Gong	ECNU, China
Lorenzo Grassi	Ruhr University Bochum, Germany
Tim Güneysu	Ruhr University Bochum, Germany
Chun Guo	Shandong University, China
Siyao Guo	NYU Shanghai, China
Fuchun Guo	University of Wollongong, Australia
Mohammad Hajiabadi	University of Waterloo, Canada
Lucjan Hanzlik	CISPA Helmholtz Center for Information Security, Germany
Xiaolu Hou	Slovak University of Technology, Slovakia
Yuncong Hu	Shanghai Jiao Tong University, China
Xinyi Huang	Hong Kong University of Science and Technology (Guangzhou), China
Tibor Jager	University of Wuppertal, Germany
Elena Kirshanova	Technology Innovation Institute, UAE and I. Kant Baltic Federal University, Russia
Eyal Kushilevitz	Technion, Israel
Russell W. F. Lai	Aalto University, Finland
Tanja Lange	Eindhoven University of Technology, Netherlands
Hyung Tae Lee	Chung-Ang University, South Korea
Eik List	Nanyang Technological University, Singapore
Meicheng Liu	Institute of Information Engineering, Chinese Academy of Sciences, China
Guozhen Liu	Nanyang Technological University, Singapore
Fukang Liu	Tokyo Institute of Technology, Japan
Shengli Liu	Shanghai Jiao Tong University, China
Feng-Hao Liu	Florida Atlantic University, USA
Hemanta K. Maji	Purdue University, USA
Takahiro Matsuda	AIST, Japan
Christian Matt	Concordium, Switzerland
Tomoyuki Morimae	Kyoto University, Japan
Pierrick Méaux	University of Luxembourg, Luxembourg

Mridul Nandi	Indian Statistical Institute, Kolkata, India
María Naya-Plasencia	Inria, France
Khoa Nguyen	University of Wollongong, Australia
Ryo Nishimaki	NTT Social Informatics Laboratories, Japan
Anca Nitulescu	Protocol Labs, France
Ariel Nof	Bar Ilan University, Israel
Emmanuela Orsini	Bocconi University, Italy
Adam O'Neill	UMass Amherst, USA
Morten Øygarden	Simula UiB, Norway
Sikhar Patranabis	IBM Research, India
Alice Pellet-Mary	CNRS and University of Bordeaux, France
Edoardo Persichetti	Florida Atlantic University, USA and Sapienza University, Italy
Duong Hieu Phan	Telecom Paris, Institut Polytechnique de Paris, France
Josef Pieprzyk	Data61, CSIRO, Australia and ICS, PAS, Poland
Axel Y. Poschmann	PQShield, UAE
Thomas Prest	PQShield, France
Adeline Roux-Langlois	CNRS, GREYC, France
Amin Sakzad	Monash University, Australia
Yu Sasaki	NTT Social Informatics Laboratories, Japan
Jae Hong Seo	Hanyang University, South Korea
Yaobin Shen	UCLouvain, Belgium
Danping Shi	Institute of Information Engineering, Chinese Academy of Sciences, China
Damien Stehlé	CryptoLab, France
Bing Sun	National University of Defense Technology, China
Shi-Feng Sun	Shanghai Jiao Tong University, China
Keisuke Tanaka	Tokyo Institute of Technology, Japan
Qiang Tang	University of Sydney, Australia
Vanessa Teague	Thinking Cybersecurity Pty Ltd and the Australian National University, Australia
Jean-Pierre Tillich	Inria, Paris, France
Yosuke Todo	NTT Social Informatics Laboratories, Japan
Alexandre Wallet	University of Rennes, Inria, CNRS, IRISA, France
Meiqin Wang	Shandong University, China
Yongge Wang	UNC Charlotte, USA
Yuyu Wang	University of Electronic Science and Technology of China, China
Qingju Wang	Telecom Paris, Institut Polytechnique de Paris, France

Benjamin Wesolowski	CNRS and ENS Lyon, France
Shuang Wu	Huawei International, Singapore, Singapore
Keita Xagawa	Technology Innovation Institute, UAE
Chaoping Xing	Shanghai Jiao Tong University, China
Jun Xu	Institute of Information Engineering, Chinese Academy of Sciences, China
Takashi Yamakawa	NTT Social Informatics Laboratories, Japan
Kang Yang	State Key Laboratory of Cryptology, China
Yu Yu	Shanghai Jiao Tong University, China
Yang Yu	Tsinghua University, Beijing, China
Yupeng Zhang	University of Illinois Urbana-Champaign and Texas A&M University, USA
Liangfeng Zhang	ShanghaiTech University, China
Raymond K. Zhao	CSIRO's Data61, Australia
Hong-Sheng Zhou	Virginia Commonwealth University, USA

Additional Reviewers

Amit Agarwal	Pedro Branco
Jooyoung Lee	Lauren Brandt
Léo Ackermann	Alessandro Budroni
Akshima	Kevin Carrier
Bar Alon	André Chailloux
Ravi Anand	Suvradip Chakraborty
Sarah Arpin	Debasmita Chakraborty
Thomas Attema	Haokai Chang
Nuttapong Attrapadung	Bhuvnesh Chaturvedi
Manuel Barbosa	Caicai Chen
Razvan Barbulescu	Rongmao Chen
James Bartusek	Mingjie Chen
Carsten Baum	Yi Chen
Olivier Bernard	Megan Chen
Tyler Besselman	Yu Long Chen
Ritam Bhaumik	Xin Chen
Jingguo Bi	Shiyao Chen
Loic Bidoux	Long Chen
Maxime Bombar	Wonhee Cho
Xavier Bonnetain	Qiaohan Chu
Joppe Bos	Valerio Cini
Mariana Botelho da Gama	James Clements
Christina Boura	Ran Cohen
Clémence Bouvier	Alexandru Cojocaru
Ross Bowden	Sandro Coretti-Drayton

Anamaria Costache

Alain Couvreur

Daniele Cozzo

Hongrui Cui

Giuseppe D'Alconzo

Zhaopeng Dai

Quang Dao

Nilanjan Datta

Koen de Boer

Luca De Feo

Paola de Perthuis

Thomas Decru

Rafael del Pino

Julien Devevey

Henri Devillez

Siemen Dhooghe

Yaoling Ding

Jack Doerner

Jelle Don

Mark Douglas Schultz

Benjamin Dowling

Minxin Du

Xiaoqi Duan

Jesko Dujmovic

Moumita Dutta

Avijit Dutta

Ehsan Ebrahimi

Felix Engelmann

Reo Eriguchi

Jonathan Komada Eriksen

Andre Esser

Pouria Fallahpour

Zhiyong Fang

Antonio Faonio

Pooya Farshim

Joël Felderhoff

Jakob Feldtkeller

Weiqi Feng

Xiutao Feng

Shuai Feng

Qi Feng

Hanwen Feng

Antonio Flórez-Gutiérrez

Apostolos Fournaris

Paul Frixons

Ximing Fu

Georg Fuchsbauer

Philippe Gaborit

Rachit Garg

Robin Geelen

Riddhi Ghosal

Koustabh Ghosh

Barbara Gigerl

Niv Gilboa

Valerie Gilchrist

Emanuele Giunta

Xinxin Gong

Huijing Gong

Zheng Gong

Robert Granger

Zichen Gui

Anna Guinet

Qian Guo

Xiaojie Guo

Hosein Hadipour

Mathias Hall-Andersen

Mike Hamburg

Shuai Han

Yonglin Hao

Keisuke Hara

Keitaro Hashimoto

Le He

Brett Hemenway Falk

Minki Hhan

Taiga Hiroka

Akinori Hosoyamada

Chengan Hou

Martha Norberg Hovd

Kai Hu

Tao Huang

Zhenyu Huang

Michael Hutter

Jihun Hwang

Akiko Inoue

Tetsu Iwata

Robin Jadoul

Hansraj Jangir

Dirmanto Jap

Stanislaw Jarecki

Santos Jha

Ashwin Jha
Dingding Jia
Yanxue Jia
Lin Jiao
Daniel Jost
Antoine Joux
Jiayi Kang
Gabriel Kaptchuk
Alexander Karenin
Shuichi Katsumata
Pengzhen Ke
Mustafa Khairallah
Shahram Khazaei
Hamidreza Amini Khorasgani
Hamidreza Khoshakhlagh
Ryo Kikuchi
Jiseung Kim
Minkyu Kim
Suhri Kim
Ravi Kishore
Fuyuki Kitagawa
Susumu Kiyoshima
Michael Klooß
Alexander Koch
Sreehari Kollath
Dimitris Kolonelos
Yashvanth Kondi
Anders Konring
Woong Kook
Dimitri Koshelev
Markus Krausz
Toomas Krips
Daniel Kuijsters
Anunay Kulshrestha
Qiqi Lai
Yi-Fu Lai
Georg Land
Nathalie Lang
Mario Larangeira
Joon-Woo Lee
Keewoo Lee
Hyeonbum Lee
Changmin Lee
Charlotte Lefevre
Julia Len

Antonin Leroux
Andrea Lesavourey
Jannis Leuther
Jie Li
Shuaishuai Li
Huina Li
Yu Li
Yanan Li
Jiangtao Li
Song Song Li
Wenjie Li
Shun Li
Zengpeng Li
Xiao Liang
Wei-Kai Lin
Chengjun Lin
Chao Lin
Cong Ling
Yunhao Ling
Hongqing Liu
Jing Liu
Jiahui Liu
Qipeng Liu
Yamin Liu
Weiran Liu
Tianyi Liu
Siqi Liu
Chen-Da Liu-Zhang
Jinyu Lu
Zhenghao Lu
Stefan Lucks
Yiyuan Luo
Lixia Luo
Jack P. K. Ma
Fermi Ma
Gilles Macario-Rat
Luciano Maino
Christian Majenz
Laurane Marco
Lorenzo Martinico
Loïc Masure
John McVey
Willi Meier
Kelsey Melissaris
Bart Mennink

Charles Meyer-Hilfiger

Victor Miller

Chohong Min

Marine Minier

Arash Mirzaei

Pratyush Mishra

Tarik Moataz

Johannes Mono

Fabrice Mouhartem

Alice Murphy

Erik Mårtensson

Anne Müller

Marcel Nageler

Yusuke Naito

Barak Nehoran

Patrick Neumann

Tran Ngo

Phuong Hoa Nguyen

Ngoc Khanh Nguyen

Thi Thu Quyen Nguyen

Hai H. Nguyen

Semyon Novoselov

Julian Nowakowski

Arne Tobias Malkenes Ødegaard

Kazuma Ohara

Miyako Ohkubo

Charles Olivier-Anclin

Eran Omri

Yi Ouyang

Tapas Pal

Ying-yu Pan

Jiaxin Pan

Eugenio Paracucchi

Roberto Parisella

Jeongeun Park

Guillermo Pascual-Perez

Alain Passelègue

Octavio Perez-Kempner

Thomas Peters

Phuong Pham

Cécile Pierrot

Erik Pohle

David Pointcheval

Giacomo Pope

Christopher Portmann

Romain Poussier

Lucas Prabel

Sihang Pu

Chen Qian

Luowen Qian

Tian Qiu

Anaïs Querol

Håvard Raddum

Shahram Rasoolzadeh

Divya Ravi

Prasanna Ravi

Marc Renard

Jan Richter-Brockmann

Lawrence Roy

Paul Rösler

Sayandeep Saha

Yusuke Sakai

Niels Samwel

Paolo Santini

Maria Corte-Real Santos

Sara Sarfaraz

Santanu Sarkar

Or Sattath

Markus Schofnegger

Peter Scholl

Dominique Schröder

André Schrottenloher

Jacob Schuldt

Binanda Sengupta

Srinath Setty

Yantian Shen

Yixin Shen

Ferdinand Sibleyras

Janno Siim

Mark Simkin

Scott Simon

Animesh Singh

Nitin Singh

Sayani Sinha

Daniel Slamanig

Fang Song

Ling Song

Yongsoo Song

Jana Sotakova

Gabriele Spini

Marianna Spyrakou

Lukas Stennes

Marc Stoettinger

Chuanjie Su

Xiangyu Su

Ling Sun

Akira Takahashi

Isobe Takanori

Atsushi Takayasu

Suprita Talnikar

Benjamin Hong Meng Tan

Ertem Nusret Tas

Tadanori Teruya

Masayuki Tezuka

Sri AravindaKrishnan Thyagarajan

Song Tian

Wenlong Tian

Raphael Toledo

Junichi Tomida

Daniel Tschudi

Hikaru Tsuchida

Aleksei Udovenko

Rei Ueno

Barry Van Leeuwen

Wessel van Woerden

Frederik Vercauteren

Sulani Vidhanalage

Benedikt Wagner

Roman Walch

Hendrik Waldner

Han Wang

Luping Wang

Peng Wang

Yuntao Wang

Geng Wang

Shichang Wang

Liping Wang

Jiafan Wang

Zhedong Wang

Kunpeng Wang

Jianfeng Wang

Guilin Wang

Weiqiang Wen

Chenkai Weng

Thom Wiggers

Stella Wohnig

Harry W. H. Wong

Ivy K. Y. Woo

Yu Xia

Zejun Xiang

Yuting Xiao

Zhiye Xie

Yanhong Xu

Jiayu Xu

Lei Xu

Shota Yamada

Kazuki Yamamura

Di Yan

Qianqian Yang

Shaojun Yang

Yanjiang Yang

Li Yao

Yizhou Yao

Kenji Yasunaga

Yuping Ye

Xiuyu Ye

Zeyuan Yin

Kazuki Yoneyama

Yusuke Yoshida

Albert Yu

Quan Yuan

Chen Yuan

Tsz Hon Yuen

Aaram Yun

Riccardo Zanotto

Arantxa Zapico

Shang Zehua

Mark Zhandry

Tianyu Zhang

Zhongyi Zhang

Fan Zhang

Liu Zhang

Yijian Zhang

Shaoxuan Zhang

Zhongliang Zhang

Kai Zhang

Cong Zhang

Jiaheng Zhang

Lulu Zhang

Zhiyu Zhang

Chang-An Zhao
Yongjun Zhao
Chunhuan Zhao
Xiaotong Zhou
Zhelei Zhou

Zijian Zhou
Timo Zijlstra
Jian Zou
Ferdinando Zullo
Cong Zuo

Sponsoring Institutions

- Gold Level Sponsor: Ant Research
- Silver Level Sponsors: Sansec Technology Co., Ltd., Topsec Technologies Group
- Bronze Level Sponsors: IBM, Meta, Sangfor Technologies Inc.

Contents – Part VIII

Quantum Cryptography

Oblivious Transfer from Zero-Knowledge Proofs
Or How to Achieve Round-Optimal Quantum Oblivious Transfer and Zero-Knowledge Proofs on Quantum States

Léo Colisson[1,3](✉) , Garazi Muguruza[2,3], and Florian Speelman[2,3]

[1] Centrum Wiskunde and Informatica, Amsterdam, The Netherlands
leo.colisson@cwi.nl
[2] Informatics Institute, University of Amsterdam, Amsterdam, The Netherlands
{g.muguruzalasa,f.speelman}@uva.nl
[3] QuSoft, Amsterdam, The Netherlands

Abstract. We provide a generic construction to turn any classical Zero-Knowledge (ZK) protocol into a composable (quantum) oblivious transfer (OT) protocol, mostly lifting the round-complexity properties and security guarantees (plain-model/statistical security/unstructured functions...) of the ZK protocol to the resulting OT protocol. Such a construction is unlikely to exist classically as Cryptomania is believed to be different from Minicrypt.

In particular, by instantiating our construction using Non-Interactive ZK (NIZK), we provide the first round-optimal (2-message) quantum OT protocol secure in the random oracle model, and round-optimal extensions to string and k-out-of-n OT.

At the heart of our construction lies a new method that allows us to prove properties on a received quantum state without revealing additional information on it, even in a non-interactive way and/or with statistical guarantees when using an appropriate classical ZK protocol. We can notably prove that a state has been partially measured (with arbitrary constraints on the set of measured qubits), without revealing any additional information on this set. This notion can be seen as an analog of ZK to quantum states, and we expect it to be of independent interest as it extends complexity theory to *quantum* languages, as illustrated by the two new complexity classes we introduce, ZKstatesQIP and ZKstatesQMA.

Keywords: Quantum Cryptography · Oblivious Transfer · Zero-Knowledge on Quantum States · Multi-Party Computing · Zero-Knowledge

1 Introduction

Oblivious Transfer (OT) is an extremely powerful primitive, as it was shown [Kil88] to be sufficient to perform multi-party computing (MPC), allowing multiple parties to jointly compute any function while keeping the input

© International Association for Cryptologic Research 2023
J. Guo and R. Steinfeld (Eds.): ASIACRYPT 2023, LNCS 14445, pp. 3–38, 2023.
https://doi.org/10.1007/978-981-99-8742-9_1

of each party secret. Since the introduction of 2-party computing in the seminal article of Yao [Yao82], followed by the famous generalisation to arbitrary many parties of Goldreich, Micali and Wigderson [GMW87], OT and
MPC received a tremendous amount of attention [Wie83, PVW08, Rab05, EGL85,
CGS02, DGJ+20, KP17, LT22].

However, all classical OT protocols need to use some structured computational assumptions providing trapdoors. Said differently, OT (classically) lives
in *Cryptomania* [Imp95], a world where public-key cryptography exists. On the
other hand, it was recently shown [GLS+21, BCK+21] that quantumly, OT lives
in *MiniQCrypt*, meaning that it is possible to obtain OT protocols using a much
weaker assumption, based only on (unstructured) one-way functions.

There are many reasons to avoid using trapdoor functions. For instance,
this additional structure can often be exploited by quantum computers, leading to attacks. As a result, many OT protocols (based on RSA, quadratic
residue, elliptic curves...) are vulnerable against quantum adversaries. While
some proposals [PVW08, BD18, Qua20] based on post-quantum assumptions like
the Learning-With-Errors problem (LWE) still seem to resist against quantum
adversaries, minimizing assumptions is an important safety-guard against potential future attacks on the computational assumptions. Understanding the minimal required assumptions is also an active field of research, with the recent
introduction of the notion of pseudo-random quantum states [JLS18], which is
an even weaker assumption than one-way functions.

However, while we know (even classical) 2-message OT protocols—optimal
in term of round complexity—achievable using trapdoors [PVW08, BD18], there
is no known round-optimal protocol requiring no structure (such protocol would
necessary be quantum unless Cryptomania collapses to MiniCrypt). The original proposal [CK88] for quantum OT (studied and improved in a long line of
research [BBC+92, MS94, Yao95, DFL+09, Unr10, BF10, GLS+21, BCK+21], see
also this review [SMP22] for quantum OT protocols based on physical assumptions, that we will not cover here) requires 7 messages, and [ABK+22] managed
to obtain a 3-message protocol (computationally secure, in the random oracle
model). However, they left the following question open:

*Does there exist two-message quantum chosen-input bit OT, that allows both
parties to choose inputs?*

They also raise the question of the existence of a 2-message string OT, even
when the bit chosen by the receiver is random. The main bottle-neck to further reduce the communication complexity of these protocols is the use of a
"cut-and-choose" approach, where the receiver sends a quantum state and some
commitments on the description of this state, gets a challenge from the sender
to ensure that the quantum states were honestly prepared, and opens some commitments. Classically, we can avoid cut-and-choose by using Non-Interactive
Zero-Knowledge proofs (NIZK) in order to prove an NP statement on a classical
string without revealing anything on that string except the fact that the statement is true. However, defining NIZK proofs on quantum states is challenging

as any measurement on a quantum state will irremediably alter it. While NIZK proofs on Quantum States (NIZKoQS) have been recently introduced [CGK21] and can be used to prove really advanced properties, they rely on trapdoor functions (LWE), and therefore live in Cryptomania, and are moreover fundamentally only computationally secure. [CGK21] actually raised two open questions:

Is it possible to do NIZKoQS without relying on LWE? Or with statistical security?

Article	Classical	Setup	Messages	MiniQCrypt	Composable	Statistical
[PVW08]	Yes	CRS	2	No (LWE)	Yes	Either
[BD18]	Yes	Plain M.	2	No (LWE)	Sender	Receiver
[CK88] + later works	No	Depends	7	Yes	Yes [DFL+09, Unr10]	Either
[GLS+21]	No	Plain M./ CRS	poly/ cte ≥ 7	Yes	Yes	No
[BCK+21]	No	Plain M./ CRS	poly/ cte ≥ 7	Yes	Yes	Sender
[ABK+22]	No	RO	3	Yes	Yes	No
[BKS23]	No	RO + Shared EPR	2	Yes	Yes	Yes
[BKS23]	No	Shared EPR	1	No (LWE)	Yes	No
This work + [Unr15]	No	RO	2	Yes	Yes	No
This work + [HSS11]	No	Plain M.	> 2	No (LWE)	Yes	No
This work + S-NIZK	No	Like ZK	2	Like ZK	Yes	Sender
This work + NIZK proof	No	Like ZK	2	Like ZK	Yes	Receiver
This work + ZK	No	Like ZK	ZK +1 or 2	Like ZK	Yes	Like ZK

Fig. 1. Comparison with related works. "RO" stands for Random Oracle, "Plain M." stands for "plain model", "Like ZK" means that the properties (mostly) inherit from the property of the underlying ZK protocol, the party in the "statistical" column represents the malicious party allowed to be unbounded to get statistical security (note that using [WW06] we can get statistical security against the other party (of course we lose the statistical security against the first party [Lo97]), at the cost of an additional message).(+1 in the Common Random String model, +2 in the plain model.)

1.1 Contributions

In this work, we answer positively all these open questions. We first state our results on OT protocols (see also Fig. 1 for a table comparing existing works):

Theorem 1.1 (informal). *There exists a (non-black-box[1]) 2-message string OT (even k-out-of-n string OT) quantum protocol composably secure in the*

---

[1] Our protocol requires the use of a hash function h: since we need to prove statements on preimages of h in a ZK protocol, this makes our protocol non-black-box with respect to h since the circuit of h must be known to the verifier. Therefore, even if the assumptions on h (collision-resistant and hiding) are trivially true if h is modelled as a random oracle, we cannot directly run the ZK protocol on an oracle since the source code of h cannot efficiently be sent to the verifier. For this reason, we do not model h itself as an oracle (this assumption is required by the ZK protocol), and only assume that h is collision-resistant and hiding.

random oracle model, assuming the existence of a collision-resistant hiding[2] function.

Actually, we provide a much more generic construction that allows us to obtain a variety of quantum OT protocols, depending on whether we want to optimize the round-complexity, the security (against unbounded sender, or unbounded verifier), the setup model (plain-model, Common Reference String (CRS), Random Oracle), or the computational assumptions (one-way functions, LWE, etc.).

Theorem 1.2 (informal). *Assuming the existence of a collision-resistant hiding one-way function, given any n-message ZK proof (or argument) of knowledge, we can obtain a $n + 1$-message OT[3] protocol (or $n + 2$ in the plain model[4]).*

Moreover, if the ZK protocol is secure against any unbounded verifier (resp. prover) and if the function is statistically hiding (resp. injective), the resulting OT protocol is secure against any unbounded sender (resp. receiver).

Note that classical ZK is a widely studied primitive as it turns out to be extremely useful in many applications, including in MPC, authentication, blockchain protocols [ELE], and more. Trapdoors are not necessary to build ZK as they can be built using only hash functions, and therefore live in Minicrypt. Many candidates have been proposed to achieve various ZK flavors: statistical security against malicious prover or malicious verifier, non-interactive or constant rounds protocols, security in the plain model, CRS, or random oracle [GMR85, Lin13, Unr15, PVW08, BD18, HSS11, PS19]... In this paper, we notably consider the non-interactive ZK protocol of Unruh [Unr15], proven secure in the random oracle model, together with the ZK protocol of Hallgren, Smith and Song [HSS11], proven secure in the plain-model assuming the hardness of LWE, but much work has been done to study ZK under many other assumptions [Wat09, AL20, Unr12, BS20, LMS21].

At the heart of our approach lies the first creation of a (potentially statistically secure when instantiated correctly) ZK protocol on *quantum* states, that can be seen as an extension of ZK and complexity theory to *quantum* languages:

Theorem 1.3 (informal). *Under the same assumptions as Theorem 1.2, a receiver can obtain a quantum state while being sure that a subset T of the qubits*

---

[2] Informally, a hiding function h is a function such that it is not possible to get any information on x given $h(x\|r)$ for sufficiently large random r (this is used for instance in commitments). Actually, we use in practice a weaker assumption called "second-bit hardcore" (the function must only hide the second bit of x), since we believe that we could use the hardcore-bit construction of Goldreich-Levin to weaken the assumptions further by only assuming that the function is one-way.

[3] This holds for all variations of OT: bit OT, string OT, and k-out-of-n OT.

[4] The model of security is the same as the ZK protocol if we want a $n + 2$-message protocol, and if we add the Common (uniform) Reference String assumption (weaker than the Random Oracle model) to provide the hash function, we can obtain a protocol with $n + 1$ messages.

has been measured, without getting any information on T beside the fact that it fulfills some arbitrary fixed constraints.

The resulting protocol is n-message (n + 1 in the plain model), and can in particular be non-interactive when using a NIZK protocol. Statistical security can also be obtained under the conditions described in Theorem 1.2 (the receiver playing the role of the prover, and the sender the verifier).

We also extend the concept of ZK on Quantum State (ZKoQS), together with the notion of *quantum* languages and we define the first two "quantum-language" based complexity classes ZKstatesQIP and ZKstatesQMA. Finally, we prove relations between ZKoQS and various ideal functionalities, we prove that we can realize them, and we show examples of quantum languages belonging to ZKstatesQIP and ZKstatesQMA.

1.2   Overview of the Main Contributions

In this section, we provide a quick, informal, overview of our approach. The OT functionality can be described as follows: a sender, Bob, owns two bits[5] m_0 and m_1, and Alice wants to learn m_b where the bit b is provided as an input. Importantly, a malicious Bob should be unable to learn the value b of Alice, and a malicious Alice should be unable to get information on both m_0 and m_1.

First Attempt: A Naive OT Protocol. A first remark we can make is that if we are given a state in the computational basis $|l\rangle$ for some bit l, rotating it by applying a Z^m gate for some bit m will leave the state unchanged (up to a global phases). On the other hand, if we are given a state in the Hadamard basis $H|r\rangle$ for some bit r, applying a Z^m gate will flip the encoded bit if $m = 1$, giving the state $H|r \oplus m\rangle$. Therefore, we can imagine a naive protocol for OT: Alice could prepare two states $|\psi^{(b)}\rangle := H|r^{(b)}\rangle$ and $|\psi^{(1-b)}\rangle := |l\rangle$ for some random bits $r^{(b)}$ and l, send $|\psi^{(0)}\rangle$ and $|\psi^{(1)}\rangle$ to Bob, Bob could rotate the i-th qubit according to Z^{m_i}, and measure them in the Hadamard basis, getting outcomes $z^{(i)}$ that will be sent back to Alice. In the light of the above comment, it is easy to see that $z^{(b)} = m_b \oplus r^{(b)}$ while $z^{(1-b)}$ is a random bit, uncorrelated with m_{1-b}. Therefore, Alice can easily recover $m_b = z^{(b)} \oplus r^{(b)}$ while she is unable to recover m_{1-b}. Moreover, because the density matrix of $\frac{1}{2}(|0\rangle\langle 0| + |1\rangle\langle 1|) = \frac{1}{2}(|+\rangle\langle +| + |-\rangle\langle -|)$ is the completely mixed state, Bob cannot recover any information on b...

Unfortunately, this protocol is not secure: Alice can easily cheat by sending two $|+\rangle$ states to learn both m_0 and m_1.

The Need for ZK on Quantum State. To avoid this trivial cheating strategy, we would like, informally, to prove to Bob that at least one of the received states is in the computational basis... without revealing the position of this qubit, and without destroying that state. So in a sense, we would like a quantum equivalent of ZK, except that the statement is on a quantum state instead of on a classical bit string.

---

[5] Our approach also works for strings or k-out-of-n OT.

As a first sight, this might seems to contradict laws of physics: it is impossible to learn the basis of a random state, and anyway any measurement would certainly disturb the state. However, we can change a bit the procedure to send $|\psi^{(0)}\rangle$ and $|\psi^{(1)}\rangle$, by sending instead bigger, more structured states encoding the original qubit: Bob would then do some (non-destructive) tests on this large state in order to check that the encoding is valid, and that at least one state is not in superposition, before collapsing it to a 2-qubit system.

At a high level, it is handy to define the encoded state as a superposition of pre-images of multiple (publicly known) images of a given hash function h: To control the number of elements allowed in the superposition, the key idea is to prove (using this time classical ZK), that the sender knows pre-images to all the publicly known images, where some of them are tagged as *dummy*, i.e. forbidden (e.g. by making sure they start with a 0). This way, if we prove that one of the two states admits only a single non-dummy preimage (without revealing which state), this state cannot be in superposition of multiple elements, or it would be possible to extract a collision of the hash function. Of course, this assume that the receiver performs some checks to ensure that the quantum state is a valid encoding and only contains non-dummy preimages of h: this can be done for instance by checking in superposition that all elements are non-dummy (e.g. by measuring the first bit and checking that it's one), and by computing h and checking (in superposition) that it belongs to the set of allowed images. This way, ZK is used on a classical string to verify, indirectly, properties on the quantum state.

More formally, instead of sending $|l\rangle$, we sample a random bit string $w_l^{(1-b)}$ starting with a 0 (this will be important later, but informally this indicates that this is a valid, non-dummy element) and send $|\psi^{(1-b)}\rangle := |l\rangle |w_l^{(1-b)}\rangle$, together with the hash $h_l^{(1-b)} := h(l\|w_l^{(1-b)})$. Similarly, we can apply this idea on states in superposition: instead of sending $|0\rangle + (-1)^{r^{(b)}}|1\rangle$, we sample similarly $w_0^{(b)}$ and $w_1^{(b)}$, and send $|\psi^{(b)}\rangle := |0\rangle |w_0^{(b)}\rangle + (-1)^{r^{(b)}}|1\rangle |w_1^{(b)}\rangle$, together with the hashes $h_0^{(b)} := h(0\|w_0^{(b)})$ and $h_1^{(b)} := h(1\|w_1^{(b)})$. Of course, now, it is relatively easy to distinguish both qubits, as the qubit in the computational basis comes with a single classical hash, while the other comes with two hashes. To avoid this issue, we add a "dummy" hash by sampling a random $w_{1-l}^{(1-b)}$ starting with a 1 (indicating that the hash is dummy), and defining $h_{1-l}^{(1-b)} := h(l\|w_{1-l}^{(1-b)})$. Importantly, given a hash, it is impossible to see if it is a dummy hash, as the hash function is hiding its input. However, Alice can prove to Bob, using classical ZK, that at least one of the provided hashes is a dummy hash, without revealing its position. Therefore, to sum-up, Alice sends the hashes, proves that she knows a preimage for all of them and that one of them is a dummy hash (i.e. its preimage has a 1 in its second position), before sending the states $|\psi^{(0)}\rangle$ and $|\psi^{(1)}\rangle$ to Bob (if the ZK proof is non-interactive, she can send everything in a single message).

Then, after verifying the ZK proof, Bob will verify that $|\psi^{(0)}\rangle$ and $|\psi^{(1)}\rangle$ are in a superposition of valid, non-dummy, preimages. More precisely, for $i \in \{0,1\}$, he applies the unitary $|x\rangle\,|w\rangle\,|0\rangle \rightarrow |x\rangle\,|w\rangle\,|w[1] = 0 \wedge h(x\|w) \in \{h_0^{(i)}, h_1^{(i)}\}\rangle$ on the i-th qubit (after adding an auxiliary qubit), and measures the last register to check if it is equal to 1. Note that for honestly prepared state, this measurement will not alter the state, as the last registers always contains a $|1\rangle$ and can therefore be factored out as the state is separable. Once the check is performed, we can shrink both states to obtain a 2-qubit state by measuring the second register containing the w's in the Hadamard basis, getting two outcomes $s^{(i)}$'s. One can easily check that since $|\psi^{(1-b)}\rangle$ is already in the computational basis, it will not alter the first qubit, resulting in the $|l\rangle$ state, i.e. a qubit in the computational basis. On the other hand, it is not hard to see that the qubit $|\psi^{(b)}\rangle$ will be turned into $|0\rangle\,|w_0^{(b)}\rangle + (-1)^{r^{(b)} \oplus \langle s, w_0^{(b)} \oplus w_1^{(b)}\rangle} |1\rangle$, i.e. the final state will be in the Hadamard basis (the encoded bit might be flipped, but Alice can easily recover that bit flip knowing the outcomes of the measurements).

This way, we are back to the original requirement of the naive oblivious transfer described above: Bob can rotate each qubit i using Z^{m_i}, measure them in the Hadamard basis, and send the outcomes $z^{(i)}$ to Alice, together with the measurements $s^{(0)}$ and $s^{(1)}$. Alice will then be able to recover the final bit m_b by computing $r^{(b)} \oplus \langle s, w_0^{(b)} \oplus w_1^{(b)}\rangle \oplus z^{(b)}$.

This protocol is summarized in Protocol 1, and can easily be generalized to string OT or k-out-of-n OT by sending one "hashed qubit" per bit to transmit, and proving via ZK the wanted properties on the number and position of the dummy hashes (e.g. either the first half of hashes are dummy, or the second half). This will be described in more details below.

Sketch of Security Proof. Interestingly, this method is significantly simpler to analyse than the interactive cut-and-choose approach used in previous works, as illustrated by the long line of research trying to prove the security of the original proposal [BBC+92, MS94, Yao95, DFL+09, Unr10, BF10]. Of course, part of this analysis is offloaded to the ZK protocol, but we like to see it as a feature: this allows us to have a more modular protocol (any improvement on ZK directly implies an improvement on OT), and the analysis only needs to be done once for the *classical* ZK protocol.

At a very high level, since the ZK protocol leaks no information on the witness, and because the hash is hiding[6], Bob learns no information on b. Note that the quantum state does not help as one can see that for any bit string x_0, x_1 the density matrix of $|x\rangle$ where $x \xleftarrow{\$} \{x_0, x_1\}$ is equal to the density matrix of $|x_0\rangle \pm |x_1\rangle$, where the sign is randomly chosen. To translate this informal argument into a composable security proof, we design our simulator by first replacing the ZK proof with a simulated proof (that does not need access to the witness), then we turn the dummy hash into a non-dummy hash (indistinguishable since h is hiding), and we sample $|\psi^{(1-b)}\rangle$ like $|\psi^{(b)}\rangle$ (indistinguishable by the above

---

[6] In practice, we ask for h to be "second-bit hardcore", meaning that it is not possible to learn the second bit of x given $h(x)$, but we could also certainly extend the construction to work for any one-way function using the Goldreich-Levin construction and rejection sampling.

argument on density matrices). This way, the simulator can extract both m_0 and m_1, and provide them to the ideal functionality for OT, that will be in charge of discarding m_{1-b} and outputting m_b. See Theorem 3.1 for more details.

On the other hand, to learn information about both m_0 and m_1, Alice needs to produce two non-collapsed states. But the tests performed by Bob force Alice to send a superposition of non-dummy preimages (in case she does not, the test might pass with some probability, but the state will be anyway projected on a superposition of non-dummy valid preimages in that case). However, by the ZK property, at least one of the classical hashes must be a dummy hash, and therefore if the corresponding qubit contains a superposition of multiple valid preimages, one of them must either collide with the dummy hash, or with the non-dummy one. This collision can even be obtained with non-negligible probability by measuring the state in the computational basis and comparing the outcome with the preimages extracted by the simulator during the ZK protocol. More details can be found in the proof of Theorem 3.1.

Note that if all the properties hold against an unbounded Alice (resp. Bob), notably by instantiating the protocol with a ZK *proof* of knowledge and an injective function h (resp. a statistical ZK and a statistically hiding function) our OT protocol is secure against an unbounded receiver (resp. sender). Note also that since our adversaries are non-uniform, we need to find a way to distribute the function h in such a way that the non-uniform advice cannot depend on h (or it might hardcode a collision). By relying on the CRS assumption (actually a uniformly random string is enough), the hash function can be distributed non-interactively by the CRS (or heuristically replaced with a fixed hash function). If we want to stay in the plain model we can instead ask Bob to sample the function and send it to Alice at the beginning of the protocol, adding an additional message (providing a $(n+2)$-message OT protocol instead of $n+1$, where n is the number of messages of the ZK protocol).

ZKoQS and Quantum Language. The above protocol internally proves a statement on a quantum state, suggesting a quantum analogue to classical Zero-Knowledge and languages. While this notion was introduced in [CGK21] ([CGK21] actually relies on the Learning-With-Error (LWE) problem while we do not require such structure, and they are fundamentally only computationally secure), we extend their definition of ZK, notably introducing the notion of sub-class needed when the protocol is composed into other protocols, and we provide a second, MPC-based point of view.

At a high level, a quantum language is, similarly to classical language $\mathcal{L} \subseteq \{0,1\}^*$, described by a set of quantum states $\mathcal{L}_Q$. Analogously to classical proof systems, where a proof should be accepted only if $x \in L$, quantumly we expect the proof to be accepted only if $\rho \in \mathcal{L}_Q$, where ρ is the obtained quantum state. Classically, we also divide $\mathcal{L}$ into subsets $\mathcal{L}_w$ where w's are called witnesses: during an honest run of the protocol we expect $x \in \mathcal{L}_w$. Similarly, quantumly we divide $\mathcal{L}_Q$ into subsets $\mathcal{L}_{\omega,\omega_s}$, where (ω, ω_s) are classical elements[7] (say bit

---

[7] For instance, you can think of ω as the basis of ρ, and ω_s as the bits encoded in these basis.

strings, we will explain later why we need two elements): like classically[8], we expect to have $\rho \in \mathcal{L}_{\omega,\omega_s} \subseteq \mathcal{L}_{\omega}$ during an honest run of the protocol. ω and ω_s can therefore be seen as a partial classical description of ρ. Finally, classically, the ZK property states that a malicious receiver should not learn w: quantumly we expect a malicious receiver to be unable to learn ω.

Remark 1.4. Despite the similarities of ZKoQS with the corresponding classical notions, there are still a few differences with the classical setting:

- First, classical ZK is typically defined in a "mono-directional" way, where the prover gets as input x and w, and where the verifier learns x and whether x belongs to $\mathcal{L}$. Quantumly, the prover does get ω as input (analog of w), but instead of receiving the classical description of ρ (the analog of x), it *outputs* ω_s, so that (ω, ω_s) (partially) describes ρ. One might wonder why ω_s is not sent as an *input*: While this would certainly be possible, because of the fundamental non-deterministic nature of quantum mechanics, the qubit obtained by the receiver will typically *not* belong to $\mathcal{L}_{\omega,\omega_s}$ after a single round of interaction (typically, while the basis is always the same, the encoded bit is random), so we would need another round of communication to correct the quantum state. In practice, the exact ω_s (encoded bit) does not really matter (but we still want to know its value of course), but we do want to optimize the number of rounds of communications.
- The second question that one might ask is why we only describe *partially* ρ with (ω, ω_s) instead of describing the full classical description of ρ (in practice we do not reveal the bit encoded in the qubit in the computational basis). This can be explained since if we send the full description of ρ, this gives too much information to the adversary (distinguisher), to the point that we are unable to prove the security of the protocol. However, in practice this is not an issue, since the discarded information on ρ is typically a useless random value, not needed in the rest of the protocol.

Extensions, and Formalisation of ZKoQS and Quantum Language. In the rest of the article, we formalize the notion of quantum language (Definition 4.3) and Zero-Knowledge on Quantum states (ZKoQS, Definition 4.5). We define the corresponding complexity classes $\mathsf{ZKstatesQIP}_S[k]$ and $\mathsf{ZKstatesQMA}_S$ (Definition 4.15). While ZKoQS is quite generic, it does not translate naturally to an ideal functionality, useful to prove the security of protocols in the simulation-based and composable quantum standalone framework [HSS11]. As a result, we define a relatively generic ideal functionality that is in charge of applying some measurement operators (Definition 4.8), and we prove that under some assumptions on the measurement operators (called postponable measurements, Definition 4.9), this functionality implies ZKoQS (Theorem 4.10). While for now we

---

[8] Note that in the formal definitions, we actually formalize them using the more general notion of simulators for various reasons, to be compatible with simulation-based proofs, but also since quantumly it is not possible to physically check if a state belongs to a set, since some distributions of quantum states are different but still indistinguishable.

do not know a realization of this functionality for any measurement operator, we consider a particular case (Definition 4.11) where the functionality is in charge of measuring a subset T of qubits (such that $\text{Pred}(T) = \top$ for an arbitrary predicate Pred) and rotating randomly the other qubits. We show in Theorem 4.12 how to realize this functionality, and we prove in Corollary 4.14 that it is a ZKoQS functionality for the language $\mathcal{L}_{\text{SemCol}}^{\text{Pred}}$ of semi-collapsed states (Definition 4.13). We provide in Corollary 4.16 the implications in term of complexity theory (e.g. $\mathcal{L}_{\text{SemCol}}^{\text{Pred}}$ is in ZKstatesQMA^{RO}). We also show in Theorem 4.17 that this functionality can be used to realize a very generic notion of OT protocol that we call Pred-OT, and in particular string-OT and k-out-of-n OT (Corollary 4.18). Finally, since our result requires the use of (NI)ZK protocols, we prove in Sect. 5 that the non-interactive protocol of [Unr15] (proven secure in the RO model) can be expressed in the quantum standalone framework, and can therefore be used in our protocol ([HSS11] already provides another interactive protocol in the plain-model).

1.3   Concurrent Work

A few months after releasing our article online, a related and independent article was posted on the ArXiV [BKS23], but as noted in [BKS23], our contributions are orthogonal, with completely different methods. They indeed assume that adversaries share EPR pairs before starting the protocol (which is a strong assumption), but they show that in this sufficient to obtain 1-message OT assuming the hardness of (sub-exponential) LWE (requiring public-key cryptography), and a 2-message OT in the random oracle setting. See Fig. 1 for a detailed comparison.

1.4   Open Problems and Ongoing Works

We expect our method used to build non-interactive OT to be of independent interest, which also raises a number of open questions. In particular, we do not know if 2-message OT without structure is possible without multi-qubit entanglement, if we can build round-efficient OT from even weaker assumptions, or what are the quantum languages that belong to ZKstatesQMA. More details can be found in the full version [CMS23].

2   Preliminaries

2.1   Notations

We assume basic familiarities with quantum computing [NC10]. For any Hermitian matrix A, we denote its trace norm as $\|A\|_1 := \text{Tr}(\sqrt{A^\dagger A}) = \sum_i |\lambda_i|$ where λ_i's are the eigen-values of A (considered with there multiplicity). We denote the trace distance between two density matrices ρ and σ as $\text{TD}(\rho, \sigma) := \frac{1}{2}\|\rho - \sigma\|_1$. A bipartite state between two registers or parties $\mathbf{A}$ and $\mathbf{B}$ will be denoted $\rho^{\mathbf{A},\mathbf{B}}$. For any bit string x and x', $x[i]$ is the i-th element of x, starting from 1, and

$\langle x, x' \rangle := \oplus_i x[i]x'[x]$. For a gate Z and a quantum state $|\psi\rangle$, $Z^{\mathbf{B},i} |\psi\rangle_{\mathbf{B},\mathcal{E}}$ represents the state obtained after applying Z on the i-th qubit of the register $\mathbf{B}$ of ψ (we might omit the register when it is clear from the context). We might abuse notations and consider that outputting true is the same as outputting 1, but for more complex formulas P it can be handy to define $\delta_P \in \{0,1\}$ such that $\delta_P = 1$ iff P is true.

2.2   Model of Security

We follow the quantum stand-alone security model defined in [HSS11] that we quickly summarize here.

This model of security follows the usual real-world/ideal-world paradigm, where a protocol Π is said to be quantum-standalone (QSA) secure[9] if no environment $\mathbf{Z}$ can distinguish this real world, where corrupted adversaries are replaced with an arbitrary adversary $\mathcal{A}$, from a so-called ideal-world where the distinguisher interacts (through a simulator $\mathbf{S}_\mathcal{A}$) with an ideal functionality $\mathcal{F}$ playing the role of a trusted third-party. More formally, we expect to have $\mathrm{REAL}^\sigma_{\Pi,\mathcal{A},\mathbf{Z}} \approx \mathrm{IDEAL}^{\sigma,\mathcal{F}}$, with $\mathrm{REAL}^\sigma_{\Pi,\mathcal{A},\mathbf{Z}} := \mathbf{Z}((\Pi \leftrightsquigarrow \mathcal{A}) \otimes I)\sigma$ and $\mathrm{IDEAL}^{\sigma,\mathcal{F}}_{\tilde\Pi,\mathbf{S}_\mathcal{A},\mathbf{Z}} := \mathbf{Z}((\tilde\Pi \overset{\mathcal{F}}{\leftrightsquigarrow} \mathbf{S}_\mathcal{A}) \otimes I)\sigma$, $\leftrightsquigarrow$ (resp. $\overset{\mathcal{F}}{\leftrightsquigarrow}$) being the interaction between multiple parties (resp. through the functionality $\mathcal{F}$), and σ being a non-uniform advice. This is pictured in Fig. 2, more details on the framework are available in the full version [CMS23].

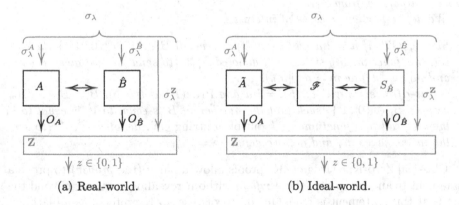

(a) Real-world.   (b) Ideal-world.

Fig. 2. Real-world and ideal-world executions when Bob is malicious.

Some Functionalities. We present here some ideal functionalities used later, starting with the main OT functionality:

Definition 2.1 (Functionality for bit oblivious transfer $\mathcal{F}_{OT}$ [HSS11]). *We define the ideal functionality $\mathcal{F}_{OT}$ for oblivious transfer as follows:*

---

[9] If the security holds against a set of unbounded parties S, we denote it as CS_s-QSA.

– *it receives two messages m_0 and m_1 from Bob's interface, or an abort message*
– *it receives one bit $b \in \{0, 1\}$ from Alice's interface, or an abort message*
– *if no party decided to abort, it sends m_b to Alice.*

We define trivially the dummy parties $\tilde{\Pi} = (\tilde{\mathbf{A}}, \tilde{\mathbf{B}})$ that forward the inputs/outputs to/from $\mathcal{F}_{OT}$.

We will then prove that our protocol can trivially be extended to more advanced OT functionalities. First, we define a generic functionality where the statements can be proven on any predicate on the bits of the message, we will then consider particular cases like string OT (to receive strings instead of bits) or k-out-of-m string OT (to receive k strings among n):

Definition 2.2 (Functionality for predicate oblivious transfer $\mathcal{F}_{OT}^{\mathrm{Pred}}$).
Let $n \in \mathbb{N}$ and $\mathrm{Pred}: \mathcal{P}([n]) \to \{0, 1\}$ be a predicate[10] on any subset of bits. We define the ideal functionality $\mathcal{F}_{OT}^{Pred}$ for predicate oblivious transfer as follows:

– *It receives n bits $(m_i)_{i \in [n]}$ from Bob's interface, or an abort message.*
– *It receive a subset $B \subseteq [n]$ from Alice's interface (we might also encode B as a bit string, where $B[x] = 1$ iff $x \in B$), or an abort message.*
– *If $B = \bot$ or $\mathrm{Pred}(B) = \bot$, it sends an abort message to Bob.*
– *If no party decided to abort and $\mathrm{Pred}(B) = \top$, it sends $(m_i)_{i \in B}$ to Alice. Otherwise it sends $\bot$ to all parties.*

We define trivially the dummy parties $\tilde{\Pi} = (\tilde{\mathbf{A}}, \tilde{\mathbf{B}})$ that forward the inputs/outputs to/from $\mathcal{F}_{OT}$.
    We define particular cases of interest:

– **String OT**: *If $n = 2m$ and $\mathrm{Pred}(B)$ is true iff $B \in \{1^m 0^m, 0^m 1^m\}$ then we call this functionality string OT, denoted $\mathcal{F}_{OT}^{str}$ (to send the two messages m_a and m_b, we define $m = m_a \| m_b$).*
– **k-out-of-m string OT**: *If $n = lm$ and $\mathrm{Pred}(B)$ is true iff $B = B_1 \| \dots B_m$ with $\forall i, B_i \in \{0^l, 1^l\}$, such that the number of B_i's equal to 1^l is equal to k, then we call this functionality k-out-of-m string OT, denoted $\mathcal{F}_{OT}^{k-m}$ (to sent the m messages m_a and m_b, we define $m = m_a \| m_b$).*

Classical Zero-Knowledge (ZK) proofs allow a party (the *prover*) to prove a statement to another party (the *verifier*) without revealing anything beyond the fact that this statement is true. Our protocols use a ZK protocol as a blackbox. We define now the functionality corresponding to ZK.

Definition 2.3 (Functionality for zero-knowledge $\mathcal{F}_{ZK}^{\mathcal{R}}$ [HSS11]). *We define the ideal functionality $\mathcal{F}_{ZK}^{\mathcal{R}}$ for zero-knowledge, where $\mathcal{R}$ is a relation describing a given language $\mathcal{L}$ ($x \in \mathcal{L} \Leftrightarrow \exists w, x\mathcal{R}w$):*

---

[10] This predicate might depend on a secret witness w known only to the prover, in which case we always replace $\mathrm{Pred}(\cdots)$ with $\mathrm{Pred}(w, \cdots)$, w being sent to the ideal functionalities and used in the ZK proofs. For simplicity, we will omit the witness from now.

– *it receives (x, w) from the prover's (a.k.a. Alice) interface or an abort message $\bot$,*
– *if $x\mathcal{R}w$ then the verifier (a.k.a. Bob) receives x otherwise it receives $\bot$.*

This functionality also implies that the ZK protocol is a *proof of knowledge* protocol (PoK, quantumly it is also know as *state-preserving* as extracting the witness should not disturb the state of the adversary) as the functionality can extract the witness. But our protocol could be proven secure in different ways:

– One of them is to assume that the protocol is a state-preserving PoK (PoK is not needed to extract m_0 and m_1 from a malicious Bob, but is handy to extract b from a malicious Alice). That's the approach taken in this paper since it has the advantage of applying also in the plain model.
– It should also be possible to obtain similar guarantees without state-preserving PoK, notably by assuming that the simulator can extract the queries made to the oracle (either by relying on Common Reference String (CRS) or on the random oracle model (ROM)). However, this approach is less modular and seems to rely heavily on CRS/RO and is therefore harder to generalize to the plain model. Moreover, we already know state-preserving NIZK PoK in the RO model [Unr15], so this second approach seems less interesting and will not be explored in this article.

Moreover, we often make the distinction between ZK arguments (computational soundness against malicious prover), ZK proofs (statistical soundness against malicious prover) and statistical ZK (ZK also holds against a malicious unbounded verifier). In the quantum stand-alone formalism, ZK proofs are protocols that $\mathsf{CS}_P\text{-}\mathsf{QSA}$ realize $\mathcal{F}^{\mathcal{R}}_{ZK}$ and statistical ZK are protocols that $\mathsf{CS}_V\text{-}\mathsf{QSA}$ realize $\mathcal{F}^{\mathcal{R}}_{ZK}$.

Note that nearly all the properties of our protocol reduce to the properties of the ZK scheme. If we use a Non-Interactive ZK (NIZK) protocol secure in the Quantum Random Oracle (OT) model or in the Common Reference String (CRS) model, then our final protocols will be optimal in term of round complexity (2-message OT, or 1-message NIZKoQS) but will rely on the RO or CRS assumption. On the other hand, we may prefer to use a n-message NIZK protocol in the plain model: in that case our protocols will be secure in the plain model, and the communication complexity will be n for the NIZKoQS protocol, resulting in an $n + 1$-message OT protocol.

There are multiple protocols realising the $\mathcal{F}^{\mathcal{R}}_{ZK}$ functionality, either in the plain model [HSS11] or non-interactively in the random-oracle model [Unr15] (this last work is not expressed in the quantum stand-alone model, but we prove in Sect. 5 that it can be reformulated in this framework).

Because we are dealing with non-uniform adversaries, we need to sample hash functions independently of the non-uniform advice, and this is usually done via a Common-Reference-String (CRS) assumption. CRS assumes that a string, honestly sampled according to a fixed procedure, can be shared among all parties (this is typically not counted in the communication as in practice we can often heuristically take a publicly known string instead, for instance by feeding the generation procedure with a known uniformly sampled string... unless the sampling needs trapdoor which is not our case here). While this adds an assumptions, it can be practical sometimes to obtain more efficient protocols (in term of communication complexity), and often can be heuristically replaced by a publicly known string (e.g. if the string contains the description of a collision resistant function like in our case, we might pick the well known SHA-256 hash function instead). Note that our protocol can also be realized without a CRS assumption at the cost of an additional message as discussed in Sect. 3.2 and in Lemma 2.10. We model CRS as an ideal functionality:

Definition 2.4. *Let* Gen *be a PPT sampling procedure. Then the ideal functionality* $\mathcal{F}_{CRS}^{Gen}$ *samples* $x \leftarrow$ Gen(1^λ) *and outputs* x *to all parties.*

2.3   Cryptographic Requirements

Before stating our security guarantees, we need to define some security definitions. A function is said to have a hardcore second-bit if it is hard to find the second bit of x given $h(x)$ (note that this notion is weaker than the more standard notion of hiding as we only need to hide a single bit). More formally:

Definition 2.5 (Hardcore second-bit). *We say that a function h has a computational (resp. statistical) hardcore second-bit property if there exists two polynomials n and m, such that for any $l \in \{0,1\}$, any QPT (resp. unbounded) adversary $\mathcal{A}$ and for any advice $\sigma = \{\sigma_\lambda\}_{\lambda \in \mathbb{N}}$:*

$$\left| \Pr\left[\mathcal{A}(\lambda, \sigma_\lambda, h(x)) = 1 \mid x \xleftarrow{\$} \{l\} \times \{0\} \times \{0,1\}^{n(\lambda)} \right] \right. \\ \left. - \Pr\left[\mathcal{A}(\lambda, \sigma_\lambda, h(x)) = 1 \mid x \xleftarrow{\$} \{l\} \times \{1\} \times \{0,1\}^{n(\lambda)} \right] \right| \leq \mathsf{negl}(\lambda)[\lambda] \tag{1}$$

We extend this definition to a family of functions $\{h_k \colon \{0,1\}^{n(\lambda)} \rightarrow \{0,1\}^{m(\lambda)}\}_{k \in \mathcal{K}}$ if for any $k \in \mathcal{K}$, h_k has a computational hardcore second-bit property, and if one can efficiently check for any k whether $k \in \mathcal{K}$ or not.

We note that many functions have (or are expected to have) a hardcore second-bit property, in particular since it can be seen as a special case of hiding. It is the case for random functions (e.g. in the RO model), where it is even possible to get statistical security if the function is lossy (i.e. many inputs map to the same output), and we expect it to be true for hash functions used nowadays since they are believed to be hiding. We note that people often consider a weaker assumption called hardcore bit predicate (even achievable from any one-way function thanks to the Goldreich-Levin construction [GL89]), where the unknown bit is a fixed predicate $b(x)$ instead of the second bit of x. While we believe that our construction could be adapted to that setting (by doing a rejection sampling to find x such that $b(x)$ has the right value), this complicates the constructions, so we leave this extension for further work. We will therefore keep this construction for future works.

Definition 2.6 (Collision resistance). *A family of functions* $\{h_k\colon \{0,$ $1\}^{l(\lambda)} \to \{0,1\}^{m(\lambda)}\}_{k\in\mathcal{K}}$ *is said to be (computationally) collision-resistant if there exists a polynomial generation algorithm* $k \leftarrow \mathsf{Gen}_h(1^\lambda)$ *such that for any* $k \in \mathcal{K}$, h_k *can be classically evaluated in polynomial time, and for any (potentially non-uniform)* QPT *adversary* $\mathcal{A}$ *and advice* $\{\sigma_\lambda\}_{\lambda\in\mathbb{N}}$:

$$\Pr\left[x \neq x' \wedge h_k(x) = h_k(x') \mid k \leftarrow \mathsf{Gen}_h(1^\lambda), (x,x') \leftarrow \mathcal{A}(k,\sigma_\lambda)\right] \leq \mathsf{negl}(\lambda) \quad (2)$$

Remark 2.7. Note that we do not directly require the functions to be collapsable [Unr16]—which is often required when considering quantum adversaries—as we can show that any attack leads to the finding of a collision. However, we do require the existence of a ZK proof of knowledge scheme, that may, in turn, require the existence of such a function. Moreover, when considering unbounded provers, the function is expected to be statistically collision-resistant, i.e. injective, and is therefore collapsing.

Note that even if we heuristically expect the protocol to stay secure when we replace h_k with a fixed hash function like SHA-256, to prove the security we need to sample the function h_k after the beginning of the protocol. The reason is that the adversaries are non-uniform (i.e. get an arbitrary advice), and the advice could contain a collision if it was chosen after h_k. As a result, one needs to decide who is going to sample h_k, leading to various tradeoffs:

- If we let a user[11] sample the function, then we need to send an additional message from Bob to Alice, but on the other side we are in the plain-model.
- Otherwise, we can assume that the circuit of h_k is provided by a CRS, which requires no additional round of communication, but we are not anymore in the plain-model.

In order to keep the proof independent of this choice, we abstract the distribution of the value of h_k in an ideal functionality:

Definition 2.8. *Let* $\{h_k\colon \{0,1\}^{l(\lambda)} \to \{0,1\}^{m(\lambda)}\}_{k\in\mathcal{K}}$ *be a family of collision resistant functions generated by* Gen, *with a hardcore second-bit property. Then, we define the ideal functionality* $\mathcal{F}_H^{\mathsf{Gen}}$ *as follows.* $\mathcal{F}_H^{\mathsf{Gen}}$ *receives an input* c *from Bob's interface, if* $c = \top$, *the functionality samples* $k \leftarrow \mathsf{Gen}(1^\lambda)$ *and sends* k *to both parties, otherwise if* $c \in \mathcal{K}$, *it forwards* c *to Alice's interface. The ideal party* $\mathbf{A}_I$ *just forwards the received* k, *while the ideal party* $\mathbf{B}_I$ *sends* $c = \top$ *to the functionality and outputs the received* k.

We prove now that this functionality can be realized in the plain-model with one message or non-interactively in the CRS model.

Lemma 2.9 ($\mathcal{F}_H$ in the CRS model). *In the CRS model (a.k.a.* $\mathcal{F}_{CRS}^{\mathsf{Gen}}$-*hybrid model), the trivial* 0-*message protocol where both Alice and Bob output the value given by* $\mathcal{F}_{CRS}^{\mathsf{Gen}}$ *realizes the functionality* $\mathcal{F}_H^{\mathsf{Gen}}$.

---

[11] Only Bob can sample the function as collision resistance must hold against Alice and a malicious Alice could cheat when generating the function.

The proof in the full version [CMS23].

Lemma 2.10 ($\mathcal{F}_H$ in the plain model). *The 1-message protocol where Bob samples $x \leftarrow \text{Gen}(1^\lambda)$ and sends x to Alice, and Alice outputs x only if $x \in \mathcal{K}$ realizes the functionality $\mathcal{F}_H^{\text{Gen}}$ in the plain model.*

The proof in the full version [CMS23].

3 Protocol for Bit OT

3.1 The Protocol

While we will define formally ZKoQS later, together with more advanced OT protocols (string-OT, k-out-of-n OT...), in this section we provide a self-contained description and security proof of our bit-OT protocol. For an intuitive explanation of our protocol, we refer to the overview in Sect. 1.2. The bit OT protocol is described in Protocol 1.

3.2 Security Proof

We prove now our main theorem, i.e. that Protocol 1 securely realizes the OT functionality.

Theorem 3.1 (Security and correctness). *Let $\{h_k\}_{k \in \mathcal{K}}$ be a family of collision resistant functions sampled by* Gen, *having the hardcore second-bit property (Definition 2.5). Let $\Pi_h = (\mathbf{A}_h, \mathbf{B}_h)$ be a protocol[12] CS_{S_h}-QSA realizing $\mathcal{F}_{CRS}^{\text{Gen}}$ and $\Pi_{zk} = (\mathbf{A}_{zk}, \mathbf{B}_{zk})$ be a protocol that CS_S-QSA realizes the ZK functionality $\mathcal{F}_{ZK}^{\mathcal{R}}$, where $(h_0^0, h_1^0, h_0^1, h_1^1)\mathcal{R}(w_0^0, w_1^0, w_0^1, w_1^1) \Leftrightarrow \forall c, d, h(d\|w_d^c) = h_d^c$ and $\exists c, d$ such that $w_d^c[1] = 1$.*

Then the Protocol 1, in which h is obtained by first running Π_h, C-QSA realizes the functionality $\mathcal{F}_{OT}$. More precisely, it $CS_{S'}$-QSA realizes $\mathcal{F}_{OT}$ for any set S' of unbounded parties such that:

- $S' \subseteq S \cap S_h$,
- $\{\mathbf{B}\} \in S'$ *only if h has the statistical hardcore second-bit property,*
- $\{\mathbf{A}\} \in S'$ *only if for any $k \in \mathcal{K}$, h_k is injective (i.e. statistically collision resistant).*

Sketch of Proof. For a first intuitive proof of the correctness and security, we refer to the corresponding paragraph in Sect. 1.2. We provide here only a sketch

---

[12] As a reminder, this protocol is sampling and distributing a function h according to Gen, and can either be done without communication in the CRS model (or heuristically if we replace h with a well known collision-resistant hash function), or with one message in the plain model.

Protocol 1: Protocol for (possibly 2-message) bit Oblivious Transfer

---

Inputs: Alice gets $b \in \{0,1\}$ as input, Bob gets $(m_0, m_1) \in \{0,1\}^2$

Assumption: $(\mathbf{A}_{zk}, \mathbf{B}_{zk})$ is a n-message ZK protocol (Definition 2.3), h is a collision-resistant (Definition 2.6) and second-bit hardcore (Definition 2.5) function distributed using $\mathcal{F}_H$ (Definition 2.8), either non-interactively via a CRS, heuristically using a fixed hash function, or sent by Bob, adding an additional message (Lemma 2.10).

Protocol:

1. **Alice** samples $l \in \{0,1\}$, $(w_0^{(b)}, w_1^{(b)}, w_l^{(1-b)}) \xleftarrow{\$} (\{0\} \times \{0,1\}^n)^3$ and $w_{1-l}^{(1-b)} \xleftarrow{\$} \{1\} \times \{0,1\}^n$, and computes for all $(c,d) \in \{0,1\}^2$, $h_d^{(c)} := h(d\|w_d^{(c)})$. Then, she sends $(h_d^{(c)})_{c\in\{0,1\},d\in\{0,1\}}$ to Bob (if the ZK protocol is non-interactive she can send it later in a single message with the NIZK proof and the quantum states) and runs the ZK protocol $\mathbf{A}_{zk}$ with Bob (running $\mathbf{B}_{zk}$) to prove that:

$$\exists (w_d^{(c)})_{c\in\{0,1\},d\in\{0,1\}}, \forall c, d, h_d^{(c)} = h(d\|w_d^{(c)})) \text{ and } \exists c, d \text{ s.t. } w_d^{(c)}[1] = 1 \quad (3)$$

Then, she samples $r^{(b)} \xleftarrow{\$} \{0,1\}$ together with:

$$|\psi^{(b)}\rangle := |0\rangle |w_0^{(b)}\rangle + (-1)^{r^{(b)}} |1\rangle |w_1^{(b)}\rangle \qquad |\psi^{(1-b)}\rangle := |l\rangle |w_l^{(1-b)}\rangle \quad (4)$$

Finally, she sends $(|\psi^{(0)}\rangle, |\psi^{(1)}\rangle)$ to Bob.

2. **Bob** verifies the ZK proof. Then, he verifies that the quantum state is honestly prepared by adding an auxiliary qubit and running the unitary:

$$|x\rangle |w\rangle |0\rangle \mapsto |x\rangle |w\rangle |w[1] \neq 1 \wedge h(x\|w) = \{h_0^{(c)}, h_1^{(c)}\}\rangle \quad (5)$$

and measuring the last auxiliary register, checking if it is equal to 1. If not, he aborts (and sends an abort message to Alice), otherwise he measures the second registers of $|\psi^{(0)}\rangle$ and $|\psi^{(1)}\rangle$ in the Hadamard basis (getting outcomes $(s^{(0)}, s^{(1)})$). Note that at that step, the first register of $|\psi^{(b)}\rangle$ contains a $|\pm\rangle$ state while $|\psi^{(1-b)}\rangle$ contains $|l\rangle$: this fact will be called ZKoQS later. Then, for any $c \in \{0,1\}$, Bob applies Z^{m_c} on $|\psi^{(c)}\rangle$ and measures it in the Hadamard basis $(\{|+\rangle, |-\rangle\})$, getting outcome $z^{(c)}$. Bob sends back $(s^{(c)}, z^{(c)})_{c\in\{0,1\}}$ to Alice.

3. **Alice** computes $\alpha := r^{(b)} \oplus \bigoplus_i s^{(b)}[i](w_0^{(b)} \oplus w_1^{(b)})[i]$ and outputs $\alpha \oplus z^{(b)}$ (that should be equal to m_b).

---

of the proof, and we refer the reader to the full security proof in the full version [CMS23].

Malicious Sender (Bob). We consider the case where the adversary $\mathcal{A} = \hat{\mathbf{B}}$ corrupts the sender Bob. Informally the goal of the simulator $\mathbf{S}_{\hat{\mathbf{B}}}$ is to extract the two values m_0 and m_1 from $\hat{\mathbf{B}}$ to provide these two values to the ideal functionality. To that end, at a high level, the simulator will interact with $\hat{\mathbf{B}}$ by providing a transcript that an honest Alice could provide, except that $|\psi^{(1-b)}\rangle$ is sampled like $|\psi^{(b)}\rangle$: since the state is now in the Hadamard basis, it can also recover m_{1-b} following the procedure used by Alice to recover m_b. However, because it is now impossible to run the ZK proof (because the statement is not even true!) the simulator will run instead the simulator of the ZK proof to convince the distinguisher that the statement is true while it is not. To prove that this simulator is valid, we write a series of hybrid games: we start from the protocol where Alice is honest, then we replace the ZK proof with the simulated proof (indistinguishable by the ZK property). In the next step we sample w_{1-b} as a non-dummy witness (i.e. starting with a 0, indistinguishable because the function h is hiding). Then we set $|\psi^{(1-b)}\rangle = |0\rangle |w_0^{(1-b)}\rangle + (-1)^{r^{(1-b)}} |1\rangle |w_1^{(1-b)}\rangle$ where $r^{(1-b)} \leftarrow \{0,1\}$ is sampled uniformly at random (indistinguishable because the density matrices are equal: for any (potentially known) string x and y, $\frac{1}{2}(|x\rangle\langle x| + |y\rangle\langle y|) = \frac{1}{4}\sum_{r \in \{0,1\}}(|x\rangle + (-1)^r |y\rangle)(\langle x| + (-1)^r \langle y|)$. Note that one might be worried that the output of Alice leaks additional information on this quantum state: however, the output of Alice is linked with the *other*, non-dummy, quantum state and any additional information regarding this dummy state are anyway discarded. Finally, we can now apply the decoding performed by Alice on both outputs and output only the one corresponding to m_b: this is exactly the role of the ideal functionality. Since nothing depends on any secret (except this very last step where the functionality discards m_{1-b} and outputs m_b), the simulator can fully run this procedure. See the full version for details.

Malicious Receiver (Alice). We consider now the case where the adversary $\mathcal{A} = \hat{\mathbf{A}}$ corrupts the receiver Alice.

Informally the goal of the simulator $\mathbf{S}_{\hat{\mathbf{A}}}$ is to extract the value b from Alice in order to provide this value to the ideal functionality, and to appropriately use the m_b provided by the functionality to fake measurement outcomes expected by Alice. At a high level, since the ZK protocol is a (state-preserving) proof (or argument) of knowledge (PoK), we can use this property to extract the witnesses $(w_d^{(c)})_{c,d}$. From this witness we can find a $w_d^{(b)}$ that starts with a 1 in order to learn b. Then, to fake the measurement outcomes, the simulator can apply exactly the same quantum operations as the one done by the honest Bob, using the m_b given by the functionality, except that the simulator will choose $m_{1-b} = 0$. Note that if the malicious Alice really sent a state $|\psi^{(1-b)}\rangle$ in the computational basis, then the $Z^{m_{1-b}}$ rotation does nothing, irrespective of the value of m_{1-b}. Now, if Alice sent a state that is in superposition of two pre-images with non-negligible amplitude, since it must pass the test checking that it contains non-dummy preimage of h, then it means that Alice "knows" a collision for h... or rather, we can measure the state to get a first preimage and compare it with the preimages extracted during the ZK protocol to get another preimage: with non-negligible probability (on the measurement outcome) they will be different, breaking the collision resistant property of h which contradicts our assumption. Note that some care must be taken as the probability of finding a collision differs across runs, but we can formalize this argument as shown is the full proof. In practice, we will define a few hybrid games, by first replacing the distribution of h and the ZK protocol by their simulated versions (since the ZK is a PoK, the simulator can learn b and the preimages of h), then we remove the $Z^{m_{1-b}}$ rotation (indistinguishable or the state is far from a state in the computational basis, in which case we can recover a collision). Finally, since this does not depend on the secret m_{1-b}, we can reorganize the elements to recover the ideal word. See the full security proof in the full version [CMS23] for more details.   □

4   (NI)ZKoQS and k-out-of-n String OT

4.1   ZKoQS

The main contribution in our main protocol (Protocol 1) is to provide a method to prove (potentially non-interactively) a statement on a received quantum state without revealing much information beside the fact that this statement is true: we call this property (Non-Interactive) Zero-Knowledge proofs on Quantum State ((NI)ZKoQS), by analogy with their classical analogue. While we have not yet introduced formally this definition in order to provide a self-contained OT protocol and proof, we will address this issue here.

NIZKoQS were introduced in [CGK21], but the protocol we present here is using a very different approach. While [CGK21] can be used to prove more advanced properties on the obtained quantum state, it also has multiple drawbacks that were left as open questions:

- First, while their protocol is purely classical, their approach is fundamentally *incompatible with statistical security* (like other potential approaches based on quantum multi-party computing [DNS12, DGJ+20, KKL+23], since these protocols build upon classical MPC, which are not only impossible to do with statistical security [Lo97], but they also require OT, which is one application of ZKoQS). A malicious unbounded verifier/receiver can always fully describe the received state. On the other hand, with our approach we can get statistical security for both parties (not as the same time).
- Secondly, [CGK21] relies on lattice based cryptography (LWE), living in Cryptomania, and the protocol is really *costly* to implement in practice as the parameters used in the LWE instance lead to very large functions. On the other side, our approach only relies on hash functions, does not exploit any structure or trapdoors, and is therefore much more efficient.

Note that the definition of ZKoQS introduced in [CGK21] is slightly too restrictive for our setting as their notion of quantum language does not allow states to be ε-close to the quantum language, the states cannot be entangled with an adversary, they omit the step where the description is given back to the sender (which is important when the protocol is used in other protocols), and their adversaries are QPT. For this last reason, we introduce different notations inspired by classical ZK proofs: when the prover is unbounded (resp. bounded) we say that we have a ZK *proof* (resp. *argument*) on quantum states, denoted ZKPoQS (resp. ZKAoQS). When the verifier is unbounded, we say that we have a statistical ZKoQS (S-ZKoQS). Note than when the protocol in Non-Interactive (a single message from the prover to the verifier), we replace the "ZK" with "NIZK" in these acronyms. We formalize now these concepts.

Quantum Language. First, we define a quantum language (we draw a parallel with classical ZK in the pictures in the full version, and illustrate this with an example in Example 4.1), which is informally speaking a set $\mathcal{L}_Q$ of bipartite quantum states on two registers V and P that characterizes all states that a malicious adversary might be able to obtain (the register V being controlled by the honest verifier, and P by the malicious prover and/or the environment[13]). Moreover, we also provide additional information on the honest expected behavior, via sets of (bipartite[14]) quantum states $\mathcal{L}_\omega \subseteq \mathcal{L}_Q$: when the prover is given as input a *class* ω (the quantum equivalent[15] of witnesses), we expect the final state to belong to $\mathcal{L}_\omega$. Because there might be many states in $\mathcal{L}_\omega$, the prover will also output a subclass ω_s to further describe the final state, interpreted as "the verifier obtained a state belonging to $\mathcal{L}_{\omega,\omega_s} \subseteq \mathcal{L}_\omega \subseteq \mathcal{L}_Q$".

Example 4.1. For instance, one might be interested in $\mathcal{L}_Q$ defined as the set of states where the registers V contains exactly two qubits, where at least one of them is non-entangled with any other qubit and collapsed in the computational basis (think "even if the prover is malicious, any state obtained by the verifier belongs to $\mathcal{L}_Q$, i.e. contains at least one qubit collapsed in the computational basis). For the honest behavior, we can for instance define $\mathcal{L}_{0,0} = \{|+\rangle|0\rangle, |+\rangle|1\rangle\}$, $\mathcal{L}_{0,1} = \{|-\rangle|0\rangle, |-\rangle|1\rangle\}$, $\mathcal{L}_{1,0} = \{|0\rangle|+\rangle, |1\rangle|+\rangle\}$, $\mathcal{L}_{1,1} = \{|0\rangle|-\rangle, |1\rangle|-\rangle\}$, $\mathcal{L}_0 = \mathcal{L}_{0,0} \cup \mathcal{L}_{0,1}$ and $\mathcal{L}_1 = \mathcal{L}_{1,0} \cup \mathcal{L}_{1,1}$: this way,

---

[13] Sometimes, we will write (P, **Z**) instead of P to denote a more precise cut between the two sub-registers owned by the prover and the environment.

[14] Contrary to $\mathcal{L}_Q$ that must represent all states potentially obtainable by a malicious party (hence the need of a second register), here $\mathcal{L}_\omega$ are only used to denote the states obtainable by honest parties, and can therefore often be seen as a set of states on a single register owned by the verifier. The reason we define it as a bipartite state here is that we might later be interested by the generation of truly bipartite states like graph states.

[15] Note that classically, we can see a witness in two different ways: it can be used to efficiently verify that $x \in \mathcal{L}$, but more abstractly it can be seen as a way to partition $\mathcal{L}$ into multiple $\mathcal{L}_w$'s: in an honest setting, given w, we expect to have $x \in \mathcal{L}_w$, where $\mathcal{L}_w = \{x \mid x\mathcal{R}w\}$. Quantumly, we will use this second point of view, as given ω (the quantum equivalent of w) we expect in an honest setting to have $\rho \in \mathcal{L}_\omega$, even if ω cannot be used directly to verify that property once ρ is generated because of the laws of physics.

Oblivious Transfer from Zero-Knowledge Proofs   23

if the prover gets input 0 and outputs 1, the verifier is expected to output a state in $\mathcal{L}_{0,1} = \{|-\rangle |0\rangle, |-\rangle |1\rangle\}$: the class ω represents the position of the state in the Hadamard basis, and the sub-class ω_s represents the value encoded in this state.

Remark 4.2 (On the choice of definition of ω and ω_s). Note that (ω, ω_s) only partially describes the state (in our example above, we remove the description of the state in the computational basis) as otherwise we are unable to prove the security of the scheme (but the lost information on ρ is anyway of no interest since it is discarded in the OT protocol). One might also ask why ω_s is sent as an output and is not part of the input ω: while in some cases it might be possible to move everything inside the input ω and remove ω_s (e.g. if we got a $|+\rangle$ instead of a $|-\rangle$ the prover could send another message "apply an additional Z gate" to flip the encoded qubit), but this comes at the cost of an additional message. In most applications, the exact value of ω_s does not really matter as it is only a random key, while saving an additional round of communication is important.

Definition 4.3 (Quantum Language). *Let $E^{\mathsf{V},\mathsf{P}} = \cup_{(n,m)\in\mathbb{N}^2}\mathcal{L}_0(\mathcal{H}_n \otimes \mathcal{H}_m)$ be the set of finite dimensional quantum states on two registers. A quantum language $(\mathcal{L}_Q, \mathcal{C}, \mathcal{C}_s, \{\mathcal{L}_{\omega,\omega_s}\}_{\omega\in\mathcal{C},\omega_s\in\mathcal{C}_s})$ is characterized by a set $\mathcal{L}_Q \subseteq E^{\mathsf{V},\mathsf{P}}$ of bipartite quantum states[16], a set $\mathcal{C} \subseteq \{0,1\}^*$ of classes (or witnesses) motivated above, a set $\mathcal{C}_s \subseteq \{0,1\}^*$ of sub-classes, and for any $\omega \in \mathcal{C}, \omega_s \in \mathcal{C}_s$, a set $\mathcal{L}_{\omega,\omega_s}$ of bipartite quantum states called quantum sub-classes. We also define for any $\omega, \mathcal{L}_\omega = \cup_{\omega_s\in\mathcal{C}_s}\mathcal{L}_{\omega,\omega_s}$ (some of these sets might be empty in case ω is not a valid class), and require $\cup_\omega\mathcal{L}_\omega \subseteq \mathcal{L}_Q$. Moreover, for any set of quantum states $\mathcal{L}$, we define $\rho \in_\varepsilon \mathcal{L} \Leftrightarrow \exists\sigma \in \mathcal{L}, \mathrm{TD}(\rho,\sigma) \leq \varepsilon$, and $\rho \notin_\varepsilon \mathcal{L} \Leftrightarrow \neg(\rho \in_\varepsilon \mathcal{L})$.*

ZKoQS. We introduce now ZKoQS, that morally provides three guarantees, similar to classical ZK:

- **Correctness**: if the parties are honest, the prover is given a class ω and ends up with the partial (cf. Remark 4.2) description (ω, ω_s) of the state ρ obtained by the verifier, i.e. such that $\rho \in \mathcal{L}_{\omega,\omega_s} \subseteq \mathcal{L}_\omega \subseteq \mathcal{L}_Q$.
- **Soundness**: if the sender is malicious, the honest receiver still ends up with a state $\rho \in \mathcal{L}_Q$.
- **Zero-Knowledge**: if the verifier is malicious, they cannot learn the value of the class/witness ω.

Example 4.4. To continue our above Example 4.1, the correctness guarantees that given an input bit $\omega \in \{0,1\}$, the ω-th qubit of ρ is $H |\omega_s\rangle$ while the other qubit is in the computational basis (we lose the information of the encoded value). The soundness mostly guarantees that even if the sender is malicious, the

---

[16] $\mathcal{L}_Q$ represents informally the set of states that any malicious party can generate, where the first register is the output of the verifier and the second register corresponds to registers potentially controlled by an adversary. Since only $\mathcal{L}_Q$ is needed to characterize the security of a protocol, it is sometimes called directly the quantum language.

received quantum state contains at least one qubit collapsed in the computational basis. The ZK property guarantees that a malicious verifier cannot learn ω, the expected position of the qubit in the Hadamard basis.

Note that the formal definition is given with respect to a "simulator", simulating the whole protocol (and not anymore a single malicious party as usual), including in the soundness and correctness part (while usually simulators are only used in the ZK part). While we could define it without any simulator to get a more restricted definition (and during a first read, it might actually be easier to replace the simulator with the original process), simulators are helpful for multiple reasons to make the definition more useful:

- **In zero-knowledge**: the typical ZK definitions already use simulators to denote the fact the we can simulate the view of the malicious verifier without access to the witness... Therefore it should come at no surprise that we also use a simulator in the ZK property.
- **In soundness**: In a real protocol, a malicious prover might be able to produce states negligibly close (in trace distance) to the quantum language $\mathcal{L}_Q$, but not strictly speaking *in* $\mathcal{L}_Q$. One might be tempted to introduce an approximate notion $\rho \in_\varepsilon \mathcal{L}_Q$ taking into account trace distance to fix this issue, unfortunately it is not sufficient as this definition does not take into account states that are statistically speaking far from $\mathcal{L}_Q$, but computationally speaking "close" to $\mathcal{L}_Q$... Indeed, sometimes provers might actually be able to produce states far (in trace distance) from any state in $\mathcal{L}_Q$, but because they are computationally bounded, they are unable to exploit that fact. This kind of false "attack" can actually be done against our protocol if the function h is not injective (explaining why we require h to be injective when considering an unbounded malicious receiver), by simply running the ZK protocol in superposition[17]: in that case the output state might be relatively close to a $|+\rangle$ or $|-\rangle$ if h is well balanced (while we expect the state to be close to $|0\rangle$ or $|1\rangle$), but a computationally bounded receiver cannot exploit this property as they need to compute all preimages of h to know if we are close to $|+\rangle$ or $|-\rangle$. Simulator are therefore useful in the soundness definition to capture this "computational distance", and discard ineffective attacks.
- **In correctness**: Perhaps surprisingly, we also use a simulator in the correctness definition. While this might not be useful when considering only a game-based security notion, we need simulator to prove for instance statements like "If a protocol Π realises a given functionality, then this protocol is a ZKoQS protocol" (see e.g. Theorem 4.10). Without further details on Π, the correctness of Π only tells us that Π is indistinguishable from a functionality that produces states in $\mathcal{L}_Q$, but it does not mean that Π itself produces such states, hence the need of a simulator.

We formalize the notion of ZKoQS:

---

[17] Of course by still measuring the classical transcript to send to the verifier.

Definition 4.5 (Zero-Knowledge Proof on Quantum State (ZKoQS)).
*Let $\mathcal{L} := (\mathcal{L}_Q, \mathcal{C}, \mathcal{C}_s, \{\mathcal{L}_{\omega,\omega_s}\}_{\omega \in \mathcal{C}, \omega_s \in \mathcal{C}_s})$ be a quantum language (Definition 4.3).
We say that a protocol $\Pi = (\mathsf{P}, \mathsf{V})$ is a ZKoQS protocol for $\mathcal{L}$, where P takes as
input a class $\omega \in \mathcal{C}$ and outputs a sub-class $\omega_s \in \mathcal{C}_s$ and[18] a quantum state ρ^{P},
and V takes no input and outputs a bit a, that is equal to 1 if V does not abort,
together with a quantum state ρ^{V} (potentially entangled with ρ^{P}), if the following
properties are respected:*

- **Correctness:** *There exists a poly-time simulator $\mathbf{S}$ and a negligible function
  ε such that $(\mathsf{P} \rightsquigarrow \mathsf{V}) \approx_c \mathbf{S}$, and for any ω such that $\mathcal{L}_\omega \neq \emptyset$:*

$$\Pr\left[a = 1 \wedge \rho^{\mathsf{V},\mathsf{P}} \in \mathcal{L}_{\omega,\omega_s} \mid ((\omega_s, \rho^{\mathsf{P}}), (a, \rho^{\mathsf{V}})) \leftarrow \mathbf{S}(\omega)\right] = 1 \qquad (6)$$

- **Soundness:** *For any malicious prover $\hat{\mathsf{P}} = \{\hat{\mathsf{P}}_\lambda\}_{\lambda \in \mathbb{N}}$, (QPT for ZKAoQS,
  unbounded for ZKPoQS) there exists a simulator $\mathbf{S}_{\hat{\mathsf{P}}} = \{\mathbf{S}_{\lambda,\hat{\mathsf{P}}}\}_{\lambda \in \mathbb{N}}$ (running
  in time polynomial in the runtime of $\hat{\mathsf{P}}$) such that $(\hat{\mathsf{P}} \rightsquigarrow \mathsf{V}) \approx_c \mathbf{S}_{\hat{\mathsf{P}}}$ ($\approx_s$ for
  ZKPoQS), and such that there exists a negligible function ε such that for any
  sequence of bipartite state $\{\sigma_\lambda^{\mathsf{P},\mathbf{Z}}\}_{\lambda \in \mathbb{N}}$ and $\lambda \in \mathbb{N}$:*

$$\Pr[a = 1 \wedge \rho^{\mathsf{V},(\mathsf{P},\mathbf{Z})} \notin \mathcal{L}_Q \mid (\rho^{\mathsf{P}}, (a, \rho^{\mathsf{V}}), \rho^{\mathbf{Z}}) \leftarrow (\mathbf{S}_{\lambda,\hat{\mathsf{P}}}^{\mathsf{P}} \otimes I^{\mathbf{Z}}) \otimes \sigma_\lambda^{\mathsf{P},\mathbf{Z}}] \leq \varepsilon(\lambda) \quad (7)$$

- **Quantum Zero-Knowledge:** *For any malicious verifier $\hat{\mathsf{V}} = \{\hat{\mathsf{V}}_\lambda\}_{\lambda \in \mathbb{N}}$ (QPT
  for ZKoQS, unbounded for S-ZKoQS), there exists a simulator $\mathbf{S}_{\hat{\mathsf{V}}}(b, \cdot)$ (where
  $b \in \{0, 1\}$ indicates if $\mathcal{L}_\omega$ is non-empty, and $\cdot$ represents an additionally
  quantum input from the environment), and an efficiently computable map $\xi.(\cdot)$
  (such that $\forall \omega, \xi_\omega$ takes one quantum register as input and outputs a classical
  message in $\mathcal{C}_s$ and a quantum state ρ^{P}), both running in polynomial time in
  the runtime of $\hat{\mathsf{V}}$, such that for any $\omega \in \mathcal{C}$:*

$$(\mathsf{P}(\omega) \rightsquigarrow \hat{\mathsf{V}}) \approx_c (\xi_\omega \otimes I)(\mathbf{S}_{\hat{\mathsf{V}}}(\mathcal{L}_\omega \neq \emptyset)) \qquad (8)$$

($\approx_s$ for ZKPoQS)

*It can sometimes be handy to cut the protocol into two phases: the honest verifier
will output the state ρ^{V} at the end of the first **send** phase, wile the output of the
honest prover will be delivered in a second **describe** phase (allowing the prover
to describe the state outputted earlier by the verifier). A ZKoQS protocol where
each phase consists of a single message is said to be non-interactive (denoted
NIZKoQS, we can similarly add the "NI" prefix to the previously seen notions,
to get NIZKPoQS, S-NIZKoQS...). Finally, for a set of parties S, we write
ZKoQS_S to denote the fact that the protocol is S-ZKoQS if $\mathsf{V} \in S$ and ZKPoQS
if $\mathsf{P} \in S$.*

Note that in ZK protocols, there is a notion of extractability, where a simulator can extract the witness w from a valid transcript (not all ZK protocols

---

[18] ρ^{P} will actually not be necessary in our main application, but we still include it in
case it turns out to be useful in future applications.

are extractable). We could define a similar notion here allowing the simulator to extract ω, but since $\mathcal{L}_Q$ might contain states not belonging to any $\mathcal{L}_\omega$ (potentially producible by malicious provers), we need to slightly update the definition of quantum language by also introducing a special "malicious" subclass $\perp$, so that $\mathcal{L}_Q = \cup_\omega (\mathcal{L}_\omega \cup \mathcal{L}_{\omega,\perp})$, and such that the simulator in the soundness property can extract the ω of the state produced by a malicious adversary:

Definition 4.6 (Extractability). *A ZKoQS protocol is said to be* extractable *with respect to* $(\mathcal{L}_{\omega,\perp})_{\omega \in \mathcal{C}}$ *($\perp$ being a special subclass not belonging to $\mathcal{C}_s$) such that $\mathcal{L}_Q = \cup_\omega (\mathcal{L}_\omega \cup \mathcal{L}_{\omega,\perp})$, and such that the soundness property is turned into:*

- **Extractability:** *For any malicious prover* $\hat{\mathsf{P}} = \{\hat{\mathsf{P}}_\lambda\}_{\lambda \in \mathbb{N}}$, *(QPT for ZKAoQS, unbounded for ZKPoQS) there exists a simulator* $\mathbf{S}_{\hat{\mathsf{P}}} = \{\mathbf{S}_{\lambda,\hat{\mathsf{P}}}\}_{\lambda \in \mathbb{N}}$ *(running in time polynomial in the runtime of* $\hat{\mathsf{P}}$*) such that* $(\hat{\mathsf{P}} \rightsquigarrow \mathsf{V}) \approx_c \mathbf{S}_{\hat{\mathsf{P}}}$ *($\approx_s$ for ZKPoQS), and such that there exists a negligible function ε such that for any sequence of bipartite state* $\{\sigma_\lambda^{\mathsf{P},\mathsf{Z}}\}_{\lambda \in \mathbb{N}}$ *and* $\lambda \in \mathbb{N}$:

$$\Pr\left[a = 1 \wedge \rho^{\mathsf{V},(\mathsf{P},\mathsf{Z})} \notin (\mathcal{L}_\omega \cup \mathcal{L}_{\omega,\perp}) \,\middle|\, (\rho^{\mathsf{P}}, (a, \rho^{\mathsf{V}}), \rho^{\mathsf{Z}}, \omega) \leftarrow (\mathbf{S}_{\lambda,\hat{\mathsf{P}}}(\sigma_\lambda^{\mathsf{P}})) \otimes \sigma_\lambda^{\mathsf{Z}}\right] \leq \varepsilon(\lambda)$$

(9)

4.2 Proof of Partial Measurement: A Generic Framework to Get ZKoQS

While the notion of ZKoQS (Definition 4.5) does not explicitly mention functionalities, it is often handy to model a ZKoQS protocol inside an ideal functionality as it is easier to interpret it and use it inside other protocols. While it is not clear how to translate the ZKoQS definition into a functionality, we provide below a few ideal functionalities that "imply" ZKoQS. We will first see what is a ZKoQS ideal functionality, then we will see a class of functionalities that are ZKoQS, and we will show that our protocol realizes a particular case of these functionalities.

Definition 4.7 (ZKoQS ideal functionality). *Let* $(\mathcal{L}_Q, \mathcal{C}, \mathcal{C}_s, \{\mathcal{L}_{\omega,\omega_s}\}_{\omega \in \mathcal{C}, \omega_s \in \mathcal{C}_s})$ *be a quantum language (Definition 4.3). We say that an ideal functionality $\mathcal{F}$ is a ZKoQS (resp. ZKoQS$_S$) ideal functionality for $\mathcal{L}_Q$ iff for any protocol $\Pi = (\mathsf{P}, \mathsf{V})$ that quantum standalone realizes $\mathcal{F}$ (resp. $\mathcal{CS}_S$-QSA-realizes $\mathcal{F}$), Π is a ZKoQS protocol (resp. ZKoQS$_S$ protocol) for $\mathcal{L}_Q$ (Definition 4.5).*

The most natural class of ideal functionalities leading to ZKoQS are the ones in which the functionality applies an operation (a partial measurement) on an arbitrary input to enforce some structures on the output state:

Definition 4.8 (Partial measurement $\mathcal{F}_{\mathsf{PartMeas}}^{M,f_0}$). *Let* $M := \{M_m\}_{m \in \mathcal{M}}$ *be a collection of measurement operators*[19] *(i.e. operators such that $\sum_m M_m^\dagger M_m = I$ [NC10, Sec. 2.2.3]), implementable in quantum polynomial time, and let $f_0: \mathcal{M} \to \mathcal{C}_s$ be an efficiently computable function*[20]. *Then, we define the proof of partial measurement* functionality $\mathcal{F}_{\mathsf{PartMeas}}^{M,f_0}$ *as follows:*

---

[19] They are the most generic way to represent a measurement.

[20] Informally, f_0 is used to filter some information on the measurement outcome m during an honest protocol.

- $\mathcal{F}^{M,f_0}_{\text{PartMeas}}$ receives a state ρ from the prover's interface, together with an abort bit a.
- If $a = \bot$, it sends $\bot$ to both parties and stops.
- Otherwise, $\mathcal{F}^{M,f_0}_{\text{PartMeas}}$ measures ρ using M, obtaining an outcome $m \in \mathcal{M}$ and a post-measured state

$$\rho' := \xi_m(\rho) := \frac{M_m \rho M_m^\dagger}{\text{Tr}(M_m^\dagger M_m \rho)} \tag{10}$$

- It sends ρ' to the verifier, and waits back for a message f, such that either $f = \bot$ (in which case the functionality sends $\bot$ to the prover to abort and stops), $f = \top$ (in which case the ideal functionality redefines $f := f_0$), or f is an efficiently computable function $f \colon \mathcal{M} \to \{0,1\}^*$.
- Finally, it sends $f(m)$ to the prover.

We would like to prove that this functionality is a ZKoQS functionality, but not all such functionalities are ZKoQS (in particular, if the post-measured state contains information on ω, it has no chance of being ZK). For this reason, we expect our functionality to have an additional property, intuitively saying that we can postpone the actual measurement *after* sending the quantum state. While this might seem counter intuitive, this can actually be realized exploiting entanglement, and similar techniques were used in previous works to prove security of protocols [DFP+14].

Definition 4.9 (Postponable measurement operator). *A measurement operator M outputting a quantum state and a classical measurement outcome is said to be postponable with respect to a collection of sampling procedures $\{G_\omega\}_{\omega \in A}$ outputting a quantum state if there exist a bipartite state $\rho^{\mathsf{V},\mathsf{F}}$ and a quantum map M' taking as input a bipartite system and outputting a measurement outcome m' such that for all $\omega \in A$, $MG_\omega \approx_s (I^{\mathsf{V}} \otimes M')(\rho^{\mathsf{V},\mathsf{F}} \otimes G_\omega)$:*

$$\boxed{G_\omega} - \boxed{M} = \begin{matrix} \rho \\ \boxed{G_\omega} \end{matrix} \boxed{M'} \tag{11}$$

We prove now that such a functionality is a ZKoQS functionality for a given quantum language and appropriately defined dummy ideal parties:

Theorem 4.10 ($\mathcal{F}_{\mathsf{PartMeas}}$ implies ZKoQS). *Let $E^{\mathsf{V}_0,\mathsf{P}} = \cup_{(n,m)\in\mathbb{N}^2}\mathcal{L}_o(\mathcal{H}_n \otimes \mathcal{H}_m)$ be the set of finite dimensional quantum states on two registers V_0 and P. Let $\mathcal{C}$ and $\mathcal{C}_s$ be two sets, and for any $\omega \in \mathcal{C}$, let $E_\omega \subseteq E^{\mathsf{V}_0,\mathsf{P}}$ be a set of bipartite quantum states. Let $M := \{M_m\}_{m\in\mathcal{M}}$ be a collection of measurement operators (and ξ_m as defined in Definition 4.8), and $f_0 : \mathcal{M} \to \mathcal{C}_s$ be a function. We define for any $\omega \in \mathcal{C}$ and $\omega_s \in \mathcal{C}_s$:*

$$\mathcal{L}_{\omega,\omega_s} := \{\rho^{\mathsf{V},\mathsf{P}} \mid \exists\rho_0^{\mathsf{V}_0,\mathsf{P}} \in E_\omega, m \in \mathcal{M}, \ s.t. \ \omega_s = f_0(m), \rho^{\mathsf{V},\mathsf{P}} = \xi_m(\rho_0^{\mathsf{V}_0,\mathsf{P}})\} \quad (12)$$

$$\mathcal{L}_\omega := \cup_{\omega_s}\mathcal{L}_{\omega,\omega_s} \quad (13)$$

$$\mathcal{L}_Q := \{((\xi_m \otimes \hat{\xi}_{f_0(m)})\rho^{\mathsf{V},(\mathsf{P},\mathbf{Z})} \mid \rho \in E^{\mathsf{V}_0,(\mathsf{P},\mathbf{Z})}, m \in \mathcal{M}, m \neq \bot,$$
$$\hat{\xi}_{f_0(m)} \ being \ an \ arbitrary \ CPTP \ map \ depending \ on \ f_0(m).\} \quad (14)$$

Then, let $\tilde{\mathsf{P}}$ and $\tilde{\mathsf{V}}$ be any poly-time ideal parties, such that:

- *If $E_\omega = \emptyset$, $\tilde{\mathsf{P}}(\omega)$ sends the abort bit $a = \bot$ to the functionality and outputs $\bot$. Otherwise, $\tilde{\mathsf{P}}(\omega)$ produces a state in E_ω according to an arbitrary sampling procedure G, sends the register V_0 to the ideal functionality, and outputs the ω_s given back from the functionality together with the register P.*
- *If $\tilde{\mathsf{V}}$ receives $\bot$ from the functionality, it outputs $a = \bot$ and stop. Otherwise, it outputs the state ρ' given by the functionality together with a bit $a = \top$ and sends back to the functionality $f = \top$.*

Then, if M are postponable measurement operators with respect to $\{G_\omega\}_{\omega,\mathcal{L}_\omega\neq\emptyset}$ (Definition 4.9), $\mathcal{F}_{\mathsf{PartMeas}}^{M,f_0}$ is a ZKoQS protocol (actually ZKoQS$_S$ for any set S, see Definition 4.7) for the language $\mathcal{L}_Q$ previously defined.

Sketch of Proof. The proof mostly derives from the definitions, and from the fact that having postponable operators allows us to push the part of the ideal functionality that depends on the secret after the interaction with the adversary, preserving the ZK property. We refer to the full security proof in the full version [CMS23] for more details. □

While the above results show that we can obtain a ZKoQS protocol from any protocol realizing the functionality $\mathcal{F}_{\mathsf{PartMeas}}^{M,f_0}$ (where M must be postponable), we show in the next section how we can realize such a functionality to prove that a state was partially collapsed (measured in the computational basis) without revealing the position of the collapsed qubit. We will then see that, as a corollary, there exists a ZKoQS protocol for the quantum language of "semi-collapsed" states.

4.3   Protocol to Prove that a State Has Been Semi-collapsed

We prove now that we can realize the functionality below, that informally measures a set T of qubits (the measured qubits, chosen by the prover, being constraint to respect $\mathrm{Pred}(T) = \top$, for an arbitrary predicate Pred), randomly rotates the other one, and provides the resulting state to the verifier.

Definition 4.11 (Semi-collapsing functionality $\mathcal{F}_{\mathsf{SemCol}}^{\mathrm{Pred}}$). *Let $n \in \mathbb{N}$, and* Pred: $\mathcal{P}([n]) \to \{\top, \bot\}$ *be an efficiently computable predicate on the subsets of* $[n]$. *We define the semi-collapsing functionality $\mathcal{F}_{\mathsf{SemCol}}^{\mathrm{Pred}}$ as $\mathcal{F}_{\mathsf{PartMeas}}^{M,f_0}$ (Definition 4.8), where:*

- *M is the measurement operator that receives a quantum state on two registers, measures (destructively) the first register[21] in the computational basis to get (an encoding of) $T \subseteq [n]$ and a sequence of bits $(r^{(i)})_{i \in [n] \setminus T}$, checks if* Pred$(T) = \top$: *if not it outputs $m = \bot$ and a dummy quantum state $|\bot\rangle$. Otherwise, it measures (non-destructively) in the computational basis all qubits in the second register whose index belongs to the set of "target" qubits T, getting outcomes $\{m^{(j)}\}_{j \in T}$, and for any $i \in [n] \setminus T$, it applies $Z^{r^{(i)}}$ on the i-th qubit. Finally it outputs $m = (T, (m^{(j)})_{j \in T}, (r^{(i)})_{i \in [n] \setminus T})$ and the post-measured state.*
- *If $m = \bot$, $f_0(m) = \bot$, otherwise if $m = (T, (m^{(j)})_{j \in T}, (r^{(i)})_{i \in [n] \setminus T})$, $f_0(m) = (r^{(i)})_{i \in [n] \setminus T}$.*

We also consider the following dummy ideal parties:

- *$\tilde{P}(T, \rho)$ samples[22] uniformly at random a sequence of bits $(r^{(i)})_{i \in [n] \setminus T}$, sends $a = $ Pred(T) and $|T, (r^{(i)})_{i \in [n] \setminus T}\rangle\langle T, (r^{(i)})_{i \in [n] \setminus T}| \otimes \rho$ to the ideal functionality $\mathcal{F}_{\mathsf{SemCol}}^{\mathrm{Pred}}$, and forwards the received message from the functionality.*
- *$\tilde{V}$ checks if it received $a = \bot$ from the functionality, or if the received quantum state is $|\bot\rangle$. If so it sends back $f = \bot$ to the functionality and aborts, and otherwise it sets $f = \top$ for the functionality and outputs the quantum state to the environment.*

We prove now that we can realize the functionality $\mathcal{F}_{\mathsf{SemCol}}^{\mathrm{Pred}}$:

Theorem 4.12 (Realization of $\mathcal{F}_{\mathsf{SemCol}}^{\mathrm{Pred}}$). *Let $\{h_k\}_{k \in \mathcal{K}}$ be a family of collision resistant functions sampled by* Gen, *having the hardcore second-bit property (Definition 2.5). Let $\Pi_h = (\mathsf{P}_h, \mathsf{V}_h)$ be a protocol[23] CS_{S_h}-QSA realizing $\mathcal{F}_{CRS}^{\mathrm{Gen}}$ and $\Pi_{zk} = (\mathbf{A}_{zk}, \mathbf{B}_{zk})$ be a protocol that CS_S-QSA realizes the ZK functionality $\mathcal{F}_{ZK}^R$, where $(h_d^{(c)})_{c \in [n], d \in \{0,1\}} \mathcal{R}(T, (w_d^{(c)})_{c \in [n], d \in \{0,1\}}) \Leftrightarrow $ Pred$(T) = \top \wedge \forall c, d, h(d \| w_d^{(c)}) = h_d^{(c)}$ and $\forall c \in T, \exists c$ such that $w_d^{(c)}[1] = 1$.*

Then, the protocol Π_{SemCol} (Protocol 2) $CS_{S'}$-QSA-realizes $\mathcal{F}_{\mathsf{SemCol}}^{\mathrm{Pred}}$ for any S' such that:

---

[21] Informally this register contains the subset of qubits in the second register to measure and a (typically random) sequence of Z rotations to apply on the remaining qubits. Since the first operation of M is to measure them, we can (and will) also consider them as classical inputs.

[22] Note that this sequence of rotations in only needed for correctness as in the real protocol the non-measured qubits will be arbitrarily rotated.

[23] As a reminder, this protocol is sampling and distributing a function h according to Gen, and can either be done without communication in the CRS model (or heuristically if we replace h with a well known collision-resistant hash function), or with one message in the plain model.

- $S' \subseteq S \cap S_h$,
- $\{P\} \in S'$ only if h has the statistical hardcore second-bit property,
- $\{V\} \in S'$ only if for any $k \in \mathcal{K}$, h_k is injective (i.e. statistically collision resistant).

Sketch of Proof. Part of the proofs of this theorem are generalizations of Theorem 3.1. Some care must be taken to show that the distributions in the honest case (ideal world versus real world) are really indistinguishable, we do so by computing the appropriate density matrices. There is also a slight difference as here we measure the state instead of applying a rotation, but it turns out that measuring is indistinguishable from rotating a state and discarding the rotation angle. We refer to the full security proof in the full version [CMS23] for more details. □

We will see that the $\mathcal{F}_{\mathsf{SemCol}}^{\mathsf{Pred}}$ functionality can be used to trivially get more advanced OT protocols, notably string OT and k-out-of-n OT for any k and n. But first, we prove that it is a ZKoQS functionality for the quantum language of "semi-collapsed" states with respect to a predicate Pred. Informally, we define the quantum language of *semi-collapsed* states as the set of states such that there exists a subset T of qubits such that $\mathrm{Pred}(T) = \top$, and such that all qubits in T are collapsed, i.e. measured in the computational basis and equal to $|0\rangle$ or $|1\rangle$ (therefore not entangled with any other system). Moreover, the identity of the set T of collapsed qubits stays hidden to a malicious verifier, and in an honest protocol the non-collapsed qubits are either a $|+\rangle$ or a $|-\rangle$, this description being known to the prover.

Definition 4.13 (Semi-collapsed states $\mathcal{L}_{\mathsf{SemCol}}^{\mathsf{Pred}}$). *The quantum language $\mathcal{L}_{\mathsf{SemCol}}^{\mathsf{Pred}}$ of semi-collapsed states relative to a predicate* $\mathrm{Pred}\colon \mathcal{P}([n]) \to \{\top, \bot\}$ *on the subsets of qubits is composed of the classes $\mathcal{C} = \mathcal{P}([n])$ (denoting the set of collapsed qubits), the sub-classes $\mathcal{C}_s = \{s \in \{0,1\}^* \mid |s| \leq n\}$ (denoting the description of the non-collapsed qubits), and the quantum (sub-)classes defined as follows, for any $T \in \mathcal{C}$ and $\omega_s \in \mathcal{C}_s$:*

- $\mathcal{L}_{T,\omega_s}$ *is the empty set if* $\mathrm{Pred}(T) = \mathsf{false}$ *or if* $|\omega_s| \neq |T|$, *and otherwise is the set of all n-qubits states where qubits in T are either $|0\rangle$ or $|1\rangle$, and other qubits i ($i \in \{1, \ldots, |T|\}$ is the index of the qubits in $[n] \setminus T$) are equal to $|+\rangle$ if $\omega_s[i] = 0$ and $|-\rangle$ otherwise.*
- $\mathcal{L}_{\mathsf{SemCol}}^{\mathsf{Pred}}$ *is the set of bipartite states on registers P and V such that V contains n qubits, and such that there exists $T \subseteq [n]$ such that $\mathrm{Pred}(T) = \bot$ and for any $i \in T$, i-th qubit of register V is not entangled with any other qubit and either $|0\rangle$ or $|1\rangle$.*

Corollary 4.14 (ZKoQS for semi-collapsed states). *Let $G'(T)$ be the procedure that samples $(r^{(i)})_{i \in [n]} \xleftarrow{\$} \{0,1\}$ and outputs the quantum state $\bigotimes_i H^{\delta_{i \notin T}} |a^{(i)}\rangle$ (i.e. all qubits in T are in the computational basis, others are in the Hadamard basis).*

Protocol 2: ZKoQS protocol to realize $\mathcal{F}_{\mathsf{SemCol}}^{\mathsf{Pred}}$

Inputs: The prover P gets $T \subseteq [n]$, a subset of qubits to measure, and the quantum state $\rho^{(1)},\ldots,^{(n)}$ to partially measure, the verifier V gets no input.

Assumption: Pred is an efficiently computable predicate on subsets of $[n]$, $(\mathsf{P}_{zk}, \mathsf{V}_{zk})$ is a n-message ZK protocol (Definition 2.3), h is a collision-resistant (Definition 2.6) and second-bit hardcore (Definition 2.5) function distributed using $\mathcal{F}_H$ (Definition 2.8), either non-interactively via a CRS, heuristically using a fixed hash function, or sent by the verifier, adding an additional message (Lemma 2.10).

Protocol:

1. **The prover** checks if $\mathrm{Pred}(T) = \top$, and abort and send $\bot$ to V otherwise. The, she samples $\forall d \in \{0,1\}, i \in [n] \setminus T, w_d^{(i)} \xleftarrow{\$} \{0\} \times \{0,1\}^n$ and for each $j \in T$, she measures (non destructively) $\rho^{(j)}$ to get outcome l, and samples $w_l^{(j)} \xleftarrow{\$} \{0\} \times \{0,1\}^n$ $l \in \{0,1\}$ and $w_{1-l}^{(j)} \xleftarrow{\$} \{1\} \times \{0,1\}^n$. Then, for each $(c,d) \in T \times \{0,1\}$ she defines $h_d^{(c)} := h(d \| w_d^{(c)})$. Then, she sends $(h_d^{(c)})_{c \in [n], d \in \{0,1\}}$ to the verifier (if the ZK protocol is non-interactive she can send it later in a single message with the NIZK proof and the quantum states) and runs the ZK protocol P_{zk} with the verifier (running P_{zk}) to prove that:

$$\exists T \subseteq [n], (w_d^{(c)})_{c \in T, d \in \{0,1\}}, \forall c, d, h_d^{(c)} = h(d \| w_d^{(c)}) \quad (15)$$

$$\text{and } \forall j \in T, \exists d \text{ s.t. } w_d^{(j)}[1] = 1, \text{ and } \mathrm{Pred}(T) = \top \quad (16)$$

   Then, she samples for each $i \in [n] \setminus T$, $r^{(i)} \xleftarrow{\$} \{0,1\}$, and applies $Z^{r^{(i)}} \rho^{(i)}$. Finally, for each $c \in [n]$, she applies on $\rho^{(c)}$ the unitary mapping $|x\rangle \mapsto |x\rangle \, |w_x^{(c)}\rangle$ (we call $\rho_1^{(1)},\ldots,^{(n)}$ the resulting state) and she sends $\rho_1^{(1)},\ldots,^{(n)}$ to the verifier.

2. **The verifier** aborts if the prover aborted or if it received a wrong ZK proof. Then, it applies on each qubit c the unitary $|x\rangle |w\rangle \mapsto |x\rangle |w\rangle |w[1] \neq 1 \wedge \exists d, h(x \| w) = h_d^{(c)}\rangle$, and measures the last auxiliary register, checking if they are all equal to 1. If not, he aborts (and sends an abort message to the prover), otherwise he measures for each $c \in [n]$ the second registers of $\rho^{(c)}$ (getting outcomes $s^{(c)}$) in the Hadamard basis. Finally, it outputs the remaining (first) qubit of each $\rho_1^{(c)}$, and sends $(s^{(c)})_{c \in [n]}$ to the prover.

3. **The prover** computes $\omega_s := (r^{(i)} \oplus \bigoplus_k s^{(i)}[k](w_0^{(i)} \oplus w_1^{(i)})[k])_{i \in [n] \setminus T}$ and outputs ω_s.

The functionality $\mathcal{F}^{\mathrm{Pred}}_{\mathrm{SemCol}}$ (where the ideal party $\tilde{\mathsf{P}}$ is slightly updated[24]: instead of receiving T and ρ, it receives $T \subseteq [n]$, and samples $\rho \leftarrow G'(T)$, before continuing as usual) is a ZKoQS ideal functionality (Definition 4.7) for the quantum language $\mathcal{L}^{\mathrm{Pred}}_{\mathrm{SemCol}}$ (Definition 4.13).

In particular, if we consider the protocol where the honest prover gets as input T, picks $\rho \leftarrow G'(T)$, and runs Protocol 2, this protocol is a ZKoQS protocol for the quantum language $\mathcal{L}^{\mathrm{Pred}}_{\mathrm{SemCol}}$.

This is mostly a corollary of Theorem 4.10. The only non-trivial statement is to prove that the measurement is postponable: this can be done by teleporting the state without applying any correction.

4.4 ZKstatesQIP$_S[k]$ and ZKstatesQMA$_S$: ZKoQS from a Complexity Theory Point of View

While we defined ZKoQS using a "cryptographic" definition, we can also consider them from the point of view of complexity theory. While classically, complexity classes involve a verifier taking an input x potentially belonging to a given classical language $\mathcal{L}$, and outputting a single accept bit (this is not an issue as the input x can anyway be copied by the verifier if it needs to be used later), for quantum languages this definition turns out to be hard (or even impossible) to use as the verification procedure will alter the input state. ([KA04] does something along that line, but needs to send many copies of the input state, which is of little interest in cryptography as it leads to polynomial security.) To overcome this issue, it is therefore natural to say that the quantum state belonging to the quantum language must be an *output* of the verifier. This is the successful point of view that we took above, and a similar approach has also been used before in [RY22] to quantify the complexity to produce a given state by defining a complexity class stateQIP. However, the class stateQIP only captures how hard it is to generate a given state, but it does not capture any notion of privacy against a malicious verifier. The following definition addresses this issue:

Definition 4.15 (ZKstatesQIP$_S[k]$ and ZKstatesQMA$_S$). *Let $\mathcal{L}$ be a quantum language (Definition 4.3), $k \in \mathbb{N}$ be a number of exchanged messages, $S \in \{\emptyset, \mathsf{P}, \mathsf{V}\}$ be a subset of parties allowed to be unbounded, and setup be a given setup assumption (e.g. CRS, Random Oracle, or plain-model). We say that $\mathcal{L}$ belongs to the complexity class ZKstatesQIP$^{\mathrm{setup}}_S[k]$ if there exists a ZKoQS$_S$ protocol for $\mathcal{L}$, secure assuming the setup assumption setup, whose send phase consists of k exchanged messages (note that we might omit S, setup, or k if we do not want to constraint this parameter).*

Similarly, we define ZKstatesQMA$^{\mathrm{setup}}_S$ = ZKstatesQIP$^{\mathrm{setup}}_S[1]$ to capture non-interactive protocols.

---

[24] $\mathcal{F}^{\mathrm{Pred}}_{\mathrm{SemCol}}$ can be used for any input quantum state, but for the ZKoQS we need to consider a particular case where the initial state is picked by the party instead of by the environment. The reason is that in ZKoQS protocols, an honest prover is only given as input a class.

For comparison with other works that introduced stateQIP, see the full version [CMS23].

We prove now that $\mathcal{L}_{\mathsf{SemCol}}^{\mathrm{Pred}}$ belongs to these classes:

Corollary 4.16 ($\mathcal{L}_{\mathsf{SemCol}}^{\mathrm{Pred}}$ is in ZKstatesQMA^{RQ}). *For any predicate* Pred, *the quantum language* $\mathcal{L}_{\mathsf{SemCol}}^{\mathrm{Pred}}$ *belong to* ZKstatesQMA^{RQ} *(where* RO *stands for Random Oracle model). Moreover, assuming the hardness of* LWE *(see [HSS11] for the exact assumptions),* $\mathcal{L}_{\mathsf{SemCol}}^{\mathrm{Pred}}$ *belongs to* ZKstatesQIP^{pm} *(where* pm *stands for plain-model).*

More generally, assuming the existence of a k-message ZK protocol CS_S-QSA *realizing* $\mathcal{F}_{ZK}$ *for any* NP *statement assuming a setup* setup, $\mathcal{L}_{\mathsf{SemCol}}^{\mathrm{Pred}}$ *belong to* ZKstatesQIP$_S^{\mathrm{setup}}[k]$.

These statements can be proven using Corollary4.14, together with the constructions of [Unr15, HSS11].

4.5   Applications to Build String and k-out-of-n OT Protocols

We prove in this section that the above functionality $\mathcal{F}_{\mathsf{SemCol}}^{\mathrm{Pred}}$ actually allows us to have string OT or k-out-of-n OT. But first, we show that we can realize this functionality:

Theorem 4.17. *Let* Pred *be a predicate on subsets of* $[n]$. *Assuming the existence of a protocol* $\Pi_{\mathsf{SemCol}} = (\mathbf{A}_{\mathsf{SemCol}}, \mathbf{B}_{\mathsf{SemCol}})$ *that* CS_S-QSA-*realises* $\mathcal{F}_{\mathsf{SemCol}}^{\mathrm{Pred}}$, *there Protocol 3* CS_S-QSA-*realises* $\mathcal{F}_{OT}^{\mathrm{Pred}}$.

This is a generalisation of the last part of the proof of Theorem 3.1.

Protocol 3: Protocol to compile a ZKoQS protocol $(\mathbf{A}_{\mathsf{SemCol}}, \mathbf{B}_{\mathsf{SemCol}})$ for the quantum language $\mathcal{L}_{\mathsf{SemCol}}^{\mathrm{Pred}}$ into a predicate OT protocol.

Alice($B \subseteq \{0,1\}^n$)		Bob($(m_1, \ldots, m_n) \in \{0,1\}^n$)
If Pred(B) = $\perp$, abort.		
$\forall i \in [n], r^{(i)} \leftarrow \{0,1\}$		
$\rho := \otimes_{i \in [n]} H^{\delta_{i \in B}} \lvert r^{(i)} \rangle$		
$(s^{(i)})_{i \in B} \leftarrow \mathbf{A}_{\mathsf{SemCol}}(B, \rho)$	$\longleftarrow \quad\quad \longrightarrow$	$\rho \leftarrow \mathbf{B}_{\mathsf{SemCol}}$
Abort if the previous step aborted.		If the previous step aborted, abort.
		$\forall c$, apply Z^{m_c} on $\rho^{(c)}$ and measure it
		in the Hadamard basis (outcome $z^{(c)}$).
return $(r^{(i)} \oplus s^{(i)} \oplus z^{(i)})_{i \in B}$	$\xleftarrow{\quad \forall c, z^{(c)} \quad}$	

Corollary 4.18. *By choosing appropriate values for* Pred *like in Definition 2.2, the protocol Protocol 3 realizes the string* OT *functionality* $\mathcal{F}_{OT}^{str}$ *and the k-out-of-n* OT *functionality* $\mathcal{F}_{OT}^{k-m}$.

This is a direct consequence of Theorem 4.17 and of the definition of $\mathcal{F}_{OT}^{k-m}$ and $\mathcal{F}_{OT}^{str}$. □

5   Composability of [Unr15]

We show now that the online extractable NIZK protocol from [Unr15] quantum stand-alone realizes the $\mathcal{F}_{ZK}^{\mathcal{R}}$ functionality in Definition 2.3, when the RO assumption is made. This is needed to instantiate Corollary 4.18 with a concrete ZK protocol.

Theorem 5.1. *Let H be a random oracle. The non-interactive protocol* $\Pi_{zk}^{H} =$ (P, V) *from [Unr15] quantum stand-alone realizes the classical zero-knowledge functionality* $\mathcal{F}_{ZK}^{\mathcal{R}}$, *were* $x \in \mathcal{L} \Leftrightarrow \exists w, x\mathcal{R}w$.

The proof in the full version [CMS23].

Corollary 5.2. *In the random oracle model, assuming the existence of a collision-resistant and second-bit hardcore hash function (which holds if h is modeled as a random oracle model, see discussion in Theorem 1.1), there exists a protocol realizing the string* OT *functionality* $\mathcal{F}_{OT}^{str}$ *and the k-out-of-n* OT *functionality* $\mathcal{F}_{OT}^{k-m}$.

Proof. This is a direct consequence of Corollary 4.18 and Theorem 5.1, where [Unr15] is used to instantiate the ZK protocol. □

Acknowledgment. The authors deeply thank Christian Schaffner for many insightful exchanges, together with Stacey Jeffery, Geoffroy Couteau and James Bartusek for precious discussions, and anonymous reviewers for many helpful comments and for pointing a mistake (now corrected) in a proof that generalizes our first result. This work is co-funded by the European Union (ERC, ASC-Q, 101040624) and supported by the Dutch National Growth Fund (NGF), as part of the Quantum Delta NL programme.

References

[ABK+22] Agarwal, A., Bartusek, J., Khurana, D., Kumar, N.: A new framework for quantum oblivious transfer. In: Hazay, C., Stam, M. (eds.) EUROCRYPT 2023. LNCS, vol. 14004, pp. 363–394. Springer, Cham (2022). https://doi.org/10.1007/978-3-031-30545-0_13

[AL20]   Ananth, P., La Placa, R.L.: Secure quantum extraction protocols. In: Pass, R., Pietrzak, K. (eds.) TCC 2020. LNCS, vol. 12552, pp. 123–152. Springer, Cham (2020). https://doi.org/10.1007/978-3-030-64381-2_5

[BBC+92] Bennett, C.H., Brassard, G., Crépeau, C., Skubiszewska, M.-H.: Practical quantum oblivious transfer. In: Feigenbaum, J. (ed.) CRYPTO 1991. LNCS, vol. 576, pp. 351–366. Springer, Heidelberg (1992). https://doi.org/10.1007/3-540-46766-1_29

[BCK+21] Bartusek, J., Coladangelo, A., Khurana, D., Ma, F.: One-way functions imply secure computation in a quantum world. In: Malkin, T., Peikert, C. (eds.) CRYPTO 2021. LNCS, vol. 12825, pp. 467–496. Springer, Cham (2021). https://doi.org/10.1007/978-3-030-84242-0_17

[BD18] Brakerski, Z., Döttling, N.: Two-message statistically sender-private OT from LWE. In: Beimel, A., Dziembowski, S. (eds.) TCC 2018. LNCS, vol. 11240, pp. 370–390. Springer, Cham (2018). https://doi.org/10.1007/978-3-030-03810-6_14

[BF10] Bouman, N.J., Fehr, S.: Sampling in a quantum population, and applications. In: Rabin, T. (ed.) CRYPTO 2010. LNCS, vol. 6223, pp. 724–741. Springer, Heidelberg (2010). https://doi.org/10.1007/978-3-642-14623-7_39

[BKS23] Bartusek, J., Khurana, D., Srinivasan, A.: Secure Computation with Shared EPR Pairs (Or: How to Teleport in Zero-Knowledge) (2023)

[BS20] Bitansky, N., Shmueli, O.: Post-quantum zero knowledge in constant rounds. In: Proceedings of the 52nd Annual ACM SIGACT Symposium on Theory of Computing, STOC 2020, pp. 269–279, New York, NY, USA. Association for Computing Machinery, 22 June 2020

[CGK21] Colisson, L., Grosshans, F., Kashefi, E.: Non-destructive Zero-Knowledge Proofs on Quantum States, and Multi-Party Generation of Authorized Hidden GHZ States, 10 April 2021

[CGS02] Crépeau, C., Gottesman, D., Smith, A.: Secure multi-party quantum computation. In: Proceedings of the Thiry-Fourth Annual ACM Symposium on Theory of Computing, STOC '02, pp. 643–652. Association for Computing Machinery, New York, NY, USA, 19 May 2002

[CK88] Crepeau, C., Kilian, J.: Achieving oblivious transfer using weakened security assumptions. In: [Proceedings 1988] 29th Annual Symposium on Foundations of Computer Science. [Proceedings 1988] 29th Annual Symposium on Foundations of Computer Science, pp. 42–52, October 1988

[CMS23] Colisson, L., Muguruza, G., Speelman, F.: Oblivious transfer from zero-knowledge proofs, or how to achieve round-optimal quantum oblivious transfer and zero-knowledge proofs on quantum states. In: ASIACRYPT 2023, 2 March 2023 (2023)

[DFL+09] Damgård, I., Fehr, S., Lunemann, C., Salvail, L., Schaffner, C.: Improving the security of quantum protocols via commit-and-open. In: Halevi, S. (ed.) CRYPTO 2009. LNCS, vol. 5677, pp. 408–427. Springer, Heidelberg (2009). https://doi.org/10.1007/978-3-642-03356-8_24

[DFP+14] Dunjko, V., Fitzsimons, J.F., Portmann, C., Renner, R.: Composable security of delegated quantum computation. In: Sarkar, P., Iwata, T. (eds.) ASIACRYPT 2014. LNCS, vol. 8874, pp. 406–425. Springer, Heidelberg (2014). https://doi.org/10.1007/978-3-662-45608-8_22

[DGJ+20] Dulek, Y., Grilo, A.B., Jeffery, S., Majenz, C., Schaffner, C.: Secure multiparty quantum computation with a dishonest majority. In: Canteaut, A., Ishai, Y. (eds.) EUROCRYPT 2020. LNCS, vol. 12107, pp. 729–758. Springer, Cham (2020). https://doi.org/10.1007/978-3-030-45727-3_25

[DNS12] Dupuis, F., Nielsen, J.B., Salvail, L.: Actively secure two-party evaluation of any quantum operation. In: Safavi-Naini, R., Canetti, R. (eds.)
CRYPTO 2012. LNCS, vol. 7417, pp. 794–811. Springer, Heidelberg
(2012). https://doi.org/10.1007/978-3-642-32009-5_46

[EGL85] Even, S., Goldreich, O., Lempel, A.: A randomized protocol for signing
contracts. Commun. ACM **28**(6), 637–647 (1985)

[ELE] ELECTRIC COIN COMPANY: Zcash: privacy-protecting digital currency. Zcash. URL: https://z.cash/. Visited 02 Oct 2023

[GL89] Goldreich, O., Levin, L.A.: A hard-core predicate for all one-way functions.
In: Proceedings of the Twenty-First Annual ACM Symposium on Theory
of Computing, STOC '89, pp. 25–32, New York, NY, USA. Association
for Computing Machinery, 1 February 1989

[GLS+21] Grilo, A.B., Lin, H., Song, F., Vaikuntanathan, V.: Oblivious transfer is
in MiniQCrypt. In: Canteaut, A., Standaert, F.-X. (eds.) EUROCRYPT
2021. LNCS, vol. 12697, pp. 531–561. Springer, Cham (2021). https://doi.
org/10.1007/978-3-030-77886-6_18

[GMR85] Goldwasser, S., Micali, S., Rackoff, C.: The knowledge complexity of interactive proof-systems. In: Proceedings of the Seventeenth Annual ACM
Symposium on Theory of Computing, STOC '85, pp. 291–304. Association for Computing Machinery, New York, NY, USA, 1 December 1985

[GMW87] Goldreich, O., Micali, S., Wigderson, A.: How to play ANY mental game.
In: Proceedings of the Nineteenth Annual ACM Symposium on Theory of
Computing, STOC '87, pp. 218–229. Association for Computing Machin-
ery, New York, NY, USA, 1 January 1987

[HSS11] Hallgren, S., Smith, A., Song, F.: Classical cryptographic protocols in a
quantum world. In: Rogaway, P. (ed.) CRYPTO 2011. LNCS, vol. 6841,
pp. 411–428. Springer, Heidelberg (2011). https://doi.org/10.1007/978-3-
642-22792-9_23

[Imp95] Impagliazzo, R.: A personal view of average-case complexity. In: Tenth
Annual IEEE Conference on Proceedings of Structure in Complexity Theory, pp. 134–147, June 1995

[JLS18] Ji, Z., Liu, Y.-K., Song, F.: Pseudorandom quantum states. In: Shacham,
H., Boldyreva, A. (eds.) CRYPTO 2018. LNCS, vol. 10993, pp. 126–152.
Springer, Cham (2018). https://doi.org/10.1007/978-3-319-96878-0_5

[KA04] Kashefi, E., Alves, C.M.: On the complexity of quantum languages, 12
April 2004

[Kil88] Kilian, J.: Founding crytpography on oblivious transfer. In: Proceedings of
the Twentieth Annual ACM Symposium on Theory of Computing, STOC
'88, pp. 20–31. Association for Computing Machinery, New York, NY,
USA, 1 January 1988

[KKL+23] Kapourniotis, T., Kashefi, E., Leichtle, D., Music, L., Ollivier, H.: Asymmetric quantum secure multi-party computation with weak clients against
dishonest majority, 15 March 2023

[KP17] Kashefi, E., Pappa, A.: Multiparty delegated quantum computing. Cryptography **1**(2), 12 (2017)

[Lin13] Lindell, Y.: A note on constant-round zero-knowledge proofs of knowledge.
J. Cryptol. **26**(4), 638–654 (2013)

[LMS21] Lombardi, A., Ma, F., Spooner, N.: Post-quantum Zero Knowledge, Revisited (Or: How to Do Quantum Rewinding Undetectably), 23 November
2021

[Lo97]   Lo, H.-K.: Insecurity of quantum secure computations. Phys. Rev. A **56**(2), 1154–1162 (1997)

[LT22]   Laud, P., Talviste, R.: Review of the State of the art in secure multiparty computation. In: Cybernetica As (2022)

[MS94]   Mayers, D., Salvail, L.: Quantum oblivious transfer is secure against all individual measurements. In: Proceedings Workshop on Physics and Computation. PhysComp '94. Proceedings Workshop on Physics and Computation. PhysComp '94, pp. 69–77, November 1994

[NC10]   Nielsen, M.A., Chuang, I.L.: Quantum Computation and Quantum Information: 10th Anniversary Edition, December 2010

[PS19]   Peikert, C., Shiehian, S.: Noninteractive zero knowledge for NP from (plain) learning with errors. In: Boldyreva, A., Micciancio, D. (eds.) CRYPTO 2019. LNCS, vol. 11692, pp. 89–114. Springer, Cham (2019). https://doi.org/10.1007/978-3-030-26948-7_4

[PVW08]   Peikert, C., Vaikuntanathan, V., Waters, B.: A framework for efficient and composable oblivious transfer. In: Wagner, D. (ed.) CRYPTO 2008. LNCS, vol. 5157, pp. 554–571. Springer, Heidelberg (2008). https://doi.org/10.1007/978-3-540-85174-5_31

[Qua20]   Quach, W.: UC-secure OT from LWE, revisited. In: Galdi, C., Kolesnikov, V. (eds.) SCN 2020. LNCS, vol. 12238, pp. 192–211. Springer, Cham (2020). https://doi.org/10.1007/978-3-030-57990-6_10

[Rab05]   Rabin, M.O.: How to exchange secrets with oblivious transfer (2005)

[RY22]   Rosenthal, G., Yuen, H.: Interactive proofs for synthesizing quantum states and unitaries. In: Braverman, M. (ed.) 13th Innovations in Theoretical Computer Science Conference, ITCS 2022, 31 January–3 February 2022, Berkeley, CA, USA of LIPIcs, vol. 215, pp. 112:1–112:4. Schloss Dagstuhl - Leibniz-Zentrum für Informatik (2022)

[SMP22]   Santos, M.B., Mateus, P., Pinto, A.N.: Quantum oblivious transfer: a short review. Entropy **24**(7), 945 (2022)

[Unr10]   Unruh, D.: Universally composable quantum multi-party computation. In: Gilbert, H. (ed.) EUROCRYPT 2010. LNCS, vol. 6110, pp. 486–505. Springer, Heidelberg (2010). https://doi.org/10.1007/978-3-642-13190-5_25

[Unr12]   Unruh, D.: Quantum proofs of knowledge. In: Pointcheval, D., Johansson, T. (eds.) EUROCRYPT 2012. LNCS, vol. 7237, pp. 135–152. Springer, Heidelberg (2012). https://doi.org/10.1007/978-3-642-29011-4_10

[Unr15]   Unruh, D.: Non-interactive zero-knowledge proofs in the quantum random oracle model. In: Oswald, E., Fischlin, M. (eds.) EUROCRYPT 2015. LNCS, vol. 9057, pp. 755–784. Springer, Heidelberg (2015). https://doi.org/10.1007/978-3-662-46803-6_25

[Unr16]   Unruh, D.: Computationally binding quantum commitments. In: Fischlin, M., Coron, J.-S. (eds.) EUROCRYPT 2016. LNCS, vol. 9666, pp. 497–527. Springer, Heidelberg (2016). https://doi.org/10.1007/978-3-662-49896-5_18

[Wat09]   Watrous, J.: Zero-knowledge against quantum attacks. SIAM J. Comput. **39**(1), 25–58 (2009)

[Wie83]   Wiesner, S.: Conjugate coding. ACM SIGACT News **15**(1), 78–88 (1983)

[WW06]   Wolf, S., Wullschleger, J.: Oblivious transfer is symmetric. In: Vaudenay, S. (ed.) EUROCRYPT 2006. LNCS, vol. 4004, pp. 222–232. Springer, Heidelberg (2006). https://doi.org/10.1007/11761679_14

[Yao82] Yao, A.C.: Protocols for secure computations. In: 23rd Annual Symposium on Foundations of Computer Science (SFCS 1982), pp. 160–164, November 1982

[Yao95] Yao, A.C.-C.: Security of quantum protocols against coherent measurements. In: Proceedings of the Twenty-Seventh Annual ACM Symposium on Theory of Computing, STOC '95, pp. 67–75. Association for Computing Machinery, New York, NY, USA, 29 May 1995

On the (Im)plausibility of Public-Key Quantum Money from Collision-Resistant Hash Functions

Prabhanjan Ananth[1], Zihan Hu[2]([envelope]), and Henry Yuen[3]

[1] UCSB, Santa Barbara, USA
prabhanjan@cs.ucsb.edu
[2] Tsinghua University, Beijing, China
huzh19@mails.tsinghua.edu.cn
[3] Columbia University, New York, USA
hyuen@cs.columbia.edu

Abstract. Public-key quantum money is a cryptographic proposal for using highly entangled quantum states as currency that is publicly verifiable yet resistant to counterfeiting due to the laws of physics. Despite significant interest, constructing provably-secure public-key quantum money schemes based on standard cryptographic assumptions has remained an elusive goal. Even proposing plausibly-secure candidate schemes has been a challenge.

These difficulties call for a deeper and systematic study of the structure of public-key quantum money schemes and the assumptions they can be based on. Motivated by this, we present the first black-box separation of quantum money and cryptographic primitives. Specifically, we show that collision-resistant hash functions cannot be used as a black-box to construct public-key quantum money schemes where the banknote verification makes classical queries to the hash function. Our result involves a novel combination of state synthesis techniques from quantum complexity theory and simulation techniques, including Zhandry's compressed oracle technique.

Keywords: Quantum Cryptography · Quantum Money · Black-Box Separations

1 Introduction

Unclonable cryptography is an emerging area in quantum cryptography that leverages the no-cloning principle of quantum mechanics [WZ82, Die82] to achieve cryptographic primitives that are classically impossible. Over the years, many interesting unclonable primitives have been proposed and studied. These include quantum copy-protection [Aar09], one-time programs [BGS13], secure software leasing [AL21], unclonable encryption [BL20], encryption with certified deletion [BI20], encryption with unclonable decryption keys [GZ20, CLLZ21], and tokenized signatures [BS16].

© International Association for Cryptologic Research 2023
J. Guo and R. Steinfeld (Eds.): ASIACRYPT 2023, LNCS 14445, pp. 39–72, 2023.
https://doi.org/10.1007/978-981-99-8742-9_2

One of the oldest and (arguably) the most popular unclonable primitives is quantum money, which was first introduced in a seminal work by Wiesner [Wie83]. A quantum money scheme enables a bank to issue digital money represented as quantum states. Informally, the security guarantee states that it is computationally infeasible to produce counterfeit digital money states. That is, a malicious user, given one money state, cannot produce two money states that are both accepted by a pre-defined verification procedure. There are two notions we can consider here. The first notion is *private-key* quantum money, where the verification procedure is private. That is, in order to check whether a money state is valid, we need to submit the state to the bank which decides its validity. A more useful notion is *public-key* quantum money, where anyone can verify the validity of money states. While private-key money schemes have been extensively studied and numerous constructions, including information-theoretic ones, have been proposed, the same cannot be said for public-key quantum money schemes.

Aaronson and Christiano [AC13] first demonstrated the feasibility of unconditionally secure public-key quantum money in the oracle model; meaning that all algorithms in the scheme (e.g., the minting and verification algorithms) query a black-box oracle during their execution. In the standard (i.e., non-oracle) model, there are two types of constructions known for building quantum money:

- In the first category, we have constructions borrowing sophisticated tools from different areas of mathematics, such as knot theory [FGH+12], quaternion algebras [KSS21] and lattices [Zha21]. The constructions in this category have been susceptible to cryptanalytic attacks as demonstrated by a couple of recent works [Rob21, BDG22, MLZ22]. We are still in the nascent stages of understanding the security of these candidates[1].
- In the second category, we have constructions based on well-studied (or perhaps *better*-studied) cryptographic primitives. In this category, we have constructions [Zha21, Shm22a, Shm22b] based on indistinguishability obfuscation (iO), first initiated by Zhandry [Zha21].

We focus on the second category. Constructions from existing primitives, especially from those that can be based on well-studied assumptions, would position public-key quantum money on firmer foundations. Unfortunately, existing constructions of indistinguishability obfuscation are either post-quantum insecure [AJL+19, JLS21, JLS22] or are based on newly introduced cryptographic assumptions [GP21, BDGM20, WW21, DQV+21] that have been subjected to cryptanalytic attacks [HJL21].

The goal of our work is to understand the feasibility of constructing public-key quantum money from fundamental and well-studied cryptographic primitives. We approach this direction via the lens of black-box separations. Black-box separations have been extensively studied in classical cryptography [Rud91, Sim98, GKM+00, RTV04, BM09, DLMM11, GKLM12, BDV17]. We say that a primitive A cannot be constructed from another primitive B in a

---

[1] A recent work by [MLZ22] presents a nice framework capturing many of the candidate constructions of public-key quantum money.

black-box manner if there exists a computational world (defined by an oracle) where B exists but A does not. Phrased another way, these separations rule out constructions of primitive A where primitive B is used in a black-box manner. In this case, we say that there is a black-box separation between A and B. Black-box separations have been essential in understanding the relationship between different cryptographic primitives. Perhaps surprisingly, they have also served as a guiding light in designing cryptographic constructions. One such example is the setting of identity-based encryption (IBE). A couple of works [BPR+08, PRV12] demonstrated the difficulty of constructing IBE from the decisional Diffie Hellman (DDH) assumption using a black-box construction which prompted the work of [DG17] who used non-black-box techniques to construct IBE from DDH.

1.1 Our Work

Black-Box Separations for Unclonable Cryptography. We initiate the study of black-box separations in unclonable cryptography. In this work, we study a black-box separation between public-key quantum money and (post-quantum secure) collision-resistant hash functions. To the best of our knowledge, our work takes the first step in ruling out certain approaches to constructing public-key quantum money from well-studied cryptographic primitives.

Model. We first discuss the model in which we prove the black-box separation. We consider two oracles with the first being a random oracle $\mathcal{R}$ (i.e., a uniformly random function) and the second being a PSPACE oracle (i.e., one that can solve PSPACE-complete problems). We investigate the feasibility of quantum money schemes and collision-resistant hash functions in the presence of $\mathcal{R}$ and PSPACE. That is, all the algorithms of the quantum money schemes and also the adversarial entities are given access to the oracles $\mathcal{R}$ and PSPACE.

There are two ways we can model a quantum algorithm to have access to an oracle. The first is *classical access*, where the algorithms in the quantum money scheme can only make classical queries to the oracle; that is, each query to the oracle is measured in the computational basis before forwarding it to the oracle. If an algorithm A has classical access to an oracle, say $\mathcal{U}$, we denote this by $A^{\mathcal{U}}$. The second is *quantum access*, where the algorithms can make superposition queries. That is, an algorithm can submit a state of the form $\sum_{x,y} \alpha_{x,y}|x\rangle|y\rangle$ to the oracle $\mathcal{O}$ and it receives back $\sum_{x,y} \alpha_{x,y}|x\rangle|\mathcal{O}(x) \oplus y\rangle$. If an algorithm A has quantum access to an oracle $\mathcal{U}$, we denote this by $A^{|\mathcal{U}\rangle}$.

Our ultimate goal is to obtain black-box separations in the quantum access model, where the algorithms in the quantum money scheme can query oracles in superposition. However, there are two major obstacles to achieving this.

First, analyzing the quantum access model in quantum cryptography has been notoriously challenging. For example, it is not yet known how to generalize to the quantum access setting black-box separations between key agreement protocols – a *classical* cryptographic primitive – and one-way functions [IR90]. Attempts to tackle special cases have already encountered significant barriers [ACC+22], and have connections to long-standing conjectures in quantum query complexity (like the Aaronson-Ambainis conjecture [AA09]).

Second, we have to contend with the difficulty that quantum money is an *inherently quantum* cryptographic primitive. A black-box separation requires designing an adversary that can effectively clone a quantum banknote given a *single* copy of it. Here one encounters problems of a uniquely quantum nature, such as the No-Cloning Theorem [WZ82, Die82] and the fact that measuring the banknote will in general disturb it.

We present partial progress towards the ultimate goal stated above by simplifying the problem and focusing exclusively on this second obstacle: we prove black-box separations where the banknote verification algorithm in the quantum money schemes makes *classical* queries to the random oracle $\mathcal{R}$ (but still can make quantum queries to the PSPACE oracle), and the minting algorithm may still make quantum queries to both $\mathcal{R}$ and PSPACE oracles. As we will see, even this special case of quantum money schemes is already challenging and nontrivial to analyze. We believe that our techniques may ultimately be extendable to the general setting (if there indeed exists a black-box impossibility in the general setting!), where all algorithms can make quantum queries to all oracles, and furthermore help prove black-box separations of other quantum cryptographic primitives.

Main Theorem. We will state our theorem more formally. A quantum money scheme consists of three quantum polynomial-time (QPT) algorithms, namely (KeyGen, Mint, Ver), where KeyGen produces a public key-secret key pair, Mint uses the secret key to produce money states and a serial number associated with money states and finally, Ver determines the validity of money states using the public key. We consider *oracle-aided* quantum money schemes, where these algorithms have access to a random oracle $\mathcal{R}$ and a PSPACE oracle, defined above.

Theorem 1 (Informal, Theorem 5). *Any public-key quantum money scheme* (KeyGen$^{|\mathcal{R}\rangle, |\mathsf{PSPACE}\rangle}$, Mint$^{|\mathcal{R}\rangle, |\mathsf{PSPACE}\rangle}$, Ver$^{\mathcal{R}, |\mathsf{PSPACE}\rangle}$) *is insecure.*

By insecurity, we mean the following. There exists a quantum polynomial-time (QPT) adversary $\mathcal{A}$ such that $\mathcal{A}^{\mathcal{R}, |\mathsf{PSPACE}\rangle}$, given a money state (pk, ρ_s, s), where pk is the public key and s is a serial number, with non-negligible probability, can produce two (possibly entangled) states that both pass the verification checks with respect to the same serial number s. The probability is taken over the randomness of $\mathcal{R}$ and also over the randomness of KeyGen, Mint, Ver and $\mathcal{A}$. We note that only KeyGen and Mint can have quantum access to $\mathcal{R}$, while Ver only has classical access. On the other hand, we show that the adversary $\mathcal{A}$ only needs classical access to $\mathcal{R}$.

Furthermore, we note that the random oracle $\mathcal{R}$ constitutes a collision-resistant hash function against quantum polynomial-time adversaries that can make queries to $(\mathcal{R}, |\mathsf{PSPACE}\rangle)$ [Zha15]. We note that $\mathcal{R}$ still remains collision-resistant even when the adversaries can make *quantum* queries to $\mathcal{R}$, not just classical ones.

Implications. Our main result rules out a class of public-key quantum money constructions that (a) base their security on collision-resistant hash functions, (b) use the hash functions in a black-box way, and (c) where the verification algorithm makes classical queries to the hash function. Clearly, it would be desirable to generalize the result to the case where the verification algorithm can make quantum queries to the hash function. However, there are some conceptual challenges to going beyond classical verification queries (which we discuss in more detail in Sect. 2.2).

The class of quantum money schemes in this hybrid classical-quantum query model is quite interesting on its own and a well-motivated setting. For example, in Zhandry's public-key quantum money scheme [Zha21], the mint procedure only needs classical access to the underlying cryptographic primitives (when the component that uses cryptographic primitives is viewed as a black-box) while the verification procedure makes quantum queries. In the constructions of copy-protection due to Coladangelo et al. [CLLZ21, CMP20], the copy-protection algorithm only makes classical queries to the cryptographic primitives in the case of [CLLZ21] and the random oracle in the case of [CMP20] whereas the evaluation algorithm in both constructions make quantum queries. Finally, in the construction of unclonable encryption in [AKL+22], all the algorithms only make classical queries to the random oracle. Given these constructions, we believe it is important to understand what is feasible or impossible for unclonable cryptosystems in the hybrid classical-quantum query model.

Secondly, we believe that the hybrid classical-quantum query model is a useful testbed for developing techniques needed for black-box separations, and for gaining insight into the structure of unclonable cryptographic primitives. Even in this special case, there are a number of technical and conceptual challenges to overcome in order to get our black-box separation of Theorem 1. We believe that the techniques developed in this paper will be a useful starting point for future work in black-box separations in unclonable cryptography.

Other Separations. As a corollary of our main result, we obtain black-box separations between public-key quantum money and many other well-studied cryptographic primitives such as one-way functions, private-key encryption and digital signatures.

Our result also gives a separation between public-key quantum money and collapsing hash functions in the same setting as above; that is, when Ver makes classical queries to $\mathcal{R}$. This follows from a result due to Unruh [Unr16] who showed that random oracles are collapsing. Collapsing hash functions are the quantum analog of collision-resistant hash functions. Informally speaking, a hash function is collapsing if an adversary cannot distinguish a uniform superposition of inputs, say $|\psi\rangle$, mapping to a random output y versus a computational basis state obtained by measuring $|\psi\rangle$ in the computational basis. Zhandry [Zha21] showed that hash functions that are collision-resistant but not collapsing imply the existence of public-key quantum money. Thus our result rules out a class of constructions of quantum money from collapsing functions, improving our understanding of the relationship between them.

Acknowledgments. We thank anonymous conference referees, Qipeng Liu, Yao Ching Hsieh, and Xingjian Li for their helpful comments. HY is supported by AFOSR award FA9550-21-1-0040 and NSF CAREER award CCF-2144219.

2   Our Techniques in a Nutshell

We present a high-level overview of the techniques involved in proving Theorem 1. But first, we will briefly discuss the correctness guarantee of *oracle-aided* public-key quantum money schemes.

Reusability. In a quantum money scheme (KeyGen, Mint, Ver), we require that Ver accepts a state and a serial number produced by Mint with overwhelming probability. However, for all we know, Ver, during the verification process, might destroy the state. A more useful correctness definition is reusability, which states that a money state can be repeatedly verified without losing its validity. In general, one can show that the gentle measurement lemma [Win99] does prove that correctness implies reusability. However, as observed in [AK22], this is not the case when Ver has only classical access to an oracle. Specifically, Ver has classical access to $\mathcal{R}$. Hence, we need to explicitly define δ_r-reusability in this setting. Roughly speaking, we require the following: the residual state obtained after we run the verification process polynomially many times should still be accepted by Ver with probability at least δ_r.

2.1   Warmup: Insecurity When $\mathcal{R}$ Is Absent

Towards developing techniques to prove Theorem 1, let us first tackle a simpler statement. Suppose we have a secure public-key quantum money scheme (KeyGen, Mint, Ver). This means that any QPT adversary cannot break the security of this scheme. But what about oracle-aided adversaries? In more detail, we ask the following question: *Does there exist a QPT algorithm, given quantum access to a* PSPACE *oracle, that violates the security of* (KeyGen, Mint, Ver)*?*

Even this seemingly simple question is challenging! Let us understand why. Classical cryptographic primitives (even post-quantum secure ones) such as encryption schemes or digital signatures can be broken by efficient adversaries who have access to even NP oracles. This follows from the fact that we can efficiently reduce the problem of breaking the scheme to the problem of determining membership in a language. For instance, in order to succeed in breaking an encryption scheme, the adversary has to decide whether the instance (pk, ct, m) $\in L$, where pk is a public key, ct is a ciphertext, m is a message and L consists of instances of the form (pk, ct, m), where ct is an encryption of m with respect to the public key pk. Implicitly, we are using the fact that pk, ct, m are binary strings. Emulating a similar approach in the case of quantum money would result in *quantum* instances and it is not clear how to leverage PSPACE, or more generally any classical oracle, to complete the reduction.

Synthesizing Witness States. Towards addressing the above question, we reduce the task of breaking the security of the quantum money scheme using PSPACE to the task of finding states accepted by the verifier in quantum polynomial space. This reduction is enabled by the following observation, due to Rosenthal and Yuen [RY21]: a set of pure states computable by a quantum polynomial space algorithm can be synthesized by a QPT algorithm with quantum access to a *classical* PSPACE oracle. Implicit in the result of [RY21] is the following important point: in order to synthesize the state using the PSPACE oracle, we need the entire description of the quantum polynomial space algorithm generating the pure states.

In more detail, we show the following statement: for every[2] verification key pk, serial number s, there exists a pure state[3] $\rho_{pk,s}$ that is accepted by $Ver(pk, s, \cdot)$ with non-negligible probability and moreover, can be generated by a quantum polynomial space algorithm.

The first attempt is to follow the classical brute-force search algorithm. Namely, we repeat the following for exponential times: guess a quantum state ρ uniformly at random and if ρ is accepted by $Ver(pk, s, \cdot)$ with non-negligible probability, output ρ and terminate. (Output an arbitrary state if all the iterations fail.) However, there are two problems with this attempt. Firstly, in general, it's not clear how to calculate the acceptance probability of $Ver(pk, s, \rho)$ in polynomial space (ρ needs exponential bits to represent). Secondly, ρ might be destroyed when we calculate the acceptance probability.

To fix the first problem, we note that an estimation of the acceptance probability is already good enough and it can be done using a method introduced by Marriott and Watrous [MW05] (called MW technique). The MW technique allows us to efficiently estimate the acceptance probability of a verification algorithm on a state with only one copy of that state. Furthermore, it does not disturb the state too much in the sense that the expected acceptance probability of the residual state does not decay too significantly, which fixes the second problem.

This brings us to our second attempt. We repeat the following process exponentially many times: apply the MW technique on a maximally mixed state and if the estimated acceptance probability happens to be non-negligible, output the residual state and terminate. (Output an arbitrary state if all the iterations fail.) As the MW technique is efficient, this algorithm only uses polynomial space. Furthermore, intuitively we can get a state that is accepted by Ver with non-negligible acceptance probability, provided that such a state exists.

A Remark About the PSPACE *Oracle.* Some readers may wonder about the significance of the PSPACE oracle – why consider this instead of (say) EXP, an oracle for exponential time? From a *query complexity* point of view, where one only cares about the number of queries made by the adversary to the random oracle $\mathcal{R}$, the choice of PSPACE oracle versus EXP oracle versus some other clas-

---

[2] Technically, we show a weaker statement which holds for almost every (pk, s).

[3] Technically, we require that the reduced density matrix of $\rho_{pk,s}$ is accepted by Ver.

sical oracle is not significant; this is because we can assume that the adversary otherwise has unlimited computational power.

On the other hand, we view our result as presenting a potential "computational world" (in the sense of Impagliazzo's worlds [Imp95]) where black-box access to a hash function (in the form of the random oracle $\mathcal{R}$) does not suffice to construct (a class of) quantum money schemes. We know that $\mathsf{P} \neq \mathsf{EXP}$, so presenting a computational world where adversaries have oracle access to EXP is irrelevant. However, we do not yet know (as of writing) whether $\mathsf{P} = \mathsf{PSPACE}$, and thus having access to a PSPACE oracle could in principle describe the "true" computational world that we live in.

2.2   Insecurity in the Presence of $\mathcal{R}$

So far, we considered the task of violating the security of a quantum money scheme where the honest algorithms did not have access to any oracle. Let us go back to the oracle-aided quantum money schemes, where, all the algorithms (honest and adversarial) have access to the random oracle and $|\mathsf{PSPACE}\rangle$. Our goal is to construct an adversary that violates the security of quantum money schemes. *But didn't we just solve this problem?* Recall that when invoking [RY21], it was crucial that we knew the entire description of the polynomial space algorithm in order to synthesize the state. However, when we are considering oracle-aided verification algorithms, denoted by $\mathsf{Ver}^{\mathcal{R},|\mathsf{PSPACE}\rangle}$, we don't have the full description of[4] $\mathsf{Ver}^{\mathcal{R},|\mathsf{PSPACE}\rangle}$. Thus, we cannot carry out the synthesizing process.

A natural approach to fix this is to replace $\mathcal{R}$ with a classical database D (that we have a full description of) and synthesize two states with respect to D. To be more specific, our QPT adversary $\mathcal{A}^{\mathcal{R},|\mathsf{PSPACE}\rangle}$ does the following: it first finds a database D (requirements and details to be stated later) and constructs another circuit $\mathsf{Ver}^{D,|\mathsf{PSPACE}\rangle}$ that runs $\mathsf{Ver}^{\mathcal{R},|\mathsf{PSPACE}\rangle}$ and when $\mathsf{Ver}^{\mathcal{R},|\mathsf{PSPACE}\rangle}$ makes a query to $\mathcal{R}$, the query is answered by D. Then, $\mathcal{A}$ synthesizes two states (s, σ_s') and (s, σ_s''), using $|\mathsf{PSPACE}\rangle$, such that both the states are accepted by $\mathsf{Ver}^{D,|\mathsf{PSPACE}\rangle}$, and outputs the two states σ_s', σ_s''.

What requirements does the database D need to satisfy in order to make the above construction work? Firstly, we should ensure that there exists a state that is accepted by $\mathsf{Ver}^{D,|\mathsf{PSPACE}\rangle}(\mathsf{pk}, s, \cdot)$ with high enough probability. Without this guarantee, the synthesizing process does not work. Secondly, the synthesizing process only guarantees that σ_s' and σ_s'' are accepted by $\mathsf{Ver}^{D,|\mathsf{PSPACE}\rangle}$ with high probability. We hope they are also accepted by $\mathsf{Ver}^{\mathcal{R},|\mathsf{PSPACE}\rangle}$ with high probability.

A good candidate for the state in the first requirement is a valid banknote ρ_s[5], which is accepted by $\mathsf{Ver}^{\mathcal{R},|\mathsf{PSPACE}\rangle}$ with high probability. Thus all we need is to ensure that $\mathsf{Ver}^{D,|\mathsf{PSPACE}\rangle}$ and $\mathsf{Ver}^{\mathcal{R},|\mathsf{PSPACE}\rangle}$ behave not too far away from each other on ρ_s and the synthesized state σ_s'.

---

[4] The fact that we don't have the description of $\mathcal{R}$ is the problem here.

[5] Actually we use the residual state after running verification polynomially many times on the valid banknote.

Towards satisfying these requirements, we first focus on a simple case when KeyGen and Mint make classical queries to $\mathcal{R}$ and we later, focus on the quantum queries case.

KeyGen and Mint: Classical Queries to $\mathcal{R}$

Compiling Out $\mathcal{R}$. Suppose we can magically find a database D, using only polynomially many queries to $\mathcal{R}$, such that all the query-answer pairs made by Ver to $\mathcal{R}$ are contained in D. In this case, $\mathsf{Ver}^{D,|\mathsf{PSPACE}\rangle}$ acts exactly the same as $\mathsf{Ver}^{\mathcal{R},|\mathsf{PSPACE}\rangle}$ on ρ_s and the synthesized state, so the requirements are satisfied.

Of course, it is wishful for us to hope that we can find a database D by making only polynomially many queries to $\mathcal{R}$ that is perfectly consistent with the queries made by Ver. Instead, we hope to recover a good enough database D. In more detail, we aim to recover a database D that captures all the relevant queries made by KeyGen and Mint.

Let D_{KeyGen} and D_{Mint} be the collection of query-answer pairs made by KeyGen and Mint respectively. A query made by Ver is called *bad* if this query is in $D_{\mathsf{KeyGen}} \cup D_{\mathsf{Mint}}$ and moreover, this query was not recorded in D. If Ver makes *bad* queries then the answers returned by D will likely be inconsistent with $\mathcal{R}$. By the lazy sampling technique, those positions outside $D \cup D_{\mathsf{KeyGen}} \cup D_{\mathsf{Mint}}$ are hidden for everyone. So those *bad* queries are the only cause for the difference between $\mathsf{Ver}^{D,|\mathsf{PSPACE}\rangle}$ and $\mathsf{Ver}^{\mathcal{R},|\mathsf{PSPACE}\rangle}$. Our hope is that the probability of Ver making bad queries on ρ_s and σ'_s is upper bounded by an inverse polynomial so that D is sufficient for successful simulation for both states.

But how do we recover this database D? To see how, we will first focus on a simple case before dealing with the general case.

State-Independent Database Simulation. Note that the queries made by Ver could potentially depend on its input state. For now, we will assume that the distribution of queries made by Ver is independent of the input state. We will deal with the state-dependent query distributions later.

The first attempt to generate D would be to rely upon techniques introduced by Canetti, Kalai and Paneth [CKP15] who, in a different context – that of proving the impossibility of obfuscation in the random oracle model – showed how to generate a database that is sufficient to simulate the queries made by the evaluation algorithm. Suppose (s, ρ_s) is the state generated by Mint. Then, run $\mathsf{Ver}^{\mathcal{R},|\mathsf{PSPACE}\rangle}(\mathsf{pk}, s, \rho_s)$ a fixed polynomially many times, referred to as *test* executions, by querying $\mathcal{R}$. In each execution of $\mathsf{Ver}^{\mathcal{R},|\mathsf{PSPACE}\rangle}$, record all the queries made by Ver along with their answers. The union of queries made in all the executions of Ver will be assigned to the database D. In the context of obfuscation for classical circuits, [CKP15] argue that, except with inverse polynomial probability, the queries made by the evaluation algorithm can be successfully simulated by D. This argument is shown by proving an upper bound on the probability that the evaluation algorithm makes bad queries.

A similar analysis can also be made in our context to argue that D suffices for successful simulation. That is, we can argue that the state we obtain after all the executions of Ver (which could be very different from the state we started off with) can be successfully simulated using D. The same holds for the synthesized state since the queries are state-independent. However, it is crucial for our analysis to go through that $D_{\sf Ver}$ (the query-answer pairs made during Ver) is *independent* of the state input to Ver.

State-Dependent Database Simulation. For all we know, $D_{\sf Ver}$ could indeed depend on the input state. In this case, we can no longer appeal to the argument of [CKP15]. At a high level, the reason is due to the fact that after each execution of Ver, the money state could potentially change and this would affect the distribution of $D_{\sf Ver}$ in the further executions of Ver in such a way that the execution of Ver on the final state (which could be different from the input state in the first execution of Ver) cannot be simulated using the database D.

Instead, we will rely upon a technique due to [AK22], who studied a similar problem in the context of copy-protection. They showed that by randomizing the number of executions, one can argue that the execution of Ver on the state obtained after all the test executions can be successfully simulated using D, except with inverse polynomial probability. That is, suppose the initial state is $(s, \rho_s^{(0)})$ and after running $\mathsf{Ver}^{\mathcal{R}, |\mathsf{PSPACE}\rangle}$, t number of times where $t \xleftarrow{\$} \{0, 1, \cdots, T\}$, let the resulting state be $(s, \rho_s^{(t)})$. Let D record all the queries during the verifications along with the answers. Then, we have the guarantee that on input $\rho_s^{(t)}$, Ver does not make any bad queries, except with inverse polynomial probability. But how does Ver work on the synthesized state?

Every Mistake We Make is Progress. Notice that each time

- either on the synthesized state, Ver does not make any bad query, in which case D suffices for successful simulation on the synthesized state
- or we will recover a new query in $D_{\sf KeyGen} \cup D_{\sf Mint}$ that is not contained in D

When the second case happens, our knowledge of $D_{\sf KeyGen} \cup D_{\sf Mint}$ improves. So we can get a better database D by adding all the queries made. That is, whenever we fail to get a successful simulation with D, we make progress in the sense that we necessarily learn a new query in $D_{\sf KeyGen} \cup D_{\sf Mint}$. Thus, with each mistake, we make progress. Since there are only a polynomial number of queries in $D_{\sf KeyGen} \cup D_{\sf Mint}$, the second case can only happen for polynomial times. So we will end up with the first case (which is what we want) except with inverse polynomial probability as long as we try a randomized large enough times.

Our Attack. In more detail, we have the following attack. On input a money state (s, ρ_s) and the public key pk, do the following:

1. $D \leftarrow \emptyset, \rho_s^{(0)} \leftarrow \rho_s, t \xleftarrow{\$} \{0, 1, \cdots, T\}, j \xleftarrow{\$} \{0, 1, \cdots, N\}$
2. **Test phase:** For $i = 0, 1, \cdots, t$, do the following
   (a) Run $\mathsf{Ver}^{\mathcal{R}, |\mathsf{PSPACE}\rangle}(\mathsf{pk}, s, \cdot)$ on $\rho_s^{(i)}$ and obtain $\rho_s^{(i+1)}$
   (b) Add the query-answer pairs to $\mathcal{R}$ into D
3. **Update phase:** For $i = 0, 1, \cdots, j$, do the following

(a) Let $\mathsf{Ver}^{D,|\mathsf{PSPACE}\rangle}$ be the verification circuit as defined earlier. Using quantum access to PSPACE, synthesize a state (s, σ_s) as per Sect. 2.1, such that the state is accepted by $\mathsf{Ver}^{D,|\mathsf{PSPACE}\rangle}$.

(b) Run $\mathsf{Ver}^{\mathcal{R},|\mathsf{PSPACE}\rangle}(\mathsf{pk}, s, \cdot)$ on σ_s and add the query-answer pairs into D.

4. **Synthesize phase:** Using quantum access to PSPACE, synthesize two states (s, σ'_s) and (s, σ''_s) such that both the states are accepted by $\mathsf{Ver}^{D,|\mathsf{PSPACE}\rangle}$ and output (s, σ'_s), (s, σ''_s).

In the technical sections, we analyze the above attack and prove that it works.

KeyGen and Mint : Quantum Queries to $\mathcal{R}$ Now let's move on to the more general case where KeyGen and Mint can make quantum queries to $\mathcal{R}$. The important point to note here is the form of our aforementioned attacker. It only takes advantage of the fact that Ver makes classical queries to $\mathcal{R}$. When KeyGen and Mint make quantum queries to $\mathcal{R}$ while Ver makes classical queries to $\mathcal{R}$, we can still run the attacker. What is left is to show that the same attacker works even when KeyGen and Mint make quantum queries to $\mathcal{R}$.

The main difficulty in carrying out the intuitions in Sect. 2.2 to the more general case is that it's difficult to define an analog of D_{KeyGen} and D_{Mint}. To give a flavour of the difficulty, let's first consider two naive attempts.

The first attempt is to define D_{KeyGen} and D_{Mint} to be those query-answer pairs asked (with non-zero amplitudes) during KeyGen and Mint. However, this attempt suffers from the problem that in this way, $D_{\mathsf{KeyGen}} \cup D_{\mathsf{Mint}}$ can have exponential elements. So even if each time we can make progress in the sense that we recover some new elements in $D_{\mathsf{KeyGen}} \cup D_{\mathsf{Mint}}$, there is no guarantee that the update phase will terminate in polynomial time.

The second attempt is to only include queries that are asked "heavily" during KeyGen and Mint. To be more specific, let D_{KeyGen} and D_{Mint} be query-answer pairs asked with inverse polynomial squared amplitudes during KeyGen and Mint. However, with this plausible definition, the claim does not hold that whenever $\mathsf{Ver}^{D,|\mathsf{PSPACE}\rangle}$ fails to simulate $\mathsf{Ver}^{\mathcal{R},|\mathsf{PSPACE}\rangle}$, we can recover a query inside $D_{\mathsf{KeyGen}} \cup D_{\mathsf{Mint}} - D$, which is a crucial idea underlying our intuitions in Sect. 2.2. This is because one can always add a random check in the scheme without enlarging $D_{\mathsf{KeyGen}} \cup D_{\mathsf{Mint}}$. In more detail, let Mint make an additional quantum query to $\mathcal{R}$ on $\frac{1}{\sqrt{2^n}} \sum_{i=0}^{2^n-1} |i\rangle|0\rangle$ to get a state $\frac{1}{\sqrt{2^n}} \sum_{i=0}^{2^n-1} |i\rangle|\mathcal{R}(i)\rangle$, measure the first register to get a value i which will be included in the serial number, and include the second register into the money state. Let Ver make an additional query on i to check whether that part of the money state is $\mathcal{R}(i)$. In this case, it is possible that $i \notin D_{\mathsf{KeyGen}} \cup D_{\mathsf{Mint}}$. But when $i \notin D$, $\mathsf{Ver}^{D,|\mathsf{PSPACE}\rangle}$ and $\mathsf{Ver}^{\mathcal{R},|\mathsf{PSPACE}\rangle}$ can behave differently even if Ver only queries i, which means the only query we learn from this failure does not give us better knowledge of $D_{\mathsf{KeyGen}} \cup D_{\mathsf{Mint}}$.

Purified View. Our insight is to consider an alternate world called the *purified view*. In this alternate world, we run everything coherently; in more detail, we consider a uniform superposition of $\mathcal{R}$, and run Mint, KeyGen and even the attacker coherently (i.e., no intermediate measurements). If the attacker is successful in this alternate world then he is also successful in the real world where $\mathcal{R}$ and the queries made by Ver to $\mathcal{R}$ are measured. We then employ the compressed oracle technique by Zhandry [Zha18] to coherently recover the database of query-answer pairs recorded during KeyGen, Mint and relate this with the database recorded during Ver. Using an involved analysis, we then show many of the insights from the case where KeyGen, Mint make classical queries to $\mathcal{R}$ can be translated to the quantum query setting.

Challenges to Handling Quantum Verification Queries. It is natural to wonder whether we can similarly use the compressed oracle technique to handle quantum queries made by Ver. Unfortunately, there are inherent limitations. Recall that in our attack, the adversary records the verifier's classical query-answer pairs in a database, uses this to produce a *classical* description of a verification circuit (that does not make any queries to the random oracle), and submits the circuit description to a PSPACE oracle in order to synthesize a money state. If the verifier instead makes quantum queries, then a natural idea is to use Zhandry's compressed oracle technique again to record the quantum queries. However, there are two conceptual challenges to implementing this idea.

First, in the compressed oracle technique, the queries are being recorded by the *oracle* itself in a "database register", and not the adversary in the cryptosystem. In our setting, we are trying to construct an adversary to record the queries, but it does not have access to the oracle's database register. In general, any attempts by the adversary to get some information about the query positions of Ver could potentially disturb the intermediate states of the Ver algorithm; it is then unclear how to use the original guarantees of Ver. Another way of saying this is that Zhandry's compressed oracle technique is typically used in the *security analysis* to show limits on the adversary's ability to break some cryptosystem. But in our case, we want to use some kind of quantum recording technique in the adversary's *attack*.

Secondly, the natural approach to using the PSPACE oracle is to leverage it to synthesize alleged banknotes. However, since the PSPACE oracle is a classical function (which may be accessed in superposition), it requires polynomial-length classical strings as input. In our approach, the adversary submits a classical description of a verification circuit with query/answer pairs hardcoded inside. On the other hand if Ver makes quantum queries, it may query exponentially many positions of the random oracle $\mathcal{R}$ in superposition, and it is unclear how to "squeeze" the relevant information about the queries into a polynomial-sized classical string that could be utilized by the PSPACE oracle.

This suggests that we may need a fundamentally new approach to recording quantum queries in order to handle the case when the verification algorithm makes quantum queries.

2.3   Related Work

Quantum Money. The notion of quantum money was first conceived in the paper by Wiesner [Wie83]. In the same work, a construction of private-key quantum money was proposed. Wiesner's construction has been well studied and its limitations [Lut10] and security guarantees [MVW12] have been well understood. Other constructions of private-key quantum money have also been studied. Ji, Liu and Song [JLS18] construct private-key quantum money from pseudorandom quantum states. Radian and Sattath [RS22] construct private-key quantum money with classical bank from quantum hardness of learning with errors.

Regarding public-key quantum money, Aaronson and Christiano [AC13] present a construction of public-key quantum money in the oracle model. Zhandry [Zha21] instantiated this oracle and showed how to construct public-key quantum money based on the existence of post-quantum iO [BGI+01]. Recently, Shmueli [Shm22a] showed how to achieve public-key quantum money with classical bank, assuming post-quantum iO and quantum hardness of learning with errors. Constructions [FGH+12, KSS21] of public-key quantum money from newer assumptions have also been explored although they have been susceptible to quantum attacks [Rob21, BDG22].

Black-Box Separations in Quantum Cryptography. So far, most of the existing black-box separations in quantum cryptography have focused on extending black-box separations for classical cryptographic primitives to the quantum setting. Hosoyamada and Yamakawa [HY20] extend the black-box separation between collision-resistant hash functions and one-way functions [Sim98] to the quantum setting. Austrin et al. [ACC+22] showed a black-box separation between key agreement and one-way functions in the setting when the honest parties can perform quantum computation but only have access to classical communication. Cao and Xue [CX21] extended classical black-box separations between one-way permutations and one-way functions to the quantum setting.

3   Preliminaries

For a string x, let $|x|$ denote its length. Let $[n]$ denote the set $\{0, 1, \cdots, n-1\}$ for any positive integer n.

3.1   Quantum States, Algorithms, and Oracles

A *register* R is a finite-dimensional complex Hilbert space. If A, B, C are registers, for example, then the concatenation ABC denotes the tensor product of the associated Hilbert spaces. For a linear transformation L and register R, we sometimes write L_R to indicate that L acts on R, and similarly we sometimes write ρ_R to indicate that a state ρ is in the register R. We write $\mathrm{Tr}(\cdot)$ to denote trace, and $\mathrm{Tr}_R(\cdot)$ to denote the partial trace over a register R.

For a pure state $|\varphi\rangle$, we write φ to denote the density matrix $|\varphi\rangle\langle\varphi|$. Let I denote the identity matrix. Let $\mathrm{TD}(\rho, \sigma)$ denote the trace distance between two density matrices ρ, σ.

Quantum Circuits. We specify the model of quantum circuits that we work with in this paper. For convenience we fix the universal gate set $\{H, CNOT, T\}$ [NC10, Chapter 4] (although our results hold for any universal gate set consisting of gates with algebraic entries). Quantum circuits can include unitary gates from the aforementioned universal gate set, as well as non-unitary gates that (a) introduce new qubits initialized in the zero state, (b) trace them out, or (c) measure them in the standard basis. The description of a circuit is a sequence of gates (unitary or non-unitary) along with a specification of which qubits they act on.

We call a sequence of quantum circuits $C = (C_x)_{x \in \{0,1\}^*}$ a *quantum algorithm*. We say that C is *polynomial-time* if there exists a polynomial p such that C_x has size at most $p(|x|)$. We say that a quantum algorithm $C = (C_x)_{x \in \{0,1\}^*}$ is *time-uniform* (or simply *uniform*) if there exists a polynomial-time Turing machine that on input x outputs the description of C_x.

Let $C = (C_x)_{x \in \{0,1\}^*}$ denote a quantum algorithm. Given a string $x \in \{0,1\}^*$ and a state ρ whose number of qubits matches the input size of the circuit C_x, we write $C(x, \rho)$ to denote the output of circuit C_x on input ρ. The output will in general be a mixed state as the circuit C_x can perform measurements.

Oracle Algorithms. *Oracle algorithms* are quantum algorithms whose circuits, in addition to having the gates as described above, have the ability to query (perhaps in superposition) a function O (called an *oracle*) which may act on many qubits. This is essentially the same as the standard quantum query model [NC10, Chapter 6], except the circuits may perform non-unitary operations such as measurement, reset, and tracing out. Each oracle call is counted as a single gate towards the size complexity of a circuit. The notion of time-uniformity for oracle algorithms is the same as with non-oracle algorithms: there is a polynomial-time Turing machine – which does *not* have access to the oracle – that outputs the description of the circuits.

Given an oracle $\mathcal{O} = (\mathcal{O}_n)_{n \in \mathbb{N}}$ where each $\mathcal{O}_n : \{0,1\}^n \to \{0,1\}$ is an n-bit boolean function, we write $C^{\mathcal{O}} = (C_x^{\mathcal{O}})_{x \in \{0,1\}^*}$ to denote an oracle algorithm where each circuit C_x can query any of the functions $(\mathcal{O}_n)_{n \in \mathbb{N}}$ (provided that the oracle does not act on more than the number of qubits of C_x).

In this paper we distinguish between classical and quantum queries. We say that an oracle algorithm $C^{\mathcal{O}}$ makes quantum queries if it can query $\mathcal{O}$ in superposition; this is akin to the standard query model. We say that $C^{\mathcal{O}}$ makes classical queries if, before every oracle call, the input qubits to the oracle are measured in the standard basis. In this case, the algorithm would be querying the oracle on a *probabilistic mixture* of inputs. For clarity, we write $C^{|\mathcal{O}\rangle}$ to denote C making quantum queries, and $C^{\mathcal{O}}$ to denote C making classical queries.

A specific oracle that we consider throughout is the PSPACE oracle. What we mean by this is a sequence of functions $(\mathsf{PSPACE}_n)_{n \in \mathbb{N}}$ where for every n, the function PSPACE_n decides n-bit instances of a PSPACE-complete language (such as Quantified Satisfiability [Pap94]).

Finally, we will consider *hybrid* oracles $\mathcal{O}$ that are composed of two separate oracles $\mathcal{R}$ and the $|\mathsf{PSPACE}\rangle$ oracle. In this model, the oracle algorithm $C^{\mathcal{O}}$ makes classical queries to $\mathcal{R}$, and quantum queries to PSPACE. We abuse the notation and refer to algorithms having access to hybrid oracles as oracle algorithms.

3.2 Public-Key Quantum Money Schemes

Definition 1 (Oracle-aided Public-Key Quantum Money Schemes). *An oracle-aided public-key quantum money scheme $\mathcal{S}^{\mathcal{O}}$ consists of three uniform polynomial-time oracle algorithms* $\left(\mathsf{KeyGen}^{\mathcal{O}}, \mathsf{Mint}^{\mathcal{O}}, \mathsf{Ver}^{\mathcal{O}}\right)$:

- $\mathsf{KeyGen}^{\mathcal{O}}(1^n)$: *takes as input a security parameter n in unary notation and generates secret key-public key pair $(\mathsf{sk}, \mathsf{pk})$.*
- $\mathsf{Mint}^{\mathcal{O}}(\mathsf{sk})$: *takes as input sk and mints banknote ρ_s associated with the serial number s.*
- $\mathsf{Ver}^{\mathcal{O}}(\mathsf{pk}, (s, \rho_s))$: *takes as inputs pk and an alleged banknote (s, ρ_s) and outputs $\rho'_s \otimes |\mathbf{x}\rangle\langle\mathbf{x}|$, where $\mathbf{x} \in \{\mathsf{Accept}, \mathsf{Reject}\}$ and ρ'_s is the residual state after the verification.*

For simplicity, when we don't care about the output ρ'_s in $\mathsf{Ver}^{\mathcal{O}}$, we sometimes denote the event that $\rho'_s \otimes |\mathsf{Accept}\rangle\langle\mathsf{Accept}| \leftarrow \mathsf{Ver}^{\mathcal{O}}(\mathsf{pk}, (s, \rho_s))$ as $\mathsf{Ver}^{\mathcal{O}}(\mathsf{pk}, (s, \rho_s))$ accepts. When we don't care about whether $\mathsf{Ver}^{\mathcal{O}}$ accepts, we write $\rho'_s \leftarrow \mathsf{Ver}^{\mathcal{O}}(\mathsf{pk}, (s, \rho_s))$ to denote that ρ'_s is the residual state after the verification.

We require the above oracle-aided public-key quantum money scheme to satisfy both correctness and security properties.

Correctness. We first consider the traditional definition of correctness. Roughly speaking, correctness states that the verification algorithm accepts the money state produced by the minting algorithm. Later, we consider a stronger notion called reusability which stipulates that the residual state after the verification is still a valid money state (not necessarily the same as before).

Definition 2 (Correctness). *An oracle-aided public-key quantum money scheme $\left(\mathsf{KeyGen}^{\mathcal{O}}, \mathsf{Mint}^{\mathcal{O}}, \mathsf{Ver}^{\mathcal{O}}\right)$ is δ-**correct** if the following holds for every $n \in \mathbb{N}$:*

$$\Pr\left[\mathsf{Ver}^{\mathcal{O}}(\mathsf{pk}, (s, \rho_s)) \text{ accepts} : \begin{array}{c} (\mathsf{sk},\mathsf{pk})\leftarrow\mathsf{KeyGen}^{\mathcal{O}}(1^n) \\ (s,\rho_s)\leftarrow\mathsf{Mint}^{\mathcal{O}}(\mathsf{sk}) \end{array}\right] \geq \delta,$$

where the probability is also over the choice of $\mathcal{O}$. We omit δ when $\delta \geq 1-\mathsf{negl}(n)$.

Reusability. In this work, we consider a stronger notion called reusability.

Definition 3 (Reusability). *An oracle-aided public-key quantum money scheme $\left(\mathsf{KeyGen}^{\mathcal{O}}, \mathsf{Mint}^{\mathcal{O}}, \mathsf{Ver}^{\mathcal{O}}\right)$ is $x\delta$-**reusable** if the following holds for every $n \in \mathbb{N}$ and for every polynomial $q(n)$:*

$$\Pr\left[\mathsf{Ver}^{\mathcal{O}}(\mathsf{pk}, (s, \rho_s^{(q(n))})) \text{ accepts} : \begin{array}{c} (\mathsf{sk},\mathsf{pk})\leftarrow\mathsf{KeyGen}^{\mathcal{O}}(1^n) \\ (s,\rho_s^{(0)})\leftarrow\mathsf{Mint}^{\mathcal{O}}(\mathsf{sk}) \\ \forall i\in[q(n)],\ \rho_s^{(i+1)}\leftarrow\mathsf{Ver}^{\mathcal{O}}(\mathsf{pk}, (s,\rho_s^{(i)})) \end{array}\right] \geq \delta,$$

where the probability is also over the choice of $\mathcal{O}$. We omit δ when $\delta \geq 1-\mathsf{negl}(n)$.

In general, gentle measurement lemma [Win99] can be invoked to prove that correctness implies reusability. However, this is not the case in our context. The reason is that the verification algorithm performs intermediate measurements whenever it makes classical queries to an oracle and these measurements cannot be deferred to the end.

Security. We consider the following security notion. Basically, it says that no efficient adversary can produce two alleged banknotes from one valid banknote with the same serial number.

Definition 4 (Security). *An oracle-aided public-key quantum money scheme $\left(\mathsf{KeyGen}^{\mathcal{O}}, \mathsf{Mint}^{\mathcal{O}}, \mathsf{Ver}^{\mathcal{O}}\right)$ is δ-secure if the following holds for every $n \in \mathbb{N}$ and for every uniform polynomial-time oracle algorithm $\mathcal{A}^{\mathcal{O}}$:*

$$\Pr\left[\mathsf{Ver}^{\mathcal{O}}(\mathsf{pk},(s,\phi_1)) \ accepts \ and \ \mathsf{Ver}^{\mathcal{O}}(\mathsf{pk},(s,\phi_2)) \ accepts : \begin{matrix} (\mathsf{sk},\mathsf{pk})\leftarrow\mathsf{KeyGen}^{\mathcal{O}}(1^n) \\ (s,\rho_s)\leftarrow\mathsf{Mint}^{\mathcal{O}}(\mathsf{sk}) \\ \phi\leftarrow\mathcal{A}^{\mathcal{O}}(\mathsf{pk},(s,\rho_s)) \end{matrix}\right] \leq \delta,$$

where the probability is also over the randomness of $\mathcal{O}$. By ϕ_i, we mean the reduced density matrix of ϕ on the ith register. We omit δ when $\delta \leq \mathsf{negl}(n)$.

3.3 Compressed Oracle Techniques

In this section, we present some basics of compressed oracle techniques introduced by Zhandry [Zha18].

For a quantum query algorithm A interacting with a random oracle, let's assume that A only queries the random oracle with n-bit input and gets binary output for simplicity. By the deferred measurement principle, without loss of generality we can write A in the form of a sequence of unitaries $U_0, U_f, U_1, \cdots, U_f, U_k$ where U_f maps $|x\rangle|y\rangle$ to $|x\rangle|y \oplus f(x)\rangle$ for a function f randomly chosen from all the functions with n-bit input and 1-bit output. Then the behavior of A when interacting with a random oracle can be analyzed in the following *purified view*:

- Initialize register A to be the input for A (along with enough ancillas $|0\rangle$) and initialize register F to be a uniform superposition of the truth tables of all functions from $[2^n]$ to $\{0,1\}$.
- Apply $U_0, U_F, U_1, \cdots, U_F, U_k$ where U_i is acting on A and U_F maps $|x\rangle|y\rangle|f\rangle_F$ to $|x\rangle|y \oplus f(x)\rangle|f\rangle_F$.

In fact, the output (mixed) state of A (we also take the randomness of f into account) equals the reduced density matrix on the output register of the state we obtain from the above procedure as U_i, U_F commute with computational basis measurement on F. More generally, the output (mixed) state of a sequence of algorithms with access to random oracle can also be analyzed in the same way.

Definition 5 (Fourier basis). $|\hat{0}\rangle := \frac{1}{\sqrt{2}}(|0\rangle + |1\rangle)$. $|\hat{1}\rangle := \frac{1}{\sqrt{2}}(|0\rangle - |1\rangle)$.

One can easily check that $\{|\hat{0}\rangle, |\hat{1}\rangle\}$ forms a basis because it's just the result of applying hermitian matrix H to $|0\rangle, |1\rangle$. We call this basis as Fourier basis.

The following fact is simple and easy to check, but crucial in compressed oracle techniques. Roughly speaking, it says that if we see *CNOT* in Fourier basis, its control bit and target bit swap.

Lemma 1. *The operator defined by $|y\rangle|y'\rangle \to |y \oplus y'\rangle|y'\rangle$ for all $y, y' \in \{0,1\}$ is the same as the operator defined by $|\hat{y}\rangle|\hat{y'}\rangle \to |\hat{y}\rangle|\widehat{y' \oplus y}\rangle$ for all $y, y' \in \{0,1\}$.*

By Lemma 1, when we view the last two registers in Fourier basis, U_F becomes

$$|x\rangle|\hat{y}\rangle|\widehat{y_0}\rangle|\widehat{y_1}\rangle \cdots |\widehat{y_{2^n-1}}\rangle \to |x\rangle|\hat{y}\rangle|\widehat{y_0}\rangle|\widehat{y_1}\rangle \cdots |\widehat{y_{x-1}}\rangle|\widehat{y_x \oplus y}\rangle|\widehat{y_{x+1}}\rangle \cdots |\widehat{y_{2^n-1}}\rangle.$$

Initially, F is $|\hat{0}\rangle|\hat{0}\rangle \cdots |\hat{0}\rangle$ and each call of U_F only changes one position when viewed in the above way. So after k calls of U_F, the state is in the form of

$$\sum_{\substack{a, y_0, y_1, \cdots, y_{2^n-1} \\ \text{such that there are at most } k \text{ non-zero} \\ \text{in } y_0, y_1, \cdots, y_{2^n-1}}} \alpha_{a, y_0, y_1, \cdots, y_{2^n-1}} |a\rangle_A |\widehat{y_0}\rangle|\widehat{y_1}\rangle \cdots |\widehat{y_{2^n-1}}\rangle.$$

We can record those non-$\hat{0}$ into a database. To be more specific, there exists a unitary that maps those $|\widehat{y_0}\rangle|\widehat{y_1}\rangle \cdots |\widehat{y_{2^n-1}}\rangle$ (perhaps along with some ancillas) to a database $|x_1\rangle|\widehat{y_{x_1}}\rangle \cdots |x_l\rangle|\widehat{y_{x_l}}\rangle$ (perhaps along with some unused space) where $x_1 < x_2 < \cdots < x_l, y_{x_i} \neq 0$ and $l \leq k$. That is, there exists a unitary that can compress the oracle into a database. Furthermore, the inverse of the unitary can decompress the database back to the oracle.

4 Our Attack: Classical Queries to the Random Oracle

In this section, we will attack the oracle-aided public-key quantum money scheme with access to a random oracle $\mathcal{R}$ and $|\text{PSPACE}\rangle$. Formally:

Theorem 2. *Reusable and secure oracle-aided public-key quantum money scheme (KeyGen$^{\mathcal{R}, |\text{PSPACE}\rangle}$, Mint$^{\mathcal{R}, |\text{PSPACE}\rangle}$, Ver$^{\mathcal{R}, |\text{PSPACE}\rangle}$) does not exist where $\mathcal{R}$ is a random oracle.*

But before we dive into the proof, let's introduce a synthesizer, which will be a building block for our attacker. The construction of the synthesizer and its analysis can be found in the full version [AHY23]. Readers can also refer to Sect. 2.1 for intuitions.

Theorem 3. *Let a (called the* guarantee*), b (called the* threshold*) be functions such that $b(n) - a(n) \geq \frac{1}{p(n)}$ for every n where p is a polynomial. Let $V^{|\text{PSPACE}\rangle}$ denote a uniform oracle algorithm. Then there exists a uniform oracle algorithm* Syn *(called the* synthesizer*) such that for every $x \in S$,*

$$\Pr\left[V^{|\text{PSPACE}\rangle}(x, \text{Syn}^{|\text{PSPACE}\rangle}(x)) \text{ accepts}\right] \geq a(|x|)$$

where $S := \left\{x : \max_\rho \Pr\left[V^{|\text{PSPACE}\rangle}(x, \rho) \text{ accepts}\right] \geq b(|x|)\right\}$.

Remark 1. In the classical setting it is easy to see that given a (classical) verifier circuit V (which may make oracle queries to PSPACE), one can find in polynomial space a witness string y that is accepted by V: one can simply perform brute-force search over all strings and check whether V^{PSPACE} accepts x. Theorem 3 shows its quantum counterpart: given the description of such a verifier circuit, with the help of $|PSPACE\rangle$, we can efficiently *synthesize* a witness state ρ that is accepted by V with probability greater than the desired guarantee (provided that there exists a witness state with acceptance probability greater than the threshold), even when the verifier circuit is quantum and can make quantum queries to the PSPACE oracle.

Our synthesizer in Theorem 3 works for uniform oracle algorithm $V^{|PSPACE\rangle}$. However, in the scheme we aim to attack, the verification algorithm has access to random oracle $\mathcal{R}$ in addition to $|PSPACE\rangle$. Inspired by [CKP15, AK22], we try to remove $\mathcal{R}$ and simulate it with a good database. Based on the ideas in Sect. 2.2, we give the following attacker.

Let $\mathcal{O}$ be the hybrid oracle composed of random oracle $\mathcal{R}$ and $|PSPACE\rangle$. For a δ_r-reusable δ_s-secure oracle-aided quantum money scheme $\left(\mathsf{KeyGen}^{\mathcal{O}}, \mathsf{Mint}^{\mathcal{O}}, \mathsf{Ver}^{\mathcal{O}}\right)$ where $\delta_r = 0.99, \delta_s = \mathsf{negl}(n)$, denote $l(n)$ to be the number of queries to $\mathcal{R}$ made by one execution of $\mathsf{KeyGen}^{\mathcal{O}}$ and $\mathsf{Mint}^{\mathcal{O}}$. By efficiency of $\mathsf{Ver}^{\mathcal{O}}$, there exists a uniform oracle algorithm $V^{|PSPACE\rangle} = (V_x^{|PSPACE\rangle})_{x \in \{0,1\}^*}$ such that running $V_{(pk,D,s)}^{|PSPACE\rangle}(\rho)$ is the same as running $\mathsf{Ver}^{D,|PSPACE\rangle}(pk, (s, \rho))$ (i.e. $\mathsf{Ver}^{\mathcal{O}}(pk, (s, \rho))$ where queries to $\mathcal{R}$ are answered by D).

Let $\epsilon = 0.01$, $b = 1 - \sqrt{1 - \delta_r + \epsilon}$, $a = 0.99b$. By Theorem 3, there exists a polynomial-time uniform oracle algorithm $\mathsf{Syn}^{|PSPACE\rangle}$ which can generate an "almost optimal" witness state of $V_{(pk,D,s)}^{|PSPACE\rangle}$ with guarantee a and threshold b. Now let's construct the adversary $\mathcal{A}^{\mathcal{O}}$.

Adversary $\mathcal{A}^{\mathcal{O}}$. It takes as input a valid banknote (s, ρ_s) and public key pk, and behaves as follows. Let $T = \lceil \frac{l}{\epsilon} \rceil$, $N = 100l / \left(1 - \sqrt{1 - \delta_r + \epsilon}\right)^2$.

1. $D \leftarrow \emptyset, t \xleftarrow{\$} [T], j \xleftarrow{\$} [N]$ and store ρ_s into a register M
2. **Test phase:** Run $\mathsf{Ver}^{\mathcal{O}}(pk, s, \cdot)$ for t times on the state in register M (the output residual state will be stored in M) while adding the query-answer pairs to $\mathcal{R}$ into D
3. **Update phase:** Do the following for j times
   (a) $\sigma_D \leftarrow \mathsf{Syn}^{|PSPACE\rangle}(pk, D, s)$
   (b) Run $\mathsf{Ver}^{\mathcal{O}}(pk, (s, \sigma_D))$ while adding the query-answer pairs to $\mathcal{R}$ into D
4. **Synthesize phase:** Output $\phi = \phi_1 \otimes \phi_2$ where $\phi_i \leftarrow \mathsf{Syn}^{|PSPACE\rangle}(pk, D, s)$

Analysis of $\mathcal{A}^{\mathcal{O}}$. The efficiency of $\mathcal{A}$ follows directly from the construction. Now let's prove that $\mathcal{A}^{\mathcal{O}}$ outputs what we want. We will use the notations defined in the construction of $\mathcal{A}^{\mathcal{O}}$.

Theorem 4. *Given input* $(\mathsf{pk}, (s, \rho_s))$ *generated by* $\mathsf{KeyGen}^{\mathcal{O}}$ *and* $\mathsf{Mint}^{\mathcal{O}}$, $\mathcal{A}^{\mathcal{O}}$ *outputs two alleged banknotes associated with the serial number* s *that will be accepted with high probability. Formally:*

$$\Pr\left[\mathsf{Ver}^{\mathcal{O}}(\mathsf{pk}, (s, \phi_i)) \text{ accepts for } i = 1, 2\right] \geq 1.8\left(1 - \sqrt{1 - \delta_r + \epsilon}\right)^2 - 1,$$

where the probability is over the randomness of $\mathcal{R}$, *the randomness of the generation of the input for* $\mathcal{A}^{\mathcal{O}}$ *(that is, the randomness of* $\mathsf{KeyGen}^{\mathcal{O}}$ *and* $\mathsf{Mint}^{\mathcal{O}}$*) and the randomness of our adversary* $\mathcal{A}^{\mathcal{O}}$.

Proof. From now on, all the probabilities are over the same randomness as the probability in the above theorem unless otherwise stated.

Let $D_{\mathsf{KeyGen}}, D_{\mathsf{Mint}}$ be the query-answer pairs made during the execution of $\mathsf{KeyGen}^{\mathcal{O}}$ and $\mathsf{Mint}^{\mathcal{O}}$. Based on the ideas from Sect. 2.2, we will first show that whenever we fail to simulate using database D, we must query a position inside $D_{\mathsf{KeyGen}} \cup D_{\mathsf{Mint}} - D$ (i.e. we make a bad query), and our knowledge of $D_{\mathsf{KeyGen}} \cup D_{\mathsf{Mint}}$ improves. Formally,

Proposition 1. *For* $\rho = \phi_i$ *or the residual state in* M *after running* $\mathcal{A}^{\mathcal{O}}$,

$$\left|\Pr\left[\mathsf{V}^{|\mathsf{PSPACE}\rangle}_{(\mathsf{pk}, D, s)}(\rho) \text{ accepts}\right] - \Pr\left[\mathsf{Ver}^{\mathcal{O}}(\mathsf{pk}, s, \rho) \text{ accepts}\right]\right|$$

$$\leq \Pr\left[\mathsf{Ver}^{\mathcal{O}}(\mathsf{pk}, s, \rho) \text{ queries } D_{\mathsf{KeyGen}} \cup D_{\mathsf{Mint}} - D\right]$$

where D *is the database of all query-answer pairs we collect during running* $\mathcal{A}^{\mathcal{O}}$.

Proof. Expand the probabilities based on whether Ver makes a bad query, and we can get

$$\left|\Pr\left[\mathsf{V}^{|\mathsf{PSPACE}\rangle}_{(\mathsf{pk}, D, s)}(\rho) \text{ accepts}\right] - \Pr\left[\mathsf{Ver}^{\mathcal{O}}(\mathsf{pk}, s, \rho) \text{ accepts}\right]\right|$$

$$= \left|\Pr\left[\mathsf{V}^{|\mathsf{PSPACE}\rangle}_{(\mathsf{pk}, D, s)}(\rho) \text{ accepts and queries } D_{\mathsf{KeyGen}} \cup D_{\mathsf{Mint}} - D\right]\right.$$

$$+ \Pr\left[\mathsf{V}^{|\mathsf{PSPACE}\rangle}_{(\mathsf{pk}, D, s)}(\rho) \text{ accepts and does not query } D_{\mathsf{KeyGen}} \cup D_{\mathsf{Mint}} - D\right]$$

$$- \Pr\left[\mathsf{Ver}^{\mathcal{O}}(\mathsf{pk}, s, \rho) \text{ accepts and queries } D_{\mathsf{KeyGen}} \cup D_{\mathsf{Mint}} - D\right]$$

$$\left.- \Pr\left[\mathsf{Ver}^{\mathcal{O}}(\mathsf{pk}, s, \rho) \text{ accepts and does not query } D_{\mathsf{KeyGen}} \cup D_{\mathsf{Mint}} - D\right]\right|$$

Notice that by lazy sampling technique, when we run $\mathsf{Ver}^{\mathcal{O}}(\mathsf{pk}, s, \rho)$, $\mathcal{R}$ can be simulated with $D \cup D_{\mathsf{KeyGen}} \cup D_{\mathsf{Mint}}$. So $\mathsf{Ver}^{\mathcal{O}}$ and $\mathsf{V}^{|\mathsf{PSPACE}\rangle}_{(\mathsf{pk}, D, s)}$ act exactly the same on ρ when they do not query $D_{\mathsf{KeyGen}} \cup D_{\mathsf{Mint}} - D$. Thus the above equation equals to

$$\left|\Pr\left[\mathsf{V}^{|\mathsf{PSPACE}\rangle}_{(\mathsf{pk}, D, s)}(\rho) \text{ accepts and queries } D_{\mathsf{KeyGen}} \cup D_{\mathsf{Mint}} - D\right]\right.$$

$$\left.- \Pr\left[\mathsf{Ver}^{\mathcal{O}}(\mathsf{pk}, s, \rho) \text{ accepts and queries } D_{\mathsf{KeyGen}} \cup D_{\mathsf{Mint}} - D\right]\right|$$

These two terms are both less or equal to $\Pr\left[\mathsf{Ver}^{\mathcal{O}}(\mathsf{pk}, s, \rho) \text{ queries } D_{\mathsf{KeyGen}} \cup D_{\mathsf{Mint}} - D\right] = \Pr\left[\mathsf{V}^{|\mathsf{PSPACE}\rangle}_{(\mathsf{pk}, D, s)}(\rho) \text{ queries } D_{\mathsf{KeyGen}} \cup D_{\mathsf{Mint}} - D\right]$ and are non-negative. Thus the above equation is not greater than $\Pr\left[\mathsf{Ver}^{\mathcal{O}}(\mathsf{pk}, s, \rho) \text{ queries } D_{\mathsf{KeyGen}} \cup D_{\mathsf{Mint}} - D\right]$, which ends the proof.

The next step is to bound the probability that Ver makes a bad query when running on the residual state in M and the synthesized state.

Lemma 2. *Let ρ be the residual state in M after running $\mathcal{A}^{\mathcal{O}}$, then*

$$\Pr\left[\mathsf{Ver}^{\mathcal{O}}(\mathsf{pk}, s, \rho) \text{ queries } D_{\mathsf{KeyGen}} \cup D_{\mathsf{Mint}} - D\right] \leq \frac{l}{T}$$

Similarly, $\Pr\left[\mathsf{Ver}^{\mathcal{O}}(\mathsf{pk}, s, \phi_i) \text{ queries } D_{\mathsf{KeyGen}} \cup D_{\mathsf{Mint}} - D\right] \leq \frac{l}{N}.$

Proof. Let $D_0 = D_{\mathsf{KeyGen}} \cup D_{\mathsf{Mint}}$. We give the proof of the first inequality here and omit the proof of the second one as it follows from a similar argument. We expand the probability based on the number of iterations t in the test phase.

$$\Pr\left[\mathsf{Ver}^{\mathcal{O}}(\mathsf{pk}, s, \rho) \text{ queries } D_{\mathsf{KeyGen}} \cup D_{\mathsf{Mint}} - D\right]$$

$$= \frac{1}{T} \sum_{t'=0}^{T-1} \Pr\left[\mathsf{Ver}^{\mathcal{O}}(\mathsf{pk}, s, \rho) \text{ queries } D_0 - D | t = t'\right]$$

$$\leq \frac{1}{T} \sum_{q \in D_0} \sum_{t'=0}^{T-1} \Pr\left[\text{the first one to query } q \text{ } textamong\{\mathsf{Ver}^{\mathcal{O}}(\mathsf{pk}, s, \rho_s^{(i)})\}_{i \geq 0} \text{ is } i = t'\right]$$

$$\leq \frac{1}{T} \cdot |D_0| \leq \frac{l}{T}$$

where $\rho_s^{(0)} = \rho_s$ and $\rho_s^{(i+1)} \leftarrow \mathsf{Ver}^{\mathcal{O}}(\mathsf{pk}, (s, \rho_s^{(i)}))$.

Combined with Proposition 1, Lemma 2 is saying that D is a good database for simulation on the residual state ρ. Thus ρ is indeed a good witness state for $\mathsf{V}^{|\mathsf{PSPACE}\rangle}_{(\mathsf{pk}, D, s)}$, and our synthesizer can find a good one. Formally,

Lemma 3. $\Pr\left[\mathsf{V}^{|\mathsf{PSPACE}\rangle}_{(\mathsf{pk}, D, s)}(\phi_i) \text{ accepts}\right] \geq 0.99 \left(1 - \sqrt{1 - \delta_r + \epsilon}\right)^2$

Proof. From Proposition 1 and Lemma 2, for the residual state ρ (which is the state after applying polynomial verifications on ρ_s),

$$\Pr\left[\mathsf{V}^{|\mathsf{PSPACE}\rangle}_{(\mathsf{pk}, D, s)}(\rho) \text{ accepts}\right] \geq \Pr\left[\mathsf{Ver}^{\mathcal{O}}(\mathsf{pk}, s, \rho) \text{ accepts}\right] - \frac{l}{T} \geq \delta_r - \epsilon$$

Define $S := \left\{(\mathsf{pk}, D, s) : \max_w \Pr\left[\mathsf{V}^{|\mathsf{PSPACE}\rangle}_{(\mathsf{pk}, D, s)}(w) \text{ accepts}\right] \geq 1 - \sqrt{1 - \delta_r + \epsilon}\right\}$ where the probability is only over the randomness of V. Then by the averaging argument,

$$\Pr\left[(\mathsf{pk}, D, s) \in S\right] \geq 1 - \sqrt{1 - \delta_r + \epsilon}$$

By Theorem 3, our synthesizer works well for all $(\mathsf{pk}, D, s) \in S$. That is, $\Pr\left[\mathsf{V}_{(\mathsf{pk},D,s)}^{|\mathsf{PSPACE}\rangle}(\mathsf{Syn}^{|\mathsf{PSPACE}\rangle}(\mathsf{pk}, D, s)) \text{ accepts}\right] \geq 0.99(1 - \sqrt{1 - \delta_r + \epsilon})$ where the probability is only over the randomness of V. Therefore,

$$\Pr\left[\mathsf{V}_{(\mathsf{pk},D,s)}^{|\mathsf{PSPACE}\rangle}(\phi_i) \text{ accepts}\right] \geq 0.99\left(1 - \sqrt{1 - \delta_r + \epsilon}\right)^2.$$

By Proposition 1 and Lemma 2, D is also a good database for simulation on ϕ_i. Thus the acceptance probability of $\mathsf{Ver}^{\mathcal{O}}$ on ϕ_i is also high. Formally,

$$\Pr\left[\mathsf{Ver}^{\mathcal{O}}(\mathsf{pk}, s, \phi_i) \text{ accepts}\right] \geq \Pr\left[\mathsf{V}_{(\mathsf{pk},D,s)}^{|\mathsf{PSPACE}\rangle}(\phi_i) \text{ accepts}\right] - \frac{l}{N} \geq 0.9\left(1 - \sqrt{1 - \delta_r + \epsilon}\right)^2$$

Then Theorem 4 follows from a union bound on ϕ_1 and ϕ_2.

Proof (Proof of Theorem 2). The proposed adversary $\mathcal{A}^{\mathcal{O}}$ is a valid attack because when $\epsilon = 0.01, \delta_r = 0.99$,

$$1.8\left(1 - \sqrt{1 - \delta_r + \epsilon}\right)^2 - 1 \geq 1.8(1 - 0.2)^2 - 1 \geq 0.1,$$

which is non-negligible.

5 Extensions to Quantum Access

In this section, we will explore a more general case where some algorithms can have quantum access to the random oracle and show our attack also works in this case. Formally:

Theorem 5. *Reusable and secure oracle-aided public-key quantum money scheme* $(\mathsf{KeyGen}^{|\mathcal{R}\rangle,|\mathsf{PSPACE}\rangle}, \mathsf{Mint}^{|\mathcal{R}\rangle,|\mathsf{PSPACE}\rangle}, \mathsf{Ver}^{\mathcal{R},|\mathsf{PSPACE}\rangle})$ *does not exist where* $\mathcal{R}$ *is a random oracle.*

Without loss of generality, we can suppose that the algorithms only make queries to the random oracle on input length $m(n)$ and receive binary output where m is a polynomial.

Let Ver make $q(n)$ classical queries to $\mathcal{R}$. Let KeyGen and Mint make $l(n)$ quantum queries to $\mathcal{R}$ in total. Denote the reusability and the security of the scheme as δ_r and δ_s respectively where $\delta_r = 1 - \mathsf{negl}(n), \delta_s = \mathsf{negl}(n)$. When it is clear from the context, we sometimes omit n for simplicity.

Recall that our attacker in Sect. 4 doesn't take advantage of the fact that KeyGen and Mint there can only make classical queries to $\mathcal{R}$. In fact, the same attacker works even when KeyGen and Mint can make quantum queries to $\mathcal{R}$ (with some modifications on the number of iterations). To be more specific, here is our construction of the attacker where $T(n), N(n)$, the guarantee a and the threshold b of Syn will be determined later.

$\mathcal{A}^{\mathcal{R},|\mathsf{PSPACE}\rangle}$ It takes as input a valid banknote (s, ρ_s) and public key pk, and behaves as follows.

1. $D \leftarrow \emptyset, t \xleftarrow{\$} [T], j \xleftarrow{\$} [N]$ and store ρ_s into a register M
2. **Test phase:** Run $\mathsf{Ver}^{\mathcal{O}}(\mathsf{pk}, s, \cdot)$ for t times on the state in register M while adding the query-answer pairs to $\mathcal{R}$ into D
3. **Update phase:** Do the following for j times
   (a) $\sigma_D \leftarrow \mathsf{Syn}^{|\mathsf{PSPACE}\rangle}(\mathsf{pk}, D, s)$
   (b) Run $\mathsf{Ver}^{\mathcal{O}}(\mathsf{pk}, (s, \sigma_D))$ while adding the query-answer pairs to $\mathcal{R}$ into D
4. **Synthesize phase:** Output $\phi = \phi_1 \otimes \phi_2$ where $\phi_i \leftarrow \mathsf{Syn}^{|\mathsf{PSPACE}\rangle}(\mathsf{pk}, D, s)$

What is left is to prove an analog of Theorem 4. That is, the output states of $\mathcal{A}$ will be accepted with high probability.

Theorem 6. *Given input* $(\mathsf{pk}, (s, \rho_s))$ *generated by* KeyGen *and* Mint, $\mathcal{A}^{\mathcal{R}, |\mathsf{PSPACE}\rangle}$ *outputs two alleged banknotes associated with the serial number* s *that will be accepted with high probability. Formally:*

$$\Pr\left[\mathsf{Ver}^{\mathcal{R}, |\mathsf{PSPACE}\rangle}(\mathsf{pk}, (s, \phi_i)) \text{ accepts for } i = 1, 2\right] \geq 1.8\left(1 - \sqrt{1 - \delta_r + \epsilon}\right)^2 - 1,$$

where the probability is over the randomness of $\mathcal{R}$, *the randomness of the generation of the input for* $\mathcal{A}^{\mathcal{R}, |\mathsf{PSPACE}\rangle}$ *(that is, the randomness of* $\mathsf{KeyGen}^{|\mathcal{R}\rangle, |\mathsf{PSPACE}\rangle}$ *and* $\mathsf{Mint}^{|\mathcal{R}\rangle, |\mathsf{PSPACE}\rangle}$) *and the randomness of our adversary* $\mathcal{A}^{\mathcal{R}, |\mathsf{PSPACE}\rangle}$.

Similar to Theorem 4, we will show that on $\phi_i \leftarrow \mathsf{Syn}^{|\mathsf{PSPACE}\rangle}(\mathsf{pk}, D, s)$, Ver accepts with high probability and then prove the theorem by union bound.

In Sect. 4, we crucially rely on the fact that whenever we make a mistake, we make progress in the sense that we make a query inside $D_{\mathsf{KeyGen}} \cup D_{\mathsf{Mint}} - D$. However, now KeyGen, Mint can make quantum queries. As a result, KeyGen and Mint could "touch" exponentially many positions. Fortunately, the compressed oracle technique introduced by Zhandry [Zha18] can be seen as a quantum analog of recording queries into a database. Basically, if we run all the algorithms in the *purified view* and see the register containing the oracle (labeled F) in Fourier basis, then all except polynomial positions are $|\hat{0}\rangle$ after polynomial quantum queries, and thus the register can be compressed using a unitary. See more details about the compressed oracle technique in Sect. 3.3. In this work, in order to better mimic $D_{\mathsf{KeyGen}} \cup D_{\mathsf{Mint}} - D$ in Sect. 4, we take advantage of the fact that Ver only makes classical queries. To be more specific, we will maintain a register to store a database D for all the classical queries and only extract those non-$|\hat{0}\rangle$ positions outside D to form our analog of $D_{\mathsf{KeyGen}} \cup D_{\mathsf{Mint}} - D$. We will elaborate on this idea in Sect. 5.2.

5.1 A Purified View of the Algorithms

From Sect. 3.3, for any sequence of algorithms that make queries to the random oracle on input length $m(n)$ and receive binary output, we can analyze the output using a pure state that we obtain by running all the algorithms in the *purified view* instead. To show what our attacker $\mathcal{A}^{\mathcal{R}, |\mathsf{PSPACE}\rangle}$ looks like in the purified view, we will start by writing its components in the purified view.

Quantum Query. Let F store the truth table of the random oracle. A quantum query to $\mathcal{R}$ in the purified view can be written as the unitary

$$U_Q : |x\rangle_Q|y\rangle_A|f\rangle_F \to |x\rangle_Q|y \oplus f(x)\rangle_A|f\rangle_F$$

where Q stores the query position and A is for the answer bit. (The subscript Q in U_Q is for Quantum queries.)

Classical Query. Without loss of generality, we can suppose for any classical query to $\mathcal{R}$, the register for query answer is always set to $|0\rangle$ before the query. Notice that a classical query to $\mathcal{R}$ is equivalent to a computational basis measurement on the query position followed by a quantum query to $\mathcal{R}$. An extra computational basis measurement on the answer of the query won't change the view. So a classical query in the purified view can be treated as applying the unitary

$$U_C : |x\rangle_Q|0\rangle_A|f\rangle_F|D_{\mathcal{R}}\rangle_{D_{\mathcal{R}}} \to |x\rangle_Q|f(x)\rangle_A|f\rangle_F|D_{\mathcal{R}}, (x, f(x))\rangle_{D_{\mathcal{R}}}$$

where $D_{\mathcal{R}}$ is a register that we will use to purify the computational basis measurements in the classical queries. By $|D_{\mathcal{R}}\rangle$, we mean a sequence of query-answer pairs $|(x_1, z_1), (x_2, z_2), \cdots (x_k, z_k)\rangle$ where $x_1, x_2, \cdots, x_k$ are not necessary to be distinct but if $x_i = x_j$, then $z_i = z_j$. Here $D_{\mathcal{R}}$ has enough space. That is, by $|(x_1, z_1), \cdots (x_k, z_k)\rangle$, we actually mean $|(x_1, z_1), \cdots (x_k, z_k), \bot, \cdots, \bot\rangle$ where $\bot$ is a special symbol that represents empty. Despite not being standard, we sometimes call $D_{\mathcal{R}}$ database. (The subscript C in U_C is for Classical queries.)

KeyGen, Mint, Ver *and* Syn We will use $U_{\text{KeyGen},n}, U_{\text{Mint},n}, U_{\text{Ver},n}$ and $U_{\text{Syn},n}$ to denote the unitary corresponding to the purified version of KeyGen, Mint, Ver and Syn on security number n respectively. Then $U_{\text{KeyGen},n}, U_{\text{Mint},n}$ and $U_{\text{Ver},n}$ are all in the form of preparing the first query and then repeatedly answering the query by applying U_Q or U_C and preparing the next query (or the final output if there is no further query). In particular, we will write $U_{\text{Ver},n}$ as $U_{q(n)}U_C U_{q(n)-1} \cdots U_C U_0$. We will omit the subscript n when it is clear from the context.

Verification While Recording. Let $U'_{\text{Ver}} := U_q U_R U_{q-1} \cdots U_R U_0$ where U_R (the subscript R is for Recording) is a unitary that in addition to a classical query U_C, it records the query-answer pair into a database register $D_{\mathcal{A}}$ held by $\mathcal{A}$. That is,

$$U_R : |x\rangle_Q|0\rangle_A|D_{\mathcal{A}}\rangle_{D_{\mathcal{A}}}|f\rangle_F|D_{\mathcal{R}}\rangle_{D_{\mathcal{R}}} \to |x\rangle_Q|f(x)\rangle_A|D_{\mathcal{A}}, (x, f(x))\rangle_{D_{\mathcal{A}}}|f\rangle_F|D_{\mathcal{R}}, (x, f(x))\rangle_{D_{\mathcal{R}}}$$

where again by $|D_{\mathcal{A}}\rangle$ and $|D_{\mathcal{R}}\rangle$, we mean a sequence of consistent query-answer pairs that are not necessary to be distinct. $D_{\mathcal{A}}$ has enough space.

It's easy to see that U'_{Ver} corresponds to running $\text{Ver}^{\mathcal{R}, |\text{PSPACE}\rangle}$ while the adversary records the query-answer pairs made by $\text{Ver}^{\mathcal{R}, |\text{PSPACE}\rangle}$.

$\mathcal{A}^{\mathcal{R}, |\text{PSPACE}\rangle}$ Given these components, the purified version of $\mathcal{A}^{\mathcal{R}, |\text{PSPACE}\rangle}$ is the following (which we will denote by $U_{\mathcal{A}}$):

1. Initialize a register T to be $\frac{1}{\sqrt{T}}\sum_{t=0}^{T-1}|t\rangle_T$ and a register J to be $\frac{1}{\sqrt{N}}\sum_{j=0}^{N-1}|j\rangle_J$.
2. **Test phase**: Conditioned on the content in T is t, apply U'_{Ver} on the banknote for t times in sequential. (Or equivalently apply unitary $U_{Test} := \sum_{t=0}^{T(n)-1}U'^t_{Ver}\otimes|t\rangle\langle t|_T$ where U'^t_{Ver} means applying U'_{Ver} for t times.)
3. **Update phase**: Conditioned on the content in J is j, apply the following for j times:
   (a) Apply U_{Syn} on all the query-answer pairs we learn so far (i.e. $D_{\mathcal{A}}$).
   (b) Apply U'_{Ver} on the state synthesized in item (a).

(Or equivalently apply unitary $U_{Upd} := \sum_{j=0}^{N(n)-1}(U'_{Ver}U_{Syn})^j\otimes|j\rangle\langle j|_J$ where $(U'_{Ver}U_{Syn})^j$ means alternatively applying U_{Syn} and U'_{Ver} for j times.)

4. **Synthesize phase**: Apply U_{Syn_1} and U_{Syn_2} on the query-answer pairs in $D_{\mathcal{A}}$ to obtain two alleged banknotes where U_{Syn_1} and U_{Syn_2} are just U_{Syn} that generates the synthesized state on different registers.

Simulated Verification. The purified version of a simulated verification $Ver^{D,|PSPACE\rangle}$ is also needed as we need to analyze the behavior of the simulated verification on the residual state after several verifications and the synthesized state.

We first define a unitary corresponding to a simulated query

$$U_D: |x\rangle_Q|0\rangle_A|D\rangle_{D_{\mathcal{A}}} \rightarrow \begin{cases} |x\rangle_Q|D(x)\rangle_A|D,(x,D(x))\rangle_{D_{\mathcal{A}}}, & x \in D \\ |x\rangle_Q\sum_{z=0}^{1}\frac{1}{\sqrt{2}}|z\rangle_A|D,(x,z)\rangle_{D_{\mathcal{A}}}, & x \notin D \end{cases}$$

where by $|D\rangle$, we mean a sequence of consistent query-answer pairs that are not necessary to be distinct. By $x \in D$, we mean there exists z such that (x,z) is a pair in D and we will denote this z as $D(x)$. By $x \notin D$, we mean for all z, (x,z) is not a pair in D. (The subscript D in U_D is for simulating with Database.)

Then applying U_D is exactly answering the query x using D (If x is in the database, then answer the query using D; Otherwise, give a random answer while recording this query-answer pair into the database for later use). Thus the purified version of $Ver^{D,|PSPACE\rangle}$ is $U_{Sim} := U_qU_DU_{q-1}\cdots U_DU_0$.

Then the difference of $Ver^{\mathcal{R},|PSPACE\rangle}$ and $Ver^{D,|PSPACE\rangle}$ can be analyzed by the difference of U_{Ver} and U_{Sim} applying on the corresponding register of the pure state we obtain after $U_{\mathcal{A}}$.

5.2   Compress and Decompress

Intuitively, $|\hat{0}\rangle$ position in F is a uniform superposition of the range and it is unentangled with all other things, so it can be seen as choosing a value from the range uniformly at random independently, which is exactly what the simulation does. It is an analog of those positions that are never asked during the sequence of algorithms in the purely classical query case.

In this subsection, we will show how to extract an analog of D and $D_{KeyGen}\cup D_{Mint}-D$ from the pure state. Roughly speaking, the recorded classical queries are an analog of D and we will compress the register F to extract those non-$|\hat{0}\rangle$ positions outside D to form our analog of $D_{\text{KeyGen}} \cup D_{\text{Mint}} - D$.

We first give a formal description of decompress unitary Decomp as it's easier to write down and analyze. Define Decomp : $|D_F\rangle_F |D_{\mathcal{R}}\rangle_{D_{\mathcal{R}}} \rightarrow |f_0, \cdots, f_{2^m-1}\rangle_F |D_{\mathcal{R}}\rangle_{D_{\mathcal{R}}}$ where $|D_F\rangle_F$ can be written as a sequence of pairs $|(x_1, \widehat{y_1}), (x_2, \widehat{y_2}), \cdots, (x_{k'}, \widehat{y_{k'}})\rangle_F$, $|D_{\mathcal{R}}\rangle_{D_{\mathcal{R}}}$ can be written as a sequence of pairs $|(x'_1, z_1), (x'_2, z_2), \cdots, (x'_k, z_k)\rangle$ and the input $|D_F\rangle_F |D_{\mathcal{R}}\rangle_{D_{\mathcal{R}}}$ satisfies

- if $x'_i = x'_j$, then $z_i = z_j$;
- $x_1 < x_2 < \cdots < x_{k'}, \widehat{y_i} \neq \hat{0}$;
- $\forall i, j, x_j \neq x'_i$;

and the output satisfies

- If $x'_j = i$, then $f_i = z_j$;
- If $x_j = i$, then $f_i = \widehat{y_j}$;
- If $\forall j, x_j \neq i, x'_j \neq i$, then $f_i = \hat{0}$.

That is, we fill $f_0, f_1, \cdots, f_{2^l-1}$ by looking at the pairs in $D_{\mathcal{R}}$ and D_F, and we fill all the remaining positions with $\hat{0}$.

As our random function has 1-bit outputs, $z_1, z_2, \cdots, z_k, y_1, \cdots, y_{k'} \in \{0, 1\}$. Recall that $|\hat{0}\rangle = \frac{1}{\sqrt{2}}(|0\rangle + |1\rangle), |\hat{1}\rangle = \frac{1}{\sqrt{2}}(|0\rangle - |1\rangle)$. One can check that each two inputs in the above form are orthogonal and they are mapped to orthogonal outputs. So we can define the outputs of other inputs that are not in the above form so that Decomp is a unitary.

For simplicity, when we write $D_{\mathcal{R}}$ or D_F, we mean a sequence of pairs that satisfies the first or second item of the input requirements above by default, respectively. The definitions of $x \in D_{\mathcal{R}}, D_F$ and $D_{\mathcal{R}}(x), D_F(x)$ are the same as those of D in Sect. 5.1. Define $D_{\mathcal{R}} \cap D_F = \{x : x \in D_{\mathcal{R}} \text{ and } x \in D_F\}$ and $D_{\mathcal{R}} \cup D_F = \{x : x \in D_{\mathcal{R}} \text{ or } x \in D_F\}$. By $D_F - x$, we mean the sequence we obtain after deleting $(x_i, \widehat{y_i})$ from D_F where $x_i = x$.

The inverse operation of the above unitary Decomp is Comp := Decomp†, which can take our database $D_{\mathcal{R}}$ and the truth table in register F as inputs and compress them into two databases $D_{\mathcal{R}}$ and D_F. From now on, for any unitary U, we denote its compressed version as $\widetilde{U} := \text{Comp} U \text{Decomp}$. Since Comp and Decomp only acts on the registers held by the oracle (F and $D_{\mathcal{R}}$), we can always analyze the output (which is not in the registers F and $D_{\mathcal{R}}$) of any sequence of unitaries $U_1, U_2, \cdots, U_k$ using its compressed version $\widetilde{U_1}, \widetilde{U_2}, \cdots, \widetilde{U_k}$.

The similarity between $D_{\mathcal{R}}, D_F$ and $D, D_{\text{KeyGen}} \cup D_{\text{Mint}} - D$ will be more clear after looking at the following compressed version of U_C, U_R and U_D from Sect. 5.1. From the description of Decomp, we can get for $D_F \cap D_{\mathcal{R}} = \emptyset$,

$$\widetilde{U_C}(|x\rangle_Q |0\rangle_A |D_F\rangle_F |D_{\mathcal{R}}\rangle_{D_{\mathcal{R}}})$$

$$= \begin{cases} |x\rangle_Q |D_{\mathcal{R}}(x)\rangle_A |D_F\rangle_F |D_{\mathcal{R}}, (x, D_{\mathcal{R}}(x))\rangle_{D_{\mathcal{R}}} & x \in D_{\mathcal{R}} \\ |x\rangle_Q \frac{1}{\sqrt{2}} \sum_{z=0}^{1} |z\rangle_A |D_F\rangle_F |D_{\mathcal{R}}, (x, z)\rangle_{D_{\mathcal{R}}} & x \notin D_{\mathcal{R}} \cup D_F \\ |x\rangle_Q \frac{1}{\sqrt{2}} \sum_{z=0}^{1} (-1)^z |z\rangle_A |D_F - x\rangle_F |D_{\mathcal{R}}, (x, z)\rangle_{D_{\mathcal{R}}} & x \in D_F \end{cases}$$

$\widetilde{U}_R(|x\rangle_Q|0\rangle_A|D_A\rangle_{D_A}|D_F\rangle_F|D_R\rangle_{D_R})$

$$= \begin{cases} |x\rangle_Q|D_R(x)\rangle_A|D_A, (x, D_R(x))\rangle_{D_A}|D_F\rangle_F|D_R, (x, D_R(x))\rangle_{D_R} & x \in D_R \\ |x\rangle_Q \frac{1}{\sqrt{2}} \sum_{z=0}^{1} |z\rangle_A|D_A, (x, z)\rangle_{D_A}|D_F\rangle_F|D_R, (x, z)\rangle_{D_R} & x \notin D_R \cup D_F \\ |x\rangle_Q \frac{1}{\sqrt{2}} \sum_{z=0}^{1} (-1)^z|z\rangle_A|D_A, (x, z)\rangle_{D_A}|D_F - x\rangle_F|D_R, (x, z)\rangle_{D_R} & x \in D_F \end{cases}$$

Since U_D does not act on F and D_R, $\widetilde{U}_D = U_D$.

By the description of $\widetilde{U}_C$ and $\widetilde{U}_R$, whenever we ask a classical query on input $x \in D_R$, we answer it with our database D_R and record $(x, D_R(x))$ for another time; whenever we ask a classical query on input $x \notin D_R \cup D_F$, we answer it with a random z and record (x, z) in our database for later use; whenever we ask a classical query on input $x \in D_F$, we actually copy the answer from the D_F, record it into D_R, and remove x from D_F. The above three cases are analogous to the classical on-the-fly simulation where the query to $\mathcal{R}$ inside D can be answered by D, the query to $\mathcal{R}$ inside $D_{\mathsf{KeyGen}} \cup D_{\mathsf{Mint}} - D$ should be answered consistently by $D_{\mathsf{KeyGen}} \cup D_{\mathsf{Mint}} - D$ and we sample a uniformly random answer to the query to outside $(D_{\mathsf{KeyGen}} \cup D_{\mathsf{Mint}} - D) \cup D$. It is worth pointing out that $\widetilde{U}_C$ and $\widetilde{U}_R$ maintain the property that $D_R \cap D_F$ is empty (analogous to $(D_{\mathsf{KeyGen}} \cup D_{\mathsf{Mint}} - D) \cap D = \emptyset$).

Furthermore, recall that $U_{\mathsf{Ver}} = U_q U_C U_{q-1} \cdots U_1 U_C U_0$ and U_i does not act on F or D_R. Thus $\widetilde{U}_i = U_i$, $\widetilde{U}_{\mathsf{Ver}} = U_q \widetilde{U}_C U_{q-1} \cdots U_1 \widetilde{U}_C U_0$. Similarly, $\widetilde{U}_D = U_D$, so $\widetilde{U}_{\mathsf{Sim}} = U_{\mathsf{Sim}} = U_q U_D U_{q-1} \cdots U_D U_0$.

5.3   Analysis of $\mathcal{A}^{\mathcal{R}, |\mathsf{PSPACE}\rangle}$

Here we analyze the acceptance probability of $\mathsf{Ver}^{\mathcal{R}, |\mathsf{PSPACE}\rangle}$ on the output of our $\mathcal{A}^{\mathcal{R}, |\mathsf{PSPACE}\rangle}$. We reuse our ideas in Sect. 4.

The following proposition can be seen as an analog of Proposition 1. It basically says that when the behavior of $\mathsf{Ver}^{\mathcal{R}, |\mathsf{PSPACE}\rangle}$ (corresponding to $\widetilde{U}_{\mathsf{Ver}} = U_q \widetilde{U}_C \cdots \widetilde{U}_C U_0$) is far from the behavior of $\mathsf{Ver}^{D, |\mathsf{PSPACE}\rangle}$ (corresponding to $\widetilde{U}_{\mathsf{Sim}} = U_q U_D \cdots U_D U_0$), the number of pairs in F (analogous to $|D_{\mathsf{KeyGen}} \cup D_{\mathsf{Mint}} - D|$) will drop a lot after the verification. The intuition is that roughly speaking, $\widetilde{U}_C$ and U_D only behave differently when given a query position $x \in D_F$, in which case x will be excluded from D_F after applying $\widetilde{U}_C$. So it results in a decrement of the number of pairs in F. Formally:

Proposition 2. *Let O denote the observable corresponding to the number of pairs in F. To be more specific, $O = \sum_{D_F} |D_F| |D_F\rangle\langle D_F|_F$ where $|D_F|$ is the number of pairs in D_F.*

For a state $|\phi\rangle$ in the following form (i.e. it's in the compressed view and the contents in D_R and D_A are the same. G is a register for any irrelevant things),

$$|\phi\rangle = \sum_{\substack{pk, s, m, D, D_F, g \\ s.t. \ D \cap D_F = \emptyset}} \alpha_{pk, s, m, D, D_F, g} |pk\rangle_{Pk} |s\rangle_S |m\rangle_M |D\rangle_{D_A} |D_F\rangle_F |D\rangle_{D_R} |g\rangle_G.$$

Let $\Pr\left[\widetilde{U_{\mathsf{Ver}}}\ accepts\ when\ running\ on\ |\phi\rangle\right]$ and $\Pr\left[\widetilde{U_{\mathsf{Sim}}}\ accepts\ when\ running\ on\ |\phi\rangle\right]$ be the acceptance probability of $\widetilde{U_{\mathsf{Ver}}}$ and $\widetilde{U_{\mathsf{Sim}}}$ when the public key, the serial number and the alleged money state are in $\mathsf{Pk, S}$ and M respectively. Then

$$\left|\Pr\left[\widetilde{U_{\mathsf{Ver}}}\ accepts\ when\ running\ on\ |\phi\rangle\right] - \Pr\left[\widetilde{U_{\mathsf{Sim}}}\ accepts\ when\ running\ on\ |\phi\rangle\right]\right|$$

$$\leq \mathrm{TD}\left(\mathrm{Tr}_{\mathsf{FD}_A \mathsf{D}_{\mathcal{R}}}(\widetilde{U_{\mathsf{Ver}}}|\phi\rangle\langle\phi|\widetilde{U_{\mathsf{Ver}}}^{\dagger}), \mathrm{Tr}_{\mathsf{FD}_A \mathsf{D}_{\mathcal{R}}}(\widetilde{U_{\mathsf{Sim}}}|\phi\rangle\langle\phi|\widetilde{U_{\mathsf{Sim}}}^{\dagger})\right)$$

$$\leq 6\sqrt{q\left(\mathrm{Tr}(O|\phi\rangle\langle\phi|) - \mathrm{Tr}(O\widetilde{U_{\mathsf{Ver}}}|\phi\rangle\langle\phi|\widetilde{U_{\mathsf{Ver}}}^{\dagger})\right)}$$

Proof. The first inequality follows immediately from the fact that we can measure a qubit (not in $\mathsf{FD}_A\mathsf{D}_{\mathcal{R}}$) of $\widetilde{U_{\mathsf{Ver}}}|\phi\rangle$ and $\widetilde{U_{\mathsf{Sim}}}|\phi\rangle$ to obtain whether they accept and the fact that we can not distinguish two states with probability greater than their trace distance.

As for the second inequality, recall that $\widetilde{U_{\mathsf{Ver}}} = U_q\widetilde{U_C}\cdots\widetilde{U_C}U_0$ and $\widetilde{U_{\mathsf{Sim}}} = U_qU_D\cdots U_DU_0$. Let U'_D be the same as U_D except that it uses the contents in $\mathsf{D}_{\mathcal{R}}$ for simulation instead of the contents in D_A. To be more specific,

$$U'_D(|x\rangle_\mathsf{Q}|0\rangle_\mathsf{A}|D_{\mathcal{R}}\rangle_{\mathsf{D}_{\mathcal{R}}}) = \begin{cases} |x\rangle_\mathsf{Q}|D_{\mathcal{R}}(x)\rangle_\mathsf{A}|D_{\mathcal{R}},(x,D_{\mathcal{R}}(x))\rangle_{\mathsf{D}_{\mathcal{R}}}, & x \in D_{\mathcal{R}} \\ |x\rangle_\mathsf{Q}\frac{1}{\sqrt{2}}\sum_{z=0}^{1}|z\rangle_\mathsf{A}|D_{\mathcal{R}},(x,z)\rangle_{\mathsf{D}_{\mathcal{R}}}, & x \notin D_{\mathcal{R}} \end{cases}$$

Define $|\phi_j\rangle = \widetilde{U_C}U_{j-1}\cdots\widetilde{U_C}U_0|\phi\rangle$ where $0 \leq j \leq q$. In order to analyze the difference of $\widetilde{U_{\mathsf{Ver}}}$ and $\widetilde{U_{\mathsf{Sim}}}$ on $|\phi\rangle$, it's enough to analyze the difference between one true query and one simulated query. Formally,

$$\mathrm{TD}\left(\mathrm{Tr}_{\mathsf{FD}_A \mathsf{D}_{\mathcal{R}}}(\widetilde{U_{\mathsf{Ver}}}|\phi\rangle\langle\phi|\widetilde{U_{\mathsf{Ver}}}^{\dagger}), \mathrm{Tr}_{\mathsf{FD}_A \mathsf{D}_{\mathcal{R}}}(\widetilde{U_{\mathsf{Sim}}}|\phi\rangle\langle\phi|\widetilde{U_{\mathsf{Sim}}}^{\dagger})\right)$$

$$=\mathrm{TD}\left(\mathrm{Tr}_{\mathsf{FD}_A \mathsf{D}_{\mathcal{R}}}(U_q\phi_qU_q^{\dagger}), \mathrm{Tr}_{\mathsf{FD}_A \mathsf{D}_{\mathcal{R}}}(U_qU'_D\cdots U'_DU_0\phi_0U_0^{\dagger}U'^{\dagger}_D\cdots U'^{\dagger}_DU_q^{\dagger})\right)$$

$$\leq\sum_{j=0}^{q-1}\mathrm{TD}\left(\mathrm{Tr}_{\mathsf{FD}_A \mathsf{D}_{\mathcal{R}}}(U_qU'_D\cdots U_{j+1}\phi_{j+1}U_{j+1}^{\dagger}U'^{\dagger}_D\cdots U_q^{\dagger}), \mathrm{Tr}_{\mathsf{FD}_A \mathsf{D}_{\mathcal{R}}}(U_qU'_D\cdots U_j\phi_jU_j^{\dagger}U'^{\dagger}_D\cdots U_q^{\dagger})\right)$$

$$\leq\sum_{j=0}^{q-1}\mathrm{TD}\left(\phi_{j+1}, U'_DU_j\phi_jU_j^{\dagger}U'^{\dagger}_D\right) = \sum_{j=0}^{q-1}\mathrm{TD}\left(\widetilde{U_C}U_j\phi_jU_j^{\dagger}\widetilde{U_C}^{\dagger}, U'_DU_j\phi_jU_j^{\dagger}U'^{\dagger}_D\right)$$

where we use the fact that $|\phi\rangle$ have the same contents on D_A and $\mathsf{D}_{\mathcal{R}}$ and thus $\mathrm{Tr}_{\mathsf{FD}_A \mathsf{D}_{\mathcal{R}}}(\widetilde{U_{\mathsf{Sim}}}|\phi\rangle\langle\phi|\widetilde{U_{\mathsf{Sim}}}^{\dagger})$ equals to $\mathrm{Tr}_{\mathsf{FD}_A \mathsf{D}_{\mathcal{R}}}(U_qU'_D\cdots U'_DU_0\phi_0 U_0^{\dagger}U'^{\dagger}_D\cdots U'^{\dagger}_DU_q^{\dagger})$.

$\widetilde{U_C}$ and U'_D act differently only when the query position is inside D_F. So intuitively, the difference between one real query and one simulated query can be bounded by the weight of queries inside D_F, which equals the decrement of the number of pairs in F after the query. Formally, we give the following lemma and defer the proof to the full version [AHY23].

Lemma 4. $\mathrm{TD}\left(\widetilde{U_C}U_j\phi_jU_j^{\dagger}\widetilde{U_C}^{\dagger}, U'_DU_j\phi_jU_j^{\dagger}U'^{\dagger}_D\right) \leq 6\sqrt{\mathrm{Tr}(O\phi_j) - \mathrm{Tr}(O\phi_{j+1})}.$

Insert Lemma 4 into the above inequality, and we can get

$$\mathrm{TD}\left(\mathrm{Tr}_{\mathsf{FD}_A D_{\mathcal{R}}}(\widetilde{U_{\mathsf{Ver}}}|\phi\rangle\langle\phi|\widetilde{U_{\mathsf{Ver}}}^{\dagger}),\mathrm{Tr}_{\mathsf{FD}_A D_{\mathcal{R}}}(\widetilde{U_{\mathsf{Sim}}}|\phi\rangle\langle\phi|\widetilde{U_{\mathsf{Sim}}}^{\dagger})\right)$$

$$\leq\sum_{j=0}^{q-1}6\sqrt{\mathrm{Tr}(O\phi_j)-\mathrm{Tr}(O\phi_{j+1})}$$

$$\leq 6\sqrt{q\sum_{j=0}^{q-1}(\mathrm{Tr}(O\phi_j)-\mathrm{Tr}(O\phi_{j+1}))}\ (\text{Cauchy-Schwarz inequality})$$

$$=6\sqrt{q\left(\mathrm{Tr}(O|\phi\rangle\langle\phi|)-\mathrm{Tr}(O\widetilde{U_{\mathsf{Ver}}}|\phi\rangle\langle\phi|\widetilde{U_{\mathsf{Ver}}}^{\dagger})\right)}$$

which ends the proof of Proposition 2.

The next lemma is an analog of Lemma 2. Basically, it argues that on average, the behaviors of $\mathsf{Ver}^{D,|\mathsf{PSPACE}\rangle}$ and $\mathsf{Ver}^{\mathcal{R},|\mathsf{PSPACE}\rangle}$ are very close on the residual state ρ after running $\mathcal{A}^{\mathcal{R},|\mathsf{PSPACE}\rangle}$ and the synthesized state even when KeyGen and Mint can make quantum queries to $\mathcal{R}$.

The intuition of the proof is the following: from Sect. 5.1, the difference between $\mathsf{Ver}^{\mathcal{R},|\mathsf{PSPACE}\rangle}$ and $\mathsf{Ver}^{D,|\mathsf{PSPACE}\rangle}$ is the difference between applying U_{Ver} and U_{Sim} on the same state, which can be transformed to the compressed view and by Proposition 2, can be bounded by the decrement of the number of pairs in F after the verification. Roughly speaking, the decrement equals the number of pairs in D_F asked during the verification. But we randomize t and j, so running another verification on the residual state and the synthesized state should not decrease the number of pairs in F too much on average. Formally:

Lemma 5. *Let ρ be the residual state of ρ_s after running $\mathcal{A}^{\mathcal{R},|\mathsf{PSPACE}\rangle}$, then*

$$\left|\Pr\left[\mathsf{Ver}^{\mathcal{R},|\mathsf{PSPACE}\rangle}(\mathsf{pk},(s,\rho))\ accepts\right]-\Pr\left[\mathsf{Ver}^{D,|\mathsf{PSPACE}\rangle}(\mathsf{pk},(s,\rho))\ accepts\right]\right|\leq 6\sqrt{\frac{ql}{T}},$$

$$\left|\Pr\left[\mathsf{Ver}^{\mathcal{R},|\mathsf{PSPACE}\rangle}(\mathsf{pk},(s,\phi_i))\ accepts\right]-\Pr\left[\mathsf{Ver}^{D,|\mathsf{PSPACE}\rangle}(\mathsf{pk},(s,\phi_i))\ accepts\right]\right|\leq 6\sqrt{\frac{ql}{N}},$$

where the probabilities are taken over the randomness of $\mathcal{R}$, the randomness of the inputs to the adversary and the randomness of the adversary.

Proof. We will focus on the proof of the first inequality. The proof of the second one is similar and we refer to the full version [AHY23] for more details.

Let $|\phi\rangle$ be the whole pure state we obtain by applying the unitaries $\widetilde{U_{\mathsf{KeyGen}}}, \widetilde{U_{\mathsf{Mint}}}$ and $\widetilde{U_{\mathcal{A}}}$ to the state $|1^n\rangle|\emptyset\rangle_{\mathsf{D}_{\mathcal{A}}}|\emptyset\rangle_{\mathsf{F}}|\emptyset\rangle_{\mathsf{D}_{\mathcal{R}}}$ along with enough ancillas. Let M be the register corresponding to the residual state ρ. From Sect. 5.1 and Sect. 5.2, these two probabilities equal to $\Pr\left[\widetilde{U_{\mathsf{Ver}}} \text{ accepts when running on } |\phi\rangle\right]$ and $\Pr\left[\widetilde{U_{\mathsf{Sim}}} \text{ accepts when running on } |\phi\rangle\right]$, respectively. It's easy to see that every classical query is recorded by the adversary (i.e. $|\phi\rangle$ has the same contents in $D_{\mathcal{A}}$ and $D_{\mathcal{R}}$). So from Proposition 2,

$$\left| \Pr\left[\mathsf{Ver}^{\mathcal{R},|\mathsf{PSPACE}\rangle}(\mathsf{pk},(s,\rho)) \text{ accepts} \right] - \Pr\left[\mathsf{Ver}^{D,|\mathsf{PSPACE}\rangle}(\mathsf{pk},(s,\rho)) \text{ accepts} \right] \right|$$

$$\leq 6\sqrt{q\left(\mathrm{Tr}(O|\phi\rangle\langle\phi|) - \mathrm{Tr}(O\widetilde{U_{\mathsf{Ver}}}|\phi\rangle\langle\phi|\widetilde{U_{\mathsf{Ver}}}^{\dagger}) \right)}$$

Denote $\widetilde{U_{\mathsf{Upd}}}$ to be unitary that describes our update phase in the compressed view. Formally, $\widetilde{U_{\mathsf{Upd}}} = \mathsf{Comp}U_{\mathsf{Upd}}\mathsf{Decomp} = \sum_{j=0}^{N(n)-1}(\widetilde{U_{\mathsf{Ver}}'}\widetilde{U_{\mathsf{Syn}}})^{j} \otimes |j\rangle\langle j|_{\mathsf{J}}$ where $\widetilde{U_{\mathsf{Ver}}'}$ is running on the state synthesized by $\widetilde{U_{\mathsf{Syn}}}$.

Let $|\psi\rangle$ be the pure state corresponding to running $\mathcal{A}$ on public key and the valid banknote until the end of the **test** phase in the compressed view. That is to say, $|\phi\rangle = U_{\mathsf{Syn}_2}U_{\mathsf{Syn}_1}\widetilde{U_{\mathsf{Upd}}}|\psi\rangle$ where U_{Syn_i} synthesizes the ith alleged banknote. Then U_{Syn_i} commutes with O and $\widetilde{U_{\mathsf{Ver}}}$. Thus

$$\mathrm{Tr}(O|\phi\rangle\langle\phi|) - \mathrm{Tr}(O\widetilde{U_{\mathsf{Ver}}}|\phi\rangle\langle\phi|\widetilde{U_{\mathsf{Ver}}}^{\dagger}) = \mathrm{Tr}(O\widetilde{U_{\mathsf{Upd}}}\psi\widetilde{U_{\mathsf{Upd}}}^{\dagger}) - \mathrm{Tr}(O\widetilde{U_{\mathsf{Ver}}}\widetilde{U_{\mathsf{Upd}}}\psi\widetilde{U_{\mathsf{Upd}}}^{\dagger}\widetilde{U_{\mathsf{Ver}}}^{\dagger})$$

It remains to prove that the above term is bounded by l/T. However, the update phase between $\widetilde{U_{\mathsf{Ver}}}$ and the test phase may bring some trouble. The following lemma shows that we can remove the update phase without decreasing the value (analogous to the fact that when all the algorithms can only make classical queries to $\mathcal{R}$, if we delete some pairs in D, the expected number of queries inside $D_{\mathsf{KeyGen}} \cup D_{\mathsf{Mint}} - D$ during verification cannot decrease). We defer the proof to the full version [AHY23].

Lemma 6. *We use the same notation as above. Then*

$$\mathrm{Tr}(O\widetilde{U_{\mathsf{Upd}}}\psi\widetilde{U_{\mathsf{Upd}}}^{\dagger}) - \mathrm{Tr}(O\widetilde{U_{\mathsf{Ver}}}\widetilde{U_{\mathsf{Upd}}}\psi\widetilde{U_{\mathsf{Upd}}}^{\dagger}\widetilde{U_{\mathsf{Ver}}}^{\dagger}) \leq \mathrm{Tr}(O\psi) - \mathrm{Tr}(O\widetilde{U_{\mathsf{Ver}}}\psi\widetilde{U_{\mathsf{Ver}}}^{\dagger})$$

Recording the queries into $D_{\mathcal{A}}$ won't influence the number of pairs in F, so $\mathrm{Tr}(O\psi) - \mathrm{Tr}(O\widetilde{U_{\mathsf{Ver}}}\psi\widetilde{U_{\mathsf{Ver}}}^{\dagger}) = \mathrm{Tr}(O\psi) - \mathrm{Tr}(O\widetilde{U_{\mathsf{Ver}}'}\psi\widetilde{U_{\mathsf{Ver}}'}^{\dagger})$.

Note that we can also write $|\psi\rangle$ as $\frac{1}{\sqrt{T(n)}}\sum_{t=0}^{T(n)-1}|\psi^{(t)}\rangle|t\rangle_{\mathsf{T}}$ where $|\psi^{(t)}\rangle$ is the state after we run t iterations in the test phase. Then $|\psi^{(t+1)}\rangle = \widetilde{U_{\mathsf{Ver}}'}|\psi^{(t)}\rangle$. Combine the above equations, and we can get

$$\left| \Pr\left[\mathsf{Ver}^{\mathcal{R},|\mathsf{PSPACE}\rangle}(\mathsf{pk},(s,\rho)) \text{ accepts} \right] - \Pr\left[\mathsf{Ver}^{D,|\mathsf{PSPACE}\rangle}(\mathsf{pk},(s,\rho)) \text{ accepts} \right] \right|$$

$$\leq 6\sqrt{q\left(\mathrm{Tr}(O\psi) - \mathrm{Tr}(O\widetilde{U_{\mathsf{Ver}}'}\psi\widetilde{U_{\mathsf{Ver}}'}^{\dagger}) \right)}$$

$$= 6\sqrt{q\left(\frac{1}{T}\sum_{t=0}^{T-1}\mathrm{Tr}\left(O\psi^{(t)}\right) - \frac{1}{T}\sum_{t=0}^{T-1}\mathrm{Tr}\left(O\widetilde{U_{\mathsf{Ver}}'}\psi^{(t)}\widetilde{U_{\mathsf{Ver}}'}^{\dagger}\right) \right)}$$

$$\leq 6\sqrt{\frac{q}{T}\mathrm{Tr}\left(O\psi^{(0)}\right)} \leq 6\sqrt{\frac{ql}{T}}$$

where we use the fact that O, $\widetilde{U'_{\text{Ver}}}$ do not act on T, and the property of compressed oracle techniques that after $l(n)$ quantum queries, there are at most $l(n)$ non-$\hat{0}$ elements in F. $|\psi^{(0)}\rangle$ is just the state we obtain after we run KeyGen and Mint (so there are at most $l(n)$ quantum queries) and then apply the unitary Comp. So there are at most $l(n)$ pairs in F of $|\psi^{(0)}\rangle$. Hence $\text{Tr}\left(O\psi^{(0)}\right) \leq l(n)$.

Now let's combine the above results to prove Theorem 6.

Proof (Proof of Theorem 6). Let $\epsilon = 0.01$, $b = 1 - \sqrt{1 - \delta_r + \epsilon}$, $a = 0.99b$. Let $T(n) = \frac{36q(n)l(n)}{\epsilon^2}$ and $N(n) = \frac{q(n)l(n)}{\epsilon^2(1-\sqrt{1-\delta_r+\epsilon})^4}$, which are both polynomial in n.

From Lemma 5, $\text{Pr}\left[\text{Ver}^{D,|\text{PSPACE}\rangle}(\text{pk}, (s, \rho) \text{ accepts}\right] \geq \delta_r - \epsilon$. Hence similar as Lemma 3, $\text{Pr}\left[\text{Ver}^{D,|\text{PSPACE}\rangle}(\text{pk}, (s, \phi_i)) \text{ accepts}\right] \geq 0.99(1 - \sqrt{1 - \delta_r + \epsilon})^2$. Again from Lemma 5, $\text{Pr}\left[\text{Ver}^{\mathcal{R},|\text{PSPACE}\rangle}(\text{pk}, (s, \phi_i)) \text{ accepts}\right] \geq 0.9(1 - \sqrt{1 - \delta_r + \epsilon})^2$. Thus by union bound, the outputs of our adversary pass two verifications simultaneously with probability at least $1.8(1 - \sqrt{1 - \delta_r + \epsilon})^2 - 1$, which is non-negligible when $\delta_r \geq 0.99$.

That is, the adversary we construct runs in polynomial time and gives a valid attack to the scheme $(\text{KeyGen}^{|\mathcal{R}\rangle,|\text{PSPACE}\rangle}, \text{Mint}^{|\mathcal{R}\rangle,|\text{PSPACE}\rangle}, \text{Ver}^{\mathcal{R},|\text{PSPACE}\rangle})$ where $\delta_r \geq 0.99$ and $\delta_s = \text{negl}(n)$, which establishes Theorem 5.

References

[AA09]   Aaronson, S., Ambainis, A.: The need for structure in quantum speedups. arXiv preprint arXiv:0911.0996 (2009)

[Aar09]   Aaronson, S.: Quantum copy-protection and quantum money. In: 24th Annual IEEE Conference on Computational Complexity, pp. 229-242. IEEE Computer Society, Los Alamitos, CA (2009). https://doi.org/10.1109/CCC.2009.42

[AC13]   Aaronson, S., Christiano, P.: Quantum money from hidden subspaces. Theory Comput. **9**, 349–401 (2013). https://doi.org/10.4086/toc.2013.v009a009

[ACC+22] Austrin, P., Chung, H., Chung, K.-M., Fu, S., Lin, Y.-T., Mahmoody, M.: On the impossibility of key agreements from quantum random oracles. Cryptology ePrint Archive (2022)

[AHY23]   Ananth, P., Hu, Z., Yuen, H.: On the (im)plausibility of public-key quantum money from collision-resistant hash functions. Cryptology ePrint Archive, Paper 2023/069. https://eprint.iacr.org/2023/069 2023. URL: https://eprint.iacr.org/2023/069 (cit. on pp. 17, 27-29)

[AJL+19] Ananth, P., Jain, A., Lin, H., Matt, C., Sahai, A.: Indistinguishability obfuscation without multilinear maps: new paradigms via low degree weak pseudorandomness and security amplification. In: Boldyreva, A., Micciancio, D. (eds.) CRYPTO 2019. LNCS, vol. 11694, pp. 284–332. Springer, Cham (2019). https://doi.org/10.1007/978-3-030-26954-8_10

[AK22]   Ananth,. P., Kaleoglu, F.: A note on copy-protection from random oracles. Cryptology ePrint Archive, Paper 2022/1109. https://eprint.iacr.org/2022/1109 (2022). https://eprint.iacr.org/2022/1109

[AKL+22] Ananth, P., Kaleoglu, F., Li, X., Liu, Q., Zhandry, M.: On the feasibility of unclonable encryption, and more. In: Dodis, Y., Shrimpton, T. (eds.) CRYPTO 2022. LNCS, vol. 13508, pp. 212–241. Springer, Cham (2022). https://doi.org/10.1007/978-3-031-15979-4_8

[AL21] Ananth, P., La Placa, R.L.: Secure software leasing. In: Canteaut, A., Standaert, F.-X. (eds.) EUROCRYPT 2021. LNCS, vol. 12697, pp. 501–530. Springer, Cham (2021). https://doi.org/10.1007/978-3-030-77886-6_17

[BDG22] Bilyk, A., Doliskani, J., Gong, Z.: Cryptanalysis of three quantum money schemes. arXiv preprint arXiv:2205.10488 (2022)

[BDGM20] Brakerski, Z., Döttling, N., Garg, S., Malavolta, G.: Factoring and pairings are not necessary for iO: circularsecure LWE suffices. Cryptology ePrint Archive (2020)

[BDV17] Bitansky, N., Degwekar, A., Vaikuntanathan, V.: Structure vs. hardness through the obfuscation lens. In: Katz, J., Shacham, H. (eds.) CRYPTO 2017. LNCS, vol. 10401, pp. 696–723. Springer, Cham (2017). https://doi.org/10.1007/978-3-319-63688-7_23

[BGI+01] Barak, B., et al.: On the (im)possibility of obfuscating programs. In: Kilian, J. (ed.) CRYPTO 2001. LNCS, vol. 2139, pp. 1–18. Springer, Heidelberg (2001). https://doi.org/10.1007/3-540-44647-8_1

[BGS13] Broadbent, A., Gutoski, G., Stebila, D.: Quantum one-time programs. In: Canetti, R., Garay, J.A. (eds.) CRYPTO 2013. LNCS, vol. 8043, pp. 344–360. Springer, Heidelberg (2013). https://doi.org/10.1007/978-3-642-40084-1_20

[BI20] Broadbent, A., Islam, R.: Quantum encryption with certified deletion. In: Pass, R., Pietrzak, K. (eds.) TCC 2020. LNCS, vol. 12552, pp. 92–122. Springer, Cham (2020). https://doi.org/10.1007/978-3-030-64381-2_4

[BL20] Broadbent, A., Lord, S.: Uncloneable quantum encryption via oracles. In: Flammia, S.T. (ed.) 15th Conference on the Theory of Quantum Computation, Communication and Cryptography (TQC 2020), vol. 158. Leibniz International Proceedings in Informatics (LIPIcs), pp. 4:1-4:22. Schloss Dagstuhl-Leibniz-Zentrum für Informatik, Dagstuhl, Germany (2020). https://doi.org/10.4230/LIPIcs.TQC.2020.4

[BM09] Barak, B., Mahmoody-Ghidary, M.: Merkle puzzles are optimal — an $O(n^2)$-query attack on any key exchange from a random oracle. In: Halevi, S. (ed.) CRYPTO 2009. LNCS, vol. 5677, pp. 374–390. Springer, Heidelberg (2009). https://doi.org/10.1007/978-3-642-03356-8_22

[BPR+08] Boneh, D., Papakonstantinou, P., Rackoff, C., Vahlis, Y., Waters, B.: On the impossibility of basing identity based encryption on trapdoor permutations. In: 2008 49th Annual IEEE Symposium on Foundations of Computer Science, pp. 283–292. IEEE (2008)

[BS16] Ben-David, S., Sattath, O.: Quantum tokens for digital signatures. arXiv preprint arXiv:1609.09047 (2016)

[CKP15] Canetti, R., Kalai, Y.T., Paneth, O.: On obfuscation with random oracles. In: Dodis, Y., Nielsen, J.B. (eds.) TCC 2015. LNCS, vol. 9015, pp. 456–467. Springer, Heidelberg (2015). https://doi.org/10.1007/978-3-662-46497-7_18

[CLLZ21] Coladangelo, A., Liu, J., Liu, Q., Zhandry, M.: Hidden cosets and applications to unclonable cryptography. In: Malkin, T., Peikert, C. (eds.) CRYPTO 2021. LNCS, vol. 12825, pp. 556–584. Springer, Cham (2021). https://doi.org/10.1007/978-3-030-84242-0_20

[CMP20] Coladangelo, A., Majenz, C., Poremba, A.: Quantum copy-protection of compute-and-compare programs in the quantum random oracle model. arXiv preprint arXiv:2009.13865 (2020)

[CX21] Cao, S., Xue, R.: Being a permutation is also orthogonal to one-wayness in quantum world: impossibilities of quantum one-way permutations from one-wayness primitives. In: Theoretical Computer Science, vol. 855, pp. 16–42 (2021)

[DG17] Döttling, N., Garg, S.: Identity-based encryption from the Diffie-Hellman assumption. In: Katz, J., Shacham, H. (eds.) CRYPTO 2017. LNCS, vol. 10401, pp. 537–569. Springer, Cham (2017). https://doi.org/10.1007/978-3-319-63688-7_18

[Die82] Dieks, D.G.B.J.: Communication by EPR devices. Phys. Lett. A **92**(6), 271–272 (1982)

[DLMM11] Dachman-Soled, D., Lindell, Y., Mahmoody, M., Malkin, T.: On the black-box complexity of optimally-fair coin tossing. In: Ishai, Y. (ed.) TCC 2011. LNCS, vol. 6597, pp. 450–467. Springer, Heidelberg (2011). https://doi.org/10.1007/978-3-642-19571-6_27

[DQV+21] Devadas, L., Quach, W., Vaikuntanathan, V., Wee, H., Wichs, D.: Succinct LWE sampling, random polynomials, and obfuscation. In: Nissim, K., Waters, B. (eds.) TCC 2021. LNCS, vol. 13043, pp. 256–287. Springer, Cham (2021). https://doi.org/10.1007/978-3-030-90453-1_9

[FGH+12] Farhi, E., Gosset, D., Hassidim, A., Lutomirski, A., Shor, P.: Quantum money from knots. In: Proceedings of the 3rd Innovations in Theoretical Computer Science Conference, pp. 276–289 (2012)

[GKLM12] Goyal, V., Kumar, V., Lokam, S., Mahmoody, M.: On black-box reductions between predicate encryption schemes. In: Cramer, R. (ed.) TCC 2012. LNCS, vol. 7194, pp. 440–457. Springer, Heidelberg (2012). https://doi.org/10.1007/978-3-642-28914-9_25

[GKM+00] Gertner, Y., Kannan, S., Malkin, T., Reingold, O., Viswanathan, M.: The relationship between public key encryption and oblivious transfer. In: Proceedings 41st Annual Symposium on Foundations of Computer Science, pp. 325–335. IEEE (2000)

[GP21] Gay, R., Pass, R.: Indistinguishability obfuscation from circular security. In: Proceedings of the 53rd Annual ACM SIGACT Symposium on Theory of Computing, pp. 736–749 (2021)

[GZ20] Georgiou, M., Zhandry, M.: Unclonable decryption keys. Cryptology ePrint Archive (2020)

[HJL21] Hopkins, S., Jain, A., Lin, H.: Counterexamples to new circular security assumptions underlying iO. In: Malkin, T., Peikert, C. (eds.) CRYPTO 2021. LNCS, vol. 12826, pp. 673–700. Springer, Cham (2021). https://doi.org/10.1007/978-3-030-84245-1_23

[HY20] Hosoyamada, A., Yamakawa, T.: Finding collisions in a quantum world: quantum black-box separation of collision-resistance and one-wayness. In: Moriai, S., Wang, H. (eds.) ASIACRYPT 2020. LNCS, vol. 12491, pp. 3–32. Springer, Cham (2020). https://doi.org/10.1007/978-3-030-64837-4_1

[Imp95] Impagliazzo, R.: A personal view of average-case complexity. In: Proceedings of Structure in Complexity Theory. Tenth Annual IEEE Conference, pp. 134–147. IEEE (1995)

[IR90] Impagliazzo, R., Rudich, S.: Limits on the provable consequences of one-way permutations. In: Goldwasser, S. (ed.) CRYPTO 1988. LNCS, vol. 403, pp. 8–26. Springer, New York (1990). https://doi.org/10.1007/0-387-34799-2_2

[JLS18] Ji, Z., Liu, Y.-K., Song, F.: Pseudorandom quantum states. In: Shacham, H., Boldyreva, A. (eds.) CRYPTO 2018. LNCS, vol. 10993, pp. 126–152. Springer, Cham (2018). https://doi.org/10.1007/978-3-319-96878-0_5

[JLS21] Jain, A., Lin, H., Sahai, A.: Indistinguishability obfuscation from well-founded assumptions. In: Proceedings of the 53rd Annual ACM SIGACT Symposium on Theory of Computing, pp. 60–73 (2021)

[JLS22] Jain, A., Lin, H., Sahai, A.: Indistinguishability obfuscation from LPN over, DLIN, and PRGs in NC. In: Dunkelman, O., Dziembowski, S. (eds.) EUROCRYPT 2022. LNCS, vol. 13275, pp. 670–699. Springer, Cham (2022). https://doi.org/10.1007/978-3-031-06944-4_23

[KSS21] Kane, D.M., Sharif, S., Silverberg, A.: Quantum money from quaternion algebras. arXiv preprint arXiv:2109.12643 (2021)

[Lut10] Lutomirski, A.: An online attack against Wiesner's quantum money. arXiv preprint arXiv:1010.0256 (2010)

[MLZ22] Montgomery, H., Liu, J., Zhandry, M.: Another round of breaking and making quantum money: how to not build it from lattices, and more. arXiv preprint arXiv:2211.11994 (2022)

[MVW12] Molina, A., Vidick, T., Watrous, J.: Optimal counterfeiting attacks and generalizations for Wiesner's quantum money. In: Iwama, K., Kawano, Y., Murao, M. (eds.) TQC 2012. LNCS, vol. 7582, pp. 45–64. Springer, Heidelberg (2013). https://doi.org/10.1007/978-3-642-35656-8_4

[MW05] Marriott, C., Watrous, J.: Quantum Arthur-Merlin games. Comput. Complex. **14**(2), 122–152 (2005)

[NC10] Nielsen, M.A., Chuang, I.L.: Quantum Computation and Quantum Information. Cambridge University Press, Cambridge (2010)

[Pap94] Papadimitriou, C.H.: Computational Complexity. Addison- Wesley, Boston (1994)

[PRV12] Papakonstantinou, P.A., Rackoff, C.W., Vahlis, Y.: How powerful are the DDH hard groups? Cryptology ePrint Archive (2012)

[Rob21] Roberts, B.: Security analysis of quantum lightning. In: Canteaut, A., Standaert, F.-X. (eds.) EUROCRYPT 2021. LNCS, vol. 12697, pp. 562–567. Springer, Cham (2021). https://doi.org/10.1007/978-3-030-77886-6_19

[RS22] Radian, R., Sattath, O.: Semi-quantum money. J. Cryptol. **35**(2), 1–70 (2022)

[RTV04] Reingold, O., Trevisan, L., Vadhan, S.: Notions of reducibility between cryptographic primitives. In: Naor, M. (ed.) TCC 2004. LNCS, vol. 2951, pp. 1–20. Springer, Heidelberg (2004). https://doi.org/10.1007/978-3-540-24638-1_1

[Rud91] Rudich, S.: The use of interaction in public cryptosystems. In: Feigenbaum, J. (ed.) CRYPTO 1991. LNCS, vol. 576, pp. 242–251. Springer, Heidelberg (1992). https://doi.org/10.1007/3-540-46766-1_19

[RY21] Rosenthal, G., Yuen, H.: Interactive proofs for synthesizing quantum states and unitaries. arXiv preprint arXiv:2108.07192 (2021)

[Shm22a] Shmueli, O.: Public-key Quantum money with a classical bank. In: Proceedings of the 54th Annual ACM SIGACT Symposium on Theory of Computing, pp. 790–803 (2022)

[Shm22b] Shmueli, O.: Semi-quantum tokenized signatures. Cryptology ePrint Archive (2022)

[Sim98] Simon, D.R.: Finding collisions on a one-way street: can secure hash functions be based on general assumptions? In: Nyberg, K. (ed.) EUROCRYPT 1998. LNCS, vol. 1403, pp. 334–345. Springer, Heidelberg (1998). https://doi.org/10.1007/BFb0054137

[Unr16] Unruh, D.: Computationally binding quantum commitments. In: Fischlin, M., Coron, J.-S. (eds.) EUROCRYPT 2016. LNCS, vol. 9666, pp. 497–527. Springer, Heidelberg (2016). https://doi.org/10.1007/978-3-662-49896-5_18

[Wie83] Wiesner, S.: Conjugate coding. In: ACM SIGACT News **15**(1), 78–88 (1983)

[Win99] Winter, A.: Coding theorem and strong converse for quantum channels. IEEE Trans. Inf. Theory **45**(7), 2481–2485 (1999)

[WW21] Wee, H., Wichs, D.: Candidate obfuscation via oblivious LWE sampling. In: Canteaut, A., Standaert, F.-X. (eds.) EUROCRYPT 2021. LNCS, vol. 12698, pp. 127–156. Springer, Cham (2021). https://doi.org/10.1007/978-3-030-77883-5_5

[WZ82] Wootters, W.K., Zurek, W.H.: A single quantum cannot be cloned. Nature **299**(5886), 802–803 (1982)

[Zha15] Zhandry, M.: A note on the quantum collision and set equality problems. Quantum Inf. Comput. **15**(7–8), 557–567 (2015)

[Zha18] Zhandry, M.: How to record quantum queries, and applications to quantum indifferentiability. Cryptology ePrint Archive, Paper 2018/276. https://eprint.iacr.org/2018/276 (2018)

[Zha21] Zhandry, M.: Quantum lightning never strikes the same state twice. Or: quantum money from cryptographic assumptions. J. Cryptol. **34**(1), Paper No. 6, 56 (2021). ISSN 0933-2790. https://doi.org/10.1007/s00145-020-09372-x

Key Exchange

Short Concurrent Covert Authenticated Key Exchange (Short cAKE)

Karim Eldefrawy[1], Nicholas Genise[2], and Stanislaw Jarecki[3(✉)]

[1] SRI International, Menlo Park, USA
karim.eldefrawy@sri.com
[2] Duality Technologies, Hoboken, USA
ngenise@dualitytech.com
[3] University of California, Irvine, Irvine, USA
sjarecki@uci.edu

Abstract. Von Ahn, Hopper and Langford introduced the notion of steganographic a.k.a. covert computation, to capture distributed computation where the attackers must not be able to distinguish honest parties from entities emitting random bitstrings. This indistinguishability should hold for the duration of the computation except for what is revealed by the intended outputs of the computed functionality. An important case of covert computation is mutually authenticated key exchange, a.k.a. mutual authentication. Mutual authentication is a fundamental primitive often preceding more complex secure protocols used for distributed computation. However, standard authentication implementations are not covert, which allows a network adversary to target or block parties who engage in authentication. Therefore, mutual authentication is one of the premier use cases of covert computation and has numerous real-world applications, e.g., for enabling authentication over steganographic channels in a network controlled by a discriminatory entity.

We improve on the state of the art in covert authentication by presenting a protocol that retains covertness and security under *concurrent composition*, has minimal message complexity, and reduces protocol bandwidth by an order of magnitude compared to previous constructions. To model the security of our scheme we develop a UC model which captures standard features of secure mutual authentication but extends them to covertness. We prove our construction secure in this UC model. We also provide a proof-of-concept implementation of our scheme.

1   Introduction

Steganography in the context of secure computation deals with hiding executions of secure computation protocols.[1] Such hiding is only possible if the participating parties have access to (public) communication channels which are *steganographic*, i.e., which naturally exhibit some entropy. Cryptographic protocols over

---

[1] The full version of this paper appears in [22].

N. Genise—This work was done while the second author was at SRI International.

J. Guo and R. Steinfeld (Eds.): ASIACRYPT 2023, LNCS 14445, pp. 75–109, 2023.
https://doi.org/10.1007/978-981-99-8742-9_3

such channels can be steganographic, a.k.a. *covert*, if all protocol messages the protocol exchanges cannot be distinguished from (assumed) a priori random behavior of the communication channels.

The study of covert secure computation was initiated by Hopper et al. [31] for the two-party case, and by Chandran et al. [15] and Goyal and Jain [29] for the multi-party case. Both [15,29,31] prove feasibility for covert computation of arbitrary circuits which tolerates passive and malicious adversaries, respectively. Subsequently, Jarecki [33] showed that general maliciously-secure two-party covert computation can be roughly as efficient as standard, i.e., non-covert, secure computation.

A flagship covert computation application is *covert authentication* and covert Authenticated Key Exchange (cAKE). In a cAKE protocol, two parties can authenticate each other as holders of mutually accepted certificates, but an entity who does not hold proper certificates, in addition to being unable to authenticate, cannot even distinguish a party that executes a covert AKE from a random beacon, i.e., from noise on the steganographic channel. In essence, cAKE allows group members to authenticate one another, but their presence on any steganographic communication channel is *entirely hidden*, i.e., they are invisible.

The application of covert computation to covert AKE has been addressed by Jarecki [32], but the state of the art in covert AKE is significantly lacking in several aspects: large bandwidth, high round complexity, and (a lack of) security under concurrent composition. Regarding security, the scheme of [32] achieves only sequential security, and does not ensure independence of keys across sessions, which is insufficient for full-fledged (covert) AKE.[2] Regarding round complexity and bandwidth, the cAKE protocol in [32] requires 6 message flows and relies on a composite-order group (and a factoring assumption), resulting in bandwidth which can be estimated as at least 3.6 kB. Recent works on random encodings of elliptic curve points, e.g. [8,47], allow for potentially dramatic bandwidth reduction if secure cAKE can be instantiated over a prime-order group.

Covert vs. Standard Authentication. Covert Authenticated Key Exchange (cAKE) can be formalized as a secure realization of functionality $\mathcal{F}_{cAKE}[C]$ shown in Fig. 1's entirety, characterized by a given *admission function* C. Let us first set the terms by explaining the standard, i.e. non-covert, AKE functionality $\mathcal{F}_{AKE}[C, L]$, characterized by C and a *leakage function* L, which is portrayed in the same figure. Reading Fig. 1 with dashed text and without greyed text defines $\mathcal{F}_{AKE}[C, L]$, and with greyed text and without dashed text defines $\mathcal{F}_{cAKE}$.

In an AKE protocol, i.e. a protocol that realizes $\mathcal{F}_{AKE}$, parties P_1 and P_2 run on inputs x_1 and x_2, which represent their *authentication tokens*, e.g. passwords, certificates, keys, etc., and if these inputs match each other's admission policy, jointly represented by circuit C, then P_1 and P_2 establish a shared random session

---

[2] In particular, [32] does not imply security against man in the middle attacks.

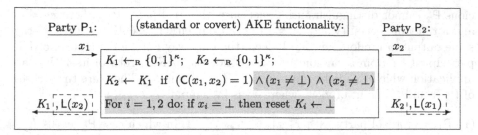

Fig. 1. Standard AKE functionality $\mathcal{F}_{\mathrm{AKE}}[C, L]$ includes dashed text & omits greyed text; Covert AKE functionality $\mathcal{F}_{\mathrm{cAKE}}[C]$ includes greyed text & omits dashed text.

key $K_1 = K_2$, otherwise their outputs K_1, K_2 are independent.[3] If L is a non-trivial function, then the protocol leaks $L(x)$ on P's input x to P's counterparty.

For example, Password Authenticated Key Exchange (PAKE) [5] can be defined as (secure realization of) $\mathcal{F}_{\mathrm{AKE}}[C_{\mathsf{pa}}]$ where C_{pa} is an equality test, i.e., $C_{\mathsf{pa}}(x_1, x_2) = 1$ if and only if $x_1 = x_2$. In another example, a standard notion of AKE, e.g. [21], which we will call here as a *Fixed Public Key* AKE (FPK-AKE) to distinguish it from other AKE types, can be defined as $\mathcal{F}_{\mathrm{AKE}}[C_{\mathsf{fpk}}, L_{\mathsf{fpk}}]$ where $C_{\mathsf{fpk}}(x_1, x_2) = 1$ iff $x_1 = (sk_1, pk_2)$ and $x_2 = (sk_2, pk_1)$ s.t. pk_1, pk_2 are the public keys corresponding to resp. sk_1, sk_2. Leakage L_{fpk} is typically omitted in the works on FPK-AKE, e.g. [3,14], because it is assumed that public keys pk_i of each P_i are public inputs. However, the implicit leakage profile in these works is $L_{\mathsf{fpk}}((sk_{\mathsf{P}}, pk_{\mathsf{CP}})) = (pk_{\mathsf{P}}, pk_{\mathsf{CP}})$ where pk_{P} is a public key corresponding to sk_{P}.[4]

We say that protocol Auth UC-realizes a *covert* AKE functionality $\mathcal{F}_{\mathrm{cAKE}}$ if it does so under a constraint that a real-world party P invoked on input $x = \bot$ does not follow protocol Auth but instead emulates a *random beacon* $\mathrm{Auth}^{\$(\kappa)}$ defined as follows: In each round, if Auth participant sends an $n(\kappa)$-bit message then $\mathrm{Auth}^{\$(\kappa)}$ sends out an $n(\kappa)$-bit random bitstring, where κ is a security parameter. In more detail, a covert AKE functionality $\mathcal{F}_{\mathrm{cAKE}}[C]$ makes the following changes to the standard AKE functionality $\mathcal{F}_{\mathrm{AKE}}[C, L]$: First, $\mathcal{F}_{\mathrm{cAKE}}$ eliminates leakage $L(x)$, equivalently $L(x) = \bot$ for all x. Second, $\mathcal{F}_{\mathrm{cAKE}}$ admits a special input $x = \bot$ which designates P as a random beacon, i.e., it tells P to run $\mathrm{Auth}^{\$(\kappa)}$ instead of Auth. Third, $\mathcal{F}_{\mathrm{cAKE}}$ adds the check that $x_1 \neq \bot$ and $x_2 \neq \bot$ to the condition for setting $K_1 = K_2$. Fourth, the functionality ensures that if P's input is $\bot$, i.e. P is a non-participant, then its output is $\bot$.

Implications of Covert AKE. The first impact of covert AKE vs. the standard AKE, is that if we disregard what P_1 does with its output key K_1, then a mali-

---

[3] Note that Fig. 1 defines AKE as a key exchange without explicit entity authentication, but the latter can be added to any AKE by testing if parties output the same key via any key confirmation protocol.

[4] In a standard FPK-AKE protocol party P can reveal either key. E.g. Sigma [36] used in TLS reveals P's own key pk_{P}, while SKEME [35] reveals key pk_{CP} which party P assumes for its counterparty, unless it employs key-private encryption [4].

cious P_2^* cannot distinguish an interaction with a real party P_1 (where $x_1 \neq \perp$) and a random beacon (where $x_1 = \perp$) because in either case $\mathcal{F}_{cAKE}$ gives P_2^* the same output, a random key K_2. Indeed, the only way P_2^* can distinguish cAKE participant P_1 from a random beacon, is not the cAKE protocol itself, but an application which P_1 might run using cAKE's output K_1. There are three cases of P_1 from P_2^*'s point of view, where x_2^* is P_2^*'s input to $\mathcal{F}_{cAKE}$:

(1) P_1 = protocol party with x_1 s.t. $C(x_1, x_2^*) = 1$, in which case P_2^* learns K_1;
(2) P_1 = protocol party with x_1 s.t. $C(x_1, x_2^*) = 0$, in which case K_1 is hidden;
(3) P_1 = random beacon, represented by $x_1 = \perp$, in which case $K_1 = \perp$.

The second property that cAKE adds to a standard AKE is that *if* the upper-layer application Π which P_1 runs on cAKE's output K_1 continues using steganographic channels, and P_1 encrypts Π's messages on these channels under key K_1, then P_2^* cannot distinguish cases (2) and (3). That is, P_2^* cannot tell a real-world P_1 who ran cAKE on inputs that didn't match x_2^* and then runs Π on cAKE output K_1, from a random beacon.[5] Detecting case (1) from a random beacon depends on the upper-layer protocol Π: If Π is non-covert than P_2^* will confirm that P_1 is a real-world party by running protocol Π on input K_1 (which P_2^* learns if $C(x_1, x_2^*) = 1$). However, if protocol Π is itself covert then P_1 will continue to be indistinguishable from a random beacon even in case (1). In other words, cAKE protocols are *composable*, e.g. running a covert PIN-authenticated KE, encrypted by a key created by a covert PAKE, ensures covertness to anyone except a party who holds both the correct password and the PIN.

Group Covert AKE (Group cAKE). In this work we target a *"group"* variant of cAKE. Namely, P's authentication token is a pair $x = (gpk, cert)$ where *gpk* is a public key identifying a group, *cert* is a certificate of membership in this group, and the admission function $C_G(x_1, x_2)$ outputs 1 if and only if $\exists\, gpk$ s.t. $x_1 = (gpk, cert_1)$, $x_2 = (gpk, cert_2)$, and $Ver(gpk, cert_1) = Ver(gpk, cert_2) = 1$, where Ver stands for certificate verification. In other words, both parties must assume the same group identified by *gpk* and each must hold a valid membership certificate in this group. We assume that key *gpk* is generated by a trusted *group manager* together with a master secret key *msk* which is used to issue valid certificates, and that the certification scheme is *unforgeable*, i.e. that an adversary which sees any number of valid certificates $cert_1, ..., cert_n$ cannot output $cert^*$ s.t. $Ver(gpk, cert^*) = 1$ and $\forall i\ cert^* \neq cert_i$.

The above setting of group cAKE is the same as that of *group signatures* [16], except that membership certificates are used to authenticate, not to sign,[6] and the authentication is covert. However, note that a straightforward usage of group signatures for authentication, e.g. where two parties sign a key exchange transcript using group signatures, can at best realize $\mathcal{F}_{AKE}[C_G, L]$ where leakage L

---

[5] This requires encryption with ciphertexts indistinguishable from random bitstrings, but this is achieved by standard block cipher modes, CBC, OFB, or RND-CTR.
[6] Using group signatures for authentication is known as an *Identity Escrow* [34].

hides P_i's certificate (and hence P_i's identity) but reveals the group public key gpk, because a group signature is verifiable under this key.[7]

In practice, a certification scheme must admit *revocation*, i.e. a group manager must be able to revoke a certificate, e.g. by distributing revocation token rt s.t. (1) there is an efficient procedure Link which links a certificate to this token, i.e. if $\mathsf{Ver}(gpk, cert) = 1$ then $\mathsf{Link}(cert, rt) = 1$ for rt associated with $cert$, and (2) certificates remain unforgeable in the presence of revocation tokens.[8] If $\mathsf{Link}(cert, \mathsf{RTset})$ stands for a procedure which outputs 1 iff $\exists rt \in \mathsf{RTset}$ s.t. $\mathsf{Link}(cert, rt) = 1$, then we define *group covert AKE (with revocation)*, or simply *group cAKE*, as $\mathcal{F}_{\mathrm{cAKE}}[\mathsf{C_{Gwr}}]$ where $\mathsf{C_{Gwr}}(x_1, x_2) = 1$ iff

1. $\exists gpk$ s.t. $x_1 = (gpk, cert_1, \mathsf{RTset}_1)$ and $x_2 = (gpk, cert_2, \mathsf{RTset}_2)$,
2. $\mathsf{Ver}(gpk, cert_1) = \mathsf{Ver}(gpk, cert_2) = 1$,
3. and $\mathsf{Link}(cert_2, \mathsf{RTset}_1) = \mathsf{Link}(cert_1, \mathsf{RTset}_2) = 0$.

In other words, parties establish a shared secret key if both assume the same group public key, both hold valid certificates under this key, and neither certificate is revoked by the revocation information held by a counterparty.

Applications of Group cAKE. Authentication and key exchange are fundamental primitives that regularly precede secure protocols used for distributed online computations. Identifying executions of such protocols is often used as a first step when blocking communication [44] or targeting it for filtering or other attacks [46,48]. *Authentication is thus a natural primitive to be protected and rendered covert to avoid such blocking or targeting.* To the best of our knowledge, there are currently no practical covert AKE protocols implemented, let alone deployed in distributed systems. If they existed, such protocols could help hide and protect communication required for authentication and key establishment in such systems. Since our work demonstrates that covert authentication can be realized with a (computation and communication) cost very close to that required for existing non-covert anonymous authentication (e.g., anonymous credentials [11]) or indeed standard non-private authentication (e.g., TLS handshake with certificate-based authentication), we argue that such protocols could become an enabling tool in large-scale resilient anonymous communication systems. Such anonymous communication systems have been the focus of the recent DARPA research program on developing a distributed system for Resilient Anonymous communication for Everyone (RACE) [45]. The RACE program objective was to develop "an anonymous, end-to-end mobile communication that would be attack-resilient and reside entirely within a contested network environment," and its targets included stenographic hiding of communication participants [45]. An efficient covert authentication could be play an essential role in such a system.

---

[7] *Secret Handshake* [2] flips this leakage, realizing $\mathcal{F}_{\mathrm{AKE}}[\mathsf{C_G}, \mathsf{L}']$ for L' that hides gpk but reveals a one-way function of P_i's certificate. To complete comparisons, standard PKI-based AKE realizes $\mathcal{F}_{\mathrm{AKE}}[\mathsf{C_G}, \mathsf{L}'']$ s.t. L'' reveals *both* a root of trust gpk *and* a one-way function of P_i's certificate, namely P_i's public key with gpk's signature.

[8] Here we follow the *verifier-local revocation* model [10], but other models are possible, e.g. using cryptographic *accumulators* [6,12].

Other Variants of Covert AKE. There are other natural variants of covert AKE which can be implemented using known techniques, but none of them imply a practical group cAKE. *Covert PAKE* corresponds to $\mathcal{F}_{cAKE}[C_{pa}]$, for C_{pa} defined above. Several known efficient PAKE schemes, e.g. EKE [5] and SPAKE2 [1], most likely realize $\mathcal{F}_{cAKE}[C_{pa}]$ after simple implementation adjustments, e.g. SPAKE2 should use an elliptic curve with a *uniform encoding*, which maps a random curve point to a random fixed-length bitstring, see Sect. 2.1. (We believe this is likely to hold because these PAKE protocols exchanges random group elements, or ideal-cipher encryptions of such elements.) The *covert Fixed Public Key AKE (FPK-AKE)* corresponds to $\mathcal{F}_{cAKE}[C_{fpk}]$, for C_{fpk} defined above. The work on *key-hiding AKE* [30] shows that several FPK-AKE protocols, namely 3DH [40], HMQV [37], and SKEME [35] instantiated with key-private and PCA-secure encryption, realize $\mathcal{F}_{AKE}[C_{fpk}]$, i.e. FPK-AKE without leakage, and after similar implementation adjustments as in the case of SPAKE2, these protocols probably realize $\mathcal{F}_{cAKE}[C_{fpk}]$. (This is likely to hold for similar reason, because these FPK-AKE protocols exchange random group elements and ciphertexts.) Another variant is an *identity based* AKE (IB-AKE), where public key *pk* is replaced by an identity and *gpk* is a public key of a Key Distribution Center. *Covert IB-AKE* can be implemented using Identity-Based Encryption (IBE) with covertly encodable ciphertexts, such as the Boneh-Franklin IBE [9] given a bilinear map group with a covert encoding.

However, it is unclear how to efficiently implement group cAKE from covert PAKE, FPK-AKE, or IB-AKE. Using any of these tools each group member would have to hold a separate token for every other group member (be it a password, a public key, or an identity), and the authentication protocol would need to involve n parallel instances of the covert PAKE/FPK-AKE/IB-AKE. Using the multiplexing technique of [17,39] such parallel execution can be done covertly at $\tilde{O}(n)$ cost, but this would not scale well. Either of these $\tilde{O}(n)$-cost implementations can be seen as implementing a *covert Broadcast Encryption (BE)* with $O(n)$-sized ciphertext. Indeed, any *covert* broadcast encryption implies cAKE. However, even though there are broadcast encryption schemes with sublinear ciphertexts, e.g. [23], to the best of our knowledge there are no sublinear BE schemes which are key-private [4], let alone covert.

1.1 Our Contributions

We show the *first practical covert group cAKE scheme*, with support for certificate revocation, with the following features:

1. *Universally composable (UC) covertness and security:* We formalize a *universally composable* (UC) [13] functionality for group cAKE, and show a scheme which realizes it. In particular, this implies that our group cAKE scheme retains covertness and security under *concurrent composition*, and that each session outputs an independent key, as expected of a secure AKE.
2. *Practically efficient:* Our group cAKE scheme is *round minimal*, using *one simultaneous flow* from each party, and *bandwidth efficient*, with a message

size of four DDH group elements and two points in a type-3 bilinear curve, resulting in bandwidth of 351B, factor of 10x improvement over state of the art. Our group cAKE scheme also has a *low computational overhead* of 14 exponentiations and $4 + n$ bilinear maps per party, where n is the size of the revocation list. Note that these parameters are a constant factor away from non-covert Group AKE, or indeed any other (A)KE. (The most significant slowdown compared to standard AKE comes from using bilinear maps.)

Furthermore, the above security and round improvements are enabled by security improvements in a crucial tool used in covert computation, namely a covert *Conditional Key Encapsulation Mechanism* (CKEM) [15,32],[9] which we construct for any language with so-called Sigma-protocol, i.e. a 3-round public-coin honest-verifier zero-knowledge proof of knowledge [20]. Covert CKEM is a covert KEM version of Witness Encryption [26]: It allows the sender to encrypt a key under a statement x, where decryption requires knowledge of a witness w for membership of statement x in a language $\mathcal{L}$ chosen at encryption. This KEM is covert if the ciphertext is indistinguishable from a random string, and in particular cannot be linked to either language $\mathcal{L}$ or statement x. The security improvements in covert CKEM are of independent interest because covert CKEM is a covert counterpart of a zero-knowledge proof, and as such it is a general-purpose tool which can find applications in other protocols.

Technical Overview. The high-level idea of our group cAKE construction follows the blueprint used for group cAKE by Jarecki [32]. Namely, it constructs group cAKE generically from a covert Identity Escrow (IE) scheme [34] and a covert CKEM: Each party sends a (covert) commitment to its IE certificate to the counterparty, and each party runs a CKEM, once as the sender (S) and once as the receiver (R), where the latter is proving ownership and validity of the committed certificate. Each party runs the CKEM once as the receiver and once as the sender, since the protocol covertly computes an AND statement: given $(gpk, cert)$ from P and $(gpk', cert')$ from P', it checks that $(cert \in \mathcal{L}^{\mathsf{IE}}(gpk')) \wedge (cert' \in \mathcal{L}^{\mathsf{IE}}(gpk))$ where $\mathcal{L}^{\mathsf{IE}}(gpk)$ is the language of valid IE certificates generated under gpk. Finally, each party checks the received committed certificate against their revocation list.[10] If the revocation check passes, each party uses the two CKEM outputs to derive a session key.

The main technical challenge is constructing provable secure group cAKE which is universally composable. To achieve this we implement several significant upgrades to the covert CKEM notion defined and constructed in [32] (for the same general class of languages with Sigma-protocols):
(1) First, we combine strong soundness of [32] and simulation-soundness of [7] to *strong simulation-soundness*. I.e., we require an efficient extractor that extracts a witness from an attacker who distinguishes S's output key from random on

---

[9] Covert CKEM was called *ZKSend* in [15]. Variants of (covert or non-covert) CKEM notion include *Conditional OT* [19], *Witness Encryption* [26], and *Implicit ZK* [7].

[10] This requires a special-purpose commitment which is hiding only in the sense of one-wayness, and which allows linking a revocation token to a committed certificate.

instance x in the presence of a simulator which plays R role on any instance $x' \neq x$. Strong simulation-soundness is needed in a concurrent group cAKE to let the reduction extract a certificate forgery from an attacker who decrypts a covert CKEM on a statement corresponding to a non-revoked certificate, while the reduction simulates all CKEM's on behalf of honest R's.

(2) Second, we amend covert CKEM with a *postponed-statement zero-knowledge* property, i.e. we require a postponed-statement simulator for simulating the CKEM on behalf of a receiver R. Such simulator must compute the same key an honest R would compute, and do so not only without knowing R's witness but also *without knowing the statement* used by R, until after all covert CKEM messages are exchanged. A group cAKE scheme requires this property because the simulator cannot know a priori the group to which a simulated party belongs, and hence cannot know the "I am a member of group [...]" statement on which this party runs as a CKEM receiver R. However, once the functionality reveals e.g. that the simulated R is a member of the same group as the attacker, the simulator must complete the R simulation on such adaptively revealed statement.

(3) The third change is that we cannot disambiguate between proof/CKEM instances using *labels*, which were used to separate between honest and adversarial CKEM instances in e.g. [33]. This change stems from the fact that whereas in many contexts protocol instances can be tied to some public unique identifiers of participating parties, we cannot use such public identifiers in the context of covert authentication. We deal with this technical challenge by strengthening the strong simulation-soundness property (1) above even further, and requiring witness extractability from adversary $\mathcal{A}$ which decrypts in interaction with a challenge $S(x)$ instance, even if $\mathcal{A}$ has access to (simulated) $R(x')$ instances for any x' values, *including $x' = x$*, with the only constraint that no $\mathcal{A}$-R transcript equals the $\mathcal{A}$-S transcript. Note that the excluded case of such transcripts being equal corresponds to a *passive attack*, i.e. $\mathcal{A}$ just transmitting messages between challenge oracles S and R, a case with which we deal separately.

We construct a covert CKEM, for any Sigma-protocol language, which satisfies this stronger covert CKEM notion, by using stronger building blocks compared to the (Sigma-protocol)-to-(Covert-CKEM) compiler of [32]. First, we rely on smooth projective hash functions (SPHF) with a property akin to PCA (plaintext checking attack) security of encryption. Using Random Oracle hash in derivation of SPHF outputs it is easy to assure this property for standard SPHF's of interest. Secondly, we use covert trapdoor commitments, with commitment instances defined by a random oracle hash applied to CKEM statements, to enable postponed-statement simulation required by property (2) above. (Intuitively, trapdoor commitments allow the simulator to open a message sent on behalf of an honest party as a CKEM ciphertext corresponding to a group membership which the functionality reveals in response to a *subsequent* active attack against this party.)

We achieve low bandwidth of the fully instantiated group cAKE by instantiating the above with the Identity Escrow scheme implied by Pointcheval-Sanders (PS) group signatures [42]. The resulting IE certificates involve only two elements of a type-3 bilinear pairing curve [25], which can be covertly encoded using the Elligator Squared encoding of Tibouchi [47], with a hash onto group due to Wahby and Boneh [50]. The CKEM part (for the language of valid IE certificates) requires sending only 4 group elements (3 for R and 1 for S), and can be implemented over a standard curve, which can be covertly encoded using e.g. the Elligator-2 encoding of Bernstein et al. [8].

Restriction to Static Corruptions. We note that our group cAKE scheme realizes the UC group cAKE model only for the case of *static* corruptions, i.e. the adversary can compromise a certificate or reveal a corresponding revocation token only if this certificate has never been used by an honest party. This is because our group cAKE scheme has no *forward privacy or covertness*. In particular, all past sessions executed by a party on some certificate become identifiable, and hence lose covertness (but only covertness, and not security), if this certificate is compromised at any point in the future. This lack of forward privacy comes from the verifier-local revocation mechanism. Enabling forward privacy in the face of revocation, and doing so covertly, introduces new technical challenges. For example, we can use our CKEM for a covert proof that a committed certificate is (or is not) included on a most recent (positive or negative) accumulator (e.g. [41]) for a given group. However, it is not clear how two group members can *covertly* deal with a possible skew between the most recent accumulator values they assume. We leave solving such challenges to future work.

Related Works. Von Ahn, Hopper, and Langford [49] introduced the notion of covert 2-party computation and achieved it by performing $O(\kappa)$ repetitions of Yao's garbled circuit evaluations. The underlying circuit was also extended by a hash function. This protocol guaranteed only secrecy against malicious participants and not output correctness. Chandran et al. [15] extended this to multiple parties while achieving correctness, but their protocol was also non-constant-round, and its efficiency was several orders of magnitude over known non-covert MPC protocols since each party covertly proves it followed a GMW MPC protocol by casting it as an instance of the Hamiltonian Cycle problem. Further, that proof internally used Yao's garbled circuits for checking correctness of committed values. Goyal and Jain [29] subsequently showed that non-constant-round protocols are necessary to achieve covert computation with black-box simulation against malicious adversaries, at least in the plain MPC model, i.e., without access to some trusted parameters. Hence, the former two constructions' inefficiencies are necessary without a trusted setup. Jarecki [32] showed a constant-round covert AKE with $O(1)$ public key operations satisfying a game-based, group-based covert AKE definition with a trusted setup. This protocol has a somewhat large communication cost: three rounds and large bandwidth since it uses composite-order groups. Recently, Kumar and Nguyen [38] gave the first post-quantum covert group-based AKE with trusted setup by adopting Jarecki's construction [32] to a lattice-based construction (three rounds in the ROM). Kumar and Nguyen do not provide bandwidth estimates, but we expect them to be somewhat large compared to Jarecki's original construction since they rely on trapdoor lattices [27].

None of the aforementioned works are proven secure in the UC framework [13]. Cho, Dachman-Soled, and Jarecki [17] achieve UC security for covert MPC of two specific functionalities, namely string equality and set intersection. The work of Jarecki [33] achieves UC secure 2PC for any function, but its efficiency is constant-round and sends $O(\kappa|C|)$ symmetric ciphertexts and $O(n\kappa)$ group elements where C is a boolean circuit with n input bits for the function to be computed. Implementing covert group-based authenticated key exchange using such generic protocol would be exceedingly costly. An open question is if the covert group-based AKE of [32] is secure as-is in the UC model despite [32] using a weaker instantiation of a covert CKEM.

Organization. Section 2 provides preliminaries. Section 3 presents a universally composable (UC) model of group covert authenticated key exchange (group cAKE). Section 4 reviews the building blocks used in our construction, namely covert trapdoor commitments, SPHF's, and an Identity Escrow (IE). Section 5 uses the first two of these tools to construct a covert CKEM, a key modular component of our group cAKE. The group cAKE scheme itself is shown in Sect. 6. For space constraint reasons, all security proofs, and an overview of our proof of concept implementation, are deferred to the full version of the paper [22].

2   Preliminaries

We reserve κ for the security parameter throughout the paper. The uniform distribution on a finite set S is denoted as $\mathcal{U}(S)$. We write $x \leftarrow_{\mathrm{R}} \mathcal{X}$ for a random variable sampled from distribution $\mathcal{X}$, and we write $x \leftarrow_{\mathrm{R}} S$ for $x \leftarrow_{\mathrm{R}} \mathcal{U}(S)$.

Standard Notation, Σ-Protocols. For lack of space, we defer the review of standard notions of computational and statistical indistinguishability, notation for groups with bilinear maps, and the review of Σ-protocols, a special form of honest-verifier zero-knowledge proof of knowledge [20], to the full version of the paper on eprint [22]. We note that in this work we assume a slightly *strengthened form of Σ-protocols* than in [20], where (1) both the verifier and the simulator use the same function to recompute the prover's first message from the rest of the transcript, (2) prover's response is a deterministic function of prior messages, and (3) the simulator samples that response from some uniformly encodable domain (see [22] for more details).

2.1   Covert Encodings and Random Beacons

We recall the covert encoding and random beacon notions used in steganography.

Definition 2.1. *Functions* (EC, DC) *form a* covert encoding *of domain* D *if there is an* l *s.t.* EC $: D \to \{0,1\}^l$, DC $: \{0,1\}^l \to D$ *is an inverse of* EC, *and* EC($\mathcal{U}(D)$) *is statistically close to the uniform distribution on* $\{0,1\}^l$. *Function* EC *can be randomized but* DC *must be deterministic. In case* EC *is randomized we require* EC($\mathcal{U}(D); r$) *to be statistically close to uniform when* EC*'s randomness* r *is a uniform random bitstring of fixed length.*

Definition 2.2. *We call a finite set S uniformly encodable if it has a covert encoding. Further, a family of sets $\mathcal{S} := \{S[\pi]\}_{\pi \in \mathcal{I}}$ indexed by some indexing set $\mathcal{I}$ is uniformly encodable if $S[\pi]$ is uniformly encodable for each $\pi \in \mathcal{I}$.*

Uniformly Encodable Domains. We use the following two uniformly encodable sets throughout the paper: (1) an integer range $[n] = \{0, ..., n-1\}$, and (2) points on an elliptic curve. For the former, if n is near a power of two then we can send an integer sampled in $\mathcal{U}([n])$ as is. Otherwise, for any t we can encode t-tuple $(a_i)_{i \in [t]}$ sampled from $\mathcal{U}([n]^t)$ as $\sum_{i=0}^{t-1} a_i \cdot n^i + r \cdot n^t$ for $r \leftarrow_R [m]$ where $m = \lceil 2^{\log_2(n)+\kappa}/n \rceil$. (See e.g. Sect. 3.4 of [47] for a proof.) For uniform encodings of elliptic curve points we require two sub-cases: (2a) a curve in Montgomery form and (2b) a pairing friendly curve. In case (2a) we can use the Elligator-2 encoding [8], which takes a random point sampled from a *subset S* of group $\mathbb{G} = E(\mathbb{F}_p)$, where $|S|/|\mathbb{G}| \approx 1/2$, and injectively maps it to integer range $[(p-1)/2]$. This map is then composed with a uniform encoding of this integer range. In the random oracle model, if H is an RO hash onto $\mathbb{G}$, see e.g. [50], a simple way to encode point P sampled from *the whole group*, i.e. $P \leftarrow_R \mathcal{U}(\mathbb{G})$ as opposed to $P \leftarrow_R \mathcal{U}(S)$, is to sample $r \leftarrow_R \{0,1\}^\kappa$ until $Q = \mathsf{H}(r) + P$ is in S, where G is a generator of $\mathbb{G}$, and output $z = \text{Elligator-2}(Q)\|r$ (see [22]). In case (2b) we can use Tibouchi's Elligator Squared encoding [47], which represents a random curve point as a pair of random elements of base field $\mathbb{F}_q$. This randomized map is then composed with a uniform encoding of $[q]^2$, implemented as above. In summary, Elligator-2 admits a more narrow class of curves than Elligator Squared, but using the above methods, the former creates slightly shorter encodings than the latter, resp. $|p| + 2\kappa$ vs. $2|q| + \kappa$ bits.

Random Beacons. The term *random beacon* refers to a network node or party which broadcasts random bitstrings. Such randomness sources are used for covert communication and here we use it for covert authentication, and, more generally, covert computation. We use $\mathsf{B}^{\$(\kappa)}$ where B is an interactive algorithm to denote a random beacon equivalent of B. Namely, if B has a fixed number of rounds and n_i is a polynomial s.t. for each i, the i-th round message of B has (at most) $n_i(\kappa)$ bits, then $\mathsf{B}^{\$(\kappa)}$ is an interactive "algorithm" which performs no computation except for sending a random bitstring of length $n_i(\kappa)$ in round i.

3   Universally Composable Model for Group Covert AKE

As discussed in the introduction, we define group covert AKE (group cAKE) as a covert *group* Authenticated Key Exchange, i.e. a scheme which allows two parties certified by the same authority, a.k.a. a *group manager*, to covertly and securely establish a session key. Covert AKE must be as secure as standard AKE, i.e. an adversary who engages in sessions with honest parties and observes their outputs cannot break the security of any session except by using a compromised but non-revoked certificate. In addition, the protocol must be *covert* in the sense that an attacker who does not hold a valid and non-revoked certificate not only cannot authenticate to an honest party but also cannot distinguish interaction with that party from an interaction with a random beacon. If such protocol is implemented over a steganographic channel [31] a party who does not have valid authentication tokens not only cannot use it to authenticate but also cannot detect if anyone else uses it to establish authenticated connections.

We define a group cAKE scheme as a tuple of algorithms (KG, CG, Auth) with the following input/output behavior:

- KG is a key generation algorithm, used by the group manager, s.t. $KG(1^\kappa)$ generates the group public key, gpk, and a master secret key, msk.
- CG is a certificate generation algorithm, used by the group manager, s.t. $CG(msk)$ generates a membership certificate $cert$ with a revocation token rt.
- Auth is an interactive algorithm used by two group members to (covertly) run an authenticated key exchange. Each party runs Auth on local input $(gpk, cert, \mathsf{RTset})$, where RTset is a set of revocation tokens representing revoked parties. Each party outputs (K, rt), where $K \in \{0,1\}^\kappa \cup \{\bot\}$ is a session key (or $\bot$ if no key is established) and $rt \in \mathsf{RTset} \cup \{\bot\}$ is a detected revocation token in RTset, or $\bot$ if Auth participant does not detect that a counterparty uses a certificate corresponding to a revocation token in RTset.

Our notion of AKE does not include *explicit entity authentication*, i.e., a party might output $K \neq \bot$ even though its counterparty is not a valid group member. However, since key K is secure, the parties can use standard key confirmation methods to explicitly authenticate a counterparty as a valid group member who computed the same session key. Moreover, Auth can remain covert even after adding key confirmation, e.g. if key confirmation messages are computed via PRF using key K. Note that in the definition above a real-world party P can output $K = \bot$, which violates the (simplified) covert mutual authentication model of Fig. 1 in Sect. 1. However, w.l.o.g. P is free to run any upper-layer protocol Π that utilizes Auth output K by replacing $K = \bot$ with a random key, thus preserving its covertness if protocol Π is covert.

Universally Composable Group cAKE. We define security of group cAKE via a universally composable functionality $\mathcal{F}_{\text{g-cAKE}}$ shown in Fig. 2, and we say that scheme $\Pi = (KG, CG, Auth)$ is a group cAKE if Π UC-realizes functionality $\mathcal{F}_{\text{g-cAKE}}$ in the standard sense of universal composability [13]. However, we adapt the UC framework [13] to the covert computation setting so that environment $\mathcal{Z}$ can pass to party P executing an AKE protocol Auth a special input $\bot$, which causes party P to play a role of a random beacon. (The same convention was adopted by Chandran et al. [15] with regards to one-shot secure computation.) For simplicity of notation we assume that protocol Auth is symmetric, i.e., the two participants act symmetrically in the protocol, and that it has a fixed number of rounds. In this case, on input (NewSession, ssid, $\bot$) from $\mathcal{Z}$, this party's session indexed by identifier ssid is replaced by a random beacon, i.e., it will run $\mathsf{Auth}^{\$(\kappa)}$ instead of Auth, see Sect. 2.

In Definition 3.1 we use the notation of [13], where $\mathbf{Ideal}_{\mathcal{F}_{\text{g-cAKE}}, \mathcal{A}^*, \mathcal{Z}}(\kappa, z)$ stands for the output of environment $\mathcal{Z}$ in the ideal-world execution defined by the ideal-world adversary (a.k.a. simulator) algorithm $\mathcal{A}^*$ and functionality $\mathcal{F}_{\text{g-cAKE}}$, for security parameter κ and $\mathcal{Z}$'s auxiliary input z, and $\mathbf{Real}_{\Pi,\mathcal{A},\mathcal{Z}}(\kappa, z)$ stands for $\mathcal{Z}$'s output in the real-world execution between a real-world adversary $\mathcal{A}$ and honest parties acting according to scheme Π, extended as specified above in case party P receives $\mathcal{Z}$'s input (NewSession, ssid, $\perp$).

Definition 3.1. *Protocol $\Pi = $ (KG, CG, Auth) realizes a UC Covert Authenticated Key Exchange if for any efficient adversary $\mathcal{A}$ there exists an efficient ideal-world adversary $\mathcal{A}^*$ such that for any efficient environment $\mathcal{Z}$ it holds that*

$$\{\mathbf{Ideal}_{\mathcal{F}_{\text{g-cAKE}},\mathcal{A}^*,\mathcal{Z}}(\kappa, z)\}_{\kappa \in \mathbb{N}, z \in \{0,1\}^*} \approx_c \{\mathbf{Real}_{\Pi,\mathcal{A},\mathcal{Z}}(\kappa, z)\}_{\kappa \in \mathbb{N}, z \in \{0,1\}^*}$$

Group cAKE Functionality. We explain how functionality $\mathcal{F}_{\text{g-cAKE}}$ operates and how it differs from a standard AKE functionality, e.g. [14,37]. Note that functionality $\mathcal{F}_{\text{g-cAKE}}$ in Fig. 2 is much more complex than functionality $\mathcal{F}_{\text{cAKE}}[\mathsf{C_{Gwr}}]$ in Fig. 1 in Sect. 1. The first difference are environment commands GInit and CertInit, which are used to initialize groups and generate membership certificates, and commands CompCert and RevealRT, which model adversarial compromise of resp. certificates and revocation tokens (which are not assumed public by default). Command NewSession models party P engaging in group cAKE on input $x = (gpk, cert, \mathsf{RTset})$, exactly as $\mathcal{F}_{\text{cAKE}}[\mathsf{C_{Gwr}}]$ of Fig. 1, except that in $\mathcal{F}_{\text{g-cAKE}}$ these real-world inputs are replaced by ideal-world identifiers, resp. gid, cid, RTcids. One aspect of functionality $\mathcal{F}_{\text{g-cAKE}}$ is that there can be many number of such sessions present, and the adversary can "connect" any pair of such sessions, by passing their messages. Secondly, the adversary can actively attack any session using some compromised group certificate, and functionality $\mathcal{F}_{\text{g-cAKE}}$ carefully delineates the effect of such attack based on whether the group assumed by the attacker matched the one used by the attacker party, and if so then whether the certificate used by the attacker was revoked by the attacked party.

Below we explain how we model secure initialization and party interactions with the group manager, and we briefly overview how we model compromise of credentials and revealing of revocation tokens, and how $\mathcal{F}_{\text{g-cAKE}}$ models key establishment and active (or passive) session attacks. For a more detailed walk through functionality $\mathcal{F}_{\text{g-cAKE}}$, see the eprint version of this paper [22].

Secure Initialization and Trusted Group Manager. A crucial difference between $\mathcal{F}_{\text{g-cAKE}}$ and standard AKE is that in the latter each party can function on its own, creating its (private, public) key pair, e.g. as in [30], maybe accessing a global certificate functionality, e.g. as in [14]. By contrast, the Covert AKE model $\mathcal{F}_{\text{g-cAKE}}$ must explicitly include a *group manager* party, denoted GM, initialized via query (GInit, gid) which models generation of a group public key indexed by a unique identifier gid. Consequently, the $\mathcal{F}_{\text{g-cAKE}}$ model assumes a *trusted party, secure channels at initialization, and secure distribution of revocation tokens*. We explain each of these assumptions in turn. Note that identifier gid in command (GInit, gid) is associated with that group instance by each party P, which can be realized if GM has a reliable authenticated connection to each party, which

$\mathcal{F}_{\text{g-cAKE}}$ interacts with parties denoted P and GM and adversary $\mathcal{A}^*$. Sets $\mathsf{CompCert}^{\text{gid}}$ and $\mathsf{RevRT}^{\text{gid}}$ store resp. revealed certificates and revocation tokens for each gid.

Keys: Initialization and Attacks

On (GInit, gid) from GM:
Save (gid, GM), reject future GInit queries for the same gid, send (GInit, GM, gid) to $\mathcal{A}^*$.

On (CertInit, gid, cid) from P:
If $\exists$ no prior record $(\cdot, \text{gid}, \text{cid})$, save tuple (P, gid, cid).

On (CompCert, P, gid, cid) from $\mathcal{A}^*$ [$\mathcal{A}^*$ needs environment permission for this action]:
If $\exists$ rec. (P, gid, cid) and $\exists$ no rec. $(P, \cdot, \text{gid}, \text{cid}, \cdot, \cdot)$ add cid to $\mathsf{CompCert}^{\text{gid}}$ and $\mathsf{RevRT}^{\text{gid}}$.

On (RevealRT, P, gid, cid) from $\mathcal{A}^*$ [$\mathcal{A}^*$ needs environment permission for this action]:
If $\exists$ record (P, gid, cid) and $\exists$ no record $(P, \cdot, \text{gid}, \text{cid}, \cdot, \cdot)$ add cid to $\mathsf{RevRT}^{\text{gid}}$.

Authentication Sessions: Initialization, Connections, Attacks

On (NewSession, ssid, $\bot$) from P:
Save record $(P, \text{ssid}, \bot, \bot, \bot, \bot)$ marked random, send (NewSession, P, ssid, $\bot$) to $\mathcal{A}^*$.

On (NewSession, ssid, gid, cid, RTcids) from P:
If $\text{RTcids} \subseteq \mathsf{RevRT}^{\text{gid}}$ and $\exists$ record (P, gid, cid) but $\exists$ no prior record $(P, \text{ssid}, \cdot, \cdot, \cdot, \cdot)$:
 − if $\text{cid} \notin \mathsf{RevRT}^{\text{gid}}$, send (NewSession, P, ssid, $\bot$) to $\mathcal{A}^*$
 − if $\text{cid} \in \mathsf{RevRT}^{\text{gid}}$, send (NewSession, P, ssid, gid, cid) to $\mathcal{A}^*$
Save record (P, ssid, gid, cid, RTcids, $\bot$) marked fresh.

On (Interfere, P, ssid) from $\mathcal{A}^*$:
If $\exists$ record $(P, \text{ssid}, \cdot, \cdot, \cdot, \bot)$ marked fresh, re-label it interfered.

On (Connect, P, ssid, P', ssid') from $\mathcal{A}^*$:
If $\exists$ record rec $= (P, \text{ssid}, \text{gid}, \text{cid}, \cdot, \bot)$ marked fresh and record $(P', \text{ssid}', \text{gid}', \text{cid}', \cdot, K')$ marked either fresh or connected(P, ssid, cid) (any of gid', cid', K' can equal $\bot$) then:
 − if $\text{gid} = \text{gid}'$ then re-label rec as connected(P', ssid', cid')
 − if $\text{gid} \neq \text{gid}'$ then re-label rec as interfered

On (Impersonate, P, ssid, gid*, cid*) from $\mathcal{A}^*$:
If $\exists$ rec $= (P, \text{ssid}, \text{gid}, \cdot, \cdot, \bot)$ marked fresh:
 − if $\text{gid} = \text{gid}^*$ and $\text{cid}^* \in \mathsf{CompCert}^{\text{gid}}$ then re-label rec as compromised(cid*)
 − if $\text{gid} = \text{gid}^*$ and $\text{cid}^* \notin \mathsf{CompCert}^{\text{gid}}$ then re-label rec as interfered(cid*)
 − if $\text{gid} \neq \text{gid}^*$ then re-label rec as interfered

Authentication Sessions: Key Establishment

On (NewKey, P, ssid, K^*) from $\mathcal{A}^*$:
If $\exists$ session record rec $= (P, \text{ssid}, \text{gid}, \text{cid}, \text{RTcids}, \bot)$ marked flag then:
1. if flag = random set $(K, \text{cid}_{\text{CP}}) \leftarrow (\bot, \bot)$
2. if flag = compromised(cid') for $\text{cid}' \notin \text{RTcids}$, set $(K, \text{cid}_{\text{CP}}) \leftarrow (K^*, \bot)$
3. if flag is either connected$(\cdot, \cdot, \text{cid}')$ or compromised(cid') or interfered(cid'), for $\text{cid}' \in$ RTcids, set $(K, \text{cid}_{\text{CP}}) \leftarrow (\bot, \text{cid}')$
4. if flag = connected(P', ssid', cid'), $\text{cid}' \notin \text{RTcids}$, and $\exists \text{ rec}' = (P', \text{ssid}', \text{gid}', \text{cid}', \cdot, K')$ s.t. $K' \neq \bot$ and rec' terminated as connected(P, ssid, cid), set $(K, \text{cid}_{\text{CP}}) \leftarrow (K', \bot)$
5. in any other case set $K \leftarrow_{\text{R}} \{0, 1\}^\kappa$ and $\text{cid}_{\text{CP}} \leftarrow \bot$
Modify rec as (P, ssid, gid, cid, RTcids, K) and output (NewKey, ssid, K, cid_{CP}) to P.

Fig. 2. $\mathcal{F}_{\text{g-cAKE}}$: Group cAKE functionality, static corruptions enforced by boxed text

allows authenticated broadcast of *gpk*. GM is assumed trusted because the model does not allow a compromise of GM or the master secret *msk* held by GM. Furthermore, when $\mathcal{Z}$'s command (CertInit, gid, cid) to party P, prompting it to generate a membership certificate with identifier cid (assumed unique within group gid), we assume that only P can later use it to authenticate. Looking ahead, we will implement CertInit relying on a secure channel between P and GM. Party GM will generate the certificate identified by cid, it will send it to P on the secure channel, and GM will be trusted not to use the certificate itself.

The above assumptions pertain to initialization procedures, but the on-line authentication will rely on the secure P-to-GM channels in one more aspect, namely for secure delivery of revocation tokens. The environment tells P to run the authentication protocol via query (NewSession, ssid, gid, cid, RTcids), which models P starting an AKE session using its certificate identified by cid within group gid, where RTcids is a set of identifiers of revoked certificates which P will use on this session. Crucially, at this step an implementation must allow P to translate this set of certificate identifiers RTcids into a set RTset of actual revocation tokens corresponding to these certificates. This can be realized e.g. if the trusted party GM stores the revocation tokens for all certificates it generates and that the P-GM channel allows for secure and authenticated transmission of the revocation tokens from GM to P whenever the environment requests it by including them in set RTcids input to P in some NewSession query. Note that the environment can set RTcids in an arbitrary way, which models e.g. parties that do not receive the revocation tokens of all compromised parties.[11]

Static Compromise Model. Adversary can compromise any certificate, using command (CompCert, gid, P, cid), and it can reveal the revocation information corresponding to any certificate, using command (RevealRT, gid, P, cid). The first command adds cid to the set CompCert^{gid} of compromised certificate identifiers in group gid, and both commands add cid to the set RevRT^{gid} of certificate identifiers whose revocation tokens are revealed to the adversary. A compromised certificate cid allows the adversary to actively authenticate to other parties using interface Impersonate, whereas a revealed revocation token implies that party P which uses it to authenticate can be identified by the adversary, and hence no longer covert (see the second clause in NewSession interface). Finally, we allow only for *static* corruptions, which is implied by marked text fragments in Fig. 2, which impose that an adversary can compromise a certificate and/or reveal a revocation token only if this certificate was never used by an honest party. This is because the group cAKE scheme we show in this work has *no forward privacy*, i.e., all past sessions executed by a party on some certificate become identifiable, and hence lose covertness, if this certificate is compromised at any point in the future. Because it appears difficult to capture a notion of "revocable covertness", i.e., that protocol instances remain covert until a certificate they use is revealed, we forego on trying to capture such property and limit the model by effectively

---

[11] To see an example of how real-world parties can use scheme $\Pi = (\mathsf{KG}, \mathsf{CG}, \mathsf{Auth})$ to implement the environment's queries to $\mathcal{F}_{\text{g-cAKE}}$, please see Fig. 5 in Sect. 6.

requiring that the adversary corrupts all certificates and reveals all revocation tokens at the beginning of the interaction.

AKE Session Establishment and Attacks. Party P starts an AKE session via command (NewSession, ssid, gid, cid, RTcids). Values gid, cid, RTcids can either form an input to a real protocol party, or they can be $\bot$, in which case this command triggers an execution of a random beacon. Crucially, if cid is not in RevRT^{gid}, i.e. a party runs on a certificate whose revocation token is not revealed, then $\mathcal{A}^*$ gets the same view of the real-world protocol as its view of the random beacon, i.e. $\mathcal{A}^*$ gets (NewSession, P, ssid, $\bot$) in either case. Below we will use a word "session" for both real sessions and random beacons. The adversary can react to sessions in 3 ways: (1) it can interfere in them, using query Interfere, which makes real sessions output random keys K on termination, modeled by query NewKey (random beacon sessions always output $K = \bot$, regardless of adversarial behavior towards them); (2) it can passively connect them to another session, using query Connect, which will make the two sessions establish a shared key at termination *if* they assume same group gid and use certificates which are not on each other's revocation lists (otherwise they output independent random keys); or (3) it can actively attack P's session using a compromised certificate cid* for some target group gid*, as modeled by query Impersonate: If gid* matches the gid used by P then $\mathcal{F}_{\text{g-cAKE}}$ marks P's session compromised(cid*), but when this session terminates via NewKey then $\mathcal{F}_{\text{g-cAKE}}$ lets $\mathcal{A}^*$ set its key to K^* only if cid* is not in RTcids used by P. Otherwise P outputs $K = \bot$ and cid* as the identifier of a revoked party which P "caught" in this interaction.

(For a more detailed walk-through of the $\mathcal{F}_{\text{g-cAKE}}$ session attack and termination interfaces see the eprint version of the paper [22].)

Note on the Environment. An environment plays a role of an arbitrary application utilizing the group cAKE scheme. The role of group cAKE is to make real AKE sessions indistinguishable from random beacons, but the two send different outputs to the environment: the former outputs keys, the latter do not. If the environment leaks that output to the adversary then the benefit of covertness will disappear. However, this is so in the real-world: If an adversary can tell that two nodes use the established key to communicate with each other, they will identify these parties on the application level and the covert property of the AKE level was "for naught", at least in that instance. However, if the upper-layer communication stays successfully hidden in some steganographic channel, then the adversary continues being unable to detect these parties. The versatility of a universally composable definition is that it implies the maximum protection whatever the strength of the upper-layer application: If the upper-layer allows some sessions to be detected (or even leaks the keys they use), this information does not help to detect other sessions, and it does not help distinguish anything from the cryptographic session-establishment protocol instances. The same goes for the revocation information the AKE sessions take as inputs: If the upper-layer detects compromised certificates and delivers the revocation information to all remaining players, the adversary will fail to authenticate to other group members and it will fail to distinguish their session instances from random beacons. If the revocation information does not propagate to some group member, the adversary can detect that party using a compromised certificate, but this inevitable outcome will not help the attacker on any other sessions.

4   Building Blocks: Commitment, SPHF, Identity Escrow

Our group cAKE construction consists of (1) each party sending out a blinded covert Identity Escrow (IE) certificate, and (2) each party verifying the counterparty's value using a covert Conditional Key Encapsulation Mechanism (CKEM). (This group cAKE construction is shown in Fig. 6 in Sect. 6.) The covert CKEM construction in turn uses a covert Trapdoor Commitment and a covert Smooth Projective Hash Function (SPHF) which must be secure against a Plaintext Checking Attack (PCA). In this section we define and show efficient instantiations for each of the three above building blocks, i.e. covert Trapdoor Commitments, in Subsect. 4.1, PCA-secure covert SPHF, in Subsect. 4.2, and covert IE, in Subsect. 4.3. (The construction of covert CKEM using trapdoor commitments and PCA-secure SPHF is shown in Sect. 5.) To fit bandwidth restrictions of steganographic channels we instantiate all tools with bandwidth-efficient schemes, using standard prime-order elliptic curve group for the Trapdoor Commitment and SPHF, and type-3 curves with bilinear pairings for IE.

4.1   Covert Trapdoor Commitment

For the reasons we explain below, we modify the standard notion of a Trapdoor Commitment [24] by splitting the commitment parameter generation into two phases. First algorithm GPG on input the security parameter κ samples global commitment parameters π, and then algorithm PG on input π samples instance-specific parameters $\overline{\pi}$. The commitment and decommitment algorithms then use pair $(\pi, \overline{\pi})$ as inputs. The trapdoor parameter generation TPG runs on the global parameters π output by GPG, but it generates instance parameters $\overline{\pi}$ with the trapdoor tk. Then, the trapdoor commitment algorithm TCom on input π generates commitment c with a trapdoor td, and the trapdoor decommitment algorithm TDecom on input $(\pi, \overline{\pi}, c, tk, td, m)$ generates decommitment d. Crucially, the trapdoor commitment TCom takes only global parameters as inputs, which allows a simulator to create trapdoor commitments independently from the instance parameters $\overline{\pi}$.

Definition 4.1. *Algorithm tuple* (GPG, PG, Com, Decom) *forms a* trapdoor commitment scheme *if there exists algorithms* (TPG, TCom, TDecom) *s.t.:*

- *GPG(1^κ) samples global parameters π and defines message space $\mathcal{M}$*
- *PG(π) samples instance parameters $\overline{\pi}$*
- *Com$(\pi, \overline{\pi}, m)$ outputs commitment c and decommitment d*
- *Decom$(\pi, \overline{\pi}, c, m, d)$ outputs 1 or 0*

- *TPG(π) outputs instance parameters $\overline{\pi}$ with trapdoor tk*

- TCom(π) *outputs commitment c with trapdoor td*
- TDecom($\pi, \overline{\pi}, c, tk, td, m$) *outputs decommimtment d*

The correctness requirement is that if $\pi \leftarrow$ GPG(1^κ), $\overline{\pi} \leftarrow$ PG(π), *and* $(c, d) \leftarrow$ Com($\pi, \overline{\pi}, m$) *then* Decom($\pi, \overline{\pi}, c, m, d$) $= 1$.

Definition 4.2. *We say that a trapdoor commitment scheme forms a* covert perfectly-binding trapdoor commitment *if it satisfies the following:*

1. Trapdoored and non-trapdoored distributions indistinguishability: *For any m tuples* $(\pi, \overline{\pi}, c, d)$ *generated by the following two processes are computationally indistinguishable: sample* $\pi \leftarrow$ GPG(1^κ) *and fix any* $m \in \mathcal{M}$,

$$P_0 : \overline{\pi} \leftarrow \mathsf{PG}(\pi), (c, d) \leftarrow \mathsf{Com}(\pi, \overline{\pi}, m)$$
$$P_1 : (\overline{\pi}, tk) \leftarrow \mathsf{TPG}(\pi), (c, td) \leftarrow \mathsf{TCom}(\pi),$$
$$d \leftarrow \mathsf{TDecom}(\pi, \overline{\pi}, c, tk, td, m)$$

2. Perfect binding: *If* $\pi \leftarrow$ GPG(1^κ) *and* $\overline{\pi} \leftarrow$ PG(π), *then for any* c, m, m', d, d' *it holds except for negligible probability over the coins of* GPG *and* PG, *that if* Decom($\pi, \overline{\pi}, c, m, d$) = Decom($\pi, \overline{\pi}, c, m', d'$) = 1 *then* $m = m'$.
3. Covertness: *There is a uniformly encodable set family S s.t. for any m, tuples* $(\pi, \overline{\pi}, c)$ *and* $(\pi, \overline{\pi}, c')$ *are computationally indistinguishable for* $\pi \leftarrow$ GPG(1^κ), $\overline{\pi} \leftarrow$ PG(π), $c \leftarrow$ Com($\pi, \overline{\pi}, m$), $c' \leftarrow_R \mathcal{U}(S[\pi])$.

Discussion. The first property is specialized for scenarios where each commitment instance $\overline{\pi}$ is used only for a single commitment. This restriction is not necessary for the implementation shown below, but we use it for simplicity because it suffices in our CKEM application. Note that *perfect binding* property holds on all non-trapdoored commitment instance parameters $\overline{\pi}$, and it is unaffected by the equivocability of commitments pertaining to any trapdoored commitment instances $\overline{\pi}'$. Observe also that the *covertness* property implies the standard *computational hiding* property of the commitment. Finally, we note that the above properties do not imply non-malleability, and we defer to Sect. 5 for the intuition why that suffices in the CKEM application.

Random Oracle Applications. In the Random Oracle Model (ROM) it can be convenient to replace the instance generator algorithm PG with a random oracle, but for that we need an additional property:

Definition 4.3. *We say that a trapdoor commitment scheme has* RO-compatible instance parameters *if each* π *output by* GPG(1^κ) *defines set* $\mathcal{C}[\pi]$ *s.t. (1) distribution* $\{\overline{\pi}\}_{\overline{\pi} \leftarrow \mathsf{PG}(\pi)}$ *is computationally indistinguishable from uniform in* $\mathcal{C}[\pi]$, *and (2) there exists an RO-indifferentiable hash function* H : $\{0, 1\}^* \rightarrow$ $\mathcal{C}[\pi]$.

The above property allows an application to set instance parameters as $\overline{\pi} :=$ H(lbl), where string lbl can be thought of as a *label* of that commitment instance. If a label can be uniquely assigned to a committing party then for all labels corresponding to adversarial instances the simulator can set $\mathsf{H}(\mathsf{lbl})$ by sampling $\mathsf{PG}(\pi)$, which makes all these instances perfectly binding, while for all labels corresponding to honest parties the simulator can set $\mathsf{H}(\mathsf{lbl})$ by sampling $\mathsf{TPG}(\pi)$, which makes all these instances equivocable.

In the CKEM application, Sect. 5, the label lbl is a *statement* x used in a given CKEM instance. In this way the simulator can "cheat" in the CKEM's on statements of the simulated parties without affecting the soundness of the CKEM's executed by the adversarial parties.[12] The same CKEM application also motivates why it is useful for the trapdoor commitment TCom to be independent of a commitment instance parameter $\bar{\pi}$. Namely, this enables the "statement-postponed zero-knowledge" property in the CKEM application, where the simulator at first does not know the statement x used by the CKEM sender on the onset of simulation, but it can use $\mathsf{TCom}(\pi)$ to create an equivocable commitment, which it can then open to an arbitrary message for any parameter $\bar{\pi} = \mathsf{H}(x)$ generated in the trapdoored way.

Instantiation. The trapdoor commitment scheme satisfying all properties of Definitions 4.1, 4.2 and 4.3, can be implemented with a "Double Pedersen" commitment in a DDH group $\mathbb{G}$ of order q with covert encoding and RO hash onto the group: Global parameters are $\pi = (g_1, g_2) \leftarrow_{\mathrm{R}} \mathbb{G}^2$, instance parameters are $\bar{\pi} = (h_1, h_2) \leftarrow_{\mathrm{R}} \mathbb{G}^2$, and the commitment is $c = (g_1^d \cdot h_1^m, g_2^d \cdot h_2^m)$ where $d \leftarrow_{\mathrm{R}} \mathbb{Z}_q$ is a decommitment. Trapdoor generators TPG and TCom set resp. $(h_1, h_2) = (g_1^{tk}, g_2^{tk})$ for $tk \leftarrow_{\mathrm{R}} \mathbb{Z}_q$ and $c = (g_1^{td}, g_2^{td})$ for $td \leftarrow_{\mathrm{R}} \mathbb{Z}_q$, and trapdoor decommitment to m opens d s.t. $td = d + tk \cdot m \bmod q$. The security proofs for this construction are deferred to the full version of the paper [22].

4.2   Covert SPHF with PCA-Security

A smooth projective hash function (SPHF) for an NP language $\mathcal{L}$, introduced by Cramer and Shoup [18], allows two parties to compute a hash on a statement $x \in \mathcal{L}$ where one party computes the hash using a random hash key hk and the statement x, and the other can recompute the same hash using a *projection* key hp corresponding to hk and a witness w for $x \in \mathcal{L}$. The smoothness property is that if $x \notin \mathcal{L}$ then the hash value computed using key hk on x is statistically independent of the projection key hp. In other words, revealing the projection key hp allows the party that holds witness w for $x \in \mathcal{L}$ to compute the hash value, but it hides this value information-theoretically if $x \notin \mathcal{L}$. In this work we require two additional properties of SPHF, namely covertness and One-Wayness under Plaintext Checking Attack (OW-PCA) security, which we define below.

Definition 4.4. *A* covert smooth projective hash function *(covert SPHF) for NP language $\mathcal{L}$ parameterized by π, is a tuple of PPT algorithms* (HKG, Hash, PHash) *and set family $\mathcal{H}$ indexed by π, where* $\mathsf{HKG}(\pi)$ *outputs* (hk, hp), *and* $\mathsf{PHash}(x, w, hp)$ *and* $\mathsf{Hash}(x, hk)$ *both compute a hash value v s.t. $v \in \mathcal{H}[\pi]$. Furthermore, this tuple must satisfy the following properties:*

---

[12] Except if an adversarial party copies a statement of the honest party, in which case CKEM security comes from the PCA security of SPHF, see Sect. 4.2.

- Correctness: *For any* (π, x, w) *s.t.* $x \in \mathcal{L}[\pi]$ *and* w *is a witness for* x, *if* $(hk, hp) \leftarrow \mathsf{HKG}(\pi)$ *then* $\mathsf{Hash}(x, hk) = \mathsf{PHash}(x, w, hp)$.
- Smoothness: *For any* π *and* $x \notin \mathcal{L}[\pi]$, *hash* $\mathsf{Hash}(x, hk)$ *is statistically close to uniform over* $\mathcal{H}[\pi]$ *even given* hp, *i.e. tuples* (hp, v) *and* (hp, v') *are statistically close for* $(hk, hp) \leftarrow \mathsf{HKG}(\pi)$, $v \leftarrow \mathsf{Hash}(x, hk)$, *and* $v' \leftarrow_R \mathcal{U}(\mathcal{H}[\pi])$. *Moreover, space* $\mathcal{H}[\pi]$ *must be super-polynomial in the length of* π.
- Covertness: *There is a uniformly encodable set* S *s.t. for any* π, *distribution* $\{hp\}_{(hk, hp) \leftarrow_R \mathsf{HKG}(\pi)}$ *is statistically close to uniform over* $S[\pi]$.

One-Wayness under Plaintext-Checking Attack (OW-PCA) for SPHF. We define OW-PCA security notion for SPHF in analogy with OW-PCA security of Key Encapsulation Mechanism (KEM). OW-PCA security of KEM [28,43] asks that for a random KEM public key pk and ciphertext c, an efficient attacker cannot, except for negligible probability, output the key k encrypted in c even given access to a Plaintext-Checking (PCA) oracle, which holds the corresponding secret key sk and for any (ciphertext,key) query (c', k') outputs 1 if $k' = \mathsf{Dec}(sk, c')$ and 0 otherwise. An SPHF can implement a KEM if $\mathcal{L}$ is hard on average, i.e. if on random $x \in \mathcal{L}$ it is hard to compute the corresponding witness w, because statement x, witness w, projection key hp, and hash value v could play the KEM roles of respectively pk, sk, c, and k. We define the OW-PCA property of SPHF as requiring that such KEM scheme is OW-PCA secure, i.e. that for a random (statement, witness) pair (x, w) in $\mathcal{L}$ and random $\mathsf{HKG}(\pi)$ outputs (hk, hp), an efficient attacker cannot output $v = \mathsf{Hash}(x, hk)$ even given access to a PCA oracle, which holds the witness w and for any query (hp', v') outputs 1 if $v' = \mathsf{PHash}(x, w, hp')$ and 0 otherwise.

Following the above parallel to the OW-PCA property of KEM, statement x, which acts like a public key, should be randomly sampled by the challenger. However, in the CKEM applications of Sect. 5, we need OW-PCA SPHF for statements chosen from a "mixed" distribution, where part the statement is arbitrarily chosen by the adversary and only part is randomly sampled by the challenger. Specifically, we will consider language $\mathcal{L}^{\mathsf{Com}}$ of valid commitments in a covert perfectly-binding trapdoor commitment scheme, see Definition 4.2, parameterized by global commitment parameters π:

$$\mathcal{L}^{\mathsf{Com}}[\pi] = \{(\overline{\pi}, m, c) \mid \exists\, d \text{ s.t. } \mathsf{Decom}(\pi, \overline{\pi}, c, m, d) = 1\} \tag{1}$$

Further, we will need OW-PCA security to hold for statements $x = (\overline{\pi}, m, c)$ where components $(\overline{\pi}, m)$ are chosen by the adversary on input π while component c together with witness d is chosen at random by the OW-PCA challenger.

In general, let $\mathcal{L}$ be parameterized by strings π sampled by alg. $\mathsf{PG}_{\mathsf{sphf}}(1^\kappa)$, let $\mathcal{L}_{\mathsf{pre}}[\pi]$ be a language of fixed-length prefixes of elements in $\mathcal{L}[\pi]$, and for any π and $x_L \in \mathcal{L}_{\mathsf{pre}}[\pi]$, let

$$\mathcal{R}_{\mathcal{L}}[\pi, x_L] = \{(x_R, w) \mid \text{s.t. } (x_L, x_R) \in \mathcal{L}[\pi] \text{ and } w \text{ is its witness}\}.$$

Notably from in Eq. 1, $x_L = (\overline{\pi}, m)$, $x_R = c$, and the witness w is the decommitment d. We define OW-PCA of SPHF for $\mathcal{L}$ as follows:

Definition 4.5. *SPHF for language $\mathcal{L}$ with parameter generation algorithm* $\mathsf{PG}_{\mathsf{sphf}}$ *and prefix language $\mathcal{L}_{\mathsf{pre}}$ is One-Way under Plaintext Checking Attack (OW-PCA) if for any efficient $\mathcal{A}$ the following probability is negligible:*

$$Pr\left[v = \mathsf{Hash}(x, hk) \mid v \leftarrow \mathcal{A}^{\mathsf{PCA}(w,\cdot)}(\pi, x, hp, st)\right]$$

where $\pi \leftarrow \mathsf{PG}_{\mathsf{sphf}}(1^\kappa)$, $(x_L, st) \leftarrow \mathcal{A}(\pi)$ *s.t.* $x_L \in \mathcal{L}_{\mathsf{pre}}[\pi]$, $(x_R, w) \leftarrow_R \mathcal{R}_{\mathcal{L}}[\pi, x_L]$, $x \leftarrow (x_L, x_R)$, $(hk, hp) \leftarrow \mathsf{HKG}(\pi)$, *and oracle* $\mathsf{PCA}(w, \cdot)$ *on queries* (hp', v') *from $\mathcal{A}$ outputs 1 if* $v' = \mathsf{PHash}(x, w, hp')$ *and 0 otherwise.*

Instantiation. Language $\mathcal{L}^{\mathsf{Com}}[\pi]$ in Eq. 1 has a well-known SPHF which satisfies all properties in Definitions 4.4 and 4.5 for the "Double Pedersen" commitment described in Sect. 4.1: The hash key is $hk = (hk_1, hk_2) \leftarrow_R \mathbb{Z}_q^2$, the projection key is $hp = (g_1)^{hk_1}(g_2)^{hk_2}$, Hash on $x = (\overline{\pi}, m, c)$ for $c = (c_1, c_2)$ sets $v \leftarrow (c_1/h_1^m)^{hk_1}(c_2/h_2^m)^{hk_2}$, and PHash on witness d for x sets $v \leftarrow hp^d$. The security proofs for this SPHF are deferred to the full version of the paper [22].

4.3 Covert Identity Escrow

We describe a *Covert Identity Escrow* (IE) scheme, an essential ingredient in our group cAKE construction of Sect. 6.

IE Syntax. An Identity Escrow (IE) scheme [34] is an entity authentication scheme with operational assumptions and privacy properties similar to a group signature scheme [16]. Namely, a designated party called a *group manager* (GM) uses a key generation algorithm KG to first generate a group public key *gpk* and a master secret key *msk*. Then, using the master secret key and a certificate generation algorithm CG, the group manager can issue each group member a membership certificate *cert* together with membership validity witness v. This pair allows a group member to authenticate herself as belonging to the group, but this authentication is anonymous in that multiple authentication instances conducted by the same party cannot be linked. In other words, the verifier is convinced that it interacts with *some* group member, in possession of some valid membership certificate, but it cannot tell which one. Following [10] we use the Verifier-Local Revocation (VLR) model for IE/group signature, where algorithm CG produces also a revocation token *rt* corresponding to certificate *cert*, and the authentication between a prover holding (*gpk*, *cert*, v) and the verifier holding *gpk* and a set of revocation tokens RTset is defined by a triple of algorithms CertBlind, Ver, Link, as follows:

1. The prover uses a certificate blinding algorithm CertBlind to create a blinded certificate *bc* from its certificate *cert*, and sends *bc* to the verifier.
2. The prover proves knowledge of witness v corresponding to the blinded certificate *bc* using a zero-knowledge proof of knowledge for relation

$$\mathcal{R}^{\mathsf{IE}} = \{((gpk, bc), v) \text{ s.t. } \mathsf{Ver}(gpk, bc, v) = 1\} \tag{2}$$

3. The verifier accepts if and only if the above proof succeeds and the tracing algorithm Link does not link the blinded certificate to any revocation token in set RTset, i.e. if $\text{Link}(gpk, bc, rt) = 0$ for all $rt \in \text{RTset}$.

The IE syntax and correctness requirements are formally captured as follows:[13]

Definition 4.6. *An identity escrow (IE) scheme is a tuple of efficient algorithms* $(\text{KG}, \text{CG}, \text{CertBlind}, \text{Ver}, \text{Link})$ *with the following syntax:*

- *Key Generation alg.* KG *picks a public key pair,* $(msk, gpk) \leftarrow \text{KG}(1^\kappa)$
- *Certificate Generation alg.* CG *generates a certificate cert, its validity witness* v, *and revocation token* rt, $(cert, v, rt) \leftarrow \text{CG}(msk)$
- *Blinding alg.* CertBlind *outputs a blinded certificate,* $bc \leftarrow \text{CertBlind}(cert)$
- *Verification alg.* Ver, *s.t. if* $(msk, gpk) \leftarrow \text{KG}(1^\kappa)$, $(cert, v, rt) \leftarrow \text{CG}(msk)$, *and* $bc \leftarrow \text{CertBlind}(cert)$, *then* $\text{Ver}(gpk, bc, v) = 1$
- *Tracing alg.* Link, *s.t. if* $(msk, gpk) \leftarrow \text{KG}(1^\kappa)$, $(cert, v, rt) \leftarrow \text{CG}(msk)$, *and* $bc \leftarrow \text{CertBlind}(cert)$, *then* $\text{Link}(gpk, bc, rt) = 1$

IE Security. Below we state the standard IE security properties [34], strengthened by covertness needed for our group cAKE construction.

The IE unforgeability property is that the adversary who receives some set of certificates, cannot create pair (bc, v) which satisfies the verification equation, i.e. $\text{Ver}(gpk, bc, v) = 1$, but which the tracing algorithm Link fails to link to the revocation tokens corresponding to the certificates received by the adversary. In the group cAKE application an adversary, in addition to holding some set of compromised certificates, can also observe revocation tokens and blinded certificates corresponding to non-compromised certificates. The definition below captures this by giving the adversary an arbitrary number of revocation tokens rt and certificates $cert$ from which it can generate blinded certificates on its own:

Definition 4.7. *We call an IE scheme* unforgeable *if for any efficient algorithm* $\mathcal{A}$ *the probability that* $b = 1$ *in the following game is negligible in* κ, *for* m, n *polynomial in* κ *s.t.* $m < n$:

1. *set* $b \leftarrow 0$ *and* $(msk, gpk) \leftarrow \text{KG}(1^\kappa)$
2. *for* $i \in [1, n]$ *set* $(cert_i, v_i, rt_i) \leftarrow \text{CG}(msk)$
3. $(bc^*, v^*) \leftarrow \mathcal{A}(gpk, \{cert_i, v_i, rt_i\}_{i \in [1, m]}, \{cert_i, rt_i\}_{i \in [m+1, n]})$
4. $b \leftarrow 1$ *if* $\text{Ver}(gpk, bc^*, v^*) = 1$ *and* $\text{Link}(gpk, bc^*, rt_i) = 0$ *for all* $i \in [1, m]$

(In the above game, tuples $(cert_i, v_i, rt_i)$ for $i \in [1, m]$ represent compromised certificates, set $\{rt_i\}_{i \in [m+1, n]}$ contains all additional revocation tokens the adversary learns, and set $\{cert_i\}_{i \in [m+1, n]}$ can be used to derive all blinded certificates the adversary receives from non-compromised parties.)

---

[13] More generally, CertBlind should take witness v along with $cert$ as input, and produce output v' along with bc as output, where v' is a validity witness for the *blinded* certificate bc. We use simpler syntax assuming that $v' = v$ because it declutters notation, and it suffices for IE instantiation from Pointcheval-Sanders signatures [42].

The IE covertness property strengthens the standard IE property of authentication anonymity [34]. Authentication anonymity asks that an adversary cannot link blinded certificate bc and decide e.g. whether they are generated from the same certificate or not. Covertness strengthens this by requiring that blinded certificates are indistinguishable from random elements in a uniformly encodable domain (hence they can be covertly encoded, see Sect. 2.1). Since each blinded certificate is indistinguishable from random domain element, it follows in particular that they are unlinkable. Similarly as in the unforgeability property, the adversary should be able to observe other certificates, hence in the definition below we hand the adversary the master secret key msk from which it can generate certificates, blinded certificates, and revocation tokens.

Definition 4.8. *We call an IE scheme* covert *if there is a uniformly encodable domain D s.t. for any efficient algorithm $\mathcal{A}$ quantity $|p_0 - p_1|$ is negligible in κ for n, m polynomial in κ, where $p_b = \Pr[b' = 1]$ in the following game:*

1. *$(msk, gpk) \leftarrow \mathsf{KG}(1^\kappa)$*
2. *for $i \in [1, n]$ set $(cert_i, v_i, rt_i) \leftarrow \mathsf{CG}(msk)$*
3. *for all $(i, j) \in [1, n] \times [1, m]$:*
   if $b = 1$ then set $bc_{ij} \leftarrow \mathsf{CertBlind}(cert_i)$ else pick $bc_{ij} \leftarrow_R D$
4. *$b' \leftarrow \mathcal{A}(msk, gpk, \{bc_{ij}\}_{i \in [1,n], j \in [1,m]})$*

We require that the zero-knowledge proof for relation $\mathcal{R}^{\mathsf{IE}}$ in Eq. (2) used is (based on) a Σ-protocol. We need this property to build a covert CKEM for the same relation using the Σ-to-CKEM compiler of Sect. 5.2.

Definition 4.9. *We call an IE scheme Σ-protocol friendly if relation $\mathcal{R}^{\mathsf{IE}}$, Eq. (2), admits a Σ-protocol with a uniformly encodable response space S_z.*

Finally, we require IE to satisfy that the same blinded certificate cannot, except for negligible probability, correspond to two different honestly generated revocation tokens created on behalf of two different groups. This property allows the AKE scheme constructed in Sect. 6 to realize the group cAKE functionality $\mathcal{F}_{\mathsf{g\text{-}cAKE}}$ of Section 3, which assumes that if the real-world adversary attempts to authenticate using some group certificate then this implies a unique choice of a certificate, and hence also a group for which it was generated.

Definition 4.10. *We call IE scheme* unambiguous *if:*

(1) the probability that $\mathsf{Link}(gpk_0, bc, rt_0) = \mathsf{Link}(gpk_1, bc, rt_1) = 1$ is at most negligible for any efficient $\mathcal{A}$, where $(msk_b, gpk_b) \leftarrow \mathsf{KG}(1^\kappa)$, $(v_b, cert_b, rt_b) \leftarrow \mathsf{CG}(msk_b)$ for $b \in \{0, 1\}$, and $bc \leftarrow \mathcal{A}(msk_0, v_0, cert_0, rt_0, msk_1, v_1, cert_1, rt_1)$;

(2) the same holds if the above experiment is adjusted by setting $(msk, gpk) \leftarrow \mathsf{KG}(1^\kappa)$ and $(v_b, cert_b, rt_b) \leftarrow \mathsf{CG}(msk)$ for $b \in \{0, 1\}$, and we measure the probability that $\mathsf{Link}(gpk, bc, rt_0) = \mathsf{Link}(gpk, bc, rt_1) = 1$.

Instantiation. An IE scheme which satisfies Definitions 4.7, 4.8, and 4.9, can be implemented using the Pointcheval-Sanders group signature [42]. (We will refer to this IE instantiation as *PS-IE*.) Sketching it briefly, if $(p, \mathbb{G}_1, \mathbb{G}_2, \mathbb{G}_T, e)$ is a bilinear pairing of type-3 with g ($\hat{g}$) a generator of $\mathbb{G}_1$ ($\mathbb{G}_2$), then (1) KG picks $x, y \leftarrow_{\mathrm{R}} \mathbb{Z}_p$ and sets $msk = (x, y)$ and $gpk = (\hat{X}, \hat{Y}) = (\hat{g}^x, \hat{g}^y)$, (2) CG($msk$) picks $\tilde{\sigma} \leftarrow_{\mathrm{R}} \mathbb{G}_1$, $v \leftarrow_{\mathrm{R}} \mathbb{Z}_p$, sets $\tilde{\omega} = \tilde{\sigma}^{x+y \cdot v}$, and outputs certificate $cert = (\tilde{\sigma}, \tilde{\omega})$, validity witness v, and revocation token $rt = \hat{Y}^v$, (3) CertBlind($cert$) picks $t \leftarrow_{\mathrm{R}} \mathbb{Z}_p$ and outputs $bc = (\tilde{\sigma}^t, \tilde{\omega}^t)$, (4) Ver($gpk, bc = (\sigma, \omega), v$) = 1 iff $e(\sigma, \hat{X} \cdot \hat{Y}^v) = e(\omega, \hat{g})$, and (5) Link($gpk, bc = (\sigma, \omega), rt$) = 1 iff $e(\sigma, \hat{X} \cdot rt) = e(\omega, \hat{g})$. The full details and security proofs are deferred to the full version of the paper [22].

5   Covert Strong Simulation-Sound Conditional KEM

Conditional Key Encapsulation Mechanism (CKEM) [32] is a KEM counterpart of Witness Encryption (WE) [26] and Conditional Oblivious Transfer (COT) [19]. A CKEM for an efficiently verifiable relation $\mathcal{R}$ (and a corresponding NP language $\mathcal{L}_\mathcal{R}$) is a protocol that allows sender S and receiver R, to establish, on input a statement x, a secure key K if R holds a witness w s.t. $(x, w) \in \mathcal{R}$. Since CKEM is an encryption counterpart to a zero-knowledge proof, we follow [7,32,33] and use ZKP terminology referring to CKEM properties, e.g. we call CKEM *sound* if S's output K_S is pseudorandom if $x \notin \mathcal{L}_\mathcal{R}$, and we call it *strong sound* [32] if w is extractable from any algorithm distinguishing K_S from random.

Benhamouda et al. [7] strengthened the notion of CKEM (called *Implicit Zero-Knowledge* therein) to include *simulatability*, i.e. that there exists an efficient simulator which for any $x \in \mathcal{L}_\mathcal{R}$ computes R's output K_R without the knowledge of witness w for x, and *simulation-soundness*, i.e. that adversarial CKEM instances remain sound even in the presence of a simulator which simulates CKEM instances performed on behalf of honest players. Jarecki [33] extended simulation-sound CKEM of [7] to *covertness*, i.e. indistinguishability of a simulation (and hence also the real receiver) from a random beacon.

Here we adopt the covert zero-knowledge and simulation-sound CKEM notion which follows the above chain of works, but we modify it in several ways. First, we combine strong soundness of [32] and simulation-soundness of [7] to *strong simulation-soundness*, i.e. we require an efficient extractor that extracts a witness from an attacker who distinguishes S's output key from random on instance x in the presence of a simulator which plays the receiver's role on any instance $x' \neq x$. This is motivated by the group cAKE application where a reduction must extract a certificate forgery from an attacker who breaks sender's security of CKEM on a statement corresponding to a non-revoked certificate.

Our second change is introducing a *postponed-statement zero-knowledge* property to CKEM, which asks that there exists a postponed-statement simulator which simulates the CKEM on behalf of the receiver, i.e. recovers the same key K_R which an honest receiver would compute, not only without knowing the witness but also *without knowing the statement* used by the real-world receiver R, except after all CKEM messages are exchanged, i.e. in the final key-computation step of the receiver. This property is crucial in an application like group cAKE, because in the ideal-world group cAKE scheme, see the group cAKE functionality in Sect. 3, the simulator does not know the group to which a simulated party belongs. Indeed, the simulator does not even know if a party whose execution it simulates is a real party which executes the group cAKE for some group or it is a random beacon. Therefore, the simulator will not know the statement x on which the real-world party performs the CKEM, except in the final step in the case that (1) the adversary performs a CKEM for some group, and (2) the functionality confirms that the honest party involved in this execution is a real-world receiver R (and not a random beacon) *and* R runs on the same group the adversary does. At this point the simulator reconstructs the correct statement x the real-world R would have used in that case, and passes x to the *postponed-statement CKEM simulator* to compute R's output K_R.

The third change is that we cannot use proof *labels*, which were used to separate between honest and adversarial proof/CKEM instances in e.g. [33]. This change stems from the fact that whereas in many applications protocol instances can be tied to unique identifiers of participating parties, we cannot do so in the case of covert authentication. Indeed, an adversary $\mathcal{A}$ interacting with a covert authentication system could forward statement x from receiver R to sender S, and forward S's CKEM for x from S to R. If in the simulation-soundness game $\mathcal{A}$ learns R's output K_R then $\mathcal{A}$ can trivially distinguish S's output K_S from random, as K_S and K_R are equal. Since this attack scenario corresponds to the case of AKE attacker who forwards protocol messages between R and S, we will handle that case separately as *eavesdropper security*, while in the simulation-soundness game we impose a restriction that the challenge $\mathcal{A}$-S interaction transcript differs from all $\mathcal{A}$-R transcripts. Note that both the relation $\mathcal{R}^{\mathsf{PS-IE}}$ for which we need this CKEM, and the SPHF tool we use to construct the CKEM scheme below, are malleable, e.g. if the adversary changes statement $x = (\sigma, \omega)$ to $x' = (\sigma^\delta, \omega^\delta)$ then $x' \in \mathcal{R}^{\mathsf{PS-IE}}$ if $x \in \mathcal{R}^{\mathsf{PS-IE}}$. However, we obtain sufficient separation between CKEM instances by deriving the CKEM key via a random oracle (RO) hash on the SPHF-derived key and an interaction transcript.

In Sect. 5.1 below we define the covert zero-knowledge strong simulation-sound CKEM, and then in Sect. 5.2 we show a CKEM construction which achieves this covert CKEM notion in ROM for any relation $\mathcal{R}$ with a Σ-protocol.

5.1 Definition of Covert CKEM with Strong Simulation-Soundness

Definition 5.1. *A conditional key encapsulation mechanism (CKEM) for relation $\mathcal{R}$ is an algorithms tuple* (GPG, Snd, Rec) *s.t. parameter generation* $\mathsf{GPG}(1^\kappa)$ *generates CRS parameter π, and the sender* Snd *and receiver* Rec *are interactive algorithms which run on local respective inputs (π, x) and (π, x, w), where each of them outputs a session key K as its local output. CKEM correctness requires that for all $(x, w) \in \mathcal{R}$ and $\pi \leftarrow \mathsf{GPG}(1^\kappa)$, if K_S, K_R are respective outputs of* $\mathsf{Snd}(\pi, x)$ *and* $\mathsf{Rec}(\pi, x, w)$ *interacting with each other, then $K_S = K_R$.*

In the definition below we use the notation $\mathsf{P}_{\&\mathsf{Out}}(x)$ for an interactive algorithm P that runs on input x and attaches its local output to its last message. (In our case this output will be a CKEM key K_S or K_R.) For notation $\mathsf{P}^{\$(\kappa)}$ refer to Sect. 2.1.

Definition 5.2. *A CKEM for relation* $\mathcal{R}$ *is* covert zero-knowledge and strong simulation-sound *if there exist efficient algorithms* TGPG *and* psTGPG *which on input* 1^κ *output parameters* π *together with trapdoor* td, *and interactive algorithms* TRec *and* psTRec *which runs on input* (π, x, td), *which satisfy the following properties:*

1. *Setup Indistinguishability:* parameters π generated by $\mathsf{GPG}(1^\kappa)$, $\mathsf{TGPG}(1^\kappa)$, and $\mathsf{psTGPG}(1^\kappa)$, are computationally indistinguishable.

2. *Zero-Knowledge:* For any efficient $\mathcal{A}$,

$$\{\mathcal{A}^{\mathsf{RecO}(\pi,\cdot)}(\pi)\} \approx_c \{\mathcal{A}^{\mathsf{TRecO}(\pi,td,\cdot)}(\pi)\}$$

   for $(\pi, td) \leftarrow \mathsf{TGPG}(1^\kappa)$, where oracle $\mathsf{RecO}(\pi, \cdot)$ runs $\mathsf{Rec}_{\&\mathsf{Out}}(\pi, x, w)$ and $\mathsf{TRecO}(\pi, td, \cdot)$ runs $\mathsf{TRec}_{\&\mathsf{Out}}(\pi, x, td)$, on any query $(x, w) \in \mathcal{R}$ sent by $\mathcal{A}$.

3. *Statement-Postponed Zero-Knowledge:* The above property must hold for $(\mathsf{psTGPG}, \mathsf{psTRec})$ replacing $(\mathsf{TGPG}, \mathsf{TRec})$ where psTRec computes all its network messages given (π, td) and only uses x for its local output.

4. *Receiver Covertness:* For any efficient $\mathcal{A}$, $\{\mathcal{A}^{\mathsf{Rec}(\pi,x,w)}(st)\} \approx_c \{\mathcal{A}^{\mathsf{Rec}^{\$(\kappa)}}(st)\}$ for $\pi \leftarrow \mathsf{GPG}(1^\kappa)$ and $(x, w, st) \leftarrow \mathcal{A}(\pi)$ s.t. $(x, w) \in \mathcal{R}$.

5. *Sender Covertness:* For any efficient $\mathcal{A}$, $\{\mathcal{A}^{\mathsf{Snd}(\pi,x)}(st)\} \approx_c \{\mathcal{A}^{\mathsf{Snd}^{\$(\kappa)}}(st)\}$ for $\pi \leftarrow \mathsf{GPG}(1^\kappa)$ and $(st, x) \leftarrow \mathcal{A}(\pi)$.

6. *Passive Security:* For any efficient $\mathcal{A}$,

$$\{\mathcal{A}(\pi, st, \mathbf{tr}, K_S)\} \approx_c \{\mathcal{A}(\pi, st, \mathbf{tr}, K')\}$$

   for $\pi \leftarrow \mathsf{GPG}(1^\kappa)$, $(x, w, st) \leftarrow \mathcal{A}(\pi)$ s.t. $(x, w) \in \mathcal{R}$, $(\mathbf{tr}, K_S, K_R) \leftarrow [\mathsf{Snd}(\pi, x) \leftrightarrow \mathsf{Rec}(\pi, x, w)]$, $K' \leftarrow \{0,1\}^\kappa$.

7. *Strong Simulation-Soundness:* There exists an efficient algorithm Ext s.t. for any deterministic efficient algorithm $\mathcal{A} = (\mathcal{A}_1, \mathcal{A}_2)$, if $\epsilon = |p_0 - p_1|$ is non-negligible, then so is ϵ', for p_b for $b = 0, 1$ and ϵ' defined as follows:

$$p_b = \Pr\left[b' = 1 : (\pi, td, x, st) \leftarrow \mathsf{Init}[\mathcal{A}_1](1^\kappa), b' \leftarrow \mathsf{Exp}_b[\mathcal{A}_2](\pi, td, x, st)\right]$$

$$\epsilon' = \Pr\left[(x, w) \in \mathcal{R} : (\pi, td, x, st) \leftarrow \mathsf{Init}[\mathcal{A}_1](1^\kappa), w \leftarrow \mathsf{Ext}^{\mathcal{A}_2(st)}(\pi, td, x, st)\right]$$

   where

   - $\mathsf{Init}[\mathcal{A}_1](1^\kappa)$ sets $(\pi, td) \leftarrow \mathsf{TGPG}(1^\kappa)$ and $(x, st) \leftarrow \mathcal{A}_1^{\mathsf{TRec}_{\&\mathsf{Out}}(\pi,\cdot,td)}(\pi)$;
   - $\mathsf{Exp}_b[\mathcal{A}_2](\pi, td, x, st)$ outputs $b' = \mathcal{A}_2^{\mathsf{SndMod}_{\&\mathsf{Out}}(b,\pi,x),\mathsf{TRec}_{\&\mathsf{Out}}(\pi,\cdot,td)}(st)$ s.t.
     - $\mathsf{SndMod}_{\&\mathsf{Out}}(1, \pi, x)$ runs $\mathsf{Snd}_{\&\mathsf{Out}}(\pi, x)$;
     - $\mathsf{SndMod}_{\&\mathsf{Out}}(0, \pi, x)$ runs $\mathsf{Snd}(\pi, x)$ and then sends $K_S' \leftarrow \{0,1\}^\kappa$;

   Moreover, Exp_b rejects if $\mathcal{A}_2$ makes the transcript of an interaction with $\mathsf{SndMod}(b, \pi, x)$ the same as that of any interaction with $\mathsf{TRec}(\pi, x, td)$.

Discussion. The most direct comparison to the above notion of covert CKEM is a covert CKEM defined in [33]. Differences from [33] include (1) lack of labels, (2) strengthening of simulation-soundness to strong simulation-soundness, and (3) requirement that the CKEM facilitates statement-postponed simulation. Furthermore, (4) we allow the adversary in the strong simulation-soundness game to interact with the receiver even on the same statement x used in the challenge sender interaction, with the only constraint of excluding the trivial attack when the adversary passes all messages between S and R, i.e. when some $\mathcal{A}$-R transcript equals the $\mathcal{A}$-S transcript. We compensate for the latter constraint with (5) a *passive security* requirement, i.e. that if the adversary passes messages between S and R then the security holds even if the attacker knows the authentication tokens these parties use.

Protocol Ingredients (see text):
- Σ-protocol $(\mathsf{P}_1, \mathsf{P}_2, \mathsf{VRec}, S_{ch}, S_z)$ for relation $\mathcal{R}$;
- covert perfectly-binding trapdoor commitment $(\mathsf{GPG}, \mathsf{PG}, \mathsf{Com}, \mathsf{Decom})$ on msg. space $\mathcal{M}$, with RO-compatible instance parameters with param. space $\mathcal{C}$;
- covert SPHF $(\mathsf{HKG}, \mathsf{Hash}, \mathsf{PHash})$ for $\mathcal{L}^{\mathsf{Com}}[\pi]$;
- CRH H and RO's $\mathsf{H}_1, \mathsf{H}_2, \mathsf{H}_{\mathsf{Com}}$ with ranges resp. $\mathcal{M}$, S_{ch}, $\{0,1\}^\kappa$, and $\mathcal{C}$;

The GPG algorithm is the same as in the commitment scheme, i.e. $\pi \leftarrow \mathsf{GPG}(1^\kappa)$.

Rec .1: On inputs $(x, w) \in \mathcal{R}$, compute:

$$(a, r) \leftarrow \mathsf{P}_1(x, w)$$
$$\overline{\pi} \leftarrow \mathsf{H}_{\mathsf{Com}}(x)$$
$$(c, d) \leftarrow \mathsf{Com}(\pi, \overline{\pi}, \mathsf{H}(a))$$
$$ch \leftarrow \mathsf{H}_1(x, c)$$
$$z \leftarrow \mathsf{P}_2(x, w, r, ch)$$

and send (c, z) to S (using covert encoding).

Snd .1: S precomputes $(hk, hp) \leftarrow \mathsf{HKG}(\pi)$ and sends hp to R (covertly encoded).

Rec .2: Given hp, compute:

$$v_R \leftarrow \mathsf{PHash}((\pi, \overline{\pi}, c, \mathsf{H}(a)), d, hp)$$
$$K_R \leftarrow \mathsf{H}_2(x, c, z, hp, v_R)$$

Snd .2: On input x and given (c, z), compute:

$$ch \leftarrow \mathsf{H}_1(x, c)$$
$$\overline{\pi} \leftarrow \mathsf{H}_{\mathsf{Com}}(x)$$
$$a \leftarrow \mathsf{VRec}(x, ch, z)$$
$$v_S \leftarrow \mathsf{Hash}((\pi, \overline{\pi}, c, \mathsf{H}(a)), hk)$$
$$K_S \leftarrow \mathsf{H}_2(x, c, z, hp, v_S)$$

Fig. 3. Covert CKEM (in ROM) for any relation $\mathcal{R}$ with a Σ-protocol

5.2   Compiler from Σ-Protocol to Covert CKEM in ROM

Our covert CKEM protocol, shown in Fig. 3, is a compiler which creates a covert CKEM for relation $\mathcal{R}$ from any Σ-protocol for $\mathcal{R}$. The two other tools this protocol requires are a *covert perfectly-binding trapdoor commitment* scheme, see Sect. 4.1, and a *covert and OW-PCA secure SPHF* for language $\mathcal{L}^{\mathsf{Com}}[\pi]$ associated with this commitment scheme, see Sect. 4.2 and Eq. (1). In addition, the compiler uses the ROM, and in particular it assumes that the commitment scheme has *RO-compatible instance parameters*, see Sect. 4.1, and it instantiates the instance parameter generation of the commitment with an RO hash $\mathsf{H}_{\mathsf{Com}}$. Usage of ROM is motivated by the goal of realizing all CKEM security properties at low cost in computation, communication, and round complexity. In particular, our CKEM has minimal round complexity: *one simultaneous flow*.

Comparison with [32]. Our CKEM construction is a modification of the Σ-to-CKEM compiler of Jarecki [32], where (1) the commitment scheme Com which R uses to compute c in step R.1 must be a *trapdoor* commitment, where the commitment parameters are derived by an RO hash of the statement x, (2) the covert SPHF has an additional property of OW-PCA security, see Definition 4.5 in Sect. 4.2, and (3) the CKEM key output is not the SPHF hash value itself, but the RO hash of that value together with the language statement and the protocol transcript. Intuitively, the first change allows the CKEM to achieve statement-postponed zero-knowledge, since the trapdoor receiver can create a commitment without knowing the instance parameter π. The second change assures security against a passive attacker. The last change allows for a stronger version of simulation-soundness, see Definition 5.2, which asks that the Sender CKEM challenge is secure in the presence of Receiver CKEM oracle that can be

---

Let $(p, g, \hat{g}_1, \mathbb{G}_1, \mathbb{G}_2, \mathbb{G}_T, e)$ be type-3 curve. Given $gpk = (\hat{X}, \hat{Y}) \in (\mathbb{G}_2)^2$ [assume gpk defines all curve parameters] and $bc = (\sigma, \omega) \in (\mathbb{G}_1)^2$, define:

$$\mathcal{R}^{\mathsf{PS-IE}} = \{ ((gpk, bc), v) \mid e(\sigma, \hat{X} \cdot \hat{Y}^v) = e(\omega, \hat{g}) \}$$

Let $(\mathbb{G}, q)$ be a DDH group, e.g. a standard curve. Let H be a CRH, and $\mathsf{H}_{\mathsf{Com}}, \mathsf{H}_1, \mathsf{H}_2$ be RO's, with ranges resp. $\mathbb{Z}_q$, $\mathbb{G}^2$, $\mathbb{Z}_q$, and $\{0,1\}^\kappa$. Messages (c_1, c_2, z) and hp below are sent using covert encodings on $\mathbb{G}$ and $\mathbb{Z}_q$.

PG: On 1^κ, set $\pi = (g_1, g_2) \leftarrow \mathbb{G}^2$ (assume $\mathbb{G}$ is chosen for sec. par. κ)
Rec .1: R on $x = (gpk, bc)$ and v picks $(r, d) \leftarrow \mathbb{Z}_p \times \mathbb{Z}_q$, sets $a \leftarrow e(\sigma, \hat{Y}^r)$, $\overline{\pi} = (h_1, h_2) \leftarrow \mathsf{H}_{\mathsf{Com}}(x)$, $(c_1, c_2) \leftarrow (g_1^d \cdot h_1^{\mathsf{H}(a)}, g_2^d \cdot h_2^{\mathsf{H}(a)})$, $z \leftarrow r + \mathsf{H}_1(x, c_1, c_2) \cdot v \bmod p$, and sends (c_1, c_2, z) to S
Snd .1: S precomputes $hk = (hk_1, hk_2) \leftarrow \mathbb{Z}_q^2$ and sends $hp = (g_1)^{hk_1}(g_2)^{hk_2}$ to R
Rec .2: On message hp, R sets $v_R \leftarrow (hp)^d$ and $K_R \leftarrow \mathsf{H}_2((gpk, bc), c_1, c_2, z, hp, v_R)$
Snd .2: On statement $x = (gpk, bc)$ and message (c_1, c_2, z), S sets $\overline{\pi} = (h_1, h_2) \leftarrow \mathsf{H}_{\mathsf{Com}}(x)$, $a' \leftarrow e(\sigma, \hat{X}^{ch}\hat{Y}^z) \cdot e(\omega, \hat{g}^{-ch})$ for $ch = \mathsf{H}_1(x, c_1, c_2)$, sets $v_S \leftarrow (c_1 \cdot h_1^{-\mathsf{H}(a')})^{hk_1} \cdot (c_2 \cdot h_2^{-\mathsf{H}(a')})^{hk_2}$, and $K_S \leftarrow \mathsf{H}_2((gpk, bc), c_1, c_2, z, hp, v_S)$

Fig. 4. Covert CKEM for Pointcheval-Sanders IE relation $\mathcal{R}^{\mathsf{PS-IE}}$.

executed *even on the same statement*, and the only restriction is that the CKEM transcripts of the adversary's interactions with the Sender and the Receiver cannot be the same. (The case of same transcripts is covered by the passive security property.) The proof of the following theorem is deferred to the full version of the paper [22]:

Theorem 5.1. *CKEM for $\mathcal{R}$ shown in Fig. 3 is covert zero-knowledge and strong simulation-sound in ROM, if $\mathcal{R}$ has a Σ-protocol with uniformly encodable response space S_z, trapdoor commitment Com is perfectly binding and covert, H is a CRH, and SPHF for $\mathcal{L}^{Com}$ is covert, smooth, and OW-PCA secure.*

Efficient Instantiation. In Fig. 4 we show an instantiation of the generic CKEM from Fig. 3, for relation $\mathcal{R}^{PS-IE}$ defined by the Covert IE based on Pointcheval-Sanders signatures (i.e. PS-IE), see Sect. 4.3, the "Double Pedersen" trapdoor commitment, see Sect. 4.1, and the associated SPHF, see Sect. 4.2.

6   Construction of Group Covert AKE Protocol

In Figs. 5 and 6 we show algorithms (KG, CG, Auth) which implement a generic group cAKE construction from covert Identity Escrow (IE) and covert CKEM. In Fig. 5 we show the group initialization algorithm KG and certificate generation algorithm CG, which implement respectively the GInit and CertInit interfaces of UC group cAKE, as defined in Sect. 3. Figure 5 also shows the "input-retrieval" step in the implementation of the NewSession command, which triggers the online authentication algorithm Auth. The algorithm Auth itself, executing between two parties, is shown in Fig. 6. Note that if a party is called with command (NewSession, ssid, $\perp$) then it executes as a random beacon, as noted in Fig. 5, instead of following the Auth protocol of Fig. 6.

The authentication protocol Auth in Fig. 6 uses the same combination of IE and CKEM as in the covert AKE of [32], i.e. each party commits to its IE certificate, and then performs a CKEM to (implicitly and covertly) prove that it knows a valid secret key issued by the group manager, corresponding to this committed certificate. (Also, similarly as in [32], since the IE supports verifier-local revocation, each party uses algorithm Link to locally verify the committed certificate against each revocation token on its revocation list.) In spite of reusing the same construction paradigm, the novel aspects of this protocol are as follows: First, thanks to stronger CKEM properties we can show that this generic protocol realizes UC group cAKE notion defined in Sect. 3. This implies that the protocol remains covert and secure under concurrent composition, e.g. that leakage of keys on any session does not endanger either covertness or security of any other session. Secondly, the strong notion of CKEM allows for minimal interaction, i.e. both receiver and sender can send only one message without waiting for their counterparty. Consequently, the generic Auth protocol in Fig. 6 has a minimally-interactive instantiation shown in Fig. 7.

The security of the above group cAKE construction is captured in the following theorem, with a proof deferred to the full version of the paper [22]:

Protocol Ingredients:
- covert IE scheme IE = (KG, CG, CertBlind, Ver, Link)
- covert CKEM scheme CKEM = (GPG, Snd, Rec) for relation $\mathcal{R}^{\mathsf{IE}}$
- secure channel between GM and each party P

Common Reference String Generation:
Sample CKEM global common reference string $\pi \leftarrow \mathsf{GPG}(1^{\kappa})$

Initialization by GM on (GInit, gid):
Sample $(msk, gpk) \leftarrow_{\mathrm{R}} \mathsf{KG}(1^{\kappa})$, broadcast (gid, GM, gpk, π) to all P's

Certificate Generation by party P on (CertInit, gid, cid):
P retrieves (gid, GM, gpk, π), sends cid to GM on a secure channel
GM sets $(v, cert, rt) \leftarrow \mathsf{CG}(msk)$, sends $(v, cert, rt)$ to P on a secure channel
P stores (gid, cid, $v, cert, rt$), GM stores $T_{rt}[\text{gid}, \text{cid}] \leftarrow rt$

Authenticated Key Exchange by party P on (NewSession, ssid, gid, cid, RTcids):
1. P retrieves (gid, GM, gpk, π) and (gid, cid, $v, cert, \cdot$)
   P sends (gid, RTcids) to GM on a secure channel
   GM sends back RTset = $\{ T_{rt}[\text{gid}, \text{cid}]$ s.t. cid $\in$ RTcids$\}$ on a secure channel
2. P runs protocol Auth$((gpk, \pi), (v, cert), \mathsf{RTset})$ in Figure 6
   P outputs (NewKey, ssid, K, cid$_{\mathsf{CP}}$) for $(K, \text{cid}_{\mathsf{CP}})$ output by protocol Auth

Random Beacon implemented by party P on (NewSession, ssid, $\perp$):
Party P runs Auth$^{\$(\kappa)}$, a random beacon of the same bandwidth as protocol Auth

Fig. 5. Generic group cAKE: Initialization and UC interface.

P on $((gpk, \pi), (v, cert), \mathsf{RTset})$	P' on $((gpk, \pi), (v', cert'), \mathsf{RTset}')$
$bc \leftarrow \mathsf{CertBlind}(cert)$ $\xrightarrow{\;bc\;}$	$\xleftarrow{\;bc'\;}$ $bc' \leftarrow \mathsf{CertBlind}(cert')$
$K_S \leftarrow \mathsf{Snd}(\pi, (gpk, bc'))\; \longleftrightarrow\; \boxed{\begin{array}{c}\mathsf{CKEM}\\(\mathsf{P}\to\mathsf{P}')\end{array}}\; \longleftrightarrow\; \mathsf{Rec}(\pi, (gpk, bc'), v') \to K_R'$	
$K_R \leftarrow \mathsf{Rec}(\pi, (gpk, bc), v)\; \longleftrightarrow\; \boxed{\begin{array}{c}\mathsf{CKEM}\\(\mathsf{P}\leftarrow\mathsf{P}')\end{array}}\; \longleftrightarrow\; \mathsf{Snd}(\pi, (gpk, bc)) \to K_S'$	
If $\exists\, rt \in \mathsf{RTset}$ s.t.	If $\exists\, rt' \in \mathsf{RTset}'$ s.t.
$\quad \mathsf{Link}(gpk, bc', rt) = 1$	$\quad \mathsf{Link}(gpk, bc, rt') = 1$
then $K \leftarrow \perp$, cid$_{\mathsf{CP}} \leftarrow$ cid$[rt]$	then $K' \leftarrow \perp$, cid$'_{\mathsf{CP}} \leftarrow$ cid$[rt']$
else $K \leftarrow \mathsf{H}(\{K_S, K_R\}_{\mathrm{ord}})$, cid$_{\mathsf{CP}} \leftarrow \perp$	else $K' \leftarrow \mathsf{H}(\{K_S', K_R'\}_{\mathrm{ord}})$, cid$'_{\mathsf{CP}} \leftarrow \perp$
H is RO with range $\{0, 1\}^{\kappa}$, notation $\{a, b\}_{\mathrm{ord}}$ stands for $(\min(a, b), \max(a, b))$	

Fig. 6. Generic group cAKE: protocol Auth, using covert encodings for bc/bc'.

We use the same parameters as CKEM for $\mathcal{R}^{\mathsf{PS-IE}}$ in Fig. 4, i.e. $(p, g, \hat{g}_1, \mathbb{G}_1, \mathbb{G}_2, \mathbb{G}_T, e)$ is a type-3 curve, $(\mathbb{G}, q)$ is a DDH group, and H is a CRH, and $\mathsf{H}_{\mathsf{Com}}, \mathsf{H}_1, \mathsf{H}_2$ are RO's, with ranges resp. $\mathbb{Z}_q, \mathbb{G}^2, \mathbb{Z}_q$, and $\{0,1\}^\kappa$.

Values $(\sigma, \omega), (c_1, c_2, z), hp$ below are sent using covert encodings on $\mathbb{G}_1, \mathbb{G}$ and $\mathbb{Z}_q$.

Common Reference String Generation:
Set $\pi = (g_1, g_2) \leftarrow_{\mathrm{R}} (\mathbb{G})^2$

Group Manager GM Initialization:
Set $msk = (x, y) \leftarrow_{\mathrm{R}} (\mathbb{Z}_p)^2$ and $gpk = (\hat{X}, \hat{Y}) \leftarrow (\hat{g}^x, \hat{g}^y)$

Certificate Generation by GM:
For P: Pick $(v, u) \leftarrow_{\mathrm{R}} (\mathbb{Z}_p)^2$, set $(\tilde{\sigma}, \tilde{\omega}) \leftarrow (g^u, g^{u(x+y \cdot v)})$, $rt \leftarrow \hat{Y}^v$
For P': Pick $(v', u') \leftarrow_{\mathrm{R}} (\mathbb{Z}_p)^2$, set $(\tilde{\sigma}', \tilde{\omega}') \leftarrow (g^{u'}, g^{u'(x+y \cdot v')})$, $rt' \leftarrow \hat{Y}^{v'}$

Authentication Protocol

P on $((gpk, \pi), (v, (\tilde{\sigma}, \tilde{\omega})), \mathsf{RTset})$:

$(\sigma, \omega) \leftarrow (\tilde{\sigma}^t, \tilde{\omega}^t)$ for $t \leftarrow_{\mathrm{R}} \mathbb{Z}_p$
$(r, d) \leftarrow_{\mathrm{R}} \mathbb{Z}_p \times \mathbb{Z}_q, a \leftarrow e(\sigma, \hat{Y}^r)$
$(h_1, h_2) \leftarrow \mathsf{H}_{\mathsf{Com}}((gpk, (\sigma, \omega)))$
$(c_1, c_2) \leftarrow (g_1^d h_1^{\mathsf{H}(a)}, g_2^d h_2^{\mathsf{H}(a)})$
$z \leftarrow r + ch \cdot v \bmod p$
  for $ch = \mathsf{H}_1(gpk, \sigma, \omega, c_1, c_2)$
$(hk_1, hk_2) \leftarrow_{\mathrm{R}} (\mathbb{Z}_q)^2$
$hp \leftarrow g_1^{hk_1} g_2^{hk_2}$

$\overline{\quad bc = (\sigma, \omega), \ (c_1, c_2, z), \ hp \quad} \longrightarrow$

$K_R \leftarrow \mathsf{H}_2(gpk, \sigma, \omega, c_1, c_2, z, (hp')^d)$
$a' \leftarrow e(\sigma', \hat{X}^{ch'} \hat{Y}^{z'}) \cdot e(\omega', \hat{g}^{-ch'})$
  for $ch' = \mathsf{H}_1(gpk, \sigma', \omega', c_1', c_2')$
$(h_1', h_2') \leftarrow \mathsf{H}_{\mathsf{Com}}((gpk, (\sigma', \omega')))$
$v_S \leftarrow (c_1' h_1'^{-\mathsf{H}(a')})^{hk_1} \cdot (c_2' h_2'^{-\mathsf{H}(a')})^{hk_2}$
$K_S \leftarrow \mathsf{H}_2(gpk, \sigma', \omega', c_1', c_2', z', v_S)$
If $\exists \, rt \in \mathsf{RTset}$ s.t.
  $e(\sigma', \hat{X} \cdot rt) = e(\omega', \hat{g})$
then $K \leftarrow \perp$, $\mathsf{cid}_{\mathsf{CP}} \leftarrow \mathsf{cid}[rt]$
else $K \leftarrow \mathsf{H}(\{K_S, K_R\}_{\mathsf{ord}}), \mathsf{cid}_{\mathsf{CP}} \leftarrow \perp$
Output $(K, \mathsf{cid}_{\mathsf{CP}})$

P' on $((gpk, \pi), (v', (\tilde{\sigma}', \tilde{\omega}')), \mathsf{RTset}')$:

$(\sigma', \omega') \leftarrow ((\tilde{\sigma}')^{t'}, (\tilde{\omega}')^{t'})$ for $t' \leftarrow_{\mathrm{R}} \mathbb{Z}_p$
$(r', d') \leftarrow_{\mathrm{R}} \mathbb{Z}_p \times \mathbb{Z}_q, a' \leftarrow e(\sigma', \hat{Y}^{r'})$
$(h_1', h_2') \leftarrow \mathsf{H}_{\mathsf{Com}}((gpk, (\sigma', \omega')))$
$(c_1', c_2') \leftarrow (g_1^{d'} h_1'^{\mathsf{H}(a')}, g_2^{d'} h_2'^{\mathsf{H}(a')})$
$z' \leftarrow r' + ch' \cdot v' \bmod p$
  for $ch' = \mathsf{H}_1(gpk, \sigma', \omega', c_1', c_2')$
$(hk_1', hk_2') \leftarrow_{\mathrm{R}} (\mathbb{Z}_q)^2$
$hp' \leftarrow g_1^{hk_1'} g_2^{hk_2'}$

$\overline{\quad bc' = (\sigma', \omega'), \ (c_1', c_2', z'), \ hp' \quad} \longleftarrow$

$K_R' \leftarrow \mathsf{H}_2(gpk, \sigma', \omega', c_1', c_2', z', (hp)^{d'})$
$a \leftarrow e(\sigma, \hat{X}^{ch} \hat{Y}^z) \cdot e(\omega, \hat{g}^{-ch})$
  for $ch = \mathsf{H}_1(gpk, \sigma, \omega, c_1, c_2)$
$(h_1, h_2) \leftarrow \mathsf{H}_{\mathsf{Com}}((gpk, (\sigma, \omega)))$
$v_S' \leftarrow (c_1 h_1^{-\mathsf{H}(a)})^{hk_1'} \cdot (c_2 h_2^{-\mathsf{H}(a)})^{hk_2'}$
$K_S' \leftarrow \mathsf{H}_2(gpk, \sigma, \omega, c_1, c_2, z, v_S')$
If $\exists \, rt' \in \mathsf{RTset}'$ s.t.
  $e(\sigma, \hat{X} \cdot rt) = e(\omega, \hat{g})$
then $K' \leftarrow \perp$, $\mathsf{cid}_{\mathsf{CP}}' \leftarrow \mathsf{cid}[rt']$
else $K' \leftarrow \mathsf{H}(\{K_S', K_R'\}_{\mathsf{ord}}), \mathsf{cid}_{\mathsf{CP}} \leftarrow \perp$
Output $(K', \mathsf{cid}_{\mathsf{CP}}')$

Fig. 7. Instantiation of Covert AKE, with IE of Sect. 4.3 and CKEM of Fig. 4

Theorem 6.1. *Protocol* $\Pi = (\text{KG}, \text{CG}, \text{Auth})$ *in Figs. 5, 6 realizes UC Covert Authenticated Key Exchange if IE is secure, covert, and Σ-protocol friendly, and CKEM is covert zero-knowledge and strong simulation-sound.*

Efficient Instantiation. Figure 7 shows a concrete instantiation of the generic group cAKE scheme shown in Figs. 5, 6. This instantiation uses the PS-IE scheme based on Pointcheval-Sanders signatures, see Sect. 4.3, and the CKEM from Sect. 5 instantiated as shown in Fig. 4. (See the full version [22] for a walk through this instantiation and an explanation of its steps.) Note that the protocol has minimal interaction, as each party sends a single message without waiting for the counterparty, and it is quite practical: Its bandwidth is 6 group elements per party (2 in a base group of a type-3 elliptic curve and 4 in a standard group), and each party computes 10 fixed-base exp's, 4 variable-base (multi-)exp's, and $4 + n$ bilinear maps, where n is the size of the revocation list.

References

1. Abdalla, M., Pointcheval, D.: Simple password-based encrypted key exchange protocols. In: Menezes, A. (ed.) CT-RSA 2005. LNCS, vol. 3376, pp. 191–208. Springer, Heidelberg (2005). https://doi.org/10.1007/978-3-540-30574-3_14
2. Balfanz, D., Durfee, G., Shankar, N., Smetters, D., Staddon, J., Wong, H.-C.: Secret handshakes from pairing-based key agreements. In: IEEE Symposium on Security and Privacy (S&P), pp. 180–196 (2003)
3. Bellare, M., Canetti, R., Krawczyk, H.: A modular approach to the design and analysis of authentication and key exchange protocols (extended abstract). In: Proceedings of the Thirtieth Annual ACM Symposium on Theory of Computing (STOC), pp. 419–428 (1998)
4. Bellare, M., Boldyreva, A., Desai, A., Pointcheval, D.: Key-privacy in public-key encryption. In: Boyd, C. (ed.) ASIACRYPT 2001. LNCS, vol. 2248, pp. 566–582. Springer, Heidelberg (2001). https://doi.org/10.1007/3-540-45682-1_33
5. Bellovin, S.M., Merritt, M.: Encrypted key-exchange: password-based protocols secure against dictionary attacks. In: IEEE Computer Society Symposium on Research in Security and Privacy, pp. 72–84 (1992)
6. Benaloh, J., de Mare, M.: One-way accumulators: a decentralized alternative to digital signatures. In: Helleseth, T. (ed.) EUROCRYPT 1993. LNCS, vol. 765, pp. 274–285. Springer, Heidelberg (1994). https://doi.org/10.1007/3-540-48285-7_24
7. Benhamouda, F., Couteau, G., Pointcheval, D., Wee, H.: Implicit zero-knowledge arguments and applications to the malicious setting. In: Gennaro, R., Robshaw, M. (eds.) CRYPTO 2015. LNCS, vol. 9216, pp. 107–129. Springer, Heidelberg (2015). https://doi.org/10.1007/978-3-662-48000-7_6
8. Bernstein, D.J., Hamburg, M., Krasnova, A., Lange, T.: Elligator: elliptic-curve points indistinguishable from uniform random strings. In: CCS, pp. 967–980. ACM (2013)
9. Boneh, D., Franklin, M.: Identity-based encryption from the Weil pairing. In: Kilian, J. (ed.) CRYPTO 2001. LNCS, vol. 2139, pp. 213–229. Springer, Heidelberg (2001). https://doi.org/10.1007/3-540-44647-8_13
10. Boneh, D., Shacham, H.: Group signatures with verifier-local revocation. In: Atluri, V., Pfitzmann, B., McDaniel, P. (eds.) ACM CCS 2004, pp. 168–177. ACM Press, October 2004

11. Camenisch, J., Lysyanskaya, A.: An efficient system for non-transferable anony-mous credentials with optional anonymity revocation. In: Pfitzmann, B. (ed.) EUROCRYPT 2001. LNCS, vol. 2045, pp. 93–118. Springer, Heidelberg (2001). https://doi.org/10.1007/3-540-44987-6_7

12. Camenisch, J., Lysyanskaya, A.: Dynamic accumulators and application to efficient revocation of anonymous credentials. In: Yung, M. (ed.) CRYPTO 2002. LNCS, vol. 2442, pp. 61–76. Springer, Heidelberg (2002). https://doi.org/10.1007/3-540-45708-9_5

13. Canetti, R.: Universally composable security: a new paradigm for cryptographic protocols. In: FOCS, pp. 136–145. IEEE Computer Society (2001)

14. Canetti, R., Krawczyk, H.: Universally composable notions of key exchange and secure channels. In: Knudsen, L.R. (ed.) EUROCRYPT 2002. LNCS, vol. 2332, pp. 337–351. Springer, Heidelberg (2002). https://doi.org/10.1007/3-540-46035-7_22

15. Chandran, N., Goyal, V., Ostrovsky, R., Sahai, A.: Covert multi-party computa-tion. In: FOCS, pp. 238–248. IEEE Computer Society (2007)

16. Chaum, D., van Heyst, E.: Group signatures. In: Davies, D.W. (ed.) EUROCRYPT 1991. LNCS, vol. 547, pp. 257–265. Springer, Heidelberg (1991). https://doi.org/10.1007/3-540-46416-6_22

17. Cho, C., Dachman-Soled, D., Jarecki, S.: Efficient concurrent covert computation of string equality and set intersection. In: Sako, K. (ed.) CT-RSA 2016. LNCS, vol. 9610, pp. 164–179. Springer, Cham (2016). https://doi.org/10.1007/978-3-319-29485-8_10

18. Cramer, R., Shoup, V.: Universal hash proofs and a paradigm for adaptive chosen ciphertext secure public-key encryption. In: Knudsen, L.R. (ed.) EUROCRYPT 2002. LNCS, vol. 2332, pp. 45–64. Springer, Heidelberg (2002). https://doi.org/10.1007/3-540-46035-7_4

19. Di Crescenzo, G., Ostrovsky, R., Rajagopalan, S.: Conditional oblivious trans-fer and timed-release encryption. In: Stern, J. (ed.) EUROCRYPT 1999. LNCS, vol. 1592, pp. 74–89. Springer, Heidelberg (1999). https://doi.org/10.1007/3-540-48910-X_6

20. Damgård, I.: On ∑-protocols (2010). https://cs.au.dk/ˢᴵᴹivan/Sigma.pdf

21. Diffie, W., Van Oorschot, P.C., Wiener, M.J.: Authentication and authenticated key exchanges. Des. Codes Crypt. **2**, 107–125 (1992)

22. Eldefrawy, K., Genise, N., Jarecki, S.: Short concurrent covert authenticated key exchange (short cAKE). Cryptology ePrint Archive, Paper 2023/xxx (2023). https://eprint.iacr.org/2023/xxx

23. Fiat, A., Naor, M.: Broadcast encryption. In: Stinson, D.R. (ed.) CRYPTO 1993. LNCS, vol. 773, pp. 480–491. Springer, Heidelberg (1994). https://doi.org/10.1007/3-540-48329-2_40

24. Fischlin, M.: Trapdoor commitment schemes and their applications. Ph.D. thesis, Goethe University Frankfurt, Frankfurt am Main, Germany (2001)

25. Galbraith, S.D., Paterson, K.G., Smart, N.P.: Pairings for cryptographers. Discret. Appl. Math. **156**(16), 3113–3121 (2008)

26. Garg, S., Gentry, C., Sahai, A., Waters, B.: Witness encryption and its applications. In: Symposium on Theory of Computing Conference, STOC 2013, pp. 467–476. ACM (2013)

27. Gentry, C., Peikert, C., Vaikuntanathan, V.: Trapdoors for hard lattices and new cryptographic constructions. In: STOC, pp. 197–206. ACM (2008)

28. Goldwasser, S., Micali, S.: Probabilistic encryption and how to play mental poker keeping secret all partial information. In: STOC, pp. 365–377. ACM (1982)

29. Goyal, V., Jain, A.: On the round complexity of covert computation. In: STOC, pp. 191–200. ACM (2010)
30. Gu, Y., Jarecki, S., Krawczyk, H.: KHAPE: asymmetric PAKE from key-hiding key exchange. In: Malkin, T., Peikert, C. (eds.) CRYPTO 2021. LNCS, vol. 12828, pp. 701–730. Springer, Cham (2021). https://doi.org/10.1007/978-3-030-84259-8_24
31. Hopper, N.J., Langford, J., von Ahn, L.: Provably secure steganography. In: Yung, M. (ed.) CRYPTO 2002. LNCS, vol. 2442, pp. 77–92. Springer, Heidelberg (2002). https://doi.org/10.1007/3-540-45708-9_6
32. Jarecki, S.: Practical covert authentication. In: Krawczyk, H. (ed.) PKC 2014. LNCS, vol. 8383, pp. 611–629. Springer, Heidelberg (2014). https://doi.org/10.1007/978-3-642-54631-0_35
33. Jarecki, S.: Efficient covert two-party computation. In: Abdalla, M., Dahab, R. (eds.) PKC 2018. LNCS, vol. 10769, pp. 644–674. Springer, Cham (2018). https://doi.org/10.1007/978-3-319-76578-5_22
34. Kilian, J., Petrank, E.: Identity escrow. In: Krawczyk, H. (ed.) CRYPTO 1998. LNCS, vol. 1462, pp. 169–185. Springer, Heidelberg (1998). https://doi.org/10.1007/BFb0055727
35. Krawczyk, H.: SKEME: a versatile secure key exchange mechanism for internet. In: 1996 Internet Society Symposium on Network and Distributed System Security (NDSS), pp. 114–127 (1996)
36. Krawczyk, H.: SIGMA: the 'SIGn-and-MAc' approach to authenticated Diffie-Hellman and its use in the IKE protocols. In: Boneh, D. (ed.) CRYPTO 2003. LNCS, vol. 2729, pp. 400–425. Springer, Heidelberg (2003). https://doi.org/10.1007/978-3-540-45146-4_24
37. Krawczyk, H.: HMQV: a high-performance secure Diffie-Hellman protocol. In: Shoup, V. (ed.) CRYPTO 2005. LNCS, vol. 3621, pp. 546–566. Springer, Heidelberg (2005). https://doi.org/10.1007/11535218_33
38. Kumar, R., Nguyen, K.: Covert authentication from lattices. In: Ateniese, G., Venturi, D. (eds.) Applied Cryptography and Network Security. ACNS 2022. LNCS, vol. 13269, pp. 480–500. Springer, Cham (2022). https://doi.org/10.1007/978-3-031-09234-3_24
39. Manulis, M., Pinkas, B., Poettering, B.: Privacy-preserving group discovery with linear complexity. In: Zhou, J., Yung, M. (eds.) ACNS 2010. LNCS, vol. 6123, pp. 420–437. Springer, Heidelberg (2010). https://doi.org/10.1007/978-3-642-13708-2_25
40. Marlinspike, M., Perrin, T.: The X3DH key agreement protocol (2016). https://signal.org/docs/specifications/x3dh/
41. Nguyen, L.: Accumulators from bilinear pairings and applications. In: Menezes, A. (ed.) CT-RSA 2005. LNCS, vol. 3376, pp. 275–292. Springer, Heidelberg (2005). https://doi.org/10.1007/978-3-540-30574-3_19
42. Pointcheval, D., Sanders, O.: Short randomizable signatures. In: Sako, K. (ed.) CT-RSA 2016. LNCS, vol. 9610, pp. 111–126. Springer, Cham (2016). https://doi.org/10.1007/978-3-319-29485-8_7
43. Rogaway, P.: Nonce-based symmetric encryption. In: Roy, B., Meier, W. (eds.) FSE 2004. LNCS, vol. 3017, pp. 348–358. Springer, Heidelberg (2004). https://doi.org/10.1007/978-3-540-25937-4_22
44. Appelbaum, J., Dingledine, R.: How governments have tried to block Tor. https://oldsite.andreafortuna.org/security/files/TOR/slides-28c3.pdf
45. Sachdeva, A.: DARPA making an anonymous and hack-proof mobile communication system. FOSSBYTES Online Article (2019). https://fossbytes.com/darpa-anonymous-hack-proof-mobile-communication-system/

46. Shbair, W.M., Cholez, T., Goichot, A., Chrisment, I.: Efficiently bypassing SNI-based https filtering. In: 2015 IFIP/IEEE International Symposium on Integrated Network Management (IM), pp. 990–995 (2015)
47. Tibouchi, M.: Elligator squared: uniform points on elliptic curves of prime order as uniform random strings. In: Christin, N., Safavi-Naini, R. (eds.) FC 2014. LNCS, vol. 8437, pp. 139–156. Springer, Heidelberg (2014). https://doi.org/10.1007/978-3-662-45472-5_10
48. Vipin, N.S., Abdul Nizar, M.: Efficient on-line spam filtering for encrypted messages. In: 2015 IEEE International Conference on Signal Processing, Informatics, Communication and Energy Systems (SPICES), pp. 1–5 (2015)
49. von Ahn, L., Hopper, N.J., Langford, J.: Covert two-party computation. In: STOC, pp. 513–522. ACM (2005)
50. Wahby, R.S., Boneh, D.: Fast and simple constant-time hashing to the BLS12-381 elliptic curve. IACR Trans. Cryptogr. Hardw. Embed. Syst. **2019**(4), 154–179 (2019)

Generalized Fuzzy
Password-Authenticated Key Exchange
from Error Correcting Codes

Jonathan Bootle[1], Sebastian Faller[1,2], Julia Hesse[1],
Kristina Hostáková[2], and Johannes Ottenhues[3]✉

[1] IBM Research Europe – Zurich, Zürich, Switzerland
[2] ETH Zurich, Zürich, Switzerland
[3] University of St. Gallen, St. Gallen, Switzerland
johannes.ottenhues@unisg.ch

Abstract. Fuzzy Password-Authenticated Key Exchange (fuzzy PAKE) allows cryptographic keys to be generated from authentication data that is both fuzzy and of low entropy. The strong protection against offline attacks offered by fuzzy PAKE opens an interesting avenue towards secure biometric authentication, typo-tolerant password authentication, and automated IoT device pairing. Previous constructions of fuzzy PAKE are either based on Error Correcting Codes (ECC) or generic multi-party computation techniques such as Garbled Circuits. While ECC-based constructions are significantly more efficient, they rely on multiple special properties of error correcting codes such as maximum distance separability and smoothness.

We contribute to the line of research on fuzzy PAKE in two ways. First, we identify a subtle but devastating gap in the security analysis of the currently most efficient fuzzy PAKE construction (Dupont et al., Eurocrypt 2018), allowing a man-in-the-middle attacker to test individual password characters. Second, we provide a new fuzzy PAKE scheme based on ECC and PAKE that provides a built-in protection against individual password character guesses and requires fewer, more standard properties of the underlying ECC. Additionally, our construction offers better error correction capabilities than previous ECC-based fuzzy PAKEs.

Keywords: Attacks on Public-Key Constructions · Key Exchange Protocols · Password-Based Cryptography · UC Framework

1 Introduction

Password-authenticated key exchange (PAKE) protocols allow two users to exchange symmetric keys from plaintext passwords only. PAKEs are a useful

J. Hesse—Author supported by the Swiss National Science Foundation (SNSF) under the AMBIZIONE grant "Cryptographic Protocols for Human Authentication and the IoT". J. Ottenhues—
Author partially funded by the EU-funded Marie Curie ITN TReSPAsS-ETN project under the grant agreement 860813.

J. Guo and R. Steinfeld (Eds.): ASIACRYPT 2023, LNCS 14445, pp. 110–142, 2023.
https://doi.org/10.1007/978-981-99-8742-9_4

tool in unlocking smartcards (e.g., German ID card [BFK09, BDFK12, BFK13], FIDO2 [BBCW21]), securing wireless networks [All22, CNPR22], and pairing IoT devices [HL19]. First formalized by Bellovin and Merrit [BM92], PAKEs provide optimal protection of potentially low-entropy passwords, a feature that is called *resistance against offline dictionary attacks*. Essentially, a PAKE does not leak any information about the password used by the counterparty in case of password mismatch. This guarantee needs to hold against network adversaries observing the protocol execution as well as active attackers playing one user in the protocol. Such strong protection is vital for use cases of PAKE. Without it, any typing of, e.g., the 6-digit PIN restricting access to a German national ID card would already expose that PIN to brute-force attacks mounted through malicious card reader hardware or software. Building secure and efficient PAKEs that even feature strong universal composability guarantees is fairly simple. The general idea is to run a Diffie-Hellman key exchange, and either encrypt the Diffie-Hellman public keys with the password [BM92, BPR00], or derive the group generator from the password [Jab96, BMP00, Mac01, HS14, HL19][1].

Unfortunately, in many application scenarios of PAKE protocols, usability can hinder their adoption. Manually entering PINs in stressful situations, such as unlocking one's smart ID card next to a waiting officer, or pairing a wearable IoT device while walking, is prone to repeated mistyping. As another example, consider IoT devices that want to automatically exchange a key with devices located in their close proximity. These devices can automatically derive passwords from sensor readings of their direct environment, but they likely end up with similar but not exactly matching bitstrings. In these situations, key exchange through PAKE fails even though the legitimate owner of the ID card was present, and even though the IoT devices were actually sitting next to each other.

In 2018, Dupont et al. [DHP+18] proposed a new cryptographic primitive called *fuzzy* PAKE (fPAKE), which allows two users to exchange a symmetric key from *similar* passwords. In addition to being a candidate to resolve the usability issues with password mistyping/mismatching in the aforementioned scenarios, fuzzy PAKE opens an interesting avenue towards secure biometric authentication, as it enables secure comparison of consecutive biometric readings *without leaking any other information about the biometric* than "match" or "no match". To date, fuzzy PAKE is the only cryptographic primitive that can provide such optimal protection of data that is both noisy *and* of low entropy.

Dupont et al. [DHP+18] gave two constructions of fuzzy PAKE, one relying on Garbled Circuits and one relying on error-correcting codes (ECC)[2] and PAKE, using Hamming distance as a metric for similarity of passwords. The ECC based construction is to the best of our knowledge the most efficient fuzzy

---

[1] [Hv22] provides an excellent overview of PAKEs in the literature, also mentioning other approaches than building PAKEs through Diffie-Hellman.

[2] Dupont et al. [DHP+18] use the terminology of *robust secret sharing* (RSS) instead of error-correcting codes, and show how to instantiate RSS with ECC. In this work, we state their construction in terms of an ECC, as it enables better comparison with our protocol.

PAKE construction in the literature [DHP+18] so far. At a high level, the protocol works as follows. One party takes the role of the sender, chooses a symmetric key s, encodes it with the error-correcting code to get $C \leftarrow \mathsf{Enc}(s)$, XORs the resulting codeword with the password to get $E \leftarrow C \oplus \mathsf{pw}$, and sends E to the receiver. The receiver XORs the received E with their own password to get $C' \leftarrow E \oplus \mathsf{pw}'$, and attempts to decode C' to retrieve s. Depending on whether pw and pw' were similar enough, the codeword C' is close enough to C to uniquely decode to s. The error correction capability of the fuzzy PAKE is hence directly related to the error correction threshold of the code. However, the protocol as described above would be prone to offline attacks: the receiver can repeatedly decode with many password guesses pw', yielding a list of candidate keys. To prevent such a dictionary attack, [DHP+18] introduce a "password expansion" step prior to the encoding of the key. Here, the two parties run a PAKE on *every character* of their passwords pw and pw', yielding key vectors K and K' that match in exactly the same entries as pw and pw', while the other entries are uniformly distributed. Because this expansion step requires active participation of both parties and the vector entries are PAKE keys that are hard to guess, one party alone cannot turn a password into a key vector. Hence, parties – malicious or honest – are limited to only one password guess per protocol run.

In fact, to prevent C from leaking information about the key s in case the receiver is malicious, C is computed by encoding s concatenated with an extra random input r. The error correcting code must satisfy multiple special properties, such as a *uniformity* property, whereby small subsets of codeword entries appear uniformly random, independently of s, and a *smoothness* property, whereby decoding an extremely noisy codeword results in a random key. Uniformity is a well-known property, satisfied by the popular Reed-Solomon codes, which has been extensively studied [CCG+07,CDBN15,Wei16,BCL22], and can be obtained via various transformations including the method presented in [DHP+18]. Smoothness is less standard, and [DHP+18] rely on maximum distance separable codes in order to achieve it.

1.1 Our Contribution

First, we identify a subtle but devastating issue in the ECC-based fuzzy PAKE construction of [DHP+18]. In a bit more detail, we give an attack that allows the adversary to make guesses on individual password bits (or characters), allowing them to extract a user's, e.g., n-bit password from only n executions of the protocol with that user. Our attack demonstrates that the measures taken by [DHP+18] to protect against such individual guesses, namely ensuring that an attacker either guesses "all-or-zero" bits of the password, subtly fails due to incorrect binding of the different protocol parts. Here, binding refers to ensuring that all messages come from the same sender. Although there exist generic techniques for binding together messages sent over unauthenticated channels

[BCL+05], they cannot be applied to the construction of [DHP+18] in black-box way due to its modular layout.[3]

The effect of our attack is that an active attacker learns one bit of an honest user's password by simply messing with an honest protocol run between two users. While the security notion of fuzzy PAKE [DHP+18] does leak information about the password, i.e., it leaks the exact password of an honest user to an attacker, we stress that this attacker must be actively running a session with the honest user *and* use close password to the one of the attacked honest user. Our attack requires much less knowledge from the adversary. In more detail, it can be executed by a network adversary essentially flipping some bits of the exchanged messages between honest clients. The attacker only needs to make an assumption about the distance of the passwords used in the execution. For example, in settings where fuzzy PAKE is usually executed without the proper passwords, e.g., mistyping happens only rarely, every honest protocol run would reveal one bit about the secret password of an honest party to a network attacker. Deriving such information from honest protocol runs is prohibited by the security model of [DHP+18].

Reference	error corr. capability	rounds	msg size	Sender	Receiver	model
[DHP+18]	$\lfloor \frac{n-k}{2} \rfloor$	1	$\mathcal{O}(n)$	2n exp	Dec + 2n exp	RO, IC, CRS
Our work, unique dec.	$\lfloor \frac{n-k}{2} \rfloor$	1	$\mathcal{O}(n)$	2n exp	Dec + 2n exp	RO, IC, CRS, SA
Our work, list dec.	$n-1-\lfloor \sqrt{(k-1)n} \rfloor$	1	$\mathcal{O}(n)$	2n exp	LDec + 2n exp	RO, IC, CRS, SA

Fig. 1. Comparison of ECC-based fuzzy PAKE constructions, using a Reed-Solomon code of rank k, and block length n equal to the size of the password. Sender and Receiver columns indicate computation complexity. Both protocols are instantiated with EKE2 [DHP+18] to derive concrete performances. RO, IC, and CRS are required for the security of EKE2. SA is split authentication. We stress that the ECC-based [DHP+18] cannot be considered a secure fuzzy PAKE (Sect. 3.2).

Our second contribution is a new fuzzy PAKE protocol based on error-correcting codes, which directly builds upon the ideas of [DHP+18] but (i) fixes the previous insecurities, (ii) provides better error-correction capabilities, and (iii) relies on fewer properties of the underlying code. These improvements come at the cost of less efficient computation and communication. We provide a high-level comparison in Fig. 1. For (i), the idea is to ensure that the transformation of Barak et al. [BCL+05] applies to the whole protocol, simply by instantiating all building blocks that require interaction between the parties *before* applying the transformation. For (ii) we investigate how the (fixed) fuzzy PAKE protocol

---

[3] More precisely, and for the reader who is familiar with the Universal Composability framework [Can01]: In Sect. 3.2, we argue that the split transformation of Barak et al. [BCL+05] cannot be meaningfully applied to transform a *hybrid* protocol that assumes authenticated channels, to a version that is secure with unauthenticated channels. In a nutshell, the reason is that the hybrid building blocks are unaffected by the transformation and do not carry any authentication guarantees.

ECC threshold	Password Length n									
$n - k + 1$	$n = 8$		$n = 32$		$n = 64$		$n = 128$		$n = 256$	
(as % of n)	[DHP+18]	Ours	[DHP+18]	Ours	[DHP+18]	Ours	[DHP+18]	Ours	[DHP+18]	Ours
10%			1	1	2	3	5	6	12	12
25%	0	1	3	4	7	8	15	17	31	34
30%	0	1	4	4	9	10	18	20	37	41
50%	1	2	7	9	15	18	31	37	63	74

Fig. 2. Error correction capability for the ECC-based PAKE constructions of [DHP+18] and in this work using list decoding, for various password lengths n and a Reed-Solomon code with rank k and block length n. The table shows the number of password errors below which key exchange will succeed. The ECC threshold refers to the percentage of errors above which key exchange will fail without leaking information about the password. Gray colored cells show parameter settings for which our construction improves upon previous works.

of [DHP+18], which applies unique decoding of the ECC, benefits from applying a non-unique decoding technique. Namely, we make use of *list decoding* which is a decoding technique that takes a codeword with errors as input, and that can produce a list of candidate codewords including the original one. When the number of errors is too large for unique decoding to work, list decoding can still produce reasonable-sized lists of codewords that still contain the original one. We give examples of the improved error correction capability of our scheme over previous works in Fig. 2, For (iii) we leverage new ingredients in our construction in order to bypass the smoothness property completely.

Intuitively, such non-unique decoding introduces a "correctness error" into the fuzzy PAKE protocol of [DHP+18], since the receiver decodes a list of key candidates and has to guess which one is the key of the sender. Moreover, it is unclear how to generalize the smoothness property and its proof in [DHP+18] to the list decoding regime, due to the higher number of errors.

Our idea is to restore perfect correctness by letting the sender give a *hint* about the correct key to the receiver. This hint, however, needs to be carefully crafted so that it benefits the correctness of the key exchange without revealing too much information about the password or the key of the sender. For example, simply using a hash of the sender's key is not possible. This is because during security proofs, the hint may have to be simulated, without knowledge of the key, against an adversary who does know the key and is able to check that whether the hint was computed correctly or not. Instead, the sender hashes the encoding C of s. Based on the uniformity of the error-correcting code, this hint contains sufficient entropy to prevent information leakage on the key. Furthermore, the fact that the hint uniquely determines the correct codeword actually allows us to dispense with the smoothness property completely. Since smoothness, which relied on maximum distance separability, is no longer needed, the space of possible codes which can be used in our construction is much larger, opening the door to codes with even better list-decoding capabilities and fuzzy PAKEs with even higher error tolerance in future.

Altogether, we are able to give a construction with better error correction capability than previous schemes in the literature. More formally, we prove the following in Theorem 2.

Our fuzzy PAKE using a Reed-Solomon code of rank k, block length n, *list* decoding, a hint as described above and signing under ephemeral public keys to achieve binding, is secure and has an error correction capability of
$$\delta = n - 1 - \sqrt{(k-1)n}.$$

We can also apply our results to obtain a fixed version of the fuzzy PAKE of [DHP+18] et al. by using unique decoding instead of list decoding, offering a trade-off between runtime (unique decoding is generally faster than list decoding) and error correction capability (see Fig. 2 for numerical examples of the error correction terms).

Corollary 1. *Our fuzzy PAKE using a Reed-Solomon code of rank k, block length n, **unique** decoding, a hint as described above and signing under ephemeral public keys to achieve binding, is secure and has an error correction capability of $\lfloor \frac{n-k}{2} \rfloor$. The computational overhead over [DHP+18] is one signature per message, and one hash by the sender.*

Roadmap. In Sect. 2 we provide preliminaries on error-correcting codes and list decoding, and on implicit PAKE which is a building block of our and previous ECC-based fuzzy PAKE protocols. Section 3 recaps fuzzy PAKE including its security model in the UC framework, explains the fuzzy PAKE of [DHP+18] and presents an attack that allows to test password bits. In Sect. 4 we give our improved fuzzy PAKE protocol and prove its security.

1.2   Related Work

Prior to the introduction of fuzzy PAKE by Dupont et al. [DHP+18], several attempts to base cryptography on low-entropy or noisy shared data have been made. Information reconciliation [BBR88] and fuzzy extractors [DORS08, RW04] let two parties identify common randomness in shared noisy bitstrings. However, the identification comes at the price of leakage, such that these techniques cannot be used when the shared data is of low entropy, such as in the case of passwords. Canetti et al. [CFP+16] construct special-purpose schemes for securely comparing the Hamming distance of, e.g., biometric readings. However, the security of their construction again relies on the data having a certain min-entropy. The PAKE-based construction for comparison of biometric readings of Boyen et al. [BDK+05] does not protect against offline attacks on the biometric data and hence cannot reach the security level of fuzzy PAKEs.

Our construction improves the parameters of [DHP+18] by using list decoding instead of unique decoding, and using a hint to select the correct codeword. In fact, Cramer et al. [CDD+15] construct robust secret-sharing schemes using a similar idea, but they ensure that the correct secret is selected using an algebraic manipulation detection (AMD) code. Putting aside the subtle issues in [DHP+18] that we address in this paper, our construction is different from using the robust secret-sharing schemes of [CDD+15] in the [DHP+18] because incorporating the hint does not constitute an AMD code, and also removes the smoothness requirement from [DHP+18].

Biometric authentication is a very active area of research. In the following we list several works that aim at providing secure biometric authentication by introducing, e.g., additional trust anchors, or by leveraging the entropy in the biometric scans. BETA [ABM+21] generates a token to be used for authenticating a client to a server, by letting three client devices communicate over authenticated channels. In the fuzzy PAKE setting, each entity only needs one device and also a fuzzy PAKE is secure even in unauthenticated channels. Agrawal et al. [ABMR20] present a protocol for authenticating a user with their biometric by letting the user's phone, an external terminal and a service provider communicate to compute the authentication result. Differences to fuzzy PAKE are that [ABMR20] has three parties instead of two, and their protocol uses cosine similarity instead of Hamming distance to compare the biometrics. Moreover, [ABMR20] focuses on authentication whereas a fuzzy PAKE achieves key exchange. Wang et al. [WHC+21] construct authenticated key change for secure messaging in which the users do not need to store their secret keys but instead derive them from their biometrics. [WHC+21] uses the biometric as an error term for LWE samples, which places very strong requirements on the biometric distribution. A fuzzy PAKE is stronger; its security cannot rely on the distribution of the authentication data, and hence our protocol is secure even when used with low entropy passwords (or biometrics). Jiang et al. [JLHG22] build key exchange from fuzzy data, which is also the goal of a fuzzy PAKE. However, similar to [WHC+21, JLHG22] relies on high entropy of that fuzzy data. A fuzzy PAKE however does not make any assumptions about the entropy of the authentication data (=passwords). The tools used in [JLHG22] such as secure sketches are known to be inherently insecure when used on low entropy data. Erwig et al. [EHOR20] leverages robust secret sharing, which previous fuzzy PAKEs and our construction also rely on. Contrary to us, [EHOR20] builds an *asymmetric* PAKE, with a client and a server party where the latter is not allowed to store the password in the clear. While this is an extremely relevant setting in practise, their solutions are computationally expensive and the authors note that it seems infeasible to go beyond passwords of 40 bits. The works of Chatterjee et al. [CAA+16, CWP+17] propose typo-tolerant password authentication systems. These password authentication systems tolerate mistyping on the user side, i.e., the user can successfully authenticate to some server even when using a password slightly different from the one they registered with. While [CAA+16] corrects a predefined set of most common typos (e.g., capitalization of first letter), the TypTop system [CWP+17] offers personalized adoption to frequent typos of users, meaning that the system will learn from past typos and apply certain rules whether to accept these errors in the future. The crucial difference to fuzzy PAKE is that both these typo-tolerant systems require the server party to learn the *cleartext* password of the user, as the password needs to be fed into the decision procedure as well as into the evolving "accepted typos" cache. The main goal of fuzzy PAKE is to prevent such transmission of clear-text passwords among the two parties. The concept of typo tolerance was subsequently carried over to PAKE [PC20]. Typo-tolerant PAKE is a system to log in to a server despite of typos in the password. The protocol in [PC20] requires storage and communication proportional to the number of close passwords, which limits the potential applications of the protocol. The storage and communication cost of our protocol only depends on the length of the password but not on the number of close passwords, which also makes it possible to use our protocol with biometrics instead of passwords.

In [RX23] it is demonstrated that the common notion of PAKE in the UC-framework does not automatically guarantee correctness. More concretely, the ideal functionality $\mathcal{F}_{\mathsf{PAKE}}$ [CHK+05] does not guarantee that two honest parties that are not maliciously attacked do output the same key when they run on the same password. Several ways to overcome these definitional issues were proposed in [RX23]. The most simple way is to demand correctness as a separate property from the protocol. This style of listing several properties is usually not desirable in UC-protocols as the additionally demanded properties might not be preserved under composition. However, [RX23, Thm. 3] shows that any PAKE protocol that is correct *and* UC-realizes $\mathcal{F}_{\mathsf{PAKE}}$ can be interpreted as a protocol that is secure in an enhanced UC PAKE formalization that ensures correctness (by modeling the man-in-the-middle adversary as a third protocol party). The observations of [RX23] rely on the way output is produced in $\mathcal{F}_{\mathsf{PAKE}}$ and not on the way how the passwords are checked. Therefore, they also apply to our $\mathcal{F}_{\mathsf{fPAKE}}$ (and $\mathcal{F}_{\mathsf{iPAKE}}$) functionality and we have to assert correctness separately.

2 Preliminaries

Notation. We denote vectors in boldface, e.g., $\boldsymbol{V} \in \mathbb{F}^n$. Let $Q \subseteq [n] := \{1, \dots, n\}$. Then, we denote with $\boldsymbol{V}|_Q := (\boldsymbol{V}_i)_{i \in Q} \in \mathbb{F}^{|Q|}$ the restriction of $\boldsymbol{V}$ to Q. We write PPT for probabilistic polynomial time.

2.1 Universal Composability (UC)

To formally define and prove security of fuzzy PAKEs, we use the UC framework of Canetti [Can01] as is standard in the PAKE literature. Our goal here is to introduce the basic terminology and notation of the UC framework at a very high level and only to the extent needed for the understanding of later sections. For a more accurate and formal explanation of the UC framework, we refer the reader to the work of Canetti [Can01].

In our case, we always consider protocols between two parties (which we typically denote $\mathcal{P}_0$ and $\mathcal{P}_1$) that are executed in the presence of a PPT adversary $\mathcal{A}$ who can corrupt any party at the beginning of the protocol execution (i.e., we consider so-called static corruption). By corruption we mean that the adversary gets a full control over the corrupt parties and learns their internal state. Parties and the adversary $\mathcal{A}$ get their inputs from a special entity, called the *environment* $\mathcal{Z}$, which represents everything external to the protocol execution. $\mathcal{Z}$ also receives outputs from both parties and the adversary. The execution of a protocol in presence of an adversary $\mathcal{A}$ is typically referred to as the "real world".

In the UC framework, security requirements of a protocol are defined via *ideal functionalities*. At a very high level, an ideal functionality $\mathcal{F}$ defines the intended input/output behaviour of parties, the allowed leakage of the protocol and the influence of an adversary on the protocol. $\mathcal{F}$ communicates with the environment through *dummy parties* $\mathcal{P}_0, \mathcal{P}_1$ that simply forward messages between $\mathcal{Z}$ and $\mathcal{F}$. The functionality additionally communicates with an adversary which is typically called the *simulator* and denoted $\mathcal{S}$. The execution of $\mathcal{F}$ in the presence of a simulator $\mathcal{S}$ is typically referred to as the "ideal world". We say that a protocol π UC-realizes (or UC-emulates) an ideal functionality $\mathcal{F}$ if for any PPT adversary $\mathcal{A}$, there exists a PPT simulator $\mathcal{S}$ such that for any PPT environment $\mathcal{Z}$ the ideal and real worlds are indistinguishable except for negligible probability. In other words, any attack possible on the protocol π can be simulated as an attack on the ideal functionality.

One of the main benefits of the UC framework is that it natively supports protocol composition and hence allows for natural modularization of protocol designs. Concretely, parties in a protocol can communicate with *hybrid* ideal functionalities $\mathcal{H}_1, \mathcal{H}_2, \ldots$. In such a case, we say that the protocol is a defined in the "$(\mathcal{H}_1, \mathcal{H}_2, \ldots)$-hybrid world". The UC composition theorem then allows to securely replace the hybrid ideal functionalities with concrete protocols that UC-realize those functionalities.

2.2 Error Correcting Codes (ECC)

A *linear error-correcting code* $\mathcal{C}$ over a finite field $\mathbb{F}_q$ of order q with rank k and block length n is a linear subspace $\mathcal{C} \subseteq \mathbb{F}_q^n$ of dimension k. We can associate $\mathcal{C}$ with an injective linear *encoding function* $\mathsf{Enc}\colon \mathbb{F}_q^k \to \mathbb{F}_q^n$, where $\mathrm{Im}(\mathsf{Enc}) = \mathcal{C}$.

– The *Hamming distance* $d(\boldsymbol{V}, \boldsymbol{V}')$ between vectors $\boldsymbol{V}, \boldsymbol{V}' \in \mathbb{F}_q^n$ is defined by

$$d(\boldsymbol{V}, \boldsymbol{V}') := |\{i \in [n]\colon \boldsymbol{V}_i \neq \boldsymbol{V}'_i\}| \ .$$

– The *minimum distance* $d(\mathcal{C})$ of a linear code $\mathcal{C}$ is defined as

$$d(\mathcal{C}) := \min_{\boldsymbol{C}, \boldsymbol{C}' \in \mathcal{C}, \boldsymbol{C} \neq \boldsymbol{C}'} d(\boldsymbol{C}, \boldsymbol{C}') \ .$$

A linear code over $\mathbb{F}_q$ with rank k, blocklength n, and minimum distance d is referred to as an $[n, k, d]_q$ code. The "q" will usually be omitted.

Error Correction. Let $e \in \mathbb{Z}$ with $0 \leq e < d/2$. A $[n, k, d]$-code $\mathcal{C}$ is said to be *e-error-correcting* if there exists a function $\mathsf{Dec}\colon \mathbb{F}_q^n \to \mathbb{F}_q^k$ such that for all $V \in \mathbb{F}_q^n$, $M \in \mathbb{F}_q^k$ with $d(V, \mathsf{Enc}(M)) \leq e$, we have $\mathsf{Dec}(V) = M$. It is well-known that an $[n, k, d]$-code is $\lfloor \frac{d-1}{2} \rfloor$-error correcting.

Further, we say that a code is *efficiently* e-error-correcting if Dec can be computed in polynomial time in n. Note that *all* linear codes are efficiently 0-error correcting, as the message associated with an error-free codeword can simply be recovered via Gaussian elimination.

List Decoding. Let $e \in \mathbb{Z}$ with $0 \leq e \leq n$. Let $\ell \in \mathbb{N}$ with $\ell \geq 1$. An $[n, k, d]$-code $\mathcal{C}$ is said to be (e, ℓ)-*list-decodable* if for all $V \in \mathbb{F}_q^n$, the list L of codewords $C \in \mathcal{C}$ with $d(V, C) \leq e$ contains at most ℓ codewords.

Further, we say that a code is *efficiently* (e, ℓ)-list-decodable if there is an algorithm LDec which computes the list of codewords in polynomial time in n. This necessarily implies that ℓ is polynomial in n. In this case, we will often simply say that $\mathcal{C}$ is efficiently e-list-decodable.

It will be convenient to use shorthand such as "$C \in \mathsf{LDec}(V)$" when a codeword C is part of the output list when LDec is run on input V.

2.3 Randomized Codes

We also consider codes with hiding properties, using terminology from [BCL22]. Let $\mathcal{C}$ be a $[n, k, d]$ code. Let $k_M, k_R \in \mathbb{N}$ with $k_M + k_R = k$. We may consider a *randomized encoding function* $\overline{\mathsf{Enc}} \colon \mathbb{F}_q^{k_M} \times \mathbb{F}_q^{k_R} \to \mathbb{F}_q^n$ defined by $\overline{\mathsf{Enc}}(M, R) := \mathsf{Enc}(M \| R)$. When considering $\overline{\mathsf{Enc}}$, we refer to $\mathcal{C}$ as a *randomized linear code*.

Uniform Codes. A randomized linear code $\mathcal{C}$ is said to be B-*query uniform* if for any set $Q \subseteq [n]$ with $|Q| \leq B$, the distribution of $\{\overline{\mathsf{Enc}}(M, R)|_Q : R \leftarrow \mathbb{F}_q^{k_R}\}$ is uniform over $\mathbb{F}_q^Q$.

Example: Reed-Solomon Codes. Let $k, n \in \mathbb{N}$. Let $\mathbb{F}_q$ be a field, let $s_1, \dots, s_n$ be distinct points in $\mathbb{F}_q$, and let $S := \{s_1, \dots, s_n\}$. The *Reed-Solomon* code $\mathcal{RS}[n, k, S]$ is defined as

$$\mathcal{RS}[n, k, S] := \{(p(s_1), \dots, p(s_n)) \mid p \in \mathbb{F}_q[X], \deg(p) \leq k - 1\} \ ,$$

with associated encoding function

$$\mathsf{Enc} \colon (M_0, \dots, M_{k-1}) \mapsto (p_M(s_1), \dots, p_M(s_n)) \ ,$$

where $p_M := \sum_{i=0}^{k-1} M_i X^i$. It is well known that $\mathcal{RS}[n, k, S]$ is a $[n, k, n-k+1]$ code and that furthermore, when considering a randomised encoding function for some $k_R < k$, the Reed-Solomon code is k_R-query uniform.

We state results on the decodability and list-decodability of Reed-Solomon codes.

Lemma 1 (Berlekamp-Welch algorithm [KR07]). *The code* $\mathcal{RS}[n, k, S]$ *is* $\lfloor \frac{n-k}{2} \rfloor$-*error correcting, and* Dec *is computable in time* $O(n^2)$.

Lemma 2 (Guruswami-Sudan algorithm [McE03, Gur06, Nie13]**).** *The code $\mathcal{RS}[n, k, S]$ is (e, ℓ)-list decodable with $e = n-1-\sqrt{(k-1)n}$ and $\ell = O(n^2)$. Moreover, the list L can be computed in time $O(n^9)$.*

Note that some references such as [McE03] allow LDec to produce codewords with distance greater than e as part of the list L as they can be easily discarded. We assume that this has already been done and L contains only codewords within Hamming distance e of the input vector.

While both decoding algorithms run in polynomial time, the asymptotic complexity of LDec in Lemma 2 is much higher than that of Dec in Lemma 1. The bound of $O(n^9)$ in Lemma 2 comes from combining Corollary 3.15 and Table 3.1 in [Nie13].

2.4 Implicit-Only PAKE

A PAKE is a cryptographic protocol π that allows two parties to agree on a shared key over an unauthenticated channel assuming that both parties know the same shared password (i.e., a potentially low entropy string), and guarantees that each party gets a freshly sampled random key if the input passwords are different. The absence of an authenticated channel and the low-entropy assumption on the shared password mean that an iPAKE has to take man-in-the-middle and offline dictionary attacks into account.

The main building block of our construction is an *implicit-only PAKE* (or iPAKE for short) put forward by Dupont et al. [DHP+18]. An iPAKE is a specific type of PAKE that only achieves *implicit* authentication with respect to the honest parties as well as the adversary. This means that at the end of the protocol execution, the two interacting parties do not know if they derived the same key or not. Moreover, an adversary launching an active attack on the protocol by trying to guess the password does not get any feedback on the correctness of their guesses. Dupont et al. [DHP+18] formally defined an iPAKE as an ideal functionality $\mathcal{F}_{iPAKE}$ which we describe in the full version of the paper.

Correctness. Roy and Xu [RX23] showed that ideal UC-functionalities for PAKE like $\mathcal{F}_{PAKE}$ by [CHK+05] do not offer correctness. This shortcoming of $\mathcal{F}_{PAKE}$ also applies to the $\mathcal{F}_{iPAKE}$ functionality. In a nutshell, all these functionalities offer an adversarial interface to *prevent* successful key exchange that is not subject to any restrictions. Since protocols that emulate a functionality can allow for the same attacks than the functionality, even a PAKE where parties always output random keys could securely realize a PAKE functionality. Further, Roy and Xu [RX23, Thm. 2] show that it is impossible to incorporate correctness into $\mathcal{F}_{PAKE}$ in the two-party setting. However, they show how to overcome this limitation by defining PAKE as a three-party protocol, where the third party is the man-in-the-middle adversary. This formulation is equivalent to demanding correctness from the PAKE protocol as a separate property [RX23, Thm. 3]. We therefore also demand that an iPAKE protocol has correctness. Let $(K, K') \leftarrow$ out$_{\mathcal{A},\pi}\langle \mathcal{P}_0(\mathsf{pw}), \mathcal{P}_1(\mathsf{pw})\rangle$ denote that $\mathcal{P}_0$ outputs K and $\mathcal{P}_1$ outputs K' when executing π on input pw $\in \mathcal{D}$, respectively and in the presence of adversary $\mathcal{A}$. Here $\mathcal{D}$ denotes a finite alphabet (or dictionary). We adapt their correctness definition to the setting of implicit-only PAKE here.

Definition 1. *We say an iPAKE protocol π is ε-correct if for all* pw $\in \mathcal{D}$, *for some finite alphabet $\mathcal{D}$, and for all passive (i.e., honest-but-curious) adversaries $\mathcal{A}$, the probability that in an execution of π with honest parties $\mathcal{P}_0, \mathcal{P}_1$ the first party $\mathcal{P}_0$ on input* pw *outputs a different key than the second party $\mathcal{P}_1$ on input* pw *in the presence of $\mathcal{A}$ is negligible, i.e.,*

$$\Pr[K \neq K' \mid (K, K') \leftarrow \mathsf{out}_{\mathcal{A},\pi} \langle \mathcal{P}_0(\mathsf{pw}), \mathcal{P}_1(\mathsf{pw}) \rangle] \leq \varepsilon(\lambda),$$

where the probability is taken over the random coins of $\mathcal{P}_0, \mathcal{P}_1$, and $\mathcal{A}$. We call ε the correctness error. *We just say π is correct if it has negligible correctness error.*

2.5 Split Authentication

Another building block in our fPAKE construction is *Split Authentication*, put forward by Barak et al. [BCL+05]. It is essentially a protocol that implements something very close to an authenticated channel in an unauthenticated setting. The adversary's only additional ability is that they can run two separate executions of an authentication protocol (one with each party) without the two communicating parties realizing it. In particular, if both parties are honest, split authentication forces the adversary to decide at the beginning of the communication whether to launch a man-in-the-middle attack and run a separate protocol with each party, or to just observe the messages being exchanged and potentially delay their delivery.

Barak et al. [BCL+05] formalized Split Authentication as an ideal functionality $\mathcal{F}_{\mathsf{SA}}$ which we describe in the full version of the paper.

3 Fuzzy Password-Authenticated Key Exchange

Fuzzy Password-Authenticated Key Exchange (fPAKE for short) is a cryptographic protocol allowing two parties to agree on a shared key in the following setting: the two parties are connected by an unauthenticated channel, but each of them holds a *noisy* version of a shared low-entropy password.

3.1 The $\mathcal{F}_{\mathsf{fPAKE}}$ Ideal Functionality

Dupont et al. [DHP+18] formalized fPAKE as a UC ideal functionality $\mathcal{F}_{\mathsf{fPAKE}}$ which we recall in Fig. 3. Here we describe $\mathcal{F}_{\mathsf{fPAKE}}$ at a high level and refer the reader to the work of Dupont et al. for a more detailed discussion.

Parties $\mathcal{P}_0, \mathcal{P}_1$ initiate a password-authenticated key exchange by sending a NEWSESSION message to the ideal functionality including their version of the password. To allow for initiator-responder-style protocols, the ideal functionality allows parties to specify their role, i.e., whether they are the Sender or the Receiver. Upon receiving a NEWSESSION message, the functionality records the received password pw and informs the adversary about the NEWSESSION request.

The adversary can then try to guess the recorded password through a TESTPWD query. This interface allows an adversary to mount an active attack on the protocol. The recorded pw is marked as compromised if adversary's guess is "close enough" and interrupted otherwise. The adversary is informed about the result of their guess. To capture the closeness formally, $\mathcal{F}_{\text{fPAKE}}$ is parametrized by *error tolerance* δ and a metric d, and two passwords pw, pw' are considered close enough for key exchange to succeed if $d(\text{pw}, \text{pw}') \leq \delta$.

The functionality outputs a secret key to a party $\mathcal{P}_i$ after receiving a NEWKEY instruction from the adversary. This captures the ability of network attackers to arbitrarily delay the termination of the protocol. $\mathcal{F}_{\text{fPAKE}}$ decides on the secret key being sent in three different ways (for a formal definition of each case, see Fig. 3.):

(i) The secret key is specified by the adversary if the adversary successfully guessed $\mathcal{P}_i$'s recorded password, which can happen either through a TESTPWD query, or by corrupting $\mathcal{P}_{1-i}$ and submitting a password on their behalf. This case captures the fact that a protocol participant with a close enough password can bias the final key.

(ii) If both parties are honest, their recorded passwords are δ-close and $\mathcal{F}_{\text{fPAKE}}$ already sent a secret key to party $\mathcal{P}_{1-i}$, then $\mathcal{P}_i$ gets the same key as $\mathcal{P}_{1-i}$. This requirement ensures the core functionality of an fPAKE; namely, that honest parties with close enough passwords output the same key.

(iii) In any other case, $\mathcal{F}_{\text{fPAKE}}$ sends a freshly sampled random key to ensures pseudorandomness of keys overall, and uniformity of keys output by parties with non-matching passwords.

Dupont et al. [DHP+18] additionally defined a modified TESTPWD interface that gives more freedom in defining the leakage to the adversary after a TESTPWD query. The functionality is now additionally parametrized by a *leakage threshold* $\gamma \geq \delta$ and three leakage functions L_c, L_m, L_f defining the leakage to the adversary depending on the closeness of their guess to the tested password. See Fig. 5 for a graphical explanation of the extended TESTPWD interface and Fig. 4 for a formal definition of the extension.

We are particularly interested in a TESTPWD interface that leaks positions at which passwords match if the passwords are sufficiently close (following [DHP+18], we call this leakage the *mask*). Our proof of security will rely on this leaked information. Formally, let $\mathcal{F}_{\text{fPAKE}}^M$ be the ideal functionality from Fig. 3 except that the TESTPWD interface is defined according to Fig. 4 with the following leakage functions (here pw = $(\text{pw}_1, \ldots, \text{pw}_n)$ and pw' = $(\text{pw}_1', \ldots, \text{pw}_n')$):

$$L_c^M(\text{pw}, \text{pw}') := (\{j \text{ s.t. } \text{pw}_j = \text{pw}_j'\}, \text{``correct guess''}),$$
$$L_m^M(\text{pw}, \text{pw}') := (\{j \text{ s.t. } \text{pw}_j = \text{pw}_j'\}, \text{``wrong guess''}),$$
$$L_f^M(\text{pw}, \text{pw}') := \text{``wrong guess''}.$$

Functionality $\mathcal{F}_{\mathsf{fPAKE}}$

The functionality $\mathcal{F}_{\mathsf{fPAKE}}$ is parameterized by a security parameter λ and error tolerance δ and leakage threshold $\gamma \geq \delta$. It interacts with an adversary $\mathcal{A}$ and two parties $\mathcal{P}_0$ and $\mathcal{P}_1$ via the following queries:

On input (NewSession, sid, $\mathsf{pw}^{\mathcal{P}_i}$, role) from party $\mathcal{P}_i$, where $\mathsf{pw}^{\mathcal{P}_i}$ is a password and role = sender implies that $\mathcal{P}_i$ wishes to initiate a key exchange, while role = receiver implies that $\mathcal{P}_i$ wishes to respond:
- Send (NewSession, sid, $\mathcal{P}_i$, role) to $\mathcal{A}$;
- If one of the following is true, record $(\mathcal{P}_i, \mathsf{pw}^{\mathcal{P}_i})$ and mark this record fresh:
  - This is the first NewSession query;
  - This is the second NewSession query and there is a record $(\mathcal{P}_{1-i}, \mathsf{pw}^{\mathcal{P}_{1-i}})$.

On (TestPwd, sid, $\mathcal{P}_i$, pw^*) from the adversary $\mathcal{A}$:
If there is a fresh record $(\mathcal{P}_i, \mathsf{pw}^{\mathcal{P}_i})$, then set $d \leftarrow d(\mathsf{pw}^{\mathcal{P}_i}, \mathsf{pw}^*)$ and do:
- If $d \leq \delta$, mark the record compromised and reply to $\mathcal{A}$ with "correct guess";
- If $d > \delta$, mark the record interrupted and reply to $\mathcal{A}$ with "wrong guess".

On (NewKey, sid, $\mathcal{P}_i$, sk) from the adversary $\mathcal{A}$:
If there is no record of the form $(\mathcal{P}_i, \mathsf{pw}^{\mathcal{P}_i})$, or if this is not the first NewKey query for $\mathcal{P}_i$, then ignore this query. Otherwise:
- If at least one of the following is true, then output (sid, sk) to player $\mathcal{P}_i$:
  - The record is compromised;
  - The record is fresh, $\mathcal{P}_{1-i}$ is corrupted, and there is a record $(\mathcal{P}_{1-i}, \mathsf{pw}^{\mathcal{P}_{1-i}})$ with $d(\mathsf{pw}^{\mathcal{P}_i}, \mathsf{pw}^{\mathcal{P}_{1-i}}) \leq \delta$.
- If this record is fresh, both parties are honest, there is a record $(\mathcal{P}_{1-i}, \mathsf{pw}^{\mathcal{P}_{1-i}})$ with $d(\mathsf{pw}^{\mathcal{P}_i}, \mathsf{pw}^{\mathcal{P}_{1-i}}) \leq \delta$, a key sk′ was sent to $\mathcal{P}_{1-i}$, and $(\mathcal{P}_{1-i}, \mathsf{pw}^{\mathcal{P}_{1-i}})$ was fresh at the time, then output (sid, sk′) to $\mathcal{P}_i$.
- In any other case, pick a new random key sk′ of length λ and send (sid, sk′) to $\mathcal{P}_i$.
- Mark the record $(\mathcal{P}_i, \mathsf{pw}^{\mathcal{P}_i})$ as completed.

Fig. 3. Ideal functionality $\mathcal{F}_{\mathsf{fPAKE}}$ [DHP+18]

On (TestPwd, sid, $\mathcal{P}_i$, pw^*) from the adversary $\mathcal{A}$:
If there is a fresh record $(\mathcal{P}_i, \mathsf{pw}^{\mathcal{P}_i})$, then set $d \leftarrow d(\mathsf{pw}^{\mathcal{P}_i}, \mathsf{pw}^*)$ and do:
- If $d \leq \delta$, mark the record compromised and reply to $\mathcal{A}$ with $L_c(\mathsf{pw}^{\mathcal{P}_i}, \mathsf{pw}^*)$;
- If $\delta < d \leq \gamma$, mark the record compromised and reply to $\mathcal{A}$ with $L_m(\mathsf{pw}^{\mathcal{P}_i}, \mathsf{pw}^*)$;
- If $\gamma < d$, mark the record interrupted and reply to $\mathcal{A}$ with $L_f(\mathsf{pw}^{\mathcal{P}_i}, \mathsf{pw}^*)$.

Fig. 4. A modified TestPwd interface to allow for different leakage [DHP+18]

Correctness of fPAKE. For the same reason as for an iPAKE protocol (see discussion in Sect. 2.4), we also additionally require that a fuzzy PAKE protocol has correctness. Let $(K, K') \leftarrow \mathsf{out}_{\mathcal{A},\pi} \langle \mathcal{P}_0(\mathsf{pw}), \mathcal{P}_1(\mathsf{pw}') \rangle$ denote that $\mathcal{P}_0$ outputs K and $\mathcal{P}_1$ outputs K' when executing π on input pw and pw′, respectively and in the presence of adversary $\mathcal{A}$.

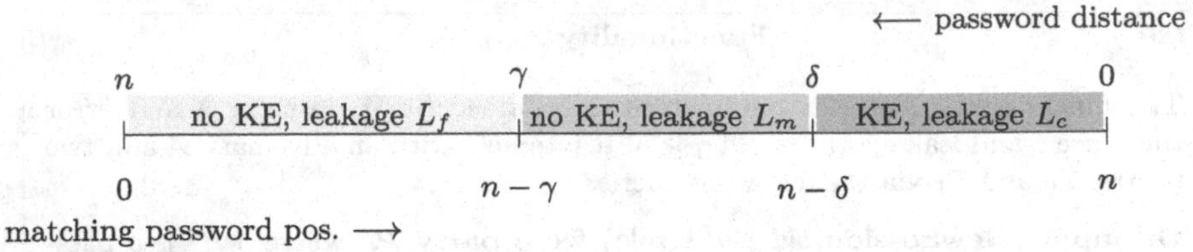

Fig. 5. A graphical explanation of the relaxed TESTPWD interface of Fig. 4. Here, "KE" stands for successful key exchange (e.g., when 0 to δ errors occur), and "no KE" stands for failure of key exchange, i.e., both parties outputting uniformly random strings.

Definition 2. *We say a fuzzy PAKE protocol π is (δ, ε)-correct if for all* pw, pw' $\in \mathcal{D}$ *with* $d(\mathsf{pw}, \mathsf{pw}') \leq \delta$, *where $\mathcal{D}$ is a finite alphabet, and for all passive (i.e., honest-but-curious) adversaries $\mathcal{A}$ the probability that in an execution of π with honest parties $\mathcal{P}_0, \mathcal{P}_1$ the first party $\mathcal{P}_0$ on input* pw *outputs a different key than the second party $\mathcal{P}_1$ on input* pw' *in the presence of $\mathcal{A}$ is bounded above:*

$$\Pr[K \neq K' \mid (K, K') \leftarrow \mathrm{out}_{\mathcal{A}, \pi} \langle \mathcal{P}_0(\mathsf{pw}), \mathcal{P}_1(\mathsf{pw}') \rangle] \leq \varepsilon(\lambda),$$

where the probability is taken over the random coins of $\mathcal{P}_0, \mathcal{P}_1$, and $\mathcal{A}$. We call ε the correctness error. *We just say π is δ-correct if it has negligible correctness error.*

3.2 On the Insecurity of Previous Fuzzy PAKE Constructions

Dupont et al. [DHP+18] proposed a concrete fPAKE protocol (which they call $\pi_{\mathsf{fPAKE}}^{\mathsf{RSS}}$) that uses an implicit PAKE (iPAKE) and an error-correcting code (ECC)[4]. In this section we explain why, in fact, the $\pi_{\mathsf{fPAKE}}^{\mathsf{RSS}}$ protocol does not realize the $\mathcal{F}_{\mathsf{fPAKE}}$ functionality. In order to do so, we first need to discuss the main ideas of $\pi_{\mathsf{fPAKE}}^{\mathsf{RSS}}$. We refer the reader to the original work [DHP+18] for more details.

Description of $\pi_{\mathsf{fPAKE}}^{\mathsf{RSS}}$. Let pw $= (\mathsf{pw}_1, \cdots, \mathsf{pw}_n) \in \mathcal{D} = \mathcal{L}^n$, for some finite alphabet $\mathcal{L}$, be the input password of the Sender and pw $= (\mathsf{pw}_1', \cdots, \mathsf{pw}_n') \in \mathcal{D} = \mathcal{L}^n$ the input password of the Receiver. We typically talk about passwords being vectors of *password characters*. In the first stage of the protocol, the two parties engage in n iPAKE protocols. In the t-th execution, the Sender's input is the t-th password character pw_t and the Receiver's input is pw_t'. Parties receive outputs $K_t, K_t' \in \mathbb{F}_q$ respectively. The iPAKE with the correctness property guarantees that if $\mathsf{pw}_t = \mathsf{pw}_t'$ and there is no attack, then $K_t = K_t'$. Otherwise the keys K_t and K_t' are independent. At the end of this stage, the parties hold *character keys* $\boldsymbol{K} := (K_t)_{t \in [n]}, \boldsymbol{K}' := (K_t')_{t \in [n]} \in \mathbb{F}_q^n$ respectively.

In the second stage, the Sender samples a random field element $U \leftarrow \mathbb{F}_q$ and encodes it using an error correcting code with a hiding property. Let $\boldsymbol{C} \in \mathbb{F}_q^n$

---

[4] As already discussed in the introduction, Dupont et al. [DHP+18] use the terminology of Robust Secret Sharing instead of ECC.

denote the resulting codeword. The Sender now performs a one-time-pad and sends $E := C + K$ to the Receiver. The Receiver computes $C' := E - K'$ and decodes the obtained codeword to U'. The idea is that if K and K' only differ at a few positions, then both codewords C and C' decode to the same value thanks to the error correcting property of the code, and hence both parties output the same key.

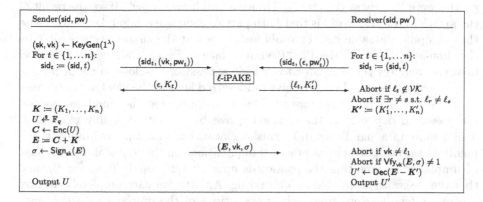

Fig. 6. Description of the $\pi_{\mathsf{fPAKE}}^{\mathsf{RSS}}$ protocol from [DHP+18] that uses n instances of an ℓ-iPAKE and a signature scheme (KeyGen, Sign, Vfy) whose verification key space is $\mathcal{VK}$ and an error-correcting code (Enc, Dec).

In order to realize the $\mathcal{F}_{\mathsf{fPAKE}}$ functionality, one needs to bind the n iPAKE executions and the final message together, as otherwise, active attacks on individual iPAKE instances allow to derive information about the corresponding password characters as observed already in [DHP+18]. To this end, the protocol $\pi_{\mathsf{fPAKE}}^{\mathsf{RSS}}$ actually makes use of a *labelled* iPAKE (or ℓ-iPAKE for short). In a nutshell, ℓ-iPAKE allows each party to additionally input a public label that serves as a public authentication string (i.e., any tampering with the label can be detected efficiently). The Sender then samples a signing key pair (sk, vk) at the beginning of the $\pi_{\mathsf{fPAKE}}^{\mathsf{RSS}}$ protocol and uses vk as their label in all ℓ-iPAKE executions. The Receiver checks that all the output labels of the ℓ-iPAKE executions are the same and aborts if this is not the case. In the last message, the Sender sends their signature $\sigma = \mathsf{Sign}_{\mathsf{sk}}(E)$ and vk to the Receiver in addition to E. The Receiver aborts if vk is not equal to the output labels of the ℓ-iPAKE instances or with the signature does not verify. See Fig. 6 for a schematic description of the protocol.

Attack on $\pi_{\mathsf{fPAKE}}^{\mathsf{RSS}}$. It turns out that the way ℓ-iPAKE instances and the last message were tightened together in the $\pi_{\mathsf{fPAKE}}^{\mathsf{RSS}}$ protocol is not sufficient to realize the $\mathcal{F}_{\mathsf{fPAKE}}$ functionality. Let us assume that both parties enter passwords pw, pw' whose distance is exactly at the threshold δ, i.e., $d(\mathsf{pw}, \mathsf{pw}') = \delta$. This means that the fPAKE would yield matching keys for both parties if there was no active attack on the protocol. The adversary can now make one of the ℓ-iPAKE key exchanges fail by making a wrong guess (without loss of generality, assume the first one). This perfectly emulates a situation where the first password values pw_1 and pw_1' mismatch. Now, imagine a simulator that ensures indistinguishability of the ideal execution of $\mathcal{F}_{\mathsf{fPAKE}}$ from the real protocol execution $\pi_{\mathsf{fPAKE}}^{\mathsf{RSS}}$ where parties make calls to the ℓ-iPAKE instances. The simulator's task is to figure out whether the described attack actually constitutes a successful DoS attack against the whole fPAKE or not, i.e., whether the passwords entered by both parties were already at the error tolerance δ and if $pw_1 = pw_1'$. If so, the result of the attack in the real world is that both parties compute random keys, otherwise they compute the same key. The only leakage about the passwords accessible by the simulator is through the TESTPWD interface of $\mathcal{F}_{\mathsf{fPAKE}}$. Calling this interface, however, requires the simulator to provide a password γ-close to pw or pw', as otherwise parties will already receive randomized keys in the ideal world because of the session getting `interrupted`. The probability that the simulator guesses the password depends on the dictionary size but is not negligibly close to 1. This results in a significant distinguishing advantage for the environment. We highlight that this attack has practical implications on the protocol. For the sake of simplicity, assume that the passwords must match exactly (i.e., $\delta = 0$), and that the password is encoded as a bit string. An attacker can completely retrieve a user's n-bit password from only n executions of the protocol with that user by guessing one bit per execution. Whenever key exchange is successful the bit was guessed correctly. For $\delta > 0$, the attack needs slightly more guesses as the attacker must ensure that the distance from his guess to the user's password is exactly at the δ boundary before the bit-wise guessing will work. We now describe the attack more formally.

Formalizing the Attack on $\pi_{\mathsf{fPAKE}}^{\mathsf{RSS}}$. To formalize the attack, we need to show that for every simulator $\mathcal{S}$ there exists an environment $\mathcal{Z}$ that can distinguish the interaction with the hybrid world adversary and the protocol from the interaction with the simulator and the ideal functionality with non-negligible probability. In fact, in Fig. 7, we describe a distinguishing environment $\mathcal{Z}$ that can distinguish the hybrid and ideal worlds with non-negligible probability *for all* PPT simulators.

Let us first look at the pseudocode in Fig. 7 and consider that $\mathcal{Z}$ interacts with the hybrid world (i.e., the protocol $\pi_{\mathsf{fPAKE}}^{\mathsf{RSS}}$ making calls to $\mathcal{F}_{\ell\text{-iPAKE}}$, and the real world dummy adversary $\mathcal{A}$ that does what $\mathcal{Z}$ tells them to do). One can easily observe that if the environment's choice bit is set to $b = 0$, then the attack results in DoS (i.e., output keys sk and sk' are chosen uniformly at random) and if $b = 1$, the attack does not disturb the key exchange (i.e. sk = sk'). Hence, if $\mathcal{Z}$ interacts with the hybrid world, they will correctly output HYBRID except with negligible probability (note that $\Pr[\mathsf{sk} = \mathsf{sk}' \mid \mathsf{sk} \xleftarrow{\$} \mathbb{F}_q, \mathsf{sk}' \xleftarrow{\$} \mathbb{F}_q] = \frac{1}{q}$, where $q \approx 2^\lambda$).

Let us now focus on the ideal world, where $\mathcal{Z}$ interacts with the ideal functionality $\mathcal{F}_{\mathsf{fPAKE}}$ and a simulator $\mathcal{S}$. The task of $\mathcal{S}$ is to make $\mathcal{F}_{\mathsf{fPAKE}}$ produce an output indistinguishable from the hybrid world described above. Let us first summarize all the information that $\mathcal{S}$ gets. From the environment, $\mathcal{S}$ receives

$\mathsf{pw}_1^* \in \mathbb{F}_p$ and we can assume that $\mathcal{S}$ knows that this character is different from pw_1. According to the definition of $\mathcal{F}_{\mathsf{fPAKE}}$, $\mathcal{S}$ gets no information about the passwords $\mathbf{pw}, \mathbf{pw}'$ from $\mathcal{F}_{\mathsf{fPAKE}}$ by default. The only way $\mathcal{S}$ could get information via $\mathcal{F}_{\mathsf{fPAKE}}$ is through the TESTPWD interface, where $\mathcal{S}$ has to guess $\mathbf{pw}$ or $\mathbf{pw}'$. If $\mathcal{S}$ guesses one of the passwords wrong, this password gets marked as `interrupted`, which means that the simulator loses all power over the keys being output to both parties (i.e. each party gets a randomly sampled key). In order to get useful information about the passwords via the TESTPWD interface without causing random keys, the simulator would have to make a close enough guess of one of the passwords. But since $\mathcal{S}$ knows only that $\mathsf{pw}_1 \neq \mathsf{pw}_1^*$ and the passwords were chosen uniformly at random, the probability that $\mathcal{S}$ succeeds in guessing is not negligibly close to 1 (the exact probability depends, of course, on the size of the dictionary and γ).

Hence, if $\mathcal{S}$ could ensure that the ideal and hybrid worlds were indistinguishable, then $\mathcal{S}$ would be able to guess b correctly with non-negligible probability. Since b was chosen uniformly at random from $\{0, 1\}$ by $\mathcal{Z}$, this is information-theoretically impossible.

---

1. Sample a bit $b \in \{0, 1\}$ uniformly at random.
2. Sample $\mathbf{pw} = (\mathsf{pw}_1, \ldots, \mathsf{pw}_n) \in \mathbb{F}_p^n$ uniformly at random.
3. Choose a random $\mathbf{pw}' = (\mathsf{pw}_1', \ldots, \mathsf{pw}_n') \in \mathbb{F}_p^n$ s.t. (1) $d(\mathbf{pw}, \mathbf{pw}') = \delta$ and (2) $\mathsf{pw}_1' = \mathsf{pw}_1$ if $b = 0$ and $\mathsf{pw}_1' \neq \mathsf{pw}_1$ if $b = 1$.
4. Choose $\mathsf{pw}_1^* \in \mathbb{F}_p \setminus \{\mathsf{pw}_1\}$.
5. Send (NEWSESSION, sid, $\mathbf{pw}$, Sender) to $\mathcal{P}_0$ and (NEWSESSION, sid, $\mathbf{pw}'$, Receiver) to party $\mathcal{P}_1$, where sid chosen arbitrarily.
6. Upon receiving (NEWSESSION, (sid, 1), $\mathcal{P}_0$, Sender) and (NEWSESSION, (sid, 1), $\mathcal{P}_1$, Receiver), instruct the adversary to send (TESTPWD, (sid, 1), $\mathcal{P}_0$, pw_1^*).
7. Instruct the adversary to send (NEWKEY, (sid, 1), $\mathcal{P}_0$, sk_1) and then (NEWKEY, (sid, 1), $\mathcal{P}_1$, sk_1) for an arbitrary key sk_1.
8. For every $t = 2, \ldots, n$:
   (a) Upon receiving (NEWSESSION, (sid, t), $\mathcal{P}_0$, Sender) and (NEWSESSION, (sid, t), $\mathcal{P}_1$, Receiver), instruct the adversary to send (NEWKEY, (sid, t), $\mathcal{P}_0$, sk_t) and then (NEWKEY, (sid, t), $\mathcal{P}_1$, sk_t) for an arbitrary key sk_t.
9. Upon receiving (sid, sk) from $\mathcal{P}_0$ and (sid, sk) from $\mathcal{P}_1$ distinguish the following two cases:
   – $b = 0$: If $\mathsf{sk} \neq \mathsf{sk}'$, output HYBRID. Otherwise, output IDEAL.
   – $b = 1$: If $\mathsf{sk} = \mathsf{sk}$, output HYBRID. Otherwise, output IDEAL.

Fig. 7. Pseudocode of an environment $\mathcal{Z}$ distinguishing the interaction with the $\pi_{\mathsf{fPAKE}}^{\mathsf{RSS}}$ protocol in the $\mathcal{F}_{\ell\text{-iPAKE}}$ hybrid world from the interaction with the $\mathcal{F}_{\mathsf{fPAKE}}$ ideal functionality.

3.3   Towards Repairing the Previous Construction

In their work, Dupont et al. mention an alternative way of binding the iPAKE instances and the last message together (see footnote 6 on page 26 of the eprint version of their paper [DHP+17]). Instead of using labels and a one-time signature scheme, they suggest letting the two parties sign every message using the split transformation put forward by Barak et al. [BCL+05]. A natural first step when trying to fix the $\pi_{\mathsf{fPAKE}}^{\mathsf{RSS}}$ protocol is hence to follow this alternative approach. Unfortunately, it turns out that applying the split transformation is not straightforward.

At a very high level, the split transformation is a generic way to transform a protocol realizing an ideal functionality $\mathcal{F}$ *assuming authenticated channels* into a protocol that achieves the same without authenticated channels.[5] Instead, the transformed protocol works in the $\mathcal{F}_{\mathsf{SA}}$-hybrid world, where $\mathcal{F}_{\mathsf{SA}}$ is the ideal functionality for split authentication recalled in Sect. 2.5.

Intuitively, this seems to be exactly what is needed to bind the iPAKE instances and the message of $\pi_{\mathsf{fPAKE}}^{\mathsf{RSS}}$ together. Let $\pi_{\mathsf{fPAKE}}^{\mathsf{plain}}$ denote the protocol which is defined exactly as $\pi_{\mathsf{fPAKE}}^{\mathsf{RSS}}$ except that it uses $\mathcal{F}_{\mathsf{iPAKE}}$ instead of $\mathcal{F}_{\ell\text{-}\mathsf{iPAKE}}$ instances and the sender does not sign the last message. Assume that the sender and the receiver have an authenticated channel available which they can use for all the communication happening during all the n iPAKE executions and parties can use the same channel for the last message. Then the $\pi_{\mathsf{fPAKE}}^{\mathsf{plain}}$ protocol would be a secure fuzzy PAKE. Unfortunately, this intuition is misleading as it does not reflect the UC formalization of the $\pi_{\mathsf{fPAKE}}^{\mathsf{RSS}}$ protocol correctly.

The core of the problem is that the result of Barak et al. does not apply to hybrid protocols like $\pi_{\mathsf{fPAKE}}^{\mathsf{plain}}$. In a bit more detail, recall that the protocol $\pi_{\mathsf{fPAKE}}^{\mathsf{plain}}$ is defined in the $\mathcal{F}_{\mathsf{iPAKE}}$-hybrid world. This, in particular, means that the only message sent between the sender and the receiver in $\pi_{\mathsf{fPAKE}}^{\mathsf{plain}}$ is the last message. The rest of the protocol consists of the communication between a party and $\mathcal{F}_{\mathsf{iPAKE}}$ ideal functionality. Sending (only) the last message over an authenticated channel would not help us to bind the n iPAKE executions together, so such a protocol could not realize $\mathcal{F}_{\mathsf{fPAKE}}$. Hence, applying the split transformation does not have the desired effect of protecting against active attacks on individual password characters, like the one described in Fig. 7, in $\pi_{\mathsf{fPAKE}}^{\mathsf{RSS}}$.

Our Approach. To address this issue, we define a protocol that does not work in the $\mathcal{F}_{\mathsf{iPAKE}}$-hybrid world. Instead, it lets the Sender and the Receiver run the code of a protocol π_{iPAKE} realizing $\mathcal{F}_{\mathsf{iPAKE}}$ directly. In a bit more detail, let us assume that the Sender received $\mathsf{pw} = (\mathsf{pw}_1, \ldots, \mathsf{pw}_n)$ as input. For every $t \in [n]$, our protocol instructs the Sender to run the code of the π_{iPAKE}-sender on input pw_t. Whenever the π_{iPAKE}-sender would have sent a message to the π_{iPAKE}-receiver instance, the Sender does so via the channel available for the two parties in our protocol. The Receiver in our protocol is defined analogously. This way,

---

[5] This is an oversimplified statement as the transformed protocol does not realize $\mathcal{F}$ but its *split variant*, denoted $s\mathcal{F}$. See the work of Barak et al. [BCL+05] for more details.

all communication happening during the iPAKE executions and the last message are sent via the same channel between the Sender and the Receiver. Hence, the split transformation will have the desired effect. We formally prove this intuitive statement in the next section, where we define our final protocol precisely.

Potential Alternative Approach. Another way to resolve the insufficient binding of the iPAKE instances and the last message together could be to define a new building block, "batched iPAKE". This new iPAKE primitive would take as input a vector $(\mathsf{pw}_t)_{t \in [n]}$ and output a vector $(K_t)_{t \in [n]}$. An adversary would be allowed to make a TESTPWD query, but would always have to test all password characters $(\mathsf{pw}_t^*)_{t \in [n]}$. Hence, the adversary would be forced to launch a man-in-the-middle attack either against all iPAKE instances, or none of them, which would guarantee the binding of the iPAKEs. In order to bind iPAKEs to the last message, we would require the "batch iPAKE" to be labelled. As in $\pi_{\mathsf{fPAKE}}^{\mathsf{RSS}}$, the sender would use their verification key as a label and then use the corresponding signing key to sign the last message.

4 Our Construction

General Idea. The idea behind our construction is very simple: we modify the fuzzy PAKE of Dupont et al. [DHP+18] by letting the receiver apply list decoding instead of unique decoding. Since now the receiver ends up with a list of potential key candidates (or codewords, more precisely), we additionally let the sender compute a "hint" on which codeword is the correct one. More formally, the sender adds the hash of the original codeword $h := H(C)$ to the last message. The receiver applies list decoding which results in a list of candidates $C^1, \ldots, C^\ell$. They then find the one that satisfies $h = H(C^j)$ and compute $U \leftarrow \mathsf{Dec}(C^j)$. The value h is a hint on which of the candidates is the correct one. The benefit of our construction is that it can correct more errors in the password: for a Reed-Solomon code of rank k and block length n, unique decoding can correct up to $\lfloor \frac{n-k}{2} \rfloor$ errors (Lemma 1), while list decoding outputs a list containing the original codeword in the presence of $n - 1 - \sqrt{(k-1)n}$ errors. Figure 2 provides several numerical examples of these terms, demonstrating that for growing password sizes, the list decoding approach yields a significantly better error correction capability than the unique decoding approach in [DHP+18].

On the other hand, it is *not* intuitively clear that the extra information passed from the sender to the receiver does not void any of the security guarantees of the protocol. To give an example, consider a different kind of hint $\bar{h} := H(\mathsf{sk})$, where sk is the output key of the sender. Such a hint helps the receiver to choose its output key just as well as the hint $h := H(C)$. However, a fuzzy PAKE protocol sending $\bar{h}$ cannot realize $\mathcal{F}_{\mathsf{fPAKE}}$. The reason is that $\bar{h}$ depends deterministically on secret information known to the sender (namely its output key sk), and hence it leaves no wiggle room for a simulator, who simply has to guess sk in order to simulate correctly. While the hint $H(C)$ does include some randomness contributed by the sender to the encoding algorithm Enc, it is not straightforward to see that the resulting fuzzy PAKE is simulatable, meaning that it does not involuntarily reveal any information about the sender's password through the hint.

Hence, in the remainder of this section, we carefully analyze the security of our fuzzy PAKE protocol given in Fig. 8.

Formal Protocol Description. The protocol is depicted in Fig. 8. To be able to fix previous issues of imperfect binding of messages, and as detailed in Sect. 3.2, we let parties send messages to each other over functionality $\mathcal{F}_{\mathsf{SA}}$ (the functionality was briefly discussed in Sect. 2.5 and is formally defined in the full version of the paper). The protocol parties take a password from a dictionary $\mathcal{D} = \mathcal{L}^n$ as input, where $\mathcal{L}$ is some finite alphabet. We write that the sender chooses $s \xleftarrow{\$} \mathbb{F}_q^k$ and encodes it using $\mathsf{Enc}(s)$. One can equivalently say that the sender chooses a message $s_0 \xleftarrow{\$} \mathbb{F}_q$ and randomness $r \xleftarrow{\$} \mathbb{F}_q^{k-1}$ and uses the randomized encoding $\overline{\mathsf{Enc}}(s_0, r)$. To make our protocol description modular, let π_j denote an instance of a protocol that UC-realizes $\mathcal{F}_{\mathsf{iPAKE}}$. We write $X \leftarrow \pi_j(\mathcal{P}_i, \mathsf{sid}, \mathsf{pw}^{\mathcal{P}_i})$ to denote that $\mathcal{P}_i$ outputs X when running π_j on sid and $\mathsf{pw}^{\mathcal{P}_i}$ and $K \leftarrow \pi_j(\mathcal{P}_i, \mathsf{sid}, X)$ to denote that $\mathcal{P}_i$ outputs K as response to input X when running π_j on sid. For the sake of simplicity, we assume that the π_j protocols are one-round protocols. For multi-round protocols, one can send every message again over $\mathcal{F}_{\mathsf{SA}}$ to the respective other party, like in the first round. Note that it is important that the receiver only continues the computation with codewords that are within distance of δ to $\boldsymbol{E} \oplus \boldsymbol{K'}$. Otherwise, the receiver might output the same key as the sender, even when the passwords were not close enough. We ensure this by letting LDec only output codewords within distance of δ to the input. As explained in Sect. 2 this can easily be guaranteed by letting LDec discard codewords with distance $> \delta$. A more formal description of the protocol, using the interfaces of $\mathcal{F}_{\mathsf{fPAKE}}$ can be found in the full version of the paper.

We start by proving the correctness of our protocol.

Theorem 1. *If $\mathcal{C}$ is a randomized linear code which is efficiently δ-list decodable, H_1 is a ε_2-collision-resistant hash function and π is ε_1-correct and UC-realizes $\mathcal{F}_{\mathsf{iPAKE}}$, then the protocol in Fig. 8 is (δ, ε_0)-correct for*

$$\varepsilon_0 = n\varepsilon_1 + \varepsilon_2.$$

Remark 1 (Implications for previous results). Note that our construction implies (a fixed version of) the original fuzzy PAKE of Dupont et al. [DHP+18] when falling back to unique decoding algorithms. Indeed, one can simply set the list size of the list decoding algorithm to 1 and thus obtain unique decoding instead of list decoding as in [DHP+18], preserving our security analysis. There are two notable differences in this "fallback" version of our fuzzy PAKE and the one of [DHP+18]. First, our version applies a proper binding mechanism by using the split functionality $\mathcal{F}_{\mathsf{SA}}$ for sending messages [BCL+05], at the cost of one signature per message (see the full version of the paper for the concrete instantiation). Second, our security proof does not rely on the smoothness property of

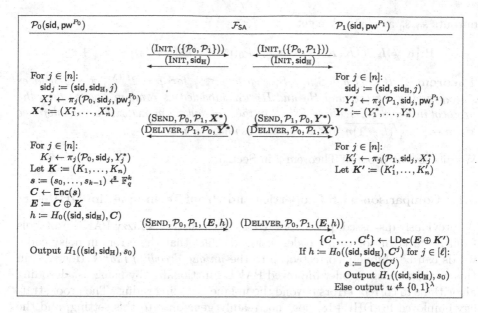

Fig. 8. The protocol in the $\mathcal{F}_{\mathsf{SA}}$-hybrid model. We drop sid from all messages for brevity. We recall $\mathcal{F}_{\mathsf{SA}}$ in the full version of the paper, but for the sake of understanding our protocol it is enough to know that $\mathcal{F}_{\mathsf{SA}}$ is used to transmit the protocol messages. With π_j we denote an instances of a protocol that UC-realizes $\mathcal{F}_{\mathsf{iPAKE}}$ (as described in the full version of the paper). We write $X \leftarrow \pi_j(\mathcal{P}_i, \mathsf{sid}, \mathsf{pw}^{\mathcal{P}_i})$ to denote that $\mathcal{P}_i$ outputs X when running π_j on sid with password $\mathsf{pw}^{\mathcal{P}_i}$ and $K \leftarrow \pi_j(\mathcal{P}_i, \mathsf{sid}, X)$ to denote that $\mathcal{P}_i$ outputs K as response to input X when running π_j on sid.

the underlying code. This enables the usage of a variety of codes for which such properties are not well researched, or do not hold at all.

Proof. Assume that two honest parties $\mathcal{P}_0, \mathcal{P}_1$ execute the protocol from Fig. 8 on inputs $\mathsf{pw}^{\mathcal{P}_0}$ and $\mathsf{pw}^{\mathcal{P}_1}$ with $d(\mathsf{pw}^{\mathcal{P}_0}, \mathsf{pw}^{\mathcal{P}_1}) \leq \delta$, respectively. Further, assume that the adversary $\mathcal{A}$ attacking this protocol is passive. Each instance π_j of π is ε_1-correct by assumption (see Definition 1). We construct a sequence of hybrids $\mathcal{H}_0, \ldots, \mathcal{H}_n$ where in the j-th hybrid, we abort the execution of the protocol if the two parties of π_j output different keys even though the respective inputs $\mathsf{pw}_j^{\mathcal{P}_0}$ and $\mathsf{pw}_j^{\mathcal{P}_1}$ are the same. By the ε_1-correctness of π, $\mathcal{H}_j$ differs from $\mathcal{H}_{j-1}$ at most by ε_1 for each $j \in \{1, \ldots, n\}$. Now in $\mathcal{H}_n$, as we have $d(\mathsf{pw}^{\mathcal{P}_0}, \mathsf{pw}^{\mathcal{P}_1}) \leq \delta$, there are at least $n - \delta$ instances of π where $\mathcal{P}_0$ and $\mathcal{P}_1$ run on matching inputs $\mathsf{pw}_j^{\mathcal{P}_0}$ and $\mathsf{pw}_j^{\mathcal{P}_1}$. Thus, we have $K_j = K_j'$ for at least $n - \delta$ keys. So the codeword $C' = E \oplus K'$ that the receiver computes differs from the sender's C on at most δ entries. As $\mathcal{C}$ is δ-list decodable, the list that is output by LDec contains the same C that the sender encoded. Now assume that there are two possible words C, C^* with $s = \mathsf{Dec}(C)$ and $s^* = \mathsf{Dec}(C^*)$ such that $H_1((\mathsf{sid}, \mathsf{sid}_H), s_0) = H_1((\mathsf{sid}, \mathsf{sid}_H), s_0^*)$ with probability ε_2. One can construct an adversary against the collision-resistance of H_1 that internally runs $\mathcal{P}_0(\mathsf{pw}^{\mathcal{P}_0})$ and $\mathcal{P}_1(\mathsf{pw}^{\mathcal{P}_1})$ and outputs s_0, s_0^* as above. We get

$$\Pr[K \neq K' \mid (K, K') \leftarrow \mathrm{out}_{\mathcal{A},\pi}\langle \mathcal{P}_0(\mathsf{pw}^{P_0}), \mathcal{P}_1(\mathsf{pw}^{P_1})\rangle] \leq n\varepsilon_1 + \varepsilon_2.$$

Theorem 2. *If $\mathcal{C}$ is a $\mathcal{RS}[n, k, S]$ code over $\mathbb{F}_q$ for $q = 2^{\Omega(\lambda)}$, π UC-realizes $\mathcal{F}_{iPAKE}$ and is correct, and H_0 and H_1 are modeled as random oracles then the protocol in Fig. 8 UC-realizes $\mathcal{F}_{fPAKE}^M$ in the $\mathcal{F}_{SA}$-hybrid model with error tolerance $\delta = n - 1 - \sqrt{(k-1)n}$ and leakage threshold $\gamma = n - k$.*

We discuss the proof of Theorem 2 in Sect. 5.

4.1 Comparison with Properties and Proof Techniques in [DHP+18]

As previously discussed, prior work [DHP+18] constructs fuzzy PAKE protocols from linear error-correcting codes, using the fact that the errors in noisy codewords can be uniquely corrected up to the *unique decoding radius*. However, in this work, we wish to offer improved PAKE functionality by using list-decoding algorithms to correct errors beyond the unique decoding radius. The proof strategy employed in [DHP+18] does not readily generalise to this setting, and the presence of the hint h becomes crucial in the proof of Theorem 2, as we will explain.

The PAKE construction of [DHP+18] builds fuzzy PAKE protocols from robust secret-sharing (RSS) schemes with various special properties, which are in turn constructed from linear error-correcting codes. First, we summarize the RSS properties used in the PAKE construction of [DHP+18] and rephrase them as properties of error-correcting codes. Then, we describe the techniques used in the proof of the *reconstruction* and *smoothness* properties, and how this proof strategy leads to challenges when we generalize to list-decoding. Finally, we explain how the inclusion of the hint h allows us to circumvent these issues.

RSS Properties in [DHP+18]. An RSS scheme consists of a sharing algorithm, which takes a message as input and produces n output shares, and a reconstruction algorithm, which, on input a list of (possibly corrupted) shares, returns a secret.

In this work, in line with our study of PAKE protocols from a decoding perspective, we phrase our algorithms in terms of randomised error-correcting codes as in Sect. 2.2, instead of RSS schemes. With this view, the randomised encoding algorithm $\overline{\mathsf{Enc}}$ simply corresponds to a share algorithm with message space generalised from $\mathbb{F}$ to $\mathbb{F}^{k_M}$, and explicit random input $\boldsymbol{R} \in \mathbb{F}^{k_R}$.

The PAKE construction of [DHP+18] uses the following properties of randomised encoding algorithms (with their corresponding RSS terminology from [DHP+18] included for clarity):

- B-query uniformity (Sect. 2.3), which corresponds to strong B-privacy for RSS;
- the existence of an efficient algorithm for e-error correction (Sect. 2.2), which corresponds to e-robustness for RSS;

– for all $E \subseteq [n]$ with $|E| \leq e$, all $M \in \mathbb{F}^{k_M}$, the distribution of

$$\left\{ \text{Dec}(V) \colon R \leftarrow \mathbb{F}^{k_R}, V|_E := \overline{\text{Enc}}(M, R)|_E, V|_{\bar{E}} \leftarrow \mathbb{F}^{\bar{E}} \right\} \tag{1}$$

is uniform over $\mathbb{F}^{k_M}$. This corresponds to e-smoothness for RSS;
– e-smoothness on random secrets. This is similar to e-smoothness except that M is also sampled uniformly at random from $\mathbb{F}^{k_M}$.

The authors of [DHP+18] give a construction of a randomised linear code with each of the above properties from a standard linear error correcting code. The construction was originally given as an RSS.

Lemma 3 ([DHP+18, **Lemma 5**], **restated**). *Given an $[n + 1, k, n - k + 2]$-linear code C_0, there is a $[n, k, n - k + 1]$ randomised linear code C with $k_M = 1$, $(k - 1)$-smoothness, $(k - 1)$-query uniformity, $\lfloor \frac{n+k}{2} \rfloor$-error correction and $(\lfloor \frac{n+k}{2} \rfloor - 1)$-smoothness on random secrets.*

Arguing Smoothness and Decoding Properties for Lemma 3. The proof of Lemma 3 in [DHP+18] starts by defining C to be the code obtained by puncturing C_0 in its last coordinate. Then, $(k - 1)$-smoothness is proved with respect to the following decoding algorithm. On input a codeword in C', the decoding algorithm selects the subvector of k entries of the codeword and then inverts the submatrix of the generator matrix of C' corresponding to these entries on the subvector to find the original message. Finally, this message vector is combined with the column of the generator matrix of C corresponding to its last coordinate.

Intuitively, in the case of Reed-Solomon codes, this is like choosing k codeword entries of a punctured codeword with the last entry missing, and then interpolating to find out what the last entry should be.

With this decoding algorithm, it is relatively easy to prove smoothness, because V in Eq. (1) has at least $n - k + 1$ random entries, so at least one entry out of the k entries is random. Based on the MDS properties of C, one can show that the "last coordinate" computed from the k selected entries must also be random.

In order for this decoding algorithm to be robust, it must be able to select k error-free positions. Otherwise, the submatrix inversion step will incorporate an error and produce an incorrect message. In the case of Reed-Solomon codes, this could be achieved by using another decoding algorithm (such as the Berlekamp-Welch algorithm) to identify these positions.

Therefore, proving the smoothness property relies heavily on the MDS properties of C and the existence of efficient decoding algorithms to allow errors in the codeword to be located.

Moving Beyond the Unique Decoding Radius. In this work, we intend to construct a PAKE scheme which works for errors beyond the unique decoding radius. In this high-error setting, the natural replacement for a decoding algorithm is a list-decoding algorithm, which produces all possible codewords within a particular radius of the transmitted word. The first challenge for our PAKE algorithm to overcome was to allow the sender and receiver to agree on the same password, even though decoding may no longer produce a unique codeword which can be used to determine the password. We solve this problem by way of the hint $h = H(C)$.

Another challenge is the fact that smoothness, an important property in the security proofs of [DHP+18], relies heavily on the special decoding strategy introduced, which must apply a linear map to error-free positions in a codeword in order to ensure robustness. In this high-error setting, it may be impossible to identify a unique set of error-free positions in a codeword. Thus, the decoding strategy above, which involves inverting the generator matrix on an error-free set of codeword entries, may not be possible either. Therefore, it seems challenging to construct a list-decoding algorithm with a generalised smoothness property via a linear decoding algorithm that still returns the correct codeword somewhere in its list, as the linear decoding step may always be applied to strings with errors instead of error-free positions.

However, amazingly, the hint that we introduce lets us circumvent this issue. In order to prove our PAKE protocol secure, we require only that the list decoding algorithm will not produce the same codeword provided by the hint after many random errors are added to it. This follows almost trivially as adding a large number of random errors produces a string which is so far away from the original codeword that the list decoding algorithm cannot produce the original codeword. This is discussed in detail in the full version of the paper.

5   Proof of Security

To prove that the protocol in Fig. 8 UC-realizes $\mathcal{F}_{\mathsf{fPAKE}}^M$, we have to show that every PPT environment $\mathcal{Z}$ has at most negligible advantage in distinguishing a real execution of the protocol from an ideal execution, with $\mathcal{F}_{\mathsf{fPAKE}}^M$ and the simulator that we show in Figs. 9 to 10. We show this using a sequence of hybrid games. In the following, we give intuition for each of the game hops and prove the necessary lemmas. We defer the full proof of Theorem 2 to the full version of the paper.

On Using Other iPAKE Protocols than EKE: The current simulator in Figs. 9 to 10 is written keeping in mind an iPAKE protocol in which each party only sends one message. However, the simulator can be easily adapted to work with any iPAKE protocol as follows: Instead of forwarding only one set of messages ($\{Z_j^*\}_{j=1}^n$) between $\mathcal{Z}$ and the iPAKE simulators, $\mathcal{S}$ would forward all iPAKE messages between $\mathcal{Z}$ and the corresponding iPAKE simulator.

Proof (Sketch) . We depict a UC execution of Fig. 8 in the full version of the paper, which makes all the interfaces of $\mathcal{F}_{\mathsf{fPAKE}}$ explicit. The general proof strategy of showing indistinguishability of this protocol from $\mathcal{F}_{\mathsf{fPAKE}}$ is to start with

On (NEWSESSION, sid, $\mathcal{P}_i$, role) from $\mathcal{F}_{\mathsf{fPAKE}}$ or (INIT, ($\{\mathcal{P}_0, \mathcal{P}_1\}$, sid)) from a corrupted $\mathcal{P}_i$ to $\mathcal{F}_{\mathsf{SA}}$:
- Create record $\langle \mathcal{P}_i, \mathsf{sid}, \mathsf{role}, \bot \rangle$ and mark it **fresh**.
- Send (INIT, ($\{\mathcal{P}_0, \mathcal{P}_1\}$, sid)) to $\mathcal{Z}$ in the name of $\mathcal{F}_{\mathsf{SA}}$.

On (INIT, sid, $\mathcal{P}_i$, $\mathbb{H}$, $\mathsf{sid}_{\mathbb{H}}$) from $\mathcal{Z}$ in the name of $\mathcal{A}$ to $\mathcal{F}_{\mathsf{SA}}$:
- Perform the same checks as $\mathcal{F}_{\mathsf{SA}}$ on $\mathsf{sid}_{\mathbb{H}}$ and $\mathbb{H}$ and ignore the message if one of them fails.
- Record $\langle \mathbb{H}, \mathsf{sid}_{\mathbb{H}} \rangle$.
- If $\mathcal{P}_i$ is corrupted then provide output (INIT, sid, $\mathsf{sid}_{\mathbb{H}}$) to $\mathcal{P}_i$. Regardless:
  - If $\mathbb{H} = \{\mathcal{P}_0, \mathcal{P}_1\}$ then set MitM $:= 0$.
  - Else if $\mathbb{H} = \{\mathcal{P}_i\}$ set MitM $:= 1$.
- Retrieve $\langle \mathcal{P}_i, \mathsf{sid}, \mathsf{role}, \bot \rangle$ and replace $\bot$ by MitM.
- If there is not already an instance of $\mathcal{S}_{\mathsf{iPAKE}}$ for session-id $(\mathsf{sid}, \mathsf{sid}_{\mathbb{H}}, j)$ for $j \in [n]$ create one. // I.e., create $\{\mathcal{S}_{\mathsf{iPAKE}}^j\}_{j=1}^n$ if MitM $= 1$ or if MitM $= 0$ and $\{\mathcal{S}_{\mathsf{iPAKE}}^j\}_{j=1}^n$ are not yet created for $\mathcal{P}_{1-i}$.
- For all $j \in [n]$ send (NEWSESSION, $(\mathsf{sid}, \mathsf{sid}_{\mathbb{H}}, j)$, $\mathcal{P}_i$, role) to $\mathcal{S}_{\mathsf{iPAKE}}^j$.
- Upon receiving output Z_j^* from all n instances of $\mathcal{S}_{\mathsf{iPAKE}}$, send $(\mathsf{sid}, \mathcal{P}_i, \mathcal{P}_{1-i}, \mathsf{msg} := (Z_1^*, \ldots, Z_n^*))$ formatted as coming from $\mathcal{F}_{\mathsf{SA}}$ to $\mathcal{Z}$ and store $\langle \mathsf{sid}, \mathcal{P}_i, \mathcal{P}_{1-i}, \mathsf{msg} \rangle$.

On instruction from $\mathcal{Z}$ to send (DELIVER, sid, $\mathcal{P}_i$, $\mathcal{P}_{1-i}$, $\mathsf{msg} := \{Z_j^*\}_{j=1}^n$) to $\mathcal{F}_{\mathsf{SA}}$:
- If MitM $= 0$:
  - If message msg is the one that $\mathcal{S}$ sent, i.e. $\mathcal{S}$ has a record $\langle \mathsf{sid}, \mathcal{P}_i, \mathcal{P}_{1-i}, \mathsf{msg} \rangle$:
    * Give instruction to $\mathcal{S}_{\mathsf{iPAKE}}^j$ to send message Z_j^* to $\mathcal{P}_{1-i}$ in the name of $\mathcal{P}_i$.
    * Remove one appearance of the record $\langle \mathsf{sid}, \mathcal{P}_i, \mathcal{P}_{1-i}, \mathsf{msg} \rangle$.
  - Else: do nothing. // message manipulated
- Else // if MitM $= 1$
  - Give instruction to $\mathcal{S}_{\mathsf{iPAKE}}^j$ to send message Z_j^* to $\mathcal{P}_{1-i}$ in the name of $\mathcal{P}_i$.

On (TESTPWD, $(\mathsf{sid}, \mathsf{sid}_{\mathbb{H}}, j)$, $\mathcal{P}_i$, pw_j') from $\mathcal{S}_{\mathsf{iPAKE}}^j$ to $\mathcal{F}_{\mathsf{iPAKE}}^j$
- store $\langle \text{test-pwd}, \mathsf{sid}, \mathcal{P}_i, j, \mathsf{pw}_j' \rangle$. // Remember the query. No need to answer

On instruction from $\mathcal{Z}$ to send (DELIVER, sid, $\mathcal{P}_{1-i}$, $\mathcal{P}_i$, $\mathsf{msg} := (E', h')$) to $\mathcal{F}_{\mathsf{SA}}$:
- Retrieve record $\langle \mathcal{P}_i, \mathsf{sid}, \mathsf{role}, \mathsf{MitM}, K \rangle$ marked **waiting**.
- If MitM $= 0$ and both parties of session sid are honest:
  - Remove one appearance of the record $\langle \mathsf{sid}, \mathcal{P}_{1-i}, \mathcal{P}_i, (E', h') \rangle$. // Record exists because no MitM attack.
  - If role $=$ receiver then send (NEWKEY, sid, $\mathcal{P}_i$, $\bot$) to $\mathcal{F}_{\mathsf{fPAKE}}$.
  - Else, ignore this message. // role $=$ sender does not expect this message
- Else // MitM $= 1$ or one of the parties is corrupted
  - If $\mathcal{P}_i$ is honest and role $=$ receiver then
    * Compute $\{C^1, \ldots, C^\ell\} \leftarrow \mathsf{LDec}(E' \oplus K)$.
    * If $h' = H_0((\mathsf{sid}, \mathsf{sid}_{\mathbb{H}}), C^j)$ for $j \in [\ell]$ then set $s := \mathsf{Dec}(C^j)$.
    * If the record $\langle \mathcal{P}_i, \mathsf{sid}, \mathsf{role}, \mathsf{MitM} \rangle$ is marked as **accident**, then choose $\widehat{\mathsf{sk}} \xleftarrow{\$} \{0,1\}^\lambda$.
    * Else if the record $\langle \mathcal{P}_i, \mathsf{sid}, \mathsf{role}, \mathsf{MitM} \rangle$ is marked as **compromised** then set $\widehat{\mathsf{sk}} := H_1((\mathsf{sid}, \mathsf{sid}_{\mathbb{H}}), s_0)$.
    * Else // record interrupted set $\widehat{\mathsf{sk}} := \bot$.
    * Regardless, send (NEWKEY, sid, $\mathcal{P}_i$, $\widehat{\mathsf{sk}}$) to $\mathcal{F}_{\mathsf{fPAKE}}$.
  - Else if $\mathcal{P}_i$ is corrupt then output (RECEIVED, sid, $\mathcal{P}_{1-i}$, $\mathcal{P}_i$, (E', h')) to $\mathcal{P}_i$.
  - Else, ignore this message. // role $=$ sender does not expect this message

On a query $((\mathsf{sid}, \mathsf{sid}_{\mathbb{H}}), s_0)$ to H_1:
- If there is a record $\langle H_1, (\mathsf{sid}, \mathsf{sid}_{\mathbb{H}}), s_0, k \rangle$ return k. Else draw $k \xleftarrow{\$} \{0,1\}^\lambda$, record $\langle H_1, (\mathsf{sid}, \mathsf{sid}_{\mathbb{H}}), s_0, k \rangle$ and return k.

On a query $((\mathsf{sid}, \mathsf{sid}_{\mathbb{H}}), C)$ to H_0:
- If there is a record $\langle H_0, (\mathsf{sid}, \mathsf{sid}_{\mathbb{H}}), C, \rho \rangle$ return ρ. Else draw $\rho \xleftarrow{\$} \{0,1\}^\lambda$. If there is another record $\langle H_0, (\mathsf{sid}, \mathsf{sid}_{\mathbb{H}}), C', \rho' \rangle$ with $C \neq C'$ but $\rho = \rho'$ abort the simulation. Else record $\langle H_0, (\mathsf{sid}, \mathsf{sid}_{\mathbb{H}}), C, \rho \rangle$ and return ρ.

Fig. 9. The first part of the simulator $\mathcal{S}$ for $\mathcal{F}_{\mathsf{fPAKE}}$ and our Fuzzy PAKE with list-decoding protocol. $\mathcal{S}$ simulates $\mathcal{F}_{\mathsf{SA}}$ and the random oracles H_0 and H_1. If we write "retrieve record" and the record does not exist, $\mathcal{S}$ ignores the message.

On $(\text{NewKey}, \text{sid}, \mathcal{P}_i, \text{sk}_j)$ from $\mathcal{S}^j_{\text{iPAKE}}$, record $\langle \text{NewKey}, \text{sid}, \mathcal{P}_i, \text{sk}_j \rangle$. If this is the n-th NewKey query for $\mathcal{P}_i$, do:

- Retrieve record $\langle \mathcal{P}_i, \text{sid}, \text{role}, \text{MitM} \rangle$ marked `fresh`.
- If MitM $= 0$ and both parties of session sid are honest: choose $K \xleftarrow{\$} \mathbb{F}_q^n$.
- Else // MitM $= 1$ or one of the parties is corrupted, then retrieve records $\langle \text{test-pwd}, \text{sid}, \mathcal{P}_i, j, \text{pw}'_j \rangle$ for any $j \in [n]$ where such a record exists. Let J be the set of j for which a record exists.
  - If there are $|J| \geq n - \gamma$ such records, choose $\text{pw}'_t \xleftarrow{\$} \{0,1\}$ for $t \in [n] \setminus J$ and send $(\text{TestPwd}, \text{sid}, \mathcal{P}_i, \text{pw}'_1 \| \ldots \| \text{pw}'_n)$ to $\mathcal{F}_{\text{fPAKE}}$.
  - Else // there are $|J| < n - \gamma$ test-pwd records, choose $K \xleftarrow{\$} \mathbb{F}_q^n$. Send $(\text{TestPwd}, \text{sid}, \mathcal{P}_i, \bot)$ to $\mathcal{F}^M_{\text{fPAKE}}$. // Interrupt the record.
  - Regardless, wait for $\mathcal{F}_{\text{fPAKE}}$'s response:
    * If $\mathcal{F}_{\text{fPAKE}}$ responds with $(T, \text{"correct guess"})$ or $(T, \text{"wrong guess"})$ check if $|T \cap J| < n - \gamma$. If that is the case, mark the record $\langle \mathcal{P}_i, \text{sid}, \text{role}, \text{MitM} \rangle$ as `accident`. Else retrieve records $\langle \text{NewKey}, \text{sid}, \mathcal{P}_i, \text{sk}_j \rangle$ and set $K_t := \text{sk}_t$ for all $t \in T \cap J$ and choose $K_t \xleftarrow{\$} \mathbb{F}_q$ for all $t \in [n] \setminus (T \cap J)$. Mark the record $\langle \mathcal{P}_i, \text{sid}, \text{role}, \text{MitM} \rangle$ as `compromised`.
    * Else // $\mathcal{F}_{\text{fPAKE}}$ responds with "wrong guess" choose $K \xleftarrow{\$} \mathbb{F}_q^n$. Mark the record $\langle \mathcal{P}_i, \text{sid}, \text{role}, \text{MitM} \rangle$ as `interrupted`.
- Regardless,
  - If role $=$ receiver then append K to the record $\langle \mathcal{P}_i, \text{sid}, \text{role}, \text{MitM} \rangle$ and mark the record as `waiting`.
  - Else // role $=$ sender
    * Choose $s \xleftarrow{\$} \mathbb{F}_q^k$. Set $C := \text{Enc}(s), E := C \oplus K$, and $h := H_0((\text{sid}, \text{sid}_\text{H}), C)$.
    * If the record $\langle \mathcal{P}_i, \text{sid}, \text{role}, \text{MitM} \rangle$ is marked as `accident`, then choose $\widehat{\text{sk}} \xleftarrow{\$} \{0,1\}^\lambda$.
    * Else if the record $\langle \mathcal{P}_i, \text{sid}, \text{role}, \text{MitM} \rangle$ is marked as `compromised` then set $\widehat{\text{sk}} := H_1((\text{sid}, \text{sid}_\text{H}), s_0)$.
    * Else // record interrupted, or fresh set $\widehat{\text{sk}} := \bot$.
    * Regardless, send $(\text{NewKey}, \text{sid}, \mathcal{P}_i, \widehat{\text{sk}})$ to $\mathcal{F}_{\text{fPAKE}}$. Store $\langle \text{sid}, \mathcal{P}_i, \mathcal{P}_{1-i}, (E, h) \rangle$ and send $(\mathcal{P}_i, \mathcal{P}_{1-i}, (E, h))$ to $\mathcal{Z}$ as message from $\mathcal{F}_{\text{SA}}$. Mark $\langle \mathcal{P}_i, \text{sid}, \text{role}, \text{MitM} \rangle$ as `completed`.

Fig. 10. The second part of the simulator $\mathcal{S}$ for $\mathcal{F}_{\text{fPAKE}}$ and our Fuzzy PAKE with list-decoding protocol. $\mathcal{S}$ simulates $\mathcal{F}_{\text{SA}}$ and the random oracles H_0 and H_1. If we write "retrieve record" and the record does not exist, $\mathcal{S}$ ignores the message.

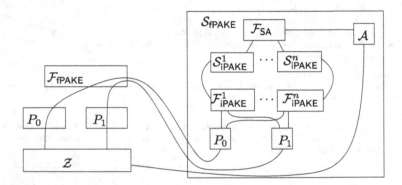

Fig. 11. This figure shows the layout of our simulator $\mathcal{S}_{\text{fPAKE}}$ in $\mathbf{G}_3$ in a setting without MitM attack.

the real-world execution of the protocol and replace parts of the protocol with simulations, step-by-step. The goal is to reach the ideal-world execution where the simulator can work without using the secret passwords of the participating parties, but with help from the ideal functionality $\mathcal{F}_{\text{fPAKE}}^M$. In the following we give intuition for every game-hop we make:

Game G_0: The proof starts with the real execution of the protocol.

Game G_1: We move the whole execution into one machine which we will call the simulator. We also add dummy parties and a functionality that merely forwards the input of the parties (i.e. NEWSESSION calls) to the simulator. Furthermore, the functionality forwards the output of the simulator to the parties as NEWKEY messages. This allows the simulator to execute the protocol on the real inputs $\text{pw}^{\mathcal{P}_i}$ and $\text{pw}^{\mathcal{P}_{1-i}}$. The goal of the remaining steps is to add and adapt interfaces of the ideal functionality until we reach $\mathcal{F}_{\text{fPAKE}}^M$ and to make the simulator independent of the input passwords $\text{pw}^{\mathcal{P}_i}$, $\text{pw}^{\mathcal{P}_{1-i}}$ until we reach the simulator as described in Figs. 9 to 10.

Game G_2: In this game the simulator aborts on collisions of H_0.

Game G_3: In this game we use the hypothesis that the iPAKE protocol π_j UC-realizes $\mathcal{F}_{\text{iPAKE}}$. There is a simulator $\mathcal{S}_{\text{iPAKE}}$ that interacts with $\mathcal{F}_{\text{iPAKE}}$ and simulates a protocol execution of π. Thus, we can replace each instance π_j of π by an instance $\mathcal{S}_{\text{iPAKE}}^j$ of $\mathcal{S}_{\text{iPAKE}}$. The simulator $\mathcal{S}$ must also simulate $\mathcal{F}_{\text{iPAKE}}$ towards $\mathcal{S}_{\text{iPAKE}}$ to make sure that the simulation works (Fig. 11). Note that $\mathcal{S}$ still needs the input passwords $\text{pw}^{\mathcal{P}_i}$, $\text{pw}^{\mathcal{P}_{1-i}}$ to internally run $\mathcal{F}_{\text{iPAKE}}$.

Game G_4: In this game we equip $\mathcal{F}_{\text{fPAKE}}^M$ with the TESTPWD interface. Also the NEWKEY and TESTPWD interfaces mark records. Also the NEWKEY interface reacts to the marked records. However, $\mathcal{S}$ does not use the TESTPWD interfaces yet.

Game G_5: $\mathcal{S}_{\text{iPAKE}}$ might send TESTPWD queries to $\mathcal{F}_{\text{iPAKE}}$. $\mathcal{S}$ still uses the input passwords to answer these. The games G_5 to G_8 will changes this. In G_5 we argue that $\mathcal{S}_{\text{iPAKE}}$ will never send a TESTPWD query to $\mathcal{F}_{\text{iPAKE}}$ if both parties are honest and no man-in-the-middle attack is mounted. In this case, $\mathcal{S}$ can ignore TESTPWD queries from $\mathcal{S}_{\text{iPAKE}}$.

Game G_6: In this game we start dealing with attacks on an honest sender. Such an attack will lead to TESTPWD queries from the $\mathcal{S}_{\text{iPAKE}}$. $\mathcal{S}$ can also send a TESTPWD query to $\mathcal{F}_{\text{fPAKE}}^M$. We leverage the fact that communication runs over the split authentication functionality. Because of $\mathcal{F}_{\text{SA}}$, the $\mathcal{F}_{\text{iPAKE}}$ instances of the sender run in a different authentication set than the iPAKE instances of the (malicious) receiver. Thus, $\mathcal{F}_{\text{iPAKE}}$ will never have a successful key exchange. Either the key is adversarially chosen or it is random. This is what mitigates the attack from Sect. 3.2.

The general idea in this game is that $\mathcal{S}$ collects the TESTPWD queries of the iPAKE simulators, concatenates the passwords and uses this to ask a TESTPWD query to $\mathcal{F}_{\text{fPAKE}}$. If the password was close enough (i.e. within distance γ), then $\mathcal{S}$ receives the position of the correct password characters as leakage from $\mathcal{F}_{\text{fPAKE}}^M$. Our simulator then uses this knowledge to simulate the $\mathcal{F}_{\text{iPAKE}}$ to $\mathcal{Z}$. If $\mathcal{S}$'s password guess was too far away, it will not receive any leakage information from $\mathcal{F}_{\mathsf{fPAKE}}^M$. In that case, $\mathcal{S}$ still uses the input passwords $\mathsf{pw}^{\mathcal{P}_i}, \mathsf{pw}^{\mathcal{P}_{1-i}}$ to produce output keys K_j for the iPAKE sessions.

The only difference to $\mathbf{G}_5$ is that in the case of an attack on an honest sender, in $\mathbf{G}_6$ the sender gets a random key as output from the functionality and not from the simulator anymore. However, by the $(k-1)$-query uniformity of the code, we can argue that the output was already independent and uniformly random in the previous game.

Game $\mathbf{G}_7$: In this game we change how $\mathcal{S}$ simulates iPAKE keys of an honest sender when there is a MitM attack or the receiver is corrupt. In the case that the adversary attacked less than $n - \gamma$ iPAKE sessions or guessed less than $n - \gamma$ characters of the password correctly, $\mathcal{S}$ just uses uniformly random iPAKE keys K_j for all $j \in [n]$. So even for the few successfully attacked iPAKE sessions the output key will be random. Again, we can use $(k-1)$-query uniformity to argue that the few correct entries of C that an adversary obtains already looked uniformly random before.

Game $\mathbf{G}_8$: In this game, we deal with attacks on honest receivers. Like in the previous game $\mathcal{S}$ can use split authentication and the TESTPWD interface of $\mathcal{F}_{\mathsf{fPAKE}}^M$ with leakage to deal with $n - \gamma$ or more attacked iPAKE sessions. In the case where less than $n - \gamma$ iPAKE sessions were attacked, $\mathcal{S}$ does not try to decode but instead interrupts the record by sending a TESTPWD query to $\mathcal{F}_{\mathsf{fPAKE}}^M$ with $\mathsf{pw} = \bot$. Then it sends a NEWKEY query with $\mathsf{sk} = \bot$ to $\mathcal{F}_{\mathsf{fPAKE}}^M$, which causes the output of the receiver to be a independent, uniformly random value. One can use Lemma 4 to see that in the case of less than $n - \gamma$ password characters the LDec algorithm will not output anything that matches the hint h and, thus, the receiver's output was an independent uniform random value already even in the previous game.

Game $\mathbf{G}_9$: This game syntactically changes $\mathcal{S}$ to remove usage of the provided input passwords $\mathsf{pw}^{\mathcal{P}_i}, \mathsf{pw}^{\mathcal{P}_{1-i}}$ in dealing with NEWSESSION and TESTPWD queries. We made sure in the previous games that $\mathcal{S}$ does not need $\mathsf{pw}^{\mathcal{P}_i}$ and $\mathsf{pw}^{\mathcal{P}_{1-i}}$ anymore for those queries.

Game $\mathbf{G}_{10}$: In this game $\mathcal{S}$ is modified such that honest and undisturbed parties produce output without $\mathcal{S}$ using the provided inputs for the parties. For this, $\mathcal{S}$ can use the NEWKEY interface of $\mathcal{F}_{\mathsf{fPAKE}}^M$. The functionality $\mathcal{F}_{\mathsf{fPAKE}}^M$ will produce output according to the input passwords. If $d(\mathsf{pw}, \mathsf{pw}') \leq \delta$ then $\mathcal{F}_{\mathsf{fPAKE}}^M$ produces matching passwords. Because of Lemma 6 the real-world protocol does the same. If $d(\mathsf{pw}, \mathsf{pw}') > \delta$ then $\mathcal{F}_{\mathsf{fPAKE}}^M$ produces independent keys. By Lemma 5, the real-world protocol does the same. We also replace the message (E, h) with a uniformly random message, which is indistinguishable for $\mathcal{Z}$ as the iPAKE keys of honest parties are hidden from $\mathcal{Z}$.

Game $\mathbf{G}_{11}$: This is the ideal-world experiment with $\mathcal{F}_{\mathsf{fPAKE}}^M$ and the simulator from Figs. 9 to 10.

The following lemma essentially says that given a target vector C, a vector $\tilde{C}$ with at least $\gamma + 1 = n - k + 1$ random entries will have $d(C, \tilde{C}) \geq \gamma + 1$. This is necessary in our protocol to make sure that a malicious sender with a far away password cannot make the key exchange succeed. In the security proof of our protocol we use this lemma in $\mathbf{G}_8$.

Lemma 4. *For* $q = 2^{\Omega(\lambda)}$, $\forall n, k \in \mathbb{N}$ *with* $n \geq k$, $\forall A \subseteq [n]$ *with* $|A| \leq k - 1$, $\forall C, \tilde{C} \in \mathbb{F}_q^n$ *with* $\tilde{C}|_{\bar{A}} \xleftarrow{\$} \mathbb{F}_q^{n-|A|}$, *we have*

$$\Pr[d(C, \tilde{C}) \geq n - k + 1] \geq 1 - \mathsf{negl}(\lambda).$$

The probability is taken over the randomness used to sample $\tilde{C}|_{\bar{A}}$.

Proof. Remember that $\gamma = n - k$. Observe that $d(C, \tilde{C}) = d(C|_A, \tilde{C}|_A) + d(C|_{\bar{A}}, \tilde{C}|_{\bar{A}})$. The statement must even hold for $d(C|_A, \tilde{C}|_A) = 0$ and A maximally large, i.e., $|A| = k - 1$ and, thus, $|\bar{A}| = n - k + 1 = \gamma + 1$. What remains to be shown is that $d(C|_{\bar{A}}, \tilde{C}|_{\bar{A}}) \geq n - k + 1 = \gamma + 1$ with overwhelming probability. For $d(C|_{\bar{A}}, \tilde{C}|_{\bar{A}}) \geq \gamma + 1$ to hold, $C|_{\bar{A}}$ and $\tilde{C}|_{\bar{A}}$ must be distinct in all $\gamma + 1$ coordinates. The probability that $C|_{\bar{A}}$ and $\tilde{C}|_{\bar{A}}$ are distinct in a specific coordinate is $1 - \frac{1}{q}$. Thus, the probability that $C|_{\bar{A}}$ and $\tilde{C}|_{\bar{A}}$ are distinct in all $\gamma + 1$ coordinates is $(1 - \frac{1}{q})^{\gamma+1}$. For constant γ and $q = 2^{\lambda}$ this probability is overwhelming in λ.

The next lemma is similar to Lemma 4. One important difference is that in Lemma 4 C was an arbitrary vector in $\mathbb{F}_q^n$, whereas in Lemma 5 C is a valid codeword. We use this lemma to guarantee that in our protocol in a session with an honest sender and an honest receiver, whose passwords mismatch in more than δ positions, both parties get independent random keys. In particular this lemma guarantees that the receiver will not be able to decode the codeword, which will make them output a random key. This is important in the transition from $\mathbf{G}_9$ to $\mathbf{G}_{10}$.

Lemma 5. *For* $s \xleftarrow{\$} \mathbb{F}_q$, $C \leftarrow \mathsf{Enc}(s)$, $\tilde{C} \in \mathbb{F}_q^n$ *and* $A \subseteq [n]$ *such that* $|A| \leq k-1$, $C|_A = \tilde{C}|_A$, *and* $\tilde{C}|_{\bar{A}} \xleftarrow{\$} \mathbb{F}_q^{n-|A|}$, *we have that* $C \in \mathsf{LDec}(\tilde{C})$ *with negligible probability.*

Proof. From Lemma 4 we get that $d(C, \tilde{C}) \geq n - k + 1$ with overwhelming probability. Because $n - k + 1 > n - 1 - \sqrt{(k-1)n} = \delta$ and $\mathsf{LDec}(\tilde{C})$ does not output candidates C with $d(C, \tilde{C}) > \delta$ by Lemma 2, we get that $C \in \mathsf{LDec}(\tilde{C})$ with negligible probability.

Lemma 6 can be seen as the counterpart of Lemma 5, as we use it to guarantee that in our protocol two honest parties that have close enough passwords (i.e. $\leq \delta$) get the same session key. In detail, this lemma guarantees that the honest receiver is able to correctly decode $C' = E \oplus K'$, which then leads to successful key exchange. We use this lemma in the transition from $\mathbf{G}_9$ to $\mathbf{G}_{10}$.

Lemma 6. *For* $s \xleftarrow{\$} \mathbb{F}_q$, $C \leftarrow \mathsf{Enc}(s)$, $\tilde{C} \in \mathbb{F}_q^n$ *and* $A \subseteq [n]$ *such that* $|A| \geq n-\delta$, $C|_A = \tilde{C}|_A$, *and* $\tilde{C}|_{\bar{A}} \xleftarrow{\$} \mathbb{F}_q^{n-|A|}$, *we have that* $C \in \mathsf{LDec}(\tilde{C})$ *with overwhelming probability.*

Proof. This follows directly from Lemma 2 with $\delta = e = n - 1 - \lceil \sqrt{(k-1)n} \rceil$.

References

[ABM+21] Agrawal, S., Badrinarayanan, S., Mohassel, P., Mukherjee, P., Patranabis, S.: BETA: biometric-enabled threshold authentication. In: Garay, J.A. (ed.) PKC 2021. LNCS, vol. 12711, pp. 290–318. Springer, Cham (2021). https://doi.org/10.1007/978-3-030-75248-4_11

[ABMR20] Agrawal, S., Badrinarayanan, S., Mukherjee, P., Rindal, P.: Game-set-MATCH: using mobile devices for seamless external-facing biometric matching. In: Ligatti, J., Ou, X., Katz, J., Vigna, G. (eds.) ACM CCS 2020, pp. 1351–1370. ACM Press (2020)

[All22] WiFi Alliance. WPA3 specification version 3.1 (2022). https://www.wi-fi.org/download.php?file=/sites/default/files/private/WPA3%20Specification%20v3.1.pdf

[BBCW21] Barbosa, M., Boldyreva, A., Chen, S., Warinschi, B.: Provable security analysis of FIDO2. In: Malkin, T., Peikert, C. (eds.) CRYPTO 2021. LNCS, vol. 12827, pp. 125–156. Springer, Cham (2021). https://doi.org/10.1007/978-3-030-84252-9_5

[BBR88] Bennett, C.H., Brassard, G., Robert, J.-M.: Privacy amplification by public discussion, vol. 17, pp. 210–229 (1988)

[BCL+05] Barak, B., Canetti, R., Lindell, Y., Pass, R., Rabin, T.: Secure computation without authentication. In: Shoup, V. (ed.) CRYPTO 2005. LNCS, vol. 3621, pp. 361–377. Springer, Heidelberg (2005). https://doi.org/10.1007/11535218_22

[BCL22] Bootle, J., Chiesa, A., Liu, S.: Zero-knowledge IOPs with linear-time prover and polylogarithmic-time verifier. In: Dunkelman, O., Dziembowski, S. (eds.) EUROCRYPT 2022. LNCS, vol. 13276, pp. 275–304. Springer, Cham (2022). https://doi.org/10.1007/978-3-031-07085-3_10

[BDFK12] Bender, J., Dagdelen, Ö., Fischlin, M., Kügler, D.: The PACE—AA protocol for machine readable travel documents, and its security. In: Keromytis, A.D. (ed.) FC 2012. LNCS, vol. 7397, pp. 344–358. Springer, Heidelberg (2012). https://doi.org/10.1007/978-3-642-32946-3_25

[BDK+05] Boyen, X., Dodis, Y., Katz, J., Ostrovsky, R., Smith, A.: Secure remote authentication using biometric data. In: Cramer, R. (ed.) EUROCRYPT 2005. LNCS, vol. 3494, pp. 147–163. Springer, Heidelberg (2005). https://doi.org/10.1007/11426639_9

[BFK09] Bender, J., Fischlin, M., Kügler, D.: Security analysis of the PACE key-agreement protocol. In: Samarati, P., Yung, M., Martinelli, F., Ardagna, C.A. (eds.) ISC 2009. LNCS, vol. 5735, pp. 33–48. Springer, Heidelberg (2009). https://doi.org/10.1007/978-3-642-04474-8_3

[BFK13] Bender, J., Fischlin, M., Kügler, D.: The PACE—CA protocol for machine readable travel documents. In: Bloem, R., Lipp, P. (eds.) INTRUST 2013. LNCS, vol. 8292, pp. 17–35. Springer, Cham (2013). https://doi.org/10.1007/978-3-319-03491-1_2

[BM92] Bellovin, S.M., Merritt, M.: Encrypted key exchange: password-based protocols secure against dictionary attacks. In: 1992 IEEE Symposium on Security and Privacy, pp. 72–84. IEEE Computer Society Press (1992)

[BMP00] Boyko, V., MacKenzie, P., Patel, S.: Provably secure password-authenticated key exchange using Diffie-Hellman. In: Preneel, B. (ed.) EUROCRYPT 2000. LNCS, vol. 1807, pp. 156–171. Springer, Heidelberg (2000). https://doi.org/10.1007/3-540-45539-6_12

[BPR00] Bellare, M., Pointcheval, D., Rogaway, P.: Authenticated key exchange secure against dictionary attacks. In: Preneel, B. (ed.) EUROCRYPT 2000. LNCS, vol. 1807, pp. 139–155. Springer, Heidelberg (2000). https://doi.org/10.1007/3-540-45539-6_11

[CAA+16] Chatterjee, R., Athayle, A., Akhawe, D., Juels, A., Ristenpart, T.: pASSWORD tYPOS and how to correct them securely. In: 2016 IEEE Symposium on Security and Privacy, pp. 799–818. IEEE Computer Society Press (2016)

[Can01] Canetti, R.: Universally composable security: a new paradigm for cryptographic protocols. In: 42nd FOCS, pp. 136–145. IEEE Computer Society Press (2001)

[CCG+07] Chen, H., Cramer, R., Goldwasser, S., de Haan, R., Vaikuntanathan, V.: Secure computation from random error correcting codes. In: Naor, M. (ed.) EUROCRYPT 2007. LNCS, vol. 4515, pp. 291–310. Springer, Heidelberg (2007). https://doi.org/10.1007/978-3-540-72540-4_17

[CDBN15] Cramer, R., Damgård, I., Nielsen, J.B.: Secure Multiparty Computation and Secret Sharing. Cambridge University Press, Cambridge (2015)

[CDD+15] Cramer, R., Damgård, I.B., Döttling, N., Fehr, S., Spini, G.: Linear secret sharing schemes from error correcting codes and universal hash functions. In: Oswald, E., Fischlin, M. (eds.) EUROCRYPT 2015. LNCS, vol. 9057, pp. 313–336. Springer, Heidelberg (2015). https://doi.org/10.1007/978-3-662-46803-6_11

[CFP+16] Canetti, R., Fuller, B., Paneth, O., Reyzin, L., Smith, A.: Reusable fuzzy extractors for low-entropy distributions. In: Fischlin, M., Coron, J.-S. (eds.) EUROCRYPT 2016. LNCS, vol. 9665, pp. 117–146. Springer, Heidelberg (2016). https://doi.org/10.1007/978-3-662-49890-3_5

[CHK+05] Canetti, R., Halevi, S., Katz, J., Lindell, Y., MacKenzie, P.: Universally composable password-based key exchange. In: Cramer, R. (ed.) EUROCRYPT 2005. LNCS, vol. 3494, pp. 404–421. Springer, Heidelberg (2005). https://doi.org/10.1007/11426639_24

[CNPR22] Cremers, C., Naor, M., Paz, S., Ronen, E.: CHIP and CRISP: protecting all parties against compromise through identity-binding PAKEs. In: Dodis, Y., Shrimpton, T. (eds.) CRYPTO 2022, Part II. LNCS, vol. 13508, pp. 668–698. Springer, Heidelberg (2022). https://doi.org/10.1007/978-3-031-15979-4_23

[CWP+17] Chatterjee, R., Woodage, J., Pnueli, Y., Chowdhury, A., Ristenpart, T.: The TypTop system: personalized typo-tolerant password checking. In: Thuraisingham, B.M., Evans, D., Malkin, T., Xu, D. (eds.) ACM CCS 2017, pp. 329–346. ACM Press (2017)

[DHP+17] Dupont, P.-A., Hesse, J., Pointcheval, D., Reyzin, L., Yakoubov, S.: Fuzzy password-authenticated key exchange. Cryptology ePrint Archive, Paper 2017/1111 (2017). https://eprint.iacr.org/2017/1111

[DHP+18] Dupont, P.-A., Hesse, J., Pointcheval, D., Reyzin, L., Yakoubov, S.: Fuzzy password-authenticated key exchange. In: Nielsen, J.B., Rijmen, V. (eds.) EUROCRYPT 2018. LNCS, vol. 10822, pp. 393–424. Springer, Cham (2018). https://doi.org/10.1007/978-3-319-78372-7_13

[DORS08] Dodis, Y., Ostrovsky, R., Reyzin, L., Smith, A.D.: Fuzzy extractors: how to generate strong keys from biometrics and other noisy data. SIAM J. Comput. 38(1), 97–139 (2008)

[EHOR20] Erwig, A., Hesse, J., Orlt, M., Riahi, S.: Fuzzy asymmetric password-authenticated key exchange. In: Moriai, S., Wang, H. (eds.) ASIACRYPT 2020. LNCS, vol. 12492, pp. 761–784. Springer, Cham (2020). https://doi.org/10.1007/978-3-030-64834-3_26

[Gur06] Guruswami, V.: Algorithmic results in list decoding. Found. Trends Theor. Comput. Sci. **2**(2), 107–195 (2006)

[HL19] Haase, B., Labrique, B.: AuCPace: efficient verifier-based PAKE protocol tailored for the IIoT. IACR TCHES **2019**(2), 1–48 (2019). https://tches.iacr.org/index.php/TCHES/article/view/7384

[HS14] Hao, F., Shahandashti, S.F.: The SPEKE protocol revisited. IACR Cryptology ePrint Archive, p. 585 (2014)

[Hv22] Hao, F., van Oorschot, P.C.: SoK: password-authenticated key exchange - theory, practice, standardization and real-world lessons. In: Suga, Y., Sakurai, K., Ding, X., Sako, K. (eds.) ASIACCS 2022, pp. 697–711. ACM Press (2022)

[Jab96] Jablon, D.P.: Strong password-only authenticated key exchange. Comput. Commun. Rev. **26**(5), 5–26 (1996)

[JLHG22] Jiang, M., Liu, S., Han, S., Gu, D.: Fuzzy authenticated key exchange with tight security. In: Atluri, V., Di Pietro, R., Jensen, C.D., Meng, W. (eds.) ESORICS 2022, Part II. LNCS, vol. 13555, pp. 337–360. Springer, Heidelberg (2022). https://doi.org/10.1007/978-3-031-17146-8_17

[KR07] Kulhandjian, M., Rudra, A.: Lecture 27: Berlekamp-welch algorithm (2007)

[Mac01] MacKenzie, P.: On the security of the SPEKE password-authenticated key exchange protocol. IACR Cryptology ePrint Archive, p. 57 (2001)

[McE03] McEliece, R.J.: The guruswami-sudan decoding algorithm for reed-solomon codes. IPN Progress Report 42-153 (2003)

[Nie13] Nielsen, J.S.R.: List decoding of algebraic codes (2013)

[PC20] Pongmorrakot, T., Chatterjee, R.: tPAKE: typo-tolerant password-authenticated key exchange. In: Batina, L., Picek, S., Mondal, M. (eds.) SPACE 2020. LNCS, vol. 12586, pp. 3–24. Springer, Cham (2020). https://doi.org/10.1007/978-3-030-66626-2_1

[RW04] Renner, R., Wolf, S.: The exact price for unconditionally secure asymmetric cryptography. In: Cachin, C., Camenisch, J.L. (eds.) EUROCRYPT 2004. LNCS, vol. 3027, pp. 109–125. Springer, Heidelberg (2004). https://doi.org/10.1007/978-3-540-24676-3_7

[RX23] Roy, L., Xu, J.: A universally composable PAKE with zero communication cost. In: Boldyreva, A., Kolesnikov, V. (eds.) PKC 2023, Part I. LNCS, vol. 13940, pp. 714–743. Springer, Cham (2023). https://doi.org/10.1007/978-3-031-31368-4_25

[Wei16] Weiss, M.: Secure computation and probabilistic checking (2016)

[WHC+21] Wang, M., He, K., Chen, J., Li, Z., Zhao, W., Du, R.: Biometrics-authenticated key exchange for secure messaging. In: Vigna, G., Shi, E. (eds.) ACM CCS 2021, pp. 2618–2631. ACM Press (2021)

A Generic Construction of Tightly Secure Password-Based Authenticated Key Exchange

Jiaxin Pan[1,2](✉) [iD] and Runzhi Zeng[2] [iD]

[1] University of Kassel, Kassel, Germany
[2] Department of Mathematical Sciences, NTNU - Norwegian University of Science and Technology, Trondheim, Norway
{jiaxin.pan,runzhi.zeng}@ntnu.no

Abstract. We propose a generic construction of password-based authenticated key exchange (PAKE) from key encapsulation mechanisms (KEM). Assuming that the KEM is oneway secure against plaintext-checkable attacks (OW-PCA), we prove that our PAKE protocol is *tightly secure* in the Bellare-Pointcheval-Rogaway model (EUROCRYPT 2000). Our tight security proofs require ideal ciphers and random oracles. The OW-PCA security is relatively weak and can be implemented tightly with the Diffie-Hellman assumption, which generalizes the work of Liu et al. (PKC 2023), and "almost" tightly with lattice-based assumptions, which tightens the security loss of the work of Beguinet et al. (ACNS 2023) and allows more efficient practical implementation with Kyber. Beyond these, it opens an opportunity of constructing tight PAKE based on various assumptions.

Keywords: Password-based authenticated key exchange · generic constructions · tight security · lattices

1 Introduction

While authenticated key exchange (AKE) protocols require a PKI to certify user public keys, password-based AKE (PAKE) protocols allow a client and a server to establish a session key, assuming that both parties share a password in advance. A password is chosen from a small set of possible strings, referred as a dictionary. Thus, a password has low-entropy and can be memorized by humans. Hence, it is very convenient, and the design and analysis of PAKE protocols have drew a lot of attention in the past few years.

After the introduction of Encrypted-Key-Exchange (EKE) protocol by Bellovin and Merritt [12], many PAKE protocols have been proposed based on variants of the Diffie-Hellman assumptions, including the well-known SPEKE [22], SPEKE2 [6], J-PAKE [20], and CPace [19]. There are only a few exception

Supported by the Research Council of Norway under Project No. 324235.

J. Guo and R. Steinfeld (Eds.): ASIACRYPT 2023, LNCS 14445, pp. 143–175, 2023.
https://doi.org/10.1007/978-981-99-8742-9_5

where PAKE is constructed based on *post-quantum assumptions*, such as lattices [13, 23, 33] and group actions [4].

SECURITY OF PAKE. The security requirements on a PAKE protocol are resistance against offline (where an adversary performs an exhaustive search for the password offline) and online (where an active adversary tries a small number of passwords to run the protocol) dictionary attacks. Similar to the classical AKE, forward secrecy is required as well, where the session keys remain secure, even if the password is corrupted at a later point in time, and also leakage of a session key should not affect other session keys. Their security is formalized by either the indistinguishability-based (IND-based) model [10] or the universal composability (UC) framework [16].

Usually, the advantage of a PAKE protocol $\varepsilon_{\text{PAKE}}$ has the form of:

$$\varepsilon_{\text{PAKE}} \leq S/|\mathcal{PW}| + L \cdot \varepsilon_{\text{Problem}}, \tag{1}$$

where S is the number of protocol sessions, $\mathcal{PW}$ is the set of all possible passwords, $\varepsilon_{\text{Problem}}$ is the advantage of attacking the underlying cryptographic hard problem, and L is called the security loss. Here we ignore the additive statistical negligible probability in Eq. (1) for simplicity. Essentially, $S/|\mathcal{PW}|$ is the success probability of online dictionary attacks and Eq. (1) shows that the best attack on the PAKE protocol is performing an online dictionary attack. This can be eliminated by restricting the online password guess in practice.

TIGHT SECURITY. We say a security proof for PAKE tight if L is a small constant. All the aforementioned PAKE protocols are non-tight. For instance, according to the analysis of [8], we estimate that the security loss L for the EKE protocol is $O(q_D \cdot (S + q_D))$, where q_D is the number of the adversary's queries to an ideal cipher. The security bound for the group-action-based protocol Com-GA-PAKE$_\ell$ in [4] is even worse, and it contains a square root of the advantage of the underlying assumption (cf. [4, Theorem 2]), due to the Reset Lemma [9]. This means even if we set up the underlying assumption with 128-bit security, Com-GA-PAKE$_\ell$ in [4] has only less[1] than 64-bit.

We note that X-GA-PAKE$_\ell$ in [4, Section 6] has tight security by restricting to weak forward secrecy, where an adversary is not allowed to perform active attacks before password corruptions. This is a rather weak security model.

In this paper, we are interested in tightly secure PAKE with perfect forward secrecy (PFS), namely, adversaries can perform active attacks before password corruptions. From a theoretical perspective, it is interesting to analyze the possibility of constructing tightly secure PAKE and under which cryptographic assumption it is possible. From a practical perspective, it is very desirable to have tightly secure PAKE (or AKE in general), since these protocols are executed in a multi-user, multi-instance scenario. In today's internet, the scenario size is often large. A non-tight protocol requires a larger security parameter to compensate the security loss and results in a less efficient protocol. Even if we

---

[1] This is because of the additional multiplicative loss factor depending on S and the length of a password in [4, Theorem 2].

cannot achieve full tightness, a tighter security proof is already more beneficial than a less tight one of the same protocol, since the tighter proof offers higher security guarantees.

OUR GOAL: TIGHT PAKE BEYOND DIFFIE-HELLMAN (DH). There are a few exceptions that construct tight PAKE protocols with PFS, and they are all based on the DH assumption. Becerra et al. [7] proved tight security of the three-move PAK protocol [25] using the Gap DH (GDH) assumption [26] in the IND-based model, where the GDH assumption states that the Computational DH (CDH) assumption is hard even if the Decisional DH (DDH) assumption is easy. Lately, Abdalla et al. [2] proved tight security of two-move SPAKE2 in the relaxed UC framework under the GDH assumption. Very recently, Liu et al. [24] carefully used the twinning technique [17] to remove the GDH assumption and proved a variant of the EKE protocol tightly based on the CDH assumption.

Our goal is to construct tightly secure PAKE protocols from post-quantum assumptions, beyond the DH assumptions. Lattice-based assumptions are the promising post-quantum ones, and it seems inherent that they do not have any Gap-like assumption or twinning techniques, since the Decisional and Computational variants of, for instance, Learning-With-Errors (LWE) assumption [30] are equivalent.

Regarding the assumption based on group actions, as we discussed earlier, the Com-GA-PAKE$_\ell$ protocol in [4] needs to rewind an adversary to argue PFS, and by using the Reset Lemma it leads to a very loose bound. Apart from that, Com-GA-PAKE$_\ell$ applies the group action in a "bit-by-bit" (wrt the bit-length of a password) fashion and sends out the resulting element, and thus it is quite inefficient in terms of both computation and communication complexity.

Finally, we note that Liu et al. [24] did not provide a formal proof on the PFS of their protocol, but rather an informal remark. In [4], we note a huge gap between the security loss of a weak FS protocol and a PFS one. Hence, in this paper we will prove the PFS of our protocol concretely.

1.1 Our Contribution

We propose a generic construction of tightly secure PAKE protocols from key encapsulation mechanisms (KEMs) in the ideal cipher and random oracle models. We require the underlying KEM to have the following security:

- Oneway plaintext-checking (OW-PCA) security in the multi-user, multi-challenge setting, namely, adversary $\mathcal{A}$'s goal is to decapsulate one ciphertext out of many given ones, and furthermore, $\mathcal{A}$ is given an oracle to check whether a key k is a valid decapsulation of a ciphertext c under some user j. It is a (slight) multi-user, multi-challenge variant of the original OW-PCA [27].
- Anonymous ciphertexts under PCA, namely, the challenge ciphertexts do not leak any information about the corresponding public keys.
- Fuzzy public keys, namely, the generated public keys are indistinguishable from a random key from all the possible public keys.

Such a KEM can be tightly constructed:

- either *generically* from pseudorandom PKE against chosen-plaintext attacks in the multi-user, multi-challenge setting (PR-CPA security[2]), which states that the given challenge ciphertexts are pseudorandom. This means, as long as we have a PR-CPA secure PKE, we have a PAKE protocol that preserves the tightness of the PKE. With lattices, we do not know a tightly PR-CPA PKE, but only a scheme (i.e. Regev's encryption [30]) tightly wrt. the number of challenges, not wrt. the number of users. This already results in a tighter PAKE protocol than the analysis from Beguinet et al. [8]. More details will be provided in "COMPARISON USING KYBER".
- or *directly* from the strong DH (stDH) assumption in a prime-order group [3]. Under this stronger assumption, our resulting PAKE protocol has $O(\lambda)$ (which corresponds to the bit-length of a group element) less than the 2DH-EKE protocol of Liu et al. [24] in terms of protocol transcripts. In fact, using the twinning technique of Cash et al. [17], we can remove the strong oracle and have our protocol under the CDH assumption, which is the same protocol as the 2DH-EKE protocol of Liu et al. Essentially, our direct instantiation abstracts the key ideas of Liu et al., and our proof for PFS gives a formal analysis of Liu et al.'s protocol.

Different to other PAKE protocol from group actions [4] and lattices as in [13], our construction is compact and does not use "bit-by-bit" approaches. Figure 1 briefly summarizes our approaches.

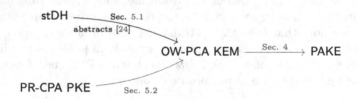

Fig. 1. Overview of our construction. All implications are tight, and the blue ones are done via generic constructions. OW-PCA security is the core for our "KEM-to-PAKE" transformation. Please find additional requirements on the KEM in the text. (Color figure online)

Our proofs are in the IND-based model (aka, the so-called Bellare-Pointcheval-Rogaway (BPR) model [10]) for readability. We are optimistic that it is tightly secure in the UC framework and briefly sketch the ideas about how to lift our proofs in the BPR model to the UC framework in our full version [28].

COMPARISON USING KYBER [32]. There are only a few efficient PAKE protocols from lattices. We focus our comparison on the very efficient one by implementing the CAKE in [8] with KYBER. The reason of not using OCAKE in [8] is because

---

[2] Our security notions are in the multi-user, multi-challenge setting. Hence, for simplicity, we do not write the 'm' in the abbreviations.

OCAKE do not have PFS, but weak FS. Our protocol is similar to CAKE, but ours has tight reductions from the KEM security.

Unfortunately, by implementing with KYBER, our protocol does not have tight security, since we cannot prove tight PR-CPA security for KYBER, but in practice one will consider using KYBER than otherwise. Our security loss is $O(S \cdot (S+q_D))$ to the Module-LWE assumption, while the security loss of CAKE is $O(q_D \cdot (S + q_D))$, where q_D is the number of decryption queries to the ideal cipher. In practice, q_D is the number of adversary $\mathcal{A}$ evaluating the symmetric cipher offline and can be large. We assume $q_D = 2^{40}$.

Very different to the standard AKE, in the PAKE setting S should be very small, since S corresponds to how many attempts an adversary can perform online dictionary attacks. We usually will limit it. We assume $S \leq 100 \approx 2^6$. Hence, although our security bound with KYBER is not tight, it is still much smaller than CAKE, since $S \ll q_D$. In fact, we have doubt on the security proof of CAKE in handling reply attacks[3], namely, $\mathcal{A}$ can reply the first round message. To fix it, we need to introduce another multiplicative factor S, but since S is relatively small we ignore it in our comparison.

Hence, implementing with KYBER-768 (corresponding to AES-192), our protocol provides about 152-bit security, while CAKE about 112-bit security.

OPEN PROBLEM. We are optimistic that our protocol can be proven tightly in the weaker and more efficient randomized half-ideal cipher model [31], and we leave the formal proof for it as an open problem.

2   Preliminaries

For an integer n, we define the notation $[n] := \{1, \ldots, n\}$. Let $\mathcal{X}$ and $\mathcal{Y}$ be two finite sets. The notation $x \xleftarrow{\$} \mathcal{X}$ denotes sampling an element x from $\mathcal{X}$ uniformly at random.

Let $\mathcal{A}$ be an algorithm. If $\mathcal{A}$ is probabilistic, then $y \leftarrow \mathcal{A}(x)$ means that the variable y is assigned to the output of $\mathcal{A}$ on input x. If $\mathcal{A}$ is deterministic, then we may write $y := \mathcal{A}(x)$. We write $\mathcal{A}^{\mathcal{O}}$ to indicate that $\mathcal{A}$ has classical access to oracle $\mathcal{O}$, and $\mathcal{A}^{|\mathcal{O}\rangle}$ to indicate that $\mathcal{A}$ has quantum access to oracle $\mathcal{O}$ All algorithms in this paper are probabilistic polynomial-time (PPT), unless we mention it.

GAMES. We use code-based games [11] to define and prove security. We implicitly assume that Boolean flags are initialized to false, numerical types are initialized to 0, sets and ordered lists are initialized to $\emptyset$, and strings are initialized to the empty string ϵ. The notation $\Pr[\mathbf{G}^{\mathcal{A}} \Rightarrow 1]$ denotes the probability that the final output $\mathbf{G}^{\mathcal{A}}$ of game $\mathbf{G}$ running an adversary $\mathcal{A}$ is 1. Let Ev be an (classical) event. We write $\Pr[\text{Ev} : \mathbf{G}]$ to denote the probability that Ev occurs during the game $\mathbf{G}$. In our security notions throughout the paper, we let N, μ be numbers

---

[3] More precisely, the argument in [8, page 41] under "*Analysis*" may not hold true for reply attacks.

of users and challenges, respectively, which are assumed to be polynomial in the security parameter λ. For simplicity, in this paper, we do not write λ explicitly. Instead, we assume every algorithm's input includes λ.

2.1 Key Encapsulation Mechanism

Definition 1 (Key Encapsulation Mechanism). *A KEM* KEM *consists of four algorithms* (Setup, KG, Encaps, Decaps) *and a ciphertext space* $\mathcal{C}$, *a randomness space* $\mathcal{R}$, *and a KEM key space* $\mathcal{K}$. *On input security parameters,* Setup *outputs a system parameter* par. KG(par) *outputs a public and secret key pair* (pk, sk). *The encapsulation algorithm* Encaps, *on input* pk, *outputs a ciphertext* $c \in \mathcal{C}$. *We also write* $c := \text{Encaps}(pk; r)$ *to indicate the randomness* $r \in \mathcal{R}$ *explicitly. The decapsulation algorithm* Decaps, *on input* sk *and a ciphertext* c, *outputs a KEM key* $k \in \mathcal{K}$ *or a rejection symbol* $\perp \notin \mathcal{K}$. *Here* Encaps *and* Decaps *also take* par *as input, but for simplicity, we do not write explicitly.*

Definition 2 (KEM Correctness). *Let* KEM := (Setup, KG, Encaps, Decaps) *be a KEM scheme and* $\mathcal{A}$ *be an adversary against* KEM. *We say* KEM *is* $(1 - \delta)$-*correct if*

$$\Pr\left[(c, k) \leftarrow \text{Encaps}(pk) \wedge k \neq \text{Decaps}(sk, c)\right] \leq \delta,$$

where par $\leftarrow$ Setup, (pk, sk) $\leftarrow$ KG(par).

Definition 3 (Implicit Rejection [14]). *A KEM scheme* KEM = (Setup, KG, Encaps, Decaps) *has implicit rejection if* Decaps(sk, $\cdot$) *behaves as a pseudorandom function when the input ciphertext is invalid, where* par $\leftarrow$ Setup, (pk, sk) $\leftarrow$ KG, *and* sk *is the key of the pseudorandom function. That is, if an input ciphertext* c *is invalid, then* Decaps(sk, c) *will output a pseudorandom key* k *instead of a rejection symbol* $\perp$. *A concrete example is shown in Fig. 18.*

OW-PCA SECURITY. Let KEM = (Setup, KG, Encaps, Decaps) be a KEM scheme with ciphertext space $\mathcal{C}$. In Definitions 4 and 5, we define two variants of one-wayness under plaintext-checking attacks (OW-PCA) security for KEM [27] in the multi-user, multi-challenge setting. They will be used for the tight security proof of our PAKE protocol and can be instantiated tightly from the Diffie-Hellman assumption and Learning-With-Errors assumption. Instead of writing 'm' in the abbreviation, we mention the explicit numbers of users and challenge ciphertexts as N and μ in the abbreviation of security.

Definition 4 (Multi-user-challenge OW-PCA security). *Let* N *and* μ *be the numbers of users and challenge ciphertexts per user, respectively. Let* $\mathcal{A}$ *be an adversary against* KEM. *We define the* (N, μ)-*OW-PCA advantage function of* $\mathcal{A}$ *against* KEM

$$\text{Adv}_{\text{KEM}}^{(N,\mu)\text{-OW-PCA}}(\mathcal{A}) := \Pr\left[\text{OW-PCA}_{\text{KEM}}^{(N,\mu),\mathcal{A}} \Rightarrow 1\right],$$

where the game OW-PCA$_{\text{KEM}}^{(N,\mu),\mathcal{A}}$ *is defined in Fig. 2. We say* KEM *is* OW-PCA *secure if* $\text{Adv}_{\text{KEM}}^{(N,\mu)\text{-OW-PCA}}(\mathcal{A})$ *is negligible for any* $\mathcal{A}$.

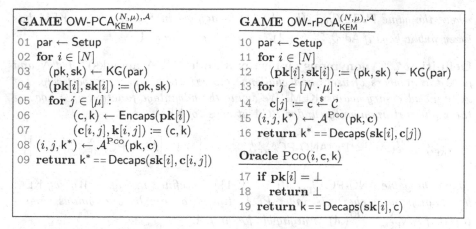

Fig. 2. Security games OW-PCA and OW-rPCA for KEM scheme KEM.

GAME ANO-PCA$_{KEM,b}^{(N,\mu),\mathcal{A}}$	GAME FUZZY$_{KEM,b}^{N,\mathcal{A}}$
01 par ← Setup	10 par ← Setup
02 for $i \in [N]$	11 for $i \in [N]$
03 $(\mathbf{pk}[i], \mathbf{sk}[i]) := (pk, sk) \leftarrow KG(par)$	12 $(\mathbf{pk}_0[i], \mathbf{sk}[i]) := (pk, sk) \leftarrow KG(par)$
04 for $j \in [\mu]$:	
05 $(c, k) \leftarrow Encaps(\mathbf{pk}[i])$	13 $\mathbf{pk}_1[i] := pk \xleftarrow{\$} \mathcal{PK}$
06 $(\mathbf{c}_0[i,j], \mathbf{k}[i,j]) := (c, k)$	14 $b' \leftarrow \mathcal{A}(par, \mathbf{pk}_b)$
07 $\mathbf{c}_1[i,j] \xleftarrow{\$} \mathcal{C}$	15 return b'
08 $b' \leftarrow \mathcal{A}^{Pco}(par, \mathbf{pk}, \mathbf{c}_b)$	
09 return b'	

Fig. 3. Security games FUZZY and ANO-PCA for KEM scheme KEM. The Pco oracle of ANO-PCA is the same as the one of OW-PCA (and OW-rPCA) in Fig. 2.

Definition 5 (OW-PCA security under random ciphertexts). *Let N and μ be the number of users and the number of challenge ciphertexts per user, respectively. Let $\mathcal{A}$ be an adversary against KEM. We define the (N,μ)-OW-rPCA advantage function of $\mathcal{A}$*

$$\mathsf{Adv}_{KEM}^{(N,\mu)\text{-OW-rPCA}}(\mathcal{A}) := \Pr\left[\text{OW-rPCA}_{KEM}^{(N,\mu),\mathcal{A}} \Rightarrow 1\right],$$

where OW-rPCA$_{KEM}^{(N,\mu),\mathcal{A}}$ is defined in Fig. 2. KEM is OW-rPCA secure if $\mathsf{Adv}_{KEM}^{(N,\mu)\text{-OW-rPCA}}(\mathcal{A})$ is negligible for any $\mathcal{A}$.

Definition 6 (Fuzzy public keys). *Let N be the number of users. Let $\mathcal{A}$ be an adversary against KEM. We define the advantage function of $\mathcal{A}$ against the fuzzyness of KEM*

$$\mathsf{Adv}_{KEM}^{N\text{-FUZZY}}(\mathcal{A}) := \left| \Pr\left[\text{FUZZY}_{KEM,0}^{N,\mathcal{A}} \Rightarrow 1\right] - \Pr\left[\text{FUZZY}_{KEM,1}^{N,\mathcal{A}} \Rightarrow 1\right] \right|,$$

where the game $\mathsf{FUZZY}_{\mathsf{KEM},b}^{N,\mathcal{A}}(b \in \{0,1\})$ is defined in Fig. 3. We say KEM has fuzzy public keys if $\mathsf{Adv}_{\mathsf{KEM}}^{N\text{-}\mathsf{FUZZY}}(\mathcal{A})$ is negligible for any $\mathcal{A}$.

Definition 7 (Anonymous ciphertexts under PCA attacks). *Let N and μ be the numbers of users and challenge ciphertexts per user, respectively. Let $\mathcal{A}$ be an adversary against* KEM. *We define the advantage function of $\mathcal{A}$ against the ciphertext anonymity (under PCA attacks) of* KEM

$$\mathsf{Adv}_{\mathsf{KEM}}^{(N,\mu)\text{-}\mathsf{ANO}}(\mathcal{A}) := \left| \Pr\left[\mathsf{ANO\text{-}PCA}_{\mathsf{KEM},0}^{(N,\mu),\mathcal{A}} \Rightarrow 1 \right] - \Pr\left[\mathsf{ANO\text{-}PCA}_{\mathsf{KEM},1}^{(N,\mu),\mathcal{A}} \Rightarrow 1 \right] \right|,$$

where the game $\mathsf{ANO\text{-}PCA}_{\mathsf{KEM},b}^{(N,\mu),\mathcal{A}}(b \in \{0,1\})$ is defined in Fig. 3. We say KEM *has anonymous ciphertexts under PCA attacks (or simply, anonymous ciphertexts) if $\mathsf{Adv}_{\mathsf{KEM}}^{(N,\mu)\text{-}\mathsf{ANO}}(\mathcal{A})$ is negligible for any $\mathcal{A}$.*

It is easy to see that if KEM is OW-PCA secure and has anonymous ciphertexts under PCA attacks, then it is also OW-rPCA secure, as stated in Lemma 1

Lemma 1 (OW-PCA + ANO-PCA $\Rightarrow$ OW-rPCA). *Let N and μ be the numbers of users and challenge ciphertexts per user, respectively. Let $\mathcal{A}$ be an adversary against* KEM. *We have*

$$\mathsf{Adv}_{\mathsf{KEM}}^{(N,\mu)\text{-}\mathsf{OW\text{-}rPCA}}(\mathcal{A}) \le \mathsf{Adv}_{\mathsf{KEM}}^{(N,\mu)\text{-}\mathsf{OW\text{-}PCA}}(\mathcal{A}) + \mathsf{Adv}_{\mathsf{KEM}}^{(N,\mu)\text{-}\mathsf{ANO}}(\mathcal{A})$$

2.2   Public-Key Encryption

PUBLIC-KEY ENCRYPTION. A PKE scheme PKE consists of four algorithms (Setup, KG, Enc, Dec) and a message space $\mathcal{M}$, a randomness space $\mathcal{R}$, and a ciphertext space $\mathcal{C}$. Setup outputs a system parameter par. KG(par) outputs a public and secret key pair (pk, sk). The encryption algorithm Enc, on input pk and a message $m \in \mathcal{M}$, outputs a ciphertext $c \in \mathcal{C}$. We also write $c := \mathsf{Enc}(\mathsf{pk}, m; r)$ to indicate the randomness $r \in \mathcal{R}$ explicitly. The decryption algorithm Dec, on input sk and a ciphertext c, outputs a message $m' \in \mathcal{M}$ or a rejection symbol $\bot \notin \mathcal{M}$.

Definition 8 (PKE Correctness). *Let* PKE $:=$ (Setup, KG, Enc, Dec) *be a* PKE *scheme with message space $\mathcal{M}$ and $\mathcal{A}$ be an adversary against* PKE. *The* COR *advantage of $\mathcal{A}$ is defined as*

$$\mathsf{Adv}_{\mathsf{PKE}}^{\mathsf{COR}}(\mathcal{A}) := \Pr\left[\mathsf{COR}_{\mathsf{PKE}}^{\mathcal{A}} \Rightarrow 1 \right],$$

where the COR *game is defined in Fig. 4. If there exists a constant δ such that for all adversary $\mathcal{A}$, $\mathsf{Adv}_{\mathsf{PKE}}^{\mathsf{COR}}(\mathcal{A}) \le \delta$, then we say* PKE *is $(1 - \delta)$-correct.*

We define fuzzyness for PKE, which is essentially the same as the one for KEM (cf. Definition 6).

```
GAME CORᴬₚₖₑ
01  par ← Setup
02  (pk, sk) ← KG(par)
03  m ← 𝒜ᴼ(par, pk, sk)
04  c ← Enc(pk, m)
05  if Dec(sk, c) ≠ m : return 1
06  return 0
```

Fig. 4. The COR game for a PKE scheme PKE and $\mathcal{A}$. $\mathcal{A}$ might have access to some oracle O (e.g., random oracles). It depends on the specific reduction.

Definition 9 (Fuzzy public key). *Let N be the number of users. We say PKE has fuzzy public keys if for any $\mathcal{A}$, the advantage function of $\mathcal{A}$ against the fuzzyness of PKE*

$$\mathsf{Adv}_{\mathsf{PKE}}^{N\text{-FUZZY}}(\mathcal{A}) := \left| \Pr\left[\mathsf{FUZZY}_{\mathsf{PKE},0}^{N,\mathcal{A}} \Rightarrow 1\right] - \Pr\left[\mathsf{FUZZY}_{\mathsf{PKE},1}^{N,\mathcal{A}} \Rightarrow 1\right] \right|$$

is negligible. The game $\mathsf{FUZZY}_{\mathsf{PKE},b}^{N,\mathcal{A}}(b \in \{0,1\})$ is defined in Fig. 3.

PSEUDORANDOM CIPHERTEXT. Let $\mathsf{PKE} := (\mathsf{KG}, \mathsf{Enc}, \mathsf{Dec})$ be a public-key encryption scheme with message space $\mathcal{M}$ and ciphertext space $\mathcal{C}$. We define PR-CPA (multi-challenge pseudorandomness under chosen-plaintext attacks) security in Fig. 5.

Definition 10 (Multi-user-challange PR-CPA security). *Let N and μ be the numbers of users and challenge ciphertexts per user. Let $\mathcal{A} = (\mathcal{A}_0, \mathcal{A}_1)$ be an adversary against PKE. Consider the games $\mathsf{PR\text{-}CPA}_{\mathsf{PKE},b}^{(N,\mu),\mathcal{A}}$ ($b \in \{0,1\}$) defined in Fig. 5. We define the (N, μ)-PR-CPA advantage function*

$$\mathsf{Adv}_{\mathsf{PKE}}^{(N,\mu)\text{-PR-CPA}}(\mathcal{A}) := \left| \Pr\left[\mathsf{PR\text{-}CPA}_{\mathsf{PKE},0}^{(N,\mu),\mathcal{A}} \Rightarrow 1\right] - \Pr\left[\mathsf{PR\text{-}CPA}_{\mathsf{PKE},1}^{(N,\mu),\mathcal{A}} \Rightarrow 1\right] \right|.$$

PKE is PR-CPA secure if $\mathsf{Adv}_{\mathsf{PKE}}^{(N,\mu)\text{-PR-CPA}}(\mathcal{A})$ is negligible for any $\mathcal{A}$.

3   Password-Based Authenticated Key Exchange

3.1   Definition of PAKE

A two-message PAKE protocol $\mathsf{PAKE} := (\mathsf{Setup}, \mathsf{Init}, \mathsf{Resp}, \mathsf{TerInit})$ consists of four algorithms. The setup algorithm Setup, on input security parameter 1^λ, outputs global PAKE protocol parameters par. For simplicity, we ignore the input of Setup and write par ← Setup.

Let U be a user, S be a server, and pw be the password shared between U and S. Since we consider the client-server setting, to initiate a session, U will send the first protocol message. U runs the client's initialization algorithm Init,

```
GAME PR-CPA_{PKE,b}^{(N,μ),A}
01 par ← Setup
02 for i ∈ N
03    (pk_i, sk_i) ← KG(par), pk[i] := pk_i
04 (m, st) ← A_0(par, pk)           // m has N × μ messages
05 for i ∈ [N]:
06    for j ∈ [μ]
07       c_0[i,j] ← Enc(pk[i], m[i,j]), c_1[i,j] ←$ C
08 b' ← A_1(st, c_b)
09 return b'
```

Fig. 5. Security game PR-CPA for PKE scheme PKE.

which takes the identities U, S and password pw as inputs and outputs a client message M_U and session state st, and then U sends M_U to S. On receiving M_U, S runs the server's derivation algorithm Resp, which takes identities U and S and the received message M_U as input, together with the password pw, to generate a server message M_S and a session key SK_S. S sends M_S to U. Finally, on receiving M_S, U runs the client's derivation algorithm TerInit which inputs U, S, the session state st generated before, the received message M_S, and password pw, to generate a session key sk'_U. In two-message PAKE protocols, the server does not need to save session state since it can compute the session key right after receiving the user's message.

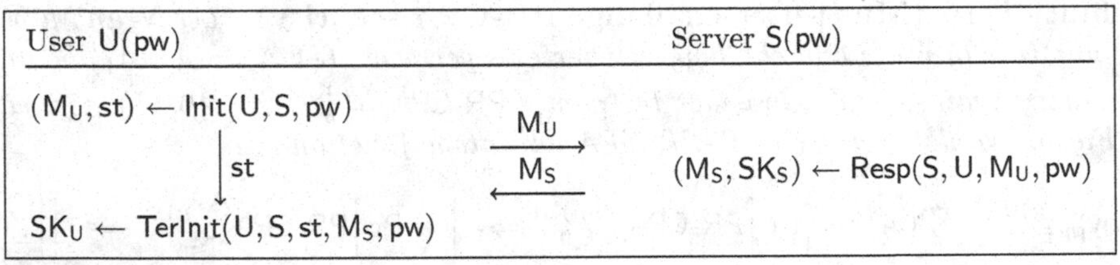

User $U(pw)$		Server $S(pw)$
$(M_U, st) ← Init(U, S, pw)$		
$\downarrow st$	$\xrightarrow{M_U}$ $\xleftarrow{M_S}$	$(M_S, SK_S) ← Resp(S, U, M_U, pw)$
$SK_U ← TerInit(U, S, st, M_S, pw)$		

Fig. 6. Illustration for a two-message PAKE protocol execution between a user U and a server S.

We define the correctness of PAKE protocols, stating that an honestly execution between user U and server S (with the same password $pw_{U,S}$) as in Fig. 6 will produce the same session key $SK_U = SK_S$.

Definition 11 (PAKE Correctness). *Let* PAKE := (Setup, Init, Resp, TerInit) *be a PAKE protocol and let* U *and* S *be a user-server pair with password* pw. *We say* PAKE *is* ρ-*correct, if for any PAKE system parameter* par ← Setup, *the following probability is at least* ρ.

$$
\Pr\left[SK_U = SK_S \,\middle|\,
\begin{array}{l}
(M_U, st) ← Init(U, S, pw) \\
(M_S, SK_S) ← Resp(S, U, M_U, pw) \\
SK_U ← TerInit(U, S, st, M_S, pw)
\end{array}
\right]
$$

3.2   Security Model of PAKE

We consider indistinguishability(IND)-based security of PAKE protocols. In this section, we define the multi-test variant of the Bellare-Pointcheval-Rogaway model [1,5,10]. We simply denoted it as the BPR model.

In the BPR model, we consider a name space of users $\mathcal{U}$ and a name space of servers $\mathcal{S}$, which are assumed to be disjoint. Oracles provided in this model rejects queries inconsistent withe these name spaces.

We denote the session key space by $\mathcal{SK}$. Password are bit strings of ℓ and the password space is defined as $\mathcal{PW} \subsetneq \{0,1\}^{\ell}$. Each pair of user and server $\mathsf{U} \times \mathsf{S} \in \mathcal{U} \times \mathcal{S}$ holds a shared password $\mathsf{pw}_{\mathsf{U},\mathsf{S}} \in \mathcal{PW}$.

Let P denotes a party (either a user or server). Each party in $\mathcal{U} \cup \mathcal{S}$ has multiple instances π_{P}^{i} (i is some index) and each instance has its internal state. The state of an instance π_{P}^{i} is a tuple $(\mathsf{e}, \mathsf{tr}, \mathsf{key}, \mathsf{acc})$ where

- e is the ephemeral secret chosen by P.
- tr is the trace of the instance, i.e., the names of user and server involved in the instance and the messages sent and received by P in the instance.
- key is the accepted session key of π_{P}^{i}.
- acc is a Boolean flag that indicates whether the instance has accepted the session key. As long as the instance did not receive the last message, $\mathsf{acc} = \bot$ (which means undefined).
- test is a Boolean flag that indicates whether the instance has been queried to the TEST oracle (which will be defined later).

To access individual components of the state, we write $\pi_{\mathsf{P}}^{i}.(\mathsf{e}, \mathsf{tr}, \mathsf{key}, \mathsf{acc})$. We define partnership via matching instance trace.

Definition 12 (Partnering). *A user instance $\pi_{\mathsf{U}}^{t_0}$ and a server instance $\pi_{\mathsf{S}}^{t_1}$ are partnered if and only if*

$$\pi_{\mathsf{U}}^{t_0}.\mathsf{acc} = \mathbf{true} = \pi_{\mathsf{S}}^{t_1}.\mathsf{acc} \quad \text{and} \quad \pi_{\mathsf{U}}^{t_0}.\mathsf{tr} = \pi_{\mathsf{S}}^{t_1}.\mathsf{tr}$$

Two user instances are never partnered, neither are two server instances. We define a partnership predicate $\mathsf{Partner}(\pi_{\mathsf{U}}^{t_0}, \pi_{\mathsf{S}}^{t_1})$ which outputs $\mathbf{true}$ if and only if $\pi_{\mathsf{U}}^{t_0}$ and $\pi_{\mathsf{S}}^{t_1}$ are partnered.

SECURITY GAME. The security game is played with an adversary $\mathcal{A}$. The experiment draws a random challenge bit $\beta \leftarrow \{0,1\}$, generates the public parameters, and outputs the public parameters to $\mathcal{A}$. $\mathcal{A}$ is allowed to query the following oracles:

- EXECUTE($\mathsf{U}, t_1, \mathsf{S}, t_2$): This oracle outputs the protocol messages of an honest protocol execution between instances $\pi_{\mathsf{U}}^{t_1}$ and $\pi_{\mathsf{S}}^{t_2}$. By querying this oracle, the adversary launches passive attacks.

- SENDINIT, SENDRESP, SENDTERINIT: These oracles model active attacks. By querying these oracles, the adversary sends protocol messages to protocol instances. For sake of simplicity, we assume that the adversary does not use these oracles to launch passive attacks (which are already captured by the EXECUTE oracle).
- REVEAL(P, t): By this oracle, the adversary reveals the session key of π_P^t.
- TEST(P, t): If π_P^t is fresh (which will be defined later), then, depending on the challenge bit β, the oracle outputs either the session key of π_P^t or a uniformly random key. Otherwise, the oracle outputs $\bot$. After this query, the flag π_P^t.test will be set as **true**.

We denote the game by $\mathsf{BPR_{PAKE}}$. The pseudocode is given in $\mathbf{G}_0$ in Fig. 8, instantiated with our PAKE protocol. Before defining PAKE security, we define freshness to avoid trivial attacks in this model.

Definition 13 (Freshness). *An instance π_P^t is fresh if and only if*

1. *π_P^t is accepted.*
2. *π_P^t was not queried to TEST or REVEAL before.*
3. *At least one of the following conditions holds:*
   (a) π_P^t accepted during a query to EXECUTE.
   (b) There exists more than one (not necessarily fresh) partner instance[4].
   (c) A unique fresh partner instance exists.
   (d) No partner instance exists and the password of P was not corrupted prior to π_P^t is accepted.

By these definitions, we are ready to define the security of PAKE protocols.

Definition 14 (Security of PAKE). *Let PAKE be a PAKE protocol and $\mathcal{A}$ be an adversary. The advantage of $\mathcal{A}$ against PAKE is defined as*

$$\mathsf{Adv}_{\mathsf{PAKE}}^{\mathsf{BPR}}(\mathcal{A}) := \left| \Pr\left[\mathsf{BPR}_{\mathsf{PAKE}}^{\mathcal{A}} \Rightarrow 1 \right] - \frac{1}{2} \right|$$

A PAKE protocol is considered secure if the best the adversary can do is to perform an online dictionary attack. Concretely, PAKE is secure if for any adversary $\mathcal{A}$, $\mathsf{Adv}_{\mathsf{PAKE}}^{\mathsf{BPR}}(\mathcal{A})$ is negligibly close to $\frac{S}{|\mathcal{PW}|}$ when passwords in the security game are drawn independently and uniformly from $\mathcal{PW}$. Here S is the number of send queries made by $\mathcal{A}$ (i.e., the number of sessions during the game $\mathsf{BPR}_{\mathsf{PAKE}}$).

4   Our Generic Construction of PAKE

CONSTRUCTION. Let $\mathsf{KEM} = (\mathsf{Setup}, \mathsf{KG}, \mathsf{Encaps}, \mathsf{Decaps})$ be a KEM scheme with public key space $\mathcal{PK}$, ciphertext space $\mathcal{C}$, and KEM key space $\mathcal{K}$. We also require KEM to have implicit rejection. Let $\mathsf{IC}_1 = (\mathsf{E}_1, \mathsf{D}_1)$ be a symmetric encryption with key space $\mathcal{PW}$, plaintext space $\mathcal{PK}$, and ciphertext space $\mathcal{E}_1$. Let $\mathsf{IC}_2 =$

Alg Init(U, S, pw)	**Alg** TerInit(U, S, st, e_2, pw)	**Alg** Resp(S, U, e_1, pw)
01 (pk, sk) $\leftarrow$	05 **let** (pk, sk, e_1) := st	11 pk := D_1(pw, e_1)
KG(par)	06 c := D_2(pw, e_2)	12 (c, k) $\leftarrow$ Encaps(pk)
02 e_1 := E_1(pw, pk)	07 k := Decaps(sk, c)	13 e_2 := E_2(pw, c)
03 st := (pk, sk, e_1)	08 ctxt := (U, S, e_1, e_2)	14 ctxt := (U, S, e_1, e_2)
04 **return** (e_1, st)	09 SK := H(ctxt, pk, c, k, pw)	15 SK := H(ctxt, pk, c, k, pw)
	10 **return** SK	16 **return** (e_2, SK)

Fig. 7. Our PAKE protocol Π.

(E_2, D_2) be a symmetric encryption with key space $\mathcal{PW}$, plaintext space $\mathcal{C}$, and ciphertext space $\mathcal{E}_2$.

We construct our two-message PAKE protocol Π = (Init, Resp, TerInit) as shown in Fig. 6, where $\mathcal{SK}$ is the session key space of PAKE and H: $\{0,1\}^* \rightarrow \mathcal{SK}$ is a hash function which is used to derive the session key. The system parameter par is generated by par $\leftarrow$ Setup.

The correctness of Π is dependent on KEM. In Fig. 7, one honest execution of Π includes one KEM encapsulation and decapsulation. So, if KEM is $(1 - \delta)$-correct, then Π is also $(1 - \delta)$-correct.

Theorem 1. *Let* H *be random oracle and* IC_1 *and* IC_2 *be ideal ciphers. If* KEM *is* $(1-\delta)$*-correct and has implicit rejection, fuzzy public keys, anonymous ciphertexts, OW-PCA security, and* OW-rPCA *security (cf. Definitions 4 to 7), then the PAKE protocol* Π *in Fig. 7 is secure (wrt Definition 14).*

Concretely, for any $\mathcal{A}$ *against* Π*, there are adversaries* $\mathcal{B}_1$-$\mathcal{B}_6$ *with* $\mathbf{T}(\mathcal{A}) \approx \mathbf{T}(\mathcal{B}_i)(1 \leq i \leq 6)$ *and*

$$
\begin{aligned}
\mathsf{Adv}_\Pi^{\mathsf{BPR}}(\mathcal{A}) \leq\ & S/|\mathcal{PW}| + \mathsf{Adv}_{\mathsf{KEM}}^{q_1\text{-FUZZY}}(\mathcal{B}_1) + \mathsf{Adv}_{\mathsf{KEM}}^{(S,q_2+S)\text{-OW-rPCA}}(\mathcal{B}_4) \\
& + \mathsf{Adv}_{\mathsf{KEM}}^{(S,1)\text{-OW-PCA}}(\mathcal{B}_2) + \mathsf{Adv}_{\mathsf{KEM}}^{(S+q_2,S)\text{-OW-PCA}}(\mathcal{B}_5) \\
& + \mathsf{Adv}_{\mathsf{KEM}}^{(S,1)\text{-ANO}}(\mathcal{B}_3) + \mathsf{Adv}_{\mathsf{KEM}}^{(S+q_1,S)\text{-ANO}}(\mathcal{B}_6) + S \cdot \delta \\
& + S^2(\eta_{pk} + \eta_{ct}) + \frac{(q_1^2 + S^2)}{|\mathcal{E}_1|} + \frac{(q_2^2 + S^2)}{|\mathcal{E}_2|} + \frac{q_1^2}{|\mathcal{PK}|} + \frac{q_2^2}{|\mathcal{C}|} + \frac{(q_{\mathsf{H}}^2 + S^2)}{|\mathcal{SK}|},
\end{aligned}
$$

where q_1, q_2, q_{H} *are the numbers of* $\mathcal{A}$ *queries to* $IC_1, IC_2,$ *and* H *respectively.* S *is the number of sessions* $\mathcal{A}$ *established in the security game.* η_{pk} *and* η_{ct} *are the collision probabilities of* KG *and* Encaps*, respectively.*

Remark 1 (Implementation of Ideal Ciphers). The implementation of IC_1 and IC_2 depends on the concrete instantiation of the underlying KEM scheme KEM. Beguinet et al. provides an implementation if KEM is instantiated with the Kyber KEM [32] in [8, Section 5.2]. More implementation for group-based schemes and lattice-based schemes can be found in [31].

---

[4] This essentially forces a secure PAKE protocol not to have more than one partner instances.

Remark 2. We require KEM to have implicit rejection (cf. Definition 3) because this simplifies our security proof. More concretely, if the underlying KEM KEM has implicit rejection, then we only require OW-PCA security to finish our tight proof. Otherwise, we need the OW-PCVA (cf. [21, Definition 2.1]) security to detect whether the c is valid in the proof.

4.1 Proof of Theorem 1

Let $\mathcal{A}$ be an adversary against PAKE in the BPR game, where N is the number of parties. Every user-server pair $(\mathsf{U}, \mathsf{S}) \in \mathcal{U} \times \mathcal{S}$ is associated with a password $\mathsf{pw}_{\mathsf{U,S}}$. The game sequences $\mathbf{G}_0$-$\mathbf{G}_{12}$ of the proof are given in Figs. 8, 9, 11, 14.

During the game sequences in this proof, we exclude the collisions of outputs of KG and Encaps in EXECUTE, SENDINIT, SENDRESP, and SENDTERINIT. We also exclude the collisions of outputs of ideal ciphers and random oracle, i.e., $\mathsf{IC}_1 = (\mathsf{E}_1, \mathsf{D}_1)$, $\mathsf{IC}_2 = (\mathsf{E}_2, \mathsf{D}_2)$, and H. If such a collision happens at any time, then we abort the game. For readability, we do not explicitly define such collision events in the codes of games sequences.

By the assumption of Theorem 1, the collision probabilities of the outputs of KG and Encaps are η_{pk} and η_{ct}, and S is the number of sessions generated (i.e., the total number of queries to EXECUTE, SENDINIT, SENDRESP, and SENDTERINIT) during the game and q_1, q_2, and q_H are the numbers of queries to IC_1, IC_2, and H, respectively. By birthday bounds and union bounds, such collision events happen within probability $S^2(\eta_{pk} + \eta_{ct}) + \frac{(q_1^2 + S^2)}{|\mathcal{E}_1|} + \frac{(q_2^2 + S^2)}{|\mathcal{E}_2|} + \frac{q_1^2}{|\mathcal{PK}|} + \frac{q_2^2}{|\mathcal{C}|} + \frac{(q_\mathsf{H}^2 + S^2)}{|\mathcal{SK}|}$. Game $\mathbf{G}_0$ is the same as $\mathsf{BPR}_\mathsf{PAKE}$ except that we define such collision events in $\mathbf{G}_0$, we have

$$\left| \Pr\left[\mathsf{BPR}_\mathsf{PAKE}^\mathcal{A} \Rightarrow 1 \right] - \Pr\left[\mathbf{G}_0^\mathcal{A} \Rightarrow 1 \right] \right|$$
$$\leq S^2(\eta_{pk} + \eta_{ct}) + \frac{(q_1^2 + S^2)}{|\mathcal{E}_1|} + \frac{(q_2^2 + S^2)}{|\mathcal{E}_2|} + \frac{q_1^2}{|\mathcal{PK}|} + \frac{q_2^2}{|\mathcal{C}|} + \frac{(q_\mathsf{H}^2 + S^2)}{|\mathcal{SK}|}$$

Moreover, excluding these collisions imply that different instances have different traces and each instance (user's or server's) has at most one partnering instance. By the construction of PAKE, different instances will have different session keys, since the hash function H take the trace of instance as input.

Game $\mathbf{G}_1$. Instead of using the Freshness procedure in the TEST oracle, we assign an additional variable $\mathtt{fr}$ to each instance π to explicitly indicate the freshness of π. Whenever $\mathcal{A}$ issues an oracle query related to π, we will update $\pi.\mathtt{fr}$ in real time according to the freshness definition (cf. Definition 13). This change is conceptual, so we have

$$\Pr\left[\mathbf{G}_0^\mathcal{A} \Rightarrow 1 \right] = \Pr\left[\mathbf{G}_1^\mathcal{A} \Rightarrow 1 \right]$$

To save space, for games $\mathbf{G}_2$ to $\mathbf{G}_x$, instead of presenting the whole codes of the game, we only present the codes of changed oracles.

Game G_0-G_1

```
01  par ← Setup
02  for (U, S) ∈ 𝒰 × 𝒮
03     pw_{U,S} ← 𝒫𝒲
04  𝒞 := ∅
05  β ← {0, 1}
06  b' ← 𝒜^{O,H,IC_1,IC_2}(par)
07  return β == b'
```

Oracle REVEAL(P, t)

```
08  if π_P^t.acc ≠ true or π_P^t.test = true
09     return ⊥
10  if ∃P' ∈ 𝒰 ∪ 𝒮, t' s.t.
11     Partner(π_P^t, π_{P'}^{t'}) = true
12     and π_{P'}^{t'}.test = true
13     return ⊥
14  for ∀(P', t') s.t. π_{P'}^{t'}.tr = π_P^t.tr      // G_1
15     π_{P'}^{t'}.fr := false                        // G_1
16  return π_P^t.key
```

Oracle TEST(P, t)

```
17  if Freshness(π_P^t) = false                       // G_0
18  if π_P^t.fr = false                               // G_1
19     return ⊥
20  SK_0^* := REVEAL(P, t), SK_1^* ←$ 𝒮𝒦
21  if SK_0^* = ⊥: return ⊥
22  π_P^t.test := true
23  return SK_β^*
```

Oracle CORRUPT(U, S)

```
24  if (U, S) ∈ 𝒞: return ⊥
25  𝒞 := 𝒞 ∪ {(U, S)}
26  return pw_{U,S}
```

Oracle E_1(pw, pk)

```
27  if ∃(pw, pk, e_1, *) ∈ ℒ_1: return e_1
28  e_1 ←$ ℰ_1\𝒯_1, ℒ_1 := ℒ_1 ∪ {e_1}
29  ℒ_1 := ℒ_1 ∪ (pw, pk, e_1, enc)
30  return e_1
```

Oracle E_2(pw, c)

```
31  if ∃(pw, c, e_2, *) ∈ ℒ_2: return e_2
32  e_2 ←$ ℰ_2\𝒯_2, 𝒯_2 := 𝒯_2 ∪ {e_2}
33  ℒ_2 := ℒ_2 ∪ (pw, c, e_2, enc)
34  return e_2
```

Oracle D_1(pw, e_1)

```
35  if ∃(pw, pk, e_1, *) ∈ ℒ_1: return pk
36  pk ←$ 𝒫𝒦, ℒ_1 := ℒ_1 ∪ (pw, pk, e_1, dec)
37  return pk
```

Oracle D_2(pw, e_2)

```
38  if ∃(pw, c, e_2, *) ∈ ℒ_2: return c
39  c ←$ 𝒞, ℒ_2 := ℒ_2 ∪ (pw, c, e_2, dec)
40  return c
```

Oracle EXECUTE(U, t_1, S, t_2)

```
41  if π_U^{t_1} ≠ ⊥ or π_S^{t_2} ≠ ⊥
42     return ⊥
43  let pw := pw_{U,S}
44  (pk, sk) ← KG(par), e_1 := E_1(pw, pk)
45  (c, k) ← Encaps(pk), e_2 := E_2(pw, c)
46  ctxt := (U, S, e_1, e_2)
47  SK := H(ctxt, pk, c, k, pw)
48  π_U^{t_1} := ((pk, sk, e_1), ctxt, SK, true)
49  π_S^{t_2} := ((c, k, e_2), ctxt, SK, true)
50  (π_U^{t_1}.fr, π_S^{t_2}.fr) := (true, true)     // G_1
51  return (U, e_1, S, e_2)
```

Oracle SENDINIT(U, t_1, S)

```
52  if π_U^{t_1} ≠ ⊥: return ⊥
53  (pk, sk) ← KG(par)
54  e_1 := E_1(pw_{U,S}, pk)
55  π_U^{t_1} := ((pk, sk, e_1), (U, S, e_1, ⊥), ⊥, ⊥)
56  π_U^{t_1}.fr := false                             // G_1
57  return (U, e_1)
```

Oracle SENDRESP(S, t_2, U, e_1)

```
58  π_S^{t_2} ≠ ⊥: return ⊥
59  if (U, S) ∈ 𝒞: π_S^{t_2}.fr := false             // G_1
60  else π_S^{t_2}.fr := true                         // G_1
61  pk := D_1(pw_{U,S}, e_1)
62  (c, k) ← Encaps(pk)
63  e_2 := E_2(pw_{U,S}, c)
64  ctxt := (U, S, e_1, e_2)
65  SK := H(ctxt, pk, c, k, pw_{U,S})
66  π_S^{t_2} := ((c, k, e_2), ctxt, SK, true)
67  return (S, e_2)
```

Oracle SENDTERINIT(U, t_1, S, e_2)

```
68  if π_U^{t_1} = ⊥ and π_U^{t_1}.tr ≠ (U, S, *, *)
69     return ⊥
70  let (pk, sk, e_1) := π_U^{t_1}.e
71  c := D_2(pw, e_2), k := Decaps(sk, c)
72  if ∃t_2 s.t. π_S^{t_2}.fr = true                  // G_1
73     and π_S^{t_2}.tr = (U, S, e_1, e_2)            // G_1
74     π_U^{t_1}.fr := true                           // G_1
75  else if (U, S) ∉ 𝒞: π_U^{t_1}.fr := true          // G_1
76  else π_U^{t_1}.fr := false                        // G_1
77  ctxt := (U, S, e_1, e_2)
78  SK := H(ctxt, pk, c, k, pw_{U,S})
79  π_U^{t_1}.(tr, key, acc) := (ctxt, SK, true)
80  return true
```

Oracle H(U, S, e_1, e_2, pk, c, k, pw)

```
81  if ℒ_H[U, S, e_1, e_2, pk, c, k, pw] = ⊥
82     SK ←$ 𝒮𝒦
83     ℒ_H[U, S, e_1, e_2, pk, c, k, pw] := SK
84  return ℒ_H[U, S, e_1, e_2, pk, c, k, pw]
```

Fig. 8. Games in proving Theorem 1. $\mathcal{A}$ has access to the set of PAKE oracles {EXECUTE, SENDINIT, SENDRESP, SENDTERINIT, CORRUPT, REVEAL, TEST}, random oracle H, and ideal ciphers $IC_1 = (E_1, D_1)$ and $IC_2 = (E_2, D_2)$.

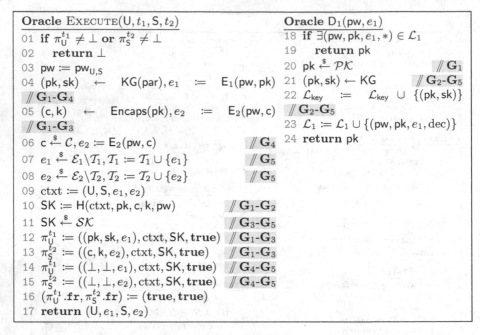

Fig. 9. Oracles Execute and D_1 in the games sequence $\mathbf{G_1}$-$\mathbf{G_5}$.

Game $\mathbf{G_2}$. We change the output of D_1. When $\mathcal{A}$ queries $D_1(\mathsf{pw}, e_1)$ where e_1 is not generated from $E_1(\mathsf{pw}, \cdot)$, we generate pk via $(\mathsf{pk}, \mathsf{sk}) \leftarrow \mathsf{KG}$ instead of $\mathsf{pk} \xleftarrow{\$} \mathcal{PK}$. Such $(\mathsf{pk}, \mathsf{sk})$ is recorded in $\mathcal{L}_{\mathsf{key}}$. cf. Lines 20 ro 22.

The difference between $\mathbf{G_1}$ and $\mathbf{G_2}$ can be bounded by using the fuzzyness of KEM. The bound is given in Lemma 2. For readability, we continue the proof of Lemma 1 and postpone the proof of Lemma 2 to our full version [28].

Lemma 2. *With notations and assumptions from $\mathbf{G_1}$ and $\mathbf{G_2}$ in the proof of Theorem 1, there is an adversary $\mathcal{B}_1$ with $\mathbf{T}(\mathcal{B}_1) \approx \mathbf{T}(\mathcal{A})$ and*

$$\left| \Pr\left[\mathbf{G_1^{\mathcal{A}}} \Rightarrow 1\right] - \Pr\left[\mathbf{G_2^{\mathcal{A}}} \Rightarrow 1\right] \right| \leq \mathsf{Adv}_{\mathsf{KEM}}^{q_1\text{-FUZZY}}(\mathcal{B}_1)$$

After this change, all pk generated by querying D_1 (i.e., there exists (pw, e_1) s.t. $(\mathsf{pw}, \mathsf{pk}, e_1, \mathsf{dec}) \in \mathcal{L}_1$) will always have a secret key sk such that $(\mathsf{pk}, \mathsf{sk}) \in \mathcal{L}_{\mathsf{key}}$. This fact is crucial for our later simulation.

Game $\mathbf{G_3}$. In this game, session keys of instances generated in Execute are all uniformly at random and independent of H (cf. Lines 10 to 11).

Let $\mathsf{Query}_{\mathsf{exec}}$ be the event that $\mathcal{A}$ queries the hash input of the session key of an instance generated in Execute. Since H is a random oracle, if $\mathsf{Query}_{\mathsf{exec}}$ does not happen, then $\mathcal{A}$ cannot detect the modification made in $\mathbf{G_3}$. We have

$$\left| \Pr\left[\mathbf{G_2^{\mathcal{A}}} \Rightarrow 1\right] - \Pr\left[\mathbf{G_3^{\mathcal{A}}} \Rightarrow 1\right] \right| \leq \Pr[\mathsf{Query}_{\mathsf{exec}}]$$

We construct an adversary $\mathcal{B}_2$ against the OW-PCA security of KEM in Fig. 10 such that $\mathbf{T}(\mathcal{B}_2) \approx \mathbf{T}(\mathcal{A})$ and $\Pr[\text{Query}_{\text{exec}}] \leq \mathsf{Adv}_{\mathsf{KEM}}^{(S,1)\text{-OW-PCA}}(\mathcal{B}_2)$. Concretely, $\mathcal{B}_2$ inputs a OW-PCA challenge $(\text{par}, \mathbf{pk}, \mathbf{c})$ and has access to a plaintext checking oracle PCO. Since $\mathcal{A}$'s number of queries to EXECUTE is S and there is only one KEM ciphertext generated per query to EXECUTE, we need at most S challenge public keys and one challenge ciphertexts per public key.

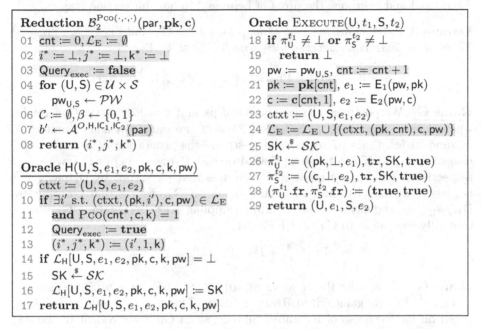

Fig. 10. Reduction $\mathcal{B}_2$ in bounding the probability difference between $\mathbf{G}_2$ and $\mathbf{G}_3$. Highlighted parts show how $\mathcal{B}_2$ uses PCO and challenge input to simulate $\mathbf{G}_3$. All other oracles (except EXECUTE and H) are the same as in $\mathbf{G}_2$.

$\mathcal{B}_2$ uses (i^*, j^*, k^*) to store its OW solution and uses $\mathcal{L}_\text{E}$ to record the intended hash input of session keys generated in EXECUTE (cf. Line 24). Although $\mathcal{B}_2$ does not have secret keys of $\mathbf{pk}$ and KEM keys of $\mathbf{c}$, it can still simulate $\mathbf{G}_3$ since this information is not required in simulating EXECUTE. Moreover, $\mathcal{B}_2$ uses $\mathcal{L}_\text{E}$ and PCO to determine whether $\text{Query}_{\text{exec}}$ happens (cf. Lines 10 to 13).

If $\mathcal{A}$ queried $\mathsf{H}(\mathsf{U}, \mathsf{S}, e_1, e_2, \mathsf{pk}, \mathsf{c}, \mathsf{k}, \mathsf{pw})$, where $(\mathsf{U}, \mathsf{S}, e_1, e_2, \mathsf{pk}, \mathsf{c}, \mathsf{k}, \mathsf{pw})$ is the intended hash input of a session key SK generated in EXECUTE, then by the construction of PAKE and Lines 21 to 24, there exists $\mathsf{cnt}^* \in [S]$ such that $(\mathsf{U}, \mathsf{S}, e_1, e_2, (\mathsf{pk}, \mathsf{cnt}^*), \mathsf{c}, \mathsf{pw}) \in \mathcal{L}_\text{E}$, $\mathsf{c} = \mathsf{c}[\mathsf{cnt}^*, 1]$, and $\mathsf{k} = \mathsf{Decaps}(\mathsf{sk}, \mathsf{c})$, where sk is the secret key of $\mathbf{pk}[\mathsf{cnt}^*]$. This means that k is the OW solution of $\mathsf{c}[\mathsf{cnt}^*, 1]$, and thus $\mathcal{B}_2$ records the OW solution (cf. Line 13) and returns it when the game ends. Therefore, we have

$$\left|\Pr\left[\mathbf{G}_2^{\mathcal{A}} \Rightarrow 1\right] - \Pr\left[\mathbf{G}_3^{\mathcal{A}} \Rightarrow 1\right]\right| \leq \Pr\left[\text{Query}_{\text{exec}}\right] \leq \mathsf{Adv}_{\mathsf{KEM}}^{(S,1)\text{-OW-PCA}}(\mathcal{B}_2).$$

Game G_4. We change the generation of c in EXECUTE (cf. Line 06). In this game, c is sampled from $\mathcal{C}$ uniformly at random instead of using Encaps. Moreover, we no longer store the information about pk, sk, c, and k in the outputting instances from EXECUTE (cf. Lines 14 to 15). The later modification is conceptual since the game does not need this information to simulate EXECUTE.

The difference between G_3 and G_4 can be bounded by using the ciphertext anonymity of KEM. The bound is given in Lemma 3. We continue the proof of Theorem 1 and postpone the proof of Lemma 3 to our full version [28].

Lemma 3. *With notations and assumptions from G_3 and G_4 in the proof of Theorem 1, there is an adversary $\mathcal{B}_3$ with $\mathbf{T}(\mathcal{B}_3) \approx \mathbf{T}(\mathcal{A})$ and*

$$\left| \Pr\left[G_3^{\mathcal{A}} \Rightarrow 1\right] - \Pr\left[G_4^{\mathcal{A}} \Rightarrow 1\right] \right| \leq \mathsf{Adv}_{\mathsf{KEM}}^{(S,1)\text{-ANO}}(\mathcal{B}_3)$$

Game G_5. We postpone the generation of pk and c in EXECUTE. Concretely, when $\mathcal{A}$ issues a query (U, t_1, S, t_2) to EXECUTE, we sample e_1 and e_2 uniformly at random (cf. Lines 07 to 08) and postpone the generation of pk and c and usage of IC_1 and IC_2 to the time that $\mathcal{A}$ queries $\mathsf{D}_1(\mathsf{pw}_{U,S}, e_1)$ or $\mathsf{D}_2(\mathsf{pw}_{U,S}, e_2)$, respectively. The change made in G_2 ensures that pk output by $\mathsf{D}_1(\mathsf{pw}_{U,S}, e_1)$ is generated using KG, and the change made in G_4 ensures that c output by $\mathsf{D}_2(\mathsf{pw}_{U,S}, e_2)$ is generated via uniformly sampling over $\mathcal{C}$. Therefore, G_5 is conceptually equivalent to G_4, which means

$$\Pr\left[G_4^{\mathcal{A}} \Rightarrow 1\right] = \Pr\left[G_5^{\mathcal{A}} \Rightarrow 1\right]$$

Game G_6. We rewrite the codes of SENDINIT, SENDRESP, and SENDTERINIT in Fig. 11. In this game, SENDRESP and SENDTERINIT compute session keys based on the freshness of instances. SENDRESP in G_6 is equivalent to the one in G_5. For SENDTERINIT in G_6, if the user instance $\pi_U^{t_1}$ has a matching server instance and such instance is fresh, then we make these two instances have the same session key (cf. Line 46). These changes are for further game transitions and they are conceptual if KEM has perfect correctness. Here we need to consider the correctness error of KEM since now we directly set up $\pi_U^{t_1}$'s session key without decapsulation. There are at most S queries to SENDTERINIT, by a union bound, we have

$$\left| \Pr\left[G_5^{\mathcal{A}} \Rightarrow 1\right] - \Pr\left[G_6^{\mathcal{A}} \Rightarrow 1\right] \right| \leq S \cdot \delta.$$

Game G_7. We use two flags $\mathsf{Guess}_{\mathsf{user}}$ and $\mathsf{Guess}_{\mathsf{ser}}$ (which are initialized as **false**) to indicate whether the following events happen:

- When $\mathcal{A}$ queries SENDRESP(S, t_2, U, e_1), if (U, S) is uncorrupted, e_1 is not generated from U's instance (cf. Line 37), and $\exists \mathsf{pk}$ such that e_1 is generated via querying $\mathsf{E}_1(\mathsf{pw}_{U,S}, \mathsf{pk})$, then we set $\mathsf{Guess}_{\mathsf{ser}}$ as **true** (cf. Lines 23 to 24).
- When $\mathcal{A}$ queries SENDTERINIT(U, t_1, S, e_2), if $\pi_U^{t_1}$ does not have matching session, (U, S) is uncorrupted, e_2 is not generated from S's instance (cf. Line 30), and $\exists c$ such that e_2 is generated via querying $\mathsf{E}_2(\mathsf{pw}_{U,S}, c)$, then we set $\mathsf{Guess}_{\mathsf{user}}$ as **true** (cf. Lines 53 to 53).

```
Game G₆-G₁₀                                    Oracle SendInit(U, t₁, S)
01 par ← Setup                                 32 if π_U^{t₁} ≠ ⊥: return ⊥
02 for (U,S) ∈ 𝒰: pw_{U,S} ← 𝒫𝒲               33 (pk,sk) ← KG(par), e₁ := E₁(pw_{U,S}, pk)
03 𝒞 := ∅, β ← {0,1}                           34 e₁ $← ℰ₁\𝒯₁, 𝒯₁ := 𝒯₁ ∪ {e₁}        // G₉-G₁₀
04 Guess_user := false          // G₇-G₁₀      35 pk := D₁(pw_{U,S}, e₁)                 // G₉-G₁₀
05 Guess_ser := false           // G₇-G₁₀      36 Retrieve sk s.t. (pk,sk) ∈ ℒ_key       // G₉-G₁₀
06 b' ← 𝒜^{O,H,IC₁,IC₂}(par)                   37 ℒ₁^U := ℒ₁^U ∪ {e₁}                    // G₇-G₁₀
07 return β == b'                              38 π_U^{t₁} := ((pk,sk,e₁),(U,S,e₁,⊥),⊥,⊥)
                                               39 π_U^{t₁}.fr := false
Oracle SendResp(S, t₂, U, e₁)                  40 return (U, e₁)

08 π_S^{t₂} ≠ ⊥: return ⊥                       Oracle SendTerInit(U, t₁, S, e₂)
09 if (U,S) ∈ 𝒞                                41 if π_U^{t₁} = ⊥ and π_U^{t₁}.tr ≠ (U,S,*,*)
10    π_S^{t₂}.fr := false                     42    return ⊥
11    pk := D₁(pw_{U,S}, e₁)                    43 (pk,sk,e₁) := π_U^{t₁}.e
12    (c,k) ← Encaps(pk)                        44 if ∃t₂ s.t. π_S^{t₂}.fr = true
13    e₂ := E₂(pw_{U,S}, c)                     45    and π_S^{t₂}.tr = (U,S,e₁,e₂)
14    ctxt := (U,S,e₁,e₂)                       46    π_U^{t₁}.fr := true, SK := π_S^{t₂}.key
15    SK := H(ctxt,pk,c,k,pw_{U,S})             47 else
16 else                                        48    ctxt := (U,S,e₁,e₂)
17    π_S^{t₂}.fr := true                       49    if (U,S) ∉ 𝒞
18    pk := D₁(pw_{U,S}, e₁)                    50       π_U^{t₁}.fr := true
19    (c,k) ← Encaps(pk)                        51       c := D₂(pw_{U,S}, e₂), k := Decaps(sk,c)
20    e₂ := E₂(pw_{U,S}, c)                     52       SK := H(ctxt,pk,c,k,pw_{U,S})
21    ctxt := (U,S,e₁,e₂)                       53       if e₂ ∉ ℒ₂^S and ∃c s.t.
22    SK := H(ctxt,pk,c,k,pw_{U,S})                        (pw_{U,S},c,e₂,enc) ∈ ℒ₂       // G₇-G₁₀
23    if e₁ ∉ ℒ₁^U and ∃pk s.t.                 54          Guess_user := true             // G₇-G₁₀
         (pw_{U,S},pk,e₁,enc) ∈ ℒ₁  // G₇-G₁₀   55       else
24       Guess_ser := true        // G₇-G₁₀     56          SK $← 𝒮𝒦                        // G₈-G₁₀
25    else                                      57    else
26       SK $← 𝒮𝒦                  // G₉-G₁₀     58       π_U^{t₁}.fr := false
27    c $← 𝒞, e₂ := E₂(pw_{U,S}, c)     // G₁₀   59       c := D₂(pw_{U,S}, e₂), k := Decaps(sk,c)
28 π_S^{t₂}.(e,tr) := ((c,k,e₂),ctxt)          60       SK := H(ctxt,pk,c,k,pw_{U,S})
29 π_S^{t₂}.(key,acc) := (SK,true)             61 π_U^{t₁}.(tr,key,acc) := (ctxt,SK,true)
30 ℒ₂^S := ℒ₂^S ∪ {e₂}            // G₇-G₁₀     62 return true
31 return (S, e₂)
```

Fig. 11. Oracles SendInit, SendResp, and SendTerInit in games $\mathbf{G_6}$-$\mathbf{G_{10}}$. For any user U, $\mathcal{L}_1^U$ records all e_1 sent by U. Similarly, $\mathcal{L}_2^S$ records all e_2 sent by server S. All these lists are initialized as $\emptyset$.

These two flags are internal and do not influence the game, and thus $\mathbf{G7}$ is equivalent to $\mathbf{G_6}$.

$$\Pr\left[\mathbf{G_6^{\mathcal{A}}} \Rightarrow 1\right] = \Pr\left[\mathbf{G_7^{\mathcal{A}}} \Rightarrow 1\right].$$

This step is crucial for our proof. Looking ahead, $\mathcal{A}$ triggered Guess_user (or Guess_ser, similarly) means that $\mathcal{A}$ queried $E_1(pw_{U,S}, pk)$ for some pk without corrupting $pw_{U,S}$. In this case, such pk is controlled by $\mathcal{A}$ (i.e., not output by the security game), and thus we cannot embed challenge public key into such pk when constructing reduction. Such events happen means that the adversary performs a successful online dictionary attack. We delay the analysis of the happening probability of such events.

Game $\mathbf{G_8}$. Fresh user instances that do not have matching session and do not trigger Guess_user will generate uniformly random session keys. Concretely, when $\mathcal{A}$ queries SendTerInit(U, t_1, S, e_2), if $\pi_U^{t_1}$ does not have matching instance,

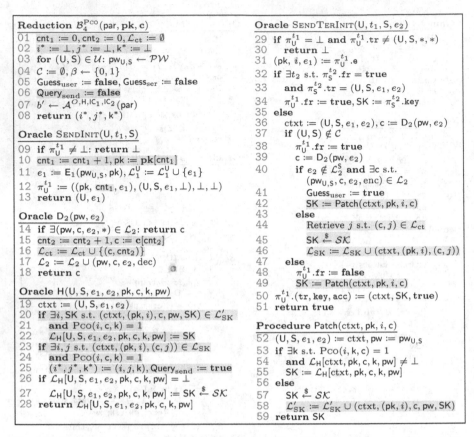

Reduction $\mathcal{B}_4^{\text{Pco}}(\text{par}, \text{pk}, c)$

01 $\text{cnt}_1 := 0, \text{cnt}_2 := 0, \mathcal{L}_{\text{ct}} := \emptyset$
02 $i^* := \bot, j^* := \bot, k^* := \bot$
03 **for** $(\mathsf{U}, \mathsf{S}) \in \mathcal{U}$: $\text{pw}_{\mathsf{U},\mathsf{S}} \leftarrow \mathcal{PW}$
04 $\mathcal{C} := \emptyset, \beta \leftarrow \{0, 1\}$
05 $\text{Guess}_{\text{user}} := \textbf{false}, \text{Guess}_{\text{ser}} := \textbf{false}$
06 $\text{Query}_{\text{send}} := \textbf{false}$
07 $b' \leftarrow \mathcal{A}^{O, \mathsf{H}, \mathsf{IC}_1, \mathsf{IC}_2}(\text{par})$
08 **return** (i^*, j^*, k^*)

Oracle $\text{SENDINIT}(\mathsf{U}, t_1, \mathsf{S})$

09 **if** $\pi_{\mathsf{U}}^{t_1} \neq \bot$: **return** $\bot$
10 $\text{cnt}_1 := \text{cnt}_1 + 1, \text{pk} := \text{pk}[\text{cnt}_1]$
11 $e_1 := \mathsf{E}_1(\text{pw}_{\mathsf{U},\mathsf{S}}, \text{pk}), \mathcal{L}_1^{\mathsf{U}} := \mathcal{L}_1^{\mathsf{U}} \cup \{e_1\}$
12 $\pi_{\mathsf{U}}^{t_1} := ((\text{pk}, \text{cnt}_1, e_1), (\mathsf{U}, \mathsf{S}, e_1, \bot), \bot, \bot)$
13 **return** (U, e_1)

Oracle $\mathsf{D}_2(\text{pw}, e_2)$

14 **if** $\exists(\text{pw}, c, e_2, *) \in \mathcal{L}_2$: **return** c
15 $\text{cnt}_2 := \text{cnt}_2 + 1, c := c[\text{cnt}_2]$
16 $\mathcal{L}_{\text{ct}} := \mathcal{L}_{\text{ct}} \cup \{(c, \text{cnt}_2)\}$
17 $\mathcal{L}_2 := \mathcal{L}_2 \cup (\text{pw}, c, e_2, \text{dec})$
18 **return** c

Oracle $\mathsf{H}(\mathsf{U}, \mathsf{S}, e_1, e_2, \text{pk}, c, k, \text{pw})$

19 $\text{ctxt} := (\mathsf{U}, \mathsf{S}, e_1, e_2)$
20 **if** $\exists i, \text{SK}$ s.t. $(\text{ctxt}, (\text{pk}, i), c, \text{pw}, \text{SK}) \in \mathcal{L}'_{\text{SK}}$
21   **and** $\text{Pco}(i, c, k) = 1$
22      $\mathcal{L}_{\mathsf{H}}[\mathsf{U}, \mathsf{S}, e_1, e_2, \text{pk}, c, k, \text{pw}] := \text{SK}$
23 **if** $\exists i, j$ s.t. $(\text{ctxt}, (\text{pk}, i), (c, j)) \in \mathcal{L}_{\text{SK}}$
24   **and** $\text{Pco}(i, c, k) = 1$
25      $(i^*, j^*, k^*) := (i, j, k), \text{Query}_{\text{send}} := \textbf{true}$
26 **if** $\mathcal{L}_{\mathsf{H}}[\mathsf{U}, \mathsf{S}, e_1, e_2, \text{pk}, c, k, \text{pw}] = \bot$
27      $\mathcal{L}_{\mathsf{H}}[\mathsf{U}, \mathsf{S}, e_1, e_2, \text{pk}, c, k, \text{pw}] := \text{SK} \xleftarrow{\$} \mathcal{SK}$
28 **return** $\mathcal{L}_{\mathsf{H}}[\mathsf{U}, \mathsf{S}, e_1, e_2, \text{pk}, c, k, \text{pw}]$

Oracle $\text{SENDTERINIT}(\mathsf{U}, t_1, \mathsf{S}, e_2)$

29 **if** $\pi_{\mathsf{U}}^{t_1} = \bot$ **and** $\pi_{\mathsf{U}}^{t_1}.\text{tr} \neq (\mathsf{U}, \mathsf{S}, *, *)$
30   **return** $\bot$
31 $(\text{pk}, i, e_1) := \pi_{\mathsf{U}}^{t_1}.\text{e}$
32 **if** $\exists t_2$ s.t. $\pi_{\mathsf{S}}^{t_2}.\text{fr} = \textbf{true}$
33   **and** $\pi_{\mathsf{S}}^{t_2}.\text{tr} = (\mathsf{U}, \mathsf{S}, e_1, e_2)$
34      $\pi_{\mathsf{U}}^{t_1}.\text{fr} := \textbf{true}, \text{SK} := \pi_{\mathsf{S}}^{t_2}.\text{key}$
35 **else**
36      $\text{ctxt} := (\mathsf{U}, \mathsf{S}, e_1, e_2), c := \mathsf{D}_2(\text{pw}, e_2)$
37   **if** $(\mathsf{U}, \mathsf{S}) \notin \mathcal{C}$
38          $\pi_{\mathsf{U}}^{t_1}.\text{fr} := \textbf{true}$
39          $c := \mathsf{D}_2(\text{pw}, e_2)$
40   **if** $e_2 \notin \mathcal{L}_2^{\mathsf{S}}$ **and** $\exists c$ s.t.
                $(\text{pw}_{\mathsf{U},\mathsf{S}}, c, e_2, \text{enc}) \in \mathcal{L}_2$
41              $\text{Guess}_{\text{user}} := \textbf{true}$
42              $\text{SK} := \text{Patch}(\text{ctxt}, \text{pk}, i, c)$
43   **else**
44   Retrieve j s.t. $(c, j) \in \mathcal{L}_{\text{ct}}$
45              $\text{SK} \xleftarrow{\$} \mathcal{SK}$
46              $\mathcal{L}_{\text{SK}} := \mathcal{L}_{\text{SK}} \cup (\text{ctxt}, (\text{pk}, i), (c, j))$
47   **else**
48          $\pi_{\mathsf{U}}^{t_1}.\text{fr} := \textbf{false}$
49          $\text{SK} := \text{Patch}(\text{ctxt}, \text{pk}, i, c)$
50 $\pi_{\mathsf{U}}^{t_1}.(\text{tr}, \text{key}, \text{acc}) := (\text{ctxt}, \text{SK}, \textbf{true})$
51 **return true**

Procedure $\text{Patch}(\text{ctxt}, \text{pk}, i, c)$

52 $(\mathsf{U}, \mathsf{S}, e_1, e_2) := \text{ctxt}, \text{pw} := \text{pw}_{\mathsf{U},\mathsf{S}}$
53 **if** $\exists k$ s.t. $\text{Pco}(i, k, c) = 1$
54   **and** $\mathcal{L}_{\mathsf{H}}[\text{ctxt}, \text{pk}, c, k, \text{pw}] \neq \bot$
55      $\text{SK} := \mathcal{L}_{\mathsf{H}}[\text{ctxt}, \text{pk}, c, k, \text{pw}]$
56 **else**
57      $\text{SK} \xleftarrow{\$} \mathcal{SK}$
58      $\mathcal{L}'_{\text{SK}} := \mathcal{L}'_{\text{SK}} \cup (\text{ctxt}, (\text{pk}, i), c, \text{pw}, \text{SK})$
59 **return** SK

Fig. 12. Reduction $\mathcal{B}_4$ in bounding the probability difference between $\mathbf{G}_7$ and $\mathbf{G}_8$. Highlighted parts show how $\mathcal{B}_4$ uses Pco and challenge input to simulate $\mathbf{G}_8$. $\mathcal{A}_4$ also uses a procedure Patch to patch H. All other oracles not shown in the figure are the same as in $\mathbf{G}_8$ (cf. Figs. 8, 9 and 11).

(U, S) is uncorrupted, and e_2 does not trigger $\text{Guess}_{\text{user}}$, then we sample the session key uniformly at random and independent of H (cf. Lines 55 ro 56).

Since session keys in $\mathbf{G}_7$ are generated via random oracle H, to distinguish $\mathbf{G}_8$ and $\mathbf{G}_7$, $\mathcal{A}$ needs to query one of the intended hash inputs of such random session keys. Let $\text{Query}_{\text{send}}$ be such querying event. To bound the happening probability of $\text{Query}_{\text{send}}$, we construct an reduction $\mathcal{B}_4$ with $\mathbf{T}(\mathcal{A}) \approx \mathbf{T}(\mathcal{B}_4)$ in Fig. 12 which attacks OW-rPCA security of KEM. $\mathcal{B}_4$ works as follows:

1. On input a OW-rPCA challenge $(\text{par}, \text{pk}, c)$, $\mathcal{B}_4$ embeds public keys in pk into queries to SENDINIT (cf. Line 02) and embeds challenge ciphertexts in D_2 (cf. Line 15). Counter cnt_1 and cnt_2 are used to record the indexes of embedded public keys and ciphertexts, respectively.
2. Since $\mathcal{B}_4$ does not have secret keys of challenge public keys (cf. Line 02), it cannot decrypt KEM ciphertexts and thus cannot directly compute session

keys of user instances or determine whether $\mathcal{A}$ has queried the hash input of such session keys (even if these keys are not fresh). To deal with it, we use RO patching technique to make the simulation consistent.

Concretely, we define a procedure Patch which uses PCO oracle to determine if $\mathcal{A}$ has queried the intended hash input of the session key of some specific user instances. If so, it returns the recorded session key. Otherwise, it samples a random session key, records this session key in $\mathcal{L}'_{\mathsf{SK}}$, and returns it. Later, if $\mathcal{A}$'s RO query matches a recorded session key, then $\mathcal{B}_4$ patches the RO and returns this key (cf. Lines 20 to 22).

When $\mathcal{A}$ queries SENDTERINIT$(\mathsf{U}, t_1, \mathsf{S}, e_2)$, where $\pi_{\mathsf{U}}^{t_1}$ does not have fresh matching instance and either e_2 triggers Guess$_{\text{user}}$ or (U, S) is corrupted, $\mathcal{B}_4$ uses the procedure to compute the session key (cf. Lines 42 and 49).

3. When $\mathcal{A}$ queries SENDTERINIT$(\mathsf{U}, t_1, \mathsf{S}, e_2)$, if $\pi_{\mathsf{U}}^{t_1}$ does not have fresh matching instance, (U, S) is corrupted, and e_2 does not trigger Guess$_{\text{user}}$, then e_2 is not generated by querying $\mathsf{E}_2(\mathsf{pw}_{\mathsf{U},\mathsf{S}}, e_2)$, which means that $\mathsf{c} = \mathsf{D}_2(\mathsf{pw}_{\mathsf{U},\mathsf{S}}, e_2)$ is one of the embedded ciphertext (cf. Line 15). $\mathcal{B}_4$ records such query in $\mathcal{L}_{\mathsf{SK}}$ (cf. Line 46) to determine whether Query$_{\text{send}}$ happens.

When $\mathcal{A}$ queried $\mathsf{H}(\mathsf{U}, \mathsf{S}, e_1, e_2, \mathsf{pk}, \mathsf{c}, \mathsf{k}, \mathsf{pw}_{\mathsf{U},\mathsf{S}})$, if this query match one record in $\mathcal{L}_{\mathsf{SK}}$ and k is the decapsulated key of a embedded challenge ciphertext c (cf. Line 23), then this RO query is the intended hash input of one of the session keys recorded in Line 46. In this case, Query$_{\text{send}}$ will be triggered, and $\mathcal{B}_4$ will use (i^*, j^*, k^*) to record the OW solution of c (cf. Line 25).

Since $\mathcal{A}$'s numbers of queries to Init and D_2 are S and q_2, respectively, $\mathcal{B}_4$ needs at most S challenge public keys and $(q_2 + S)$ challenge ciphertexts per public keys during the simulation. If Query$_{\text{send}}$ happens, then $\mathcal{B}_4$ finds the OW solution of one of the challenge ciphertexts. Therefore, we have

$$\left| \Pr\left[\mathbf{G}_7^{\mathcal{A}} \Rightarrow 1 \right] - \Pr\left[\mathbf{G}_8^{\mathcal{A}} \Rightarrow 1 \right] \right| \leq \Pr\left[\text{Query}_{\text{send}} \right] \leq \mathsf{Adv}_{\mathsf{KEM}}^{(S, q_2 + S)\text{-OW-rPCA}}(\mathcal{B}_4)$$

Game $\mathbf{G}_9$. We change SENDINIT and SENDRESP.

1. In SENDINIT, instead of generating $(\mathsf{pk}, \mathsf{sk}) \leftarrow \mathsf{KG}$ and $e_1 := \mathsf{E}_1(\mathsf{pw}_{\mathsf{U},\mathsf{S}}, \mathsf{pk})$, we firstly sample e_1 uniformly at random and then generate $(\mathsf{pk}, \mathsf{sk})$ by querying $\mathsf{D}_1(\mathsf{pw}_{\mathsf{U},\mathsf{S}}, e_1)$ (cf. Lines 34 to 36).

2. Fresh server instances that do not trigger Guess$_{\text{ser}}$ will generate uniformly random session keys. Concretely, when $\mathcal{A}$ queries SENDRESP$(\mathsf{S}, t_2, \mathsf{U}, e_1)$, if (U, S) is uncorrupted and e_1 does not trigger Guess$_{\text{ser}}$, then we sample the session key uniformly at random and independent of H (cf. Lines 25 to 26).

Similar to our argument in bounding $\mathbf{G}_7$ and $\mathbf{G}_8$, to distinguish $\mathbf{G}_8$ and $\mathbf{G}_9$, $\mathcal{A}$ needs to query one of the intended hash inputs of such random session keys. Let Query$_{\text{resp}}$ be such querying event. We construct an reduction $\mathcal{B}_5$ with $\mathbf{T}(\mathcal{A}) \approx \mathbf{T}(\mathcal{B}_5)$ in Fig. 12 to bound the happening probability of Query$_{\text{resp}}$. $\mathcal{B}_5$ attacks OW-PCA security of KEM and works as follows:

1. On input a OW-PCA challenge $(\mathsf{par}, \mathbf{pk}, \mathbf{c})$, $\mathcal{B}_5$ embeds challenge public keys $\mathbf{pk}$ into queries to D_1 (cf. Line 31). By Lines 34 to 36, public keys generated

```
Reduction B₅(par, pk, c)                    Oracle D₁(pw, e₁)
01  cnt₁ := 0, i* := ⊥, j* := ⊥, k* := ⊥     28  if ∃(pw, pk, e₁, *) ∈ L₁
02  for (U, S) ∈ U                           29    return c
03    pw_{U,S} ← PW, L₁ᵁ := ∅, L₂ˢ := ∅       30  cnt₂[cnt₁] := 0, cnt₁ := cnt₁ + 1
04  C := ∅, β ← {0, 1}                        31  pk := pk[cnt₁], L_key := L_key ∪ {(pk, cnt₁)}
05  Guess_user := false, Guess_ser := false   32  L₂ := L₂ ∪ (pw, pk, e₁, dec)
06  Query_resp := false                       33  return c
07  b' ← A^{O,H,IC₁,IC₂}(par)
08  return (i*, j*, k*)                       Oracle SendResp(S, t₂, U, e₁)
                                              34  π_S^{t₂} ≠ ⊥ : return ⊥
Oracle SendTerInit(U, t₁, S, e₂)              35  pk := D₁(pw_{U,S}, e₁)
09  if π_U^{t₁} = ⊥ and π_U^{t₁}.tr ≠ (U,S,*,*) 36  if (U, S) ∈ C
10    return ⊥                                37    π_S^{t₂}.fr := false
11  (pk, i, e₁) := π_U^{t₁}.e, c := D₂(pw, e₂) 38    (c, k) ← Encaps(pk), e₂ := E₂(pw_{U,S}, c)
12  if ∃t₂ s.t. π_S^{t₂}.fr = true            39    ctxt := (U, S, e₁, e₂)
13    and π_S^{t₂}.tr = (U, S, e₁, e₂)         40    SK := H(ctxt, pk, c, k, pw_{U,S})
14    π_U^{t₁}.fr := true, SK := π_S^{t₂}.key  41  else
15  else                                      42    π_S^{t₂}.fr := true
16    ctxt := (U, S, e₁, e₂)                   43    if e₁ ∉ L₁ᵁ and ∃pk s.t.
17    if (U, S) ∉ C                                   (pw_{U,S}, pk, e₁, enc) ∈ L₁
18      π_U^{t₁}.fr := true                    44      Guess_ser := true
19      if e₂ ∉ L₂ˢ and ∃c s.t.                45      (c, k) ← Encaps(pk), e₂ := E₂(pw_{U,S}, c)
             (pw_{U,S}, c, e₂, enc) ∈ L₂        46      SK := H(ctxt, pk, c, k, pw_{U,S})
20        Guess_user := true                   47    else
21        SK := Patch(ctxt, pk, i, c)          48      Retrieve i s.t. (pk, i) ∈ L_key
22      else SK ←$ SK                           49      cnt₂[i] := cnt₂[i] + 1, j := cnt₂[i]
23    else                                     50      c := c[i, j], e₂ := E₂(pw_{U,S}, c)
24      π_U^{t₁}.fr := false                   51      L_SK := L_SK ∪ {(ctxt, (pk, i), (c, j))}
25      SK := Patch(ctxt, pk, i, c)            52      SK ←$ SK
26  π_U^{t₁}.(tr, key, acc) := (ctxt, SK, true) 53    L₂ˢ := L₂ˢ ∪ {e₂}
27  return true                                54    π_S^{t₂} := ((c, k, e₂), ctxt, SK, true)
                                               55  return (S, e₂)
Oracle H((U, S, e₁, e₂), pk, c, k, pw)
56  ctxt := (U, S, e₁, e₂)
57  if ∃i, SK s.t. (ctxt, (pk, i), c, pw, SK) ∈ L'_SK and Pco(i, c, k) = 1
58    L_H[U, S, e₁, e₂, pk, c, k, pw] := SK
59  if ∃i, j s.t. (ctxt, (pk, i), (c, j)) ∈ L_SK and Pco(i, c, k) = 1
60    (i*, j*, k*) := (i, j, k), Query_resp := true
61  if L_H[U, S, e₁, e₂, pk, c, k, pw] = ⊥
62    L_H[U, S, e₁, e₂, pk, c, k, pw] := SK ←$ SK
63  return L_H[U, S, e₁, e₂, pk, c, k, pw]
```

Fig. 13. Reduction B_5 in bounding the probability difference between G_8 and G_9. Highlighted parts show how B_5 uses Pco and challenge input to simulate G_9. All other oracles not shown in the figure are the same as in G_8 (cf. Figs. 8, 9 and 11). Procedure Patch is the same as the one shown in Fig. 12.

in SendInit are also from **pk**. Similar to B_4, B_5 uses the Patch procedure in Fig. 12 to compute the session keys of user instances. Counter cnt_1 and vector of counters cnt_2 are used to record the indexes of embedded public keys and ciphertexts, respectively.

2. When A queries SendResp(S, t_2, U, e_1), if $\pi_S^{t_2}$ is fresh (which means that (U, S) is uncorrupted) and e_1 does not trigger $Guess_{ser}$, then by our definition of $Guess_{ser}$, e_1 is not generated by querying $E_1(pw_{U,S}, pk)$. This means that $pk = D_1(pw_{U,S}, e_1)$ is one of the embedded public key (cf. Line 31). In this case, B_5 embeds one challenge ciphertext with respect to pk (cf. Line 50)

and records such query in $\mathcal{L}_{SK}$ (cf. Line 51) to determine whether $\mathsf{Query}_{\mathrm{resp}}$ happens.

When $\mathcal{A}$ queried $\mathsf{H}(\mathsf{U}, \mathsf{S}, e_1, e_2, \mathsf{pk}, \mathsf{c}, \mathsf{k}, \mathsf{pw}_{\mathsf{U},\mathsf{S}})$, if this query match one record in $\mathcal{L}_{SK}$ and k is the decapsulated key of a embedded challenge ciphertext c (cf. Line 59), then this RO query is the intended hash input of one of the session keys recorded in Line 51. In this case, $\mathsf{Query}_{\mathrm{resp}}$ will be triggered, and $\mathcal{B}_5$ will use (i^*, j^*, k^*) to record the OW solution of the embedded challenge ciphertext c (cf. Line 60).

Since $\mathcal{A}$'s numbers of queries to $(\textsc{SendInit}, \textsc{SendResp})$ and D_2 are S and q_2 respectively, $\mathcal{B}_5$ needs at most $S + q_2$ challenge public keys and S challenge ciphertexts per public keys during the simulation. If $\mathsf{Query}_{\mathrm{resp}}$ happens, then $\mathcal{B}_5$ finds the OW solution of one of challenge ciphertexts in c. Therefore, we have

$$\left| \Pr\left[\mathbf{G}_8^{\mathcal{A}} \Rightarrow 1 \right] - \Pr\left[\mathbf{G}_9^{\mathcal{A}} \Rightarrow 1 \right] \right| \leq \Pr\left[\mathsf{Query}_{\mathrm{resp}} \right] \leq \mathsf{Adv}_{\mathsf{KEM}}^{(S+q_2,S)\text{-OW-PCA}}(\mathcal{B}_5)$$

Game $\mathbf{G}_{10}$. We sample KEM ciphertext uniformly at random for server instances that are fresh and do not trigger $\mathsf{Query}_{\mathrm{resp}}$ (cf. Line 27). Similar to the argument of bounding $\mathbf{G}_3$ and $\mathbf{G}_4$ (cf. Lemma 3), We can use the ciphertext anonymity of KEM to upper bound the probability difference between $\mathbf{G}_9$ and $\mathbf{G}_{10}$. The bound is given in Lemma 4. We continue the proof of Theorem 1 and postpone the proof of Lemma 4 to our full version [28].

Lemma 4. *With notations and assumptions from $\mathbf{G}_9$ and $\mathbf{G}_{10}$ in the proof of Theorem 1, there is an adversary $\mathcal{B}_6$ with $\mathbf{T}(\mathcal{B}_6) \approx \mathbf{T}(\mathcal{A})$ and*

$$\left| \Pr\left[\mathbf{G}_9^{\mathcal{A}} \Rightarrow 1 \right] - \Pr\left[\mathbf{G}_{10}^{\mathcal{A}} \Rightarrow 1 \right] \right| \leq \mathsf{Adv}_{\mathsf{KEM}}^{(S+q_1,S)\text{-ANO}}(\mathcal{B}_6)$$

In game transition $\mathbf{G}_{10}$-$\mathbf{G}_{12}$ (shown in Fig. 14), we bound the happening probabilities of $\mathsf{Guess}_{\mathrm{ser}}$ and $\mathsf{Guess}_{\mathrm{user}}$.

Game $\mathbf{G}_{11}$. We do not use passwords to simulate the protocol messages of fresh instances that do not trigger $\mathsf{Guess}_{\mathrm{ser}}$ and $\mathsf{Guess}_{\mathrm{user}}$. Concretely, we change $\textsc{SendInit}, \textsc{SendResp}$, and $\textsc{SendTerInit}$ as follows:

- In $\textsc{SendResp}$, if the server instance $\pi_{\mathsf{S}}^{t_2}$ is fresh and does not trigger $\mathsf{Guess}_{\mathrm{ser}}$, then we sample e_2 uniformly at random and without using $\mathsf{pw}_{\mathsf{U},\mathsf{S}}$ and c (cf. Lines 33 to 34). Moreover, we only store e_2 as the ephemeral secret of $\pi_{\mathsf{S}}^{t_2}$ (cf. Line 41). These changes are conceptual since we do not need c to compute the session key and if $\mathcal{A}$ queries $\mathsf{D}_2(\mathsf{pw}_{\mathsf{U},\mathsf{S}}, e_2)$ later, then we will return random c (which are the same as in $\mathbf{G}_{10}$).
- Similarly, in $\textsc{SendInit}$, we generate e_1 uniformly at random and without using $\mathsf{pw}_{\mathsf{U},\mathsf{S}}$ and pk (cf. Lines 49 to 52) and only store e_1 as the ephemeral secret of $\pi_{\mathsf{U}}^{t_1}$ (cf. Lines 52 to 53 and Line 59). Later, if $\mathcal{A}$ corrupts (U, S) and queries $\textsc{SendTerInit}$ to finish the user instance $\pi_{\mathsf{U}}^{t_1}$, we retrieve necessary information to compute the session key (cf. Lines 82 to 83). These changes

Game $\mathbf{G_{10}}$-$\mathbf{G_{12}}$
01 par $\leftarrow$ Setup
02 for $(U,S) \in \mathcal{U}$: $pw_{U,S} \leftarrow \mathcal{PW}$ // $\mathbf{G_{10}}$-$\mathbf{G_{11}}$
03 $\mathcal{C} := \emptyset, \beta \leftarrow \{0,1\}$
04 Guess$_{user}$:= false, Guess$_{ser}$:= false
05 $b' \leftarrow \mathcal{A}^{O,H,IC_1,IC_2}$(par)
06 for $(U,S) \in \mathcal{U} \times \mathcal{S}$ // $\mathbf{G_{12}}$
07   if $(U,S) \notin \mathcal{C}$: $pw_{U,S} \leftarrow \mathcal{PW}$ // $\mathbf{G_{12}}$
08   if $\exists S'$ s.t. $pw_{U,S'} \in \mathcal{L}_{pw}$ // $\mathbf{G_{12}}$
09   Guess$_{user}$:= true   // $\mathbf{G_{12}}$
10   if $\exists U'$ s.t. $pw_{U',S} \in \mathcal{L}_{pw}$ // $\mathbf{G_{12}}$
11   Guess$_{ser}$:= true   // $\mathbf{G_{12}}$
12 return $\beta == b'$

Oracle CORRUPT(U,S)
13 if $(U,S) \in \mathcal{C}$: return $\perp$
14 $\mathcal{C} := \mathcal{C} \cup \{(U,S)\}$
15 $pw_{U,S} \leftarrow \mathcal{PW}$ // $\mathbf{G_{12}}$
16 return $pw_{U,S}$

Oracle SENDRESP(S,t_2,U,e_1)
17 $\pi_S^{t_2} \neq \perp$: return $\perp$
18 if $(U,S) \in \mathcal{C}$
19    $\pi_S^{t_2}$.fr := false
20    $pk := D_1(pw_{U,S}, e_1), (c,k) \leftarrow$ Encaps(pk)
21    $e_2 := E_2(pw_{U,S}, c), ctxt := (U,S,e_1,e_2)$
22    $SK := H(ctxt, pk, c, k, pw_{U,S})$
23 else
24    $\pi_S^{t_2}$.fr := true
25   if $e_1 \notin \mathcal{L}_1^U$ and $\exists pk$ s.t.
        $(pw_{U,S}, pk, e_1, enc) \in \mathcal{L}_1$ // $\mathbf{G_{10}}$-$\mathbf{G_{11}}$
26   Guess$_{ser}$:= true   // $\mathbf{G_{10}}$-$\mathbf{G_{11}}$
27       $pk := D_1(pw_{U,S}, e_1)$ // $\mathbf{G_{10}}$-$\mathbf{G_{11}}$
28       $(c,k) \leftarrow$ Encaps(pk)   // $\mathbf{G_{10}}$-$\mathbf{G_{11}}$
29       $e_2 := E_2(pw_{U,S}, c)$ // $\mathbf{G_{10}}$-$\mathbf{G_{11}}$
30       $ctxt := (U,S,e_1,e_2)$ // $\mathbf{G_{10}}$-$\mathbf{G_{11}}$
31       $SK := H(ctxt, pk, c, k, pw_{U,S})$ // $\mathbf{G_{10}}$-$\mathbf{G_{11}}$
32   else   // $\mathbf{G_{10}}$-$\mathbf{G_{11}}$
33       $c \leftarrow \mathcal{C}, e_2 := E_2(pw_{U,S}, c)$ // $\mathbf{G_{10}}$
34       $e_2 \xleftarrow{\$} \mathcal{E}_2 \setminus \mathcal{T}_2, \mathcal{T}_2 := \mathcal{T}_2 \cup \{e_2\}$ // $\mathbf{G_{11}}$
35       $SK \xleftarrow{\$} \mathcal{SK}$ // $\mathbf{G_{10}}$-$\mathbf{G_{11}}$
36   if $e_1 \notin \mathcal{L}_1^U$ // $\mathbf{G_{12}}$
37   for (pw, pk) s.t.
          $(pw, pk, e_1, enc) \in \mathcal{L}_1$ // $\mathbf{G_{12}}$
38          $\mathcal{L}_{pw} := \mathcal{L}_{pw} \cup \{pw\}$ // $\mathbf{G_{12}}$
39       $e_2 \xleftarrow{\$} \mathcal{E}_2 \setminus \mathcal{T}_2, \mathcal{T}_2 := \mathcal{T}_2 \cup \{e_2\}$ // $\mathbf{G_{12}}$
40       $SK \xleftarrow{\$} \mathcal{SK}$ // $\mathbf{G_{12}}$
41    $\pi_S^{t_2}.(e, tr) := ((c,k,e_2), ctxt)$ // $\mathbf{G_{10}}$
42    $\pi_S^{t_2}.(e, tr) := ((\perp, \perp, e_2), ctxt)$ // $\mathbf{G_{11}}$-$\mathbf{G_{12}}$
43    $\pi_S^{t_2}.(key, acc) := (SK, true)$
44    $\mathcal{L}_2^S := \mathcal{L}_2^S \cup \{e_2\}$
45 return (S, e_2)

Oracle SENDINIT(U,t_1,S)
46 if $\pi_U^{t_1} \neq \perp$: return $\perp$
47 $e_1 \xleftarrow{\$} \mathcal{E}_1 \setminus \mathcal{T}_1, \mathcal{L}_1 := \mathcal{L}_1 \cup \{e_1\}$
48 $\mathcal{L}_1^U := \mathcal{L}_1^U \cup \{e_1\}$
49 $pk := D_1(pw_{U,S}, e_1)$ // $\mathbf{G_{10}}$
50 Retrieve sk s.t. $(pk, sk) \in \mathcal{L}_{key}$ // $\mathbf{G_{10}}$
51 $\pi_U^{t_1} := ((pk, sk, e_1),$
             $(U, S, e_1, \perp), \perp, \perp)$ // $\mathbf{G_{10}}$
52 $\pi_U^{t_1}.e := (\perp, \perp, e_1)$ // $\mathbf{G_{11}}$-$\mathbf{G_{12}}$
53 $\pi_U^{t_1}.tr := (U, S, e_1, \perp)$ // $\mathbf{G_{11}}$-$\mathbf{G_{12}}$
54 $\pi_U^{t_1}.fr := false$
55 return (U, e_1)

Oracle SENDTERINIT(U,t_1,S,e_2)
56 if $\pi_U^{t_1} = \perp$ and $\pi_U^{t_1}.tr \neq (U,S,*,*)$
57   return $\perp$
58 $(pk, sk, e_1) := \pi_U^{t_1}.e$ // $\mathbf{G_{10}}$
59 $(\perp, \perp, e_1) := \pi_U^{t_1}.e$ // $\mathbf{G_{11}}$
60 if $\exists t_2$ s.t. $\pi_S^{t_2}.fr = true$
61   and $\pi_S^{t_2}.tr = (U, S, e_1, e_2)$
62    $\pi_U^{t_1}.fr := true$, $SK := \pi_S^{t_2}.key$
63 else
64    $ctxt := (U, S, e_1, e_2)$
65   if $(U,S) \notin \mathcal{C}$
66       $\pi_U^{t_1}.fr := true$
67   if $e_2 \notin \mathcal{L}_2^S$ and $\exists c$ s.t.
          $(pw_{U,S}, c, e_2, enc) \in \mathcal{L}_2$ // $\mathbf{G_{10}}$-$\mathbf{G_{11}}$
68          $pk := D_1(pw_{U,S}, e_1)$ // $\mathbf{G_{11}}$
69   Retrieve sk s.t.
             $(pk, sk) \in \mathcal{L}_{key}$ // $\mathbf{G_{11}}$
70   Guess$_{user}$:= true   // $\mathbf{G_{10}}$-$\mathbf{G_{11}}$
71          $c := D_2(pw_{U,S}, e_2)$ // $\mathbf{G_{10}}$-$\mathbf{G_{11}}$
72          $k := $ Decaps(sk, c)   // $\mathbf{G_{10}}$-$\mathbf{G_{11}}$
73          $SK := H(ctxt, pk, c, k, pw_{U,S})$ // $\mathbf{G_{10}}$-$\mathbf{G_{11}}$
                                              // $\mathbf{G_{10}}$-$\mathbf{G_{11}}$
74   else   // $\mathbf{G_{10}}$-$\mathbf{G_{11}}$
75          $SK \xleftarrow{\$} \mathcal{SK}$ // $\mathbf{G_{10}}$-$\mathbf{G_{11}}$
76   if $e_2 \notin \mathcal{L}_2^S$
77   for (pw, c) s.t.
             $(pw, c, e_2, enc) \in \mathcal{L}_2$ // $\mathbf{G_{12}}$
78             $\mathcal{L}_{pw} := \mathcal{L}_{pw} \cup \{pw\}$ // $\mathbf{G_{12}}$
79          $SK \xleftarrow{\$} \mathcal{SK}$ // $\mathbf{G_{12}}$
80   else
81       $\pi_U^{t_1}.fr := false$
82       $pk := D_1(pw_{U,S}, e_1)$ // $\mathbf{G_{11}}$-$\mathbf{G_{12}}$
83   Retrieve sk s.t.
          $(pk, sk) \in \mathcal{L}_{key}$ // $\mathbf{G_{11}}$-$\mathbf{G_{12}}$
84       $c := D_2(pw_{U,S}, e_2)$
85       $k := $ Decaps(sk, c)
86       $SK := H(ctxt, pk, c, k, pw_{U,S})$
87 $\pi_U^{t_1}.(tr, key, acc) := (ctxt, SK, true)$
88 return true

Fig. 14. Oracles SENDINIT, SENDRESP, and SENDTERINIT in games $\mathbf{G_{10}}$-$\mathbf{G_{12}}$.

are also conceptual, since session keys of such instances are independently and uniformly random. We have

$$\Pr\left[\mathbf{G}_{10}^{\mathcal{A}} \Rightarrow 1\right] = \Pr\left[\mathbf{G}_{11}^{\mathcal{A}} \Rightarrow 1\right]$$

Game $\mathbf{G}_{12}$. We postpone the generation of passwords and the determination of whether $\mathsf{Guess}_{\mathsf{user}}$ or $\mathsf{Guess}_{\mathsf{ser}}$ happen. For simplicity, we define event GUESS as $\mathsf{Guess}_{\mathsf{user}} \vee \mathsf{Guess}_{\mathsf{ser}}$.

1. We generate passwords as late as possible. passwords are generated only when $\mathcal{A}$ issues CORRUPT queries or after $\mathcal{A}$ ends with output b' (cf. Lines 06, 07 to 15).
2. Since the passwords of uncorrupted parties do not exist before $\mathcal{A}$ terminates, we cannot determine whether GUESS happens when $\mathcal{A}$ is running. To deal with it, we postpone such determination. When $\mathcal{A}$ issues SENDRESP or SENDTERINIT queries, we records all potential passwords that may match the actual password of the specific user-server pair (cf. Lines 37 to 38 and Lines 76 to 78). After $\mathcal{A}$ outputs b', the passwords of uncorrupted user-server pairs are generated, and then we use these passwords to determine whether $\mathsf{Guess}_{\mathsf{user}}$ or $\mathsf{Guess}_{\mathsf{ser}}$ happen (cf. Lines 06 to 11).
3. Now all fresh instances will accept random session keys independent of H and passwords (Lines 40 and 79).

If GUESS does not happen in both game, then these changes are conceptual. We have

$$\Pr\left[\mathbf{G}_{11}^{\mathcal{A}} \Rightarrow 1 \mid \neg\text{GUESS in } \mathbf{G}_{11}^{\mathcal{A}}\right] = \Pr\left[\mathbf{G}_{12}^{\mathcal{A}} \Rightarrow 1 \mid \neg\text{GUESS in } \mathbf{G}_{12}^{\mathcal{A}}\right]$$

We claim that GUESS happens in $\mathbf{G}_{11}$ if and only if it happens in $\mathbf{G}_{12}$. It is straightforward to see that GUESS happens in $\mathbf{G}_{11}$ then it also happens in $\mathbf{G}_{12}$, since in $\mathbf{G}_{12}$ we records all potential passwords in $\mathcal{L}_{\mathsf{pw}}$ that may trigger GUESS in $\mathbf{G}_{11}$. If GUESS happens in $\mathbf{G}_{12}$, then there exists $\mathsf{pw}_{\mathsf{U},\mathsf{S}} \in \mathcal{L}_{\mathsf{pw}}$. Moreover, $\mathsf{pw}_{\mathsf{U},\mathsf{S}}$ is recorded in $\mathcal{L}_{\mathsf{pw}}$ only if (U, S) is uncorrupted. By (cf. Lines 37 to 38 and Lines 76 to 78), $\mathsf{pw}_{\mathsf{U},\mathsf{S}} \in \mathcal{L}_{\mathsf{pw}}$ means that there exists (pk, e_1) (resp., (c, e_2)) such that $e_1 \notin \mathcal{L}_1^{\mathsf{U}}$ (resp., $e_2 \notin \mathcal{L}_2^{\mathsf{S}}$) and $(\mathsf{pw}_{\mathsf{U},\mathsf{S}}, \mathsf{pk}, e_1, \mathsf{enc}) \in \mathcal{L}_1$ (resp., $(\mathsf{pw}_{\mathsf{U},\mathsf{S}}, \mathsf{c}, e_2, \mathsf{enc}) \in \mathcal{L}_2$), and thus either $\mathsf{Guess}_{\mathsf{user}}$ or $\mathsf{Guess}_{\mathsf{ser}}$ will be triggered in $\mathbf{G}_{11}$. Therefore, if GUESS happens in $\mathbf{G}_{12}$, then GUESS also happens in $\mathbf{G}_{11}$. Now we have

$$\left|\Pr\left[\mathbf{G}_{11}^{\mathcal{A}} \Rightarrow 1\right] - \Pr\left[\mathbf{G}_{12}^{\mathcal{A}} \Rightarrow 1\right]\right| \leq \Pr\left[\text{GUESS in } \mathbf{G}_{11}^{\mathcal{A}}\right] = \Pr\left[\text{GUESS in } \mathbf{G}_{12}^{\mathcal{A}}\right]$$

Furthermore, we claim that every query to SENDRESP or SENDTERINIT will add at most one password into $\mathcal{L}_{\mathsf{pw}}$. That is, at most one password will be recorded in $\mathcal{L}_{\mathsf{pw}}$ in every execution of Lines 37 to 38 or Lines 76 to 78. To see this, suppose that there are two passwords pw and pw' are recorded during a execution of Lines 37 to 38. By Line 37, we have $(\mathsf{pw}, \mathsf{c}, e_2, \mathsf{enc}) \in \mathcal{L}_2$ and $(\mathsf{pw}', \mathsf{c}', e_2, \mathsf{enc}) \in \mathcal{L}_2$ for some c and c'. This means that e_2 is generated by querying $\mathsf{E}_2(\mathsf{pw}, \mathsf{c})$ and $\mathsf{E}_2(\mathsf{pw}', \mathsf{c}')$, which is impossible since we simulate E_2 in a

Game G_{12}

01 par $\leftarrow$ Setup
02 $\mathcal{C} := \emptyset, \beta \leftarrow \{0,1\}$
03 $\text{Guess}_{user} := \text{false}, \text{Guess}_{ser} := \text{false}$
04 $b' \leftarrow \mathcal{A}^{O,H,IC_1,IC_2}(\text{par})$
05 for $(U,S) \in \mathcal{U} \times \mathcal{S}$
06   if $(U,S) \notin \mathcal{C}$: $\text{pw}_{U,S} \leftarrow \mathcal{PW}$
07   if $\exists S'$ s.t. $\text{pw}_{U,S'} \in \mathcal{L}_{pw}$
08      $\text{Guess}_{user} := \text{true}$
09   if $\exists U'$ s.t. $\text{pw}_{U',S} \in \mathcal{L}_{pw}$
10      $\text{Guess}_{ser} := \text{true}$
11 return $\beta == b'$

Oracle $\text{Execute}(U, t_1, S, t_2)$

12 if $\pi_U^{t_1} \neq \perp$ or $\pi_S^{t_2} \neq \perp$
13   return $\perp$
14 $e_1 \xleftarrow{\$} \mathcal{E}_1 \backslash \mathcal{T}_1, \mathcal{T}_1 := \mathcal{T}_1 \cup \{e_1\}$
15 $e_2 \xleftarrow{\$} \mathcal{E}_2 \backslash \mathcal{T}_2, \mathcal{T}_2 := \mathcal{T}_2 \cup \{e_2\}$
16 $\text{ctxt} := (U,S,e_1,e_2), SK \xleftarrow{\$} \mathcal{SK}$
17 $\pi_U^{t_1} := ((\perp,\perp,e_1), \text{ctxt}, SK, \text{true})$
18 $\pi_S^{t_2} := ((\perp,\perp,e_2), \text{ctxt}, SK, \text{true})$
19 $(\pi_U^{t_1}.\text{fr}, \pi_S^{t_2}.\text{fr}) := (\text{true}, \text{true})$
20 return (U, e_1, S, e_2)

Oracle $\text{Corrupt}(U, S)$

21 if $(U,S) \in \mathcal{C}$: return $\perp$
22 $\mathcal{C} := \mathcal{C} \cup \{(U,S)\}$
23 $\text{pw}_{U,S} \leftarrow \mathcal{PW}$
24 return $\text{pw}_{U,S}$

Oracle $E_1(\text{pw}, \text{pk})$

25 if $\exists(\text{pw}, \text{pk}, e_1, *) \in \mathcal{L}_1$: return e_1
26 $e_1 \xleftarrow{\$} \mathcal{E}_1 \backslash \mathcal{T}_1, \mathcal{T}_1 := \mathcal{T}_1 \cup \{e_1\}$
27 $\mathcal{L}_1 := \mathcal{L}_1 \cup (\text{pw}, \text{pk}, e_1, \text{enc})$
28 return e_1

Oracle $E_2(\text{pw}, c)$

29 if $\exists(\text{pw}, c, e_2, *) \in \mathcal{L}_2$: return e_2
30 $e_2 \xleftarrow{\$} \mathcal{E}_2 \backslash \mathcal{T}_2, \mathcal{T}_2 := \mathcal{T}_2 \cup \{e_2\}$
31 $\mathcal{L}_2 := \mathcal{L}_2 \cup (\text{pw}, c, e_2, \text{enc})$
32 return e_2

Oracle $D_1(\text{pw}, e_1)$

33 if $\exists(\text{pw}, \text{pk}, e_1, *) \in \mathcal{L}_1$
34   return pk
35 $(\text{pk}, \text{sk}) \leftarrow KG$
36 $\mathcal{L}_{key} := \mathcal{L}_{key} \cup \{(\text{pk}, \text{sk})\}$
37 $\mathcal{L}_1 := \mathcal{L}_1 \cup \{(\text{pw}, \text{pk}, e_1, \text{dec})\}$
38 return pk

Oracle $D_2(\text{pw}, e_2)$

39 if $\exists(\text{pw}, c, e_2, *) \in \mathcal{L}_2$: return c
40 $c \xleftarrow{\$} \mathcal{C}, \mathcal{L}_2 := \mathcal{L}_2 \cup (\text{pw}, c, e_2, \text{dec})$
41 return c

Oracle $\text{SendInit}(U, t_1, S)$

42 if $\pi_U^{t_1} \neq \perp$: return $\perp$
43 $e_1 \xleftarrow{\$} \mathcal{E}_1 \backslash \mathcal{T}_1, \mathcal{T}_1 := \mathcal{T}_1 \cup \{e_1\}$
44 $\mathcal{L}_1^U := \mathcal{L}_1^U \cup \{e_1\}$
45 $\pi_U^{t_1} := ((\perp,\perp,e_1), (U,S,e_1,\perp), \perp, \perp)$
46 $\pi_U^{t_1}.\text{fr} := \text{false}$
47 return (U, e_1)

Oracle $\text{SendResp}(S, t_2, U, e_1)$

48 $\pi_S^{t_2} \neq \perp$: return $\perp$
49 if $(U,S) \in \mathcal{C}$
50    $\pi_S^{t_2}.\text{fr} := \text{false}$
51    $\text{pk} := D_1(\text{pw}_{U,S}, e_1)$
52    $(c, k) \leftarrow \text{Encaps}(\text{pk})$
53    $e_2 := E_2(\text{pw}_{U,S}, c), \text{ctxt} := (U,S,e_1,e_2)$
54    $SK := H(\text{ctxt}, \text{pk}, c, k, \text{pw}_{U,S})$
55 else
56    $\pi_S^{t_2}.\text{fr} := \text{true}, SK \xleftarrow{\$} \mathcal{SK}$
57   if $e_1 \notin \mathcal{L}_1^U$
58   for (pw, pk) s.t. $(\text{pw}, \text{pk}, e_1, \text{enc}) \in \mathcal{L}_1$
59        $\mathcal{L}_{pw} := \mathcal{L}_{pw} \cup \{\text{pw}\}$
60    $e_2 \xleftarrow{\$} \mathcal{E}_2 \backslash \mathcal{T}_2, \mathcal{T}_2 := \mathcal{T}_2 \cup \{e_2\}$
61    $\pi_S^{t_2} := ((\perp,\perp,e_2), \text{ctxt}, SK, \text{true})$
62    $\mathcal{L}_2^S := \mathcal{L}_2^S \cup \{e_2\}$
63 return (S, e_2)

Oracle $\text{SendTerInit}(U, t_1, S, e_2)$

64 if $\pi_U^{t_1} = \perp$ and $\pi_U^{t_1}.\text{tr} \neq (U, S, *, *)$
65   return $\perp$
66 if $\exists t_2$ s.t. $\pi_S^{t_2}.\text{fr} = \text{true}$
67   and $\pi_S^{t_2}.\text{tr} = (U, S, e_1, e_2)$
68    $\pi_U^{t_1}.\text{fr} := \text{true}, SK := \pi_S^{t_2}.\text{key}$
69 else
70    $\text{ctxt} := (U, S, e_1, e_2)$
71   if $(U,S) \notin \mathcal{C}$
72      $\pi_U^{t_1}.\text{fr} := \text{true}, SK \xleftarrow{\$} \mathcal{SK}$
73   if $e_2 \notin \mathcal{L}_2^S$
74   for (pw, c) s.t. $(\text{pw}, c, e_2, \text{enc}) \in \mathcal{L}_2$
75        $\mathcal{L}_{pw} := \mathcal{L}_{pw} \cup \{\text{pw}\}$
76   else
77      $\pi_U^{t_1}.\text{fr} := \text{false}$
78      $\text{pk} := D_1(\text{pw}_{U,S}, e_1)$
79   Retrieve sk s.t. $(\text{pk}, \text{sk}) \in \mathcal{L}_{key}$
80      $c := D_2(\text{pw}_{U,S}, e_2), k := \text{Decaps}(\text{sk}, c)$
81      $SK := H(\text{ctxt}, \text{pk}, c, k, \text{pw}_{U,S})$
82 $\pi_U^{t_1}.(\text{tr}, \text{key}, \text{acc}) := (\text{ctxt}, SK, \text{true})$
83 return true

Oracle $H(U, S, e_1, e_2, \text{pk}, c, k, \text{pw})$

84 if $\mathcal{L}_H[U, S, e_1, e_2, \text{pk}, c, k, \text{pw}] = \perp$
85    $\mathcal{L}_H[U, S, e_1, e_2, \text{pk}, c, k, \text{pw}] := SK \xleftarrow{\$} \mathcal{SK}$
86 return $\mathcal{L}_H[U, S, e_1, e_2, \text{pk}, c, k, \text{pw}]$

Fig. 15. Final game G_{12} in proving Theorem 1. $\mathcal{A}$ has access to the set of PAKE oracles {Execute, SendInit, SendResp, SendTerInit, Corrupt, Reveal, Test}, random oracle H, and ideal ciphers $IC_1 = (E_1, D_1)$ and $IC_2 = (E_2, D_2)$. Oracles Reveal and Test are the same as in G_1 (cf. Fig. 8) so we omit their description here.

collision-free way. Similar argument applies for Lines 76 to 78. Therefore, every query to SENDRESP or SENDTERINIT will add at most one password into $\mathcal{L}_{pw}$.

Now we can bound the happening probability of GUESS in $\mathbf{G}_{12}$. A clean description of $\mathbf{G}_{12}$ is given in Fig. 15. In $\mathbf{G}_{12}$, passwords of uncorrupted user-server pairs are undefined before $\mathcal{A}$ issues CORRUPT queries or ends with output b'. Moreover, oracles EXECUTE, SENDINIT, SENDRESP, and SENDTERINIT can be simulated without using uncorrupted passwords. Therefore, uncorrupted passwords are perfectly hidden from $\mathcal{A}$'s view. Since $\mathcal{A}$ issues S queries to SENDRESP and SENDTERINIT, we have $|\mathcal{L}_{pw}| \leq S$ and

$$\Pr\left[\text{GUESS in } \mathbf{G}_{12}^{\mathcal{A}}\right] \leq \frac{S}{|\mathcal{PW}|}$$

All fresh instances in $\mathbf{G}_{12}$ will accept independently and uniformly random session keys, so we also have

$$\Pr\left[\mathbf{G}_{12}^{\mathcal{A}} \Rightarrow 1\right] = \frac{1}{2}$$

Combining all the probability differences in the games sequence, we have

$$\begin{aligned}
\mathsf{Adv}_{\Pi}^{\mathsf{BPR}}(\mathcal{A}) \leq {} & \frac{S}{|\mathcal{PW}|} + \mathsf{Adv}_{\mathsf{KEM}}^{q_1\text{-}\mathsf{FUZZY}}(\mathcal{B}_1) + \mathsf{Adv}_{\mathsf{KEM}}^{(S,q_2+S)\text{-}\mathsf{OW\text{-}rPCA}}(\mathcal{B}_4) \\
& + \mathsf{Adv}_{\mathsf{KEM}}^{(S,1)\text{-}\mathsf{OW\text{-}PCA}}(\mathcal{B}_2) + \mathsf{Adv}_{\mathsf{KEM}}^{(S+q_2,S)\text{-}\mathsf{OW\text{-}PCA}}(\mathcal{B}_5) \\
& + \mathsf{Adv}_{\mathsf{KEM}}^{(S,1)\text{-}\mathsf{ANO}}(\mathcal{B}_3) + \mathsf{Adv}_{\mathsf{KEM}}^{(S+q_1,S)\text{-}\mathsf{ANO}}(\mathcal{B}_6) + S \cdot \delta \\
& + S^2(\eta_{pk} + \eta_{ct}) + \frac{(q_1^2 + S^2)}{|\mathcal{E}_1|} + \frac{(q_2^2 + S^2)}{|\mathcal{E}_2|} + \frac{q_1^2}{|\mathcal{PK}|} + \frac{q_2^2}{|\mathcal{C}|} + \frac{(q_{\mathsf{H}}^2 + S^2)}{|\mathcal{SK}|}
\end{aligned}$$

5 Instantiations of the Underlying KEM

5.1 Direct Diffie-Hellman-Based Constructions

DIFFIE-HELLMAN ASSUMPTIONS. We recall the multi-user and multi-challenge strong Diffie-Hellman assumption. Let $\mathcal{G}$ be a group generation algorithm that on input security parameters outputs a group description $(\mathbb{G}, g, p)$, where p is an odd prime and $\mathbb{G}$ is a p-order group with generator g.

Definition 15 (Multi-Instance stDH [3]). *Let N and μ be integers. We say the stDH problem is hard on $\mathcal{G}$, if for any $\mathcal{A}$, the (N, μ)-stDH advantage of $\mathcal{A}$ against $\mathcal{G}$*

$$\mathsf{Adv}_{\mathcal{G}}^{(N,\mu)\text{-}\mathsf{stDH}}(\mathcal{A}) := \Pr\left[\mathsf{stDH}_{\mathcal{G}}^{(N,\mu),\mathcal{A}} \Rightarrow 1\right].$$

is negligible, where $\mathsf{stDH}_{\mathcal{G}}^{(N,\mu),\mathcal{A}}$ is defined in Fig. 16.

GAME stDH$_\mathcal{G}^{(N,\mu),\mathcal{A}}$	Oracle Pco(i, Y, Z)
01 par $:= (\mathbb{G}, g, p) \leftarrow \mathcal{G}$	08 if $\mathbf{X}[i] = \perp$
02 for $i \in [N]$	09 return $\perp$
03 $x_i \xleftarrow{\$} \mathbb{Z}_p, \mathbf{X}[i] := X_i := g^{x_i}$	10 return $Z == Y^{x_i}$
04 for $j \in [\mu]$:	
05 $y_j \xleftarrow{\$} \mathbb{Z}_p, \mathbf{Y}[j] := Y_j := g^{y_j}$	
06 $(i^*, j^*, Z^*) \leftarrow \mathcal{A}^{\mathrm{stDH}}(\mathrm{par}, \mathbf{X}, \mathbf{Y})$	
07 return $Z^* = Y_{j^*}^{x_{i^*}}$	

Fig. 16. Security games OW-PCA and OW-rPCA for KEM scheme KEM.

KG$_1$	Encaps$_1$(pk)	Decaps$_1$(sk, R)
01 $x \xleftarrow{\$} \mathbb{Z}_p$	06 $r \xleftarrow{\$} \mathbb{Z}_p$	11 parse $(x, \mathrm{pk}) =: \mathrm{sk}$
02 $X := g^x$	07 $R := g^r \in \mathbb{G}$	12 parse $R =: \mathrm{c}$
03 pk $:= X$	08 k $:= \mathsf{H}(\mathrm{pk}, R, X^r)$	13 k $:= \mathsf{H}(\mathrm{pk}, R, R^x)$
04 sk $:= (x, \mathrm{pk})$	09 c $:= R$	14 return k
05 return (pk, sk)	10 return (c, k)	

Fig. 17. KEM scheme KEM$_{\mathrm{stDH}}$ = (Setup$_1$, KG$_1$, Encaps$_1$, Decaps$_1$).

CONSTRUCTION BASED ON STRONG DH. In Fig. 17, we construct a KEM scheme KEM$_{\mathrm{stDH}}$ with plaintext space $\mathbb{G}$ and ciphertext space of $\mathbb{G}$. KEM$_{\mathrm{stDH}}$ is essentially the hashed ElGamal KEM [3,17].

KEM$_{\mathrm{stDH}}$ has perfect public key fuzzyness and ciphertext anonymity (even under PCA). This is because $X \xleftarrow{\$} \mathbb{G}$ is equivalent to $(x \xleftarrow{\$} \mathbb{Z}_p, X := g^x)$. Therefore, we have

$$\mathrm{Adv}_{\mathrm{KEM}_{\mathrm{stDH}}}^{(N,\mu)\text{-ANO}}(\mathcal{A}) = 0, \quad \mathrm{Adv}_{\mathrm{KEM}_{\mathrm{stDH}}}^{N\text{-FUZZY}}(\mathcal{A}) = 0$$

for any integers N and μ, and adversary $\mathcal{A}$ (even unbounded).

It is well-known that the hash ElGamal KEM is tightly IND-CCA secure (which implies OW-PCA security) if the $(1,1)$-stDH assumption holds [15]. By using the random self-reducibility of Diffie-Hellman assumption, one can show that the (N,μ)-OW-PCA security can be tightly reduced to the $(1,1)$-stDH assumption.

5.2 Generic Constructions

Let PKE$_0$ = (KG$_0$, Enc$_0$, Dec$_0$) be a PKE scheme with public key space $\mathcal{PK}$, message space $\mathcal{M}$, randomness space $\mathcal{R}$, and ciphertext space $\mathcal{C}$. Let ℓ and L be integers. Let G : $\mathcal{PK} \times \mathcal{M} \to \mathcal{R}$, H : $\mathcal{PK} \times \mathcal{M} \times \mathcal{C} \to \{0,1\}^L$, and H' : $\mathcal{PK} \times \{0,1\}^\ell \times \mathcal{C} \to \{0,1\}^L$ be hash functions. Let PKE$_0$ = (Setup$_0$, KG$_0$, Enc$_0$, Dec$_0$) be a PKE scheme. In Fig. 18, we define a generic transformation for KEM schemes. We denote such transformation as KEM = TU$^{\not\perp}$[PKE$_0$, G, H, H']. TU$^{\not\perp}$ is essentially a combination of the T transformation and the U$^{\not\perp}$ transformation in [21]. KEM has the same public key space and ciphertext space with PKE_0. The Setup algorithm of KEM is the same as the one of PKE_0.

KG(par)	Encaps(pk)	Decaps((pk, sk, s), c)
01 (pk, sk) $\leftarrow$ KG$_0$(par)	05 $m \xleftarrow{\$} \mathcal{M}'$	10 $m' := \mathsf{Dec}_0(\mathsf{sk}, \mathsf{c})$
02 $s \xleftarrow{\$} \{0,1\}^\ell$	06 $r := \mathsf{G}(\mathsf{pk}, m)$	11 **if** $m' \neq \perp$
03 sk' $:= (\mathsf{pk}, \mathsf{sk}, s)$	07 c $:= \mathsf{Enc}_0(\mathsf{pk}, m; r)$	12 **and** c $=$
04 **return** (pk, sk')	08 k $:= \mathsf{H}(\mathsf{pk}, \mathsf{c}, m)$	$\mathsf{Enc}_0(\mathsf{pk}, m'; \mathsf{G}(\mathsf{pk}, m'))$
	09 **return** (c, k)	13 k $:= \mathsf{H}(\mathsf{pk}, \mathsf{c}, m')$
		14 **else** k $:= \mathsf{H}'(\mathsf{pk}, \mathsf{c}, s)$
		15 **return** k

Fig. 18. KEM scheme KEM = (Setup, KG, Encaps, Decaps) from the generic transformation $\mathsf{TU}^{\not\perp}[\mathsf{PKE}_0, \mathsf{G}, \mathsf{H}, \mathsf{H}']$, where G, H, and H' are hash functions, $\mathsf{PKE}_0 = (\mathsf{Setup}_0, \mathsf{KG}_0, \mathsf{Enc}_0, \mathsf{Dec}_0)$ is a PKE scheme, and Setup = Setup$_0$.

CORRECTNESS OF KEM. We follow the correctness proof of [21, Theorem 3.1].

Decaps has decapsulation error if its input is c = $\mathsf{Enc}_0(\mathsf{pk}, m'; \mathsf{G}(\mathsf{pk}, m'))$ for some m' and $\mathsf{Dec}_0(\mathsf{sk}, \mathsf{c}) \neq m'$. If PKE_0 is $(1 - \delta_{\mathsf{PKE}_0})$-correct, such event happens within probability $q_\mathsf{G} \cdot \delta_{\mathsf{PKE}_0}$ if we treat G as a random oracle and assume G will be queried at most q_G times. Therefore, KEM is $(1 - q_\mathsf{G} \cdot \delta_{\mathsf{PKE}_0})$-correct.

SECURITY. In Theorems 2 to 4, we show if PKE_0 has fuzzy public keys and PR-CPA security, then KEM has fuzzy public keys, anonymous ciphertexts (under PCA attacks), and OW-(r)PCA security.

It is easy to see $\mathsf{TU}^{\not\perp}$ transformation preserves the public key fuzzyness of the underlying PKE.

Theorem 2. *Let N be the number of users. If PKE_0 has fuzzy public keys, then KEM = $\mathsf{TU}^{\not\perp}[\mathsf{PKE}_0, \mathsf{G}, \mathsf{H}, \mathsf{H}']$ in Fig. 18 also has fuzzy public keys. Concretely, for any adversary $\mathcal{A}$ against KEM, there exists an adversary $\mathcal{B}$ with $\mathbf{T}(\mathcal{A}) \approx \mathbf{T}(\mathcal{B})$ and*

$$\mathsf{Adv}^{N\text{-FUZZY}}_{\mathsf{KEM}}(\mathcal{A}) \leq \mathsf{Adv}^{N\text{-FUZZY}}_{\mathsf{PKE}_0}(\mathcal{B})$$

Theorems 3 and 4 show shat if PKE_0 is PR-CPA secure, then KEM = $\mathsf{TU}^{\not\perp}[\mathsf{PKE}_0, \mathsf{G}, \mathsf{H}, \mathsf{H}']$ has OW-CPA security and ciphertext anonymity under PCA attacks. For readability, we postpone their proofs to our full version [28].

Theorem 3. *Let N and μ be the numbers of users and challenge ciphertexts per user. If PKE_0 is PR-CPA secure and $(1 - \delta)$-correct and G, H, and H' be random oracles, then KEM = $\mathsf{TU}^{\not\perp}[\mathsf{PKE}_0, \mathsf{G}, \mathsf{H}, \mathsf{H}']$ has anonymous ciphertext under PCA attacks (cf. Definition 7).*

Concretely, for any $\mathcal{A}$ against KEM, there exists $\mathcal{B} = (\mathcal{B}_0, \mathcal{B}_1)$ with $\mathbf{T}(\mathcal{A}) \approx \mathbf{T}(\mathcal{B})$ and

$$\mathsf{Adv}_{\mathsf{KEM}}^{(N,\mu)\text{-ANO}}(\mathcal{A}) \leq 2\mathsf{Adv}_{\mathsf{PKE}_0}^{(N,\mu)\text{-PR-CPA}}(\mathcal{B}) + 2Nq_{\mathsf{G}} \cdot \delta + \frac{N\mu q_{\mathsf{G}}}{|\mathcal{M}|}$$

$$+ \frac{2N(q_{\mathsf{H}'} + q_{\mathsf{Pco}})}{2^\ell} + \frac{N^2\mu^2 + q_{\mathsf{G}}^2}{|\mathcal{R}|} + \frac{2N^2\mu^2 + q_{\mathsf{H}}^2 + q_{\mathsf{H}'}^2}{2^L},$$

where $q_{\mathsf{G}}, q_{\mathsf{H}}, q_{\mathsf{H}'}$, and q_{Pco} are the numbers of $\mathcal{A}$'s queries to $\mathsf{G}, \mathsf{H}, \mathsf{H}'$, and Pco.

Theorem 4. *Let N and μ be the numbers of users and challenge ciphertexts per user. If PKE_0 is PR-CPA secure and G, H, and H' be random oracles, then $\mathsf{KEM} = \mathsf{TU}^{\not\perp}[\mathsf{PKE}_0, \mathsf{G}, \mathsf{H}, \mathsf{H}']$ is OW-PCA secure.*

Concretely, for any $\mathcal{A}$ against KEM's (N, μ)-OW-PCA security, there exists $\mathcal{B}$ with $\mathbf{T}(\mathcal{A}) \approx \mathbf{T}(\mathcal{B})$ and

$$\mathsf{Adv}_{\mathsf{KEM}}^{(N,\mu)\text{-OW-PCA}}(\mathcal{A}) \leq 2\mathsf{Adv}_{\mathsf{PKE}_0}^{(N,\mu)\text{-PR-CPA}}(\mathcal{B}) + 2Nq_{\mathsf{G}} \cdot \delta + \frac{N\mu(q_{\mathsf{G}} + q_{\mathsf{H}})}{|\mathcal{M}|}$$

$$+ \frac{2N(q_{\mathsf{H}'} + q_{\mathsf{Pco}})}{2^\ell} + \frac{N^2\mu^2 + q_{\mathsf{G}}^2}{|\mathcal{R}|} + \frac{2N^2\mu^2 + q_{\mathsf{H}}^2 + q_{\mathsf{H}'}^2}{2^L},$$

where $q_{\mathsf{G}}, q_{\mathsf{H}}, q_{\mathsf{H}'}$, and q_{Pco} are the numbers of $\mathcal{A}$'s queries to $\mathsf{G}, \mathsf{H}, \mathsf{H}'$, and Pco.

By combining Lemma 1 and Theorems 3 and 4, we have Theorem 5.

Theorem 5. *Let N and μ be the numbers of users and challenge ciphertexts per user. If PKE_0 is PR-CPA secure and G, H, and H' be random oracles, then $\mathsf{KEM} = \mathsf{TU}^{\not\perp}[\mathsf{PKE}_0, \mathsf{G}, \mathsf{H}, \mathsf{H}']$ is OW-rPCA secure.*

Concretely, for any $\mathcal{A}$ against KEM's (N, μ)-OW-rPCA security, there exists $\mathcal{B}$ with $\mathbf{T}(\mathcal{A}) \approx \mathbf{T}(\mathcal{B})$ and

$$\mathsf{Adv}_{\mathsf{KEM}}^{(N,\mu)\text{-OW-rPCA}}(\mathcal{A}) \leq 4\mathsf{Adv}_{\mathsf{PKE}_0}^{(N,\mu)\text{-PR-CPA}}(\mathcal{B}) + 4Nq_{\mathsf{G}} \cdot \delta + \frac{N\mu(2q_{\mathsf{G}} + q_{\mathsf{H}})}{|\mathcal{M}|}$$

$$+ \frac{4N(q_{\mathsf{H}'} + q_{\mathsf{Pco}})}{2^\ell} + \frac{2(N^2\mu^2 + q_{\mathsf{G}}^2)}{|\mathcal{R}|} + \frac{2(2N^2\mu^2 + q_{\mathsf{H}}^2 + q_{\mathsf{H}'}^2)}{2^L},$$

where $q_{\mathsf{G}}, q_{\mathsf{H}}, q_{\mathsf{H}'}$, and q_{Pco} are the numbers of $\mathcal{A}$'s queries to $\mathsf{G}, \mathsf{H}, \mathsf{H}'$, and Pco.

5.3   Lattice-Based Instantiations

We discuss two lattice-based instantiations of the PAKE protocol Π (Fig. 7). The first one is the well-known Regev's encryption [29, 30] which is based on learning with error (LWE) assumption. The second one is the Kyber.PKE scheme [32], which is based on the module LWE (MLWE) assumption. For simplicity, we only discuss the security loss of these schemes (from their assumptions) and the final security loss of Π instantiated with these schemes. For more background about lattices, please refer to [18, 29, 30, 32].

Let λ the security parameter. Let S and q_{IC} be the number of session and the number of $\mathcal{A}$'s queries to ideal ciphers ($\mathsf{IC}_1, \mathsf{IC}_2$) in Fig. 7. Let ϵ_{LWE} and ϵ_{mlwe} be the best computational advantage against the LWE and MLWE assumptions, respectively. We use $\mathsf{negl}(\lambda)$ to denote negligible (about λ) statistical terms. Such terms do not influence tightness.

REGEV ENCRYPTION. We use the multi-bit version of Regev's encryption, denoted as $\mathsf{PKE}_{\mathsf{Regev}}$, in [29]. As shown in [29, Lemma 7.3, Lemma 7.4], the public keys of this scheme are indistinguishable from random by using a LWE problem instance, and the ciphertexts are pseudorandom under random public keys. Suppose this scheme encrypts $\Theta(\lambda)$ bits, then we have

$$\mathsf{Adv}_{\mathsf{PKE}_{\mathsf{Regev}}}^{N\text{-FUZZY}}(\mathcal{A}) \leq O(N\lambda) \cdot \epsilon_{\mathsf{LWE}}, \ \ \mathsf{Adv}_{\mathsf{PKE}_{\mathsf{Regev}}}^{(N,\mu)\text{-PR-CPA}}(\mathcal{A}) \leq O(N\lambda) \cdot \epsilon_{\mathsf{LWE}} + \mathsf{negl}(\lambda)$$

We can use the $\mathsf{TU}^{\not\perp}$ transformation to transform $\mathsf{PKE}_{\mathsf{Regev}}$ into a KEM scheme and then use the KEM scheme to instantiate Π (Fig. 7). By plugging these bounds into Theorems 3 to 5 and then Theorem 1, we have

$$\mathsf{Adv}_{\Pi[\mathsf{PKE}_{\mathsf{Regev}}]}^{\mathsf{BPR}}(\mathcal{A}) \leq O(\lambda \cdot (q_{\mathsf{IC}} + S)) \cdot \epsilon_{\mathsf{LWE}}$$

KYBER PKE. We consider the Kyber.CPAPKE scheme (denoted as $\mathsf{PKE}_{\mathsf{kyber}}$) in [32]. The pseudorandomness and fuzzyness proofs of $\mathsf{PKE}_{\mathsf{kyber}}$ are the same as in [8, Lemmata 1 and 2, Corollary 1]. Since the MLWE assumption does not have random self-reducibility, we can use a standard hybrid argument to extend such proofs to multi-user-challenge setting. We have

$$\mathsf{Adv}_{\mathsf{PKE}_{\mathsf{Regev}}}^{N\text{-FUZZY}}(\mathcal{A}) \leq N \cdot \epsilon_{\mathsf{mlwe}}, \ \ \mathsf{Adv}_{\mathsf{PKE}_{\mathsf{Regev}}}^{(N,\mu)\text{-PR-CPA}}(\mathcal{A}) \leq N\mu \cdot 2\epsilon_{\mathsf{mlwe}}$$

By using the $\mathsf{TU}^{\not\perp}$ transformation, we can transform $\mathsf{PKE}_{\mathsf{kyber}}$ into a KEM scheme. Then we use the KEM scheme to instantiate Π (Fig. 7). By Theorems 1 and 3 to 5, we have

$$\mathsf{Adv}_{\Pi[\mathsf{PKE}_{\mathsf{kyber}}]}^{\mathsf{BPR}}(\mathcal{A}) \leq O(S \cdot (q_{\mathsf{IC}} + S)) \cdot \epsilon_{\mathsf{mlwe}}$$

References

1. Abdalla, M., Barbosa, M.: Perfect forward security of SPAKE2. Cryptology ePrint Archive, Report 2019/1194 (2019). https://eprint.iacr.org/2019/1194
2. Abdalla, M., Barbosa, M., Bradley, T., Jarecki, S., Katz, J., Xu, J.: Universally composable relaxed password authenticated key exchange. In: Micciancio, D., Ristenpart, T. (eds.) CRYPTO 2020, Part I. LNCS, vol. 12170, pp. 278–307. Springer, Cham (2020). https://doi.org/10.1007/978-3-030-56784-2_10
3. Abdalla, M., Bellare, M., Rogaway, P.: The oracle Diffie-Hellman assumptions and an analysis of DHIES. In: Naccache, D. (ed.) CT-RSA 2001. LNCS, vol. 2020, pp. 143–158. Springer, Heidelberg (2001). https://doi.org/10.1007/3-540-45353-9_12

4. Abdalla, M., Eisenhofer, T., Kiltz, E., Kunzweiler, S., Riepel, D.: Password-authenticated key exchange from group actions. In: Dodis, Y., Shrimpton, T. (eds.) CRYPTO 2022, Part II. LNCS, vol. 13508, pp. 699–728. Springer, Heidelberg (2022). https://doi.org/10.1007/978-3-031-15979-4_24

5. Abdalla, M., Fouque, P.-A., Pointcheval, D.: Password-based authenticated key exchange in the three-party setting. In: Vaudenay, S. (ed.) PKC 2005. LNCS, vol. 3386, pp. 65–84. Springer, Heidelberg (2005). https://doi.org/10.1007/978-3-540-30580-4_6

6. Abdalla, M., Pointcheval, D.: Simple password-based encrypted key exchange protocols. In: Menezes, A. (ed.) CT-RSA 2005. LNCS, vol. 3376, pp. 191–208. Springer, Heidelberg (2005). https://doi.org/10.1007/978-3-540-30574-3_14

7. Becerra, J., Iovino, V., Ostrev, D., Šala, P., Škrobot, M.: Tightly-secure PAK(E). In: Capkun, S., Chow, S.S.M. (eds.) CANS 2017. LNCS, vol. 11261, pp. 27–48. Springer, Cham (2018). https://doi.org/10.1007/978-3-030-02641-7_2

8. Beguinet, H., Chevalier, C., Pointcheval, D., Ricosset, T., Rossi, M.: GeT a CAKE: generic transformations from key encapsulation mechanisms to password authenticated key exchanges. ACNS 2023 (2023). https://eprint.iacr.org/2023/470

9. Bellare, M., Palacio, A.: GQ and Schnorr identification schemes: proofs of security against impersonation under active and concurrent attacks. In: Yung, M. (ed.) CRYPTO 2002. LNCS, vol. 2442, pp. 162–177. Springer, Heidelberg (2002). https://doi.org/10.1007/3-540-45708-9_11

10. Bellare, M., Pointcheval, D., Rogaway, P.: Authenticated key exchange secure against dictionary attacks. In: Preneel, B. (ed.) EUROCRYPT 2000. LNCS, vol. 1807, pp. 139–155. Springer, Heidelberg (2000). https://doi.org/10.1007/3-540-45539-6_11

11. Bellare, M., Rogaway, P.: The security of triple encryption and a framework for code-based game-playing proofs. In: Vaudenay, S. (ed.) EUROCRYPT 2006. LNCS, vol. 4004, pp. 409–426. Springer, Heidelberg (2006). https://doi.org/10.1007/11761679_25

12. Bellovin, S.M., Merritt, M.: Encrypted key exchange: password-based protocols secure against dictionary attacks. In: 1992 IEEE Symposium on Security and Privacy, pp. 72–84. IEEE Computer Society Press (1992)

13. Benhamouda, F., Blazy, O., Ducas, L., Quach, W.: Hash proof systems over lattices revisited. In: Abdalla, M., Dahab, R. (eds.) PKC 2018, Part II. LNCS, vol. 10770, pp. 644–674. Springer, Cham (2018). https://doi.org/10.1007/978-3-319-76581-5_22

14. Bernstein, D.J., Persichetti, E.: Towards KEM unification. Cryptology ePrint Archive, Report 2018/526 (2018). https://eprint.iacr.org/2018/526

15. Bhattacharyya, R.: Memory-tight reductions for practical key encapsulation mechanisms. In: Kiayias, A., Kohlweiss, M., Wallden, P., Zikas, V. (eds.) PKC 2020, Part I. LNCS, vol. 12110, pp. 249–278. Springer, Cham (2020). https://doi.org/10.1007/978-3-030-45374-9_9

16. Canetti, R., Halevi, S., Katz, J., Lindell, Y., MacKenzie, P.: Universally composable password-based key exchange. In: Cramer, R. (ed.) EUROCRYPT 2005. LNCS, vol. 3494, pp. 404–421. Springer, Heidelberg (2005). https://doi.org/10.1007/11426639_24

17. Cash, D., Kiltz, E., Shoup, V.: The twin Diffie-Hellman problem and applications. In: Smart, N. (ed.) EUROCRYPT 2008. LNCS, vol. 4965, pp. 127–145. Springer, Heidelberg (2008). https://doi.org/10.1007/978-3-540-78967-3_8

18. Gentry, C., Peikert, C., Vaikuntanathan, V.: Trapdoors for hard lattices and new cryptographic constructions. In: Ladner, R.E., Dwork, C. (eds.) 40th ACM STOC, pp. 197–206. ACM Press (2008)
19. Haase, B., Labrique, B.: AuCPace: efficient verifier-based PAKE protocol tailored for the IIoT. IACR TCHES **2019**(2), 1–48 (2019). https://tches.iacr.org/index.php/TCHES/article/view/7384
20. Hao, F., Ryan, P.: J-PAKE: authenticated key exchange without PKI. Cryptology ePrint Archive, Report 2010/190 (2010). https://eprint.iacr.org/2010/190
21. Hofheinz, D., Hövelmanns, K., Kiltz, E.: A modular analysis of the Fujisaki-Okamoto transformation. In: Kalai, Y., Reyzin, L. (eds.) TCC 2017, Part I. LNCS, vol. 10677, pp. 341–371. Springer, Cham (2017). https://doi.org/10.1007/978-3-319-70500-2_12
22. Jablon, D.P.: Strong password-only authenticated key exchange. SIGCOMM Comput. Commun. Rev. **26**(5), 5–26 (1996). https://doi.org/10.1145/242896.242897
23. Katz, J., Vaikuntanathan, V.: Smooth projective hashing and password-based authenticated key exchange from lattices. In: Matsui, M. (ed.) ASIACRYPT 2009. LNCS, vol. 5912, pp. 636–652. Springer, Heidelberg (2009). https://doi.org/10.1007/978-3-642-10366-7_37
24. Liu, X., Liu, S., Han, S., Gu, D.: EKE meets tight security in the Universally Composable framework. In: Boldyreva, A., Kolesnikov, V. (eds.) PKC 2023, Part I. LNCS, vol. 13940, pp. 685–713. Springer, Heidelberg (2023). https://doi.org/10.1007/978-3-031-31368-4_24
25. MacKenzie, P.: The PAK suite: protocols for password-authenticated key exchange (2002)
26. Okamoto, T., Pointcheval, D.: The gap-problems: a new class of problems for the security of cryptographic schemes. In: Kim, K. (ed.) PKC 2001. LNCS, vol. 1992, pp. 104–118. Springer, Heidelberg (2001). https://doi.org/10.1007/3-540-44586-2_8
27. Okamoto, T., Pointcheval, D.: REACT: rapid enhanced-security asymmetric cryptosystem transform. In: Naccache, D. (ed.) CT-RSA 2001. LNCS, vol. 2020, pp. 159–174. Springer, Heidelberg (2000). https://doi.org/10.1007/3-540-45353-9_13
28. Pan, J., Zeng, R.: A generic construction of tightly secure password-based authenticated key exchange. Cryptology ePrint Archive (2023). https://ia.cr/2023/1334
29. Peikert, C., Vaikuntanathan, V., Waters, B.: A framework for efficient and composable oblivious transfer. In: Wagner, D. (ed.) CRYPTO 2008. LNCS, vol. 5157, pp. 554–571. Springer, Heidelberg (2008). https://doi.org/10.1007/978-3-540-85174-5_31
30. Regev, O.: On lattices, learning with errors, random linear codes, and cryptography. In: Gabow, H.N., Fagin, R. (eds.) 37th ACM STOC, pp. 84–93. ACM Press (2005)
31. Santos, B.F.D., Gu, Y., Jarecki, S.: Randomized half-ideal cipher on groups with applications to UC (a)PAKE. In: Hazay, C., Stam, M. (eds.) EUROCRYPT 2023, Part V. LNCS, vol. 14008, pp. 128–156. Springer, Heidelberg (2023). https://doi.org/10.1007/978-3-031-30589-4_5
32. Schwabe, P., et al.: CRYSTALS-KYBER. Technical report, National Institute of Standards and Technology (2020). https://csrc.nist.gov/projects/post-quantum-cryptography/post-quantum-cryptography-standardization/round-3-submissions
33. Zhang, J., Yu, Yu.: Two-round PAKE from approximate SPH and instantiations from lattices. In: Takagi, T., Peyrin, T. (eds.) ASIACRYPT 2017, Part III. LNCS, vol. 10626, pp. 37–67. Springer, Cham (2017). https://doi.org/10.1007/978-3-319-70700-6_2

An Efficient Strong Asymmetric PAKE Compiler Instantiable from Group Actions

Ian McQuoid and Jiayu Xu[✉]

Oregon State University, Corvallis, USA
{mcquoidi,xujiay}@oregonstate.edu

Abstract. Password-authenticated key exchange (PAKE) is a class of protocols enabling two parties to convert a shared (possibly low-entropy) password into a high-entropy joint session key. Strong asymmetric PAKE (saPAKE), an extension that models the client-server setting where servers may store a client's password for repeated authentication, was the subject of standardization efforts by the IETF in 2019–20. In this work, we present the most computationally efficient saPAKE protocol so far: a compiler from PAKE to saPAKE which costs only 2 messages and 7 group exponentiations in total (3 for client and 4 for server) when instantiated with suitable underlying PAKE protocols. In addition to being efficient, our saPAKE protocol is conceptually simple and achieves the strongest notion of universally composable (UC) security.

In addition to classical assumptions and classical PAKE, we may instantiate our PAKE-to-saPAKE compiler with cryptographic group actions, such as the isogeny-based CSIDH, and post-quantum PAKE. This yields the first saPAKE protocol from post-quantum assumptions as all previous constructions rely on cryptographic assumptions weak to Shor's algorithm.

1 Introduction

Password-authenticated key exchange (PAKE) [10] constitutes a class of protocols allowing two parties to compute a shared cryptographic key exactly when both parties hold the same (possibly low-entropy) input string, *i.e.*, a "password". Integrally, PAKE is in the "password-only" setting and does not rely on key distribution through *e.g.*, a PKI as trusted infrastructure may not always be available and additionally has a history of insecurities. Traditionally, passwords were assumed to come from some low-entropy distribution. This modeling represented the distribution of human-memorable inputs which have been estimated to only have 30 bits of entropy [27]. Because such passwords come from low-entropy or enumerable distributions, an adversary may always impersonate an honest party and perform a series of online invocations of the protocol to learn the password with non-negligible probability. A key property of PAKE is that this inevitable method should be the *only* efficient attack — with multiple

J. Guo and R. Steinfeld (Eds.): ASIACRYPT 2023, LNCS 14445, pp. 176–207, 2023.
https://doi.org/10.1007/978-981-99-8742-9_6

guesses from a single interaction computationally infeasible. A shortcoming of PAKE is that it only models symmetric roles and precludes inherent asymmetries in the client-server setting. As passwords continue to be the most common form of client-server authentication on the internet, it is incumbent on us to model password storage and, indeed, compromise of the server.

Asymmetric PAKE (aPAKE) [11,26] is a PAKE variant modeling the client-server setting where the client inputs its password pw in the clear and the server inputs a one-way function or *digest* of the password $F(pw)$. The parties then arrive at the same key if and only if the client supplies the preimage of the server's digest. Asymmetric PAKE is comparable to the model of a server storing *publicly* salted hashes of the user's password, and is vulnerable to pre-computation attacks where an adversary may pre-compute possible password files $(pw, F(pw))$ the server *could* hold and, on compromise, recover the password almost immediately by checking the server's storage against the pre-computed table to test each of its guesses.

To prevent pre-computation attacks, Jarecki, Krawczyk and Xu [31] introduced the concept of *strong* asymmetric PAKE (saPAKE), a variant of aPAKE where an adversary must spend time proportional to the number of password guesses made *after compromising the server* in order to recover the password. This is analogous to the server's password salt being *private*, and achieves the original intention of aPAKE — a PAKE that is resilient to (adaptive) server compromise. Note that as the server holds enough information to verify itself to a client, there exists an inevitable attack on the server's storage: the adversary may *locally* run the online protocol acting as both the client and as the server, testing the equality of the two output keys. Such an attack has runtime linear in the number of offline password guesses made. Strong asymmetric security guarantees that (asymptotically) this is the best possible complexity by showing a tight lower-bound on the complexity of a *post-compromise attack*.

Recent years have witnessed increasing interests in (sa)PAKE including the standardization efforts by the IETF in 2019–20. Despite this, saPAKE protocols have proven difficult to construct, and all existing protocols suffer from issues regarding either security or efficiency (see Sect. 1.2 for a detailed discussion). Furthermore, while resilience to quantum adversaries is a major concern of the PAKE community, all known constructions are based on classical assumptions and are easily broken by quantum adversaries. During the IETF's PAKE standardization process, the notion of "quantum-annoyingness" was proposed [41] and was subsequently formalized by Eaton and Stebila [23]. Roughly, a PAKE scheme is quantum-annoying if solving a discrete logarithm or integer factorization problem does not subsequently break the entire session; rather, each solution only allows the adversary an additional password guess. While quantum-annoyingness is a good stepping stone to protecting saPAKE protocols against quantum adversaries, it remains a major open problem in the area of PAKE to construct an saPAKE protocol under post-quantum assumptions.

1.1   Our Contributions

In this paper, we propose two compilers from PAKE to saPAKE. We prove the security of both compilers in the Universal Composability (UC) framework; concretely, both compilers realize the standard UC saPAKE functionality [15,31] if the underlying PAKE protocol realizes the standard UC PAKE functionality [17]. UC-security for (sa)PAKE has superseded traditional game-based definitions due to multiple advantages, including security under arbitrary composition, modeling of adversarially-chosen password distribution, and therefore modeling password reuse across different accounts.

The first of our protocols (see Sect. 3) works in a cryptographic group. It is a compiler which adds only 3 exponentiations and 1 message — which can be sent in parallel with the server's PAKE message — on top of PAKE. For instantiations of UC PAKE such as certain variants of encrypted key exchange (EKE) [24,34] this results in the most efficient saPAKE protocols to date with only 2 messages and 7 exponentiations. In addition to being computationally efficient and conceptually simple, the resulting saPAKE inherits the underlying PAKE's quantum-annoying property. The only other quantum-annoying saPAKE protocol known is CRISP [21] which additionally relies on bilinear pairings. Our protocol is proven UC-secure in the generic group model (GGM) for offline security and the algebraic group model (AGM) plus the discrete logarithm (DL) assumption for online security, in addition to the random oracle model (ROM). We note that using the GGM for offline security but not online security is standard for saPAKE protocols whose server storage is group-based [15,21]; see Sect. 2.5 for a detailed explanation.

The second compiler (see Sect. 5.2) follows the same formula as the first, but can be instantiated with cryptographic group actions [6,20,36] such as isogeny-based assumptions like CSIDH [18]. Just as the first, the second compiler only costs 3 group actions and 1 message from the server on top of PAKE. When compiling from PAKE protocols based on lattices [24], we obtain the first efficient saPAKE protocol from post-quantum assumptions realizing the standard UC functionality. Additionally, even if the assumptions on the group action fail, our protocol still provides (symmetric) PAKE security as the server's message is independent of the password. This allows our protocol to use newer assumptions like CSIDH without future breakthroughs in isogeny cryptanalysis completely invalidating security. Our protocol is UC-secure in the generic group action model with twists ($GGAM^\top$) for offline security and the algebraic group action model with twists ($AGAM^\top$) plus the group-action discrete logarithm (GA-DL) assumption for online security, in addition to the ROM. One caveat is that our protocol is proven secure under *post-quantum assumptions*, but not against *quantum adversaries*, as that would require a security analysis in the quantum-accessible random oracle model (QROM) [13], which we do not consider. We leave constructing an saPAKE secure against quantum adversaries as future work.[1]

---

[1] Constructing a UC-secure saPAKE in the QROM seems out of reach, since there has been very little work that considers a quantum adversary in the UC framework [42], and we do not know of any protocol (PAKE or not) that is proven UC-secure in the QROM.

1.2   Comparison with Previous Results

To date, there are four known saPAKE protocols. The first two, due to Jarecki, Krawczyk, and Xu, come from the original saPAKE paper [31] and are constructed from a MitM-secure oblivious pseudorandom function (OPRF) and compile (respectively) an aPAKE or authenticated key exchange (AKE) into an saPAKE protocol. The second compiler, called OPAQUE, was standardized by the IETF in 2020 [14], and when based on classical assumptions, the resultant protocols are efficient (their costs can be found in Table 1). However, OPAQUE only realizes a weak UC saPAKE functionality (which we call $\mathcal{F}^-_{\text{saPAKE}}$), which includes two significant and contrived relaxations of the standard saPAKE functionality:

- $\mathcal{F}^-_{\text{saPAKE}}$ allows for *delayed extraction*, namely the ideal adversary's password guess can happen *even after the session completes*. The password guess interface is meant to model the real-world scenario where the adversary runs an honest party's algorithm on a candidate password and interacts with the other honest party in order to test if the candidate password is the correct one. Clearly, such attacks *cannot be carried out* after the session already ends.[2]
- In $\mathcal{F}^-_{\text{saPAKE}}$, compromising one open (*i.e.*, not completed) session automatically results in compromising *all other* open sessions without any additional command from the ideal adversary. This significantly weakens saPAKE security: consider a MitM adversary that attempts to attack two open sessions in parallel, the first of which fails and the second of which succeeds (*i.e.*, resulting in a compromised session). In the real world, it should not be the case that the first session — in which *the wrong password guess is already used* — can be compromised, let alone compromised without any additional work from the adversary. However, this is exactly what $\mathcal{F}^-_{\text{saPAKE}}$ allows!

We stress that neither weakening above is inherent or "natural". Few PAKE and aPAKE protocols that were proven UC-secure need the first relaxation, and *none of them* needs the second; for saPAKE, two of the other three existing protocols (see below) need neither of the two relaxations. In fact, the two relaxations appear to be the result of tailoring the UC saPAKE functionality to fit the OPAQUE protocol, as evident in [31, p.12]:

In our context, either requirement prevents proving security of the protocols obtained via our general compiler [...], including the OPAQUE protocol [...]. For this reason we relax [$\mathcal{F}_{\text{saPAKE}}$] to obtain our definition of UC Strong aPAKE functionality [$\mathcal{F}^-_{\text{saPAKE}}$].

---

[2] This change is similar in spirit to the $\mathcal{F}_{\text{rPAKE}}$ functionality (r for "relaxed") for symmetric PAKE in [1].

By contrast, our protocol realizes the standard UC saPAKE functionality without either of the two relaxations.[3]

Finally, we note that the assumptions in OPAQUE and in our protocol are incomparable: the security of OPAQUE relies on the very strong one-more gap Diffie-Hellman (OMGDH) assumption, which has been proven in the GGM but is not equivalent to DL in the AGM [9].[4] By contrast, the online part of our protocol is proven secure in the AGM+DL, without relying on any "one-more" type assumptions.

We now compare our saPAKE protocol with the other three saPAKEs in the literature. The third protocol called strong AuCPace, due to Haase and Labrique [29], is very similar in spirit to the both previous compilers and runs a modified version of OPRF before a (symmetric) PAKE protocol. Our compiler and their protocol follow the same intuition compiling a PAKE by way of a sub-session-specific dictionary map using an ephemeral salt. Where the strong AuCPace protocol communicates the server's long-term salt by way of an OPRF, we simply blind the server's long-term salt with a random exponent. This alteration allows our compiler to use fewer exponentiations. Furthermore, strong AuCPace only realizes a weaker UC saPAKE functionality (which requires the first relaxation of the full $\mathcal{F}_{\text{saPAKE}}$ functionality as in $\mathcal{F}_{\text{saPAKE}}^-$, but not the second).

The fourth protocol, due to Bradley, Jarecki, and Xu [15], follows the "commit-and-SPHF" paradigm [32] of PAKE design and realizes the full $\mathcal{F}_{\text{saPAKE}}$ functionality. However, their protocol requires roughly *three times* as many exponentiations as ours; furthermore, it is unclear if their protocol can be converted to use post-quantum assumptions. We also note that their analysis of offline security is similar to ours, but our analysis is much more accurate; see Sect. 2.4 for a detailed explanation.

The final protocol is CRISP due to Cremers et al. [21] which is conceptually similar to our protocol and compiles a PAKE protocol into a strong identity-binding PAKE (siPAKE) — a stronger primitive than saPAKE. However, the CRISP compiler critically relies on bilinear pairings which increases the computational and communication burden of the protocol while restricting the groups over which we can implement the compiler. Further, this reliance on pairings means the CRISP compiler has no post-quantum instantiation.

Regarding security assumptions, the offline security analyses of both [15] and [21] rely on the GGM as we do ([21] additionally requires the GGM for a bilinear group with a hash-to-group operation), but their online security is based on standard group assumptions. By contrast, our protocol needs the stronger online AGM (plus the DL assumption). To the best of our knowledge, this is the first instance of applying the AGM to the UC framework since the original

---

[3] The other saPAKE construction in [31], presented as a warm-up, seems to require these two relaxations as well, and is much less efficient. An accurate comparison is difficult since the security proof of that protocol is outdated (see [31, Section 4]).

[4] [9, Section 10] shows that the one-more discrete logarithm (OMDL) assumption, which is weaker than OMGDH, cannot be proven equivalent to DL in the AGM.

Table 1. A comparison of UC-secure saPAKE schemes. (1) E denotes exponentiations, H denotes hashing into the group, P denotes pairing evaluations, and A denotes group actions; (2) although both OPAQUE and AuCPace only achieves relaxed security, AuC-Pace realizes a stronger functionality than OPAQUE; (3) on/off denotes if we require the assumption in the online or offline phases respectively; (4) GGM^+ denotes the extended generic group model [21] including hashing to the group, pairing evaluation, and isomorphism evaluation.

	client	server	rounds	security	assumption	model
CKEM-saPAKE [15]	13E	8E	2	full	2-SDH, DDH	ROM+off GGM
OPAQUE HQMV [31]	5E, 1H	4E	3	relaxed	OMGDH	ROM
JKX18 Compiler [31]	2E, 1H, aPAKE	1E, aPAKE	3C	relaxed	OMGDH	ROM
CRISP [21]	6E, 3P, 3H, PAKE	3E, 3P, 1H, PAKE	3	full (siPAKE)	CDH	off GGM$^+$
AuCPace [29]	6E, 2H	5E, 1H	3	relaxed	sSDH, OMGDH	ROM
Ours Fig. 6	E, PAKE	2E, PAKE	2	full	CDH	ROM + off GGM + on AGM
Ours Fig. 7	A, PAKE	2A, PAKE	2	full	GACDH	ROM + off GGAM$^\top$ + on AGAM$^\top$

work on UC-AGM [2]. The security of [29] relies on the ROM and a number of strong and non-standard group assumptions such as strong simultaneous CDH (sSDH) [5].

saPAKE under Post-Quantum Assumptions. Very few password-based protocols under post-quantum assumptions have been proposed. The only such aPAKE protocol that we know of is the recent one by Freitas, Gu, and Jarecki [24], which can be instantiated under lattice assumptions. However, it is not a strong aPAKE, *i.e.*, it is subject to pre-computation attacks.[5]

The recent OPRF protocol due to Basso [8] is based on isogeny assumptions, and may provide some hope for constructing an saPAKE under post-quantum assumptions — by compiling the OPRF with some suitable aPAKE/AKE, as in the paradigm of the JKX compiler [31]. However, this OPRF protocol is only claimed to realize a UC OPRF functionality that does not take into account adaptive server compromise, which is crucial for saPAKE (and even aPAKE) security. As such, it is unclear whether this OPRF yields an saPAKE under post-quantum assumptions. Even if it does, the resulting saPAKE would only achieve the weak saPAKE functionality $\mathcal{F}_{saPAKE}^-$ with the two aforementioned shortcomings; furthermore, it would be less computationally efficient, take 2

---

[5] Another possible way to construct an aPAKE from post-quantum assumptions is to take a post-quantum UC oblivious transfer (OT), use the OT-to-PAKE compiler from [16] to obtain a UC PAKE, and then use the PAKE-to-aPAKE compiler from [26]. This also yields an aPAKE but not an saPAKE.

additional rounds, and require significantly more bits of communication when compared with our protocol based on group actions.

2 Preliminaries

2.1 Notation

We use κ to denote the security parameter. For an integer n, $[n]$ denotes the set $\{1, \ldots, n\}$. For a probability distribution $\mathcal{D}$ over some set, we denote sampling an element d according to the distribution by $d \leftarrow \mathcal{D}$; we extend this notation naturally to probabilistic algorithms $a \leftarrow \mathcal{A}(x_1, x_2, \ldots)$ where the implicit distribution is defined by $\mathcal{A}$'s random coins. For a set S with no obvious accompanying distribution, we overload this notation to denote sampling from S according to the uniform distribution $s \leftarrow S$. For deterministic processes f, we denote assignment of $f(x_1, x_2, \ldots)$ to y by $y := f(x_1, x_2, \ldots)$. Finally, we use "PPT" as a shorthand for "probabilistic polynomial-time".

2.2 Computational Assumptions

Throughout this work, we use a cyclic group $\mathbb{G}$ with generator g and of prime order p, where $2^\kappa \leq p < 2^{\kappa+1}$. We assume $(\mathbb{G}, g, p)$ is public information and is omitted from all parties' inputs. We use the multiplicative notation for the group operation.

Definition 1 (The Discrete Logarithm (DL) Problem). *Let* $a \leftarrow \mathbb{Z}_p^*$. *Given* g^a, *the* Discrete Logarithm Problem *asks one to compute* a.

Definition 2 (The Computational Diffie-Hellman (CDH) Problem). *Let* $(a, b) \leftarrow (\mathbb{Z}_p^*)^2$. *Given a tuple* (g^a, g^b), *the* Computational Diffie-Hellman Problem *asks one to compute* g^{ab}.

The *advantage* of an adversary $\mathcal{A}$, denoted $\mathbf{Adv}_{\mathcal{A}}^{\mathsf{DL}}$ (resp. $\mathbf{Adv}_{\mathcal{A}}^{\mathsf{CDH}}$), is the probability that $\mathcal{A}$ solves the DL (resp. CDH) problem. The corresponding hardness assumptions state that there is no PPT adversary $\mathcal{A}$ whose advantage is non-negligible.[6] In Sect. 5.1, we use the natural extensions of these problems to group actions.

2.3 UC saPAKE Security Model

We recall the UC functionalities for PAKE [17] (Fig. 1) and saPAKE [31] (Fig. 2 and Fig. 3). Note that both functionalities only have implicit authentication,

---

[6] Note that we sample exponents from $\mathbb{Z}_p^*$ rather than $\mathbb{Z}_p$, i.e., 0 is excluded. This makes the protocol description and proof cleaner. It is obvious that our versions of DL and CDH assumptions are equivalent to the standard versions where the exponents are sampled from $\mathbb{Z}_p$.

which is standard in the PAKE literature; explicit authentication can be achieved by adding a single key confirmation flow [28].

The (Symmetric) PAKE Functionality $\mathcal{F}_{\mathsf{PAKE}}$. In a PAKE protocol, two parties run a session on their (respective) passwords in order to generate a shared key k, modeled by the NewSession interface. If the MitM adversary does not interfere with the session, the two honest parties arrive at the same key k exactly when their passwords match. The only possible attack is the inevitable *online guessing attack*, in which the MitM adversary guesses a password pw^* and interacts with an honest party by running the counterparty's algorithm on pw^*. This is modeled by the TestPwd interface, through which the ideal adversary can control an honest party's key using the NewKey interface if the password guess is correct, *i.e.*, pw^* is equal to this party's password.

Functionality $\mathcal{F}_{\mathsf{PAKE}}$

Storage:

  – two maps, sessionStatus and session

Upon receiving $(\mathsf{NewSession}, \mathsf{sid}, \mathsf{P}, \mathsf{P}', \mathsf{role}, pw)$ from P:

1. Send $(\mathsf{NewSession}, \mathsf{sid}, \mathsf{P}, \mathsf{P}', \mathsf{role})$ to $\mathcal{A}^*$.
2. If there is no record $\mathsf{session}[(\mathsf{sid}, \cdot, \cdot)]$ or exactly one record $\mathsf{sessionStatus}[(\mathsf{sid}, \mathsf{P}', \mathsf{P})]$, set $\mathsf{session}[(\mathsf{sid}, \mathsf{P}, \mathsf{P}')] := pw$ and $\mathsf{sessionStatus}[(\mathsf{sid}, \mathsf{P}, \mathsf{P}')] := \mathsf{fresh}$.

Upon receiving $(\mathsf{TestPwd}, \mathsf{sid}, \mathsf{P}, pw^*)$ from $\mathcal{A}^*$:

1. If $\mathsf{sessionStatus}[(\mathsf{sid}, \mathsf{P}, \mathsf{P}')]$ is not fresh, ignore this query.
2. Otherwise:
   1. Retrieve $pw := \mathsf{session}[(\mathsf{sid}, \mathsf{P}, \mathsf{P}')]$.
   2. If $pw = pw^*$, set $\mathsf{sessionStatus}[(\mathsf{sid}, \mathsf{P}, \mathsf{P}')] := \mathsf{compromised}$ and return "correct guess" to $\mathcal{A}^*$.
   3. Otherwise, set $\mathsf{sessionStatus}[(\mathsf{sid}, \mathsf{P}, \mathsf{P}')] := \mathsf{interrupted}$ and return "wrong guess" to $\mathcal{A}^*$.

Upon receiving $(\mathsf{NewKey}, \mathsf{sid}, \mathsf{P}, k^*)$ from $\mathcal{A}^*$ where $|k^*| = \kappa$:

1. If $\mathsf{sessionStatus}[(\mathsf{sid}, \mathsf{P}, \mathsf{P}')]$ is defined, but is not completed:
   1. If the record is compromised, set $k := k^*$.
   2. Else, if the record is fresh, (sid, k') was sent to P', $\mathsf{session}[(\mathsf{sid}, \mathsf{P}, \mathsf{P}')] = \mathsf{session}[(\mathsf{sid}, \mathsf{P}', \mathsf{P})]$, and at the time $\mathsf{sessionStatus}[(\mathsf{sid}, \mathsf{P}', \mathsf{P})]$ was fresh, set $k := k'$.
   3. Otherwise, sample $k \leftarrow \{0,1\}^\kappa$.
2. Finally, set $\mathsf{sessionStatus}[(\mathsf{sid}, \mathsf{P}, \mathsf{P}')] := \mathsf{completed}$ and send (sid, k) to P.

Fig. 1. Ideal functionality $\mathcal{F}_{\mathsf{PAKE}}$

The saPAKE Functionality $\mathcal{F}_{saPAKE}$. As (s)aPAKE is meant to model the extension of PAKE to the client-server setting, we follow convention by calling one of the parties the client C, and calling corresponding counterparty the server S. C runs an saPAKE session on a (plain) password pw' through the ClientSession interface, while S runs the session on a password file $file[(sid, C, S)]$ — representing the password underlying server's stored password digest — which is created through the StorePwdFile interface. Similar to PAKE, if the MitM adversary does not interfere with the session, the two honest parties arrive at the same key k exactly when $file[(sid, C, S)] = pw'$. The StorePwdFile interface represents client registration, but is traditionally non-interactive with the server presumably receiving the password out-of-band $e.g.$, over an authenticated and secure channel and then securely erasing the password after storing the file.[7]

In addition to the online attack interface TestPwd, $\mathcal{F}_{saPAKE}$ also models adaptive server compromise through the StealPwdFile interface. After sending StealPwdFile, the ideal adversary gains access to two additional interfaces: OfflineTestPwd and Impersonate which allow the adversary to perform an *offline dictionary attack* — i.e., make a password guess without invoking an online session — and authenticate with an honest client, respectively. To exclude precomputation attacks, *the OfflineTestPwd interface ignores all messages until StealPwdFile is sent.*

2.4 Simulation Rate

As repeatedly pointed out in prior works [15,26,30,31], the (s)aPAKE functionality alone is not enough to model the offline security guarantees expected from (s)aPAKE protocols. Roughly speaking, offline security is concerned with the runtime of an offline dictionary attack after server compromise, or equivalently, how many passwords a real adversary can test per idealized model query (in our context, generic group operation). Although not explicit in the functionality, (s)aPAKE security requires that the server's storage be a *tight one-way function* of the password: namely, there should be a linear relationship between the number of password tests and the number of idealized model queries an adversary makes. For example, if the server storage is a traditional salted hash $(s, H(pw, s))$ where H is a random oracle and s is the salt, then each post-compromise query to H tests *at most one password*.

In the saPAKE ideal functionality, the adversary's post-compromise password tests are modeled by the OfflineTestPwd interface. From the description of the functionality (Fig. 2), it is clear that each OfflineTestPwd command tests one password. However, there is an important caveat: as previously observed [26,31], the UC-modeling of (s)aPAKE requires a restriction on the simulator limiting the simulator's access to the OfflineTestPwd interface. Indeed, given unmediated access to the interface,

---

[7] In some sense this is counter to the one of the goals of saPAKE which is to prevent the server from ever seeing the client's password. Our informal description of the protocol has the client generate the password file themselves and send it over a secured channel, but formally the server will still generate the file.

Functionality $\mathcal{F}_{\mathsf{saPAKE}}$

Storage:

- Four maps: fileStatus, file, sessionStatus, session

Password Registration

Upon receiving (StorePwdFile, sid, C, pw) from S, if file[(sid, C, S)] is undefined, set file[(sid, C, S)] := pw and set fileStatus[(sid, C, S)] := uncompromised.

Stealing Password Data

Upon receiving (StealPwdFile, sid) from $\mathcal{A}^*$:

1. If file[(sid, C, S)] is undefined, return "no password file" to $\mathcal{A}^*$.
2. Otherwise:
   1. If fileStatus[(sid, C, S)] = uncompromised, set fileStatus[(sid, C, S)] := stolen.
   2. Return "password file stolen" to $\mathcal{A}^*$.

Upon receiving (OfflineTestPwd, sid, pw^*) from $\mathcal{A}^*$:

1. If fileStatus[(sid, C, S)] = stolen:
   1. Retrieve pw := file[(sid, C, S)].
   2. If $pw = pw^*$, return "correct guess" to $\mathcal{A}^*$.
   3. Otherwise, return "wrong guess" to $\mathcal{A}^*$.

Password Authentication

Upon receiving (ClientSession, sid, ssid, S, pw') from C:

1. Send (ClientSession, sid, ssid, C, S) to $\mathcal{A}^*$.
2. If sessionStatus[(sid, ssid, C, S)] is undefined, set session[(sid, ssid, C, S)] := pw' and set sessionStatus[(sid, ssid, C, S)] := fresh.

Upon receiving (ServerSession, sid, ssid) from S:

1. If file[(sid, C, S)] is undefined, ignore this query.
2. Otherwise, retrieve pw := file[(sid, C, S)] and send (ServerSession, sid, ssid, C, S) to $\mathcal{A}^*$.
3. If sessionStatus[(sid, ssid, S, C)] is undefined, set session[(sid, ssid, S, C)] := pw and set sessionStatus[(sid, ssid, S, C)] := fresh.

Fig. 2. Ideal functionality $\mathcal{F}_{\mathsf{saPAKE}}$ (part 1)

1. Protocols which realize $\mathcal{F}_{\mathsf{aPAKE}}$ also realize $\mathcal{F}_{\mathsf{saPAKE}}$ [15,21,31]: When the aPAKE simulator would send a pre-compromise OfflineTestPwd command, the saPAKE simulator instead catalogues the command and upon compromise of the server, it sends OfflineTestPwd for each catalogued command.
2. Assuming the password dictionary Dict has polynomial size, simply letting the server store the plain password is "secure" (and any PAKE is also an saPAKE) [30]: upon compromise of the server, the simulator iterates through Dict sending OfflineTestPwd for each possible password.

Active Session Attacks

Upon receiving $(\mathsf{TestPwd}, \mathsf{sid}, \mathsf{ssid}, \mathsf{P}, pw^*)$ from $\mathcal{A}^*$:

1. If $\mathsf{sessionStatus}[(\mathsf{sid}, \mathsf{ssid}, \mathsf{P}, \mathsf{P}')]$ is undefined, ignore this query.
2. Otherwise, retrieve $pw' := \mathsf{session}[(\mathsf{sid}, \mathsf{ssid}, \mathsf{P}, \mathsf{P}')]$.
3. If $\mathsf{sessionStatus}[(\mathsf{sid}, \mathsf{ssid}, \mathsf{P}, \mathsf{P}')] = \mathsf{fresh}$:
   1. If $pw' = pw^*$, return "correct guess" to $\mathcal{A}^*$ and set $\mathsf{sessionStatus}[(\mathsf{sid}, \mathsf{ssid}, \mathsf{P}, \mathsf{P}')] := \mathsf{compromised}$.
   2. Otherwise, set $\mathsf{sessionStatus}[(\mathsf{sid}, \mathsf{ssid}, \mathsf{P}, \mathsf{P}')] := \mathsf{interrupted}$ and return "wrong guess" to $\mathcal{A}^*$.

Upon receiving $(\mathsf{Impersonate}, \mathsf{sid}, \mathsf{ssid})$ from $\mathcal{A}^*$:

1. If $\mathsf{sessionStatus}[(\mathsf{sid}, \mathsf{ssid}, \mathsf{C}, \mathsf{S})] = \mathsf{fresh}$:
   1. If $\mathsf{fileStatus}[(\mathsf{C}, \mathsf{S})] = \mathsf{stolen}$ and $\mathsf{file}[(\mathsf{sid}, \mathsf{C}, \mathsf{S})] = \mathsf{session}[(\mathsf{sid}, \mathsf{ssid}, \mathsf{C}, \mathsf{S})]$, set $\mathsf{sessionStatus}[(\mathsf{sid}, \mathsf{ssid}, \mathsf{C}, \mathsf{S})] := \mathsf{compromised}$ and return "correct guess" to $\mathcal{A}^*$.
   2. Otherwise set $\mathsf{sessionStatus}[(\mathsf{sid}, \mathsf{ssid}, \mathsf{C}, \mathsf{S})] := \mathsf{interrupted}$ and return "wrong guess" to $\mathcal{A}^*$.

Key Generation

Upon receiving $(\mathsf{NewKey}, \mathsf{sid}, \mathsf{ssid}, \mathsf{P}, k^*)$ from $\mathcal{A}^*$ where $|k^*| = \kappa$:

1. If $\mathsf{sessionStatus}[(\mathsf{sid}, \mathsf{ssid}, \mathsf{P}, \mathsf{P}')]$ is defined, but is not completed:
   1. If the record is compromised, set $k := k^*$.
   2. Else, if the record is fresh, $(\mathsf{sid}, \mathsf{ssid}, k')$ was sent to P', $\mathsf{session}[(\mathsf{sid}, \mathsf{ssid}, \mathsf{P}, \mathsf{P}')] = \mathsf{session}[(\mathsf{sid}, \mathsf{ssid}, \mathsf{P}', \mathsf{P})]$, and at the time $\mathsf{sessionStatus}[(\mathsf{sid}, \mathsf{ssid}, \mathsf{P}', \mathsf{P})]$ was fresh, set $k := k'$.
   3. Otherwise, sample $k \leftarrow \{0, 1\}^\kappa$.
2. Finally, set $\mathsf{sessionStatus}[(\mathsf{sid}, \mathsf{ssid}, \mathsf{P}, \mathsf{P}')] := \mathsf{completed}$ and send $(\mathsf{sid}, \mathsf{ssid}, k)$ to P.

Fig. 3. Ideal functionality $\mathcal{F}_{\mathsf{saPAKE}}$ (part 2)

To rule out such degenerate protocols and to model the tight one-wayness of the password storage, we must restrict ourselves to simulators with limited access to the OfflineTestPwd interface. To these ends, we make explicit the ratio of the idealized model queries and the password guesses the adversary makes. We define the *simulation rate*

$$r = \frac{\#\ \mathsf{OfflineTestPwd}\ \text{commands sent by the simulator}}{\#\ \text{ideal model queries made by the adversary}}$$

of a protocol as the number of passwords that can be tested per a real adversary's ideal model query, and the "tight one-wayness" property can be expressed by requiring the simulation rate to be constant.[8] In the example above, the simulation rate of server storage $(s, H(pw, s))$ is 1. We then restrict the saPAKE simulator to only send at most r OfflineTestPwd commands *when the real adversary*

---

[8] The term "simulation rate" is borrowed from [35].

makes an idealized model query, and disallow OfflineTestPwd from the simulator otherwise.

Hesse [30] proposes a way to formalize this intuitive change by restricting the simulator so that it may access OfflineTestPwd as long as its runtime remains *locally T-bounded* [30, Definition 3]. In other words, given any real-world adversary which runs in time $T(n)$, this change restricts the simulator to run in time $T(n)$ as well, where n is the number of input bits provided by the environment and functionality minus the adversary's output bits.[9] For the sake of simplicity, in this work we instead use the equivalent intuition of a "ticketing" mechanism as is common for limiting a simulator's actions. Our simulators will (conceptually) receive r "test tickets" whenever the real world adversary would make a specific oracle query and consume one of these tickets when the simulator sends OfflineTestPwd to $\mathcal{F}_{\mathsf{saPAKE}}$. We then restrict our proofs to only consider simulators which do not send OfflineTestPwd when they have no tickets to consume.

Bradley, Jarecki, and Xu [15] prove the offline security of their saPAKE protocol in the GGM as we do; using our terminology, [15, Theorem 4] states that the simulation rate of their protocol is $O(1)$. While the offline security proof of our protocol is similar to theirs, we present a *concrete* analysis and show that our protocol has simulation rate 2. To the best of our knowledge, this is the first concrete offline security analysis of saPAKE in the GGM. We additionally show that our protocol achieves a simulation rate of 1 in the generic group action (with twists) model.

2.5 Idealized Models

The Random Oracle and Generic Group Models. Our UC random oracle and generic group functionalities can be found in Fig. 4 and Fig. 5, respectively. For simplicity, we use a variant of the GGM where the adversary is allowed to compute $A^c B^d$ for group elements A, B and integers c, d of its choice *in a single query*; such a step corresponds to at least $\log \max\{c, d\}$ steps in the standard GGM where the adversary can only perform one multiplication or division per query.[10]

The Algebraic Group Model. The algebraic group model, proposed by Fuchsbauer, Kiltz, and Loss [25], is an idealized model between the GGM and the standard model intended to analyze the security of group-based protocols.[11] Roughly speaking, the AGM requires the adversary to be *algebraic*, namely when

---

[9] [15] uses a simpler formalization that is problematic; see [30, Appendix D] for a discussion.

[10] When we say in Sect. 2.4 that the simulation rate of our protocol is 2 in the GGM, we refer to this GGM variant. It is likely that the simulation rate is smaller than 1 in the standard GGM, although we do not perform a detailed analysis in this case.

[11] While the GGM is widely used to prove lower bounds for cryptographic assumptions, it is considered problematic to use it on the protocol level; see, e.g., [40] for a discussion.

Functionality $\mathcal{F}_{\mathrm{RO}}$

Parameters:

- range $\mathcal{H}$

Storage:

- map $H : \{0,1\}^* \to \mathcal{H}$.

Upon receiving $(\mathsf{Eval}, \mathsf{sid}, x)$ from P:

1. If $H[x]$ is undefined, sample $H[x] \leftarrow \mathcal{H}$.
2. Send $(\mathsf{Eval}, \mathsf{sid}, H[x])$ to P.

Fig. 4. Ideal functionality $\mathcal{F}_{\mathrm{RO}}$

Functionality $\mathcal{F}_{\mathrm{GG}}$

Parameters:

- handle set $\mathcal{G} \subseteq \{0,1\}^\kappa$
- prime p

Storage:

- map $DL : \mathcal{G} \to \mathbb{Z}_p$.

Upon receiving $(\mathsf{Multi}, \mathsf{sid}, A, B, c, d)$ from P:

1. Retrieve $a := DL[A]$ and $b := DL[B]$; if either are undefined, sample them and set DL accordingly.
2. If there does not exist a $g' \in \mathcal{G}$ such that $DL[g'] := ca + db$, sample $g' \leftarrow \mathcal{G}$, and set $DL[g'] := ca + db$.
3. In all cases, send $(\mathsf{Multi}, \mathsf{sid}, g')$ to P.

Fig. 5. Ideal functionality $\mathcal{F}_{\mathrm{GG}}$

it outputs a group element X, it must also output its *algebraic representation* $[X]_x = (\lambda_1, \ldots, \lambda_n) \in \mathbb{Z}_p^n$ such that

$$X = X_1^{\lambda_1} \cdots X_n^{\lambda_n},$$

where $X_1, \ldots, X_n$ are group elements in the adversary's view so far.

The following lemma was proven in [25]:

Lemma 1. *The DL and CDH assumptions are equivalent in the AGM. Concretely, for any CDH solver $\mathcal{A}$, there is a DL solver $\mathcal{B}$ whose runtime is approximately equal to that of $\mathcal{A}$ such that $\mathbf{Adv}_{\mathcal{B}}^{DL} = \mathbf{Adv}_{\mathcal{A}}^{CDH}$.*

Given this lemma, we can claim that a protocol is secure in the AGM+DL while constructing a reduction to CDH, with no additional security loss. This is the approach we take in the security proof of our protocol.

Abdalla et al. [2] considered algebraic adversaries in the UC framework; in particular, they showed that the composition theorem still holds if we restrict the adversary (and the environment) to be algebraic, and as in the standard UC framework, we can still assume w.l.o.g. that the adversary is "dummy".

Offline Security in the GGM and Online Security in the AGM. As in prior works [15,21], the offline security analysis of our saPAKE protocol is done in the GGM. This seems necessary as the offline security — the server's storage is a tight one-way function of the password — is essentially a lower-bound result. However, as mentioned above, using the GGM on the protocol level (online security) might be viewed as problematic. Cremers et al. [21] state that their entire security result is in the GGM (see [21, Theorem 2]), while noting that the GGM is only used in the offline security analysis. Bradley et al. [15] state "we do not rely on GGM in the security analysis of the saPAKE protocol that uses [a tight one-way function] as the password file" (see [15, p.14]), and the authors take a more modular (yet less intuitive) approach: they abstract out the server storage as a separate primitive called salted tight one-way function (STOWF), prove that the server storage in their protocol is a UC STOWF in the GGM, and then show their protocol is a UC saPAKE without the GGM given a UC STOWF (plus some additional game-based properties). For readability, we follow the approach of Cremers et al. [21] and assume that the adversary must perform group operations via generic group queries *only while doing an offline attack*, while in online attacks the only constraint is that it must behave algebraically. However, we note that a more formal separation is straightforward by modeling the server storage as a STOWF similar to Bradley et al. [15].

3   Our saPAKE Protocol

Overview. Our starting point is the following naïve Diffie-Hellman-like protocol: The server S stores g^h where $h = H(pw)$, picks a random integer r and sends $R = g^r$ to the client C, and the two parties output g^{hr} as the session key (R^h for C and $(g^h)^r$ for S). The problem with this protocol is that g^{hr} has low entropy in the view of an eavesdropper that sees $R = g^r$. But since the two parties agree upon a low-entropy value, we can boost it into a high-entropy value by running a PAKE on top of it with g^{hr} as the input.

This yields an aPAKE but not a strong aPAKE: since the server storage is $g^{H(pw)}$, an attacker can pre-compute the table of $(x, g^{H(x)})$ for all candidate passwords x before compromising the server. To make it an saPAKE, we simply replace the fixed group base g with a variable base $S = g^s$ for a random integer s; that is, the server stores $(S, sw = S^{H(pw)})$ instead of $g^{H(pw)}$ (sw for "salted password"). This prevents the aforementioned attack as the adversary does not know S pre-compromise.

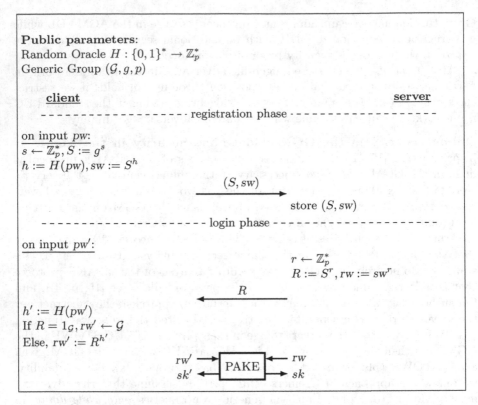

Fig. 6. Graphical representation of our protocol. See text for omitted details.

We note that using $(S, sw = S^{H(pw)})$ as server storage in saPAKE was origi-nally suggested in [15, Section 3]. However, [15] dismisses this idea because the server storage is *malleable*: an adversary that compromises the server (but with-out performing an offline dictionary attack) can impersonate the server using an alternative server storage (S^{r^*}, sw^{r^*}) for a random integer r^*, and the UC simu-lator cannot tell this is an impersonation attack if DDH is hard in the group. One of our critical observations is that *such an impersonation attack can be detected by the UC simulator in the AGM*, since the adversary must output r^* as part of the algebraic representation — so the simulator can tell that $(S, sw, S^{r^*}, sw^{r^*})$ forms a DH tuple. See the proof overview in Sect. 4 for more details.

Below we formally present our saPAKE protocol, together with a graphic illustration.

Registration Phase

On input $(\mathsf{StorePwdFile}, \mathsf{sid}, \mathsf{C}, pw)$, S

1. Samples $s \leftarrow \mathbb{Z}_p^*$.
2. Sends $(\mathsf{Eval}, \mathsf{sid}, pw)$ to $\mathcal{F}_{\mathrm{RO}}$ receiving $(\mathsf{Eval}, \mathsf{sid}, h)$.

3. Sends (Multi, sid, g, s) and (Multi, sid, g, sh) to $\mathcal{F}_{GG}$ receiving (Multi, sid, S) and (Multi, sid, sw).
4. Stores file[sid] := (S, sw).

Server Compromise

Upon receiving (StealPwdFile, sid) from $\mathcal{A}$, S retrieves file[sid] and sends it to $\mathcal{A}$. If there is no such record, S responds with "no password file".

Login Phase

1. On input (ServerSession, sid, ssid), S
   1. Retrieves (S, sw) := file[sid].
   2. Samples $r \leftarrow \mathbb{Z}_p^*$.
   3. Sends (Multi, sid, S, r) and (Multi, sid, sw, r) to $\mathcal{F}_{GG}$ receiving (Multi, sid, R) and (Multi, sid, rw).
   4. Sends (sid, ssid, R) to C and (NewSession, sid$\|$ssid$\|R$, S, C, S, rw) to $\mathcal{F}_{PAKE}$.
2. On input (ClientSession, sid, ssid, S, pw') and upon receiving (sid, ssid, R) from S, C
   1. Sends (Eval, sid, pw') to $\mathcal{F}_{RO}$ receiving (Eval, sid, h').
   2. If $R = 1_g$, samples $rw' \leftarrow \mathcal{G}$. Else, sends (Multi, sid, R, h') to $\mathcal{F}_{GG}$ receiving (Multi, sid, rw').
   3. Sends (NewSession, sid$\|$ssid$\|R$, C, S, C, rw') to $\mathcal{F}_{PAKE}$.
3. Either party, upon receiving (sid$\|$ssid$\|R, k$) from $\mathcal{F}_{PAKE}$, outputs (sid, ssid, k).

See Fig. 6 for a graphic illustration of our protocol. Note that in Fig. 6 the registration phase is done interactively, where the client computes the password file and sends it to the server via a secure channel; whereas in the formal description the server computes the password file on its own using the password (and then erases the password). Figure 6 is more likely to match real-world applications, whereas the formal description matches the UC saPAKE functionality. An additional difference is the addition of R to the sid for the PAKE session. This is needed so $\mathcal{A}$ can't test password ratios in the honest-honest case.

Correctness. As pointed out in [37], correctness of (sa)PAKE — the two parties output the same key if their passwords match and there is no active attack — is not implied by UC-security and needs to be checked separately. It is trivial to see that our saPAKE protocol is correct assuming the underlying PAKE protocol is correct: if $pw' = pw$, then $h' = h$ and thus $rw = sw^r = (S^h)^r = S^{hr}$ and $rw' = R^{h'} = R^h = (S^r)^h = S^{hr}$, so the two parties' inputs to the PAKE protocol are equal. By the correctness of PAKE, their output keys are also equal.

4   Security Proof

Theorem 1. *The protocol in Sect. 3 UC-realizes $\mathcal{F}_{saPAKE}$ (Fig. 2, Fig. 3) with simulation rate $r = 2$ in the $(\mathcal{F}_{PAKE}, \mathcal{F}_{RO}, \mathcal{F}_{GG})$-hybrid model using the AGM for online analysis and the GGM for offline analysis, in the setting where both the client and the server can be statically corrupted and assuming the DL problem is hard in group $(\mathbb{G}, g, p)$.*

Proof Overview. We provide a brief overview of the simulation strategy.

Offline security: At a high level, offline security requires that given $(S, sw = S^h)$ for h randomly chosen from a polynomial-size set $\mathbf{H}$, it takes time linear in $|\mathbf{H}|$ to find h. This "discrete logarithm over a sparse set" problem has been studied (in the GGM) by Schnorr [38, Lemma 3], of which our argument is essentially a rewrite. The simulator creates a formal variable $\mathbb{P}$ representing $\log_S sw$, and since each generic group query by the adversary computes a linear function (in the exponent), the simulator records the corresponding linear function $u_i + v_i\mathbb{P}$, and tries to solve equations

$$u_i + v_i\mathbb{P} = u_j + v_j\mathbb{P},$$

where the solutions are candidate DL values (which are then tested via OfflineTestPwd queries). The reason we solve equations of this form is because the adversary can only learn information about the discrete logarithms of group elements by string comparison (equality checking) of their handles. The difficulty here is to show a lower bound of the number of solutions when the set $\mathbf{H}$ has polynomial size, which is the main technical contribution of [38] and which we repeat here.

Online security: The simulator must detect online saPAKE password tests; in particular, when the adversary sends a TestPwd message on a certain rw^* to $\mathcal{F}_{PAKE}$, the simulator must extract the corresponding password guess pw^* on the saPAKE level. Since the PAKE-level password rw is supposed to be $S^{H(pw)\cdot r} = R^{H(pw)}$ (where R is the server's message), pw^* can be easily extracted via looking at all H queries and checking which one satisfies $R^{H(pw^*)} = rw^*$.[12]

The simulator also needs to detect impersonation attacks, i.e., the adversary executes the server's algorithm after compromising it *without knowing the saPAKE password*. Since the server's storage is $(S, sw = S^{H(pw)})$, the adversary can choose an integer r^*, send $R^* := S^{r^*}$ to client, and then send a TestPwd message for C on sw^{r^*} — which will result in "correct guess" if C's password is pw. While this seems not simulatable without the AGM, in the AGM the simulator can extract r^* from R^*, so when the adversary uses rw^* in a TestPwd message, the simulator can check if $rw^* = sw^{r^*}$ (and send Impersonate to $\mathcal{F}_{saPAKE}$ if this is the case).

---

[12] Note that if $R = 1_{\mathbb{G}}$, the adversary can make a valid password guess without making any H query by setting $rw^* = 1_{\mathbb{G}}$. While this happens with negligible probability, simply excluding this case makes the proof cleaner.

Note that in the two attacking scenarios above, only the second (the impersonation attack) needs the AGM.

The rest of the section is dedicated to the formal proof of Theorem 1. The simulator is described in Sect. 4.1, and we argue that this simulator generates an ideal-world view that is indistinguishable from the real-world view in Sect. 4.2.

4.1 Simulator

We construct the following simulator Sim for any PPT environment $\mathcal{Z}$. As standard in UC, we assume that the real adversary $\mathcal{A}$ is "dummy", *i.e.*, it merely passes messages to and from $\mathcal{Z}$. Without loss of generality, we also assume that all $\mathcal{F}_{\mathrm{RO}}$ and $\mathcal{F}_{\mathrm{GG}}$ queries are made via $\mathcal{A}$, *i.e.*, $\mathcal{Z}$ does not make these queries on its own. In the following, the session id is always included as part of a random oracle input and is omitted (*i.e.*, $H(\mathrm{sid}, x)$ is simplified to $H(x)$).

Stealing the Password File and Offline Queries

1. Upon receiving (StealPwdFile, sid) from $\mathcal{A}$ sent to S, send (StealPwdFile, sid) to $\mathcal{F}_{\mathrm{saPAKE}}$.
   A. If $\mathcal{F}_{\mathrm{saPAKE}}$ returns "password file stolen"
      I. Mark S compromised.
      II. If file[sid] is undefined
         1. Sample a pair of group handles $(S, sw) \leftarrow \mathcal{G}^2$ and return (S, sw) to $\mathcal{A}$ from S.
         2. Create a formal variable $\mathbb{P}$ representing the discrete logarithm of sw relative to base S and sample $s \leftarrow \mathbb{Z}_p^*$.
         3. Store $\mathrm{DL}[S] := s$ and $\mathrm{DL}[sw] := s\mathbb{P}$.
   B. Otherwise, return "no password file" to $\mathcal{A}$.
2. Upon receiving (Eval, sid, x) from $\mathcal{A}$ sent to $\mathcal{F}_{\mathrm{RO}}$:
   A. If $H(x)$ is undefined, sample $y \leftarrow \mathbb{Z}_p$ and record $H(x) := y$.
   B. If there exists $x' \neq x$ such that $H(x') = H(x)$, output Collision and abort.
   C. If S is marked compromised, send (OfflineTestPwd, sid, x) to $\mathcal{F}_{\mathrm{saPAKE}}$.
      I. If $\mathcal{F}_{\mathrm{saPAKE}}$ returns "correct guess", replace formal variable $\mathbb{P}$ with $H(x)$ in all future responses and store serverPW[sid] := x.
   D. Return (Eval, sid, $H(x)$) to $\mathcal{A}$.
3. Upon receiving (Multi, sid, A, B, c, d) from $\mathcal{A}$ to $\mathcal{F}_{\mathrm{GG}}$:
   A. If $\mathrm{DL}[g]$, for generator g associated with sid, is undefined, set $\mathrm{DL}[g] = 1$.
   B. If either $\mathrm{DL}[A]$ or $\mathrm{DL}[B]$ is undefined, sample the missing logarithm(s) from $\mathbb{Z}_p$.
   C. Interpret $a := \mathrm{DL}[A]$ and $b := \mathrm{DL}[B]$ as linear combinations over $\mathbb{Z}_p$ of $\{1, \mathbb{P}\}$, and record linear function $ca + db$ denoted γ:

$$a = \alpha_1 + \alpha_2 \mathbb{P}$$
$$b = \beta_1 + \beta_2 \mathbb{P}$$
$$\gamma = (c\alpha_1 + d\beta_1) + (c\alpha_2 + d\beta_2)\mathbb{P}$$

D. If S is marked compromised:
   I. Suppose this is the t-th query $\mathcal{A}$ made to $\mathcal{F}_{\text{GG}}$ post-compromise. Then let $u_1 s + v_1 s\mathbb{P}, \ldots, u_{t+2} s + v_{t+2} s\mathbb{P}$ be the $t+2$ linear equations, recorded in chronological order, after compromise such that $(u_1, v_1) = (1,0)$, $(u_2, v_2) = (0,1)$, and $u_{t+2} s + v_{t+2} s\mathbb{P}$ is the linear function recorded during the current query.
   II. Compute all solutions to the $t+1$ equations
   $$(v_i - v_{t+2}) X_{t+2,i} = u_{t+2} - u_i,$$
   where $i \in [t+1]$. Let the solutions be $h_{t+2,i}$.
   III. For any $h_{t+2,i} = H(x_{t+2,i})$, send (OfflineTestPwd, sid, $x_{t+2,i}$) to $\mathcal{F}_{\text{saPAKE}}$. If more than $2t$ OfflineTestPwd commands would be sent in total (*i.e.*, there is no "ticket" from $\mathcal{Z}$ to send an OfflineTestPwd command), output OfflineFailure and abort.
   IV. Whenever $\mathcal{F}_{\text{saPAKE}}$ returns "correct guess", replace formal variable $\mathbb{P}$ with $h_{t+2,i}$ in this and all future responses and store serverPW[sid] := $x_{t+2,i}$.
E. If γ is a fresh discrete logarithm, that is, for all previously generated handles C_i, DL[C_i] $\neq \gamma$, then sample a new handle C from the set of handles $\mathcal{G}$ and set DL[C] := γ. Otherwise there is an existing handle C_i such that DL[C_i] = γ; in this case output Collision and abort.
F. Return (Multi, sid, C) to $\mathcal{A}$.

Password Authentication

4. Upon receiving (ServerSession, sid, ssid, C, S) from $\mathcal{F}_{\text{saPAKE}}$:
   A. If file[sid] is undefined
      I. Sample a pair of group handles $(S, sw) \leftarrow \mathcal{G}^2$ and store file[sid] := (S, sw).
      II. Create a formal variable $\mathbb{P}$ representing the discrete logarithm of sw relative to base S and sample $s \leftarrow \mathbb{Z}_p^*$.
      III. Store DL[S] := s and DL[sw] := $s\mathbb{P}$.
   B. If serverSession[sid, ssid] is undefined, then set serverSession[sid, ssid] := $(C, S, \perp)$.
   C. Sample $r \leftarrow \mathbb{Z}_p^*$, compute $R := g^r$, and send (sid, ssid, R) to C from S.
   D. Send (NewSession, sid||ssid||R, S, C, S) to $\mathcal{A}$ from $\mathcal{F}_{\text{PAKE}}$, set serverSession[sid, ssid] := (C, S, R), and mark serverSession[sid, ssid] as "PAKE active".
5. Upon receiving (ClientSession, sid, ssid, C, S) from $\mathcal{F}_{\text{saPAKE}}$:
   A. If clientSession[sid, ssid] is undefined, then set clientSession[sid, ssid] := $(C, S, \perp)$.
   B. Wait to receive (sid, ssid, $[R^*]_x$) from S sent to C.[13]
   C. Send (NewSession, sid||ssid||R^*, C, S, C) to $\mathcal{A}$ from $\mathcal{F}_{\text{PAKE}}$, set clientSession[sid, ssid] := (C, S, R^*), and mark clientSession[sid, ssid] as "PAKE active".

---

[13] Formally $\mathcal{A}$ only sends (sid, ssid, R^*) to C, and additionally outputs $[R^*]_x$ as the algebraic representation of R^*. We use this compact form for brevity.

Active Session Attacks

6. Upon receiving $(\mathsf{TestPwd}, \mathsf{sid}||\mathsf{ssid}||R, \mathsf{S}, [rw^*]_x)$ from $\mathcal{A}$ sent to $\mathcal{F}_{\mathrm{PAKE}}$, if there is a record $\mathsf{serverSession}[\mathsf{sid}, \mathsf{ssid}] = (\mathsf{C}, \mathsf{S}, R)$ marked "PAKE active":
   A. Check if there exists an x such that $rw^* = R^{H(x)}$. If so, x is uniquely defined (if there were two such x, the simulator would have output Collision and aborted). Otherwise set $x := \perp$.
   B. Send $(\mathsf{TestPwd}, \mathsf{sid}, \mathsf{ssid}, \mathsf{S}, x)$ to $\mathcal{F}_{\mathrm{saPAKE}}$ and relay the response ("correct guess" or "wrong guess") to $\mathcal{A}$ from $\mathcal{F}_{\mathrm{PAKE}}$.
   C. If $\mathcal{F}_{\mathrm{saPAKE}}$ returns "correct guess", replace formal variable $\mathbb{P}$ with $H(x)$ in all future responses and store $\mathsf{serverPW}[\mathsf{sid}] := x$.
7. Upon receiving $(\mathsf{TestPwd}, \mathsf{sid}||\mathsf{ssid}||R^*, \mathsf{C}, [rw^*]_x)$ from $\mathcal{A}$ sent to $\mathcal{F}_{\mathrm{PAKE}}$, if there is a record $\mathsf{clientSession}[\mathsf{sid}, \mathsf{ssid}] = (\mathsf{C}, \mathsf{S}, R^*)$ marked "PAKE active":
   A. If (1) S is marked compromised and (S, sw) was previously given to $\mathcal{A}$ upon server compromise, and (2) $[1]_x \neq [R^*]_x = r^*[S]_x$ and $[rw^*]_x = r^*[sw]_x$, then send $(\mathsf{Impersonate}, \mathsf{sid}, \mathsf{ssid})$ to $\mathcal{F}_{\mathrm{saPAKE}}$ and relay the response ("correct guess" or "wrong guess") to $\mathcal{A}$ from $\mathcal{F}_{\mathrm{PAKE}}$.
   B. Otherwise (*i.e.*, no Impersonate command was sent):
      I. Check if there exists an x such that $rw^* = (R^*)^{H(x)}$. If so, x is uniquely defined. Otherwise set $x := \perp$.
      II. Send $(\mathsf{TestPwd}, \mathsf{sid}, \mathsf{ssid}, \mathsf{C}, x)$ to $\mathcal{F}_{\mathrm{saPAKE}}$ and relay the response ("correct guess" or "wrong guess") to $\mathcal{A}$ from $\mathcal{F}_{\mathrm{PAKE}}$.
      III. If $\mathcal{F}_{\mathrm{saPAKE}}$ returns "correct guess", replace formal variable $\mathbb{P}$ with $H(x)$ in all future responses.

Key Generation

8. Upon receiving $(\mathsf{NewKey}, \mathsf{sid}||\mathsf{ssid}||R, \mathsf{C}, k^*)$ from $\mathcal{A}$ to $\mathcal{F}_{\mathrm{PAKE}}$ such that there is a record $(\mathsf{C}, \mathsf{S}, R) := \mathsf{clientSession}[\mathsf{sid}, \mathsf{ssid}]$ marked "PAKE active":
   A. If there is a corresponding PAKE session for the server (*i.e.*, $\mathsf{serverSession}[\mathsf{sid}, \mathsf{ssid}] = (\mathsf{C}, \mathsf{S}, R^*)$) and $R^* \neq R$ (*i.e.*, $\mathcal{A}$ modifies the message before PAKE), send $(\mathsf{TestPwd}, \mathsf{sid}, \mathsf{ssid}, \mathsf{C}, \perp)$ to $\mathcal{F}_{\mathrm{saPAKE}}$.
   B. Regardless, send $(\mathsf{NewKey}, \mathsf{sid}, \mathsf{ssid}, \mathsf{C}, k^*)$ to $\mathcal{F}_{\mathrm{saPAKE}}$ and mark $\mathsf{clientSession}[\mathsf{sid}, \mathsf{ssid}]$ as "PAKE completed".
9. Upon receiving $(\mathsf{NewKey}, \mathsf{sid}||\mathsf{ssid}||R, \mathsf{S}, k^*)$ from $\mathcal{A}$ to $\mathcal{F}_{\mathrm{PAKE}}$ such that there is a record $(\mathsf{C}, \mathsf{S}, R) := \mathsf{serverSession}[\mathsf{sid}, \mathsf{ssid}]$ marked "PAKE active":
   A. If there is a corresponding PAKE session for the client (*i.e.*, $\mathsf{clientSession}[\mathsf{sid}, \mathsf{ssid}] = (\mathsf{C}, \mathsf{S}, R^*)$) and $R^* \neq R$ (*i.e.*, $\mathcal{A}$ modifies the message before PAKE), send $(\mathsf{TestPwd}, \mathsf{sid}, \mathsf{ssid}, \mathsf{S}, \perp)$ to $\mathcal{F}_{\mathrm{saPAKE}}$.
   B. Regardless, send $(\mathsf{NewKey}, \mathsf{sid}, \mathsf{ssid}, \mathsf{S}, k^*)$ to $\mathcal{F}_{\mathrm{saPAKE}}$ and mark $\mathsf{serverSession}[\mathsf{sid}, \mathsf{ssid}]$ as "PAKE completed".

4.2   Proof of Indistinguishability

We now show that the simulator in Sect. 4.1 generates a view indistinguishable from the real world for any PPT environment $\mathcal{Z}$. We will proceed by a series of hybrids starting in the real world and ending in the ideal world. We use $\mathbf{Dist}_{\mathcal{Z}}^{i,i+1}$ to denote $\mathcal{Z}$'s distinguishing advantage between *Hybrids* i and $i + 1$.

Hybrid 0: Real world

In this hybrid, the environment instructs the "dummy" adversary to play the role of a man-in-the-middle attacker between C and S. Recall that C's and S's passwords are denoted pw' and pw, respectively.

Hybrid 1: Ruling out random oracle and generic group collisions

In this hybrid, the challenger outputs Collision and aborts if there exist $x \neq x'$ such that $H(x) = H(x')$, or $A \neq A' \in \mathcal{G}$ such that their handles are equal. Assuming $\mathcal{A}$ makes q_{RO} Eval queries to $\mathcal{F}_{RO}$ and q_{GG} Multi queries to $\mathcal{F}_{GG}$, we have that

$$\mathbf{Dist}_{\mathcal{Z}}^{0,1} \leq \Pr[\text{Collision}] \leq \frac{q_{RO}^2 + q_{GG}^2}{2p},$$

which is a negligible function of κ since $2^\kappa \leq p < 2^{\kappa+1}$.

Hybrid 2: Modifying R

In this hybrid, if $R^* \neq R$ (i.e., $\mathcal{A}$ modifies the message from S to C before PAKE) and $\mathcal{A}$ does not send $(\mathsf{TestPwd}, \mathsf{sid}||\mathsf{ssid}||R, \mathsf{S}, \cdot)$ to $\mathcal{F}_{PAKE}$ (resp. $(\mathsf{TestPwd}, \mathsf{sid}||\mathsf{ssid}||R^*, \mathsf{C}, \cdot)$), then when $\mathcal{A}$ sends $(\mathsf{NewKey}, \mathsf{sid}||\mathsf{ssid}||R, \mathsf{S}, \cdot)$ to $\mathcal{F}_{PAKE}$ (resp. $(\mathsf{NewKey}, \mathsf{sid}||\mathsf{ssid}||R^*, \mathsf{C}, \cdot)$), S (resp. C) outputs a random key in $\{0,1\}^\kappa$ (independent of everything else).

In *Hybrid 1*, C's session id in $\mathcal{F}_{PAKE}$ is $\mathsf{sid}||\mathsf{ssid}||R^*$, and S's session id is $\mathsf{sid}||\mathsf{ssid}||R$. Therefore, if $R^* \neq R$ and there is no active attack on PAKE, $\mathcal{F}_{PAKE}$ will output independent random keys to C and S — exactly what *Hybrid 2* does. We have that

$$\mathbf{Dist}_{\mathcal{Z}}^{1,2} = 0.$$

Hybrid 3: Testing server's password

In this hybrid, when $\mathcal{A}$ sends $(\mathsf{TestPwd}, \mathsf{sid}||\mathsf{ssid}||R, \mathsf{S}, [rw^*]_x)$ to $\mathcal{F}_{PAKE}$ and the server PAKE sub-session is active, $\mathcal{F}_{PAKE}$ returns "correct guess" and marks the sub-session compromised if $\mathcal{A}$ has queried $H(pw) = z$ and $rw^* = R^z$. Otherwise $\mathcal{F}_{PAKE}$ returns "wrong guess" and marks the sub-session interrupted.

In *Hybrid 2*, $\mathcal{F}_{PAKE}$ returns "correct guess" (and marks the sub-session compromised) if and only if $rw^* = R^{H(pw)}$. Therefore, *Hybrid 3* and *Hybrid 2* are identical unless $\mathcal{A}$ includes $rw^* = R^{H(pw)}$ in a TestPwd message without querying $z = H(pw)$. Call this event GuessServerrw. Note that $\mathcal{A}$ only learns $R = S^r$, and potentially S and $sw = S^{H(pw)}$ (if S is compromised); (S, sw, R, rw^*) forms a DH tuple. Therefore, an environment $\mathcal{Z}$ that causes GuessServerrw can be turned into a reduction $\mathcal{B}_1$ that solves the CDH problem in $(\mathbb{G}, g, p)$: Suppose there are at most ℓ sub-sessions. $\mathcal{B}_1(A, B)$ samples $i \leftarrow [\ell]$ as a guess that GuessServerrw happens in the i-th sub-session, runs the code of the *Hybrid 3* challenger with $S := g^s$, $sw := A^s$, and $R := B^s$ where R is the S-to-C message in the i-th sub-session (note that S and sw remain the same across all sub-sessions), and upon receiving rw^*, $\mathcal{B}_1$ outputs $(rw^*)^{1/s}$.[14] Clearly $\mathcal{B}_1$ wins if and only if GuessServerrw

---

[14] Note that $\mathcal{A}$ never queries $H(pw)$ if GuessServerrw happens, so $\mathcal{B}_1$ can set S as g^s and $sw = S^{H(pw)}$ as A^s.

happens in the i-th sub-session. We have that

$$\mathbf{Dist}_{\mathcal{Z}}^{2,3} \leq \Pr[\mathsf{GuessServerrw}] \leq \ell \cdot \mathbf{Adv}_{\mathcal{B}_1}^{\mathsf{CDH}},$$

which is a negligible function of κ since the DL problem is hard in $(\mathbb{G}, g, p)$, and the CDH problem and the DL problem are equivalent in the AGM (see Lemma 1).

Hybrid 4: Impersonation attacks

In this hybrid, when $\mathcal{A}$ sends $(\mathsf{TestPwd}, \mathsf{sid}\|\mathsf{ssid}\|R^*, \mathsf{C}, [rw^*]_x)$ to $\mathcal{F}_{\mathsf{PAKE}}$ and the client PAKE sub-session is active, do the following if (1) S is compromised and (S, sw) was given to $\mathcal{A}$ upon server compromise, and (2) there exists $r \in \mathbb{Z}_p$ such that $[1]_x \neq [R^*]_x = r[S]_x$ and $[rw^*]_x = r[sw]_x$:

- If $pw' = pw$, then $\mathcal{F}_{\mathsf{PAKE}}$ returns "correct guess" and marks the sub-session compromised;
- Otherwise $\mathcal{F}_{\mathsf{PAKE}}$ returns "wrong guess" and marks the sub-session interrupted.

Note that the change from *Hybrid 3* to *Hybrid 4* is made only if both (1) and (2) hold; in other words, if either (1) or (2) does not hold, there is no change from *Hybrid 3* to *Hybrid 4*. Now assume (1) and (2) hold. Then we have:

- $R^* = S^r$ and $rw^* = sw^r$, so (S, R^*, sw, rw^*) forms a DH tuple;
- $sw = S^{H(pw)}$ and $rw' = (R^*)^{H(pw')}$, so (S, R^*, sw, rw') forms a DH tuple if and only if $pw' = pw$ (note that collisions in H have been ruled out).

Thus, $rw^* = rw'$ if and only if (S, R^*, sw, rw') forms a DH tuple, which in turn happens if and only if $pw' = pw$. In *Hybrid 3*, $\mathcal{F}_{\mathsf{PAKE}}$ returns "correct guess" if and only if $rw^* = rw'$, whereas in *Hybrid 4*, $\mathcal{F}_{\mathsf{PAKE}}$ returns "correct guess" if and only if $pw' = pw$. This means that the conditions on which $\mathcal{F}_{\mathsf{PAKE}}$ returns "correct guess" in *Hybrid 3* and in *Hybrid 4* are equivalent. Thus, *Hybrid 3* and *Hybrid 4* are identical in $\mathcal{Z}$'s view, and

$$\mathbf{Dist}_{\mathcal{Z}}^{3,4} = 0.$$

Hybrid 5: Testing client's password

In this hybrid, when $\mathcal{A}$ sends $(\mathsf{TestPwd}, \mathsf{sid}\|\mathsf{ssid}\|R^*, \mathsf{C}, [rw^*]_x)$ to $\mathcal{F}_{\mathsf{PAKE}}$ and the client PAKE sub-session is active, if either (1) or (2) defined in *Hybrid 4* does not hold, do the following: $\mathcal{F}_{\mathsf{PAKE}}$ returns "correct guess" and marks the sub-session compromised if $\mathcal{A}$ has queried $H(pw') = z$ and $rw^* = (R^*)^z$. Otherwise $\mathcal{F}_{\mathsf{PAKE}}$ returns "wrong guess" and marks the sub-session interrupted.

In *Hybrid 4*, $\mathcal{F}_{\mathsf{PAKE}}$ returns "correct guess" (and marks the sub-session compromised) if and only if $rw^* = (R^*)^{H(pw')}$. Therefore, *Hybrid 5* and *Hybrid 4* are identical unless $\mathcal{A}$ includes $rw^* = (R^*)^{H(pw')}$ in a $\mathsf{TestPwd}$ message without querying $z = H(pw')$. Call this event $\mathsf{GuessClientrw}$. If $pw' \neq pw$, then $H(pw')$ is independent of the rest of the experiment, so $\mathsf{GuessClientrw}$ happens with probability $1/p$ over the choice of random oracle outputs.

If instead $pw' = pw$, an environment $\mathcal{Z}$ that causes GuessClientrw can be turned into a reduction $\mathcal{B}_2$ that solves the DL problem in $(\mathbb{G}, g, p)$. $\mathcal{B}_2(Q)$ samples $i \leftarrow [\ell]$ as before, and runs the code of the *Hybrid 3* challenger with $S := g^s$ and $sw := Q^s$ in the i-th sub-session (so $q = \log Q$ is embedded as $H(pw)$). When $\mathcal{B}_2$ receives R^* and rw^* along with their algebraic representations $(a, b, c, t_1, \ldots, t_i)$ and $(\alpha, \beta, \gamma, \tau_1, \ldots, \tau_i)$ based on $g, S, sw, R_1, \ldots, R_i$ (where R_j is the S-to-C message in the j-th sub-session), $\mathcal{B}_2$ can obtain the expressions $R^* = g^d Q^e$ by condensing $g^a S^b \prod_j R_i^{t_j} = g^{a+sb+\sum_j sr_j t_j}$ and $sw^c = Q^{sc}$; similarly it can obtain $rw^* = g^\delta Q^\epsilon$. Combining these two equations with $rw^* = (R^*)^{H(pw')} = (R^*)^{H(pw)} = (R^*)^q$ we have

$$q^2 e + (d - \epsilon)q - \delta = 0,$$

from which $\mathcal{B}_2$ may solve for q when either $e \neq 0$ or $d - \epsilon \neq 0$. (Such equations are not generally solvable, but assuming GuessClientrw happens, there exists a solution. If there are two solutions, $\mathcal{B}_2$ may verify which one is correct by checking if $g^q = Q$ for each candidate solution.) If both are 0, we have $e = \delta = 0$ and $d = \epsilon$, so $R^* = g^d$ and $rw^* = Q^d$ which we covered in *Hybrid 4*.

We conclude that

$$\mathbf{Dist}_{\mathcal{Z}}^{4,5} \leq \Pr[\mathsf{GuessClientrw}] \leq \max\left\{\ell \cdot \mathbf{Adv}_{\mathcal{B}_2}^{\mathsf{DL}}, \frac{1}{p}\right\},$$

which is a negligible function of κ since the DL problem is hard in $(\mathbb{G}, g, p)$.

Hybrid 6: Offline attacks

In this hybrid, S defines its password file file[sid] as $(S, sw) \leftarrow \mathcal{G}^2$, rather than $S \leftarrow \mathcal{G}$ and $sw := S^{H(pw)}$. Furthermore, when $\mathcal{A}$ computes $S^{H(pw)}$ via generic group queries, program the result as sw.

The difference between *Hybrid 6* and *Hybrid 5* is that in *Hybrid 5* sw is defined as $S^{H(pw)}$, while in *Hybrid 6* it is chosen at random from $\mathcal{G}$ and when $\mathcal{A}$ computes $S^{H(pw)}$, the result is programmed to be $S^{H(pw)}$. We can see that $\mathcal{Z}$'s views in these two hybrids are identical, so

$$\mathbf{Dist}_{\mathcal{Z}}^{5,6} = 0.$$

Combining all results above, we get

$$\mathbf{Dist}_{\mathcal{Z}}^{0,6} \leq \frac{q_{\mathsf{RO}}^2 + q_{\mathsf{GG}}^2 + 4}{2p} + \ell(\mathbf{Adv}_{\mathcal{B}_1}^{\mathsf{CDH}} + \mathbf{Adv}_{\mathcal{B}_2}^{\mathsf{CDH}}),$$

which is a negligible function of κ.

Comparison Between *Hybrid 6* and the Ideal World. We now compare $\mathcal{Z}$'s views in *Hybrid 6* and in the ideal world. *Hybrid 6* is a modified real world whose challenger, among other things, includes $\mathcal{F}_{\mathsf{PAKE}}$ with modified behavior (in particular, the rules on when sessions are marked compromised or interrupted are changed); we argue that in $\mathcal{Z}$'s view this challenger is identical to the combination of $\mathcal{F}_{\text{saPAKE}}$ and the simulator Sim in the ideal world. First note that both games output Collision and abort if there is a collision in either H or the generic group. Below we assume that Collision does not happen.

We first analyze $\mathcal{F}_{\text{PAKE}}$'s response to $\mathcal{A}$ ("correct guess" or "wrong guess") upon a TestPwd command. In both *Hybrid 6* and the ideal world, we have:

- When $\mathcal{A}$ sends $(\text{TestPwd}, \text{sid}\|\text{ssid}\|R, \text{S}, [rw^*]_x)$ to $\mathcal{F}_{\text{PAKE}}$ and the server PAKE sub-session is active:
  - If $\mathcal{A}$ has queried $H(pw) = z$ and $rw^* = R^z$, then $\mathcal{F}_{\text{PAKE}}$ returns "correct guess";
  - Otherwise $\mathcal{F}_{\text{PAKE}}$ returns "wrong guess".
  This can be seen from *Hybrid 3* above and steps 6A and 6B of the simulator.[15]
- When $\mathcal{A}$ sends $(\text{TestPwd}, \text{sid}\|\text{ssid}\|R^*, \text{C}, [rw^*]_x)$ to $\mathcal{F}_{\text{PAKE}}$ and the client PAKE sub-session is active, if (1) S is compromised and (S, sw) was given to $\mathcal{A}$ upon server compromise, and (2) $\mathcal{A}$ has computed (R^*, rw^*) as (S^r, sw^r) for some $r \in \mathbb{Z}_p$:
  - If $pw' = pw$, then $\mathcal{F}_{\text{PAKE}}$ returns "correct guess";
  - Otherwise $\mathcal{F}_{\text{PAKE}}$ returns "wrong guess".
  This can be seen from *Hybrid 4* above and step 7A of the simulator.
- When $\mathcal{A}$ sends $(\text{TestPwd}, \text{sid}\|\text{ssid}\|R^*, \text{C}, [rw^*]_x)$ to $\mathcal{F}_{\text{PAKE}}$ and the client PAKE sub-session is active, if either (1) or (2) above does not hold:
  - If $\mathcal{A}$ has queried $H(pw') = z$ and $rw^* = (R^*)^z$, then $\mathcal{F}_{\text{PAKE}}$ returns "correct guess";
  - Otherwise $\mathcal{F}_{\text{PAKE}}$ returns "wrong guess".
  This can be seen from *Hybrid 5* above and steps 7B(I) and 7B(II) of the simulator.

Next, we analyze C and S's output keys when $\mathcal{A}$ sends NewKey to $\mathcal{F}_{\text{PAKE}}$. We first consider *Hybrid 6*. From *Hybrids 3–5*, we can see that whenever $\mathcal{A}$ sends a TestPwd command to $\mathcal{F}_{\text{PAKE}}$ resulting in "correct guess", $\mathcal{F}_{\text{PAKE}}$ marks the corresponding sub-session compromised. Then when $\mathcal{A}$ sends NewKey, $\mathcal{F}_{\text{PAKE}}$ lets the corresponding party output the key that $\mathcal{A}$ specifies. On the other hand, if the TestPwd command results in "wrong guess", the sub-session is marked interrupted, and when NewKey is sent, the corresponding party outputs an independent random key.

In the ideal world, when $\mathcal{A}$ sends a TestPwd command aimed at $\mathcal{F}_{\text{PAKE}}$, Sim always sends its own TestPwd command to $\mathcal{F}_{\text{saPAKE}}$ and relays $\mathcal{F}_{\text{saPAKE}}$'s answer to $\mathcal{A}$. This means that if $\mathcal{A}$ receives "correct guess", $\mathcal{F}_{\text{saPAKE}}$ marks the corresponding session compromised; after that, when $\mathcal{A}$ sends NewKey, $\mathcal{F}_{\text{saPAKE}}$

---

[15] In the ideal world, Sim checks if there exists pw^* such that $\mathcal{A}$ has queried $H(pw^*) = z$ and $rw^* = R^z$; if not, Sim defines $pw^* := \bot$. Then Sim sends $(\text{TestPwd}, \text{sid}\|\text{ssid}\|R, \text{S}, pw^*)$ to $\mathcal{F}_{\text{saPAKE}}$. $\mathcal{F}_{\text{saPAKE}}$ sends "correct guess" to Sim if and only if $pw^* = pw'$, and Sim relays the answer to $\mathcal{A}$. Since we have ruled out collisions in H, $\mathcal{A}$ receives "correct guess" if and only if $\mathcal{A}$ has queried $H(pw) = z$ and $rw^* = R^z$. The cases below can be seen similarly.

lets the corresponding party output the key that $\mathcal{A}$ specifies. Similarly, if $\mathcal{A}$ receives "wrong guess", $\mathcal{F}_{\mathrm{saPAKE}}$ marks the corresponding session interrupted, and when $\mathcal{A}$ sends NewKey, $\mathcal{F}_{\mathrm{saPAKE}}$ lets the corresponding party output an independent random key.

In other words, in both *Hybrid 6* and the ideal world, C or S outputs the key that $\mathcal{A}$ specifies if $\mathcal{A}$ has sent a TestPwd command aimed at $\mathcal{F}_{\mathrm{PAKE}}$ resulting in "correct guess", and outputs an independent random key if the TestPwd command results in "wrong guess". The remaining case is that $\mathcal{A}$ does not send a TestPwd command. We argue that in this case, when $\mathcal{A}$ sends $(\mathsf{NewKey}, \mathrm{sid}\|\mathrm{ssid}\|R, \mathsf{S}, k^*)$ and $(\mathsf{NewKey}, \mathrm{sid}\|\mathrm{ssid}\|R^*, \mathsf{C}, k^*)$ aimed at $\mathcal{F}_{\mathrm{PAKE}}$, in both *Hybrid 6* and the ideal world,

- If $R^* = R$ (*i.e.*, $\mathcal{A}$ does not modify the message before PAKE), C and S output the same random key;
- Otherwise C and S output independent random keys.

In *Hybrid 6*, if $R^* = R$, $\mathcal{F}_{\mathrm{PAKE}}$ ensures that C and S output the same random key; otherwise they output independent random keys due to *Hybrid 2*. In the ideal world, if $R^* = R$, Sim does not send any TestPwd command to $\mathcal{F}_{\mathrm{saPAKE}}$, so $\mathcal{F}_{\mathrm{saPAKE}}$ ensures that C and S output the same random key; otherwise Sim sends $(\mathsf{TestPwd}, \mathrm{ssid}, \mathsf{C}, \bot)$ and $(\mathsf{TestPwd}, \mathrm{ssid}, \mathsf{S}, \bot)$ to $\mathcal{F}_{\mathrm{saPAKE}}$ (steps 8A and 9A), and $\mathcal{F}_{\mathrm{saPAKE}}$ marks both C sub-session and S sub-session interrupted, so C and S output independent random keys — which is exactly what happens in *Hybrid 6*.

We finally consider offline attacks. In *Hybrid 6*, S's password file is $(S, sw) \leftarrow \mathcal{G}^2$, and when $\mathcal{A}$ computes $S^{H(pw)}$ via random oracle and generic group queries, the result is programmed as sw. In the ideal world, this is exactly what Sim does in steps 1–3: whenever $\mathcal{A}$ makes a post-compromise generic group query, Sim solves for all x such that $\mathcal{A}$ tests if $sw = S^{H(x)}$, sends $(\mathsf{OfflineTestPwd}, \mathrm{sid}, x)$ to $\mathcal{F}_{\mathrm{saPAKE}}$, and if $\mathcal{F}_{\mathrm{saPAKE}}$ returns "correct guess" (*i.e.*, $x = pw$), then Sim programs $sw := S^{H(x)}$. The only difference is that in the ideal world, if at any point $\mathcal{A}$ makes t generic group queries but Sim needs to send more than $2t$ OfflineTestPwd commands (*i.e.*, Sim runs out of "tickets"), then Sim outputs OfflineFailure and aborts.

In sum, we have proven that $\mathcal{Z}$'s views in *Hybrid 6* and in the ideal world are identical, unless OfflineFailure happens. Since we have also proven that $\mathcal{Z}$'s views in the real world and in *Hybrid 6* are indistinguishable, this means that $\mathcal{Z}$'s views in the real world and in the ideal world are indistinguishable as long as OfflineFailure happens with negligible probability.

Lemma 2. $\Pr[\textit{OfflineFailure}]$ *is a negligible function of* κ.

As mentioned in the proof overview, this is essentially rendering the proof of [38, Lemma 3] in the UC setting; for completeness, we include the proof of the lemma above in the full version of this paper.

5 An SaPAKE from Group Actions

In this section we extend the analysis of the compiler in Sect. 3 to the generic group action model (GGAM).

5.1 Group Actions

Until this point, our compiler has relied on classical assumptions in cryptographic groups, specifically the hardness of the DL problem. However, Shor has shown [39] that discrete logarithms can be computed in polynomial time using a sufficiently large quantum computer. Our compiled protocols are not alone in this insecurity; indeed, previous UC-secure saPAKE protocols are built from Diffie-Hellman assumptions in groups [15,21,31] and thus are vulnerable to an adversary who can compute discrete logarithms.

As a competitor to the DL assumption, Couveignes [20] proposed replacing the group operations in traditional Diffie-Hellman with *cryptographic group actions* (therein referred to as hard homogenous spaces). For a group $\mathbb{G}$ and a set $\mathcal{X}$, a group action $\star$ is a map from $\mathbb{G} \times \mathcal{X}$ to $\mathcal{X}$ — analogous to exponentiation in classical groups — which respects group operations in $\mathbb{G}$; integrally, there is no group law on $\mathcal{X}$ which makes group actions resilient to Shor's algorithm. Following Couveignes' work, group actions have been used to construct various cryptographic schemes including symmetric PAKE [4].

We recall the definition of group actions:

Definition 3 (Group Action). *A group action of a group $(\mathbb{G}, e, \cdot)$ on a set $\mathcal{X}$ is a mapping $\star : \mathbb{G} \times \mathcal{X} \to \mathcal{X}$, usually written using infix notation as $g \star x$, which satisfies the following two properties:*

1. *Identity: $e \star x = x$ for all $x \in \mathcal{X}$.*
2. *Compatibility: $g \star g' \star x = (g \cdot g') \star x$ for all $g, g' \in \mathbb{G}$ and $x \in \mathcal{X}$.*

We additionally consider three properties of group actions:

1. *Freeness*: A group action $(\mathbb{G}, \mathcal{X}, \star)$ is said to be *free* when $g \star x = x \implies g = e$ for any $x \in \mathcal{X}$.
2. *Transitivity*: A group action $(\mathbb{G}, \mathcal{X}, \star)$ is said to be *transitive* when $\mathcal{X}$ is the only orbit under $\mathbb{G}$. In other words, $\forall x, y \in \mathcal{X}, \exists g \in \mathbb{G} \mid x = g \star y$.
3. *Regularity*: A group action $(\mathbb{G}, \mathcal{X}, \star)$ is said to be *regular* when the action is both free and transitive.

For the rest of the paper, we will only consider actions which are regular and for which $\mathbb{G}$ is abelian. In the context of our protocol in Sect. 3, we can view the action of $\mathbb{Z}_p^*$ on $\mathcal{G} \setminus \{e\}$ in the natural way $a \star g = g^a$. Indeed, the only operation our protocol requires is exponentiation, so an honest party and simulator will only interact with $\mathcal{G}$ through this action. However, the additional structure $\mathcal{G}$ imposes disallows us from analyzing it as a generic group action.

As we wish to relate the security of our protocol to computational assumptions, we will further restrict our group actions to those with polynomial-time algorithms:

Definition 4 (Effective Group Action). *A group action* $(\mathbb{G}, \mathcal{X}, \star)$ *is said to be effective with respect to a computation security parameter* κ *if the following properties are satisfied:*

1. $\mathbb{G}$ *is finite and there exist polynomial-time algorithms (in* κ*) for the following:*
   (a) *Membership Testing: Decide if a given bitstring represents an element in* $\mathbb{G}$.
   (b) *Equality Testing: Decide if two given bitstrings represent the same element in* $\mathbb{G}$.
   (c) *Sampling: Sample an element* g *from* $\mathbb{G}$ *according to some distribution* $\mathcal{D}_\mathbb{G}$. *For the purpose of our protocol, we assume that* $\mathcal{D}_\mathbb{G}$ *is statistically close to the uniform distribution* $\mathcal{U}_\mathbb{G}$ *on* $\mathbb{G}$.
   (d) *Operation: Compute* $g \cdot g'$ *for any two elements* $g, g' \in \mathbb{G}$.
   (e) *Inversion: Compute* g^{-1} *for any element* $g \in \mathbb{G}$.
2. $\mathcal{X}$ *is finite (note that* $|\mathbb{G}| = |\mathcal{X}|$ *for regular actions) and there exist polynomial-time algorithms (in* κ*) for the following:*
   (a) *Membership Testing: Decide if a given bitstring represents an element in* $\mathcal{X}$.
   (b) *Unique Representation: Compute a unique bitstring* $x^!$ *canonically representing a given element* $x \in \mathcal{X}$.
3. *There exists a distinguished element* $\tilde{x} \in \mathcal{X}$ *with known representation. We will refer to* $\tilde{x}$ *as the origin.*
4. *There exists a polynomial-time algorithm (in* κ*) to evaluate the group action for any* $g \in \mathbb{G}$ *and* $x \in \mathcal{X}$.

An important category of post-quantum assumptions are those of isogeny-based cryptographic group actions, the formost of which is CSIDH [18]. Briefly, given a prime $p = 4 \cdot \ell_1 \cdots \ell_n - 1$ for ℓ_i small distinct odd primes, and elliptic curve $E_0 = y^2 = x^3 + x$ over $\mathbb{F}_p$ with $\mathbb{F}_p$-rational endomorphism ring $\mathcal{O}$, then

$$\star : \quad \mathrm{cl}(\mathcal{O}) \times \mathcal{E}\ell\ell_p(\mathcal{O}) \to \mathcal{E}\ell\ell_p(\mathcal{O})$$
$$\star : \quad ([\mathfrak{a}], E) \mapsto E/\mathfrak{a}$$

is a regular group action where $\mathrm{cl}(\mathcal{O})$ is the ideal-class group of $\mathcal{O}$ and $\mathcal{E}\ell\ell_p(\mathcal{O})$ is the set of all elliptic curves over $\mathbb{F}_p$ with $\mathbb{F}_p$-rational endomorphism ring $\mathcal{O}$ [18].

To capture actions like CSIDH, we follow Duman *et al.* 's framework [22] and extend our definitions to include an additional operation called a *twist*

$$\tau : \quad \mathcal{X} \to \mathcal{X}$$
$$\tau : \quad (g \star x) \mapsto g^{-1} \star x$$

which has a polynomial-time algorithm. As our results concern abelian groups, we will instead use additive notation and write $\tau : (g \star x) \mapsto (-g) \star x$. It is important to note that there is no corresponding operation for classical cryptographic groups assuming the inverse CDH Problem is hard (which is equivalent to the DL problem in the GGM [7]). Our protocol and simulator do not make use of the twist operation, and our proofs can readily be adapted to group actions without twists. However, to capture assumptions such as CSIDH, we provide the operation to the environment.

Finally, we assume that the structure of $\mathbb{G}$ is known including a minimal set of generators $\{g_1, \ldots, g_n\}$. Indeed, effective group actions over abelian groups are quantum-equivalent to effective group actions over known-order groups through a generalization of Shor's algorithm [19] which computes an isomorphism $\mathbb{G} \simeq \mathbb{Z}_{m_1} \times \mathbb{Z}_{m_2} \times \cdots \times \mathbb{Z}_{m_n}$ along with a minimal set of generators. CSIDH-512, for example, is known to have a cyclic group of order

$$N = 3 \cdot 37 \cdot 1407181 \cdot 51593604295295867744293584889$$
$$\cdot 31599414504681995853008278745587832204909$$

with generator $\langle 3, \pi - 1 \rangle$ i.e., $\mathbb{G} \simeq \mathbb{Z}_N$ [12].

5.2   The Protocol

Our compiler in Fig. 7 is the natural extension of our compiler in Fig. 6 replacing the group operations with group actions. As the compiler runs independently of the PAKE protocol, we may instantiate the PAKE from classical assumptions [3,34], group actions (using the generic transform [16] from OT [33] to UC PAKE), or lattice assumptions [24] with instantiations using post-quantum assumptions resulting in the first UC-secure saPAKE protocols (realizing the full functionality) from post-quantum assumptions. Note that the recent group action PAKE protocol due to Abdalla et al. [4] is not known to be compatible with our compiler as their protocol has not been proven UC-secure.

5.3   Security Analysis

Theorem 2. *The protocol in Sect. 5.2 UC-realizes $\mathcal{F}_{saPAKE}$ (Fig. 2, Fig. 3) with simulation rate $r = 1$ in the $(\mathcal{F}_{PAKE}, \mathcal{F}_{RO}, \mathcal{F}_{GA^\top})$-hybrid model using the $AGAM^\top$ for online analysis and the $GGAM^\top$ for offline analysis, in the setting where both the client and the server can be statically corrupted and assuming the GA-DL problem is hard for known-order, abelian, effective group action $(\mathbb{Z}_{m_1} \times \cdots \times \mathbb{Z}_{m_n}, \mathcal{X}, \tilde{x}, \star)$, where ℓ_2, ℓ_3, the number of m_i divisible by 2 and 3, are $O(\log(\kappa))$. (See the full version of this paper for a formal description of the GGAM functionality $\mathcal{F}_{GA^\top}$.)*

The proof of this theorem is substantially similar to that of Sect. 1, so we only provide a sketch here and defer the full proof to the full version. The main change is that when the environment would produce server-to-client messages $R^* = g^a sw^b$ and PAKE inputs $rw^* = g^c sw^d$ in the online phase, it instead produces elements of the form $a \star \tilde{x}$, $b \star sw$, or $c \star -sw$. The non-trivial change we must make is in *Hybrid 5*, when $\mathcal{A}$ produces R^* and rw^*, $\mathcal{A}$ does not query $z = H(pw')$, and $pw = pw'$. We now consider the case where R^* is of the form $(a + b(s + q)) \star \tilde{x}$ where $b \in \{-1, 0, 1\}$ and similarly rw^* is of the form

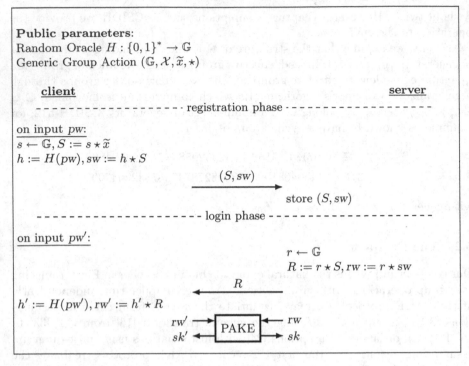

Fig. 7. Strong Asymmetric PAKE from Group Actions

$(c + d(s+q)) \star \tilde{x}$ (for $d \in \{-1, 0, 1\}$) which combined with $rw^* = H(pw') \star R^* = H(pw) \star R^* = q \star R^*$ arrives at

$$q(d - 1 - b) = a + bs - c - ds.$$

Here, we have that $(d - b) \in \{-2, -1, 0, 1, 2\}$ which means $(d - 1 - b) \in \{-3, -2, -1, 0, 1\}$. Just as before, this equivalence actually hides a system of modulo-equivalences. The i-th equivalence in the system has a single solution when $\gcd((d - 1 - b), m_i) = 1$ and at most $|d - 1 - b|$ solutions otherwise. As our reduction may verify possible solutions for q by computing $(q \star \tilde{x}) \stackrel{?}{=} Q$, we must show that the total number of solutions to this system is polynomial in κ. The total number of solutions is

$$||q|| = \prod_{i \in [N]} \gcd((d - 1 - b), m_i)$$
$$\leq 2^{\ell_2} \cdot 2^{\ell_3}$$

where ℓ_2 is the number of m_i such that $\gcd(2, m_i) \neq 1$ and ℓ_3 is the number of m_i such that $\gcd(3, m_i) \neq 1$. If both 2^{ℓ_2} and 2^{ℓ_3} are polynomial in κ then there are a polynomial number of possible solutions and the reduction may extract the correct q.

CSIDH-512, for instance, has $\ell_2 = 0, \ell_3 = 1$ and we can achieve the same bound as Lemma 2 since $|\mathbf{H}| < q_{\mathrm{RO}}$ is excluded when we remove collisions.

References

1. Abdalla, M., Barbosa, M., Bradley, T., Jarecki, S., Katz, J., Xu, J.: Universally composable relaxed password authenticated key exchange. In: Micciancio, D., Ristenpart, T. (eds.) CRYPTO 2020. LNCS, vol. 12170, pp. 278–307. Springer, Cham (2020). https://doi.org/10.1007/978-3-030-56784-2_10
2. Abdalla, M., Barbosa, M., Katz, J., Loss, J., Xu, J.: Algebraic adversaries in the universal composability framework. In: Tibouchi, M., Wang, H. (eds.) ASIACRYPT 2021. LNCS, vol. 13092, pp. 311–341. Springer, Cham (2021). https://doi.org/10.1007/978-3-030-92078-4_11
3. Abdalla, M., Barbosa, M., Rønne, P.B., Ryan, P.Y., Šala, P.: Security characterization of J-PAKE and its variants. Cryptology ePrint Archive, Report 2021/824 (2021). https://eprint.iacr.org/2021/824
4. Abdalla, M., Eisenhofer, T., Kiltz, E., Kunzweiler, S., Riepel, D.: Password-Authenticated Key Exchange from Group Actions. In: Dodis, Y., Shrimpton, T. (eds) Advances in Cryptology. CRYPTO 2022. LNCS, vol. 13508, pp. 699–728. Springer, Cham (2022). https://doi.org/10.1007/978-3-031-15979-4_24
5. Abdalla, M., Haase, B., Hesse, J.: Security analysis of CPace. In: Tibouchi, M., Wang, H. (eds.) ASIACRYPT 2021. LNCS, vol. 13093, pp. 711–741. Springer, Cham (2021). https://doi.org/10.1007/978-3-030-92068-5_24
6. Alamati, N., De Feo, L., Montgomery, H., Patranabis, S.: Cryptographic group actions and applications. In: Moriai, S., Wang, H. (eds.) ASIACRYPT 2020. LNCS, vol. 12492, pp. 411–439. Springer, Cham (2020). https://doi.org/10.1007/978-3-030-64834-3_14
7. Bao, F., Deng, R.H., Zhu, H.F.: Variations of Diffie-Hellman problem. In: Qing, S., Gollmann, D., Zhou, J. (eds.) ICICS 2003. LNCS, vol. 2836, pp. 301–312. Springer, Heidelberg (2003). https://doi.org/10.1007/978-3-540-39927-8_28
8. Basso, A.: A post-quantum round-optimal oblivious PRF from isogenies. Cryptology ePrint Archive, Paper 2023/225 (2023). https://eprint.iacr.org/2023/225
9. Bauer, B., Fuchsbauer, G., Loss, J.: A classification of computational assumptions in the algebraic group model. In: Micciancio, D., Ristenpart, T. (eds.) CRYPTO 2020. LNCS, vol. 12171, pp. 121–151. Springer, Cham (2020). https://doi.org/10.1007/978-3-030-56880-1_5
10. Bellovin, S.M., Merritt, M.: Encrypted key exchange: password-based protocols secure against dictionary attacks. In: 1992 IEEE Symposium on Security and Privacy, May 1992
11. Bellovin, S.M., Merritt, M.: Augmented encrypted key exchange: a password-based protocol secure against dictionary attacks and password file compromise. In: ACM CCS 1993, November 1993
12. Beullens, W., Kleinjung, T., Vercauteren, F.: CSI-FiSh: efficient isogeny based signatures through class group computations. In: Galbraith, S.D., Moriai, S. (eds.) ASIACRYPT 2019. LNCS, vol. 11921, pp. 227–247. Springer, Cham (2019). https://doi.org/10.1007/978-3-030-34578-5_9
13. Boneh, D., Dagdelen, Ö., Fischlin, M., Lehmann, A., Schaffner, C., Zhandry, M.: Random oracles in a quantum world. In: Lee, D.H., Wang, X. (eds.) ASIACRYPT 2011. LNCS, vol. 7073, pp. 41–69. Springer, Heidelberg (2011). https://doi.org/10.1007/978-3-642-25385-0_3

14. Bourdrez, D., Krawczyk, H., Lewi, K., Wood, C.: The opaque asymmetric PAKE protocol (2023). https://cfrg.github.io/draft-irtf-cfrg-opaque/draft-irtf-cfrg-opaque.html

15. Bradley, T., Jarecki, S., Xu, J.: Strong asymmetric PAKE based on trapdoor CKEM. In: Boldyreva, A., Micciancio, D. (eds.) CRYPTO 2019. LNCS, vol. 11694, pp. 798–825. Springer, Cham (2019). https://doi.org/10.1007/978-3-030-26954-8_26

16. Canetti, R., Dachman-Soled, D., Vaikuntanathan, V., Wee, H.: Efficient password authenticated key exchange via oblivious transfer. In: Fischlin, M., Buchmann, J., Manulis, M. (eds.) PKC 2012. LNCS, vol. 7293, pp. 449–466. Springer, Heidelberg (2012). https://doi.org/10.1007/978-3-642-30057-8_27

17. Canetti, R., Halevi, S., Katz, J., Lindell, Y., MacKenzie, P.: Universally composable password-based key exchange. In: Cramer, R. (ed.) EUROCRYPT 2005. LNCS, vol. 3494, pp. 404–421. Springer, Heidelberg (2005). https://doi.org/10.1007/11426639_24

18. Castryck, W., Lange, T., Martindale, C., Panny, L., Renes, J.: CSIDH: an efficient post-quantum commutative group action. In: Peyrin, T., Galbraith, S. (eds.) ASIACRYPT 2018. LNCS, vol. 11274, pp. 395–427. Springer, Cham (2018). https://doi.org/10.1007/978-3-030-03332-3_15

19. Cheung, K.K., Mosca, M.: Decomposing finite abelian groups. Quantum Inf. Comput. **1**(3), 26–32 (2001)

20. J.-M. Couveignes. Hard homogeneous spaces. Cryptology ePrint Archive, Report 2006/291 (2006). https://eprint.iacr.org/2006/291

21. Cremers, C., Naor, M., Paz, S., Ronen, E.: CHIP and CRISP: Protecting All Parties Against Compromise Through Identity-Binding PAKEs. In: Dodis, Y., Shrimpton, T. (eds.) Advances in Cryptology. CRYPTO 2022. LNCS, vol. 13508, pp. 668–698. Springer, Cham (2022). https://doi.org/10.1007/978-3-031-15979-4_23

22. Duman, J., Hartmann, D., Kiltz, E., Kunzweiler, S., Lehmann, J., Riepel, D.: Generic models for group actions. In: Boldyreva, A., Kolesnikov, V. (eds.) Public-Key Cryptography. PKC 2023. LNCS. vol. 13940, pp. 406–435. Springer, Cham (2023). https://doi.org/10.1007/978-3-031-31368-4_15

23. Eaton, E., Stebila, D.: The "Quantum Annoying" property of password-authenticated key exchange protocols. In: Cheon, J.H., Tillich, J.-P. (eds.) PQCrypto 2021 2021. LNCS, vol. 12841, pp. 154–173. Springer, Cham (2021). https://doi.org/10.1007/978-3-030-81293-5_9

24. Santos, B.F.D., Gu, Y., Jarecki, S.: Randomized Half-Ideal Cipher on Groups with Applications to UC (a)PAKE. In: Hazay, C., Stam, M. (eds.) Advances in Cryptology. EUROCRYPT 2023. LNCS, vol. 14008, pp. 128–156. Springer, Cham (2023). https://doi.org/10.1007/978-3-031-30589-4_5

25. Fuchsbauer, G., Kiltz, E., Loss, J.: The algebraic group model and its applications. In: Shacham, H., Boldyreva, A. (eds.) CRYPTO 2018. LNCS, vol. 10992, pp. 33–62. Springer, Cham (2018). https://doi.org/10.1007/978-3-319-96881-0_2

26. Gentry, C., MacKenzie, P., Ramzan, Z.: A method for making password-based key exchange resilient to server compromise. In: Dwork, C. (ed.) CRYPTO 2006. LNCS, vol. 4117, pp. 142–159. Springer, Heidelberg (2006). https://doi.org/10.1007/11818175_9

27. Grassi, P., Garcia, M., Fenton, J., et al.: NIST digital identity guidelines (2020). https://csrc.nist.gov/publications/detail/sp/800-63/3/final

28. A. Groce and J. Katz. A new framework for efficient password-based authenticated key exchange. In: ACM CCS 2010, October 2010

29. Hasse, B., Labrique, B.: AuCPace: efficient verifier-based PAKE protocol tailored for the IIoT. In: CHES 2019, August 2019
30. Hesse, J.: Separating symmetric and asymmetric password-authenticated key exchange. In: SCN 2020, September 2020
31. Jarecki, S., Krawczyk, H., Xu, J.: OPAQUE: an asymmetric PAKE protocol secure against pre-computation attacks. In: Nielsen, J.B., Rijmen, V. (eds.) EURO-CRYPT 2018. LNCS, vol. 10822, pp. 456–486. Springer, Cham (2018). https://doi.org/10.1007/978-3-319-78372-7_15
32. Katz, J., Ostrovsky, R., Yung, M.: Efficient password-authenticated key exchange using human-memorable passwords. In: Pfitzmann, B. (ed.) EUROCRYPT 2001. LNCS, vol. 2045, pp. 475–494. Springer, Heidelberg (2001). https://doi.org/10.1007/3-540-44987-6_29
33. Lai, Y.-F., Galbraith, S.D., Delpech de Saint Guilhem, C.: Compact, efficient and UC-secure isogeny-based oblivious transfer. In: Canteaut, A., Standaert, F.-X. (eds.) EUROCRYPT 2021. LNCS, vol. 12696, pp. 213–241. Springer, Cham (2021). https://doi.org/10.1007/978-3-030-77870-5_8
34. McQuoid, I., Rosulek, M., Roy, L.: Minimal symmetric PAKE and 1-out-of-N OT from programmable-once public functions. In: ACM CCS 2020, November 2020
35. McQuoid, I., Rosulek, M., Xu, J.: How to obfuscate MPC inputs. In: Kiltz, E., Vaikuntanathan, V. (eds.) Theory of Cryptography. TCC 2022. LNCS, vol. 13748, pp. 151–180. Springer, Cham (2022). https://doi.org/10.1007/978-3-031-22365-5_6
36. Rostovtsev, A., Stolbunov, A.: Public-Key Cryptosystem Based On Isogenies. Cryptology ePrint Archive, Report 2006/145 (2006). https://eprint.iacr.org/2006/145
37. Roy, L., Xu, J.: A universally composable PAKE with zero communication cost. In: Boldyreva, A., Kolesnikov, V. (eds.) Public-Key Cryptography. PKC 2023. LNCS, vol. 13940, pp. 714–743. Springer, Cham (2023). https://doi.org/10.1007/978-3-031-31368-4_25
38. Schnorr, C.: Small generic hardcore subsets for the discrete logarithm: short secret DL-keys. Inf. Process. Lett. **79**(2), 93–98 (2001)
39. Shor, P.W.: Polynomial-time algorithms for prime factorization and discrete logarithms on a quantum computer. SIAM Rev. **41**(2), 303–332 (1999)
40. Stern, J., Pointcheval, D., Malone-Lee, J., Smart, N.P.: Flaws in applying proof methodologies to signature schemes. In: Yung, M. (ed.) CRYPTO 2002. LNCS, vol. 2442, pp. 93–110. Springer, Heidelberg (2002). https://doi.org/10.1007/3-540-45708-9_7
41. Thomas, S.: Re: [cfrg] proposed PAKE selection process. CFRG Mailing list (2019). https://mailarchive.ietf.org/arch/msg/cfrg/dtf91cmavpzT47U3AVxrVGNB5UM
42. Unruh, D.: Universally composable quantum multi-party computation. In: Gilbert, H. (ed.) EUROCRYPT 2010. LNCS, vol. 6110, pp. 486–505. Springer, Heidelberg (2010). https://doi.org/10.1007/978-3-642-13190-5_25

New SIDH Countermeasures for a More Efficient Key Exchange

Andrea Basso[1] and Tako Boris Fouotsa[2]([✉])

[1] University of Bristol, Bristol, UK
andrea.basso@bristol.ac.uk
[2] EPFL, Lausanne, Switzerland
tako.fouotsa@epfl.ch

Abstract. The Supersingular Isogeny Diffie-Hellman (SIDH) protocol has been the main and most efficient isogeny-based encryption protocol, until a series of breakthroughs led to a polynomial-time key-recovery attack. While some countermeasures have been proposed, the resulting schemes are significantly slower and larger than the original SIDH.

In this work, we propose a new countermeasure technique that leads to significantly more efficient and compact protocols. To do so, we introduce the concept of artificially oriented curves, which are curves with an associated pair of subgroups. We show that this information is sufficient to build parallel isogenies and thus obtain an SIDH-like key exchange, while also revealing significantly less information compared to previous constructions.

After introducing artificially oriented curves, we formalize several related computational problems and thoroughly assess their presumed hardness. We then translate the SIDH key exchange to the artificially oriented setting, obtaining the key-exchange protocols binSIDH, or binary SIDH, and terSIDH, or ternary SIDH, which respectively rely on fixed-degree and variable-degree isogenies.

Lastly, we also provide a proof-of-concept implementation of the proposed protocols. Despite being implemented in a high-level language, terSIDH has very competitive running times, which suggests that terSIDH might be the most efficient isogeny-based encryption protocol.

1 Introduction

Given two elliptic curves, finding an isogeny between them is widely believed to be a computationally hard problem. This has led to the development of several cryptographic protocols, whose security relies on the hardness of some isogeny-related problem. While the first constructions date back to 1996 [22], the first practical isogeny-based protocol was the Supersingular Isogeny Diffie-Hellman (SIDH) key exchange [35]. After a decade of improvements and analysis, the protocol became the most efficient and well-known encryption scheme from isogenies, and it progressed through the four rounds of the NIST standardization process.

© International Association for Cryptologic Research 2023
J. Guo and R. Steinfeld (Eds.): ASIACRYPT 2023, LNCS 14445, pp. 208–233, 2023.
https://doi.org/10.1007/978-981-99-8742-9_7

The security of the protocol, however, did not rely on the pure isogeny problem: finding an isogeny between two supersingular elliptic curves. The problem is hard, but its lack of structure makes it hard to obtain cryptographic functionalities off it. Thus, SIDH needed to reveal additional information in the form of torsion images: not only were the domain and codomain of the secret isogenies known, but also their actions on a torsion subgroup of coprime order. This additional information has been studied over the years, and it has been shown to lead to some active attacks [33] and key-recovery attacks when the endomorphism ring of the two curves is known [33] or when the protocol uses unbalanced parameters [40,42]. However, all these attacks came short of affecting the security of SIDH. The situation changed when a series of works [9,38,43] developed a polynomial-time attack against SIDH for all possible parameters.

These attacks do not affect the security of other isogeny-based protocols, such as CSIDH [11] and SQISign [27], but they affect those protocols that reveal images of torsion points, such as SÉTA [24]. Some countermeasures against the SIDH attacks have been proposed [29]: they are based on scaling the torsion images (M-SIDH) or computing variable-degree isogenies (MD-SIDH). However, the complexity of the attacks against these protocols scale with the number of distinct primes dividing the isogeny degrees: thus, to be secure, these protocols require extremely large parameters, which lead to high running times and communication costs.

Besides M-SIDH and MD-SIDH, the only currently secure encryption protocols based on isogenies are CSIDH [11] and FESTA [5]. However, the first is vulnerable to a subexponential quantum attack [39], which makes it hard to estimate the quantum security of a given parameter set. The more conservative estimates require large primes, which lead to impractically inefficient running times [16]. The second, FESTA, is a recent public-key encryption protocol based on a constructive application of the SIDH attacks. While the initial results are promising, the protocol computes isogenies between elliptic curves of large prime degree (around 2^{16}) and isogenies between abelian varieties, which both affect the efficiency of the protocol. A third key-exchange protocol, pSIDH [37], offered interesting properties but was recently broken by Chen, Imran, Ivanyos, Kutas, Leroux and Petit [14].

In this work, we aim to fill the gap by proposing new countermeasures against the SIDH attacks that lead to a practically efficient SIDH-like key-exchange protocol. To do so, we introduce the concept of artificial orientations: an artificial A-orientation $\mathfrak{A}$ on a supersingular elliptic curve E is a pair of cyclic disjoint subgroups of $E[A]$ of order A. Given an artificial orientation $\mathfrak{A} = (G_1, G_2)$, an $\mathfrak{A}$-isogeny ϕ is an isogeny whose kernel is the direct sum of a cyclic subgroup of G_1 and a cyclic subgroup of G_2. In other words, ϕ can be written as the composition $\phi = \phi_2 \circ \phi_1$, where $\ker \phi_1 \subset G_1$, $\ker \phi_2 \subset \phi_1(G_2)$, and the degrees of ϕ_1 and ϕ_2 are coprime. While an artificial orientation does not reveal the same information as a standard orientation [18], it provides an interpolation between the original SIDH construction and the oriented protocols, such as CSIDH [11], OSIDH [18], and SCALLOP [26]. On one hand, artificial orientations and their images provide enough information to compute parallel isogenies, similarly to torsion images in SIDH; on the other, orientations always imply an artificial orientation, because given an orientation it is possible to recover the images of two cyclic disjoint groups, i.e. an artificial orientation. For example, in CSIDH, the images of the groups $\ker(\pi - 1) \cap E[\ell]$ and $\ker(\pi + 1) \cap E[\ell]$ under the secret isogeny $\phi : E \to E'$ are given by $\ker(\pi - 1) \cap E'[\ell]$ and $\ker(\pi + 1) \cap E'[\ell]$, respectively [10, Section 6.1].

Contributions. In this paper, we formalize the concept of artificial orientations and introduce some computational problems related to artificially oriented isogenies. We thoroughly assess the presumed hardness of these problems and we survey potential attacks. Then, we propose binSIDH, or binary SIDH, the first protocol that translates SIDH to the artificially-oriented setting. In other words, both parties compute an oriented isogeny, one whose kernel is the direct sum of two cyclic subgroups of the orientation, and reveal the images of a second orientation under the secret isogeny. This allows both parties to obtain a shared secret while revealing significantly less information.

As in SIDH, such a key exchange is limited to fixed-degree isogenies, which is helpful to develop constant-time implementations and zero-knowledge proofs of isogeny knowledge. Then, we generalize binSIDH to the case of variable-degree isogenies to obtain terSIDH, or ternary SIDH, which achieves smaller parameters.

The two protocols, binSIDH and terSIDH, require both parties to use artificially oriented isogenies, which results in a balanced protocol where the computational requirements of both parties is similar. We also propose a new technique that allows one party to compute SIDH-like isogenies, at the cost of the other party computing longer oriented ones. This allows one party to be significantly more efficient, which is particularly useful in advanced protocols between clients and servers with unbalanced computational power: not only can the client be more efficient than the server, but if the protocol requires proofs of isogeny knowledge, those of the client can be computed much more efficiently as well. Since the same technique can be applied to binSIDH and terSIDH, we obtain two new variants: binSIDH^{hyb} and terSIDH^{hyb}.

Lastly, we generate parameter sets for all four protocols, for all security levels, and we provide a SageMath proof-of-concept implementation of all proposed protocols. Despite being implemented in a high-level language, terSIDH has very competitive running times when compared to existing implementations of other isogeny-based encryption schemes.

2   Preliminaries

In this section, we briefly introduce the SIDH protocol and the recent key-recovery attacks. For more background information on elliptic curves and isogenies, we refer the reader to [44].

2.1 SIDH

SIDH, or Supersingular Isogeny Diffie-Hellman [35], is a key-exchange protocol based on isogenies between supersingular elliptic curves. The main protocol parameters are a prime p of the form $p = ABf - 1$, where $A = 2^a$ and $B = 3^b$, and a starting supersingular elliptic curve E_0 defined over $\mathbb{F}_{p^2}$. The protocol also specifies two bases P_A, Q_A and P_B, Q_B that generate, respectively, $E_0[A]$ and $E_0[B]$.

The first party, say Alice, generates her public key by sampling a random secret key $\mathsf{sk}_A = \alpha \in \mathbb{Z}_A$, computing the isogeny $\phi_A : E_0 \to E_A$ with kernel $\ker \phi_A = \langle P_A + [\alpha]Q_A \rangle$, and revealing $\mathsf{pk}_A = (E_A, R_A = \phi_A(P_B), S_A = \phi_A(Q_B))$. The second party, say Bob, proceeds analogously with an isogeny of degree B: he samples $\mathsf{sk}_B = \beta \in \mathbb{Z}_B$, computes the isogeny $\phi_B : E_0 \to E_B$ with kernel $\ker \phi_B = \langle P_B + [\beta]Q_B \rangle$, and reveals $\mathsf{pk}_B = (E_B, R_B = \phi_B(P_A), S_B = \phi_B(Q_A))$. Then, after exchanging public keys, both parties can obtain the same shared secret by computing the push-forward of their isogeny under the other party's isogeny. Concretely, Alice computes the isogeny $\phi'_A : E_B \to E_{AB}$ with kernel $\ker \phi'_A = \langle R_B + [\alpha]S_B \rangle = \phi_B(\ker \phi_A)$, while Bob computes the isogeny $\phi'_B : E_A \to E_{BA}$ with kernel $\ker \phi'_B = \langle R_A + [b]S_A \rangle = \phi_A(\ker \phi_B)$. The two isogenies are the correct push-forwards, and thus $\phi_A, \phi_B, \phi'_A, \phi'_B$ form a commutative diagram. Hence, the codomain curves E_{AB} and E_{BA} are isomorphic, and their j-invariant is the shared secret known to both Alice and Bob.

2.2 Polynomial Time Attacks on SIDH

The security of the SIDH protocol relies on the hardness of recovering a secret isogeny from its action on a torsion basis. In a series of works by Castryck and Decru [9], Maino, Martindale, Panny, Pope and Wesolowski [38], and Robert [43], the authors show the problem can be solved in polynomial time when the torsion information is sufficiently large compared to the degree of the isogeny. This leads to an efficient key-recovery attack on all instances of SIDH.

The attacks slightly vary in their techniques, but they all rely on Kani's theorem [36], which implies that given an SIDH square with specific properties, there exists an isogeny between the principally polarized abelian surface obtained by gluing two curves in the SIDH square to the principally polarized abelian surface obtained by gluing the other two curves in the square. It is possible to generate an SIDH square with the desired properties and compute the genus-two isogeny from the image points revealed in SIDH; evaluating such an isogeny allows an attacker to evaluate the secret isogeny on any point, which in turn can be used to recover the secret isogeny.

For the purpose of this work, the SIDH attacks can be abstracted as a generic algorithm that recovers an isogeny $\phi : E_0 \to E_1$ of degree d when it receives the curves E_0, E_1, the degree d, and the points P_0, Q_0 and $\phi(P_0), \phi(Q_0)$, where P_0, Q_0 are linearly independent points of order n and $n^2 > 4d$. There is no known technique that allows extending such attacks to a case where the image points are not known exactly: indeed, all attacks on the proposed countermeasures [29], as well as the potential attacks discussed in this work, need to recover the exact torsion images to apply the attacks.

3 Artificial Orientations

In this section, we introduce artificial orientations, the main ingredient that powers the countermeasures against the SIDH attacks. In the rest of the paper, the integers A and B are assumed to be smooth, coprime with each other, and square-free.[1] They also define a prime p of the form $p = ABf - 1$, where f is a small cofactor needed for primality; thus, the values A and B are always smaller than p and coprime with it.

Artificial orientations are composed of two independent subgroups. This is formalized in Definition 1, and we provide more information on how to explicitly compute such isogenies in Eq. (2) in Sect. 4.1.

Definition 1. *Let E be a supersingular elliptic curve defined over $\mathbb{F}_{p^2}$, and let A be an integer. An* artificial A-orientation (of E) *is a pair $\mathfrak{A} = (G_1, G_2)$ where $G_1, G_2 \subset E[A]$ are cyclic groups of order A and $G_1 \cap G_2 = \{0\}$. $(E, \mathfrak{A})$ is called an* artificially A-oriented curve.

Remark 1. Artificial orientations are known in the number theory literature as *split Cartan level structures*. We prefer the artificial orientation name as it may be more familiar to those who know isogeny-based cryptography, but the connection may lead to useful insights. For instance, see [17] for an analysis of the mixing properties of the isogeny graph with split Cartan level structures.

Given an artificially A-oriented curve $(E, \mathfrak{A})$, one can compute a range of isogenies whose kernels arise from $\mathfrak{A} = (G_1, G_2)$. We formalize this concept, which we call $\mathfrak{A}$-isogenies, in the following definition.

Definition 2. *Let $(E, \mathfrak{A})$ where $\mathfrak{A} = (G_1, G_2)$ be an artificially A-oriented curve. An isogeny $\phi : E \to E'$ is said to be an* $\mathfrak{A}$-isogeny *if $\ker \phi$ is the direct sum of a subgroup of G_1 and a subgroup of G_2, that is $\ker \phi = H_1 \oplus H_2$ where H_i is a subgroup of G_i for $i = 1, 2$.*

If $(E, \mathfrak{A})$ is an artificially A-oriented curve and $\phi : E \to E'$ is a non-trivial $\mathfrak{A}$-isogeny, then the artificial A-orientation on E cannot be carried onto E' through ϕ. In fact, since ϕ is non-trivial and $\ker \phi$ is the direct sum of a subgroup of G_1 and a subgroup of G_2, then at least one of the groups $\phi(G_1)$ and $\phi(G_2)$ has order strictly smaller than A. In order to be able to carry the artificial A-orientation on E onto E' it is necessary that the degree of the isogeny considered is coprime to A. We have the following definition for artificially A-oriented B-isogenous curves.

---

[1] The square-free property is not necessary for the correctness of the protocols, but square divisors of A and B decrease the efficiency of the protocols without increasing their security.

Definition 3. *Let $(E, \mathfrak{A})$ and $(E', \mathfrak{A}')$ be two artificially A-oriented curves and let B be an integer coprime to A. We say that $(E, \mathfrak{A})$ and $(E', \mathfrak{A}')$ are B-isogenous if there exists an isogeny $\phi : E \to E'$ of degree B such that $\mathfrak{A}' = \phi(\mathfrak{A})$, that is if $\mathfrak{A} = (G_1, G_2)$ and $\mathfrak{A}' = (G'_1, G'_2)$, then $G'_1 = \phi(G_1)$ and $G'_2 = \phi(G_2)$.*

Remark 2. Note that B-isogenous oriented curves include images of subgroups. These can be represented by choosing a random generator. Thus, if we fix generators $\langle P_1 \rangle = G_1$ and $\langle P_2 \rangle = G_2$, the subgroups G'_1 and G'_2 are represented by $[\alpha]\phi(P_1)$ and $[\beta]\phi(P_2)$ respectively, for some unknown $\alpha, \beta \in \mathbb{Z}_A$.

3.1 A Comparison of $\mathfrak{A}$-Isogenies with Existing Techniques

In this section, we discuss the main differences between artificially oriented isogenies and fully oriented isogenies, such as those used in CSIDH and SCALLOP, and between oriented isogenies and the more generic isogenies used in SIDH, M-SIDH, and MD-SIDH.

$\mathfrak{A}$-Isogenies vs Group Actions. Artificially oriented isogenies share similarities with those that arise from group actions, such as the isogenies in CSIDH, OSIDH, and SCALLOP. In both instances, isogenies are restricted to specific subsets of all possible isogenies, and the action of secret isogenies on two independent subgroups is revealed [10, Section 6.1]. However, artificially oriented isogenies are significantly different from those in CSIDH and SCALLOP: first, given any supersingular elliptic curve, it is always possible to attach an artificial orientation to it, unlike in CSIDH, where the curves need to be defined over $\mathbb{F}_p$ and the orientation is already available through the Frobenius endomorphism; or SCALLOP, where not all supersingular elliptic curves are oriented and a standard orientation needs to be provided. Most importantly, artificial orientations do not give rise to a commutative group action as the one from standard orientations, which means that the quantum subexponential attack by Childs, Jao, and Soukharev [15] does not apply. Similarly, artificial orientations are also immune to the attacks on OSIDH [23].

$\mathfrak{A}$-Isogenies vs SIDH. The main difference between SIDH-like isogenies and artificially A-oriented isogenies is the amount of information needed to compute their push-forwards. In the SIDH case, the kernel of the isogeny (say ψ) is generated by a point of the form $P + [\alpha]Q$. The kernel of the push-forward of ψ through ϕ is generated by the point $\phi(P) + [\alpha]\phi(Q)$. Therefore, the images of torsion points P and Q are needed in order to compute the push-forward of ψ through ϕ. Conversely, $\mathfrak{A}$-isogenies are limited to those that arise from $\mathfrak{A}$. Hence, only the push-forward of the artificial orientation is needed, which means only the images of two cyclic torsion groups are revealed. This prevents torsion point attacks [9, 38, 40, 42, 43].

$\mathfrak{A}$-Isogenies vs M-SIDH. In M-SIDH and MD-SIDH [29], isogenies are defined as in SIDH, but to compute their push-forwards, the torsion points images are revealed while scaled (or masked) with the same scalar β. This means that instead of revealing $\phi(P)$ and $\phi(Q)$ as in SIDH, one reveals $[\beta]\phi(P)$ and $[\beta]\phi(Q)$. This is significantly more information than what is revealed to compute the push-forwards of $\mathfrak{A}$-isogenies, since the image of an artificial orientation is equivalent, as discussed in Remark 2, to revealing $[\alpha]\phi(P)$ and $[\beta]\phi(Q)$, for independent values α and β. From a subgroup perspective, push-forwards of $\mathfrak{A}$-isogenies require the images of two cyclic disjoint subgroups, whereas M-SIDH reveals two image points scaled with the same value, which is equivalent to the images of three cyclic disjoint groups of order $\operatorname{ord}(P)$ (see [4, Lemma 1] and [30, Lemma 1]).

3.2   Security Assumptions

Having introduced artificial orientations, we now introduce three computational problems that relate to artificially oriented curves and isogenies. The first problem, which we refer to as the Supersingular Isogeny Problem for artificially A-oriented curves (SSIP-A), asks to recover an isogeny given its domain, together with an artificial orientation, and its codomain, together with a compatible orientation. This corresponds to finding a path of length B in the isogeny graph with split Cartan level structure.

Problem 1 (SSIP-A). Let $(E, \mathfrak{A})$ be an artificially A-oriented curve and let B be an integer coprime to A. Let $\phi : E \to E'$ be a cyclic isogeny of degree B and let $\mathfrak{A}' = \phi(\mathfrak{A})$. Given $(E, \mathfrak{A})$ and $(E', \mathfrak{A}')$ and the degree B, compute ϕ.

In Problem 1, there is no constraint on the isogeny ϕ, apart from its degree being B. When an artificial B-orientation $\mathfrak{B}$ is provided on E, then one may restrict to $\mathfrak{B}$-isogenies. This leads to the (supersingular) Artificially Oriented Isogeny Problem (AOIP).

Problem 2 (AOIP). Let $(E, \mathfrak{A})$ an artificially A-oriented curve and let B be an integer coprime to A. Let $\mathfrak{B}$ be an artificial B-orientation on E. Let $\phi : E \to E'$ be a cyclic $\mathfrak{B}$-isogeny of degree B and let $\mathfrak{A}' = \phi(\mathfrak{A})$. Given $(E, \mathfrak{A}, \mathfrak{B})$ and $(E', \mathfrak{A}')$, compute ϕ.

We can also study a problem that is, in some sense, the converse of Problem 1. Rather than considering general isogenies and the image of an artificial orientation, we can focus on the case where the isogeny is artificially oriented, but more torsion image information is revealed. This is summarized in the Supersingular Isogeny Problem for $\mathfrak{B}$-isogenies (SSIP-B) problem.

Problem 3 (SSIP-B). Let $(E, \mathfrak{A})$ be an artificially A-oriented curve and let B be an integer coprime to A. Let $\phi : E \to E'$ be a cyclic $\mathfrak{A}$-isogeny of degree A, with $B \ll A$. Let also P, Q be a basis of $E[B]$. Given $(E, \mathfrak{A})$, together with the points P, Q, and the curve E' with the points $\phi(P)$ and $\phi(Q)$, compute ϕ.

If $B \not\ll A$, such a problem could be solved with the techniques introduced in the SIDH attacks [9,38,43]. However, for larger choices of B (when compared to A), Problem 3 is believed to be secure, and its hardness can be used to build more efficient protocols, as we will see in Sect. 5.

3.3   Hardness Analysis

In this section, we study the computational problems that we introduced, analyze potential attacks, and justify their assumed hardness.

Finding an Isogeny from the Orientation Image. The first problem, Problem 1 is already known in the literature, as it was recently introduced with a different notation in [5, Problem 7], where it was called the Computational isogeny with scaled-torsion (CIST) problem. As argued in [5], the problem appears to be hard because the images of two subgroups do not provide enough information for the SIDH attacks to be applicable. Given two images $[\alpha]\phi(P)$ and $[\beta]\phi(Q)$, scaled by independent values α and β, an attacker can easily recover the product $\alpha\beta$ from pairing computations, but this is similarly insufficient to recover the exact images that would enable the SIDH attacks. An attacker may attempt to brute force the missing information, but this is computationally infeasible if the degree of the secret isogeny is sufficiently large, which in turn makes the order of the torsion information to be guessed large enough for the attack to be infeasible. Note that the information revealed in Problem 1 is comparable to that in CSIDH and SCALLOP, and significantly less than that in M-SIDH and MD-SIDH. It is thus likely that an attack that can solve Problem 1 in its most general form, can do so for such protocols as well.

Since not enough information is revealed for the SIDH attacks to apply, the attack on starting curves with small endomorphisms [29] does also not apply here. It is thus possible to choose a starting curve with known endomorphism ring. Very recent analysis [12] has shown it is possible to recover an isogeny from its scaled action and thus solve Problem 1 when the starting curve E_0 and the corresponding orientation has specific properties relative to the Frobenius conjugate $E_0^{(p)}$ of E_0. It is thus important to select parameters that avoid these issues; since the endomorphism ring of the starting curve can be public, this can be done in a transparent manner without the need of a trusted setup. We further expand on the choice of the artificial orientation and of the starting curve at the end of this section.

Finding an Oriented Isogeny from the Orientation Image. In Problem 2, the degree of the isogeny ϕ is not necessarily known: the degree of a $\mathfrak{B}$-isogeny can range across all values dividing the order B of the subgroups in $\mathfrak{B}$, which poses a first barrier to the application of the SIDH attacks. However, even if we restrict to isogenies of full degree, i.e. $\deg \phi = B$, the torsion information that is revealed is the same as that in Problem 1, and thus a similar analysis follows. The fact that the unknown isogeny is a $\mathfrak{B}$-isogeny does not interact in any meaningful way with the SIDH attacks or the revealed torsion information: as such, it appears to be hard for an attacker to exploit such attacks to solve Problem 2. Hence, it seems likely that any attack would have to disregard the artificial orientation and focus on recovering an isogeny between two given curves; however, since the isogeny is a $\mathfrak{B}$-isogeny, this problem is easier than the general case.

First, an attacker can simply brute force all the possible isogenies. If we restrict ourselves to isogenies of full degrees, there are 2^t possible $\mathfrak{B}$-isogenies, where t is the numbers of primes dividing B. This suggests that the degree of the isogeny should be the product of at least $t = \lambda$ distinct primes. Second, generic attacks to recover an isogeny between two given curves, such as the meet-in-the-middle (MITM), van Oorschot-Wiener (vOW) [46], Delfs-Galbraith [28] attacks, are not applicable since the prime characteristic and the isogeny degree, being the product of at least λ distinct primes, are sufficiently large to make these attacks computationally infeasible. However, it is possible to devise an enhanced MITM attack that exploits the nature of the $\mathfrak{B}$-isogenies: the attacker fixes an attack parameter $0 \leq t' \leq t$ and then computes $2^{t'}$ $\mathfrak{B}$-isogenies starting from E_0. These are chosen of the largest degree, i.e. the attacker first computes the isogenies with degree corresponding to the largest primes dividing B, so that the end curves are as close to E' as possible. The attacker stores the j-invariants of the codomain curves and starts a random walk of the correct degree from E', in the hope of finding a collision. The cost of the attack depends on the choice of t': the first part requires $2^{t'}$ computations, while the second part requires computing all the possible isogenies of a specific degree (the product of the smaller $t - t'$ primes dividing B, assuming that B is square-free) starting from E'. This technique yields a better attack than a simple brute-force approach, and thus it would require larger parameters, albeit only moderately larger ones.

Example 1. For instance, when B is the product of the first 128 primes (the case most suitable to this attack), the attack is optimal for $t = 106$, since such a value minimizes the product of the costs of the MITM attack and the brute-force attack. Setting $t = 106$ corresponds to an attack where 2^{106} isogenies are computed and 2^{106} j-invariants are stored in memory. Thus, to obtain $\lambda = 128$ bits of security, we would need the $\mathfrak{B}$-isogeny to have a degree B that is the product of the $t = 154$ smallest primes. This ensures that the optimal attack requires $t > 128$. We remark that the security estimates depend not only on the number of distinct primes dividing B, but also on the size of the specific primes.

The previous attack considers an attacker that has accesses to unbounded memory. This is far from realistic, and we can obtain better estimates of the attack possibilities when we impose an upper bound to the amount of memory available. We follow the security analysis of SIDH [1,34], and we limit our analysis to attackers with 2^{80} units of memory for any security level.[2] In this setting, the best attack is a vOW version of the enhanced MITM attack presented before, which allows the attacker to trade higher computational costs for a lower memory requirement. As shown in [1], a vOW search has a computational cost of approximately

$$N^{3/2}/w^{1/2},$$

where N is the number of collision points and w is the number of memory units available. In our case, we have $N = 2^{t'}$, and $w = 2^{80}$. This suggests that,

---

[2] More precisely, we consider attackers that can store up to 2^{80} j-invariants. Given the size of the primes used, this corresponds to more than 2^{90} bits of memory.

for $\lambda = 128$, this attack outperforms a brute-force search, but only marginally. If we set the degree B to be the product of the first t distinct primes, the enhanced vOW attack requires $t = 137$ (compared to $t = 128$, as suggested by the brute-force attack). However, for higher security levels, the brute-force attack outperforms the enhanced vOW attack, because the memory bound remains constant across all security levels, and thus it has a larger performance impact on higher security levels. Thus, for $\lambda \in \{192, 256\}$, we can choose $t = \lambda$.

The case with variable-degree isogenies follows similarly. A brute-force approach requires an attacker to compute isogenies starting from all previously visited curves, rather than just the end ones. In other words, the attack starts with a set of visited curves $\mathcal{S} = \{E_0\}$; for each prime p_i, the attacker computes two isogenies starting for all curves in $\mathcal{S}$ and adds the codomain curves to $\mathcal{S}$. We restrict ourselves to the case where the maximum degree is square free, as we will choose for the parameters of terSIDH, since higher powers decrease efficiency without improving security. In this case, the complexity of the attack is the same a brute-force attack with fixed-degree isogenies with three options at each node.

Overall, the rest of the attack proceeds similarly: as in the binSIDH case, the parameter t needs to be selected to avoid a brute-force attack, where the specific value depends on the exponents of the primes dividing B. The enhanced MITM and vOW attacks similarly apply to the variable-degree case: in this case, however, the enhanced vOW attack outperforms a brute-force attack at all commonly used security levels, and thus the parameters need to be slightly larger than what a brute-force attack would suggest.

Finding an Isogeny from the Full Torsion Image. Lastly, Problem 3 is vulnerable to the SIDH attacks, as discussed when introduced. However, the $\mathfrak{A}$-isogeny needs to have a large degree A to be secure from the attacks outlined above, and thus the torsion points would need a large order B for the SIDH attacks to be applicable. More precisely, the attacks are possible when $B^2 > 4A$, but an attacker could guess part of the isogeny so that the remaining part is short enough to be recovered through the SIDH attacks. This would suggest that if $2^{t'} B^2 \approx A$, an attacker can recover the unknown isogeny after iterating through $2^{t'}$ isogenies. This is the case for generic isogenies, but in the case of oriented ones, the attacker can brute force much longer isogenies at the same cost, since there are only limited options for any prime degree dividing A. In particular, after $2^{t'}$ computations, the attacker obtains isogenies of degree $A_{t'}$, the product of the t' largest primes dividing A. Thus, Problem 3 is secure against the SIDH attacks when $A_{t'} B^2 \leq A$.

Assuming this condition is satisfied, Problem 3 appears to be secure since the oriented-isogeny structure does not interact with the revealed torsion information, which does not make the problem easier. Lastly, before the attacks by Castryck and Decru, Maino, Martindale, Panny, Pope and Wesolowski, and Robert, SIDH with unbalanced parameters was vulnerable to torsion-point attacks [40,42] that relied on knowledge of the endomorphism ring of the starting curve. These attacks similarly do not apply to Problem 3 since the torsion information is much lower than what is needed.

3.4   On the Choice of the Artificial Orientation

As mentioned earlier in this section, a recent analysis [12] has shown it is possible to solve Problem 1 in some particular cases:

– When the starting curve E_0 is defined over $\mathbb{F}_p$ and the corresponding orientation (G_1, G_2) is such that G_1, G_2 or both are fixed by the Frobenius endomorphism.
– When the curve E_0 is not defined over $\mathbb{F}_p$, the attacks also extends to the case where the curve E_0 and its Frobenius conjugate $E_0^{(p)}$ are connected by a short isogeny $\psi : E_0 \to E_0^{(p)}$ and the artificial orientation (G_1, G_2) is such that G_1, G_2 or both are fixed by the endomorphism $\pi \circ \hat{\psi}$.
– When the starting curve admits a small endomorphism that fixes one or both groups G_1 and G_2 in a given artificial orientation.

We describe here another specific case where Problem 1 is potentially easy to solve. Assume that E_0 is defined over $\mathbb{F}_p$ (or it is close to its Frobenius conjugate; the case follows similarly) and fix an artificial orientation (G_1, G_2) where some subgroups of G_1 and G_2 are fixed by the Frobenius endomorphism. Let $\phi : E_0 \to E$ be a secret isogeny artificially oriented by (G_1, G_2); then, when the end curve E is also defined over $\mathbb{F}_p$, this indicates that the kernel of the secret isogeny is fixed by the Frobenius endomorphism, which discards any artificially oriented isogeny whose kernel is not fixed by the Frobenius. This means that one can discard several impossible secret keys just by looking at the field of definition of the end curve. In order to avoid this, either all of the end curves need to be defined over $\mathbb{F}_p$, or none of them can be defined over $\mathbb{F}_p$. In the first case, G_1 and G_2 are fixed by the Frobenius and the artificial orientation is the same as that of CSIDH. As highlighted above, this is not secure, hence the end curves should be defined over $\mathbb{F}_{p^2}$. To ensure this, no subgroup of the groups G_1 and G_2 should be fixed by the Frobenius. For any given prime ℓ, there are $\ell + 1$ cyclic groups of order ℓ, and at most two of them are fixed by the Frobenius endomorphism. Hence $\ell - 1$ cyclic groups of order ℓ are not fixed by the Frobenius, and these ones can be used in the artificial orientations. Note that when $\ell = 2$, there may be only one group that is not fixed by the Frobenius: in such a case, the isogeny degrees A and B can be selected to be both odd. This issue with this approach is that there is no guarantee that none of the attacks from [12] listed earlier does not apply. For example, there is no guarantee that the groups in the artificial orientations are not fixed by a small endomorphism (that could be exploited by an attacker). Therefore, all the strategies proposed till now do not provide enough insurance that the starting curve and the artificial orientations are secure.

In order to avoid all the problematic cases discussed above, we propose to use a uniformly random supersingular elliptic curve as a starting curve. Such a curve is defined over $\mathbb{F}_{p^2}$ with overwhelming probability ($\approx 1 - \frac{1}{\sqrt{p}}$), it is far from $\mathbb{F}_p$ curves, and it is not connected to its Frobenius conjugate by a short isogeny (with overwhelming probability). Such a curve can be generated by performing a long publicly-verifiable uniformly-random walk starting from a known supersingular elliptic curve. Practically, this walk can be computed by "nothing-up-my-sleeve" techniques: fix a seed s (say, the string `"binSIDH+terSIDH"`), compute its hash $h = \mathcal{H}(s)$ (where $\mathcal{H}$ is a cryptographically secure hash function), and pass it as input to the CGL hash function [13]. The CGL output curve is then the starting curve E_0 of binSIDH and terSIDH. The artificial orientations are then generated as $\mathcal{A} = (\langle P_A \rangle, \langle Q_A \rangle)$ and $\mathcal{B} = (\langle P_B \rangle, \langle Q_B \rangle)$, where (P_A, Q_A) and (P_B, Q_B) are canonical bases of $E_0[A]$ and $E_0[B]$, respectively. Note that this approach is publicly verifiable by anyone and does not required any trusted setup.

In the rest of this paper, we assume that the starting curve E_0 and the artificial orientations are chosen this way.

4   The binSIDH and terSIDH Protocols

In this section, we propose two new protocols: binSIDH and terSIDH. Both protocols translate the SIDH key exchange to the setting of artificially oriented curves and isogenies. The former restricts itself to fixed-degree isogenies, while the latter relies on variable-degree isogenies to improve on efficiency and compactness.

4.1   binSIDH

We first introduce binSIDH, which restricts itself to isogenies of full degree. The protocols rely on the fact that A-oriented curves provide sufficient information to compute parallel isogenies. More formally, let A be a product of t distinct primes $A = \prod_{i=1}^{t} p_i$ and write $A = A_1 A_2$ for a multiplicative splitting of A with $\gcd(A_1, A_2) = 1$. Then, given two A-oriented curves $(E, \mathfrak{A})$ and $(E', \mathfrak{A}')$ connected by a B-isogeny $\phi : E \to E'$, where $\mathfrak{A} = (\langle G_1 \rangle, \langle G_2 \rangle)$ and $\mathfrak{A}' = (\langle G_1' \rangle, \langle G_2' \rangle)$, the isogenies

$$\psi : E \to E/\langle [A_1]G_1 + [A_2]G_2 \rangle, \qquad \psi' : E' \to E'/\langle [A_1]G_1' + [A_2]G_2' \rangle$$

are parallel, i.e. we have $\ker \psi' = \phi(\ker \psi)$ and the codomain curves are also B-isogenous, connected by the isogeny ϕ' with kernel $\ker \phi' = \psi(\ker \phi)$.

The isogenies ψ and ψ' are thus determined by the splitting of A as $A = A_1 A_2$. In other words, if we represent the subgroups $\langle G_1 \rangle$ and $\langle G_2 \rangle$ as

$$\begin{aligned} \langle G_1 \rangle &= \langle G_1^1, G_1^2, \ldots, G_1^t \rangle, \\ \langle G_2 \rangle &= \langle G_2^1, G_2^2, \ldots, G_2^t \rangle, \end{aligned} \quad \text{where} \quad \begin{cases} \operatorname{ord}(G_1^i) = p_i, \\ \operatorname{ord}(G_2^i) = p_i, \end{cases} \tag{1}$$

then the kernel of ψ is determined by selectively choosing either G_1^i or G_2^i to be in the kernel of ψ, for every $i \in [t]$. The same holds for the isogeny ψ' and the generators G_1' and G_2'. This suggests the following notation: if we fix an artificial A-orientation $(E, \mathfrak{A} = (G_1, G_2))$, where $A = \prod_{i=1}^{t} p_i$, we can associate a vector $\mathbf{a} \in \{1, 2\}^t$ to any $\mathfrak{A}$-oriented isogeny ϕ by writing

$$\ker \phi = \langle G_{\mathbf{a}_1}^1, G_{\mathbf{a}_2}^2, \ldots, G_{\mathbf{a}_t}^t \rangle, \tag{2}$$

where the points G_1^i and G_2^i are defined as in Eq. (1) and $\mathbf{a}_i$ denotes the i-th element of $\mathbf{a}$. Throughout the rest of the paper, we write $\langle \mathbf{a}, \mathfrak{A} \rangle$ to denote the subgroup corresponding to the orientation $\mathfrak{A}$ with secret vector $\mathbf{a}$, as computed in Eq. (2).

We showed in Sect. 3.2 that we consider it secure to reveal artificially oriented curves since the SIDH attacks are inapplicable. Moreover, artificial orientations allow computations of parallel isogenies, and if the order A is sufficiently composite, the number of potential parallel isogenies is exponentially large. That is because the value A is the product of t distinct primes, which means there are 2^t potential splittings $A = A_1 A_2$. This suggests it is possible to replicate the SIDH key exchange with artificially oriented isogenies and to obtain a secure protocol that is immune to the SIDH attacks. We call the resulting construction binSIDH, and we represent it in Fig. 1.

Setup. Let λ be the security parameter and t an integer depending on λ. Let $p = ABf - 1$ be a prime such that $A = \prod_{i=1}^{t} \ell_i$ and $B = \prod_{i=1}^{t} q_i$ are coprime integers, ℓ_i, q_i are distinct small primes, $A \approx B \approx \sqrt{p}$ and f is a small cofactor. Let E_0 be a supersingular elliptic curve defined over $\mathbb{F}_{p^2}$ with $\#E_0(\mathbb{F}_{p^2}) = (p+1)^2$. Let $\mathfrak{A}$ be an artificial A-orientation on E_0 and let $\mathfrak{B}$ be an artificial B-orientation on E_0. The public parameters are E_0, p, A, B, $\mathfrak{A}$ and $\mathfrak{B}$.

KeyGen. Alice samples uniformly at random a vector $\mathbf{a}$ from $\{1, 2\}^t$ and computes the $\mathfrak{A}$-oriented isogeny $\phi_A : E_0 \to E_A$ of degree A defined by $\mathbf{a}$. She also computes the push forward $\mathfrak{B}'$ of $\mathfrak{B}$ on E_A through ϕ_A. Her secret key is $\mathbf{a}$ and her public key is $(E_A, \mathfrak{B}')$. Analogously, Bob samples uniformly at random a vector $\mathbf{b}$ from $\{1, 2\}^t$ and computes the $\mathfrak{B}$-oriented isogeny $\phi_B : E_0 \to E_B$ of degree B defined by $\mathbf{b}$. He also computes the push forward $\mathfrak{A}'$ of $\mathfrak{A}$ on E_B through ϕ_B. His secret key is $\mathbf{b}$ and his public key is $(E_B, \mathfrak{A}')$.

SharedKey. Upon receiving Bob's public key $(E_B, \mathfrak{A}')$, Alice checks that $\mathfrak{A}'$ is an artificial A-orientation on E_B, if not she aborts. She computes the $\mathfrak{A}'$-oriented isogeny $\phi_A' : E_B \to E_{BA}$ of degree A defined by $\mathbf{a}$. Her shared key is $j(E_{BA})$. Similarly, upon receiving $(E_A, \mathfrak{B}')$, Bob checks that $\mathfrak{B}'$ is an artificial B-orientation on E_A, if not he aborts. He computes the $\mathfrak{B}'$-oriented isogeny $\phi_B' : E_A \to E_{AB}$ of degree B defined by $\mathbf{b}$. His shared key is $j(E_{AB})$.

Fig. 1. The binSIDH protocol.

4.2   The terSIDH Variant

We now introduce terSIDH, a variant of binSIDH that is more efficient and more compact, but these improvements come at the cost of relying on variable-degree isogenies. In binSIDH, every A-oriented isogeny ϕ is determined by a binary choice for each prime p_i dividing A: the p_i-degree isogeny has kernel generated by either G_1^i or G_2^i. However, we can introduce a third option by allowing the isogeny to not have a p_i component. In other words, write ϕ as the composition of t isogenies $\phi = \phi_t \circ \ldots \phi_2 \circ \phi_1$; then, the isogeny ϕ_i has kernel generated by G_1^i, G_2^i, or $\mathcal{O}$. We thus extend the notation introduced in the previous section by letting the vector $\mathbf{a}$ have entries in $\{0, 1, 2\}$, and we set $G_0^i = \mathcal{O}$ for all $i \in [t]$. The full protocol is described in Fig. 2.

Compared to binSIDH, terSIDH introduces more choices for each prime p_i. In particular, it provides three choices, which means that every p_i dividing $p + 1$ provides $\log_2 3 \approx 1.6$ bits of security. Interestingly, terSIDH is the first countermeasure technique against the SIDH attacks that can provide more than one bit of security per prime p_i. This means that, to provide enough security, the isogeny degrees should be at least the product of $t \approx \lambda/1.6$ primes, and thus terSIDH can use significantly smaller parameters and shorter isogenies, leading to a more efficient and more compact protocol. However, to achieve this, we necessarily rely on variable-degree isogenies. This has some disadvantages: from an implementation perspective, the varying degree may make it harder to obtain constant-time implementations, as seen in the case of CSIDH implementations [2, 16]. The other issue, as argued in [3, 7], is that it appears to be hard to construct zero-knowledge proofs of variable-degree isogenies because all known approaches invariably leak the secret isogeny degree. This causes a major issue in the development of proofs of terSIDH public key correctness, and it may prevent terSIDH from being an SIDH drop-in replacement for advanced constructions.

Setup. Let λ be the security parameter and t an integer depending on λ. Let $p = ABf - 1$ be a prime such that $A = \prod_{i=1}^{t} \ell_i$ and $B = \prod_{i=1}^{t} q_i$ are coprime integers, ℓ_i, q_i are distinct small primes, $A \approx B \approx \sqrt{p}$ and f is a small cofactor. Let E_0 be a supersingular elliptic curve defined over $\mathbb{F}_{p^2}$ with $\#E_0(\mathbb{F}_{p^2}) = (p+1)^2$. Let $\mathfrak{A}$ be an artificial A-orientation on E_0 and let $\mathfrak{B}$ be an artificial B-orientation on E_0. The public parameters are E_0, p, A, B, $\mathfrak{A}$ and $\mathfrak{B}$.

KeyGen. Alice samples uniformly at random a vector $\mathbf{a}$ from $\{0, 1, 2\}^t$ and computes the $\mathfrak{A}$-oriented isogeny $\phi_A : E_0 \to E_A$ defined by $\mathbf{a}$, whose degree divides A. She also computes the push forward $\mathfrak{B}'$ of $\mathfrak{B}$ on E_A through ϕ_A. Her secret key is $\mathbf{a}$ and her public key is $(E_A, \mathfrak{B}')$. Analogously, Bob samples uniformly at random a vector $\mathbf{b}$ from $\{0, 1, 2\}^t$ and computes the $\mathfrak{B}$-oriented isogeny $\phi_B : E_0 \to E_B$ defined by $\mathbf{b}$, whose degree divides B. He also computes the push forward $\mathfrak{A}'$ of $\mathfrak{A}$ on E_A through ϕ_B. His secret key is $\mathbf{b}$ and his public key is $(E_B, \mathfrak{A}')$.

SharedKey. Upon receiving Bob's public key $(E_B, \mathfrak{A}')$, Alice checks that $\mathfrak{A}'$ is an artificial A-orientation on E_B, if not she aborts. She computes the $\mathfrak{A}'$-oriented isogeny $\phi_A' : E_B \to E_{BA}$ of degree A defined by $\mathbf{a}$. Her shared key is $j(E_{BA})$. Similarly, upon receiving $(E_A, \mathfrak{B}')$, Bob checks that $\mathfrak{B}'$ is an artificial B-orientation on E_A, if not he aborts. He computes the $\mathfrak{B}'$-oriented isogeny $\phi_B' : E_A \to E_{AB}$ of degree B defined by $\mathbf{b}$. His shared key is $j(E_{AB})$.

Fig. 2. The terSIDH protocol. This is nearly the same as Fig. 1, with the main difference being that KeyGen samples ternary secrets.

4.3   One More Variant

It is possible to define a third variant of these protocols that relies on partial artificial orientations. Rather than revealing the images of two linearly independent points G_1 and G_2, the protocol only reveals the image of one point G. Then, for each G^i of coprime order that make up G, the possible isogenies are computed by choosing whether G^i in the kernel of the isogeny or not. Using the vector notation, its entries are chosen in $\{0, 1\}$.

Since the choice is binary, such a protocol would require similar parameters as binSIDH, while also having the disadvantages of variable-degree isogenies discussed in the context of terSIDH. As such, it does not appear to have any meaningful advantage over the proposed constructions. However, the information that is revealed about the secret isogeny is less: not only its degree remains unknown, as in terSIDH, but its action on a single cyclic group is revealed. This suggests that such a variant might be relevant if further cryptanalytic breakthroughs affect the security of binSIDH and terSIDH.

5   An Oriented/Non-oriented Hybrid Approach

There are applications where it is desirable for one party to be significantly more efficient than the other. For example, this is the case for resource-constrained devices communicating to powerful servers, but it also arises in advanced constructions: for instance, in oblivious pseudorandom function protocols, it is generally desired that the client is more efficient than the server. In this section, we propose a technique that allows us to introduce trade-offs between the two parties and enable one participant to obtain more efficient zero-knowledge proofs, which makes this approach more appealing for advanced protocols that requires proofs of isogeny knowledge. This technique has the added benefit of reducing the overall prime size for binSIDH, while the ternary variant has primes of comparable size as terSIDH.

In the previously presented protocols, both parties relied on artificially oriented isogenies to avoid the SIDH attacks. However, the artificial orientation also requires to use significantly longer isogenies than those used in the original

SIDH protocol. This suggests that it may be possible to reveal some unscaled torsion information without affecting the security of the protocol, and if the isogeny is sufficiently long, the revealed torsion may be large enough to allow the computation of parallel isogenies that also guarantee sufficient security. In other words, we can build a secure protocol through a hybrid approach where one party computes binSIDH-like (or terSIDH-like) isogenies while the other party computes SIDH-like isogenies.

More formally, let Bob denote the party computing binSIDH-like isogenies, which means he computes artificially B-oriented isogenies where $B = \ell_1 \cdots \ell_n$; let Alice be the party computing SIDH-like isogenies of degree A, i.e. isogenies whose kernel is generated by $P_A + [\alpha]Q_A$, for some secret $\alpha \in \mathbb{Z}_A$ and fixed points P_A, Q_A. Fix a starting curve E_0, points P_A, Q_A, and a B-orientation $\mathfrak{B} = (G_1, G_2)$, Alice's public key consists of the codomain of her secret isogeny, together with the image of $\mathfrak{B}$ under her secret isogeny, while Bob's public key includes the codomain of his secret B-oriented isogeny, together with the images of P_A and Q_A.

Since Alice is computing SIDH-like isogenies, the degree of her secret isogeny can be very smooth (concretely, this will be a power of two); while this reduces the size of the isogeny degree of one party, the degree of the other party needs to increase to guarantee sufficient security. Thus, the resulting prime p is generally of comparable size to that used in binSIDH and terSIDH. With this setup, we can take A to be considerably smaller and smoother than B; this means that Alice

---

Setup. Let λ be the security parameter and t an integer depending on λ. Let $p = ABf - 1$ be a prime such that $A = 2^a$ ($a \approx 2\lambda$) and $B = \prod_{i=1}^{t} \ell_i$ are coprime integers, ℓ_i are distinct small odd primes, and f is a small cofactor. Let E_0 a be a supersingular elliptic curve defined over $\mathbb{F}_{p^2}$ with $\#E_0(\mathbb{F}_{p^2}) = (p+1)^2$. Let $\mathfrak{B}$ be an artificial B-orientation on E_0 and set $E_0[A] = \langle P_A, Q_A \rangle$. The public parameters are E_0, p, P_A, Q_A and $\mathfrak{B}$.

KeyGen (Alice). Alice samples uniformly at random an integer $\alpha \in \mathbb{Z}/A\mathbb{Z}$ and computes $\phi_A : E_0 \to E_A$ of kernel $\langle P_A + [\alpha]Q_A \rangle$. Her secret key is α and her public key is the artificially B-oriented curve $(E_A, \phi_A(\mathfrak{B}))$.

KeyGen (Bob). Bob samples uniformly at random a vector $\mathbf{b}$ from $\{1, 2\}^t$ and computes the $\mathfrak{B}$-oriented isogeny $\phi_B : E_0 \to E_B$ of degree B defined by $\mathbf{b}$. His secret key is $\mathbf{b}$ and his public key is $(E_B, \phi_B(P_A), \phi_B(Q_A))$.

SharedKey (Alice). Upon receiving Bob's public key (E_B, R, S), Alice checks that $e_A(R, S) = e_A(P_A, Q_A)^B$, if not she aborts. She computes the isogeny $\phi'_A : E_B \to E_{BA}$ of kernel $\langle R + [\alpha]S \rangle$. Her shared key is $j(E_{BA})$.

SharedKey (Bob). Upon receiving $(E_A, \mathfrak{B}')$, Bob checks that $\mathfrak{B}'$ is an artificial B-orientation on E_A, if not he aborts. He computes the $\mathfrak{B}'$-oriented isogeny $\phi'_B : E_A \to E_{AB}$ of degree B defined by $\mathbf{b}$. His shared key is $j(E_{AB})$.

Fig. 3. The binSIDH^{hyb} protocol. A similar variant, based on terSIDH, can be obtained by changing Bob's KeyGen algorithm to sample vectors from $\{0, 1, 2\}^t$.

can be much more efficient in computing her isogenies. Not only that, but zero-knowledge proofs of knowledge of an A-isogeny, both ad-hoc [25] and generic [20], can be much more compact and efficient. More generally, computing SIDH-like isogenies allows one party to fully reuse the range of techniques developed for SIDH. The resulting schemes are described in Fig. 3.

6   Security Analysis

In this section, we analyze the security of the proposed protocols, both binSIDH and terSIDH, as well as their hybrid variants binSIDH^{hyb} and terSIDH^{hyb}.

We analyzed the hardness assumptions relative to artificial orientations in Sect. 3.2, which guarantees it is unfeasible for an attacker to recover a secret key from a public key. In particular, the hardness of Problem 2 guarantees the security of binSIDH and terSIDH against key-recovery attacks, while the hardness of Problem 1 and 3 protects binSIDH^{hyb} and terSIDH^{hyb} from key-recovery attacks (Problem 1 for Alice's public key and Problem 3 for Bob's). However, the security of the key-exchange protocols, as well as any other protocol built on those, depends on the hardness of a different problem, which we call the Artificially Oriented Computational Diffie-Hellman (AO-CDH) problem.

Problem 4 (AO-CDH). Let the notation be as in Fig. 1. Let $\phi_A : E_0 \to E_A$ be a $\mathfrak{A}$-isogeny, and $\phi_B : E_0 \to E_B$ be a $\mathfrak{B}$-isogeny. Given $(E_A, \phi_A(\mathfrak{B}))$ and $(E_B, \phi_B(\mathfrak{A}))$, compute $j(E_{AB})$, where E_{AB} is the codomain of the push-forward of ϕ_A under ϕ_B (or vice versa).

The problem, as stated, guarantees the security of terSIDH. We can easily obtain similar problems for the remaining protocols by either requiring that the isogenies have fixed degrees (binSIDH) or allowing one party to use unoriented isogenies (binSIDH^{hyb}, terSIDH^{hyb}). We can also consider a decisional variant of these problems, where given an additional j-invariant j', the problem asks to determine whether $j' = j(E_{AB})$. While the security of the proposed protocols does not depend on such decisional problems, advanced constructions based on these protocols might require such an assumption.

The relationship between these problems and those introduced in Sect. 3.2 is similar to that between the Computational Diffie-Hellman problem and the Discrete Logarithm problem, or between the Supersingular Computational Diffie-Hellman problem and the Computational Supersingular Isogeny problem [35]. While there exists no known reduction from the problems in Sect. 3.2 to Problem 4, it is likely that any attack that breaks the proposed protocols would need to efficiently solve the problems of Sect. 3.2.

Remark 3. In binSIDH and terSIDH, the two parties reveal the codomain of their secret isogenies, together with only the images of two disjoint cyclic subgroups. This is, in some sense, optimal, as it is the minimum amount of information needed for the other party to compute the push-forwards. Thus, if any major cryptanalytic breakthrough managed to break binSIDH and terSIDH, it seems likely that any possible SIDH-like construction would equally be broken, including the existing countermeasures against the SIDH attacks [29].

6.1 The Relation with the Uber-Isogeny Problem

When proposing SÉTA [24], its authors also introduced the Uber-isogeny problem, which is the following:

Problem 5 ($\mathfrak{O}$-Uber Isogeny Problem). Let $p > 3$ be a prime and let $\mathfrak{O} = \mathbb{Z}[w]$ be a quadratic order of discriminant Δ. Let E_0 and E be two $\mathfrak{O}$-oriented supersingular curves, and let $\theta \in \mathrm{End}(E_0)$ be an endomorphism such that $\mathbb{Z}[\theta] \cong \mathfrak{O}$, that is θ allows to explicitly embed $\mathbb{Z}[\theta]$ into $\mathrm{End}(E_0)$. Given E_0, E and θ, find a power-smooth ideal $\mathfrak{a}$ of norm co-prime with Δ such that $[\mathfrak{a}] \in \mathrm{Cl}(\mathfrak{O})$ is such that $E \cong \mathfrak{a} * E_0$.

In other words, $\phi : E_0 \to E$ is an $\mathfrak{O}$-oriented isogeny, one is given the actual embedding of $\mathfrak{O}$ into $\mathrm{End}(E_0)$ but not that of $\mathfrak{O}$ into $\mathrm{End}(E)$, and one is asked to recover ϕ, or an equivalent isogeny of power-smooth degree. The authors of SÉTA [24] showed that the security of SIDH [35], CSIDH [11], OSIDH [19] and SÉTA [24] reduces to the Uber-isogeny problem. It is natural to wonder whether the security of our schemes can similarly be reduced to the Uber-isogeny problem as well. As we will show below, this is possible when the endomorphism ring of the starting curve E_0 is known, but the reduction is not trivial. In what follows, we relate Problem 4 to the Uber-isogeny problem.

A first approach proceeds as follows. Let $\phi_A : E_0 \to E_A$ be Alice's artificially oriented isogeny with respect to an artificial orientation $\mathfrak{A} = (G_1, G_2)$. If the endomorphism ring $\mathrm{End}(E_0) \cong \mathcal{O}_0$ of the starting curve E_0 is known, then one can efficiently compute an endomorphism $\theta \in \mathrm{End}(E_0)$ such that $\theta(G_1) = G_1$ and $\theta(G_2) = G_2$. Let w be a quaternion such that its norm and trace agree with θ, i.e. $w\overline{w} = N(w) = \deg\theta$ and $w + \overline{w} = tr(w) = \theta + \widehat{\theta}$, and set $\mathfrak{O} = \mathbb{Z}[w]$. Then E_0 and E_A are $\mathfrak{O}$-oriented supersingular curves, and θ provides the actual embedding of $\mathfrak{O}$ into $\mathrm{End}(E_0)$. Any algorithm that solves the Uber-isogeny problem can be used to recover a power-smooth $\mathfrak{O}$-oriented isogeny $\psi_A : E_0 \to E_A$.

Such a reduction, however, presents an issue: with high probability, the recovered isogeny $\psi_A : E_0 \to E_A$ cannot be used as the secret in binSIDH. This is because Bob only reveals $\phi_B(\mathfrak{A})$, which allows the attacker to compute only the push-forwards of isogenies oriented by (G_1, G_2) and thus whose degree divides the order A. This implies that the knowledge of ψ_A is not sufficient to compute the shared secret in the key exchange. To solve this issue, we force both Alice's artificial orientation and Bob's artificial orientation to be restrictions of the same bigger $\mathfrak{O}$-orientation on E_0.

As before, let us assume that the endomorphism ring $\mathrm{End}(E_0) \cong \mathcal{O}_0$ of the starting curve E_0 is known. Let $\mathfrak{A} = (G_1^a, G_2^a)$ and $\mathfrak{B} = (G_1^b, G_2^b)$ be Alice's and Bob's artificial orientations, respectively. Set $G_1 = G_1^a \oplus G_1^b$ and $G_2 = G_2^a \oplus G_2^b$. It is possible to efficiently compute an endomorphism $\theta \in \mathrm{End}(E_0)$ such that

$\theta(G_1) = G_1$ and $\theta(G_2) = G_2$. Let w be a quaternion such that $w + \overline{w} = tr(w) = \theta + \widehat{\theta}$ and $w\overline{w} = N(w) = \deg\theta$, and set $\mathfrak{O} = \mathbb{Z}[w]$. Then E_0, E_A and E_B are all $\mathfrak{O}$-oriented supersingular elliptic curves, and θ provides the actual embedding of $\mathfrak{O}$ into $\mathrm{End}(E_0)$. Moreover, both Alice's artificially oriented secret isogeny $\phi_A : E_0 \to E_A$ and Bob's artificially oriented secret isogeny $\phi_B : E_0 \to E_B$ are $\mathfrak{O}$-oriented. Thus, the reduction starts by first using the algorithm to solve the Uber-isogeny problem with E_0 and E_A to recover a power-smooth $\mathfrak{O}$-oriented isogeny $\psi_A : E_0 \to E_A$, and then with E_0 and E_B to recover a power-smooth $\mathfrak{O}$-oriented isogeny $\psi_B : E_0 \to E_B$. Now, since all curves are $\mathfrak{O}$-oriented the underlying binSIDH scheme can be interpreted within the framework of the OSIDH [19] protocol. To obtain the shared secret, the reduction concludes by computing the push-forward ψ_B' of ψ_B through ψ_A (or vice-versa). The j-invariant of the codomain of ψ_B' is the shared key.

6.2 Adaptive Security

SIDH has been known to be vulnerable to active adaptive attacks [30,33], i.e. attacks where the target has a long-term static key and the attacker is a participant of the key exchange. In this section, we show how the proposed protocols are unfortunately similarly vulnerable to adaptive attacks.

In binSIDH^{hyb} and terSIDH^{hyb}, one party computes SIDH-like isogenies. As such, they are vulnerable to exactly the same attacks that SIDH is. We can thus focus on active attacks against oriented isogenies, which covers the remaining cases.

Let us assume Alice is the target party, while Bob plays the role of the attacker. For simplicity, let us also assume we are in the case of binSIDH, where Alice's secret is the binary vector $\mathbf{a} \in \{1,2\}^t$. The case of terSIDH follows similarly.

Bob can use potentially malicious public keys and check whether both parties obtained the same shared secret. In other words, the attacker has access to the following oracle:

$$\mathcal{O}(E, \mathfrak{A}, j') = \begin{cases} true & \text{if } j(E/\langle \mathbf{a}, \mathfrak{A} \rangle) = j', \\ false & \text{otherwise.} \end{cases}$$

Write A, the order of the artificial orientation $\mathfrak{A}$, as $A = \prod_{i=1}^t p_i$. To target the i-th bit of the secret key $\mathbf{a}_i$, the attacker can honestly compute the curve E_B and the image orientation $\mathfrak{A} = (G_1, G_2)$ and write $G_j = H_j^1 \oplus \ldots \oplus H_j^t$ for $j \in \{1,2\}$, where each H_j^k has order p_k, which are all pairwise coprime. Then, if I_1^i is any cyclic subgroup of order p_i such that $I_1^i \cap H_1^i = \{\mathcal{O}\}$, the attacker can define $\mathfrak{A}' = (G_1', G_2)$, where G_i' is the same subgroup as G_i with H_1^i replaced by I_1^i, i.e. $G_1' = H_1^1 \oplus \ldots \oplus I_1^i \oplus \ldots \oplus H_1^t$. The attacker can also obtain the j-invariant j_{AB} corresponding to the shared secret of an honest exchange and query the oracle $\mathcal{O}(E_B, \mathfrak{A}', j_{AB})$. If the oracle returns $true$, the shared secret is unchanged: this means that modified subgroup did not affect the computations, and thus $\mathbf{a}_i = 2$. Otherwise, the modified subgroup did change the shared secret, and thus $\mathbf{a}_i = 1$.

The active attack against the proposed protocols is slightly more powerful than the GPST attack. It does not involve carefully crafted torsion points, and it allows to target any bit of the secret key without necessarily proceeding in order. In the PKE setting, one party can achieve long-term security with the use of the Fujisaki-Okamoto transform [31], while in the key exchange setting, it is possible to obtain active security for both parties, thus obtaining a non-interactive key exchange, by introducing a proof of public key correctness. For artifically oriented curves, this can be achieved by adapting the zero-knowledge proof of masked public keys from [3] to work with independently scaled points.

7 Implementation

7.1 Parameter Selection

Following the security analysis of Sect. 3.2, we generated parameter sets for the four proposed protocols at security levels $\lambda \in \{128, 192, 256\}$.

In binSIDH and terSIDH, both parties rely on oriented isogenies, and thus the degrees corresponding to both isogenies need to be quite large: in the case of binSIDH, at least the product of λ distinct primes. This is reduced to $\lambda / \log_2(3)$ for terSIDH, since each prime provides $\log_2(3)$ bits of security. To obtain a balanced trade-off between the two parties, we assign consecutive primes to different parties; in other words, the degree of Alice's isogenies is the product of t even-index primes, while the degree of Bob's isogenies is the product of t odd-index primes. Moreover, the isogeny degrees need to be coprime, and thus the underlying prime necessarily needs to be larger than the product of the first 2λ in binSIDH ($2\lambda / \log_2(3)$ in terSIDH). The resulting parameter sets for binSIDH and terSIDH are summarized in Table 1, where we also list the corresponding public key sizes.

Remark 4 (Public-key compression). As in SIDH, public keys can be compressed by expressing the torsion points with respect to a deterministically generated basis [21]. This requires three coefficients in SIDH since both points can be scaled by the same value without affecting the SIDH computations, which means that one of the four coefficients can be fixed to one. In our case, however, the two points that generate artificial orientations can be scaled independently: this means that the public keys of the proposed protocols can be compressed to only two coefficients.

The size of the primes and public keys of binSIDH and terSIDH is a stark improvement over those of the existing countermeasures M-SIDH and MD-SIDH [29]. For instance, at $\lambda = 128$, the primes of binSIDH and terSIDH are 2.5× and 8.8× smaller than those in M-SIDH and MD-SIDH, respectively.[3]

---

[3] Interestingly, in the terSIDH case, the variable-degree isogenies allow us to achieve smaller parameters, while in MD-SIDH, the variable-degree isogenies require larger parameters because of the information leakage due to pairing computations.

228   A. Basso and T. B. Fouotsa

Table 1. Parameters for binSIDH and terSIDH. The coloumn t reports the number of distinct primes dividing the degrees of Alice's and Bob's isogenies, while their smoothness bound is reported in the $\mathcal{B}$ column. The columns $|\mathsf{pk}|$ and $|\mathsf{pk}_{cmp}|$ reports the size of the public keys of both parties, respectively uncompressed and compressed.

	λ	$\log p$	Alice				Bob			
			t	$\mathcal{B}$	$|\mathsf{pk}|$	$|\mathsf{pk}_{cmp}|$	t	$\mathcal{B}$	$|\mathsf{pk}|$	$|\mathsf{pk}_{cmp}|$
binSIDH	128	2421	134	2^{11}	1816	907	134	2^{11}	1816	909
	192	3710	192	2^{12}	2783	1390	192	2^{12}	2783	1392
	256	5201	256	2^{12}	3901	1949	256	2^{12}	3901	1950
terSIDH	128	1568	93	2^{11}	1176	587	93	2^{11}	1176	588
	192	2295	128	2^{11}	1722	860	128	2^{11}	1722	861
	256	3035	162	2^{12}	2277	1137	162	2^{12}	2277	1139
binSIDH^{hyb}	128	2004	1	2	1503	937	203	2^{11}	1503	565
	192	3126	1	2	2345	1465	296	2^{11}	2345	878
	256	4267	1	2	3201	2004	387	2^{12}	3201	1195
terSIDH^{hyb}	128	1532	1	2	1149	701	156	2^{10}	1149	447
	192	2373	1	2	1780	1089	226	2^{11}	1780	690
	256	3216	1	2	2412	1479	293	2^{11}	2412	932

While terSIDH^{hyb} requires larger parameters than terSIDH, binSIDH^{hyb} manages to be smaller and more efficient than binSIDH. When compared to M-SIDH, the underlying prime in binSIDH^{hyb} is 2.9× smaller.

7.2 Implementation Results

We developed a proof-of-concept implementation of all four protocols in Sage-Math [45], based on the Kummer Line library [41] to estimate the running times of the proposed protocols[4]. We report the average running times on an Apple M1 PRO CPU in Table 2.

The results of Table 2 show that the ternary variants significantly outperforms the binary ones, especially at higher security levels. This is because binSIDH uses larger prime fields and larger-degree isogenies than terSIDH.[5] Moreover, terSIDH does not need to compute full-degree isogenies due to its varying-degree nature: it is thus likely that the benefits of this are reduced in a constant-time optimization. Nonetheless, the results of terSIDH are encouraging. At security $\lambda = 128$, the SharedKey computations take around 1.4 s, while key generation (which is run

---

[4] The source code is available at https://github.com/binary-ternarySIDH/bin-terSIDH-SageMath.

[5] The specific SageMath implementation of VéluSqrt [6] that we rely on does not outperform Vélu's formulae [47] until the isogeny degree is extremely large. We thus expect a low-level implementation to significantly improve the computation times of high-degree isogenies, more so than for lower-degree ones.

Table 2. Execution times in seconds of the SageMath proof-of-concept implementation. Since it is a PoC in a high-level language, we expect an optimized implementation of the same protocols to be several times more efficient.

	λ	$\log p$	Timings (s)			
			KeyGen$_A$	KeyGen$_B$	SharedKey$_A$	SharedKey$_B$
binSIDH	128	2421	13.69	13.86	9.40	9.46
	192	3710	48.69	49.36	27.39	27.81
	256	5201	140.79	140.57	94.13	95.67
terSIDH	128	1570	2.07	2.09	1.38	1.38
	192	2297	6.84	6.83	4.50	4.39
	256	3039	15.68	16.03	10.00	10.35
binSIDH^{hyb}	128	2004	0.23	14.33	0.22	10.66
	192	3126	0.62	56.77	0.61	42.85
	256	4267	1.41	157.58	1.34	117.07
terSIDH^{hyb}	128	1532	0.16	3.21	0.16	1.96
	192	2373	0.47	13.44	0.44	10.01
	256	3216	0.94	34.66	0.90	23.57

less often) requires about two seconds. The current implementation is only a proof of concept in a high-level language: we can thus expect it to be several times faster once optimally implemented in a low-level language.

Despite the lack of optimizations, the current implementation already outperforms optimized implementations of CSIDH with parameters sufficiently large to guarantee post-quantum security [16], which require between 2.8 and 5.8 s to compute a group action at security level one.[6] Very recently, a new implementation of CSIDH [8] achieves lower running times for a single group action, which takes between 0.9 and 4.6 s. While the CSIDH implementation with a smaller prime outperforms the SageMath implementation of terSIDH^{hyb}, the former is heavily optimized: we thus expect a similarly optimized implementation ter-SIDH^{hyb} to be significantly more efficient than CSIDH.

Comparing to other protocols, our proof-of-concept implementation outperforms the PoC implementation of FESTA [5], which is based on the same SageMath library and takes 3.5 s to encrypt and 10.1 s to decrypt. It is thus mostly likely that terSIDH provides the most efficient key exchange and encryption protocol among all isogeny-based protocols.

Moreover, the results of the hybrid variants show that it is possible to have very low running times for one party, at the cost of a slight increase in the running times of the other party. The hybrid variants significantly reduce the overall running time of a complete key exchange.

---

[6] Note, however, that the CSIDH implementations are constant-time, and that CSIDH does not require the Fujisaki-Okamoto [32] to obtain IND-CCA security.

8   Conclusion

In this work, we introduced artificial orientations, and proposed two new protocols, binSIDH and terSIDH, that translate the SIDH key exchange to the artificially oriented isogeny setting. This allows us to develop two protocols that are resistant against the SIDH attacks, while also achieving significantly smaller parameters than the previously proposed countermeasures. We also proposed binSIDH^{hyb} and terSIDH^{hyb}, hybrid variants of binSIDH and terSIDH respectively, that allow one party to have very short and efficient isogenies. To validate the concrete efficiency of the protocols, we developed a proof-of-concept implementation. Despite being far from optimal, it already outperforms existing implementations of other isogeny-based encryption protocols (both key exchanges and public-key encryption protocols), which suggests that optimized implementations of terSIDH and its hybrid variant might have practical running times.

In future work, we are interested in developing efficient and optimized implementations of binSIDH and terSIDH to accurately measure their running times. Moreover, this work opens up new possibilities that were previously closed by the SIDH attacks. In particular, it is interesting to assess the impact of the proposed protocols on the SIDH-based constructions, such as the round-optimal OPRF construction by Basso [3], where we expect binSIDH and terSIDH to have a significant impact in reducing prime size and computational costs.

Acknowlegements. We would like to express our gratitude to the anonymous reviewers of ASIACRYPT 2023 for their valuable comments that helped improve this paper. We thank Wouter Castryck and Fre Vercauteren for sharing their early draft on attacks on some instances of M-SIDH and FESTA, the attacks described in this draft were useful in the security analysis of our schemes. The first author has been supported in part by EPSRC via grant EP/R012288/1, under the RISE (http://www.ukrise.org) programme.

References

1. Adj, G., Cervantes-Vázquez, D., Chi-Domínguez, J.J., Menezes, A., Rodríguez-Henríquez, F.: On the cost of computing isogenies between supersingular elliptic curves. In: Cid, C., Jacobson, M.J., Jr. (eds.) SAC 2018. LNCS, vol. 11349, pp. 322–343. Springer, Heidelberg (2019). https://doi.org/10.1007/978-3-030-10970-7_15
2. Banegas, G., et al.: CTIDH: faster constant-time CSIDH. IACR TCHES 2021(4), 351–387 (2021). https://doi.org/10.46586/tches.v2021.i4.351-387, https://tches.iacr.org/index.php/TCHES/article/view/9069
3. Basso, A.: A post-quantum round-optimal oblivious PRF from isogenies. Cryptology ePrint Archive, Report 2023/225 (2023). https://eprint.iacr.org/2023/225
4. Basso, A., Kutas, P., Merz, S.-P., Petit, C., Sanso, A.: Cryptanalysis of an oblivious PRF from supersingular isogenies. In: Tibouchi, M., Wang, H. (eds.) ASIACRYPT 2021, Part I. LNCS, vol. 13090, pp. 160–184. Springer, Cham (2021). https://doi.org/10.1007/978-3-030-92062-3_6

5. Basso, A., Maino, L., Pope, G.: FESTA: fast encryption from supersingular torsion attacks. Cryptology ePrint Archive, Paper 2023/660 (2023). https://eprint.iacr.org/2023/660, https://eprint.iacr.org/2023/660

6. Bernstein, D.J., De Feo, L., Leroux, A., Smith, B.: Faster computation of isogenies of large prime degree. Open Book Series 4(1), 39–55 (2020). https://doi.org/10.2140/obs.2020.4.39

7. Beullens, W., Feo, L.D., Galbraith, S.D., Petit, C.: Proving knowledge of isogenies - a survey. Cryptology ePrint Archive, Paper 2023/671 (2023). https://eprint.iacr.org/2023/671, https://eprint.iacr.org/2023/671

8. Campos, F., et al.: On the practicality of post-quantum tls using large-parameter csidh. Cryptology ePrint Archive, Paper 2023/793 (2023). https://eprint.iacr.org/2023/793, https://eprint.iacr.org/2023/793

9. Castryck, W., Decru, T.: An efficient key recovery attack on SIDH. In: Hazay, C., Stam, M. (eds.) Advances in Cryptology - EUROCRYPT 2023. LNCS, vol. 14008, pp. 423–447. Springer, Cham (2023). https://doi.org/10.1007/978-3-031-30589-4_15

10. Castryck, W., Houben, M., Merz, S.P., Mula, M., van Buuren, S., Vercauteren, F.: Weak instances of class group action based cryptography via self-pairings. Cryptology ePrint Archive, Paper 2023/549 (2023). https://eprint.iacr.org/2023/549, https://eprint.iacr.org/2023/549

11. Castryck, W., Lange, T., Martindale, C., Panny, L., Renes, J.: CSIDH: an efficient post-quantum commutative group action. In: Peyrin, T., Galbraith, S. (eds.) ASIACRYPT 2018, Part III. LNCS, vol. 11274, pp. 395–427. Springer, Cham (2018). https://doi.org/10.1007/978-3-030-03332-3_15

12. Castryck, W., Vercauteren, F.: A polynomial time attack on instances of M-SIDH and FESTA. To appear in ASIACRYPT 2023 (2023)

13. Charles, D.X., Lauter, K.E., Goren, E.Z.: Cryptographic hash functions from expander graphs. J. Cryptol. 22(1), 93–113 (2009). https://doi.org/10.1007/s00145-007-9002-x

14. Chen, M., Imran, M., Ivanyos, G., Kutas, P., Leroux, A., Petit, C.: Hidden stabilizers, the isogeny to endomorphism ring problem and the cryptanalysis of psidh (2023)

15. Childs, A.M., Jao, D., Soukharev, V.: Constructing elliptic curve isogenies in quantum subexponential time. J. Math. Cryptol. 8(1), 1–29 (2014). https://doi.org/10.1515/jmc-2012-0016

16. Chávez-Saab, J., Chi-Domínguez, J.J., Jaques, S., Rodríguez-Henríquez, F.: The SQALE of CSIDH: sublinear Vélu quantum-resistant isogeny action with low exponents. J. Cryptogr. Eng. 12(3), 349–368 (2022). https://doi.org/10.1007/s13389-021-00271-w

17. Codogni, G., Lido, G.: Spectral theory of isogeny graphs (2023)

18. Colò, L., Kohel, D.: Orienting supersingular isogeny graphs. Cryptology ePrint Archive, Report 2020/985 (2020). https://eprint.iacr.org/2020/985

19. Colò, L., Kohel, D.: Orienting supersingular isogeny graphs. J. Mathematical Cryptol. 14(1), 414–437 (2020)

20. Cong, K., Lai, Y.F., Levin, S.: Efficient isogeny proofs using generic techniques. Cryptology ePrint Archive, Report 2023/037 (2023). https://eprint.iacr.org/2023/037

21. Costello, C., Jao, D., Longa, P., Naehrig, M., Renes, J., Urbanik, D.: Efficient compression of SIDH public keys. In: Coron, J.-S., Nielsen, J.B. (eds.) EUROCRYPT 2017, Part I. LNCS, vol. 10210, pp. 679–706. Springer, Cham (2017). https://doi.org/10.1007/978-3-319-56620-7_24

22. Couveignes, J.M.: Hard homogeneous spaces. Cryptology ePrint Archive, Report 2006/291 (2006). https://eprint.iacr.org/2006/291
23. Dartois, P., De Feo, L.: On the security of OSIDH. Cryptology ePrint Archive, Report 2021/1681 (2021). https://eprint.iacr.org/2021/1681
24. De Feo, L., et al.: Séta: supersingular encryption from torsion attacks. In: Tibouchi, M., Wang, H. (eds.) ASIACRYPT 2021, Part IV. LNCS, vol. 13093, pp. 249–278. Springer, Cham (2021). https://doi.org/10.1007/978-3-030-92068-5_9
25. De Feo, L., Dobson, S., Galbraith, S.D., Zobernig, L.: SIDH proof of knowledge. In: Agrawal, S., Lin, D. (eds.) ASIACRYPT 2022, Part II. LNCS, vol. 13792, pp. 310–339. Springer, Heidelberg (2022). https://doi.org/10.1007/978-3-031-22966-4_11
26. De Feo, L., et al.: SCALLOP: scaling the CSI-FiSh. In: Boldyreva, A., Kolesnikov, V. (eds.) Public-Key Cryptography - PKC 2023. LNCS, vol. 13940, pp. 345–375. Springer, Cham (2023). https://doi.org/10.1007/978-3-031-31368-4_13
27. De Feo, L., Kohel, D., Leroux, A., Petit, C., Wesolowski, B.: SQISign: compact post-quantum signatures from quaternions and isogenies. In: Moriai, S., Wang, H. (eds.) ASIACRYPT 2020, Part I. LNCS, vol. 12491, pp. 64–93. Springer, Cham (2020). https://doi.org/10.1007/978-3-030-64837-4_3
28. Delfs, C., Galbraith, S.D.: Computing isogenies between supersingular elliptic curves over $\mathbb{F}_p$. Designs Codes Cryptography **78**(2), 425–440 (2016). https://doi.org/10.1007/s10623-014-0010-1
29. Fouotsa, T.B., Moriya, T., Petit, C.: M-SIDH and MD-SIDH: countering SIDH attacks by masking information. In: Hazay, C., Stam, M. (eds.) Advances in Cryptology - EUROCRYPT 2023. LNCS, vol. 14008, pp. 282–309. Springer, Cham (2023). https://doi.org/10.1007/978-3-031-30589-4_10
30. Fouotsa, T.B., Petit, C.: A new adaptive attack on SIDH. In: Galbraith, S.D. (ed.) CT-RSA 2022. LNCS, vol. 13161, pp. 322–344. Springer, Cham (2022). https://doi.org/10.1007/978-3-030-95312-6_14
31. Fujisaki, E., Okamoto, T.: Statistical zero knowledge protocols to prove modular polynomial relations. In: Kaliski, B.S., Jr. (ed.) CRYPTO 1997. LNCS, vol. 1294, pp. 16–30. Springer, Heidelberg (1997). https://doi.org/10.1007/BFb0052225
32. Fujisaki, E., Okamoto, T.: Secure integration of asymmetric and symmetric encryption schemes. In: Wiener, M. (ed.) CRYPTO 1999. LNCS, vol. 1666, pp. 537–554. Springer, Heidelberg (1999). https://doi.org/10.1007/3-540-48405-1_34
33. Galbraith, S.D., Petit, C., Shani, B., Ti, Y.B.: On the security of supersingular isogeny cryptosystems. In: Cheon, J.H., Takagi, T. (eds.) ASIACRYPT 2016. LNCS, vol. 10031, pp. 63–91. Springer, Heidelberg (2016). https://doi.org/10.1007/978-3-662-53887-6_3
34. Jao, D., et al.: SIKE. Technical report, National Institute of Standards and Technology (2020). https://csrc.nist.gov/projects/post-quantum-cryptography/post-quantum-cryptography-standardization/round-3-submissions
35. Jao, D., De Feo, L.: Towards quantum-resistant cryptosystems from supersingular elliptic curve isogenies. In: Yang, B.-Y. (ed.) PQCrypto 2011. LNCS, vol. 7071, pp. 19–34. Springer, Heidelberg (2011). https://doi.org/10.1007/978-3-642-25405-5_2
36. Kani, E.: The number of curves of genus two with elliptic differentials. Journal für die reine undangewandte Mathematik **1997**(485), 93–122 (1997). https://doi.org/10.1515/crll.1997.485.93
37. Leroux, A.: A new isogeny representation and applications to cryptography. In: Agrawal, S., Lin, D. (eds.) ASIACRYPT 2022, Part II. LNCS, vol. 13792, pp. 3–35. Springer, Heidelberg (2022). https://doi.org/10.1007/978-3-031-22966-4_1

38. Maino, L., Martindale, C., Panny, L., Pope, G., Wesolowski, B.: A direct key recovery attack on SIDH. In: Hazay, C., Stam, M. (eds.) Advances in Cryptology - EUROCRYPT 2023. LNCS, vol. 14008, pp. 448–471. Springer, Cham (2023). https://doi.org/10.1007/978-3-031-30589-4_16

39. Peikert, C.: He gives C-sieves on the CSIDH. In: Canteaut, A., Ishai, Y. (eds.) EUROCRYPT 2020, Part II. LNCS, vol. 12106, pp. 463–492. Springer, Cham (2020). https://doi.org/10.1007/978-3-030-45724-2_16

40. Petit, C.: Faster algorithms for isogeny problems using torsion point images. In: Takagi, T., Peyrin, T. (eds.) ASIACRYPT 2017, Part II. LNCS, vol. 10625, pp. 330–353. Springer, Cham (2017). https://doi.org/10.1007/978-3-319-70697-9_12

41. Pope, G.: Kummer Isogeny SageMath Library. https://github.com/jack4818/KummerIsogeny (2023)

42. de Quehen, V., et al.: Improved torsion-point attacks on SIDH variants. In: Malkin, T., Peikert, C. (eds.) CRYPTO 2021, Part III. LNCS, vol. 12827, pp. 432–470. Springer, Cham (2021). https://doi.org/10.1007/978-3-030-84252-9_15

43. Robert, D.: Breaking SIDH in polynomial time. In: Hazay, C., Stam, M. (eds.) Advances in Cryptology - EUROCRYPT 2023. LNCS, vol. 14008, pp. 472–503. Springer, Cham (2023). https://doi.org/10.1007/978-3-031-30589-4_17

44. Silverman, J.H.: The Arithmetic of Elliptic Curves, vol. 106. Springer, New York (2009). https://doi.org/10.1007/978-0-387-09494-6

45. The Sage Developers: SageMath, the Sage Mathematics Software System (Version 9.8) (2023). https://www.sagemath.org

46. van Oorschot, P.C., Wiener, M.J.: Parallel collision search with cryptanalytic applications. J. Cryptol. 12(1), 1–28 (1999). https://doi.org/10.1007/PL00003816

47. Vélu, J.: Isogénies entre courbes elliptiques. CR Acad. Sci. Paris, Séries A 273, 305–347 (1971)

Symmetric-Key - Design

The Indifferentiability of the Duplex and Its Practical Applications

Jean Paul Degabriele[1,3]($\boxtimes$), Marc Fischlin[2] , and Jérôme Govinden[3]

[1] Cryptography Research Center, Technology Innovation Institute, Abu Dhabi, UAE
jeanpaul.degabriele@tii.ae
[2] Cryptoplexity, Technische Universität Darmstadt, Darmstadt, Germany
marc.fischlin@cryptoplexity.de
[3] CNS, Technische Universität Darmstadt, Darmstadt, Germany
jerome.govinden@tu-darmstadt.de

Abstract. The Duplex construction, introduced by Bertoni *et al.* (SAC 2011), is the Swiss Army knife of permutation-based cryptography. It can be used to realise a variety of cryptographic objects—ranging from hash functions and MACs, to authenticated encryption and symmetric ratchets. Testament to this is the STROBE protocol framework which is a software cryptographic library based solely on the Duplex combined with a rich set of function calls. While prior works have typically focused their attention on specific uses of the Duplex, our focus here is its *indifferentiability*. More specifically, we consider the indifferentiability of the Duplex construction from an *online random oracle*—an idealisation which shares its same interface. As one of our main results we establish the indifferentiability of the Duplex from an online random oracle. However indifferentiability only holds for the standard Duplex construction and we show that the full-state variant of the Duplex cannot meet this notion. Our indifferentiability theorem provides the theoretical justification for the security of the Duplex in a variety of scenarios, amongst others, its use as a general-purpose cryptographic primitive in the STROBE framework. Next we move our attention to AEAD schemes based on the Duplex, namely SpongeWrap, which is the basis for NIST's Lightweight Cryptography standard Ascon. We harness the power of indifferentiability by establishing that SpongeWrap offers security against key-dependent message inputs, related-key attacks, and is also committing.

1 Introduction

Permutation-based cryptography supplants the block cipher with an unkeyed public permutation as the central building block for realising symmetric-key cryptographic primitives. The approach has led to innovative and versatile designs in symmetric-key cryptography and is now establishing itself as a field of study in its own right. The SHA-3 standard is a prime example of its success, which brings to light the versatility of the approach in yielding a variety of primitives such as SHA-3, SHAKE, KMAC, TupleHash, and ParallelHash [30]

© International Association for Cryptologic Research 2023
J. Guo and R. Steinfeld (Eds.): ASIACRYPT 2023, LNCS 14445, pp. 237–269, 2023.
https://doi.org/10.1007/978-981-99-8742-9_8

from the same underlying construction, i.e., the Sponge [11]. The fact that the Sponge turned out to be such a versatile construct is not that surprising when one considers the central role that the random oracle [9] plays in cryptography in general. The power of the random oracle comes both from its conceptual simplicity and its ability to be a drop-in replacement for a multitude of crypto-graphic primitives. With minor cosmetic changes, a random oracle can serve as a one-way function, a collision-resistant hash, a pseudorandom generator, a ran-domness extractor, or a pseudorandom function. In turn, the Sponge inherits all these lucrative properties from the random oracle through its indifferentiability theorem, under the assumption that the underlying public permutation acts as a random permutation.

In 2011, permutation-based cryptography received a boost from the advent of the Duplex construction [12]. The Duplex construction supersedes the Sponge in that it can perfectly mimic the Sponge but allows for yet more functional-ity. Whereas the Sponge operates in two phases, an 'absorb' phase in which an input is gradually mixed into the state followed by a 'squeeze' phase in which an output is gradually extracted from the state until it is of the desired size, the Duplex is capable of absorbing input and squeezing output simultaneously. The main motivation behind the design of the Duplex is that it allows for more efficient permutation-based AEAD schemes. In principle an AEAD scheme can be constructed from two Sponge instances, one operating as a pseudorandom generator and the other serving as a message authentication code. However that would entail passing over the data twice, whereas the Duplex yields a more effi-cient scheme that can process the data in *one pass*. A one-pass AEAD scheme based on the Duplex, known as SpongeWrap, was proposed in [12]. Many candi-dates of the CAESAR competition and the NIST lightweight competition were based on SpongeWrap. This includes in particular Ascon [21], the new NIST lightweight crypto standard and CAESAR's primary choice for authenticated encryption.

More recently, the Duplex has taken a life of its own among practition-ers who, having recognised its elegance and versatility, have written crypto-graphic libraries that are based solely on this one primitive. Two such examples are the STROBE protocol framework by Mike Hamburg [29] and the State-ful Hash Object (SHO) within Trevor Perrin's Noise Protocol framework [37]. STROBE and SHO are fairly similar frameworks for realising protocols from Duplex instances. A typical scenario would have two parties maintaining one or more Duplex instances to encrypt and decrypt messages, possibly incorporating a symmetric ratchet functionality, where either party can produce or verify, a MAC tag or a hash digest, of the transcript at any point in time. The tenet behind frameworks like STROBE and SHO is that the Duplex behaves like an idealised cryptographic primitive that can be plugged into any protocol and it will retain its security. Clearly, this would hold true if the Duplex, like the Sponge, were backed by an indifferentiability theorem, but unfortunately no such result exists in the literature. In fact, it is not even clear what ideal-functionality behaviour one can expect from the Duplex.

When the Duplex was first proposed in [12], it was observed that a sequence of queries to the Duplex could be evaluated by mapping that sequence of inputs to a separate input sequence and then feeding that to the Sponge. Accordingly, it was then argued that if the Sponge is secure then the Duplex must also be secure. This argument was formalised in the security proof of SpongeWrap in that same paper, by first proving the security of SpongeWrap in the random oracle model and then invoking the indifferentiability of the Sponge. While perfectly legitimate, this security treatment is lacking in some respects. By reducing the security of SpongeWrap directly to that of the Sponge, the security of the Duplex was left uncovered. In particular, a formal security definition for the Duplex was not provided. This left unattended the question of what security one should expect from the Duplex, thereby failing to recognise its merit as a cryptographic primitive in its own right. In principle one could rely on the mapping from the Duplex to the Sponge but we contend that this approach is cumbersome, unintuitive, and error-prone. Another drawback of this approach is that the mapping from the Duplex to the Sponge entails an unnecessary degradation in the resulting security bound. Indeed, as we expand upon later, the security bound for SpongeWrap that results from applying this method is actually worse than that presented in [12], an issue that thus far seems to have gone unnoticed.

Motivated by the popularity of the Duplex and its varied applications, we provide the first treatment of the Duplex in the indifferentiability framework of Maurer, Renner, and Holenstein [34]. While there have been a number of works that consider the security of the Duplex in terms of indistinguishability, our proof of indifferentiability is beneficial for a number of reasons. First off, we provide an idealisation of the Duplex that gives a direct and intuitive way to reason about the Duplex construction and the security of its applications. We call this ideal functionality the *online random oracle*. The composition theorem then guarantees that we can replace an instance of the Duplex with the online random oracle, with the usual care regarding multi-stage games [38]. Thus our treatment provides the formal justification for employing the Duplex as a general-purpose primitive, as done in STROBE and SHO for instance. Our indifferentiability result is also useful in the case where the Duplex is endowed with a secret key, as in an AEAD scheme. In particular it allows for a simpler and more direct security analysis in the online random oracle model as opposed to a more involved analysis in the random permutation model. Besides simplifying the analysis in the standard AEAD setting, the online random oracle model also enables an easier treatment with respect to stronger security models, such as related-key and key-dependent-input security.

1.1 Summary of Our Contributions

The Online Random Oracle. Before we can delve into examining the indifferentiability of the Duplex with respect to an ideal permutation we need to identify a suitable ideal functionality. Our answer is the online random oracle (ORO), which is a natural adaptation of the random oracle to a stateful primitive that can be interacted with in an online manner, allowing to iterate over the outputs by appending new inputs. Besides enabling our treatment of indifferentiability, we believe this abstraction to be more intuitive, concise, and direct than having to map the sequence of inputs for the Duplex to a sequence of inputs for the Sponge and then replacing it with a random oracle.

A peculiarity of the ORO is that it only takes inputs of a fixed size, which in turn allows us to analyse the Duplex without padding. While this may seem more restrictive at first, since the Duplex can only take inputs of a certain size, it actually renders our treatment more general. In the Sponge construction, padding is not only required to allow for arbitrary-length inputs but it is also necessary for security and indifferentiability to hold. In particular, padding is required to delineate the boundary between input and output, thereby excluding the possibility of two inputs (say x and $x \| 0^r$) having related outputs. Now, in order to map the Duplex to the Sponge, the Duplex needs to include 'Sponge-compliant' padding in every round as in [12]. Consequently, a security treatment based on this mapping relies crucially on the presence of this padding. Lifting the need for sponge-compliant padding removes this extra layer of complexity, reducing padding from a matter of security to one of functionality, and allows practitioners the freedom to use the padding that best fits their application. While some AEAD constructions include sponge-compliant padding, e.g., Ketje [13], others do not, e.g. Ascon [21]. Accordingly our treatment serves in part to justify this latter type of constructions. Finally, we provide the ORO with a more pragmatic API that supports multiple concurrent sessions and the ability to switch easily between them. This serves to bring the ORO closer to practice, and although it may seem like a superficiality the specifics of the API have an effect on the simulator's efficiency used to prove indifferentiability.

Indifferentiability of the Duplex. We start by considering a variant of the Duplex that appeared in [20, 22, 35, 36], known as the full-state Duplex, and show that indifferentiability is out of reach for this variant. This result justifies our choice of restricting our attention to the Duplex without full state absorption, requiring that the encoding functions cannot affect the entire input. We then go on to prove our main result of indifferentiability between the Duplex and the ORO. This result can be leveraged in a variety of settings. For instance, an immediate consequence is that the Duplex yields an online randomness extractor [24]. Alternatively, by lifting constructions based on the Duplex to the ORO model one can employ proof techniques similar to the random oracle model, like 'programmability' and 'extractability'. We emphasize that we obtain a fairly good indifferentiability bound and that our simulator is very efficient. This serves to make our result all the more usable and meaningful in practice, resulting in good bounds when composability is invoked.

Stronger Security for SpongeWrap. Our indifferentiability theorem is profitable also for the case where the Duplex is used as keyed primitive, its most popular application being the realisation of one-pass AEAD schemes. We use it to revisit the security of SpongeWrap in more demanding settings that, to the best of our knowledge, have not been considered so far: key-dependent message (KDM) security, related-key attacks (RKA), and commitment (CMT). KDM security guarantees security when an AEAD scheme is used to encrypt a message that depends on the key or an application where a number of keys are used to encrypt each other in the form of a cycle. Such cases arise in disk encryption, hardware security modules, and key management/distribution systems. RKA security models scenarios such as fault-injection attacks where an adversary may obtain ciphertexts evaluated under modified key values which is a concern when an adversary gets access to the hardware the scheme is running on. Recent works [1, 28, 32] have highlighted several practical issues, in relation to message franking, password-based AEAD, key rotation, and envelope encryption, that arise when an AEAD is non-committing.

We prove SpongeWrap to be KDM-AEAD secure as defined by Bellare and Keelveedhi [7]. To this end we first prove that the (nonce-based SpongeWrap version of the) ORO achieves KDM-AEAD security. Then we can apply the composition theorem of Barbosa and Farshim [5] for indifferentiable Authenticated Encryption to conclude that the nonce-based SpongeWrap of the Duplex is also secure. We provide a similar treatment covering security against related-key attacks (RKA-AEAD) and committing security (CMT-AEAD). Our analysis serves to highlight the fact that AEAD schemes based on the Duplex automatically offer these attractive properties without requiring any alteration that would detriment their efficiency or any additional assumption beyond what is already required.

2 Preliminaries

Notation. Unless otherwise stated, an algorithm may be randomised. For any algorithm A we use $y \leftarrow \mathsf{A}(x_1, x_2, \ldots)$ to denote the process of running A on the indicated inputs and fresh random coins, and assigning the output to y. By convention the running time of an adversary refers to the sum of its actual running time and the size of its description. We generically refer to the resources of an adversary as any subset of the following quantities: its running time, the number of queries that it makes to its oracles, and the total length (in bits) of its oracle queries. We write $\mathsf{B.sub1}, \mathsf{B.sub2}, \ldots$ to denote a group of algorithms that share state and refer to them collectively as B.

If S is a set then $|S|$ denotes its size, and $z \leftarrow S$ denotes the process of selecting an element from S uniformly at random and assigning it to z. When assigning a value y to variable x or table entry $T[x]$ we write $x \leftarrow y$ or $T[x] \leftarrow y$. We assume throughout that tables are initialized to $\bot$ entries and sets are initially empty. When T is a table, we write $x \in T$ to indicate that the table entry $T[x] \neq \bot$. For sets X and Y, the set of all functions mapping from X to Y is denoted by $\mathsf{Func}(X, Y)$.

For a bit b and a positive integer n, we denote by b^n the string composed of b repeated n times. With $\{0, 1\}^n$ we denote the set of all binary strings of length n, and $\{0, 1\}^*$ denotes the set of all binary strings of finite length. The empty string is represented by ε. For any two strings u and v, $|u|$ denotes the length of u in bits, $u \parallel v$ denotes their concatenation, and $u \oplus v$ denotes their bitwise XOR operation. For $n \in \mathbb{N}$ and $u \in \{0,1\}^*$, $(u_1, \ldots, u_\ell) \xleftarrow{n} u$ denotes the n-bit parsing of u where $|u_i| = n$ for all $1 \leq i < \ell$ and $0 < |u_i| \leq n$. For a boolean expression exp, we denote its encoding into a single bit as $\langle \text{exp} \rangle$. We use $u[i,j]$ to denote the substring of u from bit i to bit j inclusive, where the indexes start at 1. For a positive integer $n \leq |u|$, we use $\lfloor u \rfloor_n$ to denote the strings obtained by truncating u to its leftmost n bits. We denote by $[t]$ the set $\{1, \ldots, t\}$, $t \in \mathbb{N}$.

We will at times make use of the code-based game-playing framework by Bellare and Rogaway [10]. Here the interaction between a game and the adversary is implicit, whereby the adversary is given as its input the output of the initialize procedure, it has oracle access to the other procedures described in the game, and its output is fed into the finalize procedure. The output of the finalize procedure is the output of the game. For a game Gm and an adversary $\mathcal{A}$, $\text{Gm}^{\mathcal{A}} \Rightarrow x$ denotes the event that Gm outputs x when interacting with $\mathcal{A}$. Similarly, $\mathcal{A}^{\text{Gm}} \Rightarrow y$ denotes the event that $\mathcal{A}$ outputs y when interacting with Gm.

AEAD Syntax. An authenticated encryption scheme with associated data $\text{SE} = (\text{K}, \text{E}, \text{D})$ is a triple of efficient algorithms such that:

- The key generation algorithm K is randomised, takes no input, and samples k-bit strings according to some distribution.
- The encryption algorithm $\text{E} : \{0,1\}^k \times \{0,1\}^n \times \{0,1\}^* \times \{0,1\}^* \to \{0,1\}^*$ is deterministic and takes as input a secret key K, a nonce N, associated data A, and a message M to return a ciphertext C.
- The decryption algorithm $\text{D} : \{0,1\}^k \times \{0,1\}^n \times \{0,1\}^* \times \{0,1\}^* \to \{0,1\}^* \cup \{\bot\}$ is deterministic and takes as input a secret key K, a nonce N, associated data A, and a ciphertext C to return a message $M \in \{0,1\}^*$ or $M = \bot$ indicating an invalid set of inputs.

We require that an authenticated encryption scheme be both *correct* and *tidy*. Correctness requires that for all K, N, A, M it hold that if $\text{E}(K, N, A, M) = C$ then $\text{D}(K, N, A, C) = M$. In a similar manner, tidiness requires that for all K, N, A, C it hold that if $\text{D}(K, N, A, C) = M \neq \bot$ then $\text{E}(K, N, A, M) = C$. Moreover, encryption must be length regular, i.e., we assume a function $\text{cl}(\cdot, \cdot)$ such that $|C| = \text{cl}(|A|, |M|)$ for any C returned by $\text{E}(\cdot, \cdot, A, M)$.

2.1   The Duplex

The Duplex is a construction similar to the Sponge that is based on some public permutation p over b-bit strings. A user can interact with the Duplex either via an initialisation call Dup.init or a next call Dup.next. An initialisation call starts a session which sets the initial state to some fixed value IV and processes the given input. The session can then be updated via one or more next calls. Both type of calls take an input of size r bits and return an output of r bits. The

Dup.init(X)	Dup.next(X, id)
if $\|X\| \neq r$	**if** $\|X\| \neq r$
return $\perp$	**return** $\perp$
$id \leftarrow \mathsf{GenID}$	$Y_{id} \leftarrow S_{id} \oplus \mathsf{encode}(X)$
$S_{id} \leftarrow IV$	$S_{id} \leftarrow \mathsf{p}(Y_{id})$
$Y_{id} \leftarrow S_{id} \oplus \mathsf{encode}(X)$	$Z \leftarrow \mathsf{decode}(S_{id})$
$S_{id} \leftarrow \mathsf{p}(Y_{id})$	**return** Z
$Z \leftarrow \mathsf{decode}(S_{id})$	
return (Z, id)	

Fig. 1. The Duplex construction from a public permutation p, where r is the (input) rate and encode maps the r-bit input X to $b = r + c$ bits resp. decode maps the permutation's output to r bits again. Algorithm GenID generates a unique identifier in order to be able to handle multiple sessions simultaneously.

value r is called the rate of the Duplex. A detailed pseudocode description of the Duplex is shown in Fig. 1.

The internal working of the Duplex is also described pictorially in Fig. 2. The function encode works by appending the bits 0^c to its inputs and decode reverses this operation by truncating the rightmost c bits of its input. The quantity c is known as the capacity where $c = b - r$. At any point the state of the Duplex consists of a b-bit string S. We use S_R and S_C to denote the leftmost r bits and the right most c bits of S respectively. We will slightly abuse terminology by referring to S_R and S_C as the rate component and capacity component of S.

Typically, constructions based on the Duplex will need to use some form of padding to handle variable length inputs. Our formulation of the Duplex does not consider such padding to be part of it. This increases the generality of our treatment, in that security, specifically indifferentiability, will not rely on the particular type of padding being used as long as the input is of the right size. In contrast, note that for the Sponge to be indifferentiable from a random oracle it requires a specific type of padding, even if the input size is restricted to be an integral multiple of the rate.

Finally, note that we let the Duplex support multiple sessions. We do so by extending the interface to return a session identifier after each initialisation call and require that every subsequent next call refer to a specific session. Past formulations of the Duplex could support only a single session at any point in time where an initialisation call would automatically erase the state of the prior session. In contrast our interface allows one to easily switch between sessions without having to repeat the prior inputs in order to advance the Duplex to its last state. This reflects a more realistic implementation of the Duplex that relieves its users from making unnecessary queries.

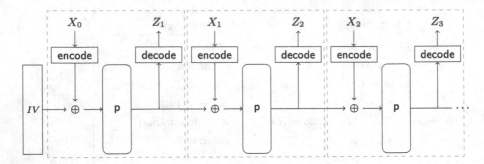

Fig. 2. Duplex based on permutation p. Note that the encoding and decoding functions in each round only access the same rate part of the intermediate state, i.e., the same bit positions, independent of the round. Subscripts in inputs and outputs denote the number of p applications which have been made so far.

2.2   Prior Security Treatments of the Duplex

The Duplex construction first appeared in [12] as a way of 'duplexing' the Sponge in order to realise *one-pass* AEAD schemes, like SpongeWrap, from public permutations. The crucial observation behind the design of the Duplex was that a call to Duplex could be mapped to a call to the Sponge, thereby reducing an instance of the Duplex to a sequence of Sponge calls. This was stated as the Duplexing-Sponge lemma (cf. [12, Lemma 3]), and was then used to analyse the AEAD security of SpongeWrap. Namely, in the AEAD game, Duplex queries were translated to Sponge queries to allow for an analysis of SpongeWrap in the random oracle model. The result was then translated to the random permutation model by leveraging the indifferentiability of the Sponge.

While this observation was very insightful and valuable in leading to the creation of the Duplex, there are significant limitations in resting the security of the Duplex on this approach. To begin with, it lacks a compact and intuitive security definition for the Duplex. This limits our understanding of the Duplex as well as our ability to use it correctly and securely. For instance, there are fundamental differences between the Duplex and the Sponge, which are easy to overlook if we restrict ourselves to think of the former in terms of the latter. One case in point is the fact that the Duplex is a stateful construction whereas the Sponge is in contrast stateless. Moreover, mapping from Duplex to Sponge introduces an additional step in the analysis which adds unnecessarily to its complexity. Secondly, by viewing the Duplex in terms of the Sponge we are implicitly imposing any limitation that may be specific to the Sponge onto the Duplex. For instance, a subtle condition for this mapping work is the inclusion of 'Sponge-compliant' padding in *every* permutation call within the Duplex— see [12,13] for details. While such padding is necessary in the case of the Sponge for indifferentiability to hold true, as we will show, this turns out not to be the case for the Duplex.

Subsequent works on the Duplex, namely [20,22,35,36], have focused on the Full-State Keyed Duplex (FSKD)—a variant of the Duplex which is always keyed and that can admit inputs covering the full width b of the permutation. Exploiting the fact that this primitive is always keyed, these treatments focus on security in terms of *indistinguishability*. An overview of the Duplex variants and their security in the sense of indistinguishability can be found in [35]. Instead we focus here on the *indifferentiability* of the Duplex. As mentioned before, indifferentiability is impossible to achieve for the full-state keyed Duplex.

2.3   Other Related Work

Barbosa and Farshim have introduced the notion of indifferentiable Authenticated Encryption (iAE) [5]. Moreover they show that indifferentiable Authenticated Encryption automatically guarantees security against Key-Dependent Messages, Related-Key Attacks, and is committing. They present two ideal functionalities for AEAD corresponding to the offline and online syntaxed. Both are based on random injections, as introduced by Rogaway and Shrimpton [39]. Both idealisations, have appealing properties but they also result in rather strong objects. Unfortunately, as we explain in Sect. 7.2, it is not possible for a Duplex-based single-pass AEAD scheme, like SpongeWrap, to be indifferentiable from either of these functionalities. Our work addresses this gap by showing that SpongeWrap achieves these advanced security properties based on the indifferentiability of the Duplex, even if SpongeWrap is itself not iAE secure.

3   The Online Random Oracle

We propose the *Online Random Oracle* (ORO) as an idealisation of the Duplex construction. This functionality is similar in spirit to the Ideal Extendible Input Function (IXIF) described in [20] for the Full-State Keyed Duplex. However, there are some important differences between the two—which we explain below. As the name suggests, the ORO functionality can be viewed as an online adaptation of the well-known random oracle functionality. A *session* is initiated with a call to ORO.init, after which the input and output of the ORO can be extended by r bits at a time via calls to ORO.next. The ORO is not forgetful, in the sense that distinct sessions are subject to the condition that a common prefix across their input sequences will result in a common prefix in their corresponding output sequences. A pseudocode description of the online random oracle is presented in Fig. 3. Internally, for each session id, the corresponding input sequence is mapped to a path (a string) P_{id}, where for each path a corresponding output is sampled uniformly at random and stored in a table.

ORO.init(X)	ORO.next(X, id)
if $\lvert X \rvert \neq r$	**if** $\lvert X \rvert \neq r$
return $\perp$	**return** $\perp$
$id \leftarrow$ GenID	$P_{id} \leftarrow P_{id} \parallel X$
$P_{id} \leftarrow X$	**if** Tab$[P_{id}] = \perp$
if Tab$[P_{id}] = \perp$	Tab$[P_{id}] \leftarrow \{0,1\}^r$
Tab$[P_{id}] \leftarrow \{0,1\}^r$	**return** Tab$[P_{id}]$
return (Tab$[P_{id}], id$)	

Fig. 3. A lazy-sampled view of the Online Random Oracle functionality. Here, r is the input and output size and Tab is a table, initialized as empty by setting all entries to $\perp$. Algorithm GenID generates a unique identifier to support multiple sessions.

Sessions and Identifiers. Unlike a random oracle, the ORO is a stateful object which introduces some additional complexity in modelling it as a shared resource. Namely the output to a query depends on prior queries and when shared among multiple algorithms we need to ensure that the queries of one algorithm do not interfere with another algorithm's queries. We use sessions precisely to circumvent this issue. At each ORO.init call a unique session identifier is created and returned together with the output. A session identifier is simply a string and we do not impose any further restriction on its format except the existence of some algorithm GenID that can generate them uniquely and efficiently. Accordingly GenID can simply increment a counter value or a random string. Then in each ORO.next call the algorithm specifies which session should be updated. We require that any algorithm with access to the ORO only make ORO.next calls to session which it obtained from calls to ORO.init. Note that this requirement does not limit access to the ORO in any way, it simply ensures that distinct parties cannot interfere in each other's sessions. Moreover, all sessions, irrespective of which entity initiates them, are answered using the same randomness which can alternatively be viewed as being sampled all at once at the beginning of the game.

Differences Between the ORO and the IXIF. First let us observe that the ORO and the IXIF serve different purposes: the former one is tailored for *indifferentiability* whereas the other is intended for *indistinguishability*. Besides targeting distinct security notions, they also model different constructions. While the IXIF is intended as an idealisation of the full-state keyed Duplex, the ORO is an idealisation of the unkeyed Duplex without full-state absorption, and, accordingly, the two present different interfaces. A more subtle discrepancy is that the full-state keyed Duplex described in [20] is "phased" differently from the standard Duplex [12], in that the input is *not* inserted at the same point where the output is extracted.

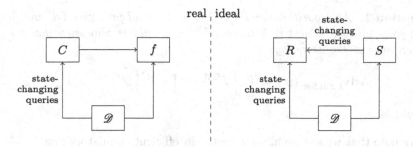

Fig. 4. Issues with stateful constructions in the indifferentiability framework: The state changes by the simulator S in the ideal world may be detectable by the distinguisher $\mathscr{D}$.

In addition to the main input the IXIF takes a flag and during an initialisation call it additionally takes a key handle and an initialisation vector. The flag determines how the internal path is constructed. If the flag is set, the path is constructed such that it also depends on the output that the IXIF returns. Otherwise the path is constructed as in the case of the ORO. The different phasing and flag introduced in [20] is meant to reflect applications where the the adversary's ability to overwrite the Duplex input is limited thereby allowing for a better security bound in such cases. Follow-up works have introduced yet other ways of phasing the Duplex, see [35] for a recent summary. In this work we stick with the original Duplex phasing and reflect the more conservative setting where the distinguisher can adaptively choose its input based on the prior output.

In the IXIF, the key handle reflects a multi-user setting where the distinguisher can query multiple instances of the IXIF—each instance corresponding to a distinct pair of key and initialisation vector. Clearly the key handle serves a very different purpose from that of a session identifier in the ORO, but they also present a different interface. In contrast to the ORO, only one IXIF instance exists at any point in time and thus one cannot progress two or more instances simultaneously. That is, any sequence of inputs to a particular instance have to be evaluated consecutively from start to end. While this is without loss of generality a construction such as NORX [4] that requires two or more simultaneous instances is forced to repeat all prior queries when switching from one instance to another.

4   Indifferentiability

In this section we recall the basic definitions of indifferentiability and discuss some peculiarities relevant to out results. Indifferentiability has been defined by Maurer et al. [34] in terms of random systems; we use here the algorithmic approach of Coron et al. [19]:

Definition 1. *An algorithm* C *with access to an ideal primitive* f *is indifferentiable from an ideal object* R *if there exists a simulator* Sim *such that for any distinguisher* $\mathscr{D}$ *the advantage*

$$\mathbf{Adv}^{indiff}_{\mathsf{C,f,R,Sim}}(\mathscr{D}) = \left| \Pr\left[\mathscr{D}^{\mathsf{C^f,f}} = 1 \right] - \Pr\left[\mathscr{D}^{\mathsf{R,Sim^R}} = 1 \right] \right|$$

is negligible.

We note that we are usually interested in efficient simulators Sim.

4.1 Indifferentiability of Stateful Constructions

Our online random oracle functionality is stateful, it keeps the path P_{id} of previous queries for next calls. Indifferentiability has so far been mostly used for stateless ideal objects such as (plain) random oracles and ideal ciphers. But the framework also allows for stateful constructions such as our online random oracle. This switch, however, may cause inconsistencies in the state of the construction if we carelessly move from the real world to the ideal world (see Fig. 4). In the real world only the distinguisher queries the construction and alters the state. In the ideal world both the distinguisher and the simulator may query the ideal object, and in most solutions the simulator actually does query the ideal primitive to ensure matching answers. But then the distinguisher may be able to detect such state changes via calls to the construction.

Consider our scenario with the online random oracle. We argue that it is necessary to distinguish between the paths under control of the distinguisher $\mathscr{D}$ and the simulator Sim, otherwise no construction can be indifferentiable. Suppose that the distinguisher $\mathscr{D}$ and the simulator Sim have access to the same instance id and state P_{id}. Then the distinguisher (in either world) first queries $\mathsf{init}(X_0)$ and then $\mathsf{next}(X_1, id)$ and $\mathsf{next}(X_2, id)$ for random X_0, X_1, X_2 to the construction oracle. Let Z be the result of the final call. Afterwards it "resets" the state of the online random oracle by another call $\mathsf{init}(X_0)$ followed by $\mathsf{next}(X_1)$ to $P_{id} = X_0 \| X_1$. Now the distinguisher makes a call $IV \oplus \mathsf{encode}(X_0)$ to the primitive oracle. Afterwards it makes a query $\mathsf{next}(X_2, id)$ to the construction oracle and then checks that it obtains once more the same result Z.

In the real world the state $P_{id} = X_0 \| X_1$ of the construction before $\mathscr{D}$'s final call $\mathsf{next}(X_2, id)$ will be sound and make the oracle return the same result Z as earlier. In contrast, in the ideal world our simulator will have changed the state to $P_{id} = X_0$ when simulating the primitive call about X_0, in order to provide a consistent answer. It is conceivable that any simulator would need to change the state, and if this happens then reconstructing the expected state $P_{id} = X_0 \| X_1$ is impossible, because the random value X_1 is unknown to the simulator. But then, with overwhelming probability, the distinguisher gets a mismatching value in the final call $\mathsf{next}(X_2, id)$.

We note that the indifferentiability framework already assumes different interfaces for distinguisher and simulator such that one could keep one state for $\mathscr{D}$ and a separate one for Sim to avoid the problems above. We have chosen the version with identifiers *id* since it is closer to real-life scenarios of various instances. In terms of our indifferentiability proof for Duplex it also allows the simulator to minimize the calls to the online random oracle to simulate answers for the primitive.

4.2   Indifferentiability and Multistage Games

Indifferentiability comes with compositional guarantees in the sense that, instead of using a construction C^f based on ideal primitive f in so-called single-stage security game, one can securely use the indifferentiable ideal construction in the game. However, as pointed out by Ristenpart et al. [38] the composition theorem of indifferentiability does not necessarily provide security for multistage security games. Following the terminology in [5] we can view multistage security games $\mathcal{G}^{C^f, \mathscr{A}_1^f, \mathscr{A}_2^f, \ldots, \mathscr{A}_n^f}$ as games in which several adversarial instances $\mathscr{A}_1^f, \mathscr{A}_2^f, \ldots, \mathscr{A}_n^f$ with access to the ideal primitive f communicate with each other (through the game) in restricted form. The problem for the indifferentiability simulator Sim is that it usually needs to keep larger state for consistent simulations of the primitive, which it may not be able to pass along if we join the simulator and adversary into a single adversary against the game according to the composition theorem.

Key-dependent message security and security against related-key attacks for AEAD schemes are two prominent examples of multistage games where the general composition results cannot be applied. For key-dependent message security the adversary can see encryptions under message which may depend on the key. In the most simple form the adversary picks a function ϕ for the encryption scheme, one applies $\phi(K)$ to the key to derive the message M, and then encrypts M under this key and returns the ciphertext to the adversary $\mathscr{A}$. In the model with ideal primitives the function ϕ (and other algorithms) may depend on f. As discussed in [26] we can then view the attack as a two-stage game in which $\mathscr{A}_1^f$ chooses ϕ^f and $\mathscr{A}_2^f$ picks the key, evaluates ϕ^f, and returns the ciphertext back to $\mathscr{A}_1$. Now we have two adversarial instances with restricted communication, such that simulating the local instances by a single simulator is infeasible (and even impossible, as [38] shows).

Barbosa and Farshim [5] discuss that one can resurrect compositional guarantees if one can virtually reduce the adversarial instances to a single stage. This is the case if only one of the adversarial instances has access to primitive f, but the other instances can only access C^f. Since the game has access to C^f, too, one can execute the other instances via the game directly. More generally, they present the following theorem:

Theorem 1 ([5, **Theorem 2**]). *Let* (C, f) *be indifferentiable from* R *via some simulator* Sim. *Let* $\mathcal{G}^{C^f, \mathscr{A}_1^f, \mathscr{A}_2^{C^f}, \ldots, \mathscr{A}_n^{C^f}}$ *be a security game for adversary* $(\mathscr{A}_1, \ldots, \mathscr{A}_n)$. *Then there exists an adversary* $(\mathscr{B}_1, \ldots, \mathscr{B}_n)$ *and a distinguisher* $\mathscr{D}$ *such that*

$$\Pr\left[\mathcal{G}^{C^f, \mathscr{A}_1^f, \mathscr{A}_2^{C^f}, \ldots, \mathscr{A}_n^{C^f}}\right] \leq \Pr\left[\mathcal{G}^{R, \mathscr{B}_1^R, \mathscr{B}_2^R, \ldots, \mathscr{B}_n^R}\right] + \mathbf{Adv}_{C, f, R, Sim}^{indiff}(\mathscr{D}).$$

For key-dependent message security we can thus guarantee composition if we let ϕ not depend on the primitive f but on the construction C^f only. Similar restrictions apply to our other applications.

5   Differentiability of Full-State Duplex

In this section we show that one cannot achieve *indifferentiability* of the full-state duplex where the round inputs X_i may affect the entire state. This is in sharp contrast to the *indistinguishability* results in [20,22,35,36] and shows that one cannot prove the stronger security guarantees of indifferentiability for this duplex version.

Recall that indifferentiability [34] allows to compare ideal objects. More concretely, assume that we have a construction C based on some ideal primitive f, like the duplex construction Dup based on the ideal permutation p. We would like to argue that the construction C^f looks like another ideal object R, say, our online random oracle ORO. The distinguisher $\mathscr{D}$ against the construction may also have access to the primitive f (and even the inverse permutation p^{-1} in case of the duplex), running an attack $\mathscr{D}^{\mathsf{C}^f,f}$. This is contrasted with the setting where $\mathscr{D}$ communicates with the ideal object R and a simulator Sim^R simulating the absent primitive in this setting. Indifferentiability then says that

$$\mathbf{Adv}^{\mathrm{indiff}}_{\mathsf{C},f,R,\mathsf{Sim}}(\mathscr{D}) = \left| \Pr\left[\mathscr{D}^{\mathsf{C}^f,f} = 1 \right] - \Pr\left[\mathscr{D}^{R,\mathsf{Sim}^R} = 1 \right] \right|$$

is negligible.

Below we argue that the full-state duplex cannot achieve indifferentiability from an online random oracle. Our result holds even under very mild assumptions, namely when the round-outputs Z_i only consists of a single bit and if $\mathscr{D}$ does not have access to the inverse permutation p^{-1}. To capture the full-state property in our generalised duplex setting we assume that for some round i, given any string $Y_i \in \{0,1\}^{r+c}$, one can (efficiently) determine an X_i such that $Y_i = \mathsf{encode}(X_i)$. In the attack below we describe for simplicity how the attack works if $i = 1$. It can be easily adapted for other values of $i \geq 1$.

Our distinguisher $\mathscr{D}^{l_1,l_2}$, described in Fig. 5, has access to two oracle interfaces, either instantiated with Dup^p and p in the real world, or with ORO and $\mathsf{Sim}^{\mathsf{ORO}}$ in the ideal world. For the analysis first assume that we are in the real world and l_1 is the duplex construction and l_2 the permutation p. Then the first call to l_1 about $X||W$ in Line 4 computes

$$\mathsf{p}(\ \mathsf{p}(IV \oplus \mathsf{encode}(X))\ \oplus \mathsf{encode}(W)\ ) = \mathsf{p}(\ Y \oplus \mathsf{encode}(W)\ )$$

such that

$$Z = \mathsf{decode}(\mathsf{p}(\ Y \oplus \mathsf{encode}(W)\ )).$$

$\mathscr{D}^{l_1,l_2}$

---

1 :   // let $X \neq X'$, W be arbitrary round inputs

2 :   query l_2 about $IV \oplus \mathsf{encode}(X)$ to get Y

3 :   query l_2 about $IV \oplus \mathsf{encode}(X')$ to get Y'

4 :   query l_1 about $X\|W$ to get Z // via two calls, init and next

5 :   compute W' with $\mathsf{encode}(W') = \mathsf{encode}(W) \oplus Y \oplus Y'$

6 :   query l_1 about $X'\|W'$ to get Z' // via two calls, init and next

7 :   output 1 iff $Z = Z'$

Fig. 5. Distinguisher $\mathscr{D}^{l_1,l_2}$ against Full-State Duplex.

The second call to l_1 in Line 6 about $X'\|W'$ is processed as:

$$\mathsf{p}(\, \mathsf{p}(IV \oplus \mathsf{encode}(X')) \,\oplus\, \mathsf{encode}(W')\,) = \mathsf{p}(Y' \oplus \mathsf{encode}(W) \oplus Y \oplus Y'\,)$$
$$= \mathsf{p}(Y \oplus \mathsf{encode}(W))$$

such that

$$Z' = \mathsf{decode}(\mathsf{p}(Y \oplus \mathsf{encode}(W))).$$

In this case both calls thus yield the same value $Z = Z'$ such that our distinguisher outputs 1.

Assume now that we are in the ideal setting and l_1 is an (online) random oracle ORO and l_2 the simulator Sim instead. Since the inputs $X\|W$ and $X'\|W'$ are distinct by assumption about $X \neq X'$, the random oracle returns the same values $Z = Z'$ with probability at most $2^{-|Z|} \leq \frac{1}{2}$. It follows that the distinguisher returns 1 with probability at most $\frac{1}{2}$ in this case. The overall advantage of the distinguisher is therefore at least $\frac{1}{2}$, showing that it successfully tells both cases apart.

While the attack we described exploits the full state absorption that happens just after the first round of the Duplex, it can be easily adapted to exploit full state absorption of the later rounds. When the full state absorption happens at the initial round, the attack can be adapted by using in addition l_2^{-1} to construct X', W' differently. Instead of choosing X' different from X and computing W' such that $\mathsf{encode}(W') = \mathsf{encode}(W) \oplus l_2(IV \oplus \mathsf{encode}(X)) \oplus l_2(IV \oplus \mathsf{encode}(X'))$, we can choose W' different from W and compute X' such that $\mathsf{encode}(X') = IV \oplus l_2^{-1}(\mathsf{encode}(W') \oplus \mathsf{encode}(W) \oplus l_2(IV \oplus \mathsf{encode}(X)))$. The attack then proceeds similarly as above with the same advantage.

6   Indifferentiability of Duplex from ORO

In this section we show, via a code-based argument, that the Duplex construction is indifferentiable from ORO.

6.1 Security Statement

As we have seen in the previous section, the security of the Duplex depends on the encoding and decoding functions. In the following we consider the basic case where all round functions are of the form $\mathsf{encode}(X) = X \parallel 0^c$ for all rounds such that the leading r bits form the rate part, and to which the input is simply added in the Duplex iterations. Each decoding function $\mathsf{decode}(S)$ truncates the capacity component and outputs the rate part of r bits in clear. Call these functions *plain*.

Theorem 2. *Let* Dup *be the Duplex construction described in Fig. 1 with plain encoding and decoding functions, composed from a random permutation* p *over* b*-bit strings, and let* c *denote its capacity. Further let* ORO *be the online random oracle with rate* $r = b - c$. *Then there exists a simulator* Sim *such that for every distinguisher* $\mathscr{D}$ *making* q_p *queries to its permutation oracle and* q_c *queries to its construction oracle, where* $q_p, q_c \leq 2^{c-2}$, *its advantage in differentiating* Dup *from* ORO *is bounded by*

$$\mathbf{Adv}^{indiff}_{\mathsf{Dup},\mathsf{p},\mathsf{ORO},\mathsf{Sim}}(\mathscr{D}) \leq \frac{(q_p + q_c + 1)^2 + 6q_p q_c}{2^c}.$$

Let $(r \cdot \ell)$ *be a bound on the maximum number of bits queried in an* ORO *session. Then for each of the* q_p *queries it receives,* Sim *runs in time proportional to* ℓ *and makes at most* ℓ *calls to the* ORO.

Proof Overview. The proof proceeds via a sequence of games, **G0**–**G7**. We start from the real-world game where the distinguisher $\mathscr{D}$ interacts with a random permutation p and the Duplex construction instantiated with this same random permutation. We then transform this game, step by step, to the ideal-world game, where the distinguisher has access to the online random oracle ORO and a simulator Sim, and argue that any two consecutive games can only be distinguished with (at most) negligible probability. Note that we build our simulator gradually as we progress through the game sequence, and accordingly we define several distinct simulator algorithms in the process. However, the simulator that the indifferentiability theorem refers to, is the one in the final game (**G7**). We also remark that the strategy of this simulator is independent of the distinguisher in question, as required by the standard notion of strong indifferentiability.

Analogous to the proof of indifferentiability for the Sponge [11], we associate to our simulator a directed graph, that evolves as $\mathscr{D}$ and Dup query the simulator. In this directed graph each node represents a string of size b, and an edge (U, V) represents the mapping $U \rightarrow V$. Accordingly, a forward query to the simulator on input U returns V, denoted as $V \leftarrow \mathsf{Sim}(U, +)$, and similarly, an inverse query to the simulator on input V returns U, denoted as $U \leftarrow \mathsf{Sim}(V, -)$. The simulator maintains this directed graph in a data structure G, where for any node U, $\mathsf{G.in}(U)$ identifies the predecessor of U and $\mathsf{G.out}(U)$ its successor. From this directed graph of input-output mappings, we can derive a second directed graph, which we refer to as the *capacity graph*, by collapsing all nodes sharing the same capacity component into a single node identified by that capacity component. The simulator will ensure that no two adjacent nodes share the same capacity component, and thus all edges in the graph of input-output mappings will transfer to the capacity graph. The reason we care about the capacity graph is that every session evaluated by the Duplex will correspond to a unique path on the capacity graph. More specifically, calls to $\mathsf{Dup}^{\mathsf{Sim}}$ will result in a directed tree, rooted at IV_C, where each session corresponds to a path between the root and a leaf node. Consequently, the simulator must ensure that if the queries it receives from $\mathscr{D}$ correspond to edges on this tree they must be consistent with the online random oracle as otherwise $\mathscr{D}$ would be able to differentiate the real world from the ideal world. To accomplish this, our simulator will maintain its own copy of this tree and only extend it through forward $(+)$ queries for which the queried node is already in the tree and then add a freshly sampled node adjacent to the queried node. The ability to detect when a query extends a path in the tree allows the simulator to recover the path corresponding to the relevant session on the online random oracle and sample the new node consistently with it. In addition the simulator will ensure that queries involving nodes outside the tree and inverse queries do not interfere with the tree structure.

A key requirement of the simulator is that it needs to simulate p from ORO without any knowledge of $\mathscr{D}$'s queries to ORO. A natural approach to prove indifferentiability, which is also the approach we adopt, is to start from p and transform it gradually into the desired simulator. However in the real world p has an interface to the construction which indirectly informs it of the distinguisher's queries to the construction. Consequently, the central challenge in the proof, when transitioning from p to the final simulator, is in dropping the simulator's interface to the construction. The reason this is problematic is that removing the construction interface can alter the simulator's internal state, as it is no longer affected by the distinguisher's queries to the construction. This was also noted in [17], pointing out that the original indifferentiability proof of the Sponge [11] overlooked this step. In turn, [17] provided its own indifferentiability proof of the Sponge. We note, however, that we handle this transition quite differently from [17], and, in fact, our proof strategy turns out to be significantly different from that in [17] or [11]. Moreover, we are obviously considering a different construction (the Duplex instead of the Sponge) from these prior works, and, because we adopt a code-based proof approach, we also delve deeper into the implementation details of the simulator which allows us to better quantify its resources.

Below is an outline of the game transitions in our proof. Some of the games have a boxed (or unboxed) variant which is a reformulation of the prior game that is mainly intended for better exposition. In this outline we only list the game variant in which the substantive alteration occurs.

Game G0: This is the real-world game where the distinguisher $\mathscr{D}$ is given access to the Duplex $\mathsf{Dup}^{\mathsf{p}}$ via its construction oracle, as well as direct oracle access to the random permutation p.

Game G1: In this game, instead of sampling the random permutation at the start of the game we implement p through lazy-sampling where we store the input-output mappings as a directed graph in the data structure G. As this is merely a syntactic change, **G**0 and **G**1 are perfectly indistinguishable.

Game G2: We now replace p with a simulator Sim_{fc} that samples nodes in the graph according to a different distribution. Specifically, it ensures that all sampled nodes have a *fresh capacity component* and samples the rate component uniformly at random. To accomplish this, Sim_{fc} maintains a list C of the capacity component of every node that is added to G and IV_C, and samples the capacity component uniformly from the set $\{0,1\}^c \setminus \mathsf{C}$.

Note that distinct nodes in G can still share the same capacity component, as queried nodes are also added to G and there is no restriction on which nodes can be queried. However this modification ensures that no two adjacent nodes share the same capacity component and consequently the capacity graph contains no loops. Moreover since all sampled nodes have a fresh capacity component, there will also be no cycles in the capacity graph.

We also introduce some labeling that leaves the game functionally unaltered, but which will become handy later on. Everytime a node is added to G, we mark it with '\$' or '*' to indicate whether the node was added via sampling or as a query input, respectively. Note that, due to the fresh-capacity sampling, for each capacity component stored in C there exists at most one node with that capacity component and the mark \$. We call such a node the *representative* of that capacity component and we additionally store it alongside each entry in C (if it exists).

Game G3: We now adapt the simulator's behaviour to take into account the interface from which it receives a query. We do so by providing two separate interfaces: Sim_p which handles direct primitive queries from the distinguisher, and Sim_c which handles internal calls from the construction. We also introduce new labelling and in this game the interface-dependent behaviour of the simulator differs only in how this labelling is applied. Every node that is added to G is additionally labelled with 'd' or 't', where 't' represents nodes on a computation path of the duplex (starting with "root" IV and potentially branching of from an earlier computation path, thus forming a tree of paths), and 'd' marks disconnected nodes through direct primitive queries. This labelling extends to the corresponding entries in C and is applied as follows. Nodes added by Sim_c are always labelled with 't', whereas nodes added by Sim_p are labelled with 'd' except when (1) there already exists another node in G with the same capacity component labelled 't', or (2) the node's predecessor is labelled 't'. In addition the node IV is labelled 't' before any query is made.

Through this labelling we have effectively subdivided C into two disjoint sets C_d and C_t. Thus, the capacity graph can now be subdivided into two subgraphs whose nodes correspond to these two sets. Of particular note is the capacity subgraph corresponding to C_t, which represents Duplex evaluations carried out by the distinguisher either through its construction oracle or computed locally via its primitive oracle. Specifically, this capacity subgraph is a directed tree (hence the label 't') with IV_C as its root, and every path from the root to any other node corresponds to a unique sequence of Duplex queries. While the two subgraphs can be connected in general, edges can only be directed from C_d to C_t and not vice versa.

At this point we have a two-part simulator which imposes enough structure on the graph to allow it to discern queries that relate to a Duplex session from ones that do not. In the remaining game transitions we further separate Sim_p from Sim_c, and we gradually transform Dup^{Sim_c} into the ORO and Sim_p into our final simulator.

Game G4: In this game we introduce an ORO instance, but we only make it accessible to the simulator and not the distinguisher. That is, the construction oracle continues to be the Duplex construction, which makes primitive queries to the simulator, which in turn can now query the ORO. The simulator will now use the ORO to sample the rate component of nodes labelled ($\$$,t) rather than sampling them uniformly at random. The sampling of the capacity components remains unchanged.

Now, every node labelled ($\$$,t) corresponds to a distinct node in the tree within the capacity graph. In turn every node in the tree identifies a distinct sequence of Duplex queries determined by the path from the root to that node. Thus, for every new node labelled ($\$$,t) the simulator will determine this sequence of Duplex queries, submit them to the ORO, and assign its final output as the rate component of that node. Intuitively, we have adjusted the simulator to sample the nodes in the graph so that the output of the Duplex matches that of the ORO. In addition, we have not altered the output distribution of the simulator because every node identifies a distinct sequence of Duplex queries, and accordingly the corresponding ORO output is guaranteed to be uniformly distributed.

Game G5: In the previous game we have aligned the output of the construction oracle with the ORO. Looking ahead, we ultimately want that the current combination of the Duplex accessing Sim_p which in turn accesses the ORO be replaced with the ORO directly. Although the construction oracle is already reproducing the output of the ORO, we are not yet ready to make this swap. The main reason is that Sim_c and Sim_p share memory, and thus the presence of Sim_c heavily affects the operation of Sim_p. In this and the next game hop, we work towards lifting the influence that Sim_c has on Sim_p in preparation for that last step.

In this game we make four main changes. The first one is that we remove any internal calls that Sim_p makes to Sim_c, so that they are separate algorithms, although they still share memory. The second change is to let Sim_p keep track of "its own copy" of C_t. Technically, we introduce another label p to identify the nodes marked 't' that are sampled by Sim_p. We store the capacity components of these nodes in a new data structure L_p, initialised to $\{IV_C\}$, and it clearly follows that $L_p \subseteq C_t$. Moreover the set $C_t \setminus L_p$ identifies the capacity components of the nodes sampled by Sim_c. The third change is that we replace the lines which test for membership in C_t with a membership test in L_p. This change makes partial progress in making Sim_p rely on the data that it generates itself. The fourth, and perhaps the most important part of this game hop, is to limit the possibility of Sim_p outputting a node with a capacity component contained in $\mathsf{L}_p \subseteq \mathsf{C}_t$. The most direct way in which the distinguisher can cause this, is by reproducing the internal Duplex calls corresponding to prior construction queries. To avoid this, we change Sim_p so that it overwrites these capacity components, previously set by Sim_c, by resampling them anew. Since construction queries do not reveal the capacity components of the nodes that they sample, this resampling will ensure that they remain hidden from the distinguisher with high probability. As a result of this modification, the distinguisher will then be unlikely to query these values to Sim_p. The technical challenge of this game hop lies in showing that this resampling leaves the distribution of Sim_p's outputs largely unaffected.

Game G6: We now adjust the sampling procedures in Sim_p so that it is not affected by data structures which Sim_c writes to. More specifically, it will now sample capacity components from $\{0,1\}^c \setminus \mathsf{C}_d \cup \mathsf{L}_p$ instead of $\{0,1\}^c \setminus \mathsf{C}$. Note that we now sample from a slightly larger set, and by using the fundamental lemma of game playing, it can be shown that this modification is only detectable if at any point the sampled value lies in their set difference, i.e., $\mathsf{C}_t \setminus \mathsf{L}_p$. This happens only with small probability.

Game G7: We are finally ready to replace the combination of the Duplex construction, Sim_c, and the ORO, directly with the ORO itself. We can make this change because at this point Sim_c is for the most part acting as a relay forwarding calls to the ORO and forwarding back its replies. The only side effect is that Sim_c adds nodes into the data structure G when forwarding queries between the Duplex and the ORO. When we replace the Duplex with the ORO these values will no longer be added to G, which is still used by Sim_p. However this would only affect the operation of Sim_p if it is ever queried on the nodes added by Sim_c. Once again, these are the nodes whose capacity components are contained in $\mathsf{C}_t \setminus \mathsf{L}_p$, and most importantly, are hidden from the distinguisher. Thus this swap will only be noticeable with negligible probability and Sim_p now serves as the final indifferentiability simulator.

The full details of the proof can be found in the full version of this paper.

7   Revisiting the Security of SpongeWrap

Having shown the Duplex to be indifferentiable from the ORO we now put this result to use by analysing the security of constructions based on the Duplex. Specifically, we can now leverage the indifferentiability of the Duplex to translate security proofs in the ORO model to security proofs in the random permutation model. One reason why this is advantageous is that we generally expect security proofs in the ORO model to be simpler and more intuitive than ones in the random permutation model. The target of our analysis will be SpongeWrap [12], which is arguably the most direct approach for constructing an AEAD scheme from the Duplex, and it also served as the basis for several other Duplex-based AEAD constructions—such as NIST's Lightweight Cryptography standard Ascon [21]. Towards proving stronger security for SpongeWrap, one avenue would be to prove it indifferentiable from one of the ideal AEAD primitives put forth by Barbosa and Farshim [5]. As shown therein, this would automatically imply that SpongeWrap retains security under related-key attacks and key-dependent messages, offers misuse resistance, and is suitable for message franking applications. Unfortunately, for reasons that we explain in Sect. 7.2, SpongeWrap, and generally most Duplex-based AEAD schemes, are unable to meet the idealised AEAD notions put forth in [5]. Nevertheless, with the exception of misuse-resistance, all security properties implied by ideal AEAD are still perfectly within reach. In the rest of this section, we show, in the ORO model, that SpongeWrap benefits from these advanced security properties and then use Theorem 2 to translate these results to the random permutation model.

7.1 A Nonce-Based Variant of SpongeWrap

SpongeWrap was introduced in [12] as a one-pass AEAD scheme based on the Duplex where its security was argued based on the indifferentiability of the Sponge. As explained in Sect. 2.2, this approach has some drawbacks. Most notably, it results in an effective security bound on the order of $\mathcal{O}(N^4)$ when the total query count entails N permutation calls. In contrast, our analysis will result in a bound on the order of $\mathcal{O}(N^2)$. This quantitative improvement is a direct consequence of basing the security analysis in the online random oracle model as opposed to the random oracle model.

A pseudocode description of SpongeWrap ($\mathsf{nSW[Dup]}$), expressed as a function of the Duplex is shown in Fig. 6, together with a pictorial description of the encryption and decryption procedures in Figs. 7 and 8. It is assumed that $\mathsf{pad}(\cdot, r-1)$ only appends bits at the end of its first input such that it constitutes an injective mapping to strings of size $a(r-1)$ for some integer $a \geq 1$. In every Duplex call, a bit is appended to each input in order to delineate the boundary between the associated data and the message and between the ciphertext and the tag. Specifically, this bit is always set to zero except for the last block of the associated data and the last block of the message. This variant of SpongeWrap differs from its original formulation in two ways. It explicitly exposes a fixed-size nonce, whereas in the original version, the associated data was required to be non-empty and non-repeating, thereby filling the role of a variable-length nonce. Thus our adaptation of SpongeWrap makes it compliant with the standard nonce-based AEAD syntax. Secondly, it does away with Sponge-compliant padding at every permutation call since it is not needed for the indifferentiability of the Duplex.

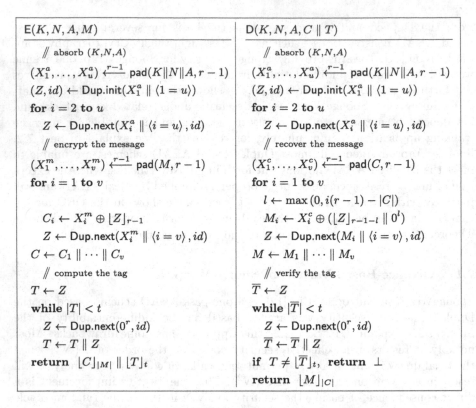

$\mathsf{E}(K, N, A, M)$	$\mathsf{D}(K, N, A, C \parallel T)$
// absorb (K,N,A)	// absorb (K,N,A)
$(X_1^a, \ldots, X_u^a) \xleftarrow{r-1} \mathsf{pad}(K\|N\|A, r-1)$	$(X_1^a, \ldots, X_u^a) \xleftarrow{r-1} \mathsf{pad}(K\|N\|A, r-1)$
$(Z, id) \leftarrow \mathsf{Dup.init}(X_1^a \parallel \langle 1 = u \rangle)$	$(Z, id) \leftarrow \mathsf{Dup.init}(X_1^a \parallel \langle 1 = u \rangle)$
for $i = 2$ **to** u	**for** $i = 2$ **to** u
$\quad Z \leftarrow \mathsf{Dup.next}(X_i^a \parallel \langle i = u \rangle, id)$	$\quad Z \leftarrow \mathsf{Dup.next}(X_i^a \parallel \langle i = u \rangle, id)$
// encrypt the message	// recover the message
$(X_1^m, \ldots, X_v^m) \xleftarrow{r-1} \mathsf{pad}(M, r-1)$	$(X_1^c, \ldots, X_v^c) \xleftarrow{r-1} \mathsf{pad}(C, r-1)$
for $i = 1$ **to** v	**for** $i = 1$ **to** v
	$\quad l \leftarrow \max\left(0, i(r-1) - |C|\right)$
$\quad C_i \leftarrow X_i^m \oplus \lfloor Z \rfloor_{r-1}$	$\quad M_i \leftarrow X_i^c \oplus (\lfloor Z \rfloor_{r-1-l} \parallel 0^l)$
$\quad Z \leftarrow \mathsf{Dup.next}(X_i^m \parallel \langle i = v \rangle, id)$	$\quad Z \leftarrow \mathsf{Dup.next}(M_i \parallel \langle i = v \rangle, id)$
$C \leftarrow C_1 \parallel \cdots \parallel C_v$	$M \leftarrow M_1 \parallel \cdots \parallel M_v$
// compute the tag	// verify the tag
$T \leftarrow Z$	$\overline{T} \leftarrow Z$
while $|T| < t$	**while** $|\overline{T}| < t$
$\quad Z \leftarrow \mathsf{Dup.next}(0^r, id)$	$\quad Z \leftarrow \mathsf{Dup.next}(0^r, id)$
$\quad T \leftarrow T \parallel Z$	$\quad \overline{T} \leftarrow \overline{T} \parallel Z$
return $\lfloor C \rfloor_{|M|} \parallel \lfloor T \rfloor_t$	**if** $T \neq \lfloor \overline{T} \rfloor_t$, **return** $\perp$
	return $\lfloor M \rfloor_{|C|}$

Fig. 6. Pseudocode description of SpongeWrap (nSW[Dup]) expressed as a function of the Duplex.

We analyse SpongeWrap with respect to KDM, RKA and context commitment security. Being already a fairly efficient scheme (it is the basis for several CAESAR candidates) it is noteworthy that nSW[Dup] achieves KDM, RKA and context commitment security without any additional overhead or assumptions. In comparison, other AEAD constructions that achieve KDM-AEAD security are the ideal AEAD constructions by Barbosa and Farshim [5] and the generic transformation by Bellare and Keelveedhi [7]. The fastest construction from [5] is a *three-pass* scheme, where each pass can be implemented via a Sponge evaluation, and the construction from [7] augments an AEAD scheme with a pre-computation step requiring a hash evaluation and re-keying the AEAD scheme for every encryption/decryption call. For RKA-AEAD security, the construction from Barbosa and Farshim [5] and the construction N* from Faust et al. [27] are both three-pass schemes. Finally, for context commitment, the different existing constructions (cf. [18, Table 2]) require an additional function evaluation that could be a hash, a MAC or a PRF.

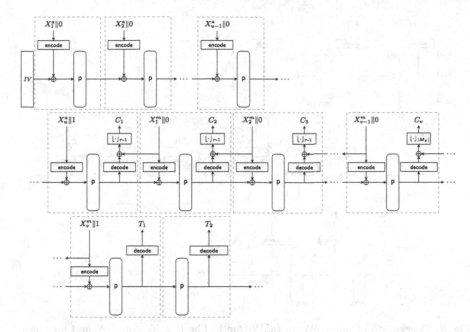

Fig. 7. Encryption of SpongeWrap (nSW[Dup]). The key K, nonce N and associated data A gets padded into u blocks as $(X_1^a, \ldots, X_u^a) \xleftarrow{r-1} \mathrm{pad}(K\|N\|A, r-1)$ and the plaintext gets padded into v blocks as $(X_1^m, \ldots, X_v^m) \xleftarrow{r-1} \mathrm{pad}(M, r-1)$ with $u, v \geq 1$.

7.2 SpongeWrap Is Differentiable from Ideal AEAD

In [5] Barbosa and Farshim put forth two ideal AEAD functionalities corresponding to the online and offline syntaxes. In broad terms, the offline functionality corresponds to a tweakable length-expanding random injection, and the online (encryption) functionality processes each call through a tweakable random injection where its output additionally yields a state that is fed back into the tweak of the next call, but its input and output are expanded to also carry a state. Being a random injection with sufficient expansion, it directly follows that the offline ideal AEAD functionality is misuse-resistant [39]. On the other hand, it is well known that a single-pass scheme, like SpongeWrap, cannot be misuse-resistant. Accordingly, indifferentiability with respect to the offline functionality is unattainable. As for the online functionality, it is not misuse-resistant when considering the aggregate ciphertext over multiple calls. However, it still guarantees that the first encryption call of two distinct messages under the same nonce-key pair will yield totally uncorrelated ciphertexts. Clearly, SpongeWrap does not meet this requirement since a repeated nonce-key pair will always xor the message with the same string.

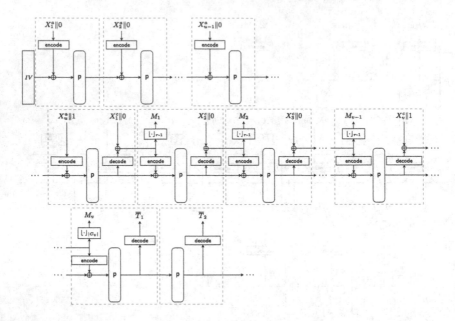

Fig. 8. Decryption of SpongeWrap (nSW[Dup]). The key K, nonce N and associated data A gets padded into u blocks as $(X_1^a, \ldots, X_u^a) \xleftarrow{r-1} \mathsf{pad}(K\|N\|A, r-1)$ and the ciphertext gets padded into v blocks as $(X_1^c, \ldots, X_v^c) \xleftarrow{r-1} \mathsf{pad}(C, r-1)$ with $u, v \geq 1$.

7.3   KDM-AEAD Security

Key-dependent-message security in the context of symmetric encryption was first studied by Black, Rogaway, and Shrimpton in [16]. Subsequently, Bellare and Keelveedhi [7] extended this security notion to nonce-based AEAD schemes. By means of generic attacks, they showed that key-dependent-data security is only possible when nonces are sampled at random and the header is independent of the key. Accordingly, only one of the four security definitions that they considered is satisfiable—reproduced here as Definition 2 and its corresponding game is described in Fig. 9. In order to constrain the nonce to be sampled uniformly at random, it is sampled by the ENC oracle and then returned to the adversary rather than being chosen directly by the adversary. Also note that the DEC oracle returns either the $\frac{1}{4}$ symbol to indicate a prohibited input, or a bit indicating whether decryption succeeded or failed. As noted in [7], this latter choice is without loss of generality.

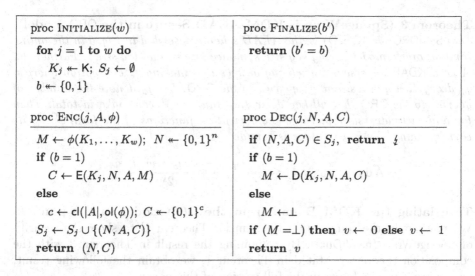

proc INITIALIZE(w)	proc FINALIZE(b')
for $j = 1$ **to** w **do**	**return** $(b' = b)$
$\quad K_j \twoheadleftarrow \mathsf{K}; \ S_j \leftarrow \emptyset$	
$b \twoheadleftarrow \{0,1\}$	

proc ENC(j, A, ϕ)	proc DEC(j, N, A, C)
$M \leftarrow \phi(K_1, \ldots, K_w); \ N \twoheadleftarrow \{0,1\}^n$	**if** $(N, A, C) \in S_j,$ **return** $\maltese$
if $(b = 1)$	**if** $(b = 1)$
$\quad C \leftarrow \mathsf{E}(K_j, N, A, M)$	$\quad M \leftarrow \mathsf{D}(K_j, N, A, C)$
else	**else**
$\quad c \leftarrow \mathsf{cl}(|A|, \mathsf{ol}(\phi)); \ C \twoheadleftarrow \{0,1\}^c$	$\quad M \leftarrow \perp$
$\quad S_j \leftarrow S_j \cup \{(N, A, C)\}$	**if** $(M = \perp)$ **then** $v \leftarrow 0$ **else** $v \leftarrow 1$
return (N, C)	**return** v

Fig. 9. The KDAE game for defining AEAD security in the presence of key-dependent messages.

Definition 2 (KDM-AEAD Security). *Let* $\mathsf{SE} = (\mathsf{K}, \mathsf{E}, \mathsf{D})$ *be an AEAD scheme with key size* k *and the* KDAE *game be as defined in Fig. 9. Further let* $\mathcal{A}$ *be any adversary whose queries are such that* $\phi : (\{0,1\}^k)^w \to \{0,1\}^{\mathsf{ol}(\phi)}$*, where the output length* $\mathsf{ol}(\phi)$ *of* ϕ *is constant and* w *is its input to* INITIALIZE*. Then its corresponding* KDAE *advantage is given by:*

$$\mathbf{Adv}^{\mathsf{kdae}}_{\mathsf{SE}}(\mathcal{A}) = 2 \cdot \Pr\left[\mathsf{KDAE}^{\mathcal{A}} \Rightarrow \mathsf{true}\right] - 1.$$

If we work with idealised schemes such as the Duplex with the permutation p then the message-derivation function ϕ, chosen by the adversary in each encryption query, may depend on the idealised primitives as well. Formally, the description of the function ϕ may entail oracle gates, where we write $\phi^{(\cdot)}$ to denote such functions. However, as noted in [38], if we allow ϕ to call p directly, then we demonstrably cannot apply the composition theorem for indifferentiability anymore. On the other hand, as pointed out by Barbosa and Farshim [5], compositional guarantees luckily still hold if ϕ only makes calls to the construction instead of direct calls to the primitive. See also Sect. 4.2 for a more comprehensive discussion. In particular, if we transfer the compositional result in [5] to our setting, it suffices to consider KDM security with respect to the online random oracle (where each function ϕ may call ORO). Then the security of SpongeWrap (nSW[Dup]) in the p-model with respect to key-derivation functions of the form $\phi^{\mathsf{Dup}[\mathsf{p}]}$ follows, where the difference in the advantages between the two settings is bounded by the indifferentiability advantage $\mathbf{Adv}^{\mathrm{indiff}}_{\mathsf{Dup},\mathsf{p},\mathsf{ORO},\mathsf{Sim}}(\mathscr{D})$ for the distinguisher $\mathscr{D}$ consisting of the security game running $\mathcal{A}^{\mathsf{Sim}}$. The KDM-AEAD security of SpongeWrap in the online random oracle model is stated formally in Theorem 3 below, and its proof can be found in the full version of this paper.

Theorem 3 (SpongeWrap is KDM-AEAD Secure in the ORO-model).
Let nSW[ORO] = (K, E, D) *be the AEAD scheme described in Fig. 6 in the online random oracle model having key size k, nonce size n, and tag size t. Further, let $\mathcal{A}$ be a KDAE adversary initialising w keys and making q_e encryption queries, q_d decryption queries, and q_o queries to the ORO. Let q_ϕ denote the number of queries to the ORO that all key derivation function ϕ can make in total. Then for any such adversary querying key-derivation functions of the form ϕ^{ORO}, its corresponding KDAE advantage is bounded by:*

$$\mathbf{Adv}^{kdae}_{nSW[ORO]}(\mathcal{A}) \leq \frac{q_e^2 + q_e q_\phi}{2^n} + \frac{wq_o + w^2}{2^k} + \frac{q_d}{2^t}.$$

Translating the KDM Bound from the ORO-model to the p-model
We now apply the composition theorem [5, Theorem 1] to show the security of SpongeWrap (nSW[Dup]). By combining the result in Theorem 3 with the composition theorem re-stated in Theorem 1, we obtain the following result, whose proof can be found in the full version of this paper.

Theorem 4 (SpongeWrap is KDM-AEAD Secure in the p-model). *Let* nSW[Dup] = (K, E, D) *be the AEAD scheme described in Fig. 6 in the p-model having key size k, nonce size n, and tag size t. Further, let $\mathcal{A}$ be a KDAE adversary initialising w keys and making q_e encryption queries, q_d decryption queries, q_p primitive queries. Let q_ϕ denote the maximum number of construction queries that all key derivation function ϕ can make in total. Then for any such adversary querying key-derivation functions of the form ϕ^{Dup}, its corresponding KDAE advantage is bounded by:*

$$\mathbf{Adv}^{kdae}_{nSW[Dup]}(\mathcal{A}) \leq \frac{q_e^2 + q_e q_\phi}{2^n} + \frac{wq_p + w^2}{2^k} + \frac{q_d}{2^t} + \frac{(q_p + \ell(q_e + q_d) + q_\phi + 1)^2}{2^c}$$
$$+ \frac{6q_p(\ell(q_e + q_d) + q_\phi)}{2^c}.$$

where $\ell \cdot r$ is a bound on the maximum input bit length made to the duplex construction during an encryption/decryption query.

7.4 RKA-AEAD Security

Related-key attacks were first introduced as a cryptanalysis tool for block cipher [15,31]. Motivated by real attacks, related-key security was then formally studied by Bellare and Kohno [8] for pseudorandom permutations and functions. From then, the notion was extended to other primitives such as encryption schemes [3] and MACs [14]. For authenticated encryption, Lu et al. [33] defined RKA security for probabilistic schemes as a combination of two security notions: indistinguishability security against related-key attacks (IND-RKA) and integrity security against related-key attacks (INT-RKA). Later, Faust et al. [27] defined an all-in-one RKA security notion for nonce-based AEAD schemes, which we reproduce in Definition 3 and denote RKA-AEAD security. This security

proc INITIALIZE	proc FINALIZE(b')
$K \leftarrow \mathsf{K}; \ S \leftarrow \emptyset$	**return** ($b' = b$)
$b \leftarrow \{0, 1\}$	
proc ENC(φ, N, A, M)	proc DEC(φ, N, A, C)
if ($b = 1$)	**if** ($\varphi, N, A, C) \in S$, **return** $\lightning$
$\quad C \leftarrow \mathsf{E}(\varphi(K), N, A, M)$	**if** ($b = 1$)
else	$\quad M \leftarrow \mathsf{D}(\varphi(K), N, A, C)$
$\quad c \leftarrow \mathsf{cl}(|A|, |M|); \ C \leftarrow \{0, 1\}^c$	**else**
$S \leftarrow S \cup \{(\varphi, N, A, C)\}$	$\quad M \leftarrow \perp$
return C	**return** M

Fig. 10. The RKAE game for defining AEAD security under related keys.

notion implies the classical all-in-one AEAD security notion from [39] by considering the identity function as the only related-key-deriving (RKD) function allowed.

Definition 3 (RKA-AEAD Security). *Let* SE $= (\mathsf{K}, \mathsf{E}, \mathsf{D})$ *be an AEAD scheme,* $\Phi \subset$ Func(K, K) *and the RKAE game be defined as in Fig. 10. Further, let* $\mathcal{A}$ *be any adversary whose queries are such that* $\varphi \in \Phi$ *and* (φ, N) *never repeats across their encryption queries. Then its corresponding* RKAE *advantage is given by:*

$$\mathbf{Adv}_{\mathsf{SE}}^{\mathsf{rkae}}(\mathcal{A}, \Phi) = 2\Pr\left[\mathsf{RKAE}^{\mathcal{A}} \Rightarrow \mathsf{true}\right] - 1.$$

In the previous definition, the RKAE advantage depends on a set Φ of related-key deriving functions. This restriction is necessary, as Bellare and Kohno [8] showed that RKA security is only achievable for restricted sets of related-key deriving functions. For the ideal cipher to be RKA secure, they showed that output-unpredictability (Definition 4) and collision resistance (Definition 5) are sufficient conditions on the set of related-key deriving functions.

Definition 4 (Output-unpredictability for Φ.). *Let* K *be a set of keys and* $\Phi \subset$ Func(K, K). *Let* r, r' *be positive integers. Then*

$$\boldsymbol{InSec}_{\Phi}^{up}(r, r') = \max_{F \subseteq \Phi, X \subseteq \mathsf{K}, |F| \leq r, |X| \leq r'} \Pr_{K \leftarrow \mathsf{K}}[\{\varphi(K) : \varphi \in F\} \cap X \neq \emptyset]$$

is defined as the (r, r')-output-unpredictability of Φ.

In the previous definition, the maximum is over all multisets F of at most r elements of Φ.

Definition 5 (Collision resistance for Φ.). *Let* K *be a set of keys and* $\Phi \subset$ $\mathsf{Func}(\mathsf{K}, \mathsf{K})$. *Let* r *be a positive integer. Then*

$$\boldsymbol{InSec}_{\Phi}^{cr}(r) = \max_{F \subseteq \Phi, |F| \leq r} \Pr_{K \leftarrow \mathsf{K}} [|\{\varphi(K) : \varphi \in F\}| < |F|]$$

is defined as the r-*collision resistance of* Φ.

Similarly as in the KDM case, when working with idealised schemes such as the Duplex with an ideal permutation p, the key-derivation functions φ, chosen by the adversary in each encryption/decryption query, can call the idealised primitive. We again write $\varphi^{(\cdot)}$ to denote such functions with access to an oracle $(\cdot)$ and $\Phi^{(\cdot)}$ to denote a set of them. To be able to leverage the indifferentiability of the Duplex from ORO and apply the composition theorem, we restrict our analysis to RKD functions that can make only calls to the construction and cannot make calls to the primitive. As shown by Albrecht et al. [2], new restrictions must be added on the set of related key-derivation functions when the key derivation function is dependent on the cipher. In the case of RKA security of the ideal cipher, they introduced the notion of oracle-independence for a set of RKD functions. We adapt this notion to the duplex construction in Definition 6 and call it query independence.

Definition 6 (Query independence for Φ^{Dup}.). *Let* K *be a set of keys and* Φ^{Dup} *be a set of related-key-deriving functions on the key space* K.
Then $\boldsymbol{InSec}_{\Phi^{\mathsf{Dup}}}^{qi}(r, r')$ *is defined as the maximum probability that for any multi-set* F *of at most* r *elements of* Φ^{Dup} *and making at most* r' *queries to the duplex construction* Dup, *when running successively all elements* φ^{Dup} *of* F *over a random input key* K, *one of the key derived by a* φ^{Dup} *hits one of the path queried to* Dup *by another or the same* φ^{Dup}, *i.e.,*

$$\boldsymbol{InSec}_{\Phi^{\mathsf{Dup}}}^{qi}(r, r') = \max_{F \subseteq \Phi^{\mathsf{Dup}}, |F| \leq r, \sum_{\varphi \in F} |\mathrm{Qry}[\varphi^{\mathsf{Dup}}(K)]| \leq r'} \Pr_{K \leftarrow \mathsf{K}} [\exists \varphi_1^{\mathsf{Dup}}, \varphi_2^{\mathsf{Dup}}$$
$$\in F, \exists P \in \mathrm{Qry}[\varphi_2^{\mathsf{Dup}}(K)], \varphi_1^{\mathsf{Dup}}(K) = [P]^K],$$

where $\mathrm{Qry}[\varphi^{\mathsf{Dup}}(K)]$ *denotes the set of queries placed to* Dup *by* φ^{Dup} *when run on input* K. *We call* $\boldsymbol{InSec}_{\Phi^{\mathsf{Dup}}}^{qi}(r, r')$ *the* (r, r')-*query independence of* Φ^{Dup}.

In the previous definition, the maximum is over all multisets F of at most r elements of Φ^{Dup}. Note that any set Φ of oracle-free related-key-deriving functions is query independent.

Similarly as in previous works analysing the RKA security of a scheme with RKD functions dependent on the cipher, when restricting the set of RKD functions to be output-unpredictable, collision resistant and query independent, we can show that SpongeWrap is RKA-AEAD secure. The RKA-AEAD security of SpongeWrap in the online random oracle model is stated formally in Theorem 5 below, and its proof can be found in the full version of this paper.

proc FINALIZE$((K_1, N_1, A_1, M_1), (K_2, N_2, A_2, M_2))$
return $(((K_1, N_1, A_1) \neq (K_2, N_2, A_2)) \wedge (\mathsf{E}(K_1, N_1, A_1, M_1) = \mathsf{E}(K_2, N_2, A_2, M_2)))$

Fig. 11. The CMT game defining context-commiting AEAD security.

Theorem 5 (SpongeWrap is RKA-AEAD Secure in the ORO-model).
Let $\mathsf{nSW[ORO]} = (\mathsf{K}, \mathsf{E}, \mathsf{D})$ *be the AEAD scheme described in Fig. 6 in the online random oracle model having tag size* t *and* Φ^{ORO} *be a set of related-key-deriving functions on the key space* K. *Further, let* $\mathcal{A}$ *be a RKAE adversary making* q_e *encryption queries,* q_d *decryption queries, and* q_o *queries to the ORO. Let* q_φ *denote the number of queries to the ORO that all key derivation function* φ *can make in total. Then for any such adversary querying key-derivation functions of the form* $\varphi^{\mathsf{ORO}} \in \Phi^{\mathsf{ORO}}$ *and never repeating a pair* $(\varphi^{\mathsf{ORO}}, N)$ *across their encryption queries, its corresponding RKAE advantage is bounded by:*

$$\mathbf{Adv}^{rkae}_{\mathsf{nSW[ORO]}} (\mathcal{A}, \Phi^{\mathsf{ORO}}) \leq \mathbf{InSec}^{up}_{\Phi^{\mathsf{ORO}}}(q_e + q_d, q_o) + \mathbf{InSec}^{cr}_{\Phi^{\mathsf{ORO}}}(q_e + q_d)$$
$$+ \mathbf{InSec}^{qi}_{\Phi^{\mathsf{ORO}}}(q_e, q_\varphi) + \frac{q_d}{2^t} .$$

Similarly as done in Theorem 4 for the KDM case, combining the composition Theorem 1 with the result from Theorem 5 yields the RKA-AEAD security of SpongeWrap in the p-model, where the related-key-deriving functions have only access to the Duplex construction.

7.5   CMT-AEAD Security

Following previous works on commitment of authenticated encryption schemes [1,23,25,28], Bellare and Hoang [6] proposed multiple security notions for committing AEAD. The strongest notion for tidy AEAD schemes, denoted CMT-3 originally, and called context-committing here, is reproduced in Definition 7 with its associated game in Fig. 11. It says that the adversary wins if it creates distinct inputs to the AEAD scheme resulting in the same ciphertext. Since the adversary has full control over the input to the AEAD scheme, including the key, the security game only consists of the FINALIZE procedure checking the adversary's choice for a collision.

Definition 7 (CMT-AEAD Security). *Let* $\mathsf{SE} = (\mathsf{K}, \mathsf{E}, \mathsf{D})$ *be an AEAD scheme and the CMT game be as defined in Fig. 11. Then the CMT advantage of an adversary* $\mathcal{A}$ *is given by:*

$$\mathbf{Adv}^{cmt}_{\mathsf{SE}} (\mathcal{A}) = \Pr \left[\mathsf{CMT}^{\mathcal{A}} \Rightarrow \mathsf{true} \right] .$$

CMT-AEAD security notably implies r-BIND security [28], making CMT-AEAD secure schemes suitable for message franking applications. The CMT-AEAD security of SpongeWrap in the online random oracle model stated in Theorem 6, follows immediately from the collision resistance of ORO, assuming a sufficiently long tag. The proof of the following theorem can be found in the full version of this paper.

Theorem 6 (SpongeWrap is CMT-AEAD Secure in the ORO-model). *Let* $\mathsf{nSW[ORO]} = (\mathsf{K}, \mathsf{E}, \mathsf{D})$ *be the AEAD scheme described in Fig. 6 in the online random oracle model and having tag size* t. *Further, let* $\mathcal{A}$ *be a* CMT *adversary making* q_o *oracle queries to the* ORO. *Then for any such adversary, its corresponding* CMT *advantage is bounded by:*

$$\mathbf{Adv}^{\mathsf{cmt}}_{\mathsf{nSW[ORO]}}(\mathcal{A}) \leq \frac{q_o^2}{2^{t+1}}.$$

As CMT-AEAD security is modelled as a single-stage game, simply combining the composition Theorem 1 with the result from Theorem 6 yields the CMT-AEAD security of SpongeWrap in the p-model.

Acknowledgments. We thank Aishwarya Thiruvengadam for her input during earlier stages of this work. We are grateful to the anonymous ASIACRYPT 2023 reviewers for their constructive comments. This research was supported by the German Federal Ministry of Education and Research and the Hessen State Ministry for Higher Education, Research and the Arts within their joint support of the National Research Center for Applied Cybersecurity ATHENE.

References

1. Albertini, A., Duong, T., Gueron, S., Kölbl, S., Luykx, A., Schmieg, S.: How to abuse and fix authenticated encryption without key commitment. In: Butler, K.R.B., Thomas, K. (eds.) USENIX Security 2022, pp. 3291–3308. USENIX Association (2022)
2. Albrecht, M.R., Farshim, P., Paterson, K.G., Watson, G.J.: On cipher-dependent related-key attacks in the ideal-cipher model. In: Joux, A. (ed.) FSE 2011. LNCS, vol. 6733, pp. 128–145. Springer, Heidelberg (2011). https://doi.org/10.1007/978-3-642-21702-9_8
3. Applebaum, B., Harnik, D., Ishai, Y.: Semantic security under related-key attacks and applications. In: Innovations in Computer Science - ICS 2011, pp. 45–60 (2011)
4. Aumasson, J.P., Jovanovic, P., Neves, S.: NORX: parallel and scalable AEAD. In: Kutylowski, M., Vaidya, J. (eds.) ESORICS 2014, Part II. LNCS, vol. 8713, pp. 19–36. Springer, Heidelberg (2014). https://doi.org/10.1007/978-3-319-11212-1_2
5. Barbosa, M., Farshim, P.: Indifferentiable authenticated encryption. In: Shacham, H., Boldyreva, A. (eds.) CRYPTO 2018, Part I. LNCS, vol. 10991, pp. 187–220. Springer, Heidelberg (2018). https://doi.org/10.1007/978-3-319-96884-1_7
6. Bellare, M., Hoang, V.T.: Efficient schemes for committing authenticated encryption. In: Dunkelman, O., Dziembowski, S. (eds.) EUROCRYPT 2022, Part II. LNCS, vol. 13276, pp. 845–875. Springer, Heidelberg (2022). https://doi.org/10.1007/978-3-031-07085-3_29

7. Bellare, M., Keelveedhi, S.: Authenticated and misuse-resistant encryption of key-dependent data. In: Rogaway, P. (ed.) CRYPTO 2011. LNCS, vol. 6841, pp. 610–629. Springer, Heidelberg (2011). https://doi.org/10.1007/978-3-642-22792-9_35
8. Bellare, M., Kohno, T.: A theoretical treatment of related-key attacks: RKA-PRPs, RKA-PRFs, and applications. In: Biham, E. (ed.) EUROCRYPT 2003. LNCS, vol. 2656, pp. 491–506. Springer, Heidelberg (2003). https://doi.org/10.1007/3-540-39200-9_31
9. Bellare, M., Rogaway, P.: Random oracles are practical: a paradigm for designing efficient protocols. In: Denning, D.E., Pyle, R., Ganesan, R., Sandhu, R.S., Ashby, V. (eds.) ACM CCS 93, pp. 62–73. ACM Press (1993). https://doi.org/10.1145/168588.168596
10. Bellare, M., Rogaway, P.: The security of triple encryption and a framework for code-based game-playing proofs. In: Vaudenay, S. (ed.) EUROCRYPT 2006. LNCS, vol. 4004, pp. 409–426. Springer, Heidelberg (2006). https://doi.org/10.1007/11761679_25
11. Bertoni, G., Daemen, J., Peeters, M., Van Assche, G.: On the indifferentiability of the sponge construction. In: Smart, N.P. (ed.) EUROCRYPT 2008. LNCS, vol. 4965, pp. 181–197. Springer, Heidelberg (2008). https://doi.org/10.1007/978-3-540-78967-3_11
12. Bertoni, G., Daemen, J., Peeters, M., Van Assche, G.: Duplexing the sponge: single-pass authenticated encryption and other applications. In: Miri, A., Vaudenay, S. (eds.) SAC 2011. LNCS, vol. 7118, pp. 320–337. Springer, Heidelberg (2012). https://doi.org/10.1007/978-3-642-28496-0_19
13. Bertoni, G., Daemen, J., Peeters, M., Van Assche, G., Van Keer, R.: Ketje v2. Submission to the CAESAR Competition (2016). https://keccak.team/files/Ketjev2-doc2.0.pdf
14. Bhattacharyya, R., Roy, A.: Secure message authentication against related-key attack. In: Moriai, S. (ed.) FSE 2013. LNCS, vol. 8424, pp. 305–324. Springer, Heidelberg (2014). https://doi.org/10.1007/978-3-662-43933-3_16
15. Biham, E.: New types of cryptanalytic attacks using related keys (extended abstract). In: Helleseth, T. (ed.) EUROCRYPT'93. LNCS, vol. 765, pp. 398–409. Springer, Heidelberg (1994). https://doi.org/10.1007/3-540-48285-7_34
16. Black, J., Rogaway, P., Shrimpton, T.: Encryption-scheme security in the presence of key-dependent messages. In: Nyberg, K., Heys, H.M. (eds.) SAC 2002. LNCS, vol. 2595, pp. 62–75. Springer, Heidelberg (2003). https://doi.org/10.1007/3-540-36492-7_6
17. Canteaut, A., Fuhr, T., Naya-Plasencia, M., Paillier, P., Reinhard, J.R., Videau, M.: A unified indifferentiability proof for permutation- or block cipher-based hash functions. Cryptology ePrint Archive, Report 2012/363 (2012). https://eprint.iacr.org/2012/363
18. Chan, J., Rogaway, P.: On committing authenticated-encryption. In: Atluri, V., Di Pietro, R., Jensen, C.D., Meng, W. (eds.) ESORICS 2022, Part II. LNCS, vol. 13555, pp. 275–294. Springer, Heidelberg (2022). https://doi.org/10.1007/978-3-031-17146-8_14
19. Coron, J.S., Dodis, Y., Malinaud, C., Puniya, P.: Merkle-Damgård revisited: how to construct a hash function. In: Shoup, V. (ed.) CRYPTO 2005. LNCS, vol. 3621, pp. 430–448. Springer, Heidelberg (2005). https://doi.org/10.1007/11535218_26
20. Daemen, J., Mennink, B., Assche, G.V.: Full-state keyed duplex with built-in multi-user support. In: Takagi, T., Peyrin, T. (eds.) ASIACRYPT 2017, Part II. LNCS, vol. 10625, pp. 606–637. Springer, Heidelberg (2017). https://doi.org/10.1007/978-3-319-70697-9_21

21. Dobraunig, C., Eichlseder, M., Mendel, F., Schläffer, M.: Ascon v1.2. Submission to the CAESAR Competition (2016). http://competitions.cr.yp.to/round3/asconv12.pdf
22. Dobraunig, C., Mennink, B.: Leakage resilience of the duplex construction. In: Galbraith, S.D., Moriai, S. (eds.) ASIACRYPT 2019, Part III. LNCS, vol. 11923, pp. 225–255. Springer, Heidelberg (2019). https://doi.org/10.1007/978-3-030-34618-8_8
23. Dodis, Y., Grubbs, P., Ristenpart, T., Woodage, J.: Fast message franking: from invisible salamanders to encryptment. In: Shacham, H., Boldyreva, A. (eds.) CRYPTO 2018, Part I. LNCS, vol. 10991, pp. 155–186. Springer, Heidelberg (2018). https://doi.org/10.1007/978-3-319-96884-1_6
24. Dodis, Y., Pointcheval, D., Ruhault, S., Vergnaud, D., Wichs, D.: Security analysis of pseudo-random number generators with input: /dev/random is not robust. In: Sadeghi, A.R., Gligor, V.D., Yung, M. (eds.) ACM CCS 2013, pp. 647–658. ACM Press (2013). https://doi.org/10.1145/2508859.2516653
25. Farshim, P., Orlandi, C., Roşie, R.: Security of symmetric primitives under incorrect usage of keys. IACR Trans. Symm. Cryptol. 2017(1), 449–473 (2017). https://doi.org/10.13154/tosc.v2017.i1.449-473
26. Farshim, P., Procter, G.: The related-key security of iterated even-mansour ciphers. In: Leander, G. (ed.) FSE 2015. LNCS, vol. 9054, pp. 342–363. Springer, Heidelberg (2015). https://doi.org/10.1007/978-3-662-48116-5_17
27. Faust, S., Krämer, J., Orlt, M., Struck, P.: On the related-key attack security of authenticated encryption schemes. In: Security and Cryptography for Networks: 13th International Conference, SCN 2022, Amalfi (SA), Italy, September 12–14, 2022, Proceedings, pp. 362–386. Springer (2022)
28. Grubbs, P., Lu, J., Ristenpart, T.: Message franking via committing authenticated encryption. In: Katz, J., Shacham, H. (eds.) CRYPTO 2017, Part III. LNCS, vol. 10403, pp. 66–97. Springer, Heidelberg (2017). https://doi.org/10.1007/978-3-319-63697-9_3
29. Hamburg, M.: The STROBE protocol framework. Cryptology ePrint Archive, Report 2017/003 (2017). https://eprint.iacr.org/2017/003
30. Kelsey, J., Chang, S.J., Perlner, R.: SHA-3 derived functions: cSHAKE, KMAC, TupleHash, and ParallelHash. NIST SP 800–185 (2016). https://nvlpubs.nist.gov/nistpubs/SpecialPublications/NIST.SP.800-185.pdf
31. Knudsen, L.R.: Cryptanalysis of loki91. In: Advances in Cryptology - AUSCRYPT 1992, vol. 718, pp. 196–208 (1992). https://doi.org/10.1007/3-540-57220-1_62
32. Len, J., Grubbs, P., Ristenpart, T.: Partitioning oracle attacks. In: Bailey, M., Greenstadt, R. (eds.) USENIX Security 2021, pp. 195–212. USENIX Association (2021)
33. Lu, X., Li, B., Jia, D.: KDM-CCA security from RKA secure authenticated encryption. In: Oswald, E., Fischlin, M. (eds.) EUROCRYPT 2015, Part I. LNCS, vol. 9056, pp. 559–583. Springer, Heidelberg (2015). https://doi.org/10.1007/978-3-662-46800-5_22
34. Maurer, U.M., Renner, R., Holenstein, C.: Indifferentiability, impossibility results on reductions, and applications to the random oracle methodology. In: Naor, M. (ed.) TCC 2004. LNCS, vol. 2951, pp. 21–39. Springer, Heidelberg (2004). https://doi.org/10.1007/978-3-540-24638-1_2
35. Mennink, B.: Understanding the duplex and its security. Cryptology ePrint Archive, Report 2022/1340 (2022). https://eprint.iacr.org/2022/1340

36. Mennink, B., Reyhanitabar, R., Vizár, D.: Security of full-state keyed sponge and duplex: applications to authenticated encryption. In: Iwata, T., Cheon, J.H. (eds.) ASIACRYPT 2015, Part II. LNCS, vol. 9453, pp. 465–489. Springer, Heidelberg (2015). https://doi.org/10.1007/978-3-662-48800-3_19

37. Perrin, T.: Stateful hash objects: API and constructions (2018). https://github.com/noiseprotocol/sho_spec/blob/master/output/sho.pdf

38. Ristenpart, T., Shacham, H., Shrimpton, T.: Careful with composition: limitations of the indifferentiability framework. In: Paterson, K.G. (ed.) EUROCRYPT 2011. LNCS, vol. 6632, pp. 487–506. Springer, Heidelberg (2011). https://doi.org/10.1007/978-3-642-20465-4_27

39. Rogaway, P., Shrimpton, T.: A provable-security treatment of the key-wrap problem. In: Vaudenay, S. (ed.) EUROCRYPT 2006. LNCS, vol. 4004, pp. 373–390. Springer, Heidelberg (2006). https://doi.org/10.1007/11761679_23

Populating the Zoo of Rugged Pseudorandom Permutations

Jean Paul Degabriele[1]([⊠]) and Vukašin Karadžić[2]

[1] Technology Innovation Institute, Abu Dhabi, UAE
`jeanpaul.degabriele@tii.ae`
[2] Technische Universität Darmstadt, Darmstadt, Germany
`vukasin.karadzic@tu-darmstadt.de`

Abstract. A Rugged Pseudorandom Permutation (RPRP) is a variable-input-length tweakable cipher satisfying a security notion that is intermediate between tweakable PRP and tweakable SPRP. It was introduced at CRYPTO 2022 by Degabriele and Karadžić, who additionally showed how to generically convert such a primitive into nonce-based and nonce-hiding AEAD schemes satisfying either misuse-resistance or release-of-unverified-plaintext security as well as Nonce-Set AEAD which has applications in protocols like QUIC and DTLS. Their work shows that RPRPs are powerful and versatile cryptographic primitives. However, the RPRP security notion itself can seem rather contrived, and the motivation behind it is not immediately clear. Moreover, they only provided a single RPRP construction, called UIV, which puts into question the generality of their modular approach and whether other instantiations are even possible. In this work, we address this question positively by presenting new RPRP constructions, thereby validating their modular approach and providing further justification in support of the RPRP security definition. Furthermore, we present a more refined view of their results by showing that strictly weaker RPRP variants, which we introduce, suffice for many of their transformations. From a theoretical perspective, our results show that the well-known three-round Feistel structure achieves stronger security as a permutation than a mere pseudorandom permutation—as was established in the seminal result by Luby and Rackoff. We conclude on a more practical note by showing how to extend the left domain of one RPRP construction for applications that require larger values in order to meet the desired level of security.

Keywords: Tweakable Wide-Block Ciphers · Rugged Pseudorandom Permutations · Hash-Encipher-Counter · Three-Round Feistel · Domain Extension

1 Introduction

A Rugged Pseudorandom Permutation (RPRP) is a tweakable variable-input-length cipher satisfying a security notion intermediate between a tweakable Pseudorandom Permutation (PRP) and a tweakable Strong Pseudorandom Permutation (SPRP). It was introduced in [13] where it was shown how to generically

J. Guo and R. Steinfeld (Eds.): ASIACRYPT 2023, LNCS 14445, pp. 270–300, 2023.
https://doi.org/10.1007/978-981-99-8742-9_9

convert such a primitive into nonce-based and nonce-hiding AEAD schemes that are either misuse-resistant [22] or secure under the release of unverified plaintext [3]. That work revisited the classical encode-then-encipher paradigm [5,23] and showed analogous constructions that can be instantiated with a weaker primitive—a Rugged PRP instead of a tweakable Strong PRP. Although the encode-then-encipher paradigm is more than twenty years old, it is often dismissed because variable-length tweakable SPRPs are rather inefficient to construct. However, Rugged PRPs can be constructed more efficiently, and their introduction extends the encode-then-encipher paradigm with a new set of trade-offs between security and efficiency. In addition, Degabriele and Karadžić introduced Nonce-Set AEAD as a conceptual building block from which a variety of order-resilient secure channels, such as QUIC and DTLS, can be easily realised. Indeed they presented a generic way of transforming any Nonce-Set AEAD scheme into an order-resilient channel with any desired functionality, and, in addition, it is simpler than QUIC. Thus, another application of Rugged PRPs is that they can easily be transformed into Nonce-Set AEAD schemes with the added benefit of yielding more compact ciphertexts than alternative constructions. The Authenticate-with-Nonce (AwN) construction, presented in [13], does exactly this. It outperforms other constructions by 'overloading' the use of the nonce to additionally provide authentication without introducing further redundancy in the ciphertext. Another important application of Rugged PRPs is that they suffice to construct onion encryption schemes that can be used in Tor [12].

Taking a closer look at Rugged Pseudorandom Permutations, one of their salient features is the asymmetry in the security required from the encipher and decipher algorithms. Roughly speaking, the security definition requires the encipher algorithm to be pseudorandom, but it only imposes a strictly weaker requirement on the decipher algorithm. In the security game, the adversary is given three oracles: an Encipher oracle, a Decipher oracle, and a Guess oracle. The Encipher oracle is equivalent to that in the tweakable (S)PRP games. The Decipher oracle works analogously, but the adversary is significantly restricted in what it can query to this oracle. Finally, the Guess oracle provides an alternative way of interacting with the decipher algorithm. Namely, the adversary can attempt to guess part of the output of the decipher algorithm for an input of its choice, and the oracle returns a single bit indicating success or failure. In contrast to the Decipher oracle, there are no restrictions on the adversary besides that it does not query an input for which it already knows the corresponding output of the decipher algorithm, which is necessary as it would allow for trivial win conditions. This way, the two oracles offer different tradeoffs in how the adversary can interact with the decipher algorithm. Nevertheless, the combination of these two oracles still exposes the decipher algorithm significantly less than the tweakable SPRP game—which is why the RPRP notion is strictly weaker.

As can be noted from the above, the RPRP definition is more involved than the better-known tweakable PRP and SPRP definitions, and the intuition behind it is not immediately clear. Degabriele and Karadžić state that the RPRP definition is tailored to capture the features needed by the encode-then-encipher paradigm and other transforms while at the same time being within reach of more efficient constructions. However, they only present *a single* RPRP construction, called UIV [13], which raises the question of whether this is a contrived security definition that revolves around this single construction. That is, is the abstract notion of a Rugged PRP really justified and is it natural enough for it to be instantiable by other constructions? Their work exposes several applications of RPRPs where they present several transformations for realising higher-level primitives generically from any RPRP. However, the value of their modular approach is rather limited if there exists no other instantiation thereof. In that case, we could just as well focus our attention on this single construction and ignore the security definition. Another limitation of the UIV construction, and [13] more generally, is its rigid security parameterisation. The quantitative security of the UIV construction is closely tied to the block size of the underlying tweakable blockcipher. In the AwN construction, which is used to construct order-resilient channels like QUIC and DTLS, this block size corresponds to a security budget that has to be divided between the overall bit-level security and the amount of reordering that the channel can tolerate. Accordingly, the AES-based instantiation of UIV suggested in [13], while offering good performance on hardware with AES-NI support, may be incapable of delivering the required tradeoff between (multi-user) security and tolerance to reordering that is required in practice by protocols like QUIC and DTLS.

NIST has recently renewed its interest in blockcipher modes of operation with the potential goal of standardising constructions of tweakable variable-length ciphers [19]. In this work, we take a deeper look into Rugged PRPs by revisiting their security definition and presenting new constructions that address the above limitations. Our results complement the work of Degabriele and Karadžić by making a stronger case for the general applicability of Rugged PRPs and their potential role in the upcoming NIST standardisation effort. More specifically, we make contributions in the following directions:

Security Definitions. The asymmetry between the encipher and decipher algorithms gives rise to a broader set of possibilities when applying the encode-then-encipher paradigm. Namely, one could naturally use the encipher algorithm to encrypt and decipher to decrypt, or alternatively, use the decipher algorithm to encrypt and encipher to decrypt. These correspond to the EtE and EtD transforms presented in [13], which have two variants each—yielding either nonce-based AEAD or nonce-hiding AEAD. Compared to the classical encode-then-encipher paradigm (relying on an SPRP), the restrictions on the decipher algorithm render the analysis of these transforms more challenging. A notable feature of these transforms is that their security proofs do not require all three oracles at once. More specifically, the EtE security proofs do not make any use of the Decipher oracle, whereas the EtD ones do not make any use of the Guess oracle. This prompts us to consider two natural relaxations of the RPRP notion, which were not considered in [13], but which still suffice to enable these transforms. By dropping access to the Guess oracle, we obtain the RPRPd notion, and similarly, removing access to the Decipher oracle yields the RPRPg notion. We study the relation between the three notions and present separations showing that these two relaxations result in strictly weaker notions. We will show that introducing these relaxed notions allows us to instantiate the EtE and EtD transforms with a wider class of constructions. That said, there are other applications—such as onion encryption [12]—which still require a full-fledged RPRP, and thus we do not consider our notions to be a replacement but rather a more refined characterisation.

New Constructions. We present three new variable-length tweakable cipher constructions that meet on the three Rugged PRP notions. The first construction, and the one that achieves the strongest of the three notions, namely the RPRP security, is the **H**ash–**E**ncipher–**C**ounter (HEC) construction. It is based on the HCTR construction [24], which achieves tweakable SPRP security and can be seen as a lightweight version of it. It improves over UIV by making do with just a blockcipher rather than a tweakable blockcipher and requiring only a single blockcipher key rather than two, thereby reducing the key-scheduling time. This latter aspect is beneficial, for instance, when it (or the corresponding RPRP-based AEAD scheme) is used in a ratcheted configuration where its key is updated after every message that is encrypted. The other two constructions are based on the classical Feistel construction. More specifically, they consist of three rounds of an unbalanced Feistel structure, which we refer to as **E**xpand-**C**ompress-**E**xpand (ECE) and **C**ompress-**E**xpand-**C**ompress (CEC), where the naming refers to the order in which the underlying pseudorandom functions appear in the construction. Here, we supersede the classical result of Luby and Rackoff by showing that each of these three-round Feistel constructions achieves one of the two restricted RPRP variants (each of which is strictly stronger than tweakable PRP) but not the other. We note that the Feistel constructions are not of mere theoretical interest as they can be instantiated quite efficiently, even if they require three rounds. In particular, recent work has shown efficient instantiations using permutation-based cryptography with very competitive performance [4].

Left-Domain Extension. The security definition of Rugged PRPs requires the tweakable cipher to be defined over a split domain. In [13], the authors assume a split domain of the form $\{0,1\}^n \times \{0,1\}^{\geq m}$ and refer to the two strings that compose an element in this domain as the left and right components. Indeed, their UIV construction, as well as the constructions we introduce, satisfy this syntax. In their transforms, the security of the resulting scheme is always dependent on the size of the left part of the domain n. In the UIV construction as well as our HEC construction the value of n is fixed by the block size of the underlying (tweakable) blockcipher, which is typically 128 bits. As mentioned earlier, in the Nonce-Set AEAD construction presented in [13], the value n has to be divided between the overall bit-level security and the amount of reordering that the channel can tolerate. In a setting like QUIC and DTLS, where an adversary may have multiple forgery attempts and a high degree of reordering should be tolerated, the resulting quantitative security for $n = 128$ may not be satisfactory, especially when considering multi-user security.

One advantage of the Feistel constructions, especially when instantiated with permutation-based primitives, is that they allow for a high degree of freedom in tuning the value of n. In the case of UIV and HEC, adjusting n is not as straightforward, however. Domain extension for blockciphers and tweakable blockciphers has been studied in several prior works. In HEC, there is a single blockcipher instance used throughout various parts of the construction, and replacing all instances would be rather detrimental to performance. On the other hand, in UIV, the tweakable blockcipher whose blocksize determines n is keyed with a separate key, allowing us to replace it with other constructions. We identify two suitable constructions and show how they can be used to extend the left domain of UIV and improve its security when used to construct Nonce-Set AEAD and order-resilient channels like QUIC and DTLS.

1.1 Related Work

The HCTR construction, which our RPRP scheme HEC is based on, was introduced in 2005 by Wang, Feng and Wu. A THCTR [14] is a "tweakable HCTR" construction that appeared in 2019. The authors claimed it achieves beyond-birthday-bound security. However, that was disproven in [2]. The HCTR2 construction [9] is another recent direct "descendant" of HCTR. The HCTR2 mitigates two minor bugs in HCTR specification by changing the hash function and introducing one more masking value in the construction. In addition, HCTR2 construction has a smaller key size than HCTR and a tighter bound. Minematsu and Iwata proposed a beyond-birthday-bound scheme called LargeBlock1 that is similar to HCTR [18]. A more interesting point about this construction is the extended size of the left input, which makes it related to the domain extender idea we deal with in Sect. 6. However, the LargeBlock1 construction in question is neither a tweakable cipher, nor is it VIL.

As mentioned before, the UIV construction from [13] is the only other construction proved so far to be a RPRP. It has the same number of keys as our HEC construction, though it needs one more key-scheduling setup step. The constructions are similar in the sense that both have a 2-round pass, but they differ in the underlying building blocks (e.g., UIV uses a tweakable blockcipher, HEC a blockcipher).

Using Feistel schemes to build PRPs or SPRPs is an idea that dates back to the seminal work of Luby and Rackoff [16]. Since then, there has been much work on this conceptual idea. We are interested in more recent work, namely that of [1,4]. The unbalanced Feistel schemes we present in this work closely resemble the schemes based on the three-round unbalanced Feistel that appear in those works. First of our unbalanced three-round Feistel schemes, the ECE scheme, looks similar to Deck-JAMBO [4]. The other, CEC constructions, is similar to Deck-BOREE [4] and could be seen as an abstraction of the RIV scheme [1]. However, there is one crucial distinction between our work and theirs. The target cryptographic primitive and security notion they target is AE(AD). We treat the aforementioned schemes ECE and CEC in the setting of VIL tweakable ciphers.

2 Preliminaries

Notation. For any string X we denote its length in bits by $|X|$ and ε denotes the empty string. For any integer $0 < a \le |X|$, $\lfloor X \rfloor_a$ denotes the substring consisting of the first a bits of X, and $\lceil X \rceil_a$ denotes the substring consisting of the last a bits of X. For any two integers a and b, $\langle a \rangle_2$ denotes a's representation as a binary string, and if $0 < b \le a$ we denote the falling factorial $a(a-1)\cdots(a-b+1)$ by $(a)_b$. For a real number $r > 0$, $\lceil r \rceil$ denotes the first integer that is greater than or equal to r.

For any set $\mathcal{S}$, $s \leftarrow\!\!\$\, \mathcal{S}$ denotes the process of uniformly sampling an element from the set $\mathcal{S}$ and assigning it to s. We use $\mathsf{IC}(\mathcal{K}, \mathcal{X})$ to denote the set of all ciphers over the domain $\mathcal{X}$ and key space $\mathcal{K}$. Similarly $2\text{-Func}(\mathcal{T}, \mathcal{X})$ denotes the set of all functions $\{+, -\} \times \mathcal{T} \times \mathcal{X} \to \mathcal{X}$. Sampling uniformly at random from $2\text{-Func}(\mathcal{T}, \mathcal{X})$ yields what is sometimes referred to as a two-sided random function, that can alternatively be viewed as a pair of independent random functions $\mathcal{T} \times \mathcal{X} \to \mathcal{X}$.

For an event E and process P, we denote with $\Pr[P : E]$ the probability of event E occuring after running process P.

Tweakable Ciphers. A tweakable cipher is an algorithm

$$\widetilde{\mathsf{EE}} : \mathcal{K} \times \mathcal{T} \times \mathcal{X} \to \mathcal{X}$$

that, for $(K, T) \in \mathcal{K} \times \mathcal{T}$, identifies a permutation $\widetilde{\mathsf{EE}}(K, T, \cdot)$ over the domain $\mathcal{X}$. We refer to $\mathcal{K}$ and $\mathcal{T}$ as key space and tweak space, respectively. We write the inverse of $\widetilde{\mathsf{EE}}$ as $\widetilde{\mathsf{EE}}^{-1}(K, T, \cdot)$. We define $\widetilde{\mathsf{EE}}_K(T, \cdot) := \widetilde{\mathsf{EE}}(K, T, \cdot)$ and $\widetilde{\mathsf{EE}}_K^{-1}(T, \cdot) := \widetilde{\mathsf{EE}}^{-1}(K, T, \cdot)$. One of the two classical security definitions for tweakable ciphers is the *strong tweakable pseudorandom permutation* (STPRP) security notion. Intuitively the notion implies that an adversary cannot distinguish between a STPRP-secure cipher keyed with a random key and an ideal cipher with key space $\mathcal{T}$. The definition of STPRP advantage is given below.

Definition 1 (STPRP Advantage). *Let $\widetilde{\mathsf{EE}}$ be a tweakable cipher defined over $(\mathcal{K}, \mathcal{T}, \mathcal{X})$. Then for any adversary $\mathcal{A}$ its STPRP advantage is defined as:*

$$\mathbf{Adv}_{\widetilde{\mathsf{EE}}}^{\mathrm{stprp}}(\mathcal{A}) = \left| \Pr\left[K \leftarrow\!\!\$\, \mathcal{K} : \mathcal{A}^{\widetilde{\mathsf{EE}}_K(\cdot,\cdot), \widetilde{\mathsf{EE}}_K^{-1}(\cdot,\cdot)} \Rightarrow 1 \right] \right.$$

$$\left. - \Pr\left[\widetilde{\Pi} \leftarrow\!\!\$\, \mathsf{IC}(\mathcal{T}, \mathcal{X}) : \mathcal{A}^{\widetilde{\Pi}(\cdot,\cdot), \widetilde{\Pi}^{-1}(\cdot,\cdot)} \Rightarrow 1 \right] \right|.$$

In the weaker TPRP notion the adversary only has access to the encipher oracle, and the advantage is then defined analogously.

If the tweak set is a singleton, then a tweakable cipher becomes just a *cipher*. Furthermore, if $\mathcal{X} = \{0, 1\}^n$, we call the cipher a *blockcipher*. The security notion for (block)ciphers adjust accordingly, and we denote them with PRP and SPRP.

Hash Functions. A hash function is a function

$$H : \mathcal{H} \times \{0,1\}^* \to \mathcal{Y}$$

taking as an input a hash key $h \in \mathcal{H}$ and a string $X \in \{0,1\}^*$ and outputting an element from output space $\mathcal{Y}$. In this work, we will mainly use hash functions with output space $\{0,1\}^n$.

Security. There are many security notions a hash function can satisfy. We are interested in the *almost-XOR-universal* (AXU) hash functions, the definition of which follows.

Definition 2. *Let* H *be a hash function with key space* $\mathcal{H}$ *and output space* $\mathcal{Y}$. *We call* H ϵ_1-*AXU if for all bit string pairs* (X_1, X_2), *with* $X_1 \neq X_2$, *and* $Y \in \mathcal{Y}$ *it holds*

$$\Pr_{h \leftarrow \$ \mathcal{H}} [H_h(X_1) \oplus H_h(X_2) = Y] \leq \epsilon_1.$$

PRFs. Let $FE : \{0,1\}^k \times \{0,1\}^{\geq n} \times \{0,1\}^l \to \{0,1\}^*$ be a variable-input-length (VIL) variable-output-length (VOL) function with key of size k bits. The first input is $X \in \{0,1\}^{\geq n}$ and the second input $L \in \{0,1\}^l$ is the size of output the function should produce.

We expect the function FE to behave as an independent PRF for every output length L. The PRF security definition of FE uses a VOL random function R^∞. For an input (X, L), function R^∞ outputs a uniformly random string of length L bits. Formally, the security is then defined as follows.

Definition 3. *For an adversary* $\mathcal{A}$, *the PRF advantage of VOL function* $FE :$ $\{0,1\}^k \times \{0,1\}^{\geq n} \times \{0,1\}^l \to \{0,1\}^*$ *is defined as*

$$\mathbf{Adv}_{FE}^{prf}(\mathcal{A}) = \left| \Pr \left[K \leftarrow \$ \mathcal{K} : \mathcal{A}^{FE_K(\cdot,\cdot)} \Rightarrow 1 \right] - \Pr \left[\mathcal{A}^{R^\infty(\cdot,\cdot)} \Rightarrow 1 \right] \right|.$$

We also make use of VIL functions with fixed output size. Let $FC : \{0,1\}^k \times \{0,1\}^{\geq m} \to \{0,1\}^n$ VIL function with output size n. The key is k bits long and m the minimum size of the function input.

Definition 4. *For an adversary* $\mathcal{A}$, *the PRF security of VIL function* $FC :$ $\{0,1\}^k \times \{0,1\}^{\geq m} \to \{0,1\}^n$ *is defined as*

$$\mathbf{Adv}_{FC}^{prf}(\mathcal{A}) = \left| \Pr \left[K \leftarrow \$ \mathcal{K} : \mathcal{A}^{FC_K(\cdot)} \Rightarrow 1 \right] - \Pr \left[\mathcal{A}^{R^\infty(\cdot,n)} \Rightarrow 1 \right] \right|.$$

H-Coefficient Technique. In all of the proofs in this paper, we utilize the H-coefficient technique. The H-coefficient technique [6,20] is a tool used for bounding the advantage of a computationally unbounded adversary $\mathcal{A}$, which is trying to distinguish whether it is interacting with the real or the ideal world. The adversary $\mathcal{A}$ can make oracle queries to either the real construction (in the real world) or its ideal equivalent (in the ideal world). The list of $\mathcal{A}$'s queries and corresponding answers is contained in a *transcript* τ. A transcript τ is called *attainable* if the probability that τ is generated during $\mathcal{A}$'s interaction with the ideal world is greater than 0.

A rough tutorial for the application of the H-coefficient technique goes as follows. We define what the transcript looks like. Then, one defines what it means for a transcript to be *bad*. After that, we need to calculate the probability that some transcript is bad. Finally, one should calculate the interpolation probabilities of some *good* attainable transcript appearing in the real world and it appearing in the ideal world. A transcript is called good if it is not bad. By applying the theorem we give below, one obtains a bound on the adversary's distinguishing advantage.

Letting X_r and X_i denote random variables corresponding to the transcript generated during $\mathcal{A}$'s interaction with the real and ideal world, the H-Coefficient technique is applied using the following theorem.

Theorem 1. *Let $\mathcal{A}$ be a computationally unbounded adversary trying to distinguish between a real world, represented by the game $\mathbf{G}_{\mathrm{real}}$, and an ideal world, represented by the game $\mathbf{G}_{\mathrm{ideal}}$. Let $\mathcal{T}$ be the set of all attainable transcripts and let $\mathcal{T}_{bad}$ be a set of transcripts deemed to be bad. Define $\mathcal{T}_{good} := \mathcal{T} \setminus \mathcal{T}_{bad}$. If there exist $\epsilon_{\mathrm{bad}}, \epsilon_{\mathrm{ratio}} \geq 0$ such that for all transcripts $\tau' \in \mathcal{T}_{good}$*

$$\frac{\Pr\left[X_r = \tau'\right]}{\Pr\left[X_i = \tau'\right]} \geq 1 - \epsilon_{\mathrm{ratio}} \quad and \quad \Pr\left[X_i \in \mathcal{T}_{bad}\right] \leq \epsilon_{\mathrm{bad}},$$

then it holds

$$\left|\Pr\left[\mathcal{A}^{\mathbf{G}_{\mathrm{real}}} \Rightarrow 1\right] - \Pr\left[\mathcal{A}^{\mathbf{G}_{\mathrm{ideal}}} \Rightarrow 1\right]\right| \leq \epsilon_{\mathrm{bad}} + \epsilon_{\mathrm{ratio}}.$$

3   RPRPs, Its Derivatives and Relations Among Them

The RPRP security notion for VIL tweakable ciphers over a split domain was introduced by Degabriele and Karadžić [13]. The RPRP security game they present offers the adversary access to the decipher algorithm via two oracles. One is a *"restricted" decipher* oracle DE, and the other is an oracle GU they call *guess* oracle. The game in question is given in Fig. 1 together with games RPRPd and RPRPg, which are our contributions. We present two subvariants of the RPRP game, namely these RPRPd and RPRPg games. In the RPRPd game, the adversary has access to EN and DE oracles, while in the RPRPg game, the adversary has access to EN and GU oracles. The restrictions imposed by the RPRP game are also present in the subvariant games. We aim to investigate the relations between the RPRP security notion and the security notions corresponding to the subvariants. For completeness, we reiterate the definition of RPRP advantage in the following and present analogous advantage definitions for RPRPd and RPRPg notions.

Game RPRP$_{\widetilde{EE}}^{\mathcal{A},v}$ / $\boxed{\text{RPRPd}_{\widetilde{EE}}^{\mathcal{A}}}$ / RPRPg$_{\widetilde{EE}}^{\mathcal{A},v}$

$K \leftarrow_\$ \mathcal{K}$
$b \leftarrow_\$ \{0,1\}$
$\mathcal{F}, \mathcal{R}, \mathcal{U} \leftarrow \emptyset, \emptyset, \emptyset$
$\widetilde{\Pi} \leftarrow_\$ \mathsf{IC}(\mathcal{T}, \mathcal{X}_L \times \mathcal{X}_R)$
$b' \leftarrow \mathcal{A}^{\text{EN,DE,GU}}$ / $\boxed{\mathcal{A}^{\text{EN,DE}}}$ / $\mathcal{A}^{\text{EN,GU}}$
return $b = b'$

$\text{EN}(T, X_L, X_R)$

if $b = 0$
$\quad (Y_L, Y_R) \leftarrow \widetilde{\Pi}(T, X_L, X_R)$
else
$\quad (Y_L, Y_R) \leftarrow \widetilde{EE}_K(T, X_L, X_R)$
$\quad \mathcal{F} \overset{\cup}{\leftarrow} \{Y_L\}; \mathcal{U} \overset{\cup}{\leftarrow} \{(T, Y_L, Y_R)\}$
return (Y_L, Y_R)

$\text{DE}(T, Y_L, Y_R)$

if $Y_L \in \mathcal{F} \cup \mathcal{R}$
$\quad$return $\frac{l}{2}$
if $b = 0$
$\quad (X_L, X_R) \leftarrow \widetilde{\Pi}^{-1}(T, Y_L, Y_R)$
else
$\quad (X_L, X_R) \leftarrow \widetilde{EE}_K^{-1}(T, Y_L, Y_R)$
$\quad \mathcal{R} \overset{\cup}{\leftarrow} \{Y_L\}; \mathcal{U} \overset{\cup}{\leftarrow} \{(T, Y_L, Y_R)\}$
$\quad$return (X_L, X_R)

$\text{GU}(T, Y_L, Y_R, \boldsymbol{V})$

if $((T, Y_L, Y_R) \in \mathcal{U}) \vee (|\boldsymbol{V}| > v)$
$\quad$return $\frac{l}{2}$
if $b = 0$
$\quad$return false
else
$\quad (X_L, X_R) \leftarrow \widetilde{EE}_K^{-1}(T, Y_L, Y_R)$
$\quad$return $X_L \in \boldsymbol{V}$

Fig. 1. The games used to define RPRP, RPRPd and RPRPg security for a tweakable cipher $\widetilde{EE}$.

Definition 5 (RPRP / RPRPg Advantage). *Let $\widetilde{EE}$ be a tweakable cipher over a split domain $(\mathcal{X}_L \times \mathcal{X}_R)$. Then for a positive integer v and an adversary $\mathcal{A}$ attacking the RPRP / RPRPg security of $\widetilde{EE}$ the corresponding advantage is defined as*

$$\mathbf{Adv}_{\widetilde{EE}}^{\text{rprp/rprpg}}(\mathcal{A}, v) = \left| 2\Pr\left[\text{RPRP}_{\widetilde{EE}}^{\mathcal{A},v} / \text{RPRPg}_{\widetilde{EE}}^{\mathcal{A},v} \Rightarrow 1\right] - 1 \right|.$$

Definition 6 (RPRPd Advantage). *Let $\widetilde{EE}$ be a tweakable cipher over a split domain $(\mathcal{X}_L \times \mathcal{X}_R)$. Then for an adversary $\mathcal{A}$ attacking the RPRPd security of $\widetilde{EE}$ the corresponding advantage is defined as*

$$\mathbf{Adv}_{\widetilde{EE}}^{\text{rprpd}}(\mathcal{A}) = \left| 2\Pr\left[\text{RPRPd}_{\widetilde{EE}}^{\mathcal{A}} \Rightarrow 1\right] - 1 \right|.$$

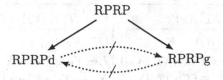

Fig. 2. Relations between RPRP notions. Solid arrows indicate trivial implications. Dotted, stroke-out arrows indicate separations.

3.1 Relations Between RPRP Notions

Now that we have defined the RPRP subvariants, we can continue showing the relations between RPRP, RPRPd, and RPRPg notions. It is obvious that RPRP security implies both RPRPd and RPRPg notions since in the games of the latter notions, the adversary has one oracle access less than in the RPRP game. Therefore, if it cannot distinguish while having access to all three oracles, it cannot distinguish having access to just two.

The interesting relations are those between RPRPg and RPRPd notions. As we will show next, neither implies the other notion. We show the RPRPg $\not\Rightarrow$ RPRPd separation in a general way. In contrast, for the other way around, we show the separation with the help of a concrete construction. In Fig. 2 we give an overview of the established relations.

3.1.1 RPRPg $\not\Rightarrow$ RPRPd.
Let $\widetilde{\mathsf{EE}}$ be a RPRPg-secure tweakable cipher and assume $k = n$. We construct a tweakable cipher $\widetilde{\mathsf{EE}}'$ that is not RPRPd secure. The cipher $\widetilde{\mathsf{EE}}'$ has the same key and tweak space, domain and range, and is defined as follows.

$$\widetilde{\mathsf{EE}}'_K(T, X_L, X_R) = \begin{cases} (0^n, 0^n), & \text{if } (T, X_L, X_R) = (0^n, K, 0^n) \\ \widetilde{\mathsf{EE}}_K(0^n, K, 0^n), & \text{if } (X_L, X_R) = \widetilde{\mathsf{EE}}_K^{-1}(0^n, 0^n, 0^n) \wedge T = 0^n \\ \widetilde{\mathsf{EE}}_K(T, X_L, X_R), & \text{otherwise.} \end{cases}$$

Now in the RPRPd game, an adversary can correctly guess the bit b by first querying $\mathrm{DE}(0^n, 0^n, 0^n)$ and taking the left output X_L as a key guess. It then checks if it is interacting with the real world by making some enciphering queries and checking if the answers are equal to the outputs it could calculate itself with the key guess.

The attack can easily be adapted to the cases where $k < n$ or $k > n$.

$\widetilde{\mathsf{EE}}'$ *is RPRPg Secure.* We argue informally why this reduction holds. Our "rewired" $\widetilde{\mathsf{EE}}'$ differs from $\widetilde{\mathsf{EE}}$ only for two values. Problematic queries are the ones where the cipher $\widetilde{\mathsf{EE}}'$ would be queried on these differing values. If the adversary does not make problematic queries, the reduction is obvious. If the adversary makes a problematic query, it could break the security of $\widetilde{\mathsf{EE}}'$. However, the probability of the adversary making a problematic query is small.

$\widetilde{\mathsf{EE}}_K(T, X_L, X_R)$	$\widetilde{\mathsf{EE}}_K^{-1}(T, Y_L, Y_R)$
$(K_1, K_2, K_3) \leftarrow K$	$(K_1, K_2, K_3) \leftarrow K$
$I \leftarrow X_R \oplus \mathsf{FE}_{K_1}(X_L, |X_R|)$	$I \leftarrow Y_R \oplus \mathsf{FE}_{K_3}(Y_L, |Y_R|)$
$Y_L \leftarrow X_L \oplus \mathsf{FC}_{K_2}(T, I)$	$X_L \leftarrow Y_L \oplus \mathsf{FC}_{K_2}(T, I)$
$Y_R \leftarrow I \oplus \mathsf{FE}_{K_3}(Y_L, |X_R|)$	$X_R \leftarrow I \oplus \mathsf{FE}_{K_1}(X_L, |Y_R|)$
return (Y_L, Y_R)	**return** (X_L, X_R)

Fig. 3. Pseudocode description of 3-round Feistel construction ECE.

The probability that the adversary queries the encipher oracle with $(0^n, K, 0^n)$ is equal to the probability that it guesses a secret random key. The probability that the adversary queries the encipher oracle with $(0^n, X_L, X_R)$, where $(X_L, X_R) = \widetilde{\mathsf{EE}}_K^{-1}(0^n, 0^n, 0^n)$ is also small, since $\widetilde{\mathsf{EE}}_K$ is by assumption indistinguishable from an ideal cipher.

As for the guess oracle, the problematic queries would be $\mathrm{Gu}(0^n, 0^n, 0^n, \{K\})$, and $\mathrm{Gu}(0^n, Y_L, Y_R, \{X_L\})$, where $(Y_L, Y_R) = \widetilde{\mathsf{EE}}_K(0^n, K, 0^n)$ and $(X_L, X_R) = \widetilde{\mathsf{EE}}_K^{-1}(0^n, 0^n, 0^n)$. Since it is by assumption hard to guess the left deciphering output in $\widetilde{\mathsf{EE}}$, the probability of the adversary making successful guess queries will be small.

Hence, the RPRPg security of $\widetilde{\mathsf{EE}}'$ reduces to the RPRPg security of $\widetilde{\mathsf{EE}}$, except for the small probability of these problematic queries occurring.   □

3.1.2 RPRPd $\not\Rightarrow$ RPRPg. In proving the separation in the other direction we do not have the generality we had in the previous case. Here we give a concrete construction and show it is RPRPd secure, but not RPRPg secure. The construction in question is an unbalanced three-round Feistel construction. We present it, together with the separation result, in the following Sect. 4.

4   3-Round Feistel Construction

For an unbalanced 3-round Feistel construction, it is natural to consider two variants. The first one is **E**xpand-**C**ompress-**E**xpand (ECE) variant, where in the first and third round, the left part is expanded and added to the right part, and in the second round, the right part is compressed and added to the left part.

The expanding and compressing are realised using a VOL PRF $\mathsf{FE} : \{0,1\}^k \times \{0,1\}^n \times \{0,1\}^l \to \{0,1\}^{\geq m}$ and VIL PRF $\mathsf{FC} : \{0,1\}^k \times \{0,1\}^{\geq m} \to \{0,1\}^n$, respectively. We sometimes call FE an *expanding* PRF, and FC a *compressing* PRF. The graphical representation of the ECE encipher algorithm is given in Fig. 4 and pseudocode description of its encipher and decipher algorithms in Fig. 3. The second variant of an unbalanced 3-round Feistel we consider is **C**ompress-**E**xpand-**C**ompress (CEC) construction, where the first and third

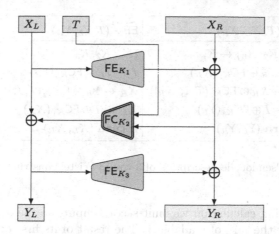

Fig. 4. Graphical representation of 3-round Feistel construction ECE, realized from expanding PRF FE and compressing PRF FC.

rounds are compressing, and the second one is expanding. The graphical representation of the CEC encipher algorithm is given in Fig. 6 and pseudocode description of its encipher and decipher algorithms in Fig. 5. The expanding PRF admits, in this case, three inputs, where the first two are the values the PRF should be evaluated on, and the third one is the output length[1].

One may wonder why only the second rounds in the constructions admit the tweak T. The reason is that in both ECE and CEC constructions, tweaking just the second round is enough to make them RPRPd and RPRPg secure, respectively. Going further, we show, as a negative result, that a three-round Feistel cipher is not a RPRP. Specifically, in the following, we present an attack against RPRPg security of the ECE variant. The same attack works in the RPRP game, where one does not use the deciphering oracle. This attack makes the first step of showing the RPRPd $\not\Rightarrow$ RPRPg separation.

ECE is not RPRPg Secure. To break the RPRPg security of ECE, the adversary $\mathcal{A}$ executes the following steps.

1. Query $(Y_L^1, Y_R^1) \leftarrow \text{EN}(T, X_L, X_R)$, with $X_L \neq X_R$.
2. Query $(Y_L^2, Y_R^2) \leftarrow \text{EN}(T, X_L, Y_R^1)$
3. Query $o \leftarrow \text{GU}(T, Y_L^1, X_R, \{Y_L^1 \oplus Y_L^2 \oplus X_L\})$
4. **output** 1 if $o = \textbf{true}$, otherwise **output** 0.

---

[1] One can equivalently write $\text{FE}_{K_2}(T, I, |X_R|)$ as $\text{FE}_{K_2}(T\|I, |X_R|)$.

$\widetilde{\mathsf{EE}}_K(T, X_L, X_R)$	$\widetilde{\mathsf{EE}}_K^{-1}(T, Y_L, Y_R)$
$(K_1, K_2, K_3) \leftarrow K$	$(K_1, K_2, K_3) \leftarrow K$
$I \leftarrow X_R \oplus \mathsf{FC}_{K_1}(X_R)$	$I \leftarrow Y_L \oplus \mathsf{FC}_{K_3}(Y_R)$
$Y_R \leftarrow X_R \oplus \mathsf{FE}_{K_2}(T, I, \lvert X_R \rvert)$	$X_R \leftarrow Y_R \oplus \mathsf{FE}_{K_2}(T, I, \lvert Y_R \rvert)$
$Y_L \leftarrow I \oplus \mathsf{FC}_{K_3}(Y_L)$	$X_L \leftarrow I \oplus \mathsf{FC}_{K_1}(X_R)$
return (Y_L, Y_R)	**return** (X_L, X_R)

Fig. 5. Pseudocode description of 3-round Feistel construction CEC.

In the following calculation we omit second inputs to the expanding PRFs, $\lvert X_R \rvert$ or $\lvert Y_R \rvert$, for the sake of readability. The result of its first query is

$$Y_L^1 = X_L \oplus \mathsf{FC}_{K_2}(T, X_R \oplus \mathsf{FE}_{K_1}(X_L))$$

and

$$Y_R^1 = X_R \oplus \mathsf{FE}_{K_1}(X_L) \oplus \mathsf{FE}_{K_3}(X_L \oplus \mathsf{FC}_{K_2}(T, X_R \oplus \mathsf{FE}_{K_1}(X_L)))$$

Similarly, the output of its second query is

$$Y_L^2 = X_L \oplus \mathsf{FC}_{K_2}(T, Y_R^1 \oplus \mathsf{FE}_{K_1}(X_L))$$

and

$$Y_R^2 = Y_R^1 \oplus \mathsf{FE}_{K_1}(X_L) \oplus \mathsf{FE}_{K_3}(Y_L^2)$$

The last query $\mathcal{A}$ makes is a guess oracle query, and $\mathcal{A}$ outputs that result as its final guess (real or ideal world). Suppose the adversary has access to the real cipher, and let us look at the guess oracle query. Left part of the deciphered input inside the Gu oracle would be

$$X_L^3 = Y_L^1 \oplus \mathsf{FC}_{K_2}(T, X_R \oplus \mathsf{FE}_{K_3}(Y_L^1)).$$

On the other hand, the guessed value is equal to

$$\underbrace{X_L \oplus \mathsf{FC}_{K_2}(T, X_R \oplus \mathsf{FE}_{K_1}(X_L))}_{Y_L^1} \oplus \underbrace{X_L \oplus \mathsf{FC}_{K_2}(T, Y_R^1 \oplus \mathsf{FE}_{K_1}(X_L))}_{Y_L^2} \oplus X_L$$

$$= Y_L^1 \oplus \mathsf{FC}_{K_2}(T, Y_R^1 \oplus \mathsf{FE}_{K_1}(X_L)) = Y_L^1 \oplus \mathsf{FC}_{K_2}(T, X_R \oplus \mathsf{FE}_{K_3}(Y_L^1)),$$

which is exactly equal to X_L^3. Therefore, the adversary $\mathcal{A}$ always outputs 1 if the bit b in the RPRP game is 1. On the other hand, in the ideal world ($b = 0$), the guess oracle returns **true** with very small probability. Overall, $\mathcal{A}$ wins the RPRPg game with high probability.

ECE is RPRPd Secure. The other part of the separation comes next. In Theorem 2, we give the result for RPRPd security of ECE. The proof utilizes the H-coefficient technique, focusing on finding collisions in the input of inner PRFs.

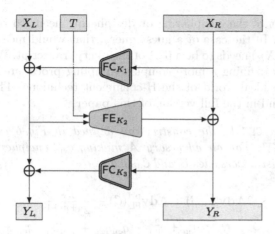

Fig. 6. Graphical representation of 3-round Feistel construction CEC, realized from compressing PRF FC and expanding PRF FE.

There already exist proofs for 3-round Feistel being a secure PRP. However, our proof required a different analysis since we are trying to prove a stronger notion (and a tweakable one at that). There is no reference proof for the 3-round Feistel that considers decipher queries, and that is what we needed to take care of in our analysis. The full, detailed proof can be found in the full version of this paper.

Theorem 2. *Let* ECE *be the construction defined in Fig. 3 over the domain* $\{0,1\}^n \times \{0,1\}^{\geq m}$. *For an adversary* $\mathcal{A}$ *making* q_{en} *encipher and* q_{de} *decipher queries, there exist adversaries* $\mathcal{B}$ *and* $\mathcal{C}$ *such that*

$$\mathbf{Adv}_{\mathrm{ECE}}^{\mathrm{rprpd}}(\mathcal{A}) \leq 2\mathbf{Adv}_{\mathrm{FE}}^{\mathrm{prf}}(\mathcal{B}) + \mathbf{Adv}_{\mathrm{FC}}^{\mathrm{prf}}(\mathcal{C}) + \frac{q^2}{2^{n+m}} + \frac{q^2}{2^{m+1}} + \frac{q_{\mathrm{en}}^2}{2^n} + \frac{q_{\mathrm{en}}q_{\mathrm{de}}}{2^{n-1}},$$

under the assumption that $q_{\mathrm{en}} + q_{\mathrm{de}} \leq \frac{1}{2^{n+m-1}}$, *and where* $q = q_{\mathrm{en}} + q_{\mathrm{de}}$. *The resulting PRF adversary* $\mathcal{B}$ *makes at most* $q_{\mathrm{en}} + q_{\mathrm{gu}}$ *queries, whereas the resulting PRF adversary* $\mathcal{C}$ *makes at most* $q_{\mathrm{en}} + q_{\mathrm{gu}}$ *queries.*

As it can be seen from the bound, in order for ECE to have meaningful security, the minimal size of the right input m needs to be large enough (i.e., $m \geq n$).

We can now continue with analyzing the security of the CEC construction. The results for the CEC construction are the opposite of those for ECE. The CEC construction is not RPRPd secure, and an attack against RPRPd security of CEC can be found in the full version of this paper. On the other hand, CEC does achieve RPRPg security.

CEC is RPRPg Secure. We present the result for RPRPg security of CEC in Theorem 3. The proof utilizes the H-coefficient technique, and it was challenging to incorporate the analysis of guess oracle queries. The peculiarities of the guess oracle, namely the fact that the only thing leaked to the adversary is whether $X_L \in V$, contrast the conventional approach in the H-coefficient technique where the whole output of the enciphering or deciphering needs to be included in a query transcript. In the case of a guess query, that would mean the internally deciphered (X_L, X_R) needs to be a part of the query transcript. We "circumvent" this challenge by defining a more complex sampling procedure that builds the transcript in the ideal world of the H-coefficient technique. The full, detailed proof can be found in the full version of this paper.

Theorem 3. *Let* CEC *be the construction defined in Fig. 6 over the domain* $\{0,1\}^n \times \{0,1\}^{\geq m}$. *For an adversary* $\mathcal{A}$ *making* q_{en} *encipher and* q_{gu} *guess queries, there exist adversaries* $\mathcal{B}$ *and* $\mathcal{C}$ *such that*

$$\mathbf{Adv}_{\mathsf{CEC}}^{\mathrm{rprpg}}(\mathcal{A}, v) \leq 2\mathbf{Adv}_{\mathsf{FC}}^{\mathrm{prf}}(\mathcal{B}) + \mathbf{Adv}_{\mathsf{FE}}^{\mathrm{prf}}(\mathcal{C}) + \frac{q_{\mathrm{en}}^2}{2^{n+m+1}}$$
$$+ \frac{q_{\mathrm{en}}^2 + q_{\mathrm{gu}}^2}{2^{n+1}} + \frac{q_{\mathrm{en}}q_{\mathrm{gu}} + q_{\mathrm{gu}}v}{2^n} + \frac{q_{\mathrm{en}}^2 + q_{\mathrm{gu}}^2}{2^{m+1}} + \frac{3q_{\mathrm{en}}q_{\mathrm{gu}}}{2^m}.$$

The resulting PRF adversary $\mathcal{B}$ *makes at most* $q_{\mathrm{en}} + q_{\mathrm{gu}}$ *queries, whereas the resulting PRF adversary* $\mathcal{C}$ *makes at most* $q_{\mathrm{en}} + q_{\mathrm{gu}}$ *queries.*

As the security bound shows, in order for CEC to have meaningful security, the minimal size of the right input m needs to be large enough (i.e., $m \geq n$).

4.1 Instantiating ECE and CEC

Instantiating the constructions ECE and CEC reduces to how one instantiates the expanding and compressing round functions. For the compressing PRF FC, one could use the Hash-then-PRF paradigm and instantiate the function with an efficient almost-universal hash function together with a fixed-input-size PRF that could be AES or the ChaCha20 block function. The FE could be instantiated using AES in Counter mode or the stream cipher ChaCha20.

Another option would be to instantiate FC with Xoofff [10], a so-called deck function. A deck function is a variable-input and variable-output length PRF, so it is also an excellent candidate for instantiating the expanding FE. Using Xoofff for both FE and FC enables us to instantiate our 3-round Feistel schemes with a single permutation-based primitive, which would also offer very competitive performance [4,10].

5 HEC

We now present one of our main contributions, a construction called HEC (Hash–Encipher–Counter), which we base on a tweakable VIL cipher HCTR [24], originally proven to be STPRP secure. Our goal is to construct a cipher satisfying the weaker notion of RPRP security and a natural step in achieving that is to try and reduce the complexity of HCTR. The original HCTR construction consists of three layers, the first and the third one being an AXU hash function "compressing" layers that process the right part of the plaintext. The middle

$\widetilde{\mathsf{EE}}_{K,h}(T, X_L, X_R)$	$\widetilde{\mathsf{EE}}_{K,h}^{-1}(T, Y_L, Y_R)$
$LL \leftarrow X_L \oplus \mathsf{H}_h(T, X_R)$	$Y_L' \leftarrow Y_L \oplus K_C$
$Y_L' \leftarrow \mathsf{E}_K(LL)$	$LL \leftarrow \mathsf{E}_K^{-1}(Y_L')$
$IV \leftarrow LL \oplus Y_L' \,;\; k \leftarrow \lceil \lvert X_R \rvert / n \rceil$	$IV \leftarrow LL \oplus Y_L' \,;\; k \leftarrow \lceil \lvert Y_R \rvert / n \rceil$
$S \leftarrow \lfloor \mathsf{E}_K(IV \oplus 1) \Vert \cdots \Vert \mathsf{E}_K(IV \oplus k) \rfloor_{\lvert X_R \rvert}$	$S \leftarrow \lfloor \mathsf{E}_K(IV \oplus 1) \Vert \cdots \Vert \mathsf{E}_K(IV \oplus k) \rfloor_{\lvert Y_R \rvert}$
$Y_R \leftarrow X_R \oplus S$	$X_R \leftarrow Y_R \oplus S$
$Y_L \leftarrow Y_L' \oplus K_C$	$X_L \leftarrow LL \oplus \mathsf{H}_h(T, X_R)$
return (Y_L, Y_R)	**return** (X_L, X_R)

Fig. 7. Pseudocode description of HEC[H, E].

"expanding" layer is a simple counter mode. We modify HCTR in two ways to arrive at our construction HEC.

The first step is removing the lower hash layer. The second step is introducing a n-bit key K_C that is used for masking the left output value Y_L. The pseudocode of the HEC construction encipher and decipher algorithm is presented in Fig. 7. A graphical representation of it is given in Fig. 8.

Just removing the lower layer in HCTR is not enough to achieve RPRP security, the masking key needs to be present. We give in the full version of this paper an attack against RPRPd security of the variant that does not have the masking key K_C, therefore showing such construction would not satisfy RPRP security as well. The attack exploits the fact that one can make such a query to the construction's DE oracle so that the decipher algorithm of the underlying blockcipher is queried with a value that has already been output by its encipher algorithm.

Note that the alteration we made to the HCTR construction to arrive at the HEC construction makes HEC insecure against an STPRP adversary. Querying (T, Y_L, Y_R) and (T, Y_L, Y_R') to the decipher oracle, for $Y_R \neq Y_R'$, leads to the respective outputs (X_L, X_R) and (X_L', X_R'). It will hold $X_R \oplus Y_R = X_R' \oplus Y_R'$, which would be true in the ideal world with a very small probability.

HEC *Security.* Continuing, we prove HEC is a secure RPRP. We use the H-coefficient technique in our proof, and the proof takes care of inputs of all valid lengths, i.e., inputs with a length that is not a multiple of blocksize n. Other relevant works on tweakable cipher constructions prove the security for inputs that end on a full block. Compared to the proof of other known RPRP scheme, namely that of the UIV scheme, the proof we give is much more involved since HEC construction is concrete, as opposed to the more abstract UIV. The HEC security theorem and the corresponding proof follow.

Theorem 4. *Let HEC be the construction defined in Fig. 7 over the domain* $\{0,1\}^n \times \{0,1\}^{\geq m}$, *with* H *being an* ϵ_1-*AXU hash function. For any positive integer* v *and an adversary* $\mathcal{A}$ *making* q_{en} *encipher queries,* q_{de} *decipher queries and* q_{gu} *guess queries, such that every query input is at most* ln *bits long, there exists an adversary* $\mathcal{B}$ *such that*

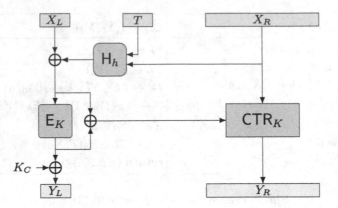

Fig. 8. Graphical representation of the HEC enciphering algorithm.

$$\mathbf{Adv}_{\mathsf{HEC}}^{\mathrm{rprp}}(\mathcal{A}, v) \leq \mathbf{Adv}_{\mathsf{E}}^{\mathrm{sprp}}(\mathcal{B}) + \frac{q^2}{2^{n+m}} + q_1 q \epsilon_1 + \frac{q_1 q l^2}{2^{n-2}} + \frac{q_1 q l}{2^{n-1}}$$

$$+ \frac{q_1^2}{2^n} + 2 q_{\mathrm{gu}} v \max\{\frac{1}{2^{n-1}}, \epsilon_1\},$$

where $q = q_{\mathrm{en}} + q_{\mathrm{de}} + q_{\mathrm{gu}}$, $q_1 = q_{\mathrm{en}} + q_{\mathrm{de}}$ and under the assumption $q \leq 2^{n+m-1}$. The resulting SPRP adversary $\mathcal{B}$ makes at most ql oracle queries in total to its own encipher and decipher oracle.

Proof. Without loss of generality, we assume that the adversary does not make redundant queries. That is, the adversary does not repeat queries to either of the oracles or make queries that the game will restrict.

Our starting game is the real world ($b = 1$) of the RPRP game. Using the standard argument, we first replace the blockcipher E in the construction with a random permutation Π. This adds a SPRP advantage term of E to the bound. We have

$$\mathbf{Adv}_{\mathsf{HEC}}^{\mathrm{rprp}}(\mathcal{A}, v) \leq \mathbf{Adv}_{\mathsf{E}}^{\mathrm{sprp}}(\mathcal{B}) + \mathbf{Adv}_{\mathsf{HEC^*}}^{\mathrm{rprp}}(\mathcal{A}, v), \tag{1}$$

where HEC* is the HEC construction having a random permutation Π instead of a blockcipher. We now aim to apply the H-coefficient technique and Theorem 1 in order to bound $\mathcal{A}$'s distinguishing advantage between HEC* and the ideal world ($b = 0$) of HEC's RPRP game.

The first step in doing that is defining the real and ideal worlds in the H-coefficient technique. In the real world, the adversary interacts with HEC* via oracles EN, DE and GU. In the ideal world, the adversary has access to EN, DE and GU oracles given in Fig. 9. In words, for each tweak T and input length $n + |X_R|$ (or $n + |Y_R|$), a separate random permutation is lazily sampled with the help of the table $\widetilde{\Pi}$. Note that the ideal world corresponds to the ideal world of the RPRP game.

$\mathrm{EN}(T, X_L, X_R)$	$\mathrm{DE}(T, Y_L, Y_R)$	$\mathrm{GU}(T, Y_L, Y_R, \boldsymbol{V})$
if $\widetilde{\Pi}(T, X_L, X_R) \neq \perp$ **then**	**if** $\widetilde{\Pi}^{-1}(T, Y_L, Y_R) \neq \perp$ **then**	**return false**
$\quad (Y_L, Y_R) \leftarrow \widetilde{\Pi}(T, X_L, X_R)$	$\quad (X_L, X_R) \leftarrow \widetilde{\Pi}^{-1}(T, Y_L, Y_R)$	
else	**else**	
$\quad S \leftarrow \mathrm{rng}(\widetilde{\Pi}(T, \cdot, \cdot))$	$\quad S \leftarrow \mathrm{dom}(\widetilde{\Pi}(T, \cdot, \cdot))$	
$\quad (Y_L, Y_R) \leftarrow\!\!\$\ \{0,1\}^{n+|X_R|} \setminus S$	$\quad (X_L, X_R) \leftarrow\!\!\$\ \{0,1\}^{n+|Y_R|} \setminus S$	
$\quad \widetilde{\Pi}(T, X_L, X_R) \leftarrow (Y_L, Y_R)$	$\quad \widetilde{\Pi}(T, X_L, X_R) \leftarrow (Y_L, Y_R)$	
$\quad \widetilde{\Pi}^{-1}(T, Y_L, Y_R) \leftarrow (X_L, X_R)$	$\quad \widetilde{\Pi}^{-1}(T, Y_L, Y_R) \leftarrow (X_L, X_R)$	
return (Y_L, Y_R)	**return** (X_L, X_R)	

Fig. 9. The ideal world for H-coefficient technique application in Theorem 4 (HEC is RPRP).

The transcript τ is structured as follows

$$\tau = (\tau', h, K_C),$$

where τ' contains the queries adversary made during the interaction with the real or ideal world. The h and K_C in the real world correspond to the real hash and masking key appearing in HEC*. On the other hand, in the ideal world, the two keys are sampled at the end, the exact sampling procedure being explained later.

As for τ', two types of queries are stored there:

1. Queries $(T^i, X_L^i, X_R^i, Y_L^i, Y_R^i, R^i)$, corresponding to the queries to EN and DE oracles. If the input (or output) length is a multiple of blockcipher size, then $R^i = \varepsilon$. Otherwise, for X_R^i that has k full blocks and r more bits, where $r < n$, R^i in the real world contains the last $n - r$ bits of the last blockcipher (permutation) output in counter mode. That is,

$$R^i := \lceil \Pi(IV \oplus \langle k+1 \rangle_2) \rceil_{n-r}$$

In the ideal world R^i is sampled by the simulator S at the end. We define S shortly.

2. Queries $(T^i, Y_L^i, Y_R^i, \boldsymbol{V}^i, o^i, X_L^i, X_R^i, R^i)$, corresponding to the queries to GU oracle. The variable o^i corresponds to the answer of the guess oracle, and for a query from an attainable transcript, its value will always be **false**. In the real world, (X_L^i, X_R^i) corresponds to (X_L, X_R) that would internally be deciphered on input (T^i, Y_L^i, Y_R^i). The value R^i is defined analogously as in the case of encipher and decipher query. As for the ideal world, the simulator defined below samples these values.

The simulator S runs in the ideal world after the adversary has finished its interaction with the oracles, and executes the following steps (in the given order).

i. It uniformly samples the hash key h and the masking key K_C.

ii. It iterates through all EN and DE queries and for each query $(T^i, X_L^i, X_R^i, Y_L^i, Y_R^i)$, it sets $R^i := \epsilon$ if X_R^i has k full blocks. Otherwise, X_R^i does not end on a full block, but it has k full blocks and r more bits, where $r < n$. The simulator S in that case sets $R^i \leftarrow\!\!\$ \{0,1\}^{n-r}$.

iii. It iterates through all GU queries and for each query $(T^i, Y_L^i, Y_R^i, \boldsymbol{V}^i)$ it first determines if the triple (T^i, Y_L^i, Y_R^i) is fresh.

- (T^i, Y_L^i, Y_R^i) *appears for the first time in a guess query*: The simulator checks if Y_L^i is *new*. We call Y_L^i new if there is no EN or DE query (occurring either before or after this i-th guess query) or an earlier GU query in τ' that contains Y_L^i.
  If Y_L^i is new, then (X_L^i, X_R^i) is sampled according to the permutation $\widetilde{\Pi}^{-1}(T^i, \cdot, \cdot)$. The variable $R^i := \epsilon$ if $r = 0$, otherwise $R^i \leftarrow\!\!\$ \{0,1\}^{n-r}$.
  If Y_L^i is not new, let j-th query be the first EN, DE query $(T^j, X_L^j, X_R^j, Y_L^j, Y_R^j, R^j)$ or the first GU query[2] $(T^j, Y_L^j, Y_R^j, \boldsymbol{V}^j, \textsf{false}, X_L^j, X_R^j, R^j)$ such that $Y_L^i = Y_L^j$. Then set $X_R^i := X_R^j \oplus Y_R^j \oplus Y_R^i$, $X_L^i := X_L^j \oplus \mathsf{H}_h(T^j, X_R^j) \oplus \mathsf{H}_h(T^i, X_R^i)$ and $R^i := R^j$. Note that the term $X_R^j \oplus Y_R^j$ would be the key stream produced by the counter mode if we were in the real world.
- (T^i, Y_L^i, Y_R^i) *does not appear for the first time in a guess query*: The simulator takes the values (X_L^j, X_R^j, R^j) from some previous j-th guess query with the same (T^i, Y_L^i, Y_R^i) and sets

$$(X_L^i, X_R^i, R^i) := (X_L^j, X_R^j, R^j).$$

In the rest of the proof, we assume that l_i denotes the length of the input of the i-th query. We will sometimes write the right value X_R^i of length $kn + r$ as

$$x_1^i \| x_2^i \| \cdots \| x_k^i \| x_{k+1}^i,$$

where $0 \leq r < n$. For $1 \leq j \leq k$, $x_j^i \in \{0,1\}^n$. If $r \neq 0$, then $x_{k+1}^i \in \{0,1\}^r$, otherwise $x_{k+1}^i = \varepsilon$. We do the same for right value Y_R^i and write it as

$$y_1^i \| y_2^i \| \cdots \| y_k^i \| y_{k+1}^i.$$

Defining and Bounding the Bad Transcripts. We now define what it means for an attainable transcript to be *bad*. The intuition for the following bad transcript conditions is as follows. The [B1.*] conditions ensure that for two EN/DE queries, there will be no collisions in the input or the output of the underlying blockcipher, that is, permutation. The [B2.*] conditions are similar to [B1.*] conditions. They ensure that for one EN/DE and one GU query that has new Y_L, there will be no collisions in the input or the output of the underlying blockcipher, that is, permutation. The condition [B3] excludes guess oracle queries that would be deemed successful in the real world.

Definition 7. *A transcript $\tau = (\tau', h, K_C)$ is called bad, if in τ' there exist:*

---

[2] In case of a GU query, it will hold $j < i$.

[B1] *Two* EN / DE *queries* $(T^i, X_L^i, X_R^i, Y_L^i, Y_R^i, R^i)$ *and* $(T^j, X_L^j, X_R^j, Y_L^j, Y_R^j, R^j)$, *with* $|X_R^i| = k_i n + r_i$, $|X_R^j| = k_j n + r_j$ *and* $0 \leq r_i, r_j < n$, *such that one of the following conditions hold:*

[B1.1] $X_L^i \oplus \mathsf{H}_h(T^i, X_R^i) = X_L^j \oplus \mathsf{H}_h(T^j, X_R^j)$, *with* $i \neq j$.

[B1.2] $IV^i \oplus \langle \mathrm{ctr}_i \rangle_2 = IV^j \oplus \langle \mathrm{ctr}_j \rangle_2$ *with* $\mathrm{ctr}_i \in \{1, \dots, k_i + 1\}$, $\mathrm{ctr}_j \in \{1, \dots, k_j + 1\}$ *and* $i \neq j$.

[B1.3] $X_L^i \oplus \mathsf{H}_h(T^i, X_R^i) = IV^j \oplus \langle \mathrm{ctr}_j \rangle_2$ *with* $\mathrm{ctr}_j \in \{1, \dots, k_j + 1\}$.

[B1.4] $Y_L^i \oplus K_C = Y_L^j \oplus K_C$, *with* $i \neq j$.

[B1.5] $Y_L^i \oplus K_C = x_{\mathrm{ctr}_j}^j \oplus y_{\mathrm{ctr}_j}^j$ *with* $\mathrm{ctr}_j \in \{1, \dots, k_j\}$, *or, if* $r_j > 0$, $Y_L^i \oplus K_C = (x_{k_j+1}^j \oplus y_{k_j+1}^j) \| R^j$

[B1.6] $x_{\mathrm{ctr}_i}^i \oplus y_{\mathrm{ctr}_i}^i = x_{\mathrm{ctr}_j}^j \oplus y_{\mathrm{ctr}_j}^j$ *with* $\mathrm{ctr}_i \in \{1, \dots, k_i\}$ *and* $\mathrm{ctr}_j \in \{1, \dots k_j\}$, *or, if* $r_j > 0$, $x_{\mathrm{ctr}_i}^i \oplus y_{\mathrm{ctr}_i}^i = (x_{k_j+1}^j \oplus y_{k_j+1}^j) \| R^j$ *with* $\mathrm{ctr}_i \in \{1, \dots, k_i\}$, *or, if* $i \neq j$, $r_i > 0$ *and* $r_j > 0$, $(x_{k_i+1}^i \oplus y_{k_i+1}^i) \| R^i = (x_{k_j+1}^j \oplus y_{k_j+1}^j) \| R^j$.

[B2] *One* EN / DE *query and one* GU *query with new* Y_L, *such that one of the following conditions hold:*

[B2.1] $X_L^i \oplus \mathsf{H}_h(T^i, X_R^i) = X_L^j \oplus \mathsf{H}_h(T^j, X_R^j)$, *with* i *being* EN/DE *query and* j *being* GU *query or vice versa.*

[B2.2] $IV^i \oplus \langle \mathrm{ctr}_i \rangle_2 = IV^j \oplus \langle \mathrm{ctr}_j \rangle_2$ *with* $\mathrm{ctr}_i \in \{1, \dots, k_i + 1\}$ *and* $\mathrm{ctr}_j \in \{1, \dots, k_j + 1\}$, *and with* i *being* EN/DE *query and* j *being* GU *query or vice versa.*

[B2.3] $X_L^i \oplus \mathsf{H}_h(T^i, X_R^i) = IV^j \oplus \langle \mathrm{ctr}_j \rangle_2$ *with* $\mathrm{ctr}_j \in \{1, \dots, k_j + 1\}$, *and with* i *being* EN/DE *query and* j *being* GU *query or vice versa.*

[B2.4] i *being* EN/DE *query and* j *being* GU *query, or vice versa, and:* $Y_L^i \oplus K_C = x_{\mathrm{ctr}_j}^j \oplus y_{\mathrm{ctr}_j}^j$ *with* $\mathrm{ctr}_j \in \{1, \dots, k_j\}$, *or, if* $r_j > 0$, $Y_L^i \oplus K_C = (x_{k_j+1}^j \oplus y_{k_j+1}^j) \| R^j$.

[B2.5] i *being* EN/DE *query and* j *being* GU *query, or vice versa, and:* $x_{\mathrm{ctr}_i}^i \oplus y_{\mathrm{ctr}_i}^i = x_{\mathrm{ctr}_j}^j \oplus y_{\mathrm{ctr}_j}^j$ *with* $\mathrm{ctr}_i \in \{1, \dots, k_i\}$ *and* $\mathrm{ctr}_j \in \{1, \dots k_j\}$, *or, if* $r_j > 0$, $x_{\mathrm{ctr}_i}^i \oplus y_{\mathrm{ctr}_i}^i = (x_{k_j+1}^j \oplus y_{k_j+1}^j) \| R^j$ *with* $\mathrm{ctr}_i \in \{1, \dots, k_i\}$, *or, if* $i \neq j$, $r_i > 0$ *and* $r_j > 0$, $(x_{k_i+1}^i \oplus y_{k_i+1}^i) \| R^i = (x_{k_j+1}^j \oplus y_{k_j+1}^j) \| R^j$.

[B3] *One* GU *query* $(T^i, Y_L^i, Y_R^i, V^i, o^i, X_L^i, X_R^i, R^i)$ *such that* $X_L^i \in V^i$.

Now, let τ be some attainable transcript in the ideal world. We bound the probabilities of above defined conditions holding true in the ideal world.

[B1.1] We rewrite the condition as

$$\mathsf{H}_h(T^i, X_R^i) \oplus \mathsf{H}_h(T^j, X_R^j) = X_L^i \oplus X_L^j.$$

The equation above holds, by the AXU property of H, with probability at most ϵ_1. Summing over all i and j, with $i \neq j$, we get the term

$$\binom{q_1}{2} \epsilon_1 \leq \frac{q_1^2 \epsilon_1}{2}. \tag{2}$$

[B1.2] Without loss of generality, assume $i < j$. By expanding IV^i and IV^j, the condition becomes

$$X_L^i \oplus H_h(T^i, X_R^i) \oplus Y_L^i \oplus \langle \mathrm{ctr}_i \rangle_2 = X_L^j \oplus H_h(T^j, X_R^j) \oplus Y_L^j \oplus \langle \mathrm{ctr}_j \rangle_2$$

We fix some ctr_i and ctr_j. If j-th query was an encipher query, we bound the equation above over the distribution of Y_L^j. Otherwise j-th query was a decipher query and then we bound the equation over the distribution of X_L^j. Assuming $q_1 \leq 2^{n+m-1} \leq 2^{l_j-1}$, the upper bound for the equation above holding true is

$$\frac{2^{l_j-n}}{2^{l_j} - (j-1)} \leq \frac{2^{l_j-n}}{2^{l_j} - q_1} \leq \frac{2^{l_j-n}}{2^{l_j-1}} = \frac{1}{2^{n-1}}.$$

Summing up over all i and j, with $i \neq j$, we arrive at the term

$$\binom{q_1}{2} \frac{l^2}{2^{n-1}} \leq \frac{q_1^2 l^2}{2^n}. \tag{3}$$

[B1.3] There are two possibilities here. The first one is, $i \neq j$. The equation, when IV^j is expanded, becomes

$$X_L^i \oplus H_h(T^i, X_R^i) = X_L^j \oplus H_h(T^j, X_R^j) \oplus Y_L^j \oplus K_C \oplus \langle \mathrm{ctr}_j \rangle_2.$$

For a fixed ctr_j, the probability of the equation being true is $\frac{1}{2^n}$, taken over the randomness of K_C. Summing up over all i, j and ctr_j, with $i \neq j$, the total probability for condition [B1.3] in this case is at most $\frac{q_1(q_1-1)l}{2^n}$.

The other option is that $i = j$. The condition equation is then reduced to $Y_L^i \oplus \langle \mathrm{ctr}_i \rangle_2 = K_C$. The probability of the equation being true is $\frac{1}{2^n}$ in this case as well, taken over the randomness of K_C. There are q possibilities for i, therefore summing over i and ctr_j, the bound becomes $\frac{q_1 l}{2^n}$.

Adding up the bounds of both cases, the total term for bounding the probability of this condition holding true is

$$\frac{q_1^2 l}{2^n}. \tag{4}$$

[B1.4] Without loss of generality, assume $i < j$. The condition of [B1.4] is equivalent to $Y_L^i = Y_L^j$. We differentiate 4 subcases here.

- *Both queries are encipher queries.* The probability of the condition being true is $\frac{1}{2^{n-1}}$, taken over the draw of Y_L^j and assuming $q_1 \leq 2^{n+m-1}$.
- *Both queries are decipher queries.* The probability of the condition being true is 0, since the adversary would not make j-th query with Y_L^j repeating.
- *i-th query is encipher query, j-th query is decipher query.* The probability of the condition being true is 0, since the adversary would not make j-th query with Y_L^j repeating.

- *i-th query is decipher query, j-th query is encipher query.* The probability of the condition being true is $\frac{1}{2^{n-1}}$, taken over the draw of Y_L^j and assuming $q_1 \leq 2^{n+m-1}$.

Summing up over all i and j, the total bound for condition [B1.4] becomes

$$\binom{q_1}{2} \frac{1}{2^{n-1}} \leq \frac{q_1^2}{2^n}. \tag{5}$$

[B1.5] We differentiate here two subcases.

- $l_j = k_j n$. For a fixed ctr_j, the probability of the equation being true is $\frac{1}{2^n}$, taken over the randomness of K_C.
- $l_j = k_j n + r_j$, for $r_j > 0$. The probability of bad condition occurring can be rewritten as

$$\Pr\left[\lfloor Y_L^i \oplus K_C \rfloor_{r_j} = (x_{k_j+1}^j \oplus y_{k_j+1}^j) \wedge \lceil Y_L^i \oplus K_C \rceil_{n-r_j} = R^j \right].$$

The probability of the first equation holding true can be bounded by $\frac{1}{2^{r_j}}$, taken over randomness of K_C, and the probability of second equation being true is $\frac{1}{2^{n-r_j}}$, since R^j is sampled uniformly at random. In total, the probability is bounded by

$$\frac{1}{2^n}.$$

Summing up over all i, j and ctr_j, the total bound for condition [B1.5] holding true is

$$\frac{q_1^2 l}{2^n}. \tag{6}$$

[B1.6] We differentiate three subcases here.

- $r_i = r_j = 0$. Assume first that $i = j$. In that case the, probability of a condition being true for some fixed $\mathrm{ctr}_{i_1} \neq \mathrm{ctr}_{i_2}$ is at most $\frac{1}{2^{n-1}}$, taken over the sampling of y^i's in case the query was an encipher query, or x^i's in case the query was a decipher query.
  In case of $i \neq j$, the probability is calculated analogously and one gets the same bound $\frac{1}{2^{n-1}}$.
- $r_j > 0$. We fix some ctr_i. The probability of bad condition occurring can be rewritten as

$$\Pr\left[\lfloor x_{\mathrm{ctr}_i}^i \oplus y_{\mathrm{ctr}_i}^i \rfloor_{r_j} = (x_{k_j+1}^j \oplus y_{k_j+1}^j) \wedge \lceil x_{\mathrm{ctr}_i}^i \oplus y_{\mathrm{ctr}_i}^i \rceil_{n-r_j} = R^j \right].$$

The equation above is bounded by $\frac{1}{2^{r_j-1}} \frac{1}{2^{n-r_j}} = \frac{1}{2^{n-1}}$, taken over the distribution of R^j and $x_{\mathrm{ctr}_i}^i / y_{\mathrm{ctr}_i}^i$ or $x_{k_j+1}^j / y_{k_j+1}^j$.
- *Both $r_i > 0$ and $r_j > 0$.* Without loss of generality assume $r_i \leq r_j$. The probability of bad condition occurring can be rewritten as

$$\Pr\left[\lfloor x_{k_i+1}^i \oplus y_{k_i+1}^i \rfloor_{r_i} = \lfloor x_{k_j+1}^j \oplus y_{k_j+1}^j \rfloor_{r_i} \wedge R^i = \lceil x_{k_j+1}^j \oplus y_{k_j+1}^j \rceil_{n-r_i}^{r_i} \right].$$

This is bounded by $\frac{1}{2^{r_i-1}} \frac{1}{2^{n-r_i}} = \frac{1}{2^{n-1}}$, where the calculation is analogous to the calculation from the previous subcase.

Summing up over all i, j, ctr$_i$ and ctr$_j$, the final bound for condition [B1.6] occurring is

$$\frac{q_1^2 l^2}{2^{n-1}}. \tag{7}$$

[B2.1] This condition holds true with probability at most

$$q_1 q_{gu} \epsilon_1, \tag{8}$$

where the probability is calculated similarly as in condition [B1.1].
[B2.2] This condition holds true with probability at most

$$\frac{q_1 q_{gu} l^2}{2^{n-1}}, \tag{9}$$

where the probability is calculated similarly as in condition [B1.2] and assuming $q \le 2^{n+m-1}$.
[B2.3] This condition holds true with probability at most

$$\frac{q_1 q_{gu} l}{2^n}, \tag{10}$$

where the probability is calculated similarly as in condition [B1.3].
[B2.4] This condition holds true with probability at most

$$\frac{q_1 q_{gu} l}{2^n}, \tag{11}$$

where the probability is calculated similarly as in condition [B1.5].
[B2.5] This condition holds true with probability at most

$$\frac{q_1 q_{gu} l^2}{2^{n-1}}, \tag{12}$$

where the probability is calculated similarly as in condition [B1.6] and assuming $q \le 2^{n+m-1}$.
[B3] Let us fix some $X_L^* \in V^i$. We immediately differentiate two cases. The first one is when Y_L^i is new. In that case, (X_L^i, X_R^i) is sampled according to $\widetilde{\Pi}$ and it holds

$$\Pr\left[X_L^i = X_L^*\right] \le \frac{2^{l_i-n}}{2^{l_i} - (q_1 + q_{gu})} \le \frac{1}{2^{n-1}},$$

assuming $q \le 2^{n+m-1} \le 2^{l_i-1}$. The second case is when Y_L^i is *not* new. Then it holds $X_L^i = X_L^j \oplus H_h(T^j, X_R^j) \oplus H_h(T^i, X_R^i)$, where the j-th query is the one in which Y_L^i appears in for the first time. If $(T^i, X_R^i) \ne (T^j, X_R^j)$, we can reduce the probability of the equation $X_L^* = X_L^i$ holding true to ϵ_1. Otherwise $(T^i, X_R^i) = (T^j, X_R^j)$ and the equation reduces to $X_L^* = X_L^j$, which can again be bounded by $\frac{1}{2^{n-1}}$. The bound, for the case when Y_L^i is not new, is then $\max\{\frac{1}{2^{n-1}}, \epsilon_1\}$. Summing up over all X_L^* in V^i and then over all guess oracle queries, we have that the probability of the condition [B3] being true is at most

$$2q_{gu}v\max\{\frac{1}{2^{n-1}},\epsilon_1\}. \tag{13}$$

Adding up the bounds in (2)–(13) we have that the probability of an attainable transcript τ in the ideal world being bad is bounded by

$$\epsilon_{bad} \le q_1 q\epsilon_1 + \frac{q_1 q l^2}{2^{n-2}} + \frac{q_1 q l}{2^{n-1}} + \frac{q_1^2}{2^n} + 2q_{gu}v\max\{\frac{1}{2^{n-1}},\epsilon_1\}.$$

Bounding the Ratio of Good Transcripts. Fix some good and an attainable transcript (τ', h, K_C). We split the encipher, decipher and guess queries that have new Y_L in τ' into two disjoint sets τ_1' and τ_2'. The set τ_1' contains queries whose length is a multiple of n and τ_2' contains all other EN, DE and GU queries (with new Y_L). We note here that we defined the term of "new Y_L" in the ideal world, but the "new Y_L" has the same meaning in the real world. Furthermore, each of τ_1' and τ_2' is further "decomposed" into smaller disjoint subsets that only contain queries of the same length. That is, for $l_{1,1}, l_{1,2}, ..., l_{1,c_1}$, where every $l_{1,i}$ is a multiple of n, we have disjoint sets $\tau_{1,1}, ..., \tau_{1,c_1}$, with $\tau_{1,i}$ containing queries of length $l_{1,i}$. Therefore, it holds

$$\tau_1' = \tau_{1,1} \cup \cdots \cup \tau_{1,c_1}.$$

Similarly, for $l_{2,1}, ..., l_{2,c_2}$, where every $l_{2,i}$ is not a multiple of n, we have disjoint sets $\tau_{2,1}, ..., \tau_{2,c_2}$, with $\tau_{2,i}$ containing queries of length $l_{2,i}$. It holds

$$\tau_2' = \tau_{2,1} \cup \cdots \cup \tau_{2,c_2}.$$

In addition, for queries in τ_1' we let $k_{1,i}'$ denote the number of blocks in the whole input[3], i.e. $l_{1,i} = k_{1,i}'n$. With $k_{2,i}'$ we denote the number of full blocks for a query in τ_2' with length $l_{2,i}$, i.e. $l_{2,i} = k_{2,i}'n + r_{2,i}$. We denote the cardinality of set $\tau_{b,i}$ with $t_{b,i}$. We also introduce an equivalence relation $\sim_T$, where two queries from set $\tau_{b,i}$ are related if and only if they have the same tweak T. This equivalence relation partitions the set $\tau_{b,i}$ into equivalence classes by the tweak T, and there will be $w[b,i]$ classes with j-th equivalence class having $t_{b,i,j}$ number of queries in it. It then holds $t_{b,i} = t_{b,i,1} + \cdots + t_{b,i,w[b,i]}$, for $w[b,i]$ being the number of queried tweaks for queries in $\tau_{b,i}$. Finally, with uyl we denote the number of guess oracle queries that contain new Y_L and we let $\mathcal{H}$ denote the key space of the HEC's AXU hash function H.

Ideal World. The interpolation probability for the hash key h and the masking key K_C is $\frac{1}{|\mathcal{H}|}\frac{1}{2^n}$. The interpolation probabilities of queries in τ_1' and τ_2' are

$$\prod_{i=1}^{c_1} \frac{1}{(2^{l_{1,i}})_{t_{1,i,1}} \cdots (2^{l_{1,i}})_{t_{1,i,w[1,i]}}} \text{ and } \prod_{i=1}^{c_2} \frac{1}{(2^{l_{2,i}})_{t_{2,i,1}} \cdots (2^{l_{2,i}})_{t_{2,i,w[2,i]}}} \frac{1}{2^{(n-r_{2,i})t_{2,i}}},$$

---

[3] Following the previous notation, it holds $k_{1,i}' = k_{1,i} + 1$, where $k_{1,i}$ is the number of full blocks in the right part of the input.

respectively. As for the interpolation probability of guess oracle queries that do not contain a new Y_L, we fix some such query $(T^i, Y_L^i, Y_R^i, \mathbf{V}^i, \mathsf{false}, X_L^i, X_R^i, R^i)$. Since Y_L is not new, there exists some EN, DE or GU query with the same Y_L. The variables X_L^i, X_R^i and R^i then have the following value

$$X_R^i = X_R^j \oplus Y_R^j \oplus Y_R^i, \ X_L^i = X_L^j \oplus \mathsf{H}_h(T^j, X_R^j) \oplus \mathsf{H}_h(T^i, X_R^i), \ R^i = R^j.$$

The values in the right-hand side of the three equations above are already fixed, so the interpolation probability for the triple (X_R^i, X_L^i, R^i) is equal to 1.
In total, the interpolation probability for a transcript τ in the ideal world $\Pr[X_i = \tau]$ is

$$\frac{1}{|\mathcal{H}|} \frac{1}{2^n} \times \prod_{i=1}^{c_1} \frac{1}{(2^{l_{1,i}})_{t_{1,i,1}} \cdots (2^{l_{1,i}})_{t_{1,i,w[1,i]}}}$$

$$\times \prod_{i=1}^{c_2} \frac{1}{(2^{l_{2,i}})_{t_{2,i,1}} \cdots (2^{l_{2,i}})_{t_{2,i,w[2,i]}}} \frac{1}{2^{(n-r_{2,i})t_{2,i}}} \times 1^{q_{\mathsf{gu}} - \mathsf{uyl}}.$$

Real World. The interpolation probability for the hash key h and the masking key K_C is $\frac{1}{|\mathcal{H}|} \frac{1}{2^n}$ in the real world as well. For queries in τ_1' and τ_2' we know there are no input and output collisions to the underlying blockcipher (permutation). Then, for example for some j-th query in τ_1' that has $k_{1,i}'$ blocks, the interpolation probability that its input maps to its output is

$$\frac{1}{(2^n - \sigma)(2^n - \sigma - 1) \cdots (2^n - \sigma - (k_{1,i}' - 1))},$$

where σ represents the number of blocks processed in all the queries preceding the i-th query. By the above, the interpolation probability in total for queries in τ_1' and τ_2' is

$$\frac{1}{(2^n)_{t_{1,1}k_{1,1}' + \cdots + t_{1,c_1}k_{1,c_1}' + t_{2,1}(k_{2,1}' + 1) + \cdots + t_{2,c_2}(k_{2,c_2}' + 1)}}.$$

As for the guess oracle queries that do not have a new Y_L, considering we have already "fixed" the values related to this Y_L (e.g., the $IV = \Pi^{-1}(Y_L \oplus K_C) \oplus Y_L \oplus K_C$ and with that the keystream produced by the counter mode), the interpolation probability for X_R^i appearing in that guess query transcript will be 1. Similarly for $X_L^i = \Pi^{-1}(Y_L \oplus K_C) \oplus \mathsf{H}_h(X_R^i)$, everything on the right-hand side has already been fixed and therefore the X_L^i appears in that transcript with probability 1. In total, the interpolation probability for a transcript τ in the real world $\Pr[X_r = \tau]$ is

$$\frac{1}{|\mathcal{H}|} \frac{1}{2^n} \times \frac{1}{(2^n)_{t_{1,1}k_{1,1}' + \cdots + t_{1,c_1}k_{1,c_1}' + t_{2,1}(k_{2,1}' + 1) + \cdots + t_{2,c_2}(k_{2,c_2}' + 1)}} \times 1^{q_{\mathsf{gu}} - \mathsf{uyl}}.$$

Interpolation Ratio. Finally, the interpolation ratio $\frac{\Pr[X_r = \tau]}{\Pr[X_i = \tau]}$ for a good transcript τ is

$$\frac{\prod_{i=1}^{c_1}(2^{l_{1,i}})_{t_{1,i,1}}\cdots(2^{l_{1,i}})_{t_{1,i,w[1,i]}} \times \prod_{i=1}^{c_2}(2^{l_{2,i}})_{t_{2,i,1}}\cdots(2^{l_{2,i}})_{t_{2,i,w[2,i]}} 2^{(n-r_{2,i})t_{2,i}}}{(2^n)_{t_{1,1}k'_{1,1}+\cdots+t_{1,c_1}k'_{1,c_1}+t_{2,1}(k'_{2,1}+1)+\cdots+t_{2,c_2}(k'_{2,c_2}+1)}}.$$

Going further, by applying simple theorems about falling factorials, that can be found in the full version of this paper, both in the enumerator and the denominator, it follows that the term above is greater or equal than

$$\frac{\prod_{i=1}^{c_1}(2^{l_{1,i}})_{t_{1,i}}}{(2^n)_{t_{1,1}k'_{1,1}+\cdots+t_{1,c_1}k'_{1,c_1}}} \times \frac{\prod_{i=1}^{c_2}(2^{l_{2,i}})_{t_{2,i}} 2^{(n-r_{2,i})t_{2,i}}}{(2^n)_{t_{2,1}(k'_{2,1}+1)+\cdots+t_{2,c_2}(k'_{2,c_2}+1)}}.$$

Another application of the theorems about falling factorials, that we present in the full version of this paper, tells us the expression above is greater or equal than

$$\prod_{i=1}^{c_2} \frac{(2^{k_{2,i}n+r_{2,i}})_{t_{2,i}} 2^{(n-r_{2,i})t_{2,i}}}{(2^n)_{t_{2,i}(k_{2,i}+1)}}.$$

Finally, with some more calculation and applying the Weierstrass inequality we get

$$\frac{\Pr[X_r = \tau]}{\Pr[X_i = \tau]} \geq \prod_{i=1}^{c_2} \frac{(2^{k_{2,i}n+r_{2,i}} - q)^{t_{2,i}} 2^{(n-r_{2,i})t_{2,i}}}{2^{nt_{2,i}(k_{2,i}+1)}}$$

$$= \prod_{i=1}^{c_2} \left(\frac{(2^{k_{2,i}n+r_{2,i}} - q)2^{n-r_{2,i}}}{2^{n(k_{2,i}+1)}} \right)^{t_{2,i}} = \prod_{i=1}^{c_2} \left(1 - \frac{q}{2^{k_{2,i}n+r_{2,i}}} \right)^{t_{2,i}}$$

$$\geq 1 - q \sum_{i=1}^{c_2} \frac{t_{2,i}}{2^{k_{2,i}n+r_{2,i}}} \geq 1 - q \sum_{i=1}^{c_2} \frac{t_{2,i}}{2^{n+m}} \geq 1 - \frac{q^2}{2^{n+m}},$$

therefore $\epsilon_{\text{ratio}} = \frac{q^2}{2^{n+m}}$.

Summing up (1), ϵ_{bad} and ϵ_{ratio} one achieves the bound from the theorem statement. □

6 RPRP Domain Extension

In the case of UIV and HEC, the size of the left domain $\mathcal{X}_L$ is inherently equal to the size of the underlying (tweakable) blockcipher. Typical (tweakable) blockciphers have a block size of at most 128 bits, as is the case for AES, for instance. This can be a limiting factor in some RPRP applications, namely, in using RPRPs as a building block to arrive at the order-resilient secure channel. Namely, if one considers the order-resilient secure channel construction from [13, Section 6], instantiated with the nonce-set AEAD scheme AwN, the overall security of the channel reduces to the security of the underlying RPRP scheme. The RPRP advantage term of the UIV scheme is bounded by

$$\mathbf{Adv}^{\mathrm{stprp}}_{\widetilde{\mathsf{E}}^*}(\mathcal{B}) + \mathbf{Adv}^{\mathrm{prf}}_{\mathsf{F}}(\mathcal{C}) + \frac{q_{\mathrm{gu}}v}{2^{n-1}} + \frac{q(q-1)}{2^{n+1}} + \frac{q_{\mathrm{en}}(q_{\mathrm{en}}-1)}{2^{n+1}} + \frac{q_1(q_1-1)}{2^{n+m+1}},$$

where $\widetilde{\mathsf{E}}^*$ and F are the underlying tweakable blockcipher and PRF, respectively.

The term $\frac{q_{\mathrm{gu}}v}{2^{n-1}}$ in that bound corresponds to the integrity term of the order-resilient secure channel, where the q_{gu} would be the number of forgery attempts the channel adversary makes. The product $q_{\mathrm{gu}}v$ can grow quickly in specific use cases. Firstly, certain application will "embed" information in the nonce, consequently making the v large (i.e. up to 2^{64}). Secondly, some applications with long-lived channels that cannot be rekeyed easily could need to withstand unlimited adversarial forgery attempts. Because of the two reasons above, the integrity term $\frac{q_{\mathrm{gu}}v}{2^{n-1}}$ can quickly become large, leading to a need to extend the left domain of the underlying RPRP. If one doubles the size of $\mathcal{X}_L$ from $\{0,1\}^n$ to $\{0,1\}^{2n}$, the term above becomes $\frac{q_{\mathrm{gu}}v}{2^{2n-1}}$.

In addition, we also get an interesting "side effect" of the domain extension. Namely, the other three independent terms in the bound improve as well, e.g. the term $\frac{q_{\mathrm{en}}(q_{\mathrm{en}}-1)}{2^{n+1}}$ becomes $\frac{q_{\mathrm{en}}(q_{\mathrm{en}}-1)}{2^{2n+1}}$. Assuming that the STPRP security of $\widetilde{\mathsf{E}}^*$ and PRF security of F can also be strengthened, the overall security of the UIV construction (and thus the order-resilient secure channel it builds) would improve. However, we do not investigate this "side effect" further in this work.

In the following subsections, we present two possible black-box solutions for extending the left domain of the UIV construction [13]. The graphical representations of the UIV enciphering algorithm and these extender constructions are given in Fig. 10. We will call the UIV using one of these extender constructions an *extended UIV*.

We do not consider domain extenders for HEC in this work since the blockcipher used in the left part is also used throughout the whole construction. Therefore, replacing all appearances of it in a black-box manner would damage the performance. However, we leave finding specific domain extender options for HEC as an avenue for future work.

6.1   CDMS Extender

For our first extender, we use the construction of Coron et al. [8] that transforms a n-bit tweakable blockcipher into a $2n$-bit tweakable cipher using a 3-round Feistel scheme. We denote this construction with CDMS. The idea of using CDMS for domain extension inside a VIL cipher is not new. Shrimpton and Terashima utilized the same approach to instantiate their PIV construction [23].

The CDMS construction assumes the tweakable blockcipher admits tweaks of size ω. The size of the "outer" tweak, which is here (T, X_R), is then $\omega - n$. Denoting the underlying tweakable blockcipher with $\widetilde{\mathsf{E}}$, we can express the security of the UIV construction extended with CDMS using the following theorem, which is an adaptation of the original theorem for RPRP security of UIV [13, Theorem 1], using the result of Coron et al. [8] transform.

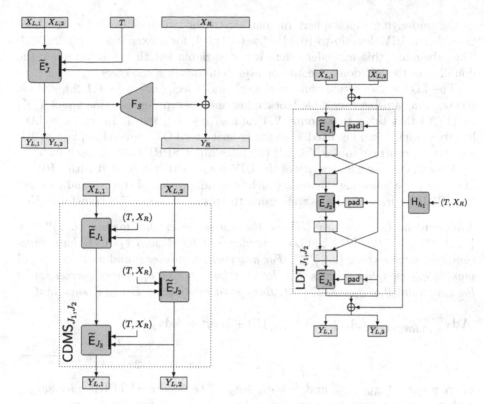

Fig. 10. Top left: Extended UIV construction with a black-box tweakable blockcipher $\widetilde{\mathsf{E}}$; **Bottom left:** CDMS extender; **Right:** LRW2 + LDT extender.

Theorem 5. *Let extended UIV be the scheme over the domain* $\{0,1\}^{2n} \times \{0,1\}^{\geq m}$ *using the CDMS extender. For any positive integer* v *and an adversary* $\mathcal{A}$ *making* q_{en} *encipher queries,* q_{de} *decipher queries and* q_{gu} *guess queries under the constraint that* $q_{\mathrm{gu}}v \leq 2^{2n-1}$, *there exist adversaries* $\mathcal{B}$ *and* $\mathcal{C}$ *such that*

$$\mathbf{Adv}^{\mathrm{rprp}}_{\mathrm{UIV[CDMS]}}(\mathcal{A}, v) \leq 3\mathbf{Adv}^{\mathrm{stprp}}_{\widetilde{\mathsf{E}}}(\mathcal{B}) + \frac{q^2}{2^{2n}} + \mathbf{Adv}^{\mathrm{prf}}_{\mathsf{F}}(\mathcal{C})$$

$$+ \frac{q_{\mathrm{gu}}v}{2^{2n-1}} + \frac{q^2}{2^{2n+1}} + \frac{q^2_{\mathrm{en}}}{2^{2n+1}} + \frac{q^2_1}{2^{2n+m+1}},$$

where $q = q_{\mathrm{en}} + q_{\mathrm{de}} + q_{\mathrm{gu}}$ *and* $q_1 = q_{\mathrm{en}} + q_{\mathrm{de}}$. *The resulting STPRP adversary* $\mathcal{B}$ *makes at most* q_{en} *encipher queries and* $q_{\mathrm{de}} + q_{\mathrm{gu}}$ *decipher queries, whereas the resulting PRF adversary* $\mathcal{C}$ *makes at most* $q_{\mathrm{en}} + q_{\mathrm{de}} + q_{\mathrm{gu}}$ *queries.*

6.2 LRW2 + LDT Extender

For our second extender we use the LRW2 [15] instantiation of $\widetilde{\mathsf{E}}^*$ with the 3-round length doubler construction LDT [7] by Chen, Mennink and Nandi serving as the underlying blockcipher. In contrast to the previous extender, the LDT extends the UIV domain to $\{0,1\}^{n+s} \times \{0,1\}^{\geq m}$, for a fixed $s \in [n+1, 2n-1]$. The advantage this extender offers is the variable length extension since the doubling of the left domain could be overabundant in some cases.

The LDT construction can "encipher" and "decipher" a $[n+1, 2n-1]$-bit string, using a n-bit tweakable blockcipher and a swapping function $\mathsf{swap}(X, Y) := (Y, X)$ that takes two inputs X, Y of size $1 \leq s \leq n-1$. In our case, LDT has fixed input size, i.e. fixed s, so the security for LDT we need is plain SPRP security, in contrast to the VSPRP (variable-input SPRP) notion used in [7].

We can express the security of the UIV construction extended with LRW2+ LDT using the following theorem, which is an adaptation of the original theorem for RPRP security of UIV as well, using the result of the LRW2 transform [15].

Theorem 6. *Let extended UIV be the scheme over the domain $\{0,1\}^{n+s} \times \{0,1\}^{\geq m}$ using the LRW2+LDT extender and let H be a ϵ_1-AXU hash function with output space $\{0,1\}^{n+s}$. For any positive integer v and an adversary $\mathcal{A}$ making q_{en} encipher queries, q_{de} decipher queries and q_{gu} guess queries under the constraint that $q_{gu} v \leq 2^{n+s-1}$, there exist adversaries $\mathcal{B}$ and $\mathcal{C}$ such that*

$$\mathbf{Adv}^{\mathrm{rprp}}_{\mathrm{UIV[LRW2+LDT]}}(\mathcal{A}, v) \leq \mathbf{Adv}^{\mathrm{sprp}}_{\mathrm{LDT}}(\mathcal{B}) + 3\epsilon_1 q^2 + \mathbf{Adv}^{\mathrm{prf}}_{\mathsf{F}}(\mathcal{C})$$

$$+ \frac{q_{gu} v}{2^{n+s-1}} + \frac{q^2}{2^{n+s+1}} + \frac{q_{en}^2}{2^{n+s+1}} + \frac{q_1^2}{2^{n+s+m+1}},$$

where $q = q_{en} + q_{de} + q_{gu}$ and $q_1 = q_{en} + q_{de}$. The resulting STPRP adversary $\mathcal{B}$ makes at most q_{en} encipher queries and $q_{de} + q_{gu}$ decipher queries, whereas the resulting PRF adversary $\mathcal{C}$ makes at most $q_{en} + q_{de} + q_{gu}$ queries.

Interpreting Corollary 2 from [7], the SPRP advantage of the LDT construction in the bound above gives at least $\frac{2n}{3}$ bits of security.

One should take care when instantiating the LRW2 AXU hash function H since it needs to have a non-standard output size. One natural approach is concatenating and truncating two independently keyed AXU hash functions. Start with a n-bit AXU H' and construct a $2n$-bit AXU by concatenating two instances of H' keyed with two independent keys. After that, truncate the output to the desired output size $n' \in [n+1, 2n-1]$, which would incur a security loss of $2n - n'$ bits. Examples of concatenating and truncating AXU hash functions can be found in these works [11,17,21].

7   Conclusion

In this work, we gave multiple new results on rugged pseudorandom permutations. The first group of results introduced the RPRPd and RPRPd variations of the main RPRP definition. Then, we showed two interesting results about the 3-round unbalanced Feistel scheme. First, that the ECE scheme satisfies the RPRPd but not the RPRPg security, and second, that the CEC scheme satisfies the RPRPg but not the RPRPd security.

After that, we presented the HEC scheme and proved it RPRP secure, making it, together with the UIV scheme, the only other construction proven to be RPRP secure so far. In the end, we showed that the left domain of the UIV construction could be extended using the 3-round CDMS and LDT schemes in a black-box manner, providing better security than the "plain" UIV, which furthermore can be beneficial for order-resilient channels that are instantiated with UIV as presented in [13, Section 6].

Collectively, these findings contribute to a deeper understanding of the RPRP notion and show that it is more natural than it may seem.

Acknowledgments. We thank the anonymous ASIACRYPT 2023 reviewers for their constructive comments. This research was supported by the German Federal Ministry of Education and Research and the Hessen State Ministry for Higher Education, Research and the Arts within their joint support of the National Research Center for Applied Cybersecurity ATHENE.

References

1. Abed, F., Forler, C., List, E., Lucks, S., Wenzel, J.: RIV for robust authenticated encryption. In: Peyrin, T. (ed.) FSE 2016. LNCS, vol. 9783, pp. 23–42. Springer, Heidelberg (2016). https://doi.org/10.1007/978-3-662-52993-5_2
2. Andreeva, E., Bhati, A.S., Preneel, B., Vizár, D.: 1, 2, 3, fork: Counter mode variants based on a generalized forkcipher. IACR Trans. Symm. Cryptol. **2021**(3), 1–35 (2021)
3. Andreeva, E., Bogdanov, A., Luykx, A., Mennink, B., Mouha, N., Yasuda, K.: How to securely release unverified plaintext in authenticated encryption. In: Sarkar, P., Iwata, T. (eds.) ASIACRYPT 2014, Part I. LNCS, vol. 8873, pp. 105–125. Springer, Heidelberg (2014). https://doi.org/10.1007/978-3-662-45611-8_6
4. Bacuieti, N., Daemen, J., Hoffert, S., Assche, G.V., Keer, R.V.: Jammin' on the deck. In: Agrawal, S., Lin, D. (eds.) ASIACRYPT 2022, Part II. LNCS, vol. 13792, pp. 555–584. Springer, Heidelberg (2022). https://doi.org/10.1007/978-3-031-22966-4_19
5. Bellare, M., Rogaway, P.: Encode-then-encipher encryption: how to exploit nonces or redundancy in plaintexts for efficient cryptography. In: Okamoto, T. (ed.) ASIACRYPT 2000. LNCS, vol. 1976, pp. 317–330. Springer, Heidelberg (2000). https://doi.org/10.1007/3-540-44448-3_24
6. Chen, S., Steinberger, J.: Tight security bounds for key-alternating ciphers. In: Nguyen, P.Q., Oswald, E. (eds.) EUROCRYPT 2014. LNCS, vol. 8441, pp. 327–350. Springer, Heidelberg (2014). https://doi.org/10.1007/978-3-642-55220-5_19
7. Chen, Y.L., Mennink, B., Nandi, M.: Short variable length domain extenders with beyond birthday bound security. In: Peyrin, T., Galbraith, S. (eds.) ASIACRYPT 2018, Part I. LNCS, vol. 11272, pp. 244–274. Springer, Cham (2018). https://doi.org/10.1007/978-3-030-03326-2_9
8. Coron, J.-S., Dodis, Y., Mandal, A., Seurin, Y.: A domain extender for the ideal cipher. In: Micciancio, D. (ed.) TCC 2010. LNCS, vol. 5978, pp. 273–289. Springer, Heidelberg (2010). https://doi.org/10.1007/978-3-642-11799-2_17
9. Crowley, P., Huckleberry, N., Biggers, E.: Length-preserving encryption with HCTR2. Cryptology ePrint Archive, Report 2021/1441 (2021). https://eprint.iacr.org/2021/1441

10. Daemen, J., Hoffert, S., Assche, G.V., Keer, R.V.: The design of Xoodoo and Xoofff. IACR Trans. Symm. Cryptol. **2018**(4), 1–38 (2018)
11. Degabriele, J.P., Govinden, J., Günther, F., Paterson, K.G.: The security of ChaCha20-Poly1305 in the multi-user setting. In: Vigna, G., Shi, E. (eds.) ACM CCS 2021, pp. 1981–2003. ACM Press, November 2021
12. Degabriele, J.P., Karadžić, V., Melloni, A., Münch, J.-P., Stam, M.: Rugged pseudorandom permutations and their applications. Presented at the IACR Real World Crypto Symposium (2022)
13. Degabriele, J.P., Karadžić, V.: Overloading the nonce: rugged PRPs, nonce-set AEAD, and order-resilient channels. In: Dodis, Y., Shrimpton, T. (eds.) CRYPTO 2022, Part IV. LNCS, vol. 13510, pp. 264–295. Springer, Heidelberg (2022). https://doi.org/10.1007/978-3-031-15985-5_10
14. Dutta, A., Nandi, M.: Tweakable HCTR: a BBB secure tweakable enciphering scheme. In: Chakraborty, D., Iwata, T. (eds.) INDOCRYPT 2018. LNCS, vol. 11356, pp. 47–69. Springer, Cham (2018). https://doi.org/10.1007/978-3-030-05378-9_3
15. Liskov, M., Rivest, R.L., Wagner, D.: Tweakable block ciphers. J. Cryptol. **24**(3), 588–613 (2011)
16. Luby, M., Rackoff, C.: How to construct pseudorandom permutations from pseudorandom functions. SIAM J. Comput. **17**(2), 373–386 (1988)
17. McGrew, D.A., Viega, J.: The security and performance of the galois/counter mode of operation (full version). Cryptology ePrint Archive, Report 2004/193 (2004). https://eprint.iacr.org/2004/193
18. Minematsu, K., Iwata, T.: Building blockcipher from tweakable blockcipher: extending FSE 2009 proposal. In: Chen, L. (ed.) IMACC 2011. LNCS, vol. 7089, pp. 391–412. Springer, Heidelberg (2011). https://doi.org/10.1007/978-3-642-25516-8_24
19. National Institute of Standards and Technology (NIST): The Third NIST Workshop on Block Cipher Modes of Operation (2023). https://csrc.nist.gov/Events/2023/third-workshop-on-block-cipher-modes-of-operation
20. Patarin, J.: The "Coefficients H" technique. In: Avanzi, R.M., Keliher, L., Sica, F. (eds.) SAC 2008. LNCS, vol. 5381, pp. 328–345. Springer, Heidelberg (2009). https://doi.org/10.1007/978-3-642-04159-4_21
21. Rogaway, P.: Bucket hashing and its application to fast message authentication. In: Coppersmith, D. (ed.) CRYPTO 1995. LNCS, vol. 963, pp. 29–42. Springer, Heidelberg (1995). https://doi.org/10.1007/3-540-44750-4_3
22. Rogaway, P., Shrimpton, T.: A provable-security treatment of the key-wrap problem. In: Vaudenay, S. (ed.) EUROCRYPT 2006. LNCS, vol. 4004, pp. 373–390. Springer, Heidelberg (2006). https://doi.org/10.1007/11761679_23
23. Shrimpton, T., Terashima, R.S.: A modular framework for building variable-input-length tweakable ciphers. In: Sako, K., Sarkar, P. (eds.) ASIACRYPT 2013, Part I. LNCS, vol. 8269, pp. 405–423. Springer, Heidelberg (2013). https://doi.org/10.1007/978-3-642-42033-7_21
24. Wang, P., Feng, D., Wu, W.: HCTR: a variable-input-length enciphering mode. In: Feng, D., Lin, D., Yung, M. (eds.) CISC 2005. LNCS, vol. 3822, pp. 175–188. Springer, Heidelberg (2005). https://doi.org/10.1007/11599548_15

Generic Security of the SAFE API
and Its Applications

Dmitry Khovratovich[1], Mario Marhuenda Beltrán[2(✉)] [iD], and Bart Mennink[2] [iD]

[1] Ethereum Foundation, Luxembourg City, Luxembourg
[2] Radboud University, Nijmegen, The Netherlands
{m.marhuenda,b.mennink}@cs.ru.nl

Abstract. We provide security foundations for SAFE, a recently introduced API framework for sponge-based hash functions tailored to prime-field-based protocols. SAFE aims to provide a robust and foolproof interface, has been implemented in the Neptune hash framework and some zero-knowledge proof projects, but despite its usability and applicability it currently lacks any security proof. Such a proof would not be straightforward as SAFE abuses the inner part of the sponge and fills it with protocol-specific data.

In this work we identify the SAFECore as versatile variant sponge construction underlying SAFE, we prove indifferentiability of SAFECore for all (binary and prime) fields up to around $|\mathbb{F}_p|^{c/2}$ queries, where $\mathbb{F}_p$ is the underlying field and c the capacity, and we apply this security result to various use cases. We show that the SAFE-based protocols of plain hashing, authenticated encryption, verifiable computation, non-interactive proofs, and commitment schemes are secure against a wide class of adversaries, including those dealing with multiple invocations of a sponge in a single application. Our results pave the way of using SAFE with the full taxonomy of hash functions, including SNARK-, lattice-, and x86-friendly hashes.

Keywords: SAFE · sponge · API · field elements · indifferentiability

1 Introduction

The sponge construction is a permutation-based mode for cryptographic hashing. It was first introduced by Bertoni et al. [13], and it quickly gained in popularity, in particular in light of the SHA-3 competition [34], which was won by the Keccak sponge function [11]. The sponge operates on a b-bit state, which is split into a c-bit inner part, where c is called the "capacity", and an r-bit outer part, where r is called the "rate". On input of a message, the sponge first injectively pads this message and splits it into r-bit chunks. These chunks are then absorbed one by one by adding them to the outer part of the state, where each addition is interleaved with an evaluation of a b-bit permutation of the state. After the message is absorbed, digests are squeezed r bits at a time by extracting them from the outer part.

© International Association for Cryptologic Research 2023
J. Guo and R. Steinfeld (Eds.): ASIACRYPT 2023, LNCS 14445, pp. 301–327, 2023.
https://doi.org/10.1007/978-981-99-8742-9_10

Under the assumption that the permutation is random, Bertoni et al. [13] proved that the sponge behaves like a random oracle up to around $2^{c/2}$ queries in the indifferentiability framework [30]. Naito and Ohta proved a similar result for a slightly more general setting where the initial message block can be $r + c/2$ bits, and the squeezing is performed with around $r + c/2 - \log_2(c)$ bits at a time [33].

These are powerful results: they imply that the sponge construction behaves like a random oracle and can replace it as such in many applications, as long as less than $2^{c/2}$ evaluations of the permutation are made. They imply that finding collisions, preimages, or second preimages is not easier than finding them for a random oracle (up to this bound),[1] but they can also be used in keyed applications [11]. Improved but comparable results for keyed applications are derived by using the sponge's sibling, namely the duplex construction [9,10,18, 20,32]. A thorough account of the duplex can be found in the work by Mennink [31].

1.1   Field-Based Sponges and SAFE API

Both the sponge and the duplex specification, however, see their inputs and outputs as raw bits, and leave application-specific encoding to the users. The exact encoding, as long as it is injective and reasonably simple, does not pose a performance problem for regular hash functions such as SHA-2/3 as they are usually not a bottleneck in applications. The situation is drastically different in protocols that operate on prime field elements rather than on bits, and particularly in those that deal with verifiable computation of hash functions – e.g. private cryptocurrencies and mixers [2,26], recursive proof systems [15,27], and zero-knowledge virtual machine (ZKVM) computations [39]. The infamous example of Zcash's transaction requiring 40 s to be generated triggered the design of field-oriented hash functions Poseidon [23], Rescue [4], MiMC [3], and Reinforced Concrete [22]. With many of these functions designed in the sponge framework, it became crucial to utilize as much throughput of the sponge as possible, ideally removing all possible overhead such as padding. Indeed, a sponge-based hash function with a rate of $r = 2$ elements spends one permutation to hash a pair of unpadded field elements, but two permutation calls if the input is padded. For obvious reasons, a straightforward removal of padding or building a hash function directly from the inner permutation rather than the sponge framework has led to terrible bugs [1] and, in general case, to bad practices. Extensive use of a sponge function may also incur domain-separation issues or even cross-oracle collisions, i.e. collisions between the implementations of two different random oracles in the same protocol.

Another problem, not specific to sponge functions, arises in the context of the interactive protocols and the Fiat-Shamir heuristic [21] to make them noninteractive. Researchers have found several critical bugs in the implementations of Fiat-Shamir [8,17,19,25], which are partly attributed to the fact that the

---

[1] For preimage resistance, an improved result is derived, cf. [28].

protocol state is stateful and interactive whereas the older hash functions from the SHA family are not interactive and few implementations are stateful. It is natural to implement Fiat-Shamir via sponges, but no concrete design has been proposed so far.

To salvage this issue, Aumasson et al. [5] proposed SAFE (Sponge API for Field Elements), a generic API for sponge functions specifically tailored towards its use on field elements. They also provided a production-ready reference implementation. SAFE has already been implemented in Filecoin's Neptune hash framework and has been integrated in other zero-knowledge proof projects [29,37]. A sponge call in SAFE takes as input an input-output (IO) pattern IO, that among others contains the particular order of the absorb calls and squeeze calls, and optionally a domain separator D. The IO and D are then hashed onto $c/2$ elements of the inner part of the state (using a general collision resistant hash function like SHA-3). Then, it operates a sponge in an online mode, where data is absorbed as it comes and squeezed as it is needed, provided the absorbing and squeezing happen in accordance with the IO pattern IO. At first sight, this IO pattern seems to limit the generality as it encodes the upcoming hash *in advance*, but this is not a problem for most applications of SAFE: e.g. Merkle trees, interactive protocols, and verifiable encryption of cryptocurrency transactions all know how much data and in which order should be hashed. On the other hand, the usage of the IO avoids the need to use padding, eliminates misuse patterns by limiting the set of callable operations, and contributes to avoiding collisions between instantiations of different oracles. As such, SAFE forms a versatile API for many protocols that use hash functions under the hood, and would like to do it securely.

One may wonder the choice of using two different hash functions, a regular one for absorbing the IO pattern and the domain separator, and a field-oriented one for the online mode. However, there are multiple reasons to do so. First, since IO and D are usually protocol constants, it makes sense to precompute the initial state of SAFE. If IO and D were simply absorbed into the sponge, the size of the precomputation would be b field elements. By hashing them into the inner part, we reduce this to $c/2$ field elements. Second, since D is optional and of variable length, it would require an extra padding (and a specification of it) to make sure it does not overlap with the future absorptions. This extra padding can be costly if working over large fields. Third, the hashing of IO and D is currently independent of the sponge used within SAFE. This allows us to reuse hashed states across different sponges while still providing the same security. This also emphasizes that the processing of IO is different from processing the data as those are inputs that are generated by different roles: protocol designer and protocol party, respectively.

1.2 Generic and Improved Security of SAFE API

It is clear that SAFE API is a versatile API with many potential applications. For example, it has already found employment in the Filecoin's Neptune[2] hash framework. However, despite all its utility, a rigorous analysis of SAFE API, providing a tight bound on its security, is missing. It is possible to argue security of SAFE in the random oracle model using the indifferentiability result of Naito and Ohta [33], but the resulting bound is not quite as good. Most importantly, Naito and Ohta apply an injective padding to the message, which is absent in SAFE. In addition, as in SAFE the encoding of the IO and D are hashed into only $c/2$ field elements of the inner part, an adaptation of the security proof of Naito and Ohta to this setting would give $c/4$ field element security at best. For authenticated encryption applications, i.e. where absorbing rounds and squeezing rounds are interleaved, an additional point of concern is raised as one uses the same IO pattern for different message lengths.

These issues leave us with an undesired situation: (i) the security proof is not rigorous, and (ii) even if it were correct, only security up to $|\mathbb{F}_p|^{c/4}$ evaluations is guaranteed due to possible hash function collisions.

In order to both derive a rigorous analysis and to improve this $|\mathbb{F}_p|^{c/4}$ bound, we first describe a variant sponge construction, called `SAFECore`, on top of a cryptographic hash function H and a permutation P. It gets as input an IO pattern $IO \in (\mathbb{N}_+)^*$, optionally a domain separator $D \in \{0,1\}^*$, and a message M of appropriate length. The IO pattern is required to be of even length, and alternatingly describes the number of field elements absorbed and squeezed. Note that this definition is slightly different from the IO pattern in the SAFE API, but the changes are only cosmetic and are made to make the security proof easier to construct and process. Besides, a translation between the two is clear. The `SAFECore` construction then operates by first hashing the IO pattern and the domain separator onto the *entire inner part* (as opposed to half of it) using hash function H, and processing a sponge as usual using permutation P. The message is required to be of appropriate length as dictated by the IO pattern IO, and the number of squeezed blocks will be determined by the *next* element in IO. We stress that this seems like a restriction compared to the original SAFE API, but this restriction is solely to make the proof convenient; after all, `SAFECore` will be used as a *building block* to argue security of the SAFE API. A detailed description of `SAFECore` is given in Sect. 3, including our security result (proof in Sect. 4) guaranteeing indifferentiability up to $|\mathbb{F}_p|^{c/2}$ queries. Here, we stress that we have improved security compared to what was suggested for the SAFE API based on the work of Naito and Ohta. This is because of our observation that one can hash the IO pattern and the domain separator onto the *entire* inner part, without any risk and thus with a free security improvement from $|\mathbb{F}_p|^{c/4}$ to $|\mathbb{F}_p|^{c/2}$. The observation is comparable to the truncated permutation without initial value construction of Grassi and Mennink [24] with significant difference that their construction only makes one permutation call on input of a partially random partially chosen state, instead of a full-fledged sponge.

[2] https://github.com/filecoin-project/neptune/tree/master/src/sponge.

Our proof is field-agnostic, which extends the domain of SAFE from the originally envisioned 256-bit fields to both bigger and smaller ones: processing 380-bit curve coordinates [14], 64-bit hashes for verifiable computation based on FRI commitments [35], 12-bit hashes for aggregating post-quantum signatures [36], and other lattice-based scenarios.

1.3 Applications

We stress that SAFECore is not made to be run only in isolation, it rather serves as a building block to argue security of the much more versatile and user-friendly SAFE API. In more detail, the specification of the SAFE API [5] (discussed in Sect. 5) is very general, but to assure generality in a foolproof interface, it follows strict rules with respect to the IO pattern IO and the upcoming absorbing and squeezing evaluations. SAFECore, in turn, is defined in such a way that it is possible to describe any correct application of the SAFE API in terms of the SAFECore construction. This immediately implies generic security of the application in light of our indifferentiability result of Theorem 2.

To exemplify this, we discuss in Sects. 5.1–5.4 various applications of SAFE based on those given by the designers [5]: plain hashing, commitment schemes, interactive protocols, and authenticated encryption. For each of these applications, we describe *exactly* how they can be built by using SAFECore internally, and we derive generic security in the appropriate model for the application. We demonstrate that all applications achieve 128-bit security in their respective model, provided $c \geq \mu$ elements and provided they output μ elements, where μ is the number of field elements that correspond to 256 bits (or a little less). For example, for prime fields stemming from elliptic curve groups, we typically set $\mu = 1$. Likewise, for 64-bit Goldilocks prime field [35], we would have $\mu = 4$.

Our results, in fact, imply something stronger. Each particular application defines for the underlying protocols which kind of adversaries it protects against. As SAFE requires the protocol that uses it to specify the length of input and output messages, in many real-world scenarios the application does not bother with collisions or preimages that violate the specification. We call this setting *single-oracle security*. A less frequent case is when the application needs protection against inputs of other lengths too. This case may arise when a protocol employs different random oracles that take different inputs. We call this scenario *cross-oracle security*. We show that when all the oracles are implemented with SAFECore, and the adversary has only limited control on how these oracles are initialized using the IO pattern and the domain separation, then the security still holds up to 128-bit security.

Theorem 1. *(Informal) Let $\mathcal{P}$ be a cryptographic protocol that employs random oracles $\mathcal{R}_1, \mathcal{R}_2, \ldots, \mathcal{R}_k$ and is secure in the random oracle model against adversaries that make up to 2^λ queries to the oracles. Then, the implementation of this protocol with oracle $\mathcal{R}_i$ instantiated with the SAFE API using a field of size at least $2^{2\lambda}$ and a domain separator D_i (pairwise distinct) is secure against adversaries that make up to 2^λ queries to underlying hash H and permutation P.*

A more detailed statement can be found in Sect. 5.

1.4 Outline

Section 2 introduces the notation we will use and the necessary context, such as the sponge construction and the indifferentiability framework. Section 3 describes the SAFECore construction in detail and its generic security result (Theorem 2). In Sect. 4 we give a formal proof of the security result. We discuss the SAFE API in detail in Sect. 5, where we also demonstrate how the security of SAFECore implies the security of any proper evaluation of the SAFE API. In Sects. 5.1–5.4 this fundamental observation is applied to various use cases of the SAFE API in order to derive simple and meaningful security claims. The work is concluded in Sect. 6.

2 Preliminaries

2.1 Notation

We use machine typographic fonts to denote functions (e.g. A, a), upper case bold to denote sets (e.g. $\mathbf{A}, \mathbf{B}$), and case sans-serif to denote variables (e.g. a, b). To denote the set of natural numbers, we use $\mathbb{N}$. We use $\emptyset$ to denote the empty set and $\mathbf{S}^* = \cup_{i=0}^{\infty} \mathbf{S}^i$ for a set $\mathbf{S}$. Given $x \in \mathbf{S}^*$, there exists a unique n so that $x \in \mathbf{S}^n$, we denote it by $\mathtt{len}(x) = n$. Abusing notation, we denote the empty string by $\emptyset$ as well. For a finite set $\mathbf{S}$, we say that $x \xleftarrow{\$} \mathbf{S}$ when x is sampled uniformly from $\mathbf{S}$. Throughout, we will use r to denote the rate and c to denote the capacity. For an explanation of their meaning see Sect. 3.1.

Given a tuple $x = (x_1, x_2, \dots) \in \mathbf{S}^*$, we also denote it $x = x_1 \| x_2 \| \dots$ and we use both notations interchangeably. We denote $x[1 : k] = (x_1, \dots, x_k)$. We denote by $\mathtt{left}_r : \mathbf{S}^* \to \mathbf{S}^r$ and $\mathtt{right}_c : \mathbf{S}^* \to \mathbf{S}^c$ the functions defined by $\mathtt{left}_r(m_r \| m_{\text{rest}}) = m_r$ and $\mathtt{right}_c(m_{\text{rest}} \| m_c) = m_c$.

Given $M \in \mathbf{S}^*$, we denote $\mathtt{cut}_r(M) = (M_1, \dots, M_\ell)$, where:

$$M_1 = M[1 : r],$$
$$M_2 = M[r + 1 : 2r],$$
$$M_3 = M[2r + 1 : 3r],$$
$$\vdots$$
$$M_\ell = M[(\ell - 1)r + 1 : \mathtt{len}(M)] \| 0^{-M \bmod r},$$

where 0^ℓ denotes the all 0's string of bits of length ℓ. We denote by $\mathtt{pad}_r(\cdot)$ an injective padding, e.g. an injective function $\mathbf{S}^* \to (\mathbf{S}^r)^*$. A usual padding is the 10-padding, which works by appending one 1 and filling the rest with 0's, in the case elements $\mathbf{S}$ can be represented by a string of bits, e.g. when $\mathbf{S}$ is a finite field.

We use RO to denote a random oracle [6].

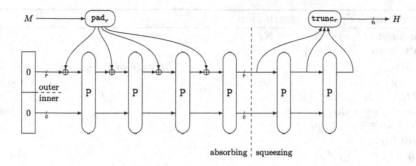

Fig. 1. Sponge construction, with a requested output of n bits.

2.2 Security Model

In this paper, we use the indifferentiability framework, first introduced by Maurer et al. [30] and refined to the context of hash functions by Coron et al. [16]. We introduce the indifferentiability framework below. We will use it to analyze the SAFECore construction in Sect. 3.

Consider a construction C, relying on an ideal primitive P: $C^P : S^* \rightarrow S^*$. Then consider a simulator, S, with the same interface as P. Finally, we consider a distinguisher D, which is an algorithm having access to either (RO, S^{RO}) or (C^P, P). In the first case we say that D is in the ideal world, denoted by W_I, whereas in the second case, it is said to be in the real world, denoted by W_R. The goal of D is to determine in which world it was placed. If D determines it is in W_R, it outputs 0, and 1 otherwise.

The advantage of D is defined as:

$$\mathbf{Adv}_{C,S}^{iff}(D) = \left| \Pr\left[D^{W_I} \Rightarrow 1\right] - \Pr\left[D^{W_R} \Rightarrow 1\right] \right|. \tag{1}$$

2.3 Sponge Construction

In this section, we give a description of the standard sponge construction operating on bits. Let $b, r, c \in \mathbb{N}$ such that $b = r + c$. Let $P : \{0,1\}^b \rightarrow \{0,1\}^b$ be a permutation.

First, the sponge gets an input, $(M, n) \in \{0,1\}^* \times \mathbb{N}_+$. It *absorbs* the message M and then it *squeezes* n bits as output. A formal description is given in Fig. 1 and Algorithm 1.

2.4 Limitations in Application

The sponge construction is a powerful versatile tool. In particular, it can be used to argue security of the duplex construction and security of keyed applications of the sponge (e.g. the keyed sponge [12]) or keyed applications of the duplex (e.g. SpongeWrap [10]).

Algorithm 1. Sponge construction
___
Data: input $(M, n) \in \{0,1\}^* \times \mathbb{N}_+$
Result: output $Z \in \{0,1\}^\infty$
1: $S = 0^b$ ▷ State of the sponge construction
2: $Z = \emptyset$ ▷ Output string
3: $(M_1, \ldots, M_\ell) = \text{pad}_r(M)$
4: **for** $1 \le i \le \ell$ **do**   ▷ Absorb
5:      $S \leftarrow \text{P}(S \oplus (M_i \| 0^c))$
6: **end for**
7: **for** $1 \le i \le \lceil \frac{n}{r} \rceil$ **do**   ▷ Squeeze
8:      $Z \leftarrow Z \| \text{left}_r(S)$
9:      $S \leftarrow \text{P}(S)$
10: **end for**
11: **return** $Z[1 : n]$ ▷ $Z[1 : n]$ means the first n <u>bits</u>
___

On the downside, however, the sponge requires an injective padding. A typical choice for this is the 10-padding, which on input of a message $M \in \{0,1\}^*$ appends a single 1 and a sufficient number of 0's such that the resulting string is in $(\{0,1\}^r)^*$. Although in most use cases this is fine, it is problematic if the sponge is not applied on raw bits but rather on (large) field elements where we take a low value for r. For example, if one uses a permutation on top of two field elements, one simply takes $c = r = 1$, and padding *always* incurs an extra permutation call.

We stress that one cannot simply discard the 10-padding. The reason for this is that ending with a 0^r-block could be problematic. Consider, for the sake of example, a simplified setting where the sponge is evaluated for two padded messages, $M \in \{0,1\}^{3r}$ with a requested digest of $2r$ bits and $M' = M\|0^r \in \{0,1\}^{4r}$ with a requested digest of r bits. In this case, we will necessarily have

$$\text{Sponge}(M, 2r)[r + 1 : 2r] = \text{Sponge}(M', r)[1 : r],$$

which would happen for a RO with negligible probability.

We stress that it *is* possible to have padded messages ending with a 0^r-block, but only in very restricted settings, where in particular overlapping squeeze/absorb evaluations are avoided. This case is, however, not supported by the current sponge indifferentiability proofs [13,33].

3   SAFECore Construction

In this section, we will describe the SAFECore construction, which will be a building block that we will use in Sect. 5 to argue security of the full SAFE API. We first describe the construction in Sect. 3.1, we give an extensive example use case in Sect. 3.2, and we discuss the security of SAFECore in Sect. 3.3.

3.1 Construction

In this section we give a description of the SAFECore construction. Consider a finite field $\mathbb{F}_p$. Let $b, r, c \in \mathbb{N}$ such that $b = r + c$. Let $\mathsf{P} : \mathbb{F}_p^b \to \mathbb{F}_p^b$ be a permutation, and let $\mathsf{H} : (\mathbb{N}_+)^* \times \{0,1\}^* \to \mathbb{F}_p^c$ be a hash function. Given $X = (X_r, X_c) \in \mathbb{F}_p^b$, we reuse the previous notation: $\texttt{left}_r(X) = X_r$ and $\texttt{right}_c(X) = X_c$.

SAFECore takes an input $(IO, D, M) \in (\mathbb{N}_+)^* \times \{0,1\}^* \times (\mathbb{F}_p)^*$. Here, IO is the input-output (IO) pattern, D, an optional domain separator that will mostly be of use in the applications in Sect. 5, and message, M, which is expected to obey to IO in a certain way. To be precise, IO is a tuple of even length, that we decompose as $IO = (I_1, O_1, \ldots, I_\ell, O_\ell)$, where the I_i correspond to the number of elements of $\mathbb{F}_p$ absorbed and the O_i correspond to the number of elements of $\mathbb{F}_p$ squeezed. Looking ahead, the SAFE API alternates absorbing phases with squeezing phases as prescribed by IO. As SAFECore will be used as a building block, it is more restricted. To be precise, in SAFECore the message M is restricted to the condition that its length $\texttt{len}(M)$ should be equal to $I_1 + I_2 + \cdots + I_k$ for some $k \leq \ell$. In this case, the number of squeezed elements will be O_k.

Formally, we define the set of acceptable inputs:

$$
\mathbf{I} = \left\{ (IO, D, M) \in (\mathbb{N}_+)^* \times \{0,1\}^* \times (\mathbb{F}_p)^* \;\middle|\; \begin{array}{l} IO = (I_1, O_1, \ldots, I_\ell, O_\ell), \\[2mm] \exists\, k \text{ such that } \texttt{len}(M) = \sum_{j=1}^{k} I_j \end{array} \right\}. \tag{2}
$$

For any $(IO, D, M) \in \mathbf{I}$, we define $\mathsf{absrnds}(IO, M)$ as the unique number k such that $\texttt{len}(M) = \sum_{j=1}^{k} I_j$.

On input of a tuple $(IO, D, M) \in \mathbf{I}$, SAFECore evaluates H on input of (IO, D) to obtain a value $H \in \mathbb{F}_p^c$, which it uses to initialize the inner part of the sponge. Then, a variant of the sponge is used to absorb M *in accordance with the IO pattern IO*. For this, a specific padding function SAFECorePad (Algorithm 2), will be employed. SAFECorePad properly pads each absorption round (noting that I_j is expressed in terms of elements and not in terms of r-element blocks) and for blank evaluations of in-between squeezing rounds. Then, at the end, it squeezes $O_{\mathsf{absrnds}(IO,M)}$ elements in $\mathbb{F}_p$. We stress that this last step is *not* in accordance with how the SAFE API works, recalling that it alternates absorbing and squeezing phases, but after all, SAFECore is defined more restrictively as being an easy-to-analyze building block for the SAFE API. A full description of the SAFECore construction is given in Fig. 2 and Algorithm 3.

3.2 Example

Consider an instantiation of SAFECore with parameters $c = 2, r = 2$. A typical IO pattern could be $IO = (8, 6, 5, 3, 4, 7)$. In the SAFE API (that we will discuss

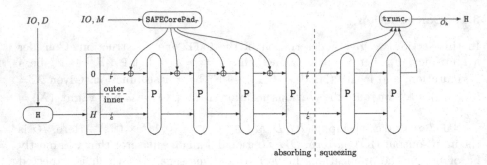

Fig. 2. SAFECore construction, where the input message M is of length $I_1 + \cdots + I_k$ elements and the digest consists of O_k elements. The function SAFECorePad is described in Algorithm 3.

Algorithm 2. Description of SAFECorePad

Data: input $(IO, M) \in \mathbf{I}$
Result: output $M' \in (\mathbb{F}_p^r)^*$
 1: $k = \mathtt{absrnds}(IO, M)$
 2: $M' = \emptyset$ ▷ Output string
 3: **for** $1 \le i \le k-1$ **do**
 4:     $M' \leftarrow M' \| M[I_1 + \cdots + I_{i-1} + 1 : I_1 + \cdots + I_i] \| 0^{-I_i \bmod r}$
 5:     $M' \leftarrow M' \| 0^{r \lceil O_i / r \rceil}$
 6: **end for**
 7: $M' \leftarrow M' \| M[I_1 + \cdots + I_{k-1} + 1 : I_1 + \cdots + I_k] \| 0^{-I_k \bmod r}$
 8: **return** M'

---

in Sect. 5), this pattern means that we start with absorbing 8 elements in $\mathbb{F}_p$ (which happens in 4 rounds, as $r = 2$), followed by squeezing 6 elements in $\mathbb{F}_p$ (which happens in 3 rounds), followed by absorbing 5 elements (which happens in 3 rounds), and so on. However, SAFECore is more restrictive than that, in order to be able to have an easy-to-analyze building block for the SAFE API. Concretely, for the example IO, there are three permissible message lengths:

- 8 elements from $\mathbb{F}_p$, in which case the output consists of 6 elements from $\mathbb{F}_p$;
- 13 elements from $\mathbb{F}_p$, in which case the output consists of 3 elements from $\mathbb{F}_p$;
- 17 elements from $\mathbb{F}_p$, in which case the output consists of 7 elements from $\mathbb{F}_p$.

We remark that, although IO puts restrictions on the length of M, one may allow arbitrary-length squeezing at the end. We have not included this option in our formalization in order to stay close to the SAFE API, but the security analysis in our work would allow this.

3.3   Security of SAFECore Construction

When D is in the real world, we count the cost of queries by how many times H and P are called, where duplicate queries are only counted once. For our running

Algorithm 3. Description of SAFECore

Data: input $(IO, D, M) \in \mathbf{I}$
Result: output $Z \in (\mathbb{F}_p)^*$

1: $S = 0^r \| \mathrm{H}(IO, D)$ ▷ State of the SAFECore construction
2: $Z = \emptyset$ ▷ Output string
3: $M' = \mathtt{SAFECorePad}(IO, M)$ ▷ See Algorithm 2
4: **for** $1 \le i \le \mathtt{len}(M')/r$ **do**   ▷ Absorb
5:     $S \leftarrow \mathrm{P}(S \oplus (M'[r \cdot (i-1) + 1 : r \cdot i] \| 0^c))$
6: **end for**
7: $k = \mathtt{absrnds}(IO, M)$
8: **for** $1 \le i \le \lceil O_k/r \rceil$ **do**   ▷ Squeeze
9:     $Z \leftarrow Z \| \mathtt{left}_r(S)$
10:     $S \leftarrow \mathrm{P}(S)$
11: **end for**
12: **return** $Z[1 : O_k]$ ▷ $Z[1 : O_k]$ means the first O_k elements

---

example of Sect. 3.2, if one makes three evaluations of SAFECore as suggested, where the three message inputs are prefixes of each other, the total cost is the total number of unique permutation evaluations, which happens to be as much as the cost of the longest query of the three.

When D is in the ideal world, we likewise count the cost of queries by how many times H and P would have been called, had the same query been made in the real world.

We now state the main security result.

Theorem 2 (Security of SAFECore). *Let* C *be the* SAFECore *construction based on a random oracle* H *and random permutation* P. *There exists a simulator* S, *such that for any distinguisher* D *making at most* Q_{H} *unique hash queries and* Q_{P} *unique primitive queries:*

$$Adv_{\mathrm{C,S}}^{\mathrm{iff}}(\mathrm{D}) \le \frac{3 \cdot \binom{Q_{\mathrm{H}}}{2} + 2 \cdot \binom{Q_{\mathrm{P}}}{2} + 4 \cdot Q_{\mathrm{P}} \cdot Q_{\mathrm{H}}}{|\mathbb{F}_p|^c} + \frac{3 \cdot \binom{Q_{\mathrm{P}}}{2}}{|\mathbb{F}_p|^b}. \tag{3}$$

The proof is given in Sect. 4.

4 Proof of Theorem 2

Let C be the SAFECore construction based on a random oracle H and random permutation P. Our goal is to construct a simulator S such that for any distinguisher D, the following distance is "small", in a precise way:

$$\mathbf{Adv}_{\mathrm{C,S}}^{\mathrm{iff}}(\mathrm{D}) = \left| \Pr\left[\mathrm{D}^{\mathrm{RO,S^{RO}}} \Rightarrow 1 \right] - \Pr\left[\mathrm{D}^{\mathrm{C^{H,P},H,P}} \Rightarrow 1 \right] \right|. \tag{4}$$

Here, S simulates both the hash function H, and the construction P in both directions, i.e., it simulates both P and P^{-1}. Abusing notation, we denote S =

(S_H, S_P, S_{P-1}).[3] The world (RO, S^{RO}) is called the ideal world and $(C^{H,P}, H, P)$ is called the real world. These worlds are depicted in Fig. 3.

First, in Sect. 4.1, we will describe our simulator. In Sect. 4.2 we will describe an intermediate world and apply the triangle inequality to derive two easier-to-bound distances from (4). These two distances are then bounded in Sects. 4.4 and 4.5, using bad events introduced in Sect. 4.3. The proof is inspired by that of Naito and Ohta [33], but in addition taking into account the hashing functionality and its related bad events.

4.1 Simulator

We first define $\mathbf{I}_{ext}$ (read $\mathbf{I}$ extended):

$$
\mathbf{I}_{ext} = \bigcup_{(IO,D,M)\in\mathbf{I}} \left\{ (IO, D, M'\|M'') \;\middle|\; \begin{array}{l} M' = \texttt{SAFECorePad}(IO, M), \\ M'' \in \{\emptyset, 0^r, \dots, 0^{r(\lceil O_k/r\rceil - 1)}\}, \\ \text{where } k = \texttt{absrnds}(IO, M) \end{array} \right\},
$$

where the function SAFECorePad is defined in Algorithm 3. Intuitively $\mathbf{I}_{ext}$ covers all tuples for which the simulator knows that, if it receives an input value X to S_P "completing" $(IO, D, M) \in \mathbf{I}_{ext}$, it will have to output a value consistent with the random oracle. However, it will also need to know *which* bits of the output of the (variable output length) RO it has to select. Therefore, for any $(IO, D, M) \in \mathbf{I}_{ext}$, we define $\texttt{Oelts}(IO, M)$ as the total number of elements (i.e. the length of $\texttt{len}(M'')$) attached to M'.

The simulator can be queried through three interfaces: S_H, S_P, and S_P^{-1}. It maintains tables $\mathbf{C}_H$ and $\mathbf{C}_P$ recording the query-response pairs of each query: any input-output tuple $S_H(IO, D) \mapsto H$ is stored as (IO, D, H) in $\mathbf{C}_H$, and any input-output tuple $S_P(X) \mapsto Y$ or $S_P^{-1}(Y) \mapsto X$ is stored as (X, Y) in $\mathbf{C}_P$. Furthermore, we define:

$$
\begin{aligned}
\mathbf{D}_H &= \{(IO, D) \in (\mathbb{N}_+)^* \times \{0,1\}^* \mid \exists H \in \mathbb{F}_p^c \text{ s.t. } (IO, D, H) \in \mathbf{C}_H\}, \\
\mathbf{R}_H &= \{H \in \mathbb{F}_p^c \mid \exists (IO, D) \in (\mathbb{N}_+)^* \times \{0,1\}^* \text{ s.t. } (IO, D, H) \in \mathbf{C}_H\}, \\
\mathbf{D}_P &= \{X \in \mathbb{F}_p^b \mid \exists Y \in \mathbb{F}_p^b \text{ s.t. } (X, Y) \in \mathbf{C}_P\}, \\
\mathbf{R}_P &= \{Y \in \mathbb{F}_p^b \mid \exists X \in \mathbb{F}_p^b \text{ s.t. } (X, Y) \in \mathbf{C}_P\}.
\end{aligned}
$$

The simulator maintains a graph that it uses to avoid discrepancies that D might detect. We adopt the graph representation from Bertoni et al. [13].

The nodes are elements of $\mathbb{F}_p^b$. Two nodes $X, Y \in \mathbb{F}_p^b$ are joined by an edge if $\exists M \in \mathbb{F}_p^r$ such that $(X \oplus (M\|0^c), Y) \in \mathbf{C}_P$. Then M is the label of the edge joining X and Y, which we denote as $X \xrightarrow{M} Y$. We write $X \to Y$ to denote that X and Y are linked through a 0-string label. We say that X is a root node if there exists $(IO, D, H) \in \mathbf{C}_H$ so that $X = 0^r\|H$. For simplicity, we denote $X \xrightarrow{M_1} Y \xrightarrow{M_2} Z$ by $X \xrightarrow{M_1\|M_2} Z$. The graph is initialized by the simulator as

---

[3] Here, we omit the superscript RO on S to simplify notation.

Algorithm 4. Simulator S

Function S_H:
Data: input $(IO, D) \in (\mathbb{N}_+)^* \times \{0,1\}^*$
Result: output $H \in \mathbb{F}_p^c$

1: $H \xleftarrow{\$} \mathbb{F}_p^c$
2: $\mathbf{C_H} \leftarrow \mathbf{C_H} \cup \{(IO, D, H)\}$
3: **return** H

Function S_P:
Data: input $X \in \mathbb{F}_p^b$
Result: output $Y \in \mathbb{F}_p^b$

1: **if** $\exists (IO, D, M\|u) \in \mathbf{I}_{\text{ext}}, H \in \mathbb{F}_p^c : (IO, D, H) \in \mathbf{C_H} \wedge \left(0^r\|H \xRightarrow{M} X \oplus (u\|0^c) \right)$ **then**
2: $\quad \alpha \leftarrow \texttt{0elts}(IO, M\|u)$
3: $\quad M' \leftarrow \texttt{left}_{\texttt{len}(M\|u)-\alpha}(M\|u)$
4: $\quad Y_r \leftarrow \texttt{RO}(IO, D, M')[\alpha + 1 : \alpha + r]$
5: $\quad Y_c \xleftarrow{\$} \mathbb{F}_p^c$
6: $\quad Y \leftarrow Y_r \| Y_c$
7: **else**
8: $\quad Y \xleftarrow{\$} \mathbb{F}_p^b$
9: **end if**
10: $\mathbf{C_P} \leftarrow \mathbf{C_P} \cup \{(X, Y)\}$
11: **return** Y

Function S_P^{-1}:
Data: input $Y \in \mathbb{F}_p^b$
Result: output $X \in \mathbb{F}_p^b$

1: $X \xleftarrow{\$} \mathbb{F}_p^b$
2: $\mathbf{C_P} \leftarrow \mathbf{C_P} \cup \{(X, Y)\}$
3: **return** Y

---

being empty, then it is updated lazily in the following way: When a query is made, it is added to the table, and the proper edges and labels are added to the graph.

The three simulator interfaces are formally described in Algorithm 4. Here, we recall that the distinguisher does not make redundant queries.

4.2 Intermediate World

We will use an intermediate world, which we denote W_S. This world behaves like the real world, with the exception that the ideal primitives, i.e. H and P, are replaced by the simulator interfaces. The world is depicted in Fig. 3.

By the triangle inequality, we have:

$$(4) \le \left| \mathbf{Pr}[\mathsf{D}^{W_I} \Rightarrow 1] - \mathbf{Pr}[\mathsf{D}^{W_S} \Rightarrow 1] \right| \tag{5}$$
$$+ \left| \mathbf{Pr}[\mathsf{D}^{W_S} \Rightarrow 1] - \mathbf{Pr}[\mathsf{D}^{W_R} \Rightarrow 1] \right|. \tag{6}$$

Distance (5) is bounded in Sect. 4.4 and distance (6) is bounded in Sect. 4.5. Before doing so, we define bad events in Sect. 4.3.

W_I: Ideal World	W_S: Intermediate World	W_R: Real World
RO	C^{S_H, S_P}	$C^{H,P}$
S_H	S_H	H
S_P	S_P	P
S_P^{-1}	S_P^{-1}	P^{-1}
Game 1	Game 2	Game 3

Fig. 3. Worlds involved in the security proof.

4.3 Bad Events

When the distinguisher makes a query, the simulator will try to maintain consistency with the ideal world. However, it is possible that an earlier response is such that the simulator cannot guarantee consistency anymore. To capture these cases, we will define additional bad events. Note that the distinguisher can make Q queries, Q_H of which to the hash interface and Q_P of which to the permutation interface. Consider $i \in \{1, \ldots, Q\}$. We define the following bad events:

- **CollH$_i$**: the i-th query is a query (IO, D, H) to S_H and there exists $(IO', D', H') \in \mathbf{C_H}$ such that $(IO, D) \neq (IO', D')$ and $H = H'$.
- **CollP$_i$**: the i-th query is a query (X, Y) to S_P or S_P^{-1} and there exists $(X', Y') \in \mathbf{C_P}$ such that either[4]
  - $X \neq X'$ and $Y = Y'$, or
  - $Y \neq Y'$ and $X = X'$.
- **ConnectP$_i$**: either
  - the i-th query is a query (X, Y) to S_P and there exists $(X', Y') \in \mathbf{C_P}$ such that $\mathtt{right}_c(Y) = \mathtt{right}_c(X')$, or
  - the i-th query is a query (X, Y) to S_P^{-1} and there exists $(X', Y') \in \mathbf{C_P}$ such that $\mathtt{right}_c(X) = \mathtt{right}_c(Y')$.
- **ConnectPH$_i$**: either
  - the i-th query is a query (X, Y) to S_P and there exists $(IO, D, H) \in \mathbf{C_H}$ such that $\mathtt{right}_c(Y) = H$, or
  - the i-th query is a query (X, Y) to S_P^{-1} and there exists $(IO, D, H) \in \mathbf{C_H}$ such that $\mathtt{right}_c(X) = H$, or
  - the i-th query is a query (IO, D, H) to S_H and there exists $(X, Y) \in \mathbf{C_P}$ such that $H = \mathtt{right}_c(X)$ or $H = \mathtt{right}_c(Y)$.

We furthermore define:

$$\mathbf{Bad}_i = \mathbf{CollH}_i \vee \mathbf{CollP}_i \vee \mathbf{ConnectP}_i \vee \mathbf{ConnectPH}_i.$$

---

[4] Here, we remark that the distinguisher never makes a redundant query, so it can never set the former condition in an inverse query or the latter condition in a forward query.

For each of the bad events $\mathbf{Event}_i \in \{\mathbf{Bad}_i, \mathbf{CollH}_i, \mathbf{CollP}_i, \mathbf{ConnectP}_i,$ $\mathbf{ConnectPH}_i\}$, we write:

$$\mathbf{Event} = \bigcup_{i=1}^{Q} \mathbf{Event}_i .$$

Bad event $\mathbf{CollH}$ registers hash collisions, which are problematic as they would allow different IO patterns and domain separators leading to the same root in the graph. Bad event $\mathbf{CollP}$ registers collisions in the permutation interface. Bad event $\mathbf{ConnectP}$ registers the case that a permutation query accidentally extends a path in the graph. Finally, bad event $\mathbf{ConnectPH}$ registers accidentally making a non-rooted path rooted and registers accidental collisions at the H-value.

For each of these events, if relevant, we add a superscript (like $\mathbf{Bad}^{(1)}$, $\mathbf{Bad}^{(2)}$, or $\mathbf{Bad}^{(3)}$) to indicate to which of the games (see Fig. 3) it applies.

The bad events are quite straightforward to bound, and we can obtain the following lemma. In this lemma, we consider both the general bad event $\mathbf{Bad}$ as the isolated bad event $\mathbf{CollP}$, as both results are needed separately.

Lemma 1. *For any distinguisher* D *making at most* Q_H *unique hash queries and* Q_P *unique primitive queries, the following holds for* $j = 1, 2$:

$$\Pr[\mathbf{CollP}^{(j)}] \leq \frac{\binom{Q_P}{2}}{|\mathbb{F}_p|^b}, \tag{7}$$

$$\Pr[\mathbf{Bad}^{(j)}] \leq \frac{\binom{Q_H}{2} + \binom{Q_P}{2} + 2 \cdot Q_P \cdot Q_H}{|\mathbb{F}_p|^c} + \frac{\binom{Q_P}{2}}{|\mathbb{F}_p|^b}, \tag{8}$$

and the following holds for $j = 1, 2, 3$:

$$\Pr[\mathbf{CollH}^{(j)}] \leq \frac{\binom{Q_H}{2}}{|\mathbb{F}_p|^c}. \tag{9}$$

Proof. The bad events can in fact be easily bounded in isolation:

$$\Pr[\mathbf{Bad}] \leq \Pr[\mathbf{CollH}] + \Pr[\mathbf{CollP}] + \Pr[\mathbf{ConnectP}] + \Pr[\mathbf{ConnectPH}].$$

For each of these four events, $\mathbf{Event} \in \{\mathbf{CollH}, \mathbf{CollP}, \mathbf{ConnectP}, \mathbf{ConnectPH}\}$, we observe that:

$$\Pr[\mathbf{Event}] \leq \sum_{i=1}^{Q} \Pr[\mathbf{Event}_i \mid \neg\mathbf{Event}_{i-1}] \leq \sum_{i=1}^{Q} \Pr[\mathbf{Event}_i].$$

We will now consider the events separately, where the reasoning for $\mathbf{CollH}$ holds for $j = 1, 2, 3$ and the reasoning of the other events for $j = 1, 2$. In the rest of this proof we omit the superscript.

$\mathbf{CollH}$. Note that this bad event only involves hash queries, so w.l.o.g. i runs from 1 to Q_H. At the point of the i-th query, there are at most $i - 1$ tuples in $\mathbf{C}_H$.

316 D. Khovratovich et al.

As the response H of the i-th query is uniformly randomly selected from $\mathbb{F}_p^c$, it sets the bad event with probability $(i-1)/|\mathbb{F}_p|^c$. We thus obtain that:

$$\Pr[\mathbf{CollH}] \leq \sum_{i=1}^{Q_{\mathrm{H}}} \frac{i-1}{|\mathbb{F}_p|^c} \leq \frac{\binom{Q_{\mathrm{H}}}{2}}{|\mathbb{F}_p|^c} .$$

CollP. Note that this bad event only involved primitive queries, so w.l.o.g. i runs from 1 to Q_{P}. At the point of the i-th query, there are at most $i-1$ tuples in $\mathbf{C_P}$. If the i-th query is a forward query, since the b elements of Y are uniformly randomly selected from $\mathbb{F}_p$, it sets the bad event with probability $(i-1)/|\mathbb{F}_p|^b$. The same holds in case the i-th query is an inverse query. As any query is either a forward or an inverse query (not both), we obtain that:

$$\Pr[\mathbf{CollP}] \leq \sum_{i=1}^{Q_{\mathrm{P}}} \frac{i-1}{|\mathbb{F}_p|^b} \leq \frac{\binom{Q_{\mathrm{P}}}{2}}{|\mathbb{F}_p|^b} .$$

ConnectP. Note that this bad event only involves primitive queries, so w.l.o.g. i runs from 1 to Q_{P}. At the point of the i-th query, there are at most $i-1$ tuples in $\mathbf{C_P}$. If the i-th query is a forward query, as the c inner elements of Y are uniformly randomly selected from $\mathbb{F}_p^c$, it sets the bad event with probability $(i-1)/|\mathbb{F}_p|^c$. The same holds in case the i-th query is an inverse query. As any query is either a forward or an inverse query (not both), we obtain that

$$\Pr[\mathbf{ConnectP}] \leq \sum_{i=1}^{Q_{\mathrm{P}}} \frac{i-1}{|\mathbb{F}_p|^c} \leq \frac{\binom{Q_{\mathrm{P}}}{2}}{|\mathbb{F}_p|^c} .$$

ConnectPH. Any query to $\mathsf{S_P}/\mathsf{S_P}^{-1}$ may set the bad event if its response (either Y in forward queries or X in inverse queries) has its c inner elements equal to H for an earlier query to $\mathsf{S_H}$. Likewise, any query to $\mathsf{S_H}$ may set the bad event if its response H equals the c inner elements of any X or Y for an earlier query to $\mathsf{S_P}/\mathsf{S_P}^{-1}$. As all fresh inner values and all fresh values H are uniformly randomly selected from $\mathbb{F}_p^c$, and there are at most Q_{P} queries to $\mathsf{S_P}/\mathsf{S_P}^{-1}$ and at most Q_{H} queries to $\mathsf{S_H}$, and any pair sets bad with probability $2/|\mathbb{F}_p|^c$. We thus obtain that:

$$\Pr[\mathbf{ConnectPH}] \leq \frac{2 \cdot Q_{\mathrm{P}} \cdot Q_{\mathrm{H}}}{|\mathbb{F}_p|^c} .$$

Conclusion. The lemma immediately follows by adding the individual bad events. □

4.4 Bound of (5)

We will use the following lemma, which informally states that the simulator in game 2 operates consistently with the random oracle in game 1 as long as no bad event occurs.

Lemma 2. *Unless a bad event happens in game 1 or game 2, we always have the following result. For any rooted path in the simulator graph of the following form*

$$0^r \| H \xrightarrow{\texttt{SAFECorePad}(M)} Y_1 \to \cdots \to Y_\ell, \qquad (10)$$

where $(IO, D, H) \in \mathbf{C_H}$, $(IO, D, M) \in \mathbf{I}$, *and where* $\ell \leq \lceil O_k/r \rceil$ *for* $k = \texttt{absrnds}(IO, M)$,

$$\texttt{left}_r(Y_1) \| \cdots \| \texttt{left}_r(Y_\ell) = \texttt{RO}(IO, D, \texttt{SAFECorePad}(M))[1 : r \cdot \ell]. \qquad (11)$$

Proof. We proceed by induction on the number of queries the distinguisher D makes. Clearly, $\mathbf{Bad}_1^{(j)}$ never happens. Assume that the lemma holds for any simulator performing $Q - 1$ queries. Consider distinguisher D making its Q-th query, where $\mathbf{Bad}_i^{(j)}$ has not occurred for $i < Q$. By hypothesis,

$$\texttt{left}_r(Y_1) \| \cdots \| \texttt{left}_r(Y_\ell) = \texttt{RO}(IO, D, \texttt{SAFECorePad}(M))[1 : r \cdot \ell], \quad \ell < Q$$

for any path on the simulator's graph.

Assume $\mathbf{Bad}_Q^{(j)}$ does not occur in the Q-th query and suppose there is a path on the simulator's graph contradicting (10). In other words, there is a path:

$$0^r \| H \xrightarrow{\texttt{SAFECorePad}(M)} Y_1 \to \cdots \to Y_{\ell-1} \to Y_\ell,$$

where necessarily

$$\texttt{left}_r(Y_1) \| \cdots \| \texttt{left}_r(Y_{\ell-1}) = \texttt{RO}(IO, D, \texttt{SAFECorePad}(M))[1 : r \cdot (\ell - 1)]$$

but

$$\texttt{left}_r(Y_l) \neq \texttt{RO}(IO, D, \texttt{SAFECorePad}(M))[r \cdot (\ell - 1) + 1 : r \cdot \ell].$$

By the construction of the simulator, we know there must be another path from $0^r \| H$ to Y_ℓ satisfying (10). This implies that in the simulator's graph there is a node with two out-going (or two in-going) edges, in which case $\mathbf{CollP}_Q$ must have occurred, there is a rooted node with an in-going edge, in which case $\mathbf{ConnectPH}_Q$ must have occurred, there is a cycle, in which case $\mathbf{ConnectP}_Q$ must have occurred, or the selection of (IO, D) was ambiguous in the first place, in which case $\mathbf{CollH}_Q$ must have occurred. Since by hypothesis, neither of those occurred, we conclude that the result holds. □

From Lemma 2, we can conclude that W_I and W_S are identical, i.e. their outputs are identically distributed, as long as **Bad** does not happen in either world. More formally, by the fundamental lemma of game playing [7] (or by [38]) we have:

$$\mathbf{Pr}[\mathsf{D}^{W_I} \Rightarrow 1 \mid \neg \mathbf{Bad}^{(1)}] = \mathbf{Pr}[\mathsf{D}^{W_S} \Rightarrow 1 \mid \neg \mathbf{Bad}^{(2)}].$$

Similar to Naito and Ohta [33, Section 3.4], we obtain from (8) of Lemma 1:[5]

$$(5) \leq \mathbf{Pr}[\mathbf{Bad}^{(1)}] + \mathbf{Pr}[\mathbf{Bad}^{(2)}] \leq \frac{2 \cdot \binom{Q_H}{2} + 2 \cdot \binom{Q_P}{2} + 4 \cdot Q_P \cdot Q_H}{|\mathbb{F}_p|^c} + \frac{2 \cdot \binom{Q_P}{2}}{|\mathbb{F}_p|^b} . \tag{12}$$

4.5   Bound of (6)

The intermediate world W_S and the real world W_R (see Fig. 3) are identical, except for the fact that P/P^{-1} is a permutation whereas S_P/S_P^{-1} is a random function. First note that S_P queries its oracle on input of a tuple $(IO, D, \mathtt{SAFECorePad}(M))$, which is always distinct for each evaluation. Thus, the outputs of S_P/S_P^{-1} are always uniformly randomly drawn. In the real world, it may happen that P is evaluated twice for the same value for a different construction evaluation, while this would not happen in the intermediate world. However, this would only happen in case of event $\mathbf{CollH}^{(3)}$. Assuming that this never happens, the two oracles P/P^{-1} and S_P/S_P^{-1} are identical as long as the latter does not output colliding values, which would in turn trigger event $\mathbf{CollP}^{(2)}$. From (7) and (9) of Lemma 1:

$$(6) \leq \mathbf{Pr}[\mathbf{CollH}^{(3)}] + \mathbf{Pr}[\mathbf{CollP}^{(2)}] \leq \frac{\binom{Q_H}{2}}{|\mathbb{F}_p|^c} + \frac{\binom{Q_P}{2}}{|\mathbb{F}_p|^b} .$$

5   SAFE API

The SAFE API [5] considers a sponge with a state of $b = r + c$ field elements in $\mathbb{F}_p^b$, where r is the rate and c the capacity. The sponge operates on a permutation $P : \mathbb{F}_p^b \to \mathbb{F}_p^b$. In addition, a hash function $H : (\mathbb{N}_+)^* \times \{0,1\}^* \to \mathbb{F}_p^c$ is involved upon initialization. A sponge object exposes four operations:

- START. This operation officially marks the start of a sponge life. It receives as input an IO pattern, IO, and a domain separator D. The input, IO, prescribes exactly the sequence of future calls and their respective lengths in the form of a string of 32-bit words (the exact encoding is slightly different from that of Sect. 3, but the difference is irrelevant for the current discussion), and D is an arbitrary domain separator which could for instance be used to distinguish between different use cases. It feeds IO and D into the hash function to obtain a c-element tag $T = H(IO, D)$. This tag is then used to initialize the inner part of the state.
- ABSORB. It receives as input a length L and an array $X[L]$ of L field elements, and absorbs them r elements at a time, interleaved with a call of P. The function also checks if the input matches the IO pattern.

---

[5] In their work, Naito and Ohta omitted a factor 2, which is included here. Our bound can also be derived from [38, Lemma 1].

- SQUEEZE. It receives as input a length L stating the requested number of blocks, and squeezes them r elements at a time, interleaved with a call of P. The function also checks if the input matches the IO pattern.
- FINISH. This operation officially marks the end of a sponge life. It receives no input and outputs 'OK' or 'NOK', depending on whether the sponge evaluation was correctly executed.

It is important to note that the functions ABSORB and SQUEEZE can be evaluated element-wise, and they only evaluate the permutation once they exhausted the entire outer part, i.e. once they absorbed/squeezed r elements. In addition, a transition from ABSORB to SQUEEZE is always made through a permutation evaluation, even if they did not exhaust the outer part. The other way around, this is not the case: one can e.g. squeeze r elements and then absorb r elements before the next permutation call is made. Details on this, and how it is implemented, can be found in [5].

Example 1. We will explain how the example of Sect. 3.2 would appear in the SAFE API, with parameters $c = 2, r = 2$. We have an IO pattern $IO = (8, 6, 5, 3, 4, 7)$, and any domain separator D. Let $M = M[1 : 17]$ be any input of the correct length. We describe two different ways to process this IO pattern, domain separator, and message using the SAFE API in Algorithms 5 and 6. The two evaluations are, in fact, equivalent. For example, in Algorithm 5, line 3 incurs 4 evaluations of P (recall that $r = 2$), whereas in Algorithm 6, line 3 incurs 2 evaluations of P and line 4 incurs 2 evaluations of P. The two evaluations in Algorithms 5 and 6 succeed upon finishing; if there were a mismatch between the number of absorbed/squeezed elements and what was prescribed by the IO pattern, finish would fail.

Algorithm 5. Example evaluation of SAFE API

```
1: Z = ∅
2: START(IO, D)
3: ABSORB(8, M[1 : 8])
4: Z ← Z‖SQUEEZE(6)
5: ABSORB(5, M[9 : 13])
6: Z ← Z‖SQUEEZE(3)
7: ABSORB(4, M[14 : 17])
8: Z ← Z‖SQUEEZE(7)
9: return FINISH() ? Z : ⊥
```

Algorithm 6. Example evaluation of SAFE API

```
1: Z = ∅
2: START(IO, D)
3: ABSORB(5, M[1 : 5])
4: ABSORB(3, M[6 : 8])
5: Z ← Z‖SQUEEZE(3)
6: Z ← Z‖SQUEEZE(3)
7: ABSORB(4, M[9 : 12])
8: ABSORB(1, M[13])
9: Z ← Z‖SQUEEZE(3)
10: ABSORB(4, M[14 : 17])
11: Z ← Z‖SQUEEZE(3)
12: Z ← Z‖SQUEEZE(4)
13: return FINISH() ? Z : ⊥
```

By definition, these evaluations of the SAFE operations are covered almost exactly by SAFECore, with the crucial difference that SAFE for efficiency and implementation reasons allows element-wise data processing whereas in SAFECore all inputs are basically absorbed at once before the first squeezing starts. It turns out that this does not restrict the generality of SAFECore, and in particular, we can argue security of any use case of the SAFE API. For example, for Example 1, we have

$$Z \leftarrow \text{SAFECore}(IO, D, M[1:8]) \tag{13a}$$
$$\| \text{SAFECore}(IO, D, M[1:13]) \tag{13b}$$
$$\| \text{SAFECore}(IO, D, M[1:17]) \,. \tag{13c}$$

Note that in SAFECore, the function SAFECorePad assures proper padding of M to account for squeezing rounds in (13b) and (13c). Because in Theorem 2 we proved that SAFECore is indifferentiable from a random oracle up to bound (4), we can obtain that the output string (13) is indistinguishable from random, provided $Q_H, Q_P \ll |\mathbb{F}_p|^{c/2}$.

This result can be straightforwardly generalized to the observation that all outputs of an evaluation of the SAFE API are indistinguishable from random, except in case two evaluations have a common prefix. To understand this, let us first consider the example case above, where we query the SAFE API on input of $IO = (8, 6, 5, 3, 4, 7)$, any domain separator D, and on two different messages $M = M[1:17]$ and $M' = M'[1:17]$ satisfying that $M[1:8] = M'[1:8]$. Then, in the evaluation of the SAFE API in Algorithm 5 or 6, the first 6 squeezed elements will be equal in the two evaluations, the remaining 10 elements may be either equal or independently distributed depending on the values $M[9:17]$ and $M'[9:17]$. This can in fact also be concluded from (13).

More formally, we say that two tuples (IO, D, M) and (IO', D', M') have a common prefix of k phases if

$$(IO, D, M[1:I_1 + I_2 + \cdots + I_k]) = (IO', D', M'[1:I_1 + I_2 + \cdots + I_k])$$

but

$$M[I_1 + I_2 + \cdots + I_k + 1 : I_1 + I_2 + \cdots + I_{k+1}] \neq$$
$$M'[I_1 + I_2 + \cdots + I_k + 1 : I_1 + I_2 + \cdots + I_{k+1}] \,.$$

Then, in the SAFE API, the first $O_1 + O_2 + \cdots + O_k$ squeezed elements will be identical but the future squeezes will be mutually independent. Obviously, common digests for common prefixes is not a bug, but rather a feature that is also present in duplex constructions [9,10,18,20,32]. By using different IO patterns $IO \neq IO'$, different domain separators $D \neq D'$, or a nonce that initializes M, the problem is avoided all the way.

We can conclude the following for the SAFE API.

Corollary 1 (Security of SAFE API). *Under the assumption that* H *is a random oracle and* P *a random permutation, and as long as the total number of* *primitive evaluations Q_H, Q_P are less than $|\mathbb{F}_p|^{c/2}$, outputs of SAFE are indistinguishable from random up to common prefix.*

This corollary, in turn, has immediate consequences for many practical use cases of the SAFE API. In the remainder of this section, we discuss various examples in more detail. In each of these applications, $\mu \in \mathbb{N}$ is the number of field elements that correspond to 256 bits (or a little less), and we take $c \geq \mu$.

5.1 Fixed-Length Hashing

In order to hash an array of $\ell \in \mathbb{N}$ field elements $M = M[1 : \ell] \in \mathbb{F}_p^\ell$ and obtain a digest of μ elements, one can evaluate the SAFE operations as follows. First, we fix IO pattern $IO = (\ell, \mu)$ and arbitrary domain separator D. Then, the hash digest is generated as follows:

1: START(IO, D)
2: ABSORB($\ell, M[1 : \ell]$)
3: $Z \leftarrow$ SQUEEZE(μ)
4: **return** FINISH() ? Z : $\bot$

By definition, this is exactly the same as evaluating SAFECore:

$$Z \leftarrow \text{SAFECore}(IO, D, M), \tag{14}$$

where M is restricted to match the IO pattern IO and the length of Z is prescribed by IO as well. Note that, just like in the comparison of Algorithms 5 and 6, for hashing the consumer is allowed to absorb and squeeze element-wise, but it does not matter much. We obtain the following corollary.

Corollary 2. *Under the assumption that H is a random oracle and P a random permutation, above fixed-length hashing construction outputs Z that is indistinguishable from random as long as the total number of START calls and the total number of permutation calls do not exceed $|\mathbb{F}_p|^{c/2}$. In particular, for $c \geq \mu = \log_p 2^{256-\epsilon}$ the fixed-length hashing construction is preimage resistant against an adversary that makes at most $\min\{|\mathbb{F}_p|^{c/2}, |\mathbb{F}_p|^\mu\}$ queries and collision resistant against an adversary that makes at most $\min\{|\mathbb{F}_p|^{c/2}, |\mathbb{F}_p|^{\mu/2}\}$ queries implying security up to $128 - \epsilon/2$ bits.*

Merkle tree hashing is a subclass of this scenario.

5.2 Commitment Schemes

In order to commit to ℓ d-tuples of field elements $X_1, X_2, \ldots, X_\ell \in \mathbb{F}_p^d$ and randomness $R \in \mathbb{F}_p$ and obtain a digest of μ elements, one can evaluate the SAFE operations as follows. First, we fix IO pattern $IO = (\ell \cdot d + 1, \mu)$ and arbitrary domain separator D. Then, the commitment is generated as follows:

1: START(IO, D)
2: ABSORB($\ell \cdot d + 1, X_1 || X_2 || \ldots || X_\ell || R$)
3: $Z \leftarrow$ SQUEEZE(μ)

4: **return** FINISH() ? Z : $\perp$

By definition, this is exactly the same as evaluating SAFECore:

$$Z \leftarrow \texttt{SAFECore}(IO, D, X_1 \| X_2 \| \cdots \| X_\ell \| R), \tag{15}$$

just like for the example of Sect. 5.1. In fact, the application is merely identical, but the security model is different. Here, we do not aim for collision or preimage resistance as in Corollary 2, but rather to binding and hiding. Moreover, as our adversary can freely choose IO and D, our security results applies not to a single invocation of a commitment scheme but also to protocols where *several commitment schemes are used in parallel*.

Corollary 3. *Under the assumption that* H *is a random oracle and* P *a random permutation, above commitment scheme construction outputs Z that is indistinguishable from random as long as the total number of* START *calls and the total number of permutation calls do not exceed $|\mathbb{F}_p|^{c/2}$. In particular, for $c \geq \mu = \log_{|\mathbb{F}_p|} 2^{256-\epsilon}$ the commitment scheme construction is computationally binding and hiding against an adversary that makes at most $\min\{|\mathbb{F}_p|^{c/2}, |\mathbb{F}_p|^\mu\}$ queries to* H *and* P, *implying security up to $128 - \epsilon/2$ bits.*

Note that the IO pattern will be the same for committing $\ell \cdot d$ 1-field elements. If this difference matters for an application, a domain separator should be used.

5.3   Multi-round Interactive Protocols

A non-interactive argument of knowledge is often based on a multi-round interactive protocol, where a verifier is replaced by a hash function within the Fiat-Shamir paradigm. SAFE is suitable for implementing such a hash with minimum overhead. As an example, consider a 5-round protocol. Let $n \in \mathbb{N}$ be the length of the common input, and let $\lambda_1, \lambda_2, \lambda_3 \in \mathbb{N}$ be the lengths of proof elements:

- Prover and verifier agree on the common input $N \in \mathbb{F}_p^n$;
- Prover prepares and sends proof elements $\pi_1 \in \mathbb{F}_p^{\lambda_1}$ and $\pi_2 \in \mathbb{F}_p^{\lambda_2}$;
- Verifier responds with challenge $C_1 \in \mathbb{F}_p^\mu$;
- Prover prepares and sends proof element $\pi_3 \in \mathbb{F}_p^{\lambda_3}$;
- Verifier responds with challenges $C_2, C_3 \in \mathbb{F}_p^\mu$;
- Prover sends final proof π_4.

Here the prover sends a proof of knowledge in three steps while getting verifier's challenges in-between. To make the protocol non-interactive we apply the Fiat-Shamir transformation where the challenges are generated as follows. First, we fix IO pattern $IO = (n + \lambda_1 + \lambda_2, \mu, \lambda_3, 2\mu)$ and arbitrary domain separator D. Then, the challenges are generated as follows:

1: START(IO, D)
2: ABSORB($n + \lambda_1 + \lambda_2, N \| \pi_1 \| \pi_2$)
3: $C_1 \leftarrow$ SQUEEZE(μ)
4: ABSORB(λ_3, π_3)

5: $C_2 \leftarrow$ SQUEEZE(μ)
6: $C_3 \leftarrow$ SQUEEZE(μ)
7: **return** FINISH() ? (C_1, C_2, C_3) : $\perp$

By definition, this is exactly the same as evaluating SAFECore:

$$C_1 \leftarrow \text{SAFECore}(IO, D, N\|\pi_1\|\pi_2), \tag{16a}$$

$$C_2\|C_3 \leftarrow \text{SAFECore}(IO, D, N\|\pi_1\|\pi_2\|\pi_3). \tag{16b}$$

We obtain, by security of SAFECore, that this non-interactive version of the protocol is as secure as the interactive one up to the security of SAFECore. We note that as our adversary is powerful enough to choose arbitrary IO and D, the security holds when *several such protocols co-exist in one application*, whether in parallel or recursively.

Corollary 4. *Suppose the multi-round interactive protocol construction is computationally sound against an adversary that makes up to 2^t calls to H and P assuming H is a random oracle and P a random permutation. Then the non-interactive protocol (above) outputs (C_1, C_2, C_3) that are indistinguishable from random as long as the total number of START calls and the total number of permutation calls do not exceed $|\mathbb{F}_p|^{c/2}$. In particular, for $c \geq \mu = \log_{|\mathbb{F}_p|} 2^{256-\epsilon}$ the non-interactive protocol construction is sound against an adversary that makes at most $\min\{2^t, |\mathbb{F}_p|^{c/2}, |\mathbb{F}_p|^{\mu}\}$ queries, implying security up to $128 - \epsilon/2$ bits.*

5.4 Authenticated Encryption

SAFE allows to perform authenticated encryption using the SpongeWrap mode [10], with subtle differences that the 1-padding (present in the original SpongeWrap) can be avoided by using the IO pattern de facto as prefix. Let k be the key length, n the nonce length, and t the tag length. In order to encrypt and authenticate ℓ blocks of data $M_1, M_2, \ldots, M_\ell$ each of length λ_i with key $K \in \mathbb{F}_p^k$ and nonce $N \in \mathbb{F}_p^n$ in order to obtain ciphertext blocks $C_1, C_2, \ldots, C_\ell$ and tag $T \in \mathbb{F}_p^\mu$, we proceed as follows. First, we fix IO pattern

$$IO = (k + n, \lambda_1, \lambda_1, \lambda_2, \lambda_2, \ldots, \lambda_\ell, \lambda_\ell, \mu)$$

and an arbitrary domain separator D. Then, the message is encrypted and authenticated as follows:

1: START(IO, D)
2: ABSORB($k + n, K\|N$)
3: $Z_1 \leftarrow$ SQUEEZE(λ_1)
4: ABSORB(λ_1, M_1)
5: $Z_2 \leftarrow$ SQUEEZE(λ_2)
6: ABSORB(λ_2, M_2)
7: $\cdots$
8: $Z_\ell \leftarrow$ SQUEEZE(λ_ℓ)
9: ABSORB(λ_ℓ, M_ℓ)

10: $T \leftarrow \text{SQUEEZE}(\mu)$
11: $(C_1, C_2, \ldots, C_\ell) \leftarrow (Z_1 + M_1, Z_2 + M_2, \ldots, Z_\ell + M_\ell)$
12: **return** FINISH() ? $(C_1, \ldots, C_\ell, T)$: $\bot$

By definition, this is exactly the same as evaluating SAFECore:

$$Z_1 \leftarrow \text{SAFECore}(IO, D, K\|N), \tag{17a}$$
$$Z_2 \leftarrow \text{SAFECore}(IO, D, K\|N\|M_1), \tag{17b}$$
$$\vdots$$
$$Z_\ell \leftarrow \text{SAFECore}(IO, D, K\|N\|M_1\|\cdots\|M_{\ell-1}), \tag{17c}$$
$$T \leftarrow \text{SAFECore}(IO, D, K\|N\|M_1\|\cdots\|M_\ell), \tag{17d}$$

with the final output being $(Z_1 + M_1, Z_2 + M_2, \ldots, Z_\ell + M_\ell, T)$. We obtain, by security of SAFECore, that this authenticated encryption scheme is secure.

Corollary 5. *Under the assumption that* H *is a random oracle and* P *a random permutation, above authenticated encryption construction outputs Z that is indistinguishable from random as long as the total number of* START *calls and the total number of permutation calls do not exceed* $|\mathbb{F}_p|^{c/2}$. *In particular, for* $c \geq \mu = \log_{|\mathbb{F}_p|} 2^{256-\epsilon}$ *the authenticated encryption construction offers confidentiality and authenticity against an adversary that makes at most* $\min\{|\mathbb{F}_p|^{c/2}, |\mathbb{F}_p|^\mu\}$ *queries, implying security up to* $128 - \epsilon/2$ *bits.*

This construction is the most efficient when $\lambda_i \equiv 0 \mod r$, that is, all blocks fit the rate parameter of the sponge. This mode can be adapted to support associated data (authenticated but not encrypted), in the same vein as the SpongeWrap mode. Note that there is no padding overhead, nor we spend unneeded calls to the inner permutation.

6   Conclusion

We have formally proven the security of the SAFE API with applications to many use cases, from hashing to interactive protocols. A number of typical applications have been highlighted in Sects. 5.1–5.4, but extensions to protocol composition, variable-length hashing, PRNGs, and support of multiple fields are possible. The most important observation is that it is possible to get rid of the padding schemes at the (arguably smaller) cost of pre-declaring the pattern of absorptions and squeezes. As the majority of applications of the SAFE API know this pattern in advance, we have placed no significant burden on the designers. Our results, perhaps surprisingly, demonstrated that SAFE API is better than it was originally considered. In particular, our results demonstrate that the full inner part of the sponge can be used to hash the IO pattern onto, without any security loss. This principle can be used in the future applications of sponges, which may put all the application/run metadata (properly processed) into the capacity, and then run the sponge in a simple but flexible and foolproof way.

Acknowledgements. We would like to thank Mary Maller for fruitful discussions on the applications of our result. Mario Marhuenda Beltrán and Bart Mennink are supported by the Netherlands Organisation for Scientific Research (NWO) under grant VI.Vidi.203.099.

References

1. Longsight faulty design (2018). https://github.com/zcash/zcash/issues/2233# issuecomment-416648993
2. Tornado Cash Privacy Solution Version 1.4 (2021). https://tornado.cash/Tornado. cash_whitepaper_v1.4.pdf
3. Albrecht, M., Grassi, L., Rechberger, C., Roy, A., Tiessen, T.: MiMC: efficient encryption and cryptographic hashing with minimal multiplicative complexity. In: Cheon, J.H., Takagi, T. (eds.) ASIACRYPT 2016, Part I. LNCS, vol. 10031, pp. 191–219. Springer, Heidelberg (2016). https://doi.org/10.1007/978-3-662-53887-6_7
4. Aly, A., Ashur, T., Ben-Sasson, E., Dhooghe, S., Szepieniec, A.: Design of symmetric-key primitives for advanced cryptographic protocols. IACR Trans. Symmetric Cryptol. **2020**(3), 1–45 (2020). https://doi.org/10.13154/tosc.v2020.i3.1-45
5. Aumasson, J., Khovratovich, D., Quine, P.: SAFE: Sponge API for Field Elements. Cryptology ePrint Archive, Paper 2023/522 (2023). https://eprint.iacr.org/2023/522
6. Bellare, M., Rogaway, P.: Random oracles are practical: a paradigm for designing efficient protocols. In: Denning, D.E., Pyle, R., Ganesan, R., Sandhu, R.S., Ashby, V. (eds.) CCS 1993, Proceedings of the 1st ACM Conference on Computer and Communications Security, Fairfax, Virginia, USA, 3–5 November 1993, pp. 62–73. ACM (1993). https://doi.org/10.1145/168588.168596
7. Bellare, M., Rogaway, P.: Code-based game-playing proofs and the security of triple encryption. Cryptology ePrint Archive, Paper 2004/331 (2004). https://eprint.iacr.org/2004/331
8. Bernhard, D., Pereira, O., Warinschi, B.: How not to prove yourself: pitfalls of the Fiat-Shamir heuristic and applications to helios. In: Wang, X., Sako, K. (eds.) ASIACRYPT 2012. LNCS, vol. 7658, pp. 626–643. Springer, Heidelberg (2012). https://doi.org/10.1007/978-3-642-34961-4_38
9. Bertoni, G., Daemen, J., Hoffert, S., Peeters, M., Van Assche, G., Van Keer, R.: Farfalle: parallel permutation-based cryptography. IACR Trans. Symmetric Cryptol. **2017**(4), 1–38 (2017). https://tosc.iacr.org/index.php/ToSC/article/view/801
10. Bertoni, G., Daemen, J., Peeters, M., Van Assche, G.: Duplexing the sponge: single-pass authenticated encryption and other applications. In: Miri, A., Vaudenay, S. (eds.) SAC 2011. LNCS, vol. 7118, pp. 320–337. Springer, Heidelberg (2012). https://doi.org/10.1007/978-3-642-28496-0_19
11. Bertoni, G., Daemen, J., Peeters, M., Assche, G.V.: Keccak. In: International Conference on the Theory and Application of Cryptographic Techniques (2013)
12. Bertoni, G., Daemen, J., Peeters, M., Van Assche, G.: Sponge Functions (2007)
13. Bertoni, G., Daemen, J., Peeters, M., Van Assche, G.: On the indifferentiability of the sponge construction. In: Smart, N. (ed.) EUROCRYPT 2008. LNCS, vol. 4965, pp. 181–197. Springer, Heidelberg (2008). https://doi.org/10.1007/978-3-540-78967-3_11
14. Bowe, S.: BLS12-381: New zk-SNARK elliptic curve construction (2017). https://electriccoin.co/blog/new-snark-curve

15. Chiesa, A., Ojha, D., Spooner, N.: FRACTAL: post-quantum and transparent recursive proofs from holography. In: Canteaut, A., Ishai, Y. (eds.) EUROCRYPT 2020, Part I. LNCS, vol. 12105, pp. 769–793. Springer, Cham (2020). https://doi.org/10.1007/978-3-030-45721-1_27

16. Coron, J.-S., Dodis, Y., Malinaud, C., Puniya, P.: Merkle-Damgård revisited: how to construct a hash function. In: Shoup, V. (ed.) CRYPTO 2005. LNCS, vol. 3621, pp. 430–448. Springer, Heidelberg (2005). https://doi.org/10.1007/11535218_26

17. Cortier, V., Gaudry, P., Yang, Q.: How to fake zero-knowledge proofs, again. In: E-Vote-Id 2020-The International Conference for Electronic Voting (2020). https://hal.inria.fr/hal-02928953/document

18. Daemen, J., Mennink, B., Van Assche, G.: Full-state keyed duplex with built-in multi-user support. In: Takagi, T., Peyrin, T. (eds.) ASIACRYPT 2017, Part II. LNCS, vol. 10625, pp. 606–637. Springer, Cham (2017). https://doi.org/10.1007/978-3-319-70697-9_21

19. Dao, Q., Miller, J., Wright, O., Grubbs, P.: Weak Fiat-Shamir Attacks on Modern Proof Systems. Cryptology ePrint Archive, Paper 2023/691 (2023). https://eprint.iacr.org/2023/691.pdf

20. Dobraunig, C., Mennink, B.: Leakage resilience of the duplex construction. In: Galbraith, S.D., Moriai, S. (eds.) ASIACRYPT 2019, Part III. LNCS, vol. 11923, pp. 225–255. Springer, Cham (2019). https://doi.org/10.1007/978-3-030-34618-8_8

21. Fiat, A., Shamir, A.: How to prove yourself: practical solutions to identification and signature problems. In: Odlyzko, A.M. (ed.) CRYPTO 1986. LNCS, vol. 263, pp. 186–194. Springer, Heidelberg (1987). https://doi.org/10.1007/3-540-47721-7_12

22. Grassi, L., Khovratovich, D., Lüftenegger, R., Rechberger, C., Schofnegger, M., Walch, R.: Reinforced concrete: a fast hash function for verifiable computation. In: Proceedings of the 2022 ACM SIGSAC Conference on Computer and Communications Security, CCS 2022, pp. 1323–1335. Association for Computing Machinery, New York (2022). https://doi.org/10.1145/3548606.3560686

23. Grassi, L., Khovratovich, D., Rechberger, C., Roy, A., Schofnegger, M.: Poseidon: a new hash function for zero-knowledge proof systems. In: Bailey, M., Greenstadt, R. (eds.) 30th USENIX Security Symposium, USENIX Security 2021, 11–13 August 2021, pp. 519–535. USENIX Association (2021). https://www.usenix.org/conference/usenixsecurity21/presentation/grassi

24. Grassi, L., Mennink, B.: Security of truncated permutation without initial value. In: Agrawal, S., Lin, D. (eds.) ASIACRYPT 2022, Part II. LNCS, vol. 13792, pp. 620–650. Springer, Cham (2022). https://doi.org/10.1007/978-3-031-22966-4_21

25. Haines, T., Lewis, S.J., Pereira, O., Teague, V.: How not to prove your election outcome. In: 2020 IEEE Symposium on Security and Privacy, SP 2020, San Francisco, CA, USA, 18–21 May 2020, pp. 644–660. IEEE (2020). https://doi.org/10.1109/SP40000.2020.00048

26. Hopwood, D., Bowe, S., Hornby, T., Wilcox, N.: ZCash protocol specification (2023). https://github.com/zcash/zips/blob/master/protocol/protocol.pdf

27. Kothapalli, A., Setty, S., Tzialla, I.: Nova: recursive zero-knowledge arguments from folding schemes. In: Dodis, Y., Shrimpton, T. (eds.) CRYPTO 2022, Part IV. LNCS, vol. 13510, pp. 359–388. Springer, Cham (2022). https://doi.org/10.1007/978-3-031-22966-4_21

28. Lefevre, C., Mennink, B.: Tight preimage resistance of the sponge construction. In: Dodis, Y., Shrimpton, T. (eds.) CRYPTO 2022, Part IV. LNCS, vol. 13510, pp. 185–204. Springer, Cham (2022). https://doi.org/10.1007/978-3-031-15985-5_7

29. Maller, M., Khovratovich, D.: Baloo: open source implementation (2022). https://github.com/mmaller/caulk-dev/tree/main/baloo

30. Maurer, U., Renner, R., Holenstein, C.: Indifferentiability, impossibility results on reductions, and applications to the random oracle methodology. In: Naor, M. (ed.) TCC 2004. LNCS, vol. 2951, pp. 21–39. Springer, Heidelberg (2004). https://doi.org/10.1007/978-3-540-24638-1_2

31. Mennink, B.: Understanding the duplex and its security. IACR Trans. Symmetric Cryptol. **2023**(2), 1–46 (2023). https://tosc.iacr.org/index.php/ToSC/article/view/10976

32. Mennink, B., Reyhanitabar, R., Vizár, D.: Security of full-state keyed sponge and duplex: applications to authenticated encryption. In: Iwata, T., Cheon, J.H. (eds.) ASIACRYPT 2015, Part II. LNCS, vol. 9453, pp. 465–489. Springer, Heidelberg (2015). https://doi.org/10.1007/978-3-662-48800-3_19

33. Naito, Y., Ohta, K.: Improved indifferentiable security analysis of PHOTON. In: Abdalla, M., De Prisco, R. (eds.) SCN 2014. LNCS, vol. 8642, pp. 340–357. Springer, Cham (2014). https://doi.org/10.1007/978-3-319-10879-7_20

34. NIST: SHA-3 competition. In: International Conference on the Theory and Application of Cryptographic Techniques (2007–2012)

35. Polygon Team: Introducing Plonky2 (2017). https://polygon.technology/blog/introducing-plonky2

36. Prest, T., et al.: Falcon: fast-Fourier lattice-based compact signatures over NTRU. Submission NIST's Post-quantum Cryptogr. Standardization Process **36**(5), 1–75 (2018)

37. Setty, S.: Nova: open source implementation

38. Shoup, V.: Sequences of games: a tool for taming complexity in security proofs. Cryptology ePrint Archive, Paper 2004/332 (2004). https://eprint.iacr.org/2004/332

39. Zhang, Y.: Introducing zkEVM (2022). https://scroll.io/blog/zkEVM

Author Index

© International Association for Cryptologic Research 2023
J. Guo and R. Steinfeld (Eds.): ASIACRYPT 2023, LNCS 14445, p. 329, 2023.
https://doi.org/10.1007/978-981-99-8742-9

Printed in the United States
by Baker & Taylor Publisher Services

Printed in the United States
by Baker & Taylor Publisher Services